ELEVENTH EDITION

Intercultural Communication

A READER

Larry A. Samovar
San Diego State University,
Emeritus

Richard E. Porter
California State University,
Long Beach, Emeritus

Edwin R. McDaniel
Aichi Shukutoku University

• Mexico • Singapore • Spain • United Kingdom • United States

Intercultural Communication: A Reader

ELEVENTH EDITION

Larry A. Samovar, Richard E. Porter, Edwin R. McDaniel

Publisher: Holly J. Allen
Editor: Annie Mitchell
Assistant Editor: Aarti Jayaraman
Editorial Assistant: Trina Enriquez
Senior Technology Project Manager: Jeanette Wiseman
Senior Marketing Manager: Kimberly Russell
Marketing Assistant: Andrew Keay
Advertising Project Manager: Shemika Britt
Project Manager, Editorial Production: Mary Noel
Art Director: Maria Epes

Printed in the United States of America
1 2 3 4 5 6 7 09 08 07 06 05

Library of Congress Control Number: 2004117748

ISBN 0-534-64440-6

Print Buyer: Karen Hunt
Permissions Editor: Chelsea Junget
Production Service: Melanie Field, Strawberry Field Publishing
Text Designer: Adriane Bosworth
Copy Editor: Margaret C. Tropp
Cover Designer: Laurie Anderson
Cover Images: basketry detail, Jim Wehtje/Getty Images; colored tiles, Mark Hibbard/Getty Images
Compositor: Interactive Composition Corporation
Printer: Malloy Incorporated

Thomson Higher Education
10 Davis Drive
Belmont, CA 94002-3098
USA

Asia (including India)
Thomson Learning
5 Shenton Way
#01-01 UIC Building
Singapore 068808

Australia/New Zealand
Thomson Learning Australia
102 Dodds Street
Southbank, Victoria 3006
Australia

Canada
Thomson N
1120 Birchn
Toronto, Or
Canada

UK/Europe
Thomson L
High Holbo
50–51 Bedf
London WC
United King

Latin Amer
Thomson L
Seneca, 53
Colonia Pol
11560 Mex
D.F. Mexico

Spain (incl
Thomson P
Calle Magall
28015 Madr

Contents

Preface

Wonder is the beginning of wisdom.

GREEK PROVERB

PHILOSOPHY

It would not be an overstatement to assert that the ability to successfully engage in intercultural communication may be one of the most important skills you will ever develop. You need only look around to see a challenging future in which you will interact with people from a wide range of dissimilar cultural backgrounds. Those people may include your neighbor next door who speaks with a foreign accent, someone a thousand miles away who considers you an enemy, or your classmate who has just arrived from another country. Regardless of the specifics, it behooves you to prepare to meet this new challenge. This book is designed to assist you with that assignment. We begin, however, by noting it will not be easy. First, because your view of the world is shaped by the perspective of your own culture, it is often difficult to understand and appreciate many of the actions originating in other people, groups, and nations. Your cultural perception tends to condition you to see people and events through a highly selective prism. Second, to be a successful intercultural communicator you must be open to new communication experiences, have empathy toward cultures different from your own, develop a universalistic, realistic worldview, and learn to be tolerant of views that differ from your own.

The preceding characteristics are easy to read about but difficult to translate into action. Yet intercultural communication training offers an arena in which to work on these skills. In short, it is your ability to change, to make adjustments in your communication habits and behaviors, that gives you the potential to engage in successful and effective intercultural contacts. We should add that part of that success requires you to rid yourself of racism and ethnocentrism and in its place learn to reflect an attitude of mutual respect, trust, and common worth. Intercultural communication will not be successful if, by actions or words, communicators evince an arrogant attitude or exhibit a condescending manner. Every individual wants to believe that his or her culture is equal to, and as important as, any other. Behaviors and attitudes that convey a feeling of one's own superiority will stifle meaningful interaction. To be racist or ethnocentric is to preordain any intercultural communication event to failure. The reward for adopting the behaviors and attitudes necessary to overcome racism and ethnocentrism is the exhilaration that comes when you have connected successfully with someone far removed from your own sphere of experience.

We moved toward this new edition with feelings of exhilaration and prudence. The excitement was because we have been received with enough recognition to warrant another new edition. With some degree of modesty we note that very few books thrive long enough to justify eleven editions. Yet our delight was tempered with a degree of caution. As we proceeded, we wanted to preserve the basic framework and philosophy that has sustained us through the previous ten editions, while also including what was new to the field. This is to say, it would have been imprudent of us to abandon, just for the sake of change, an orientation to intercultural communication that has found wide acceptance for more than three decades. The field, however, has continued to evolve, and hence so has this new edition.

This eleventh edition grants us the opportunity to combine two complementary positions. First, it reflects our continued belief that the basic core of the field should not be changed for the sake of simply being novel; such change would deprive the book of those concepts that have infused all of the previous editions. Second, it reflects our belief that as our intercultural contacts change in number and intensity, there is a need to present essays that mirror that change. We have perceived each new edition as an opportunity to examine that change and to stake out new territory for the field—territory that takes into account the complexities of communicating in the 21st century.

As the field of intercultural communication has grown, we have attempted to grow with it and to fuse the old with the new. In 1972, the first edition contained 34 articles and essays. In this new edition we included 44—23 of which are new to this volume. Twelve of these were written especially for this edition. In an attempt to broaden our base, we have also incorporated the work of 12 authors from a wide array of countries and cultures.

NEW FEATURES

In one sense we would say that the tallying of 23 new essays constitutes "new features." But that count is obvious. There are however two other significant changes deserving the title of "new features." First is the adding of a new coeditor—Dr. Edwin R. McDaniel. We are delighted to have Ed join us for a variety of reasons. His extensive research agenda and teaching experience bring a fresh infusion of new ideas to the book. In addition, Ed spent more than 20 years traveling throughout the world. This firsthand knowledge of different cultures gives him a unique point of view toward cultural diversity.

Another new feature is the inclusion of a new chapter examining the topic of *cultural identity* and its role in human interaction. Your identity is composed of a host of factors, ranging from where you live to the clubs you belong to, but it is your cultural identity that tells you something about who you are, where you belong, and how you "fit in." What cultural identity attempts to do is strike a balance between your current picture of yourself (self-concept) and your past ancestry. As we have indicated, the synthesis of these various identities has an impact on communication. That is why we have included the subject in this edition.

APPROACH

The basic energizing motive for this book has remained the same since we became interested in the topic of intercultural communication almost 40 years ago. We sincerely believe that the ability to communicate effectively with people from diverse cultures and co-cultures benefits each of us as individuals and has the potential to benefit the more than 6.5 billion people with whom we share this planet. We have intentionally selected materials that will assist you in understanding those intercultural communication principles that are instrumental to success when you interact with people from diverse cultures.

Fundamental to our approach is the conviction that communication is a social activity; it is something people do to and with one another. The activity might begin in our heads, but it is manifested in our behaviors, be they verbal or nonverbal. In both explicit and implicit ways, the information and the advice contained in this book are usable; the ideas presented can be translated into action.

USE

As in the past, we intend this anthology to be for the general reader, so we have selected materials that are broadly based, comprehensive, and suitable for both undergraduate and graduate students. Although the level of difficulty varies from essay to essay, we have not gone beyond the level found in most textbooks directed toward college and university students.

Intercultural Communication: A Reader is designed to meet three specific needs. The first comes from a canon that maintains that successful intercultural communication is a matter of highest importance if humankind and society are to survive. Events during the past 30 years have created a world that sees us linked together in a multitude of ways. From pollution to economics to health care, what happens to one culture potentially happens to all other cultures. This book, then, is designed to serve as a basic anthology for courses concerned with the issues associated with human interaction. Our intention is to make this book theoretical and practical so that the issues associated with intercultural communication can be first understood and then acted upon.

Second, the book may be used as a supplemental text to existing service and basic communication skill courses and interpersonal communication courses. The rationale is a simple one: Understanding other cultures is indispensable in this age of cross-cultural contact. It matters very little if that contact is face-to-face or on the public platform.

Third, the book provides resource material for courses in communication theory, small group communication, organizational and business communication, and mass communication, as well as for courses in anthropology, health care, sociology, social psychology, social welfare, social policy, business, and international relations. The long list of possible uses only underscores the increased level of intercultural interaction that is characteristic of what is often now called the "global village."

ORGANIZATION

The book is organized into eight closely related chapters. In Chapter 1, "Approaches to Understanding Intercultural Communication," our purpose is twofold: We hope to acquaint you with the basic concepts of intercultural communication while at the same time arousing your interest in the topic. Hence, the essays in this chapter are both theoretical and philosophical. The selections explain what intercultural communication is and why it is important.

Chapter 2, "Cultural Identity: Issues of Belonging," has five essays that demonstrate how different cultural and ethnic identities influence role expectations, perceptions, and intercultural interaction. Through various stories you will be able to get an appreciation of how a person's identity helps shape his or her view of the world.

Chapter 3, "International Cultures: Understanding Diversity," deals with the communication patterns of five specific cultures. These cultures represent East Asia, India, and Africa, including Egypt. We should add that in many other chapters of the book we examine additional international cultures in specific settings.

Chapter 4, "Co-Cultures: Living in Two Cultures," moves us from the international arena to co-cultures that operate within the United States. Here again space constraints have limited the total number of co-cultures we could include. Yet we believe that through the selection of groups such as Native Americans, African Americans, Asian Americans, the disabled, homosexuals, and women, you will get an idea of the cultural diversity found in those groups with whom most of you have regular contact. As is the case with international cultures, many other co-cultures will appear in other chapters.

In Chapter 5, "Intercultural Messages: Verbal and Nonverbal Communication," we study how verbal and nonverbal symbols are used in intercultural communication. We offer readings that will introduce you to some of the difficulties you might encounter when your intercultural partner uses a different verbal or nonverbal coding system. We will look at how verbal idiosyncrasies and distinctions influence problem solving, speaking, perception, translation, interpreting, and understanding. As noted, this chapter is also concerned with nonverbal symbols and explains some of the cultural differences in movement, facial expressions, eye contact, silence, space, time, and the like.

Chapter 6, "Cultural Contexts: The Influence of Setting," continues with the theme of how culture modifies interaction. This time, however, the interaction is examined in a specific context. The assumption is that culturally diverse rules influence how members of a culture behave in certain settings. To clarify this important issue, we have selected "places" where cultures often follow rules that differ from those found in North America. More specifically, we look at settings related to business, groups, negotiations, health care, and education.

In Chapter 7, "Communicating Interculturally: Becoming Competent," readings are offered that are intended to provide you with knowledge about and suggestions for improving intercultural communication. Each essay presents practical recommendations.

Chapter 8, "Ethical Considerations: Prospects for the Future," presents essays that deal with ethical and moral issues as well as the future directions and challenges of intercultural communication. It is also the intent of this chapter to ask you not to conclude your study of intercultural communication with the reading of a single book or the completion of one course. We believe that the study of intercultural communication is a lifetime endeavor. Each time we want to share an idea or feeling with someone from another culture, we face a new and exhilarating learning experience. We urge everyone to seek out as many of these experiences as possible. A philosopher once wrote, "Tomorrow, when I know more, I'll recall that piece of knowledge and use it better."

ASSISTANCE

As in the past, many people have helped us rethink and reshape this project. We express appreciation to our editor Annie Mitchell, who offered sound advice and positive direction. We also wish to thank Trina Enriquez, who was always there to handle both major and minor problems. And, as we do with each edition, we must call attention to our first editor, Rebecca Hayden. Becky had enough courage and insight 35 years ago to decide that intercultural communication should and would become a viable discipline.

In a culture that values change, this collection would not have survived for more than 30 years if we had not been fortunate enough to have so many scholars willing to contribute original essays to each edition. Here, in the eleventh edition, we acknowledge the work of Polly A. Begley, Dawn O. Braithwaite, Charles A. Braithwaite, Julia T. Wood, Mary Fong, Wenshan Jia, Peter A. Andersen, Young Yun Kim, Mary Jane Collier, Stella Ting-Toomey, Sheryl Lindsley, Donald G. Ellis, Ifat Maoz, Carolyn Roy, Nagesh Rao, Aaron Castelan Cargile, Robert Krizek, Jolanta A. Drzewiecka, Nancy Draznin, A. L. Zimmerman, Patricia Geist-Martin, Donna M. Stringer, Nina M. Reich, William F. Eadie, Ann Neville Miller, and Hua Wang. We thank all of you for letting us expose your work to thousands of other people who share your commitment to intercultural matters.

For their helpful comments and suggestions on the revision of this edition of the text, sincere thanks go to Barbara Blackstone, Slippery Rock University of Pennsylvania; Carol Bruess, University of St. Thomas; John Chetro-Szivos, Fitchburg State College; Kathleen Clark, University of Akron; Glenda Dianne Crossman, Baldwin-Wallace College; Melbourne S. Cummings, Howard University; Qingwen Dong, University of the Pacific; Martine Harvey, Minnesota State University, Mankato; Michael Hecht, Pennsylvania State University; Mary Hinchcliff-Pelias, Southern Illinois University at Carbondale; Edwin L. Isley, Ohio Dominican University; Wenshan Jia, The State University of New York at New Paltz; Jeremy Lipschultz, University of Nebraska at Omaha; Carmen Mendoza, Trinity International University; Owen Mordaunt, University of Nebraska at Omaha; George Musambira, Western Kentucky University; Judy C. Nixon, University of Tennessee at Chattanooga; Richard Paine, North Central College; Jill Pinkney Pastrana, California State University, Long Beach; Linda Rea, Hiram College; Carole Warshaw, Lynn University; and Dennis L. Wignall, Saginaw Valley State University.

Finally, we express our gratitude to the countless users of previous editions who have allowed us to "talk to them" about intercultural communication. Although it may have been a rather intangible connection, we have greatly appreciated it all the same.

Approaches to Intercultural Communication

1

Every tale can be told in a different way.

GREEK PROVERB

Intercultural communication is an important form of human interaction that has been practiced for as long as people from different cultures have encountered one another. Intercultural contacts are now a normal occurrence for most people, and cultural diversity is a fact of life. As obvious as intercultural interaction may be, only during the past 40 or so years has there been a serious and systematic study of the dynamics inherent in intercultural communication. Cultural diversity is now recognized as a crucial factor when the communication process involves people from different cultures.

A major impetus behind the quest to understand intercultural communication is the recognition that science and technology have produced the means for humankind's self-destruction. Historically, intercultural communication, more often than not, employed a rhetoric of force rather than reason. But with the recognition that the effect of force is severely limited, people increasingly seek to achieve their goals through communication rather than force. A second important reason to study intercultural communication is also pragmatic. Easy mobility, increased contact among cultures, a global marketplace, and multinational business organizations and workforces have led to the development of communication skills appropriate to life in a multicultural global village.

Before the mid-20th century, intercultural communication was limited to a small portion of the world's populace. Government representatives, merchants and traders, missionaries, explorers, and tourists were the primary visitors to foreign cultures. Historically, people in the United States had little contact with other cultures, even within their own country. Members of nonwhite races were generally segregated. Only since the mid-1960s have laws been changed to require integrated schools, workforces, and, to some extent, neighborhoods. In addition, those who made up the vast, white, Euro-America remained at home, rarely leaving their own county. This situation, of course, has changed markedly; the United States is now a mobile society interacting regularly with other mobile societies.

This increased contact with other cultures and domestic co-cultures makes it imperative that you make a concerted effort to understand and get along with people who may be significantly different from you. Your ability to coexist peacefully with people who do not necessarily share your background, views, beliefs, values, customs, habits, or lifestyle can benefit you in your own neighborhoods and can be a decisive factor in forestalling international conflict.

Before we begin our inquiry, we must specify the nature of intercultural communication and recognize that people who hold various viewpoints see it somewhat differently. From what we have already said, you should suspect that the topic of intercultural communication can be explored in a variety of ways. Scholars who look at it from a mass media perspective are concerned with such issues as international broadcasting, worldwide freedom of expression, the West's domination of information, and the use of modern electronic technologies for instantaneous worldwide transmission of information. Other groups investigate international communication with an emphasis on communication between nations and governments; this is the communication of diplomacy and propaganda. Still others are interested in the communication inherent in worldwide business, which includes such diverse concerns as international marketing and negotiations as well as day-to-day communication within multinational organizations.

Our concern is with the more personal aspects of communication: What happens when people from different cultures interact face-to-face? Hence, our approach examines the interpersonal dimensions of intercultural communication in a variety of contexts. The essays we have selected for this collection focus on those variables of both culture and communication that most affect the intercultural communication encounter—those occasions on which you are attempting to share information, ideas, and feelings with someone from a different culture.

Inquiry into the nature of intercultural communication has raised many questions, and has produced some theories. But knowledge about intercultural communication is far from complete. Much inquiry has been associated with fields other than communication: anthropology, international relations, sociology, social psychology, and socio- and psycholinguistics. Although the range of research topics has been wide, the acquired knowledge has not been fully integrated. Much that has emerged has been more a reaction to current sociological, racial, and ethnic concerns than an attempt to define and explain intercultural communication. It is clear, however, that knowledge of intercultural communication can temper communication problems before they arise. Schoolteachers who understand cultural diversity in motivation and learning styles are more likely to be successful in their multicultural classrooms. Teachers who recognize something as simple as cultural differences in the nonverbal use of eye contact can experience improvement in multicultural classroom communication. And health care workers who understand that some people treat illness as an invoked curse may be able to deliver better health care. In essence, we believe that many problems can be avoided by understanding the components of intercultural communication. This book, by applying those components to numerous cultures, seeks to contribute to that understanding.

We begin this exploration of intercultural communication with a series of diverse articles that will (1) introduce the philosophy underlying our concepts of intercultural communication; (2) provide a general orientation to, and overview of, intercultural communication; (3) theorize about the analysis of intercultural transactions; (4) provide insight into cultural diversity; and (5) demonstrate the relationship between culture and perception. Our purpose at this point is to give you a sufficient introduction to the many diverse dimensions of intercultural communication so that you will be able to approach the remainder of this volume in an appropriate frame of mind to make further inquiry interesting, informative, and useful.

We begin with an essay by the three editors of this book titled "Understanding Intercultural Communication: An Overview," which will introduce you to many of the specific subjects and issues associated with the study of intercultural communication. As a preface to the essay, we remind you of the importance of intercultural communication both at home and aboard. Next we discuss the purpose of communication, define it, and offer a review of its characteristics. Third, we examine the purpose of culture. We then turn our attention to the specific dimensions of culture that are most germane to human communication—those aspects of culture that form the field of intercultural communication. We examine these major variables—perceptual elements, verbal and nonverbal behavior, patterns of cognition, and social contexts—so you will better understand what happens when people of diverse cultural backgrounds engage in communication. By knowing at the outset of the book what the study of intercultural communication entails, you should have a greater appreciation for the essays that follow.

Thus, the first essay will introduce you to the concepts of intercultural communication and give you some notion of what is encompassed by the term *culture*. The problem here, however, is that the meaning of culture is somewhat "fuzzy." In the next essay, "Imagining Culture with a Little Help from the Pushmi-Pullyu," Aaron Castelan Cargile attempts to remedy this situation. Cargile reviews definitions of culture and demonstrates how they have developed into rather lengthy lists of components and characteristics that are symbolic, learned, transmitted, changing, and ethnocentric. To this list, Cargile adds the characteristic that culture is dialectical in nature, and he proceeds to imagine culture through the lens of dialectics.

A dialectical approach to understanding is, as Cargile points out, "one of the oldest of philosophic concepts, dating back to 900 B.C." Its early roots are identified with Heraclitus, Lao Tzu, Plato, and Aristotle. In more recent times, Kant, Hegel, Marx, and Bakhtin have added to the idea. From this perspective, culture exists as part of a larger whole in a dynamic, push-pull relationship.

Cargile uses the pushmi-pullyu metaphor to focus on the complex, dynamic, and sometimes contradictory interplay between the various facets of culture. He shows, for instance, that American culture "has been the site of movements toward justice for all [while] it has sponsored movements reinforcing the power structure." From a dialectical point of view, he sees this as unsurprising because equality and hierarchy are two faces of the same coin. At times the forces are balanced, and other times they move in one direction or the other. Neither will "finally dominate this (or any other) culture because they are eternal partners in the ongoing labor of group life."

Cargile uses his dialectical perspective to examine the influence of individualism and collectivism within cultures. Because of the "pushmi-pullyu" nature of culture, "no culture is completely free of the influence of either individualism or collectivism." He sees these as ubiquitous forces in a constant pushing and pulling in unique dynamic configurations that characterize a culture. He applies this notion to such issues as equality/hierarchy, tolerance/intolerance, and assimilation/differentiation among cultural groups. In each instance he demonstrates the dialectical dynamic between these cultural characteristics.

The next essay, by Harry C. Triandis, introduces you to another way of approaching intercultural communication. Triandis begins by underscoring one of the propositions of this book—that culture and communication are linked. But he goes on to show that cultural distances often lead to and cause miscommunications and conflict.

You will see this connection when he speaks of culture as including "the knowledge that people need to have in order to function effectively in their social environment."

To help you identify what "knowledge" is most useful when interacting with another culture, Triandis examines what he calls *cultural syndromes*. A cultural syndrome "is a shared pattern of beliefs, attitudes, self-definitions, norms, and values organized around a theme." In his discussion, Triandis includes the following syndromes: *complexity, tightness, individualism and collectivism, vertical and horizontal cultures, active-passive cultures, universalism-particularism, diffuse-specific, instrumental-expressive, emotional expression or suppression,* and the *weights given to different attributes in social perception*. Miscommunications occur because people are not aware of these syndromes. Because effective intercultural communication is so dependent on mutual knowledge of the prevalent diversity, we ask you to learn about these syndromes as part of your training in intercultural communication.

Triandis believes that when people come into contact with members of other cultures, they pass through four stages of communication competence. He calls the first stage, in which people are not aware there are problems, *unconscious incompetence.* As the realization grows that miscommunication is occurring, people move into the state of *conscious incompetence,* in which they realize something is wrong but do know what it is. As shared cultural knowledge increases, people begin to communicate correctly, but it requires an effort on their part. This is the stage of *conscious competence.* The final stage of *unconscious competence* occurs when communication becomes effortless and is correct.

We extend our study of culture with an essay, written by Satoshi Ishii, Donald Klopf, and Peggy Cooke, that uses the concept of *worldview* as a means of looking at culture. In "Our Locus in the Universe: Worldview and Intercultural Communication," you will see that worldview is a systemized totality of beliefs about the world. Thus, a culture's worldview represents a collective description of how the cosmos and universe function and how each individual fits into that religious and philosophical scheme. More specifically, worldview helps each person find answers to questions about pain, suffering, death, and the meaning of life. The basic premise the authors express is that worldview shapes a culture's psyche and helps the members of that culture make sense of the world. Worldview also, as the authors note, distinguishes one culture from another.

Although worldviews can take a variety of forms (scientific, metaphysical, and religious), most scholars agree with the assertion by Ishii, Klopf, and Cooke that religion is the most "pervasive determinant of worldview." Even a secular person is touched by the writings, attitudes, beliefs, and ethics advanced by the great religious traditions. To help you appreciate the influence of religion on culture, the authors highlight the major dimensions of Eastern and Western religions. As a means of connecting religion to culture and communication, the authors end their essay with a discussion of some of the problems that might occur when Eastern and Western worldviews collide.

The last essay in this chapter is "The Practice of Intercultural Communication: Reflections for Professionals in Cultural Meetings" by Ibsen Jensen. Jensen argues that globalization has two major implications for intercultural communication. The first is the emergence of a group of professional practitioners of intercultural communication within multiethnic societies. The second issue is that of cultural identity. Jensen holds that cultural identity is one of the most important concepts in intercultural research. So, in fact, do we, hence the next chapter is devoted to that topic.

Jensen divides his essay into three parts. In the first, he discusses how intercultural communication research can assist professional practitioners in multiethnic societies. In the second, he presents four analytical tools for intercultural communication as seen from a poststructuralist perspective. Finally, Jensen discusses the concepts of cultural identity in relation to intercultural communication.

A major portion of Jensen's essay deals with his model of intercultural communication. Here he posits "positions of experiences," which refers to the fact that all perceptual interpretations are bounded by individual experiences that are related to the person's social position. For Jensen, positions of experiences encompass cultural presuppositions and cultural self-perception. In addition, Jensen discusses "cultural fix points," the requirement that both parties to an intercultural communication situation identify with the topic. The next major component of Jensen's model involves cultural identity in intercultural communication.

Jensen ends his essay with a discussion of cultural identity as an analytical tool. He proposes that cultural identity is not determined only by race, ethnicity, or nation but incorporates a wide variety of different kinds of identity such as gender, work, and leisure pursuits.

Understanding Intercultural Communication: An Overview

Edwin R. McDaniel
Larry A. Samovar
Richard E. Porter

INTERCULTURAL COMMUNICATION IN CONTEMPORARY SOCIETY

The origins of intercultural communication are as old as humankind. The earliest historical records report periodic interactions between peoples from different tribes and varying geographical regions. All too frequently the encounters were hostile, with one group intent on subjugating or destroying the other. Fortunately, there were also meetings motivated by trade, which necessitated a more civil mode of interaction and required that both parties arrive at common agreements, always using the medium of communication.

The passage of time brought increased contact between peoples from different cultures. Conflicts and disagreements continued to plague many of these meetings, just as they do today, and other encounters were dominated by economic interests. War and commerce, however, concurrently provided a forum for broad cultural exchange. For example, religious prelates accompanying or close behind invading armies and merchants helped promote the spread of the world's three largest religions—Islam, Buddhism, and Christianity. Languages, arts, and technology were also expanded across cultures by the growing number of contacts with other societies. Alliances and treaties provided yet another form for cultural exchange and the practice of intercultural communication.

The rise of nation states, coupled with technological advances, prompted developed countries to begin voyages of exploration in search of new lands for acquisition of natural resources, trade, and religious conversion. These explorations also increased the need for treaties and alliances, expanding the requirement for intercultural communication. The age of discovery ultimately gave way to an era of colonialism, with the great powers subjugating less developed nations in order to control and extract raw materials to feed the European and U.S. industrial economies. Colonialism continued in various forms, sometimes virulent and sometimes benign, until after World War II.

World War II created a new world political and economic order, with nations divided into three camps: (1) those countries dominated by the communist political system and the attendant planned economies; (2) the states advocating democracy and a free market economy; and (3) the unaligned nations, which often served as the battleground for the two contending ideologies. This volatile geopolitical environment fostered a growing need for intercultural communication as international tensions ebbed and flowed, frequently moving to the brink of nuclear war. Behind these political polemics, however, international commerce continued to grow in size and importance.

The fall of the Berlin Wall in 1989 ended the era of bipolar power relations and concomitantly opened the door to a multipolar political order. No longer is the world divided into communist, democratic, and nonaligned nation blocs. We now live in a world of political multipolarism and economic convergence, driven by technological advances. Dismemberment of the former communist bloc released long suppressed forces of nationalism and gave rise to numerous new and renascent political demarcations. Concurrently, modern transportation, production, and telecommunications technologies significantly reduced time- and distance-related barriers, expanding political interconnectedness and creating greater economic interdependencies. Contemporary international business has greatly reduced the influence and significance of national borders and fostered a growing number of government-orchestrated regional alliances—NAFTA, APEC, EU, MERCOSUR—based on economics, rather than national security considerations.

These continually evolving changes, accompanied by a new wave of immigration from less developed to industrialized nations, have produced a global setting

---

 Edwin R. McDaniel teaches at Aichi Shukutoku University, Aichi, Japan. Larry Samovar is Professor Emeritus at San Diego State University. Richard E. Porter is Professor Emeritus at California State University, Long Beach.

characterized by increased contact among peoples from different cultural settings. The contacts, which take a variety of forms ranging from diplomatic, political, and military missions to international commerce and increased social interactions, are sometimes conflictive but more frequently mutually beneficial.

The forces coalescing to form a new world order have also brought change to the U.S. domestic population. The civil rights legislation of the 1960s encouraged minority groups to demand equal treatment under the law. The value of diversity in the workforce is now recognized and promoted. A new wave of immigration has brought people from the south, east, and west to the U.S. in search of enhanced economic opportunity, freedom from political oppression, and the opportunity to live life beyond the threat of armed conflict. As a result, the U.S. demographics have shifted dramatically. For example, in Southern California, minority groups now collectively outnumber the white majority. The new arrivals bring with them their cultural values, perspectives, and languages, which must be integrated with U.S. cultural traditions. Not infrequently, this mixing creates misunderstanding and conflict, but more often, it offers a rich medium for exchange and growth.

Although there is no crystal ball to help forecast the future, it is saliently clear that globalization is increasing the interactions between peoples of different cultures and that these exchanges, both domestic and international, will continue to grow in frequency and importance. The meeting of peoples from diverse national and ethnic cultures will certainly produce tensions and even conflicts—political, organizational, and personal—that can only be resolved by effective communication that bridges the differences.

The United States and China are now competing for oil to drive their respective economic engines. Human rights organizations are demanding that all nations adhere to a similar standard. Environmental agencies are lobbying for international acceptance and adherence to agreements that will reduce pollution. Mass communication makes media accessible from any part of the world, but some nations and cultures object to the values reflected in Western entertainment media. Ideological differences continue to create conflict and harbor the prospect of future clashes. Willingly or not, we are all thrust into a new world order characterized by increasing levels of contact and communication with people of other cultures. This evolving social setting has created a mandate for greater understanding and improved communication across cultural boundaries. In sum, we must learn how to become effective intercultural communicators.

As the first step on our path to learning how to employ effective intercultural communication, we will begin with a fundamental definition: *Intercultural communication occurs whenever a message produced in one culture must be processed in another culture.* Although this definition may seem simple and undemanding, it requires a thorough understanding of two key ingredients—communication and culture. Thus, we will first examine communication and its various components. Then, culture will be explained. Finally, we will explore how these two concepts are fused into intercultural communication.

UNDERSTANDING COMMUNICATION

We live in a communication-saturated environment. Frequently, the first thing we do in the morning is turn on the TV or radio. Commuting to class, we are exposed to signs and billboards, often while continuing to listen to the radio or playing a CD. The classroom is filled with communicative interactions such as lectures, group projects, reading a textbook, or even sitting in the back of the room talking with a classmate. Time between classes is used for such activities as meeting with a study group, talking with friends over coffee, or arranging plans for a weekend party. After class, many students have jobs where they use communication to interact with other employees or customers. Evenings are taken up with study, watching TV, catching a movie, meeting a significant other, calling a friend, or phoning home in hopes of getting help with the latest credit card bill. Finally, at day's end, we might spend a few moments with the TV or listening to music to relax before drifting off to sleep.

These are simply a few of the instances of communication encountered on a daily basis. To function normally in our information-driven society, we cannot avoid communicating. Moreover, we seem to have an innate need to associate with, and connect to, other people through communication. Thus, the motives for entering into communicative interactions can be classified into one of three categories. When we communicate, regardless of the situation, we are trying either to persuade, to inform, or to entertain. In other words, we communicate for a purpose; we have an objective.

Communication Defined

We have argued and attempted to demonstrate that communication is instrumental to daily life, something that cannot readily be avoided or escaped. But what exactly is communication? What happens when we communicate? To answer these questions, we need to define and explain the phenomenon.

Communication has been defined variously, often depending on the writer's objective or the specific scenario. Indeed, one could consult a wide variety of communication textbooks and journal articles without uncovering two identical definitions. Often the definitions are long and cumbersome, as the author attempts to encompass as many aspects of communication as possible. In other places, the definition is narrow and precise, designed to explain a specific type or instance of communication. For understanding the union of culture and communication, however, a succinct, clearly comprehensible definition best serves everyone's interests. Thus, for us, *communication is the management of messages with the objective of creating meaning* (Griffin, 2003). This definition is somewhat all-encompassing, yet is precise in specifying what takes place in every communicative event. Nor does it attempt to ascertain what constitutes successful or unsuccessful communication, which is actually determined by the participants, can vary from one person to the next, and is often scenario dependent. The only qualifiers we place on communication are intentionality and interaction. In other words, if communication is considered to be purposeful—to persuade, inform, or entertain—then we communicate intentionally, and we achieve these objectives only through interaction with another person or persons.

The Components of Communication

Using our definition of communication, we are now ready to examine the eight major structural components used to manage messages in the creation of meaning. The first and most obvious component is the **sender**—the individual or group originating the message. A sender is someone with a need or desire, be it social, occupational, or information driven, to communicate with others. To sate this motivation, the sender formulates and transmits the message via a channel to the receiver(s).

The **message** consists of the information the sender desires to have understood—what is used to create meaning. Messages characteristically take the form of verbal or nonverbal behaviors, which are encoded and transmitted via a **channel** to the receiver. The channel is any means that provides a path for moving the message from the sender to the receiver. For example, an oral message may be sent directly when in the immediate presence of the receiver or mediated through a cell phone. A visual, or nonverbal, message can be transmitted by waving good-bye to a friend as you drive away or mediated through a video camera or a picture.

The **receiver** is the intended recipient of the message and the locus for creating the meaning. Because the receiver interprets the message and assigns a meaning, which may or may not be what the receiver proposed, communication is often characterized as *receiver based*. You may formulate a message designed to have a friend meet you at the local coffee shop before class. However, the receiver may (mis)interpret the message and show up after class. After interpreting the message and assigning a meaning, the receiver will formulate a **response.** This is the action taken by the receiver as a result of the meaning he or she assigns to the message. A response can be benign, such as simply ignoring a provocative remark, or, at the other extreme, a physically aggressive act of violence.

Feedback is an important component of communication related to, yet separate from, the response. Feedback is what allows us to assign a qualitative evaluation to the effectiveness of a message. Perhaps the receiver smiles, or frowns, after decoding our message. This gives us a clue as to how the message has been interpreted and facilitates adjustment of our behavior to the developing situation. Depending on the feedback, we may rephrase or amplify our message to provide greater clarity, or even retract the statement.

Every communicative interaction takes place in an **environment,** both physical and contextual. The physical environment refers to the actual place where the communication takes place, such as a classroom, library, business office, or restaurant. The contextual, or social, environment is more abstract and influences the style of communication employed. Think about the different styles of communication employed during an interview or when applying for a student loan, asking a friend for a favor, visiting your professor during office hours, or apologizing for being late on a date. We vary our communicative style in response to the occasion—the contextual environment.

The final component of communication, **noise,** relates to the different types of interference or distractions that plague every communication event. *Physical noise* is apart from the communication participants and can take many forms, such as a classmate tapping her pencil on the desktop, a skateboarder rolling past the open classroom door, the sounds of ongoing construction across the street, or static from the instructor's microphone.

Noise that is intrinsic to the people participating in the communication episode can take a variety of forms. Suppose during a Friday afternoon class you find yourself concentrating more on an upcoming weekend road trip than on the lecture. Perhaps you had a fight with your roommate and are trying to think of a way to apologize, or the midterm test scheduled for next week has you worried. These are all examples of *psychological noise* that diminishes your understanding of the classroom communication. *Physiological noise* relates to the physical well-being of the people engaged in the communication activity. Coming to class with too little sleep, feeling hungry, or dealing with a head cold will interfere with the ability to comprehend the classroom lesson.

The final type of noise is the one most common to intercultural communication and most likely to produce misunderstandings. For effective communication in an intercultural event, the participants must employ a common language, which often means that one or more individuals will not be using their native tongue. Total fluency in a second language is difficult and somewhat rare. Most people who use another language will commonly demonstrate an accent or perhaps misuse a word or phrase, which can adversely influence understanding of the message. This type of distraction, referred to as *semantic noise,* also encompasses jargon, slang, and even specialized professional terminology (West & Turner, 2004).

Collectively, these eight components provide an overview of factors that facilitate and shape ongoing communication encounters. Also of importance is the role of culture in each component, which is especially influential in intercultural communication. To appreciate culture's impact on communication, we must first have an understanding of culture itself.

UNDERSTANDING CULTURE

Culture is a popular and widely used, often overused, word in contemporary society. Terms such as *cultural differences, cultural diversity, multiculturalism, corporate culture, cross-culture,* and other variations continually appear in the popular media. Culture has been tied to such fields as management, health care, psychology, education, public relations, marketing, and advertising. We often hear how U.S. forces operating in Iraq and Afghanistan are hampered by insufficient awareness and understanding of the local culture. The pervasive use of the term attests to the increased role that culture plays in today's social order. Seldom, however, are we provided a definition of exactly what culture is, what it does, or what it encompasses. This section will answer those questions.

Culture Defined

Similar to the treatment of communication, culture has been the topic of numerous and often complex, abstract definitions as writers have endeavored to incorporate a broad array of cultural components and objectives. For example, the noted social anthropologist Clifford Geertz defined culture as "a historically transmitted pattern of meaning embodied in symbols, a system of inherited conceptions expressed in symbolic forms by means of which men communicate, perpetuate, and develop their knowledge about and attitudes toward life" (1973, p. 89). Definitions commonly mention shared values, attitudes, beliefs, behaviors, norms, and material objects (e.g., Brislin, 1990; Martin & Nakayama, 2005; Neuliep, 2003; Rogers & Steinfatt, 1999; Triandis, 1995), and all are quite correct. Indeed, the many and varied definitions attest to the complexity of this social concept called culture.

For our purposes, however, we offer a more applied definition. For a moment, think about what the word *football* brings to mind. Most U.S. Americans will picture two teams of 11 men each in helmets and pads, but someone in Montréal, Canada, would imagine 12 men per team. A resident of Sidney, Australia, may think of two 18-man teams in shorts and jerseys endeavoring to kick an oblong ball between two uprights, while a young woman in Sao Palo, Brazil, would probably envision two teams of 11 men, or women, attempting to kick a round ball into a net. In each case, the contest is referred to as "football," but the playing fields and rules of each game are quite different.

Now recall your first visit to an ethnic restaurant that was completely different from any previous experience. When sitting down at the sushi counter, did you know what to order? At the South Indian vegetarian buffet, did you wonder why they provided a large tray and many small bowls of varying size and shape instead of plates? Were you surprised that there was no menu at the Chinese *dim sum* restaurant? Yet you probably saw Japanese, Indians, and Chinese ordering and eating in these respective establishments without hesitation or difficulty. They knew the proper rules for obtaining and enjoying their food.

We can draw on these two examples for an applied definition of culture. Simply stated, *culture is the rules for living and functioning in society*. In other words, culture provides the rules for playing the game of life (Gudykunst, 2004; Yamada, 1997). The rules will differ from society to society, and to function and be effective in a particular society, one must know how to apply the rules. We learn the rules of our own culture as a matter of course, beginning at birth and continuing throughout life. As a result, the rules are ingrained in our subconscious, enabling us to react to familiar situations without thinking. It is when we enter another culture, with different rules, that problems begin to arise.

The Purpose of Culture

If we accept that culture can be considered as a set of rules, culture's purpose becomes somewhat evident. Cultural rules provide a framework for imparting meaning to events, objects, and people. The rules enable us to make sense of our surroundings and reduce uncertainty about the social environment. Recall your first date in high school. No doubt there was a degree of nervousness because you wanted to make a good impression and have things go well. During the date you may have had a few thoughts about what to do and what not to do. Overall, however, you had a good idea of the proper courtesies, what to talk about, and generally how to behave. This is because you had learned the proper rules of behavior by listening to and observing others. Now, take that same situation and imagine going out on a date for the first time with someone from a different country, such as Korea or Indonesia. Would you know what to say and do? Would those cultural rules you had been learning since birth be applicable in this new social situation?

Culture also functions to instill in us an identity, or sense of self. From childhood, we are inculcated with the idea of belonging to a variety of groups—family, community, church, sports teams, schools—and these memberships form our different identities. Our cultural identity is derived from our "sense of belonging to a particular cultural or ethnic group" (Lustig & Koester, 2000, p. 3), which may be Chinese, Mexican American, African American, Greek, Egyptian, Jewish, or one or more of many, many other possibilities. Growing up, we learn the rules of social deportment appropriate to our specific cultural group, or groups in the case of multicultural families such as Vietnamese American, Italian American, or Russian American. Cultural identity becomes especially salient in interactions between people from different cultural groups who have been taught different sets of rules for social interaction. Thus, cultural identity can be a significant factor in the practice of intercultural communication.

The Characteristics of Culture

Although definitions are many and varied, there is a community of agreement on what constitutes the major characteristics of culture. An exploration of these characteristics will provide increased understanding of the amorphous, complex concept called culture and also give insight into how communication is influenced.

Culture Is Learned. At birth, we have no knowledge of the many cultural rules necessary for functioning in society, but we very quickly begin to internalize this information. Through interactions, observations, and imitation, the proper ways of thinking and behaving are communicated to us. Being taught to eat with a fork, a pair of chopsticks, or even our fingers is learning culture behavior. Attending a Catholic mass or praying at a mosque is learning cultural behaviors and values. Celebrating Christmas, Kwanza, Ramadan, or Passover is learning cultural traditions. Culture is also learned from art, proverbs, folklore, history, and a multiplicity of other sources. This learning, often called enculturation, occurs at both conscious and subconscious levels, with the common objective of teaching us how to function properly within our cultural milieu.

Culture Is Transmitted Intergenerationally. The Spanish philosopher George Santayana wrote, "Those who cannot remember the past are condemned to repeat it." Clearly he was not referring to culture, which exists only because it is remembered and repeated by people. Your culture was learned from family members, teachers, peers, books, personal observations, and a host of additional sources. The appropriate way to act, what to say, and things to value were communicated to the members of your generation by a variety of sources. You are a source for communicating these cultural expectations, with little or no variation, to succeeding generations. Culture represents our link to past and future generations, and communication is the critical factor in this equation.

Culture Is Symbolic. Words, gestures, and images are merely symbols used to convey meaning. It is this ability to use symbols that allows us to engage in the many forms of social intercourse necessary for constructing and conveying culture. Our symbol-making ability enables learning and facilitates transmission from one person to another, group to group, and generation to generation. In addition to transmission, the portability of symbols facilitates the storage of information, which allows cultures to preserve what is considered important. The preservation of culture provides each new generation with a road map to follow and a reference library to consult when unknown situations are encountered. This depository of knowledge gives culture a historical characteristic. Succeeding generations may advance new behaviors or values, but the accumulation of past traditions is what we know as culture.

Culture Is Dynamic. Despite its historical nature, culture is by no means static. Within a culture, new ideas and inventions bring about change. One has only to look at discoveries like the stirrup, gunpowder, the nautical compass, penicillin, or nuclear power to understand culture's susceptibility to innovation and new ideas. More recently, advances made by minority groups and the women's movement since the early 1970s have significantly altered the fabric of U.S. society. Invention of the computer chip has brought profound changes not only to U.S. culture but also to that of most developed countries and many underdeveloped nations.

Diffusion, or cultural borrowing, is also a source of change. Despite the impression conveyed in the movie *The Last Samurai,* the Japanese adopted and began manufacturing firearms almost immediately after they were introduced to the islands by the Portuguese, in the late 1500s. Proliferation of the Internet has produced global cultural change by giving people access to new knowledge and insights. Immigrants bring their own cultural practices, traditions, and artifacts, some of which become incorporated into the culture of their new homeland—for example, Vietnamese noodle shops in the United States, Indian restaurants in England, or Japanese foods in Brazil.

Cultural calamity, such as war, political upheaval, or large-scale natural disasters, can also bring about change. U.S. intervention in Afghanistan is bringing greater equality to the women of that nation. The traditional culture of Zimbabwe is being eroded as a result of a repressive political dictatorship. Citizen outcry about government failures in the wake of the Great Hanshin Earthquake, which devastated Kobe, Japan, in 1995, produced changes lessening the traditional power of the bureaucracy (Hendry, 2003).

Most of the changes affecting culture are somewhat topical, such as dress, food preference, modes of transportation, or housing, and remain attached to the underlying cultural value system. Values, ethnics, morals, the importance of religion, or attitudes toward gender, age, and sexual orientation, which constitute the deep structures of culture, are far more resistant to major change and tend to endure from generation to generation. This resistance was exemplified during the most recent presidential campaign when both candidates' continually promised to preserve "traditional U.S. values."

Culture Is Ethnocentric. The strong sense of group identity, or attachment, produced by culture can also lead to ethnocentrism, the tendency to value or place one's own culture in a superior position relative to other cultures. Ethnocentrism can be a product of enculturation. Being continually told that that you live in the greatest country in the world or that your way of life is better than those of other nations or ethnic groups can lead to feelings of cultural superiority, especially among children. Ethnocentrism can also be a result of underexposure to other cultures. If exposed only to a U.S. cultural orientation, it is likely that you would develop the idea that our country is the center of the world, and you would tend to view the rest of the world from the perspective of U.S. culture.

An inability to understand or accept different ways and customs can also provoke feelings of ethnocentrism. It is quite natural to feel at ease with people who are like us and adhere to the same social norms and protocols. It is also normal to feel uneasy when confronted with new and different social values, beliefs, and behaviors. However, to view or evaluate those dissimilarities negatively simply because they are different from your expectations is a product of ethnocentrism. It should be self-evident that a disposition toward ethnocentrism would be especially detrimental to effective intercultural communication.

COMMUNICATION AND CULTURE

As we have demonstrated, culture is an extremely complex, abstract, and amorphous concept that exerts a pervasive influence on every aspect of our lives. A number of cultural components are particularly relevant to the study of intercultural communication. These include (1) perceptual elements, (2) patterns of cognition, (3) verbal behaviors, (4) nonverbal behaviors, and (5) the influence of context. Although each of these components will be discussed separately, in an intercultural situation all of them function concurrently.

Perceptual Elements

We are daily bombarded with a wide variety of stimuli that must be processed and assigned meaning. This process of selecting, organizing, and evaluating stimuli is referred to as perception. The volume of environmental stimuli is far too large for us to attend to everything, so we select only what is considered relevant or interesting. After determining what we will pay attention to, the next step is organizing the selected stimuli so they can be evaluated. Just as in this text, the university library, or CNN news, information must be given a structure before it can be interpreted. The third step of perception then becomes a process of evaluating and assigning meaning to the stimuli.

A commonly accepted assumption is that people conduct their lives in accordance with how they perceive the world, and these perceptions are strongly influenced by culture. In other words, we see, hear, feel, taste, and even smell the world through the criteria that culture has placed on our perceptions. Thus, one's idea of beauty, attitude toward the elderly, and concept of self in relation to others are culturally influenced and can vary between social groups. Perception is an important aspect of intercultural communication, because people from separate cultures frequently perceive the world differently. Thus, it is important to be aware of the more important sociocultural elements that have a significant and direct influence on the meanings we assign to stimuli. These elements represent our belief, value, and attitude systems and our worldview.

Beliefs, Values, and Attitudes. **Beliefs** may be defined as individually held subjective ideas about the nature of an object or event. These subjective ideas are, in large part, a product of culture, and they directly influence our behaviors. If you believe that horses are intended to be used only for work or pleasure, the thought of eating horsemeat may well be repulsive. Some people believe in only one god, and others pay homage to multiple deities.

Values are what we hold important in life and include such qualities as morality, ethics, and aesthetics. We use values to distinguish between the desirable and the undesirable. Each person has a set of unique, personal values and a set of cultural values. The latter are a reflection of the rules a culture has established to reduce uncertainty, mitigate conflict, help in decision making, and provide structure to social organization and interactions. Cultural values are a motivating force behind behaviors. Someone from a culture that places a high value on harmonious social relations, such as Japan, will likely employ an indirect communication style. In contrast, a U.S. American can be expected to use a more direct communication style, because frankness, honesty, and openness are admired.

Our beliefs and values push us to hold certain **attitudes,** which can be defined as learned tendencies to act or respond in a specific way to events, objects, people, or orientations. Culturally instilled beliefs and values exert a strong influence on attitudinal dispositions. Thus, people tend to embrace what is liked and avoid what is disliked. Someone from a culture that reveres cows will take a negative attitude toward eating beef.

Worldview. Though quite abstract, worldview is among the most import elements of the perceptual attributes influencing intercultural communication. Simply stated, a culture's worldview forms people's orientation toward such philosophical concepts as god, the universe, nature, and the like. Normally, worldview is deeply imbedded in one's psyche and usually operates on a subconscious level. This can be problematic in an intercultural environment, where conflicting worldviews may come into play. As an example, many Asian and Native North American cultures possess a worldview that people should have a harmonious, symbiotic relationship with nature. In contrast, Euro-Americans are imbued with the concept that people must conquer and shape nature to conform to personal needs and desires. Individuals from nations possessing these incongruent worldviews could well encounter difficulties when working to develop an international environmental protection accord.

Patterns of Cognition

Another important consideration in intercultural communication is the influence of culture in cognitive thinking patterns, which includes reasoning and approaches to problem solving. Culture can often produce variant ways of knowing and doing. Nisbett (2003) has verified that Northeast Asians (Chinese, Japanese, and Koreans) employ a holistic thinking pattern, whereas Westerners use a linear, cause-and-effect model. To be more explicit, Westerners place considerable value on logical reasoning and rationality. Thus, problems can best be solved by a systematic, in-depth analysis of individual components, progressing individually from the simple to the more complex. Northeast Asians, however, see problems as much more complex and interrelated, requiring a greater understanding of, and emphasis on, the collective rather than focusing on individual parts.

Thought patterns common to a culture affect the way individuals of that culture communicate and interact with people from another culture. To illustrate the potential of this problem, in Japanese–U.S. business negotiations, the Japanese have a tendency to revisit or reopen issues that the U.S. side considers concluded (McDaniel, 2000). U.S. negotiators find this practice to be frustrating and time-consuming, believing that once a point has been agreed to, it is completed. From the Japanese perspective, however, as new issues are examined, they can have an influence on previously discussed points. This example demonstrates the importance of understanding that variant patterns of cognition exist and learning to accommodate them in an intercultural communication encounter.

Verbal Behavior

The role of language in intercultural communication is self-evident in that all of the participants must, to some degree, share a language, be it their first or second. What is not so self-evident is the symbiosis that exists between culture and language, because one cannot exist without the other. Without a common language, a group of people would not be able to establish and perpetuate a culture. They would be unable to share their beliefs, values, social norms, and worldview with one another or to transmit these cultural characteristics to succeeding generations. In turn, culture helps people to establish, evolve, and preserve their language.

Language itself is merely a set of symbols that a cultural group has arbitrarily agreed upon in order to bring meaning to objects, events, emotions, experiences, places, and the like. Different cultures have, of course, decided to use different sets of symbols. However, the use of symbol systems to construct and express meaning is an inexact process, because the meanings for words are open to a variety of translations by both individuals and cultures. In an earlier example, the word *horse* was used to illustrate that someone from France or Japan may be stimulated to think of food, whereas someone from the United States or the United Kingdom may picture work or pleasure animals. The word *parallel* can also be used to demonstrate how culture influences meaning and leads to misunderstandings in intercultural communication. In the United States, telling someone they are on a "parallel" course implies agreement. In Japanese, however, "parallel" (*heikōsen*) is used to indicate that the parties disagree, because parallel lines never converge.

Nonverbal Behavior

Another critical factor in intercultural communication is nonverbal behavior, which encompasses gestures, facial expressions, eye contact and gaze, posture and movement, touch, dress, silence, the use of space and time, objects and artifacts, and paralanguage. These nonverbal behaviors are inextricably intertwined with verbal behaviors and often communicate as much or more meaning than the actual spoken words. As with language, culture also directly influences the use of, and meanings assigned to, nonverbal behavior. In intercultural communication, inappropriate or misused nonverbal behaviors can easily lead to misunderstandings and sometimes result in insults. Comprehensive treatment of all nonverbal behaviors is beyond the scope of this chapter, but we will draw on a few cultural-specific examples to demonstrate their importance in intercultural communication exchanges.

Nonverbal greeting behaviors show remarkable variance across cultures. In the United States, a firm handshake among men is the norm, but among some Middle Eastern cultures, a gentle grip is used. In Mexico, acquaintances will normally embrace (*abrazo*) each other after shaking hands. People from Japan and India traditionally bow to greet each other. Japanese men will place their hands to the side of the body and bow from the waist, with the subordinate individual bowing before and lower than the other person. Indians will perform the *namaste,* which entails holding the hands together in a prayer-like fashion at mid-chest and slightly bowing the head and shoulders (Axtell, 1991).

Another important culturally influenced nonverbal communication behavior is eye contact. Recently a student related the following incident to one of the authors. A young Euro-American elementary school teacher, in her first year, was assigned a class of predominantly minority-culture students. One minority student, while being addressed by the teacher, continually averted his eyes downward. The teacher felt the student was being disrespectful for not maintaining eye contact with her. Only later did the she learn that avoiding eye contact was a demonstration of respect in the student's culture. Among some Native Americans, children are taught to show adults respect by avoiding eye contact. When giving a presentation in Japan, it is common to see many people in the audience with their eyes shut, as this is thought to facilitate listening.

Nonverbal expressions, like language, comprise a coding system for constructing and expressing meaning, and these expressions are culture bound. Through culture, we learn which nonverbal behavior is proper for a particular social interaction. But what is appropriate and polite in one culture may be disrespectful or even insulting in another culture. Therefore, people engaging in intercultural communication should try to maintain a continual awareness of how body behaviors may influence the interaction.

The Role of Context

We have defined culture as a set of rules that have been established for conducting social intercourse among people of a cultural group. These rules determine what is considered correct communicative behavior, including both verbal and nonverbal elements, for both physical and social (situational) contexts. For example, you would not normally go to a job interview (social context) in the employer's office (physical context) dressed in beachwear or use profanity when addressing the interviewer. Your culture has taught you that these behaviors are contextually inappropriate, and they will not help you get the job.

Context is also an important consideration in intercultural communication meetings, where the rules for specific situations usually vary. What is appropriate in one culture is not necessarily correct in another. In the United States, funerals are traditionally a solemn occasion, but an Irish wake can be a boisterous gathering of family and friends (Brislin, 2000). In graduate seminars at U.S. universities, students are expected to actively discuss and critically examine the lesson material, with the professor serving as a moderator. In Japan, however, the professor will lecture the students, who listen attentively and seldom ask questions. Imagine the reaction of an international student who goes to his or her first seminar not knowing these differences.

In these two examples, we see the importance of having an awareness of the cultural rules governing the context of an intercultural communication exchange. Unless both parties in the exchange are sensitive to how culture affects the contextual aspects of communication, difficulties will most certainly arise and could negate effective interaction.

CONCLUSION

We began with a discussion of how the forces of contemporary geopolitics, technology, economics, and immigration have coalesced to produce an ever shrinking world community, making interaction among people from different cultures increasingly common and necessary. We will end with a reflection on the requirement and urgency of increased tolerance of cultural differences generated by this new world order.

The world population, as well as U.S. domestic demographics, is moving toward a pluralistic, multicultural society at a quickstep pace. The social forces behind this movement will not easily or soon abate. The resulting cultural mixing requires that we, both individually and as a society, become more tolerant of the beliefs, worldviews, values, and behaviors of people from other cultures. Acceptance or tolerance may not be appropriate in every situation, nor is universal, unquestioning acquiescence advocated. We do, however, have to become willing to "live and let live" on a broader scale. That we do not yet seem able or prepared to do this is demonstrated by ongoing international and domestic struggles.

The international community is riven with sectarian violence arising from ideological, cultural, and racial differences. As we write this chapter, in the western region of Sudan, people are being killed and driven from their homes as a result of cultural and racial differences. The conflict in Chechnya is motivated, in part, by religious ideology. Peace in the Balkan nations is maintained only through the presence of UN and U.S. peacekeeping forces. The contending religious factions in Northern Ireland have settled into an uneasy peace, but have not yet resolved their historically embedded cultural differences. The ongoing war on terrorism, a product of variant ideological and cultural perspectives, promises to be protracted and violent.

Intolerance of differences is also an issue in the United States, where we are divided over such culturally based issues as stem cell research, same-sex marriage, school prayer, affirmative action, assisted suicide, right to life versus freedom of choice, and how to deal with immigration problems. The demands of coping with diverse customs, values, views, and behaviors inherent in a multicultural society are producing increased levels of personal frustration, social stress, and often violence.

As the flow of immigrants and refugees continues to arrive in the United States and other developed nations, we will be confronted with increased cultural diversity. If we continue to assert that cultural diversity is a valuable, desirable asset and embrace the concept of a global village, we must quickly learn to accept and tolerate the resulting differences. We do not profess to have the solution for these problems. However, as a means of better preparing you for life in the global village, we do hope to stimulate thought and discussion about the advantages and difficulties of multiculturalism and the need for effective intercultural communication.

References

Axtell, R. E. (1991). *Gestures*. New York: John Wiley & Sons.

Brislin, R. W. (Ed.). (1990). Applied cross-cultural psychology: An introduction. In R. W. Brislin (Ed.), *Applied cross-cultural psychology* (pp. 9–33). Newbury Park, CA: Sage.

Brislin, R. W. (2000). *Understanding culture's influence on behavior* (2nd ed.). Fort Worth, TX: Harcourt.

Geertz, C. (1973). *The interpretation of cultures*. New York: Basic Books.

Griffin, E. (2003). *A first look at communication* theory (5th ed.). Boston: McGraw-Hill.

Gudykunst, W. B. (2004). *Bridging differences* (4th ed.). Thousand Oaks, CA: Sage.

Hendry, J. (2003). *Understanding Japanese society* (3rd ed.). London: Routledge Curzon.

Lustig, M. W., & Koester, J. (2000). The nature of cultural identity. In M. W. Lustig & J. Koester (Eds.), *Among us: Essays on identity, belonging, and intercultural competence* (pp. 3–8). New York: Longman.

Martin, J. N., & Nakayama, T. K. (2005). *Experiencing intercultural communication: An introduction* (2nd ed.). Boston: McGraw-Hill.

McDaniel, E. R. (2000). *Japanese negotiation practices: Low-context communication in a high-context culture.* Unpublished doctoral dissertation, Arizona State University.

Neuliep, J. W. (2003). *Intercultural cultural communication: A contextual approach* (2nd ed.). Boston: Houghton Mifflin.

Nisbett, R. (2003). *The geography of thought*. New York: Free Press.

Rogers, E. M., & Steinfatt, T. M. (1999). *Intercultural communication*. Prospect Heights, IL: Waveland.

Triandis, H. C. (1995). *Individualism and collectivism*. Boulder: CO: Westview Press.

West, R., & Turner, L. H. (2004). *Introducing communication theory: Analysis and application* (2nd ed.). Boston: McGraw-Hill.

Yamada, H. (1997). *Different games, different rules: Why Americans and Japanese misunderstand each other.* New York: Oxford University Press.

Concepts and Questions

1. Do you believe that most people are prepared to engage in intercultural communication?
2. In how many circumstances do you find yourself in situations where increased facility in intercultural communication would be useful?
3. How can knowledge of the basic principles of communication be useful in day-to-day life?
4. How do the authors define culture? Can you think of other definitions of culture that might serve you in understanding intercultural communication?
5. What is the purpose of culture?
6. What do the authors mean by the statement that "culture is learned"? Can you think of instances in your life that demonstrate the learning dynamic of culture?
7. Suggest several relationships between culture and communication.
8. What are cultural values? How do they relate to individual values?
9. Distinguish several ways in which verbal behavior may differ between cultures.
10. What role does context play in communication? How does context affect intercultural communication?

Imagining Culture with a Little Help from the Pushmi-Pullyu

AARON CASTELAN CARGILE

Pushmi-pullyus are now extinct. That means there aren't any more. But long ago, when Doctor Dolittle was alive, there were some of them still left. . . . They had no tail, but a head at each end, and sharp horns on each head. . . . [Most animals are caught] by sneaking up behind them while they are not looking. But you could not do this with the pushmi-pullyu—because, no matter which way you came toward him, he was always facing you. And besides, only one half of him slept at a time.

LOFTING, 1920/1988, p. 73

Just what is this "thing" called culture? Although nearly everyone has some sense of the concept, hardly anyone agrees as to what it is exactly, least of all cultural scholars. When the field of intercultural communication first began after World War II, there were at least 164 definitions of culture (Kroeber & Kluckhohn, 1952), and there are no fewer than 300 around today (Baldwin, Faulkner, Hecht, & Lindsley, in press). This begs the question, how are we supposed to learn something about culture when we're not even sure of what it is we are studying? Well, I believe that there is something to be learned if we can first appreciate a little bit of fuzziness and a lot of contradiction when it comes to culture. To do this, we will need a little help from the pushmi-pullyu.

The "problem" of the fuzziness of culture has been present from the beginning, when Tylor first defined the concept in 1871 as "that complex whole which includes knowledge, belief, art, morals, law, custom, and any other capabilities and habits acquired by man [sic] as a member of society" (1871/1958). The notion of a complex whole set many scholars down the path of itemizing everything that culture could include. Quite predictably, then, they ended up with

---

 Aaron Castelan Cargile teaches at California State University, Long Beach.

lists that looked a little bit different, one from the other. For example, Small stated that "culture is our whole body of technical equipment" (1905, p. 59), Harms suggested it is "the learning acquired by the members of a group in the process of living as they live" (1973, p. 32), and Glenn defined it as "the sum of total meanings shared by [a] population" (1966, p. 251).

Over the years, scholars have tried to prune down the concept for the sake of clarity (culture includes this but not that; e.g., Weiss, 1973), but like a plant, the idea of culture has grown back more fully than before. This is because we have all been romanced by Tylor; we concur that the root essence of culture is some sort of complex whole. Thus, how can any one definition, no matter how precise, ever take hold? It is highly unlikely. Consequently, most textbooks have given up on picking a single definition for culture and have focused instead on describing its general features. According to Samovar and Porter, "regardless of the definition employed, most people agree about the major characteristics of culture" (2003, p. 8). As they describe it, culture is widely agreed to be symbolic, learned, transmitted, changing, and ethnocentric. To this list I propose adding a sixth characteristic: Culture may also be considered dialectical in nature. Although not yet widely agreed to, imagining culture through the lens of dialectics will help us understand Tylor's notion of a complex whole more richly, thereby adding to our appreciation of this "thing" we call culture.

Before we go to such effort, however, it is useful to ask, why bother? Don't we understand culture well enough with the characteristics already listed? Indeed, we do understand quite a bit about culture, but our grasp of some important aspects of the complex whole remains underdeveloped. In particular, our desire to know something definite about a group of people and their culture has gotten in the way. Few of us want to end up seemingly uncertain about culture after having studied it, so most of us content ourselves with knowing only the unmistakable patterns. For example, you might "know" that the national culture of the United States is individualistic or that the national culture of Japan is collectivistic.

In many ways, this sort of clear, descriptive knowledge is both valid and valuable. However, culture is called a *complex* whole for good reason; there is more to it than that. As you may have noticed, the national culture of the United States is also collectivistic in many respects, just as that of Japan is individualistic as well. Indeed, some textbooks point out that cultural patterns are often contradictory. For example, Samovar and Porter note that "in the United States, we speak of 'all people being created equal,' yet we observe pervasive racial prejudice" (2004, p. 51). Researchers have also recognized these inconsistencies (e.g., Triandis, 1995). Thus, we are left to wonder how much we really understand culture by describing it using only the five widely agreed upon characteristics. It is this lack of appreciation for cultural contradiction that leads us back to dialectics and the pushmi-pullyu.

A DIALECTICAL PERSPECTIVE

The idea of dialectics is hardly new. In fact, it is one of the oldest of philosophic concepts, dating back to 900 B.C. (Lavine, 1984). In antiquity, Heraclitus, Lao Tzu, Socrates, Plato, and Aristotle were among those who wrote about it; more recently, Kant, Hegel, Marx, and Bakhtin have further developed the idea. Although each philosopher has defined dialectics in unique ways, the basic notion is one of *opposition.* Much like the four elements of antiquity (earth, air, fire, and water), things exist as part of a larger whole, and more specifically, in dynamic, push-pull relationships. For example, water was believed to offset the force of fire, and air balanced earth. In this manner, constant opposition, as symbolized by the pushmi-pullyu, is seen as a necessary and defining characteristic of dialectics.

Although important in many ancient philosophies, dialectics did not develop into a full philosophical worldview until the nineteenth century, thanks in large part to the work of Hegel. Hegel believed that all concepts are based within a structure of opposition that requires specification of what things *are not* in order to define what things *are.* In his words, "Every concept is rational, is abstractly opposed to another, and is united in comprehension together with its opposites. This is the definition of dialectic" (Hegel, 1959). For example, understanding the concept of "up" depends upon delimiting its negative—either "not up" or "down." Similarly, the notion of whiteness as a racial category depends upon the marking of nonwhiteness or "color." As Loewen reminds us, "there were no 'white' people in Europe before 1492. With the transatlantic slave trade, first Indian, then African, Europeans increasingly saw 'white' as a race and race as an important human characteristic" (1995, p. 67).

According to Hegel, although human concepts are grounded in opposition, people are nonetheless drawn to reconcile such opposition through a *synthesis* of contradictory positions (*thesis* and *antithesis*). Ideally, synthesis preserves the respective truths embodied within the thesis and antithesis while transcending their opposition. For example, head and heart are conceived as independent and opposing forces within Western thought; as a business executive once explained, "a good leader needs to have a compass in his [sic] head and a bar of steel in his heart" (Townsend, 1997). Even so, there is a rich history of philosophers and laypersons alike who have their own explanations as to how head and heart may work together (i.e., a synthesis; see Lakoff & Johnson, 1999). Such attempts at synthesis illustrate that dialectics are defined not only by opposition, but equally by *time* and *transformation*. Dialectics are *never* static, in part because a final, perfect synthesis of forces such as the head and the heart is unachievable in a world where contradiction and change structure rational thought itself.

Following Hegel, Marx subsequently developed dialectics, perhaps most famously with his notion of dialectical materialism. Seeing Hegel's dialectical worldview as too idealistic, Marx sought to locate it in a material world defined by social class. Rather than treat human consciousness abstractly, Marx viewed consciousness as both a product of social structure and a means of transforming it. Because capitalism alienated and oppressed workers, the state of consciousness that came about as a result of this material oppression was the very vehicle to change it (i.e., let the workers rise up!). According to Baxter and Montgomery (1996), Marx's application of dialectics to concrete practices of society provided a systematic explanation of *praxis*—a dialectical characteristic whereby people's prospects are constrained, though not determined, by previous actions and conditions. As one saying goes, we are all our own ancestors and heirs—devising our future while inheriting our past.

As is apparent in the preceding discussion, dialectics in its most general sense is a meta-theory about the process of relating entailed in human activity (Georgoudi, 1983). As such, it has been widely applied within many academic traditions, such as anthropology (e.g., Karp, 1976), psychology (e.g., Adams, 1977), sociology (e.g., Valverde, 1996), and interpersonal communication (e.g., Rawlins, 1992). Although not as common, it has also been applied to understanding culture (e.g., Peng & Nisbett, 1999). From a dialectical perspective, contradiction is not a characteristic of culture to be ignored or explained away; it is instead a defining feature. As Baxter and Montgomery clarify, "contradictions are inherent in social life and not evidence of failure or inadequacy in a person or in a social system" (1996, p. 7). In this light, culture is seen as "a problem that cannot be solved" (Nuckolls, 1998).

DIALECTICAL CHARACTERISTICS OF CULTURE

So what do the pushmi-pullyu and culture have in common? In order to best appreciate both of them, we should focus not only on the faces that they present, but also on the complex and dynamic interplay between the faces. Returning to the example of equality and racial prejudice in U.S. American national culture, historian James Horton points out,

> African-American history raises the blatant contradiction in American society. . . . How can we be a people committed to [equality], believing in [the Bill of Rights and the Constitution] when, at the same time, the people who wrote those documents, who articulated those beliefs, were themselves the holders of human beings in human bondage? (Dyer, 2001)

When we use dialectics as a tool for imagining culture, we transcend the trap presented by this example. The status of African Americans does not represent an exception to the "rule" of equality within the United States, nor does it signify a complete disregard for fairness. Instead, the struggle of African Americans (and others) illustrates that the tides of equality and inequality ebb and flow in an interconnected manner. While this culture has been the site of movements toward justice for all, it has also sponsored movements reinforcing the power structure (e.g., see Harris, 1993). From a dialectical perspective, this is unsurprising because equality and hierarchy are viewed as two faces of the same coin. These forces may be evenly balanced at times, or the scales may tip in one direction or the other, in either small or large measure. Regardless, neither the practices of equality nor of inequality will ever finally dominate this (or any other) culture because they are eternal partners in the ongoing labor of group life.

Perhaps one area where the dialectical nature of culture can be seen most clearly is at its core. Because all cultures are built around group life, every one of them must address the paradox of individuals living collectively. On the one hand, human beings operate in physically sovereign bodies and thus naturally develop some sense of independence and autonomy. On the other hand, we are also social creatures whose very survival and development demand connection. As a result, none of us can ever be entirely independent from, nor entirely dependent upon, other human beings. Instead, we must all manage the unavoidable tension between the pushes of individualism (autonomy) and the pulls of collectivism (interdependence).

Describing culture dialectically thus means that no society is completely free of the influence of either individualism or collectivism. Rather, these forces are present everywhere, the constant pushing and pulling of which result in unique and dynamic configurations that we may use to characterize a culture. For example, as mentioned earlier, the mainstream culture of the United States is both individualistic and collectivistic, with a historically heavy emphasis on the former. Because of the political context in which this country was established (Europeans seeking religious and other freedoms), as well as the material circumstances that were provided (low population density and great economic wealth; see Murphy & Margolis, 1995), the national culture has tilted, very heavily at times, toward individualism. This tilt has been so great that the culture is frequently characterized almost exclusively in individualistic terms (e.g., Hofstede, 1980; Rogers & Steinfatt, 1999; Ting-Toomey, 1988). Despite this, collectivistic currents remain, often rising and falling in response to practices of individualism itself.

From the beginning, U.S. American individualism has been intertwined with two important collectivist traditions, religion and civic republicanism (see Bellah, Madsen, Sullivan, Swidler, & Tipton, 1985). Religious traditions have been the center of countless communities throughout the nation, drawing people together in both worship and personal relationship. Similarly, the national culture has always extolled the virtues of civic responsibility, encouraging citizens to take responsibility for the welfare of their fellows and for the common good.

Collectivism has also manifested itself in countless other ways (and to various degrees) throughout U.S. history. The New Deal introduced many important programs and policies to support the general populace in times of economic depression, including social security. During World War II, victory gardens were planted in empty lots and tended to by entire neighborhoods in an effort to support the war. People also gathered in community around the radio to hear President Roosevelt's fireside chats, updating them about the fighting abroad. Much more recently, select articles (e.g., Marma, 2003) and programs (e.g., A Force More Powerful) have featured ways in which, despite the onslaught of individualistic forces, the communal spirit is still very much alive in the United States through practices such as volunteerism and habitat protection. As the producer of one such series, *Humankind,* commented regarding his inspiration for the show, "American culture has unfortunately gotten very fragmented. People feel disconnected in their cars and in their living rooms. . . . We need some way to forge deeper bonds with community" (Matsumoto, 1999, p. F2).

The push and pull of culture are experienced as a contest not only between individualism and collectivism, or equality and hierarchy, but also between divergent resolutions of any issue fundamental to group life. Such issues include the tolerance/intolerance of "nontraditional" cultural practices and the assimilation/differentiation of cultural (sub)groups. In the United States, the tolerance issue has played out on the political stage as the continuous engagement of conservative and liberal forces. The modern religious right emerged as a political power in the 1970s primarily as a response to the social movements of the '60s that promoted feminism and civil rights for homosexuals, among other things. As they have effectively championed the restriction and even prohibition of "nontraditional" practices in arenas such as marriage and birth control, the very recent revitalization of liberal forces is unsurprising; it is a direct response to conservative success. When viewed dialectically, we can appreciate that this struggle will never finally end.

Another issue that will be forever deliberated is the ideal degree of assimilation or differentiation among cultural groups. Because the existence of culture depends on the existence of groups, the regulation of membership—who is included and who is not—is always a central concern. The borders between cultural groups are rarely defined clearly and are always subject to negotiation. One reason people never settle completely in their groups is our psychological need to fit in, but only to a point; Brewer (1991) calls this our desire for "optimal distinctiveness." We belong to groups in order to feel connected, yet when too many people are granted membership, the benefits of connection diminish. Thus, we are constantly changing our affiliations as large groups splinter into small ones and then possibly merge with other similar groups (e.g., does someone born in the Philippines and raised in the United States identify as "Asian," "Asian American," "Asian/Pacific Islander," "Filipino," "Malay," or "American"?).

A second reason that we will always push and pull over group membership is that our groups are located in a changing material world. As the world changes, so too do our ideas of what makes up a cultural group. For example, even though we take the idea of a national culture for granted in this day and age, there was a time before the development of nation-states when people identified only with those who lived locally. Moreover, there may be a time in the near future when nation-states are largely meaningless cultural categories, when people are socialized instead by a variety of transnational groups, including networks such as al Qaeda. Changes in technology undoubtedly play a large role in shifts such as these. Indeed the U.S. culture that binds people from diverse places such as Lafayette, Indiana, and Los Angeles, California, would not be possible without television. As Poniewozik writes, "mass culture flattened out dialects and provided new Americans with a quick if superficial means of assimilation" (2003, p. 150). Because the technology of mass choice has now finally been adapted for mass communication (we have moved from "broadcasting" to "narrowcasting" as consumers select from hundreds of media options), it remains to be seen in what ways our ideas of nationhood, and who qualifies as a real "American," will be affected.

As dialectics encourages us to imagine opposition, time, and transformation as fundamental features of culture, it also helps reveal our own capacity for action. The idea of praxis suggests that although we are influenced by cultural prescriptions, we are not trapped by them. Instead, culture is like a well-worn path through the woods; we may often follow the markers but may sometimes blaze our own trial. Consider, for example, the case of the woman who climbed up the house. A local woman arrived at a house in Nepal to be interviewed by several foreign researchers. As the host went downstairs to greet her, she "somehow crawled up the vertical outside wall, made her way around the balcony to an opening in the railing, came through the opening, and sat down" (Holland, Lachiotte, Skinner, & Cain, 1998, p. 10). In dialectical terms, we could say that the woman was praxically constrained: In the usual circumstances of community life, she would not be allowed to enter the house because it belonged to a higher-caste person, yet she needed to get to the second-floor balcony. In response, she came up with a spectacular improvisation that reflected both her own agency and the restrictions of culture. Seen in this light, culture comes to be an important source from which to fashion the stuff of action. "One's history-in-person is the sediment from past experiences upon which one improvises, using the cultural resources available" (Holland et al., 1998, p. 18).

Recognizing that there are no "right" answers when it comes to defining the complex whole of culture, it is my hope that the brief appreciation of dialectics developed here will prove useful in your continued journey toward understanding human groups, including your own. Don't forget that according to the dialectics of culture, what comes around will go around, and around, and around because contradiction is fundamental to group life, not something to ever be irrevocably resolved. Maybe that's why at the height of the U.S. infatuation with sport utility vehicles, the following billboard could be spotted on the streets of Los Angeles: "Someday we'll look back at big cars and laugh. The Mini."

References

Adams, G. R. (1977). Physical attractiveness research: Toward a developmental social psychology of beauty. *Human Development, 20,* 217–239.

Baldwin, J. R., Faulkner, S. L., Hecht, M. L., & Lindsley, S. L. (2005). *Conceptualizing culture across the disciplines.* Mahwah, NJ: Erlbaum.

Baxter, L. A., & Montgomery, B. M. (1996). *Relating: Dialogues and dialectics.* New York, Guilford.

Bellah, R. N., Madsen, R., Sullivan, W. M., Swidler, A., & Tipton, S. M. (1985). *Habits of the heart: Individualism and commitment in American life.* Berkeley: University of California Press.

Brewer, M. B. (1991). The social self: On being the same and different at the same time. *Personality and Social Psychology Bulletin, 17,* 475–482.

Dyer, J. (2001). A world apart. *Shaping America: U.S. history to 1877*. Public Broadcasting System.

Georgoudi, M. (1983). Modern dialectics in social psychology: A reappraisal. *European Journal of Social Psychology, 13,* 77–93.

Glenn, E. S. (1966). Meaning and behavior: Communication and culture. *Journal of Communication, 16,* 248–272.

Harms, L. S. (1973). *International communication*. New York: Harper and Row.

Harris, C. (1993). Whiteness as property. *Harvard Law Review, 106,* 1709–1791.

Hegel, G. W. F. (1959). *Encyclopedia of philosophy*. New York: Philosophical Library.

Hofstede, G. (1980). *Culture's consequences*. Newbury Park, CA: Sage.

Holland, D., Lachiotte, W., Jr., Skinner, D., & Cain, C. (1998). *Identity and agency in cultural worlds*. Cambridge, MA: Harvard University Press.

Karp, L. (1976). Good man for the anthropologist: Structure and anti-structure in *Duck Soup*. In W. Arens & S. P. Montague (Eds.), *The American dimension: Cultural myths and social realities* (pp. 53–68). Port Washington, NY: Alfred.

Kroeber, A. L., & Kluckhohn, C. (1952). *Culture: A critical review of concepts and definitions*. Cambridge, MA: Harvard University Press.

Lakoff, G., & Johnson, M. (1999). *Philosophy in the flesh*. New York: Basic Books.

Lavine, T. Z. (1984). *From Socrates to Sartre: The philosophic quest*. New York: Bantam Books.

Loewen, J. L. (1995). *Lies my teacher told me: Everything your American history textbook got wrong*. New York: Simon & Schuster.

Lofting, H. (1988). *The Story of Doctor Dolittle*. New York: Bantam Doubleday Dell. (Original work published 1920)

Marma, S. (2003, May 9). Driving force in the community. *San Diego Union–Tribune,* p. B1.

Matsumoto, J. (1999, December 27). "Humankind" series of inspiring, surprising stories. *Los Angeles Times,* pp. F2, F7.

Murphy, M. F., & Margolis, M. L. (Eds.). (1995). Science, materialism, and the study of culture. Gainesville: University Press of Florida.

Nuckolls, C. W. (1998). *Culture: A problem that cannot be solved*. Madison: University of Wisconsin Press.

Peng, K., & Nisbett, R. E. (1999). Culture, dialectics, and reasoning about contradiction. *American Psychologist, 54,* 741–754.

Poniewozik, J. (2003, December 29). Has the mainstream run dry? *Time, 162,* 148–160.

Rawlins, W. K. (1992). *Friendship matters: Communication, dialectics, and the life course*. New York: Aldine de Gruyter.

Rogers, E. M., & Steinfatt, T. M. (1999). *Intercultural communication*. Prospect Heights, IL: Waveland.

Samovar, L., & Porter, R. (2003). Understanding intercultural communication: An introduction and overview. In L. Samovar & R. Porter (Eds.), *Intercultural communication: A reader* (10th ed., pp. 6–17). Belmont, CA: Wadsworth.

Samovar, L., & Porter, R. (2004). *Communication between cultures*. Belmont, CA: Wadsworth.

Small, A. (1905). *General sociology: An exposition of the main development in sociological theory from Spencer to Ratzenhofer*. Chicago: University of Chicago.

Ting-Toomey, S. (1988). Intercultural conflict styles: A face-negotiation theory. In Y. Y. Kim & W. B. Gudykunst (Eds.), *Theories in intercultural communication* (pp. 213–238). Newbury Park, CA: Sage.

Townsend, R. (1997). *The ultimate success quotations library*.

Triandis, H. C. (1995). *Individualism and collectivism*. Boulder, CO: Westview Press.

Tylor, E. B. (1958). *Primitive culture*. New York: Harper. (Original work published 1871)

Valverde, M. (1996). The dialectic of the familiar and the unfamiliar: *The Jungle* in early slum travel writing. *Sociology, 30,* 493–509.

Weiss, G. (1973). A scientific concept of culture. *American Anthropologist, 75,* 1376–1413.

Concepts and Questions

1. What does Cargile mean when he refers to culture as being fuzzy?
2. How would you define culture?
3. What does Cargile imply when he states that culture is dialectical?
4. How does the use of a dialectical perspective permit understanding of the inconsistencies present in any culture?
5. How does Hegel's concept of synthesis apply to understanding culture?
6. What does Cargile mean when he says that dialectics is a meta-theory about human relationships?
7. Discuss how a dialectical approach helps us understand the presence of both individualism and collectivism in a culture.
8. How does the pushmi-pullyu metaphor help explain the dialectical perspective advanced by Cargile?
9. What does Cargile mean when he states that "we will always push and pull over group membership"?

Culture and Conflict

Harry C. Triandis

A report that appeared in the *New York Times* claimed that on January 9, 1991, at a meeting where the Foreign Minister of Iraq, Tariq Aziz, met the Secretary of State of the United States, James Baker, they miscommunicated. According to the report, Baker was very clear that the United States would attack if Iraq did not leave Kuwait. But he said it calmly. The miscommunication occurred because next to Aziz was seated Saddam Hussein's brother, who paid attention only to *how* Baker talked, rather than to *what* he said. He reported back to Baghdad "the Americans will not attack. They are weak. They are calm. They are not angry. They are only talking."

We do know that Western individualist cultures sample mostly the *content* of communications, whereas Eastern collectivist cultures sample mostly the *context* of communication (Gudykunst, 1993; Triandis, 1994). Thus, it is plausible that Hussein's brother, who had little exposure to the West, did not sample the conversation correctly. Also, Baker did not throw anything at Aziz, to show that he was angry. He acted calmly. It is doubtful that Baker could have thrown anything. People cannot change their behavior that drastically, just because they are interacting with members of other cultures. We do not know what report Aziz gave to Hussein, but it is plausible that Hussein paid special attention to his brother's assessment, because trust in collectivist cultures is much greater within the intimate in-group than within the outer in-group. In any case, we do know that a war took place after that meeting. Cultural differences often cause miscommunications and conflict.

Conflict is greater when the two cultures are very different than when they are similar. Technically this difference is called "cultural distance" (Triandis, 1994).

From *The International Journal of Psychology*. Copyright © 2000, 35 (2), 145–152, www.psypress.co.uk. Reprinted by permission. Harry Triandis is Professor Emeritus at the University of Illinois, Urbana-Champaign, Department of Psychology in the Social-Personality-Organizational Division.

CULTURAL DISTANCE

Cultural distance is greater when people speak different languages. Even speaking languages that are related can be a problem. For example the ancient Greek root of *sympathetic* is "to feel together." That is fairly close to the English meaning. But modern Greek, Italian, Spanish, and French use terms that are derived from that root yet mean "a nice, pleasant person." So, "I am sympathetic" does not translate correctly into "Je suis sympatique!"

Triandis (1994) listed many funny examples of mistranslations. For instance, at the office of an Italian physician: "Specialist in women and other diseases." Of course, what happens when languages are members of the same language family (say, Indo-European) can be even more of a problem when the languages have very different structures (e.g., tonal or click languages).

Cultural distance is also greater when people have different social structures, such as family structures. Todd (1983) has identified eight types of family structure, and simple terms like "aunt" may convey different meanings when the family structure is different.

Religion, of course, can be a great source of differences in points of view. Even when one knows that the other person believes something different, there is the problem that humans use themselves as the anchors for such judgments. The diplomat may not believe that it is possible for the other diplomat to have such "outlandish" beliefs. A well-established social psychological phenomenon is called the "false consensus" effect (Mullen et al., 1985). Even when people know about this bias, they cannot wipe it out (Krueger & Clement, 1994). The phenomenon is that if we agree with a particular position, we believe that most other people also agree with it; if we disagree with a particular position, we believe that most people disagree with it. The phenomenon is even stronger when we interact with people who are similar to us in dress, profession, and other characteristics.

Differences in standards of living can create cultural distance. When the cost of sending a letter is a substantial fraction of one's budget, one may not be as likely to send the letter as when the cost is trivial in relation to one's budget.

Values differ substantially between cultures (Schwartz, 1992, 1994). These values are related to the cultural syndromes that we will discuss here.

MEANING OF CULTURE

Culture is a shared meaning system, found among those who speak a particular language dialect, during a specific historic period, in a definable geographic region (Triandis, 1994). It functions to improve the adaptation of members of the culture to a particular ecology, and it includes the knowledge that people need to have in order to function effectively in their social environment.

Cultures differ drastically in the amount of aggression that is found both within and between them. For example, the Lepcha of the Indian Himalayas had one murder two centuries ago (Segall, Ember, & Ember, 1997). Homicide rates in some segments of U.S. society are extremely high. There is evidence that the absence of fathers during socialization is a factor in high rates (Segall et al.). There is some evidence that high between-cultures aggression is related to high within-culture aggression (Segall et al.). Warfare is associated with the unpredictability of resources and conflicts over territory; it is found most usually in societies where aggression within the family is permitted, where the media of communication portray aggression, where there are warlike sports, and where wrongdoing is severely punished (Segall et al.). There is evidence that democracies do not fight with each other (Ember, Ember, & Russett, 1992), so much so that some analysts have argued that it is "counterproductive to support any undemocratic regimes, even if they happen to be enemies of our enemies" (Ember & Ember, 1994).

Shared patterns of elements of subjective culture constitute subjective cultural syndromes (Triandis, 1996). A cultural syndrome is a shared pattern of beliefs, attitudes, self-definitions, norms, roles, and values organized around a theme.

Cultural differences are best conceptualized as different patterns of sampling information found in the environment (Triandis, 1989). In collectivist cultures (most traditional cultures, most Asian and Latin American cultures), people are more likely (a) to sample the collective self (reflecting interdependence with others) and to think of themselves as interdependent with their groups (family, coworkers, tribe, coreligionists, country), rather than to sample the individual self (reflecting an independent self) and to see themselves as autonomous individuals who are independent of their groups (Markus & Kitayama, 1991); (b) to give more priority to the goals of their in-group than to their personal goals (Triandis, 1995); (c) to use in-group norms to shape their behavior more than personal attitudes (Abrams, Ando, & Hinkle, 1998; Suh, Diener, Oishi, & Triandis, 1998); and (d) to conceive of social relationships as communal (Mills & Clark, 1982) rather than in exchange theory terms (Triandis, 1995). That is, they pay attention to the needs of others and stay in relationships even when that is not maximally beneficial to them. There is evidence that these four aspects are interrelated (Triandis & Gelfand, 1998).

The sampling of collectivists focuses on groups, with people seen as appendages of groups; the sampling of individualists focuses on individuals. A recent example is the coverage of the Kosovo war: CNN and BBC cover the refugees (individuals) in great detail. The Russian and the Serbs present nothing about the refugees on their television. The *Times* of London (April 7, 1999) had a story about a member of the Russian Duma who was so upset that the Russian TV did not mention the refugees at all that he went on a hunger strike. Finally, 12 days into the war, an independent Russian station mentioned the refugees. We called a friend in Belgrade and asked her if she knew why NATO was bombing her city. She did not! Of course, such control of information is part of the war effort, but when it is consistent with the culture, it is a natural bias.

Culture shapes us, so we pay more attention to individuals and to the internal processes of individuals (attitudes, beliefs) if we are raised in an individualist culture, and more attention to groups, roles, norms, duties, and intergroup relationships if we are raised in a collectivist culture. Collectivist cultures have languages that do not require the use of "I" and "you" (Kashima & Kashima, 1997, 1998). They also have many culture-specific relational terms that are not found in individualist cultures, such as *philolimo* in Greek (Triandis, 1972), which is a positive attribute of an individual who does what the in-group expects; *amae* in Japanese, which reflects tolerance of deviation from norms by a dependent person (Yamaguchi, 1998); and *simpatia* among Latin Americans (Triandis, Marin, Lisansky, & Betancourt, 1984), which reflects the expectation that social relationships will include mostly positive and very few negative behaviors.

Collectivists use action verbs (e.g., he offered to help) rather than state verbs (e.g., he is helpful). This is because they prefer to use context in their communications. Zwier (1997), in four studies, obtained support for this cultural difference. Specifically, she found that the accounts of events given by Turkish and Dutch students show this difference. She content-analyzed the radio commentaries of Turkish and Dutch radio personalities and found the same difference. She asked Turkish and Dutch students to write a letter requesting a favor, and content-analyzed the letters. She examined the writing of Turkish/Dutch bilinguals when writing in the two languages, and found the same pattern.

The contrasting cultural pattern is individualism. Here people tend to (a) sample the individual self—this pattern is very common in North and Western Europe, North America (except Mexico), Australia, and New Zealand, where the self is conceived as independent of in-groups; (b) give priority to personal goals; (c) use attitudes much more than norms as determinants of their social behavior; and (d) pay attention only to their own needs and abandon interpersonal relationships that are not optimally beneficial to them. Individualist cultures have languages that require the use of "I" and "you" (Kashima & Kashima, 1997, 1998). English is a good example. It would be difficult to write a letter in English without using these words. Individualists are very positive about "me" and "we," whereas collectivists are sometimes ambivalent about "me" but very positive about "we."

CULTURAL SYNDROMES

Complexity

Some cultures (e.g., hunters and gatherers) are relatively simple, and other cultures (e.g., information societies) are relatively complex. The organizing theme of the syndrome is complexity. For example, in complex societies one finds subgroups with different beliefs and attitudes, whereas in simple societies individuals are in considerable agreement about their beliefs and attitudes. In fact, cultural uniformity and conformity are higher in simple than in complex societies. Simple cultures have few jobs; if we take into account specialties such as urologist and general practitioner, complex cultures have a quarter of a million different jobs (see *Dictionary of Occupational Titles,* 1977). The size of settlements is one of the best ways to index cultural complexity (Chick, 1997).

Tightness

Tight cultures have many rules, norms, and ideas about what is correct behavior in each situation; loose cultures have fewer rules and norms. In tight cultures, people become quite upset when others do not follow the norms of the society, and may even kill those who do not behave as expected, whereas in loose cultures people are tolerant of many deviations from normative behaviors.

Thus, conformity is high in tight cultures. In Thailand, which is a loose culture, the expression *"mai bin rai"* (never mind) is used frequently. In Japan, which is a tight culture, people are sometimes criticized for minor deviations from norms, such as having too much suntan, or having curly hair (Kidder, 1992). Most Japanese live in fear that they will not act properly (Iwao, 1993).

Tightness is more likely when the culture is relatively isolated from other cultures, so that consensus about what is proper behavior can develop. It is also more likely that tightness will occur in situations where people are highly interdependent (when the other deviates from norms it hurts the relationship) and where there is a high population density (high density requires norms so that people will not hurt each other; also, when the other deviates one notices it).

When cultures are at the intersection of great cultures (e.g., Thailand is at the intersection of China and India), contradictory norms may be found, and people cannot be too strict in imposing norms. Also, when the population density is low, it may not even be known that a person who is miles away has behaved improperly. Cosmopolitan cities are loose, except when they have ethnic enclaves, which can be very tight, whereas small communities are relatively tight.

Individualism and Collectivism

Triandis (1994) has suggested that individualism emerges in societies that are both complex and loose; collectivism, in societies that are both simple and tight. For example, theocracies or monasteries are both tight and relatively poor; Hollywood stars live in a culture that is both complex and loose. This speculation has not been tested rigorously, but the data seem to hang together reasonably well. It may be the case, for instance, that contemporary Japan, which is now quite complex, is less collectivist than the Japan of the

19th century. In fact, reports of 19th-century travelers to Japan (see Edgerton, 1985) mentioned hundreds of rules for how to laugh, sit, and so on, that apparently no longer operate in modern Japan.

Bond and Smith (1996) did a meta-analysis of studies of conformity that used the Asch paradigm, and found that collectivist cultures were higher in conformity than individualist cultures. This is what we would expect if tightness and collectivism were closely linked.

Kim and Markus (1998) showed that in the West people see "uniqueness" as desirable, whereas in East Asia it is often seen as "deviance"; in the West "conformity" is sometimes seen as undesirable, but in East Asia it is seen as "harmony." For example, content analyses of advertisements from the United States and Korea show different frequencies of uniqueness and conformity themes. Conformity themes were used by 95% of the Korean and 65% of the American advertisements; uniqueness themes were used by 89% of the American and 49% of the Korean advertisements.

Vertical and Horizontal Cultures

Vertical cultures accept hierarchy as a given. People are different from each other. Hierarchy is a natural state. Those at the top "naturally" have more power and privileges than those at the bottom of the hierarchy. Horizontal cultures accept equality as a given. People are basically similar, and if one is to divide any resource it should be done equally (Triandis, 1995).

Active–Passive Cultures

In active cultures, individuals try to change the environment to fit them; in passive cultures, people change themselves to fit into the environment (Diaz-Guerrero, 1979). The active cultures are more competitive and action-oriented, and emphasize self-fulfillment; the passive ones are more cooperative, emphasize the experience of living, and are especially concerned with getting along with others. In general, individualist cultures are more active than collectivist cultures, though the relationship between the two cultural syndromes is not strong.

Universalism–Particularism

In universalist cultures, people try to treat others on the basis of universal criteria (e.g., all competent persons, regardless of who they are in terms of sex, age, race, etc., are acceptable employees); in particularist cultures, people treat others on the basis of who the other person is (e.g., I know Joe Blow and he is a good person, so he will be a good employee; Parsons, 1968). In general, individualists are universalists and collectivists are particularists.

Diffuse–Specific

Diffuse cultures respond to the environment in a holistic manner (e.g., I do not like your report means I do not like you). Specific cultures discriminate different aspects of the stimulus complex (e.g., I do not like your report says nothing about liking you; Foa & Chemers, 1967).

Instrumental–Expressive

People may sample more heavily attributes that are instrumental (e.g., get the job done) or expressive (e.g., enjoy the social relationship). In general, individualists are more instrumental and collectivists are more expressive. When Latin Americans meet a friend in the street, they are likely to stop and chat, even when they are late for an appointment. The importance of the social relationship eclipses the importance of the instrumental relationship (Levine & Norenzayan, 1999).

Emotional Expression or Suppression

People may express their emotions freely, no matter what the consequences, or they may control the expression of emotion. The free expression of negative emotions can disrupt relationships, so collectivists tend to control such emotions. Individualists are often high in emotional expression. For example, Stephan, Stephan, and de Vargas (1996) tested the hypothesis that people in collectivist cultures would feel less comfortable expressing negative emotions than people in individualist cultures, and found strong support for that hypothesis.

In addition, the instigation of emotion is often culture specific. Stipek, Weiner, and Li (1989) found that when Americans were asked to recall what made them angry, they remembered mostly events that happened to them personally; when Chinese were given that task, they remembered mostly events that occurred to other people. This self-focus versus other-focus is an important contrast between individualism and collectivism (Kagiteibasi, 1997).

The Weights Given to Different Attributes in Social Perception

In addition to sampling different attributes, members of different cultures give different weights to the attributes that they sample. For example, in a conflict situation, an individual might sample the ethnicity of the other person, his profession, and his competence. Members of some cultures will give most of the weight to ethnicity and react to the other person on the basis of ethnicity; members of other cultures will give most of the weight to competence and profession, and disregard ethnicity. Triandis (1967) reviewed many cross-cultural studies showing differences in the weights used in social perception. In general, members of collectivist cultures tend to sample and weigh ascribed attributes more heavily, whereas members of individualist cultures sample and weigh achieved attributes more heavily.

One can identify many more syndromes, such as those reflected in the Kluckhohn and Strodtbeck (1961) value orientations, the culture of honor (Nisbett & Cohen, 1996), and others. This introduction is sufficient for our purposes.

CULTURAL SYNDROMES AND THE SITUATION

Humans have a predisposition to respond that can be traced to culture, but their behavior depends very much more on the situation. For example, all humans have both collectivist and individualist cognitions, but they sample them with different probabilities depending on the situation. When the in-group is being attacked, for instance, most humans become collectivists.

The larger the in-group, the less effective it is likely to be in calling for individuals to do what the in-group authorities want done. A call to arms by a clan leader is more likely to be effective than a call to arms by a state, though penalties may make the latter effective in many countries.

Certain factors increase the probability that the collectivist cognitive system will be activated. This is most likely to happen when (a) the individual knows that most other people in the particular situation are collectivists, which makes the norm that one must act as a collectivist more salient; (b) the individual's membership in a collective is especially salient—for instance, the individual represents a country; (c) within an in-group, the situation emphasizes what people have in common—for instance, common goals; (d) within an in-group, the situation emphasizes that people are in the same collective—for instance, people wear the same uniforms; and (e) within an in-group, the task is cooperative.

Certain factors increase the probability that the individualistic cognitive system will be activated. This is most likely to happen when (a) others in the situation are and behave like individualists, which makes individualist norms more salient; (b) the situation makes the person focus on what makes him or her different from others (Trafimow, Triandis, & Goto, 1991)—for instance, the person is dressed very differently from the rest of the group; and (c) the task is competitive.

Culture is relevant for understanding conflict in at least two domains: how conflict starts and how conflict evolves. Problems of poor communication are the major causes of the first, and problems of the way members of different cultures treat out-groups are relevant for understanding the second of these domains.

CULTURAL SYNDROMES AND COMMUNICATION

When people come into contact with members of other cultures, they are often not aware of their miscommunications, because they think that the others are more or less like they are. This is the stage of *unconscious incompetence.* After some interpersonal difficulties, people realize that they are miscommunicating, but they do not know exactly what is wrong. That is the stage of *conscious incompetence.* As they get to know more and more about the culture of the other, they begin communicating correctly, but they have to make an effort to communicate in a different way. That is the stage of *conscious competence.* Finally, after they develop habits of correct communication with members of the other culture, they reach the stage of *unconscious competence,* where the communication is effortless and correct.

A very serious problem in communication is that people do not perceive the same "causes" of behavior (Miller, 1984; Morris & Peng, 1994). We call these *attributions.* When the actor thinks that a behavior is due to one cause and the observer thinks that the behavior is due to a different cause, they each give a different meaning to the behavior. For instance, a diplomat may invite another diplomat to dinner. The inviter may do so because he likes the other diplomat. The invitee, however, may use the cause "his boss told him to invite me." Obviously, the meaning of the invitation is different for the two diplomats.

There are training procedures called "culture assimilators" (Fiedler, Mitchell, & Triandis, 1971), which consist of 100 or so episodes involving interactions between members of the two relevant cultures, with each episode followed by four attributions. Usually three attributions are "incorrect" from the point of view of the culture the trainee is learning about, and one is "correct." The trainee selects one attribution, and gets feedback as to whether it is the correct one from the point of view of the culture the trainee is trying to learn about. People who go through this training gradually learn to make the correct attributions from the point of view of the other culture. This reduces miscommunications (Bhawuk, 1998).

There is a well-researched phenomenon regarding attributions. When two groups, A and B, are in conflict, if a member of group B does something "nice," members of group A attribute the behavior to external factors (e.g., he was forced to do it by the circumstances); when a member of group B does something "nasty," members of group A attribute it to internal factors (e.g., they are nasty "by nature"). The attributions that group B makes about the behavior of group A are exact mirror images; that is, when A does something nice it is due to external factors, and when A does something nasty it is due to internal factors. When a member of group A makes attributions about the actions of members of group A, if the action is positive it is attributed to internal factors and if it is negative it is attributed to external factors.

In all cultures, when we ask actors why they did something, they report external causes, but observers of these actions tend to use causes internal to the actor. This is called the "fundamental attribution error." In short, people all over the world have a tendency to make attributions incorrectly. However; those from individualistic cultures are even worse in this bias than those from collectivist cultures.

Another factor in miscommunications is the tendency of collectivists to sample the context of communications more than individualists, which results in their paying more attention to gestures, eye contact, level of voice, the direction of the two bodies, touching, the distance between the bodies, and the like. There is a large opportunity for errors and misinterpretations in the way people interpret paralinguistic cues. Also, the way people use time can result in misunderstandings, because people from monochronic time cultures are used to carrying out one conversation at a time, whereas people who use polychronic time carry several conversations simultaneously, which confuses and frustrates the users of monochronic time.

The structure of messages can be another source of difficulties. Western people tend to organize their thoughts and messages in a linear fashion: fact 1, fact 2, and so on; generalization; conclusion. In many other cultures, people start with the conclusion, then find facts that fit the conclusion, and permit deviations from a straight line. In some cases, the argument is like a spiral, starting from general ideological or mystical considerations and gradually zeroing to a conclusion (Triandis, 1994). The extent to which ideology versus pragmatic matters are sampled also varies with culture. Glenn (1981) gave an interesting example. At a UN conference, the Russians advocated the use of reinforced concrete structures (ideal for all), whereas the American delegates said that "it depends on what works best" (pragmatic). Delegates from the Third World interpreted the exchange in favor of the Russians. They thought that the Americans were saying that "we are not good enough to use what they are using."

When a universalist meets a particularist, there can be interpersonal difficulties. For example, when presenting a position, the universalist may expect that all the facts will "fit in" with the position, whereas the particularist may not consider this necessary. When such expectations are present, the particularist might need to start the presentation with a universalist position (e.g., "we are all in favor of peace") and then present the particularist view.

Another source of miscommunication is that in some cultures communication is "associative" and in others "abstractive." In the West, it is typically abstractive; that is, one abstracts the most important elements of the argument and organizes them for the presentation. An associative presentation can present anything that is vaguely related to the point, which can frustrate the Westerner (Szalay, 1993). For example, in 1932, the finance minister of Japan was assassinated after agreeing to a 17% revaluation of the yen. In 1971, the American Treasury Secretary Connaly, oblivious to Japanese history, demanded a 17% revaluation of the yen. His Japanese counterpart rejected it without explanation. When Connaly suggested a 16.9% upward revaluation, the Japanese minister accepted it (Cohen, 1991).

Examples of associative communications abound. The *Los Angeles Times,* on February 12, 1977, published a conversation between two Egyptians. One was Westernized, and the other was traditional. The communication of the traditional was not understood by the Westernized. Another example was the presentation of the Egyptian ambassador to the UN in 1967, in which he accused the Americans of actively helping the Israelis. The American ambassador asked for proof, but the Egyptian answered that no proof was needed because it was "obvious that the Americans had intervened. How else could one explain that three quarters of the Egyptian air force was destroyed in a few hours? Only a large, powerful country could do this."

In sum, cultural distance can result in miscommunications, which may lead to international conflict. We now turn to the way the conflict is carried out, and look at the role of cultural syndromes in this area.

CULTURAL SYNDROMES AND CONFLICT

We need to distinguish conflict within the in-group from conflict between groups. Individualism is associated with conflict inside a culture, such as crime or divorce. Collectivism is associated with conflict between groups, such as ethnic cleansing or war.

Factors that have been found to increase aggression (see Triandis, 1994) include biological factors (e.g., high levels of testosterone), social structural factors (such as low family cohesion, few intimate relationships, low father involvement in the upbringing of sons, isolation from kin, and anonymity, all of which are associated with individualism), high levels of arousal (because of frustration, competition), hot weather, modeling (aggressive models, aggressive people receive more status in the society), gender marking (men and women are seen as very different), retaliation, economic inequality, few resources (associated with collectivism), social stress (e.g., high levels of inflation), ease of being aggressive (e.g., availability of weapons), and low costs (aggression does not lead to punishment). Clearly there are many factors, many of which do not have much to do with cultural patterns. Yet culture is important for many of these factors (Segall et al., 1997). Some of the factors, such as weak families, are associated with individualism and lead to within-group aggression; others are associated with collectivism.

When interacting with in-group members, people from collectivist cultures tend to be unusually sensitive to the needs of the others, supportive, helpful, and even self-sacrificing. However, when interacting with out-group members, they are usually indifferent and, if the two groups have incompatible goals, even hostile.

Once the in-group has been called to action against an out-group by in-group authorities, vertical collectivists are especially likely to become aggressive. This pattern leads to especially high levels of hostility when a "culture of honor" is present. Such cultures are found in situations where there are no police (or other authorities that can resolve conflict), so that people have to protect themselves against intruders by means of their personal efforts (Nisbett & Cohen, 1996). To extrapolate to the international scene, conflict would be higher if international bodies such as the United Nations did not exist.

Certain combinations of cultural syndromes can lead to treating the out-group inhumanely. In simple cultures, the distinction between different kinds of "others" is unlikely to occur. In vertical cultures, there is likely to be a perception that "others" are very different, just as people at the top and bottom of a hierarchy are seen as very different. In active cultures, the elimination of out-groups (e.g., ethnic cleansing) is likely to be seen as an especially good way to change the sociopolitical environment. In universalist cultures, treating all out-group members the same fits the cultural pattern. If one enemy is to be killed, all should be killed. In diffuse cultures, making distinctions between different kinds of enemies is not likely, so that all out-group members are likely to be treated badly. Instrumental cultures may be particularly effective in eliminating their enemies. Thus, when a particular combination of cultural syndromes is found—namely active, universalistic, diffuse, instrumental, vertical collectivism—inhumane treatment of out-groups is likely to occur.

All humans are ethnocentric (Triandis, 1994). That means that they think of their in-group as the standard of what is good and proper, and of other groups as good only to the extent that they are similar to the in-group. Ethnocentrism also results in members of a culture seeing their own norms and behavior as "natural" and "correct" and those of members of other cultures as "unnatural" and "incorrect." Ethnocentrism leads people to see their norms as universally valid; to avoid questioning norms, role definitions, and values; and to help in-group members feel proud of the in-group and, simultaneously, to reject out-groups (Triandis, 1994).

The rejection of out-groups is especially likely to occur in collectivist cultures. In extreme collectivist cultures, out-groups are often seen as "not quite human" and "not deserving any rights." Although individualists are capable of dealing with out-groups in an inhuman way (e.g., the My Lai incident during the Vietnam War), collectivists are even more extreme in dealing with out-groups (e.g., the rape of Nanking, where an estimated 300,000 civilians were killed, Chang, 1997; the Holocaust). Fortunately, the particular combination of active, universalistic, diffuse, instrumental, vertical collectivism is rare, so that such incidents do not occur frequently.

Furthermore, as indicated earlier, typical collectivism is usually incompatible with the active, universalistic, and instrumental syndromes so that the above-mentioned combination is really rare. Nevertheless, in the 20th century we have witnessed many cases of genocide and ethnic cleansing, so we cannot ignore the data.

One way to avoid these inhuman actions would be to monitor cultures that tend toward this undesirable combination of syndromes and to change them to reduce the probability of occurrence of the particular combination of syndromes. There is very little research about the factors that result in the various syndromes mentioned earlier, but we do know something about the occurrence of collectivism.

PREVALENCE OF COLLECTIVISM

Collectivism is found in societies that are not affluent (Hofstede, 1980), especially where there is only one normative system—that is, a single culture that is not cosmopolitan. There is a fair amount of evidence about the attributes of collectivism and the causes of the development of this cultural pattern (Triandis, 1990).

Collectivism is also high among the lower social classes of any society (Kohn, 1969; Marshall, 1997), among those who have not traveled (Gerganov, Dilova, Petkova, & Paspalanova, 1996) or been socially mobile, and among those who have not been exposed to the modern mass media (McBride, 1998). When the major economic activity is based on agriculture, rather than on hunting, fishing, industry, or service, collectivism is often high.

Collectivism is thus found in societies that are relatively homogeneous (so that in-group norms can be widely accepted); where population density and job interdependence are high (because they require the development of and adherence to many rules of behavior); among members of the society who are relatively old (Noricks et al., 1987) and who are members of large families (because it is not possible for every member to do his or her own thing); and in groups that are quite religious (Triandis & Singelis, 1998). When the in-group is under pressure from the outside, collectivism increases. Thus, one consideration in international relations is whether the advantages of putting pressure on a country outbalance the disadvantages of increasing the collectivism of the country.

CONCLUSION

We examined two major ways in which culture is related to conflict. One is that cultural distance increases the probability of miscommunication. There are training programs that can overcome this problem. The second is the way a combination of cultural syndromes results in the inhuman treatment of out-groups.

References

Abrams, D., Ando, K., & Hinkle, S. (1998). Psychological attachment to groups: Cross-cultural differences in organizational identification and subjective norms as predictors of workers' turnover intentions. *Personality and Social Psychology Bulletin, 24,* 1027–1039.

Bhawuk, D. P. S. (1998). The role of culture theory in cross-cultural training: A multimethod study of culture specific, culture general, and culture theory-based assimilators. *Journal of Cross-Cultural Psychology, 29,* 630–655.

Bond, R., & Smith, P. B. (1996). Culture and conformity: A meta-analysis of studies using Asch's (1952b, 1956) line judgement task. *Psychological Bulletin, 119,* 111–137.

Chang, I. (1997). *The rape of Nanking: The forgotten holocaust of World War II.* New York: Basic Books.

Chick, G. (1997). Cultural complexity: The concept and its measurement. *Cross-Cultural Research, 31,* 275–307.

Cohen, R. (1991). *Negotiating across cultures.* Washington, DC: United States Institute of Peace.

Diaz-Guerrero, R. (1979). The development of coping style. *Human Development, 22,* 320–331.

Dictionary of Occupational Titles (4th ed.). (1977). [Supplements in 1986]. Washington, DC: U.S. Government Publications Office.

Edgerton, R. B. (1985). *Rules, exceptions, and social order.* Berkeley: University of California Press.

Ember, M., & Ember, C. R. (1994). Prescriptions for peace: Policy implications of crosscultural research on war and interpersonal violence. *Cross-Cultural Research, 28,* 343–350.

Ember, C. R., Ember, M., & Russett, B. (1992). Peace between participatory polities: A cross-cultural test of the "Democracies rarely fight each other" hypothesis. *World Politics, 44,* 573–599.

Fiedler, F. E., Mitchell, T., & Triandis, H. C. (1971). The culture assimilator: An approach to cross-cultural training. *Journal of Applied Psychology, 55,* 95–102.

Foa, U., & Chemers, M. M. (1967). The significance of role behaviour differentiation for crosscultural interaction training. *International Journal of Psychology, 2,* 45–57.

Gerganov, E. N., Dilova, M. L., Petkova, K. G., & Paspalanova, E. P. (1996). Culture-specific approach to the study of individualism/collectivism. *European Journal of Social Psychology, 26,* 277–297.

Glenn, E. (1981). *Man and mankind: Conflicts and communication between cultures.* Norwood, NJ: Ablex.

Gudykunst, W. (Ed.). (1993). *Communication in Japan and the United States.* Albany: State University of New York Press.

Hofstede, G. (1980). *Culture's consequences.* Beverly Hills, CA: Sage.

Iwao, S. (1993). *The Japanese woman: Traditional image and changing reality.* New York: Free Press.

Kagiteibasi, C. (1997). Individualism and collectivism. In I. W. Berry, M. H. Segall, & C. Kagiteibasi (Eds.), *Handbook of cross-cultural psychology* (2nd ed., pp.1–50). Boston: Allyn & Bacon.

Kashima, E. S., & Kashima, Y. (1997). Practice of the self in conversations: Pronoun drop, sentence co-production and contextualization of the self. In K. Leung, U. Kim, S. Yamaguchi, & Y. Kashima (Eds.), *Progress in Asian social psychology* (Vol. 1, pp. 165–180). Singapore: Wiley.

Kashima, E. S., & Kashima, Y. (1998). Culture and language: The case of cultural dimensions and personal pronoun use. *Journal of Cross-Cultural Psychology, 29,* 461–486.

Kidder, L. (1992). Requirements for being "Japanese": Stories of returnees. *International Journal of Intercultural Relations, 16,* 383–394.

Kim, H., & Markus, H. R. (1998). *Deviance or uniqueness, harmony or conformity? A cultural analysis.* Unpublished manuscript.

Kluckhohn, F., & Strodtbeck, F. (1961). *Variations in value orientation.* Evanston, IL: Row, Peterson.

Kohn, M. K. (1969). *Class and conformity.* Homewood, IL: Dorsey Press.

Krueger, I., & Clement, R. W. (1994). The truly false consensus effect: An ineradicable egocentric bias in social perception. *Journal of Personality and Social Psychology, 67,* 596–610.

Levine, R. V., & Norenzayan, A. (1999). The pace of life in 31 countries. *Journal of Cross-Cultural Psychology, 30,* 178–205.

Markus, H., & Kitayama, S. (1991). Culture and self: Implications for cognition, emotion and motivation. *Psychological Review, 98,* 224–253.

Marshall, R. (1997). Variances in levels of individualism across two cultures and three social classes. *Journal of Cross-Cultural Psychology, 28,* 490–495.

McBride, A. (1998). Television, individualism, and social capital. *Political Science and Politics, 31,* 542–555.

Miller, J. G. (1984). Culture and the development of everyday social explanation. *Journal of Personality and Social Psychology, 46,* 961–978.

Mills, J., & Clark, M. S. (1982). Exchange and communal relationships. In L. Wheeler (Ed.), *Review of personality and social psychology,* (Vol. 3, pp. 121–144). Beverly Hills, CA: Sage.

Morris, M. W., & Peng, K. (1994). Culture and cause: American and Chinese attributions for social and physical events. *Journal of Personality and Social Psychology, 67,* 949–971.

Mullen, B., Atkins, J. L., Champion, D. S., Edwards, C., Handy, D., Story, J. E., & Venderklok, M. (1985). The false consensus effect: A meta-analysis of 115 hypothesis tests. *Journal of Experimental Social Psychology, 21,* 262–283.

Nisbett, R. E., & Cohen, D. (1996). *Culture of honor.* Boulder, CO: Westview Press.

Noricks, J. S., Agler, L. H., Bartholomew, M., Howard-Smith, S., Martin, D., Pyles, S., & Shapiro, W. (1987). Age, abstract things and the American concept of person. *American Anthropologist, 89,* 667–675.

Parsons, T. (1968). *The structure of social action.* New York: Free Press.

Schwartz, S. H. (1992). Universals in the content and structure of values: Theoretical advances and empirical tests in 20 countries. In M. Zanna (Ed.), *Advances in experimental social psychology* (Vol. 25, pp. 1–166). New York: Academic Press.

Schwartz, S. H. (1994). Beyond individualism and collectivism: New cultural dimensions of value. In U. Kim, H. C. Triandis, C. Kagiteibasi, S. C. Choi, & O. Yoon (Eds.),

Individualism and collectivism: Theory, method and applications (pp. 85–122). Newbury Park, CA: Sage.

Segall, M. H., Ember, C. R., & Ember, M. (1997). Aggression, crime, and warfare. In J. W. Berry, M. H. Segall, & C. Kagiteibasi (Eds.), *Handbook of cross-cultural psychology,* (2nd ed., Vol.3, pp. 213–254). Boston: Allyn & Bacon.

Stephan, W. G., Stephan, C. W., & de Vargas, M. C. (1996). Emotional expression in Costa Rica and United States. *Journal of Cross-Cultural Psychology, 27,* 147–160.

Stipek, D., Weiner, B., & Li, K. (1989). Testing some attribution-emotion relations in the People's Republic of China. *Journal of Personality and Social Psychology, 56,* 109–116.

Suh, E., Diener, E., Oishi, S., & Triandis, H. C. (1998). The shifting basis of life satisfaction judgements across cultures: Emotions versus norms. *Journal of Personality and Social Psychology, 74,* 482–493.

Szalay, L. B. (1993). The *subjective worlds of Russians and Americans: A guide for mutual understanding.* Chevy Chase, MD: Institute of Comparative Social and Cultural Studies.

Todd, E. (1983). *La troisième planète.* Paris: Editions du Scuil.

Trafimow, D., Triandis, H. C., & Goto, S. (1991). Some tests of the distinction between private and collective self. *Journal of Personality and Social Psychology, 60,* 649–655.

Triandis, H. C. (1967). Toward an analysis of the components of interpersonal attitudes. In C. Sherif & M. Sherif (Eds.), *Attitudes, ego-involvement, and change* (pp. 227–270). New York: Wiley.

Triandis, H. C. (1972). *The analysis of subjective culture.* New York: Wiley.

Triandis, H. C. (1989). The self and social behaviour in differing cultural contexts. *Psychological Review, 96,* 506–520.

Triandis, H. C. (1990). Crosscultural studies of individualism and collectivism. In I. Berman (Ed.), *Nebraska Symposium on Motivation* (pp. 41–133). Lincoln: University of Nebraska Press.

Triandis, H. C. (1994). *Culture and social behaviour.* New York: McGraw-Hill.

Triandis, H. C. (1995). *Individualism and collectivism.* Boulder, CO: Westview Press.

Triandis, H. C. (1996). The psychological measurement of cultural syndromes. *American Psychologist, 51,* 407–415.

Triandis, H. C., & Gelfand, M. (1998). Converging measurement of horizontal and vertical individualism and collectivism. *Journal of Personality and Social Psychology, 74,* 118–128.

Triandis, H. C., Marin, G., Lisansky, J., & Betancourt, (1984). *Simpatia* as a cultural script of Hispanics. *Journal of Personality and Social Psychology, 47,* 1363–1374.

Triandis, H. C., & Singelis, T. M. (1998). Training to recognize individual differences in collectivism and individualism within culture. *International Journal of Intercultural Relations, 22,* 35–48.

Yamaguchi, S. (1998, August). The *meaning of amae.* Paper presented at the Congress of the International Association of Cross-Cultural Psychology, Bellingham, WA.

Zwier, S. (1997). *Patterns of language use in individualistic and collectivist cultures.* Unpublished doctoral dissertation, Free University of Amsterdam, The Netherlands.

Concepts and Questions

1. Differentiate between message *content* and message *context.* How do different cultures react to content and context? How might cultural diversity in attending to content and context affect intercultural communication?
2. What does Triandis mean by cultural distance? How does language affect cultural distance?
3. What is Triandis referring to when he discusses different patterns of sampling information found in the environment? How might these differences affect intercultural communication between an individual from a collectivist culture and someone from an individualistic culture?
4. What differences may be found in the use of "I" and "you" in collectivistic and individualistic cultures?
5. What is cultural tightness? How might cultural diversity in tightness affect intercultural communication?
6. Differentiate between vertical and horizontal cultures.
7. How is culture relevant for understanding conflict?
8. Triandis holds that a very serious problem in communication is that people do not perceive the same "causes" of behavior. How does culture diversity affect the perception of causes?
9. How does culture affect interpersonal aggression? What cultures do you believe would be least prone to violence?
10. What are the characteristics of a collectivistic culture?

Our Locus in the Universe: Worldview and Intercultural Communication

SATOSHI ISHII
DONALD KLOPF
PEGGY COOKE

Worldview shapes cultures and serves to distinguish one culture from another. Its importance stems from the role it plays in defining reality or explaining the purpose of human life. Worldview thus represents one of the most fundamental qualities of culture, affecting all aspects of how a culture perceives the environment. Nurius (1994) reflects that the propensity for individuals to establish and sustain an image of a comprehensive, orderly, and predictable world fulfills one of the most fundamental human needs. Pennington (1985) proclaims that worldview must be given high, if not first, priority in the study of culture because it permeates all other components of culture. She further suggests that by understanding a culture's worldview, it is possible to attain reasonable accuracy in predicting behaviors and motivations in other dimensions. As such, worldview becomes a critical element of successful intercultural communication.

The worldview concept deserves the comprehension of communication scholars; in this paper we delineate its qualities, types, and religious perspectives.

WORLDVIEW DEFINED

Although the term *worldview* probably originated in German philosophy as *Weltanschauung,* literally "worldview," it has come to represent a variety of approaches to understanding the underpinnings of cultural diversity. It consists of the most general and comprehensive concepts and unstated assumptions about life.

Anthropologists Spradley and McCurdy (1980) define worldview as the way people characteristically look out on the universe. To communication educationalists Paige and Martin (1996), worldview is one of the lenses through which people view reality and the rest of the world. Sociologists Cosner, Nock, Steffan, and Rhea (1987) define it as a definition of reality. The psychologist Harriman (1947) relates worldview's association with *Weltanschauung* and considers it to be a total frame of reference.

Reflecting a religious perspective, Helve (1991) characterizes worldview as a systemized totality of beliefs about the world. In the same vein, Emerson (1996) conceives it as a set of assumptions about how the world is and ought to be organized. Nurius (1994), operating from a social work orientation, takes a tack at odds with other worldview advocates. She uses the term *assumptive worlds* to describe clusters of fundamental assumptions that individuals hold about themselves and the world around them. And, in the simplest of terms, psychologist Furnham (1993) describes worldview as "just world beliefs."

Samovar, Porter, and Stefani (1998) offer a more inclusive view in their definition: "Worldview is culture's orientation toward God, humanity, nature, questions of existence, the universe and cosmos, life, death, sickness, and other philosophical issues that influence how its members see the world."

Klopf (1998) also offers an inclusive perspective that relates to many fields of study. He perceives worldview as providing a frame of reference for understanding a culture's ways of perceiving, thinking, and speaking—a system of beliefs about the nature of the universe and its effects on the environment. Worldview deals with a culture's orientation toward ontological matters such as God, humankind, lower forms of life, inanimate objects, supernatural beings, nature, and matters concerning the relations of humans to one another. Worldview thus serves to explain how and why things got to be the way they are and why they continue that way. It assists people during crises and helps them adjust to environmental conditions.

Satoshi Ishii, Donald Klopf, and Peggy Cooke. Our Locus in the Universe: Worldview and Intercultural Communication. From the *Dokkyo International Review,* No. 12, (1999), 302–317. Reprinted by permission of the publisher. Satoshi Ishii teaches at Dokkyo University, Japan. Donald Klopf teaches at the University of Hawaii and West Virginia University. Peggy Cooke teaches at the University of Washington.

ELEMENTS OF WORLDVIEW

What constitutes worldview? The definitions given above included some of the elements. We add others, beginning with an anthropological analysis extended by Redfield (1953). He argues that the framework is the same for every culture's interpretation of worldview. His system includes 12 general conceptions of these elements:

1. The self or principal actor on humankind's stage
2. The others, those within the purview of the self
3. Other people, the unidentifiable mass
4. Differences between men and women
5. Distinctions between "we" (our own people) and "they" (other people)
6. Distinctions between what is human and what is not
7. Invisible beings, forces, principles
8. Animals
9. Concepts of human nature
10. A spatial orientation
11. A temporal orientation
12. Ideas about birth and death

Pennington's (1985) conception of worldview elements appear in the form of ten questions. The salient characteristics of her list are:

1. The culture's dominant beliefs and attitudes about a human's place in nature and society
2. The general pattern of relationships between humans and nature
3. The relationship between humans and the culture's supreme being
4. The supreme being's power over life and events
5. Humans' competitive or cooperative nature
6. Humans' expressions of their beliefs
7. Humans' myths about the origins of people
8. Humans' beliefs in the supernatural
9. The living patterns as group practices
10. The ways a group uses rituals, prayers, and other ceremonies

Psychologists Gilgen and Cho (1979) perceive worldview in an East–West dichotomy, the East based on religions associated with the Eastern world, and the West with European and American thought. These are compared as follows.

East	*West*
Humans are one with nature and perceive the spiritual and physical as one.	Humans are separate from nature and overshadowed by a personal God.
Mind and body are one.	Humans consist of mind, body, and soul.
Humans should accept their basic oneness with nature rather than try to control it.	Humans have to manipulate and control nature to survive.
Humans are one with nature; they should feel comfortable with anyone.	Humans should reward actions competitive in spirit.
Science and technology create an illusion of progress.	Science and technology provide the good life.
Enlightenment causes differences to disappear and brings oneness with the universe through meditation.	No such belief.

Dodd (1987) categorizes worldview elements into nine groupings, some of which tend to contrast the East and West.

Shame/Guilt. An Easterner bringing shame to a group is likely to be cast out of it. Westerners consider the individual more important than the group. Saving face is essential in the East; not so in the West.

Task/People. The East accentuates people relationships. The West stresses task accomplishment.

Secular/Spiritual. Eastern spiritual cultures rely on intuition and introspection. Secular Western cultures are analytical and logical.

Dead/Living. The East believes the dead can influence the living, bringing them luck or harm. The West is less prone to think that way.

Humans/Nature. Humans are either subject to nature, in harmony with nature, or should control nature. The East favors harmony; the West control.

Doing/Being. The East prefers harmonious relations, being rather than doing. The West wants to do things.

Linear/Cyclical. In the East, life is birth, life, death, and rebirth. In the West, life is birth, life, death.

Good/ Evil. Humans are either good or evil, or a mix of good and evil.

Fatalism/Control. To the fatalist, what happens is beyond a person's control, which tends to be an Eastern view. In the control view, people are masters of their own destiny, which tends to be a Western view.

FORMATION OF WORLDVIEWS

Worldview is implicit, implied but not verbally expressed. Helve (1991) believes it is improbable that people would be aware of their worldview. How it is formed, therefore, is a matter of speculation.

Worldview evidently develops in early childhood. Helve determined through empirical research that its actual growth can be comprehended by applying one or all of the theories identified as *cognitive development, social learning,* and *socialization.* She concluded each extended a sensible explanation.

Rubin and Peplau (1975) credit the child's parents, religious instruction, and instruction in the schools attended as contributors. Each child's maturation, experiences in the physical environment, and activities in the social environment contribute to worldview's formation. Then, too, children draw conclusions from their own experiences about what the world is like. Each child is a product of a social community, and the child's way of seeing the world is shaped by shared images and constructions of the child's social group or class.

Children and young people conceptualize the world in various ways at different stages in their growth according to their own mental development. Infancy, childhood, and adolescence involve distinct stages in thinking and learning. The shaping of their needs, values, beliefs, and attitudes varies from stage to stage, and so too will their worldview undergo change as they mature.

Emerson (1996) places stress on religion in developing worldview. By outlining what ought to be and by creating and reinforcing group norms through interaction, religion has a substantial influence on a person's worldview. Religion shapes reasoning. It also provides the meaning, importance, and properness of different social arrangements and institutions. Religion infuses all of these with universal if not transcendent significance.

Religious beliefs and practices differ, of course, and that is why, Emerson contends, people possess different worldviews. Those with conservative worldviews base their moral authority in the transcendent. Those holding more liberal views participate in the religious and secular cultures that root moral authority in humans. They stress reason and revelation.

Even though Emerson emphasizes religion's role in worldview development, he recognizes a person's position in the social structure as significant, even though he perceives it as only secondary. Reasonable people who live in dissimilar parts of the world are exposed to unlike realities. This dissimilar exposure leads each to arrive at separate worldviews.

Emerson's point is substantiated by Cooke (1992), who measured worldview among university students in Japan, Korea, Puerto Rico, and the United States. Her findings reveal significant differences among the four groups. Each group arrived at different conceptions of the worldview.

Chamberlain and Zika (1992) attribute the meaning of worldview to numerous sources, religion being just one. They argue that worldview stems from a variety of sources and that it is inappropriate to constrain it to a purely religious dimension.

TYPES OF WORLDVIEW

Helve (1991) classifies worldview into three types. In doing so, she appears to endorse the Chamberlain and Zika position. Helve's types are *scientific, metaphysical,* and *religious.*

The *scientific* worldview is based on the rules laid down by the exact sciences. It is open and self-correcting in accordance with new systematic and methodical findings. Helve found it to appear most clearly among scientific scholars. A quasi-scientific worldview results from television, magazine, and newspaper influences, she notes; it is more "information based" than scientific. Those with a scientific bent do not harbor this quasi-scientific worldview.

A *metaphysical* worldview tends to be based on abstract general reasoning without an empirical base. For example, the metaphysical worldview of young children may contain beliefs in imaginary beings such as Santa Claus, ghosts, witches, fairies, and elves. Older children may include elements of magic and superstition. Teenagers might construct their worldviews around horoscopes and act in accordance with the advice they give. The metaphysical worldview is apt to consist of certain types of unnatural beings, their characteristics, and their relationships. These beings originate partly in the traditions of religion and partially in folklore, some of which is created by the mass media.

The third type of worldview is *religious*. For most people, religion serves as the foundation of their worldview. The content of their beliefs will vary from person to person depending upon their religious perspective. A Catholic's worldview will undoubtedly differ from that of a Jew, a Protestant's from a Buddhist's, a Muslim's from a Taoist's, and a Shintoist's from a Confucianist's.

DIMENSIONS OF RELIGION

Religion, as we have related, is a deep and pervasive determinant of worldview. Even the most secular of people feel religion's influence. Those who reject religious faith still follow much of the religious heritage that influences their culture. Most people, theists and atheists alike, adhere to the commandment "Thou shalt not kill"—a tenet virtually all cultures respect.

Religion, Emerson (1996) attests, is multidimensional. He conceptualizes it along two dimensions, religiosity and orthodoxy, each with two subdivisions, public and private. Religiosity refers to the intensity and consistency of religious practices. Orthodoxy is the degree to which one's beliefs center on a guiding authority—for example, the Scriptures of the Church.

Private religiosity is one's own personal, undisclosed religious practice. Examples include the frequency of prayer and holy scripture reading as well as a doubt-free faith. Public religiosity describes the religious activities practiced with other people. It is manifest in frequent church attendance and participation in membership functions.

Private orthodoxy refers to held beliefs that rely on a transcendent authority, a god, or a supernatural being. Heavy reliance on Holy Scripture while verbalizing and making decisions is an example. Public orthodoxy is the sharing of beliefs in the company of others.

EASTERN AND WESTERN RELIGIONS

As a more manageable way of thinking about the world's diverse faiths, Smart (1988) groups them into two major divisions: Eastern and Western. Each can help increase an understanding of the impact religion has on the content and development of one's worldview. Eastern and Western religious traditions account for about 90% of the world's population. The remaining 10% consists of shamanists, animists, atheists, and the like.

Religious Similarities

Although the two divisions have few common teachings, they do possess similarities typical of all religions. Samovar, Porter, and Stefani (1998) identify five such similarities, the most important being *sacred writings*. All of the world's major religions have writings revered by believers. These writings are the vehicles for dissemination of the religion's knowledge and wisdom. Included are the Bible, the written centerpiece for the Christian religion; the Hebrew Bible or Old Testament, the sacred book of the Jews; the Koran, the Muslim writings; the Vedas, the sacred writings of the Hindus; and the Pali Canon, where the teachings of the Buddha are inscribed.

Another similarity is an *authority figure*. God, Allah, Jesus as the Son of God, or the Buddha is an authority figure who is someone greater than the religion's members, one they turn to for guidance.

Rituals are the third similarity. They are practices required of the membership or acts that are forbidden to the members. For example, believers must be baptized or circumcised. They must fast on certain days or pray at special times. They may not eat pork or perhaps beef. These acts embody humility, restraint, and awareness, behaviors of great significance.

Speculation typifies all religions. Humans seek answers to life's mysteries—what is life, death, suffering, origins of the universe—and religions supply answers, speculative at best.

Religion also includes an *ethic*, a set of moral principles for the membership to observe. For most religions, the set contains items such as marital fidelity, paying honor to mother and father, and prohibitions against killing, stealing, and lying.

Eastern

The countries of Eastern and Southern Asia (Korea, China, Japan, India, and others) embrace religious traditions that feature harmony as the ultimate good (Smart, 1988). Harmony is the major tenet found in

Hinduism, Shintoism, Buddhism, Confucianism, and Taoism.

Although these religions differ considerably, their foundations are similar. Deity is in every place in every form, rather than in a single place or form. Harmony affects behavior because everything is benign, nothing is worth worrying about. True believers respond to crucial issues with a smile. Being pleasant helps keep things in perspective because nothing is going to mean much in the long run anyway.

Ethically, Eastern religions do not hold with an absolute right. Everything is relative to the situation. Then, too, life is circular. One's essence takes another form at death, termed *reincarnation*. This goes on and on without end. What is desirable is in every thing in the world, not just in special places or acts called sacred. What is important is the here and now.

In Figure 1, Ishii (1990) characterizes Eastern and Western worldviews. The polytheistic represents the East and the monotheistic the West. In the polytheistic view, the gods/goddesses/deities, human beings, and natural beings are all relative to each other. They are changeable, not absolute or rigid. Deities can reside anywhere, in rocks, animals, and humans. In the figure, the triangular relationship of the three entities symbolizes this relative relationship. No hierarchy is present among the three. Their domains are relative and flexible, as implied by the broken ovals connected by lines within the world/universe circle.

Western

The West's capsulation of religion, and hence worldview, is in sharp contrast to the Eastern. The Western religions perceive the ultimate good as transformation. Members of the Jewish, Islamic, and Christian faiths believe that divine grace is the desired end, whether in this life or the next. Differences among these religions are obvious, yet they have a common foundation. They are monotheistic, believing in one God who is "out there" and everything else is here, with a great gulf in between. The world is split in two—the way it was intended to be versus the way it is. There is the good and desirable, and there is sin.

In the Western religions, Smart (1988) informs us, everything is headed somewhere, to the Kingdom of God or to heaven, to an end. At the end of an individual's life will be an accounting or payoff, either life or death or resurrection of the body. At the end of all human life will be an apocalypse, a disclosure.

The things that belong to God and religion are sacred. They are special, to be treated with awe and reverence. What is important is felicity—happiness or bliss—beyond this earthly life.

In Figure 1, the monotheistic worldview depicts the existence of one almighty God who ranks first above all else. Human beings rank next in the hierarchy, and natural beings last. These rankings are absolute and unchangeable, as shown by the solid circles

Figure 1 *Contrastive Worldviews (Ishii, 1990)*

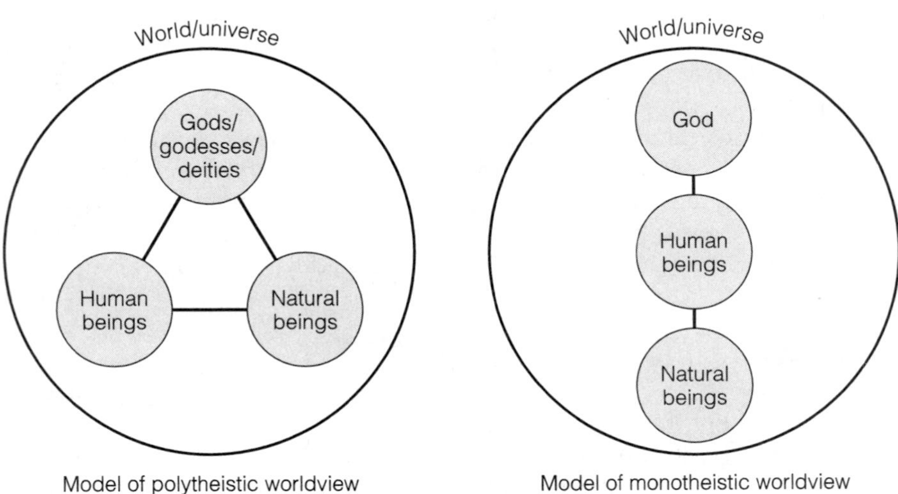

vertically aligned within the world/universe circle. The domains of the three are not related one to the other.

COLLIDING WORLDVIEWS

Figure 1 also reveals two distinct worldviews, ones clearly at odds with each other. The separation is immortalized in the words of Rudyard Kipling: "Oh, East is East, and West is West, and never the twain shall meet." The two are so unlike they will never be capable of sharing their ideas and feelings about anything. Nevertheless, Kipling's next lines in his *Ballad of East and West* extend hope. He thinks that strong men and women when standing face to face regardless of their breed, birth, or border can interact successfully. Whether one's view is Eastern or Western, Kipling holds out hope for satisfying verbalizing.

Unfortunately, fruitful intercultural relations are not always the norm even when strong men and women meet together. Too often, imbroglios like Captain Cook's Hawaiian adventure bring out the worst in people. Misunderstandings and occasional serious consequences result.

No less contentious are the frequent encounters between developers and environmentalists, those who want to conquer and direct the forces of nature and those who maintain that humans are subject to nature. Those conflicts are being fought at every level, local, national, and international.

Clark (1998) warns us that environmental destruction is accelerating, not decelerating. At the local level, the loss of forests, soil erosion, and overdrafts of groundwater are common occurrences. Increased yields of timber and food crops are unsustainable. People worldwide are mining nature's resource base. Human-induced global warming, overgrazing, and deforestation are compounding droughts. Pollution problems are multiplying as waters are poisoned or salinated, as forests and lakes are decimated by acid rain, and as cities worldwide suffer from foul air.

Recall that Dodd (1987) reminded us about our relationship with nature. Either we are subject to nature, in harmony with it, or should control it. Today's state suggests that harmony is absent, control is not working, and soon we will be subject to total natural disaster. Worldviews are colliding as we communicate more and more closely with our fellow humans throughout the world.

Clark (1989) points a finger at the Western worldview, placing blame for environmental conditions directly on the West. Although major polluters, soil eroders, and deforesters are prevalent in the East as well, Clark believes it is the Western worldview that is destroying the environment. She suggests that the Western worldview lacks proper values and goals and has grown obsolete. All worldviews, she claims, require adjustment if humans are to survive. But the most in need of redoing is that of the West, whose enormous military, technological, and economic power impinges upon the entire globe.

UNTYING THE GORDIAN KNOT

In her book, *Ariadne's Thread: The Search for New Modes of Thinking* (1989), Clark gives us a thread with which we might find our way out of the labyrinth created by colliding worldviews. Her way may help untie the Gordian knot in which disparate worldviews are enmeshed as they attempt to exist together in the 21st century.

In ages past, she argues, worldviews evolved gradually, often imperceptibly. With today's enormous powers unleashed by science and technology from the Western worldview creating excessive environmental change, humankind can no longer rely on the old, indiscernible thinking. Human goals need to be reordered.

All worldviews require some degree of adjustment if the species is to survive. Tracing the beliefs and assumptions underlying them is the first step in making social change possible. This first step is one that students of communication can undertake, learning to understand the differences in worldview globally and to comprehend the beliefs and assumptions on which they are based.

Clark cautions that imposing a new worldview will certainly fail unless it comes from within the cultural context. A culture's people must actively participate in the change making. For a new worldview to evolve, everyone must participate in the change process.

In her 1998 *Zygon* article, Clark expounds on her new worldview in detail. Her plan may be far too esoteric for students in intercultural courses to consider. They can exit their courses with the rudiments of the worldview concept. If they do, as Pennington (1985) believes, reasonable preciseness can be reached in predicting behaviors and motivations in the social, economic, and political lives of the globe's cultures. As Smart (1988) prompts us, we ignore at our peril the worldview dimensions of our interactions with other cultures.

References

Chamberlain, K., & Zika, S. (1992). Religiosity, meaning in life, and psychological well being. In J. F. Schumacher (Ed.), *Religion and mental health.* New York: Oxford University Press.

Clark, M. E. (1989). *Ariadne's thread: The search for new modes of thinking.* New York: St. Martin's Press.

Clark, M. E. (1998). Human nature: What we need to know about ourselves in the twenty first century. *Zygon, 333,* 645–659.

Cooke, P. (1992). *The relationship between culture and worldview: A cross cultural comparison of Japan, Korea, Puerto Rico, and the United States.* Unpublished master's thesis, West Virginia University, Morgantown, VA.

Cosner, L., Nock, S., Steffan, P., & Rhea, B. (1987). *Introduction to sociology* (2nd ed.). San Diego, CA: Harcourt Brace.

Dodd, C. H. (1987). *Dynamics of intercultural communication* (2nd ed.). Dubuque, IA: W. C. Brown.

Emerson, M. O. (1996). Through tinted glasses: Religion, worldviews, and abortion attitudes. *Journal for the Scientific Study of Religion, 35,* 41–55.

Furnham, A. (1993). Just world beliefs in twelve societies. *Journal of Social Psychology, 133,* 317–329.

Gilgen, A., & Cho, I. (1979). Questionnaire to measure Eastern and Western thought. *Psychological Reports, 44.*

Harriman, P. L. (1947). *The new dictionary of psychology.* New York: Philosophical Library.

Helve, H. (1991). The formation of religious attitudes and worldviews: A longitudinal study of young Finns. *Social Compass, 38,* 373–392.

Ishii, S., Okabe, R., Kume, T., & Hirai, K. (1990). *Ibunks komyunikeshon kiwado.* Tokyo: Yuhikaku.

Klopf, D. W. (1998). *Intercultural encounters:* The *fundamentals of intercultural communication.* Englewood, NJ: Morton.

Nurius, P. S. (1994). Assumptive worlds, self-definition, and striving among women. *Basic and Applied Social Psychology, 15,* 311–327.

Paige, R. M., & Martin, J. N. (1996). Ethics in intercultural training. In D. Landis & R. S. Bhagat (Eds.), *Handbook of intercultural training,* (2nd ed.). Thousand Oaks, CA: Sage.

Pennington, U. L. (1985). Intercultural communication. In L. Samovar & R. E. Porter (Eds.), *Intercultural communication: A reader* (4th ed.). Belmont, CA: Wadsworth.

Redfield, R. (1953). The *primitive world and its transformation.* Ithaca, NY: Cornell University Press.

Rubin, Z., & Peplau, L. A. (1975). Who believes in a just world? *Journal of Social Issues, 31,* 65–89.

Samovar, L., Porter, R. E., & Stefani, L. A. (1998). *Communication between cultures.* Belmont, CA: Wadsworth.

Smart, R. (1988). Religion-caused complications in intercultural communication. In L. Samovar & R. E. Porter (Eds.), *Intercultural communication: A reader* (5th ed., pp. 62–76). Belmont, CA: Wadsworth.

Spradley, J. P., & McCurdy, U. W. (1980). *Anthropology: The cultural perspective* (2nd ed.). Prospect Heights, IL: Waveland.

Concepts and Questions

1. Ishii, Klopf, and Cooke assert that worldview shapes culture. How does your worldview contribute to your culture?
2. What is the most significant aspect of worldview? How does cultural diversity in this dynamic lead to differing worldviews?
3. Sumarize in general terms how worldview differs between Eastern and Western cultures.
4. How does shame/guilt affect worldview? In which cultures might this factor be most prevalent?
5. How is worldview formed? Are there cultural differences in the mechanisms by which worldview is formed?
6. What is a scientific worldview? What cultures are most likely to have a scientific-based worldview?
7. What does a metaphysical view tend to contribute to a worldview?
8. What is religiosity? How does it contribute to shaping a worldview?
9. Differentiate between Eastern and Western religious perspectives regarding ethics.

The Practice of Intercultural Communication: Reflections for Professionals in Cultural Meetings

Iben Jensen

Intercultural communication research has a new target group, thanks to the globalization process: professional practitioners in multiethnic societies—nurses, social workers, lawyers, teachers, and others who in respect of their professionalism are responsible for successful intercultural communication. Traditionally, professional practitioners have been left with handbooks and readers based mainly upon functionalistic theories (Martin & Nakayama, 2000; Samovar, Porter, & Jain, 1981; Asante & Gudykunst, 1989; Hofstede, 1980; Okabe, 1983; Prosser, 1978). Lots of answers have been given. However, more and more professional practitioners have found that simple answers to cultural differences do not work in multiethnic societies.

The complexity in society demands more complex questions and answers. I will argue that a poststructural approach can handle the complexity of the concepts that are necessary to describe multiethnic societies. I will also argue that it is both necessary and possible from a poststructuralist approach to develop analytical tools that refer to the practitioner's everyday experiences. The functionalistic approach has already proved that practitioners want practical tools they can use in praxis in everyday life. In respect to this need, I find that one of the challenges in the field of intercultural communication is to develop analytical tools on the basis of complex concepts describing complex societies (Bauman, 1999; Jensen, 1998/2001).

This article is divided into three parts. In the first part, I will discuss how the field of intercultural communication research can contribute to professional practitioners in multiethnic societies. In the second part, I will present four analytical tools for intercultural communication as seen from a poststructuralist perspective. These analytical tools add up to a model for intercultural communication. In the third part, I will discuss the concept of cultural identity in relation to intercultural communication.

INTERCULTURAL COMMUNICATION IN A GLOBAL CONTEXT

Intercultural communication research has by definition been related to the understanding of national cultures as the fundamental principle. Cultures were nations. Apart from the curiosity that most intercultural readers began with a short passage saying that sometimes people inside a nation could be more different from one another than people across cultures (Samovar et al., 1981), the whole idea of intercultural communication was linked to national culture.

Twelve years ago, however, Ulf Hannerz (1992) argued that rather than talking about different national cultures, we should see all cultures as creolized societies. Hannerz grasped early the discourse that has continued in new discussions about globalization. Globalization normally refers to two opposite processes: (a) the globalization process, in which we are all getting closer and closer to each other through consumerism, ideology, and knowledge about each other; and (b) the localization process, which makes us focus intensively on our local nation or local ethnic group (Featherstone, 1990; Hylland Eriksen, 1993).

In the debates about globalization, it is intensively discussed whether globalization is a new process or not. Jonathan Friedman (1994) suggests that there is nothing new. He argues that the mobility that is seen as central to globalization applies primarily to the elite (p. 23). Zygmunt Bauman (1999) agrees, but he adds that it makes sense to see mobility as the *idea* of society. Bauman also argues that the mobile society is not open to everybody. Globalization has, according to Bauman, caused a new polarization in societies that divides people into two groups: tourists and vagabonds. The tourists can travel freely with few restrictions. The vagabonds are forced to travel because of war, poverty,

From *The Journal of Intercultural Communication,* no. 6 (2003). http://www.immi.se/intercultural/nr6/jensen.rtf. Iben Jensen, Associate Professor, teaches at the University of Roskilde, Denmark. Reprinted by permission.

or hunger. The vagabonds are not welcomed like tourists, but are met with high walls of customs duties and barbed wire. Although Bauman can be criticized for painting a too simplistic picture, I think he points to some of the most important discourses in Western societies, significant to the intercultural communication process: the discourses telling whom to include and whom to exclude, which I find is a social practice crucial to research in intercultural communication.

It is often argued that there is no difference between intercultural communication and other kinds of communication (Gudykunst, 1994; Sarbaugh, 1979). However, in multiethnic societies, one of the differences is exactly that in intercultural communication it is legitimate discourse to discuss who of the participants in a communication process "really" belongs to the majority culture. Intercultural communication in a globalized world is forced to take that circumstance into account and include questions of globalization and cultural identity.

WHAT DOES THE "CLASSIC" RESEARCH FIELD OFFER PRACTITIONERS?

In short, the field of intercultural communication research can be divided in two main traditions: a tradition based on a functionalistic approach and a tradition based on a poststructuralist approach. The functionalist research tradition has tried to *predict* how culture would influence communication. The focus has been on identifying *culture as a barrier* against more effective communication (Samovar et al., 1981[1]; Samovar & Porter, 1991; Brislin et al., 1986; Gudykunst, 1983, 1994, 1995; Hall, 1959; Sarbaugh, 1979). In these works, practitioners are offered tools to describe how they can expect the intercultural communication to appear. The functionalist research tradition also includes competence research that tries to establish criteria to determine which characteristics a person needs in order to acquire intercultural competence (Gertsen, 1990; Søderberg, 1994; Kincaid, 1987).

The Dutch management researcher Geert Hofstede's work *Culture's Consequences* (1980) has had an enormous influence on the research tradition in intercultural communication. Hofstede investigated the relationship between employees and management in 40 different cultures, and on this basis he developed four dimensions: power/ distance (small/large), uncertainty avoidance/anxiety, individualism/collectivism, and masculinity/ femininity. The dimensions are all based on the idea that cultures are homogenous national cultures that do not change in time worth mentioning. Most often Hofstede's dimensions are used uncritically, in spite of the fact that they were developed more than 20 years ago. William B. Gudykunst is one of the influential researchers who have legitimized the use of Hofstede's work in recent times. Gudykunst (1995) presents a new theory of intercultural communication in which he builds upon Hofstede's dimensions, developed from the perspective of nations as homogeneous static societies. However, Hofstede's model is an offer—an offer to categorize the world in some very simple categories that we can recognize from everyday life. Hofstede offers all interested in intercultural communication an immediate explanation of how communication in management is influenced by culture.

William B. Gudykunst and Young Yun Kim, in their book *Communicating with Strangers* (1984), took a very important step in their attempt to describe the intercultural communication process. They argued that we should see intercultural communication as a dialogical process in which both persons involved are both addressee and addressed. Their model describes interpersonal intercultural communication in terms of person A and B message/feedback influences with psychocultural, sociocultural, and cultural filters. Framing the whole communication process are environmental influences (p. 14). The authors explain their model as follows: "Without understanding the strangers' filters, we cannot accurately interpret or predict their behaviours" (p. 35). Related to the poststructural approach, the model is missing the aspect of power. You could argue that the aspect of power could be in every part of the model, yet somehow it is not mentioned at all. The model offers the possibility of thinking in terms of social differences, but it still leaves the possibility of categorization with national cultures as the dominant and most relevant in every communication process.

POSTSTRUCTURAL OFFERS?

Compared to the functionalists' offers, the poststructuralist approach at first glimpse does not appear very useful. Most of the researchers working with a poststructuralist approach are either philosophical

(Applegate & Sypher, 1983, 1988; González & Tanno, 1999; Jandt & Tanno, 1994, 1996) or discussing issues related to theory of intercultural communication (Collier & Thomas, 1988). Collier and Thomas, for example, discuss intercultural communication from the perspective of the individual. They define intercultural communication as involving those "who identify themselves as distinct from one another in cultural terms" (p. 100). This definition differs from the then dominant thinking by taking its point of departure in the actor rather than in the culture. It is the interpretations of the participant that determine what culture the person belongs to.

Taking a poststructuralist approach, Jandt and Tanno (1996) wrote some important theoretical and philosophical articles about ethics and methods that address the importance of labeling and constructing "the other" in intercultural research. In 1995, Jandt published a reader in intercultural communication in which students were introduced to a poststructuralist approach. Jandt's reader is the first and most competent reader about intercultural communication from a critical perspective. Jandt takes a portion of the functionalistic perspective into account but relates it to context and research methods.

From another tradition, but as part of constructionist thinking, the Japanese American Muneo Yoshikawa has done a study of intercultural dialogue. Yoshikawa (1987) presents what he calls the "double swing model." The model looks like a sign of infinity.[2] Yoshikawa was inspired by Martin Buber, who worked with a duality in the relationship between "you" and "I." With this model, Yoshikawa emphasizes that both partners in communication play both roles as addresser and addressee. In the double swing model, communication is seen as an infinite process, and the two participants will both change in the meeting. Yoshikawa underlines that the goal in communication is not to eliminate differences, but to use the dynamics that arise through the meeting.

INTERCULTURAL COMMUNICATION MODEL

In a study of intercultural communication in complex, multiethnic societies (Jensen, 1998), I developed a model for intercultural communication from a poststructuralist approach using four analytical tools: positions of experience, cultural presuppositions, cultural self-perception, and cultural fix points. This model, illustrated in Figure 1, (1) describes an intercultural communication process between two actors,

Figure 1 *Communication Model from Jensen (1988) and Yoshikawa (1987)*

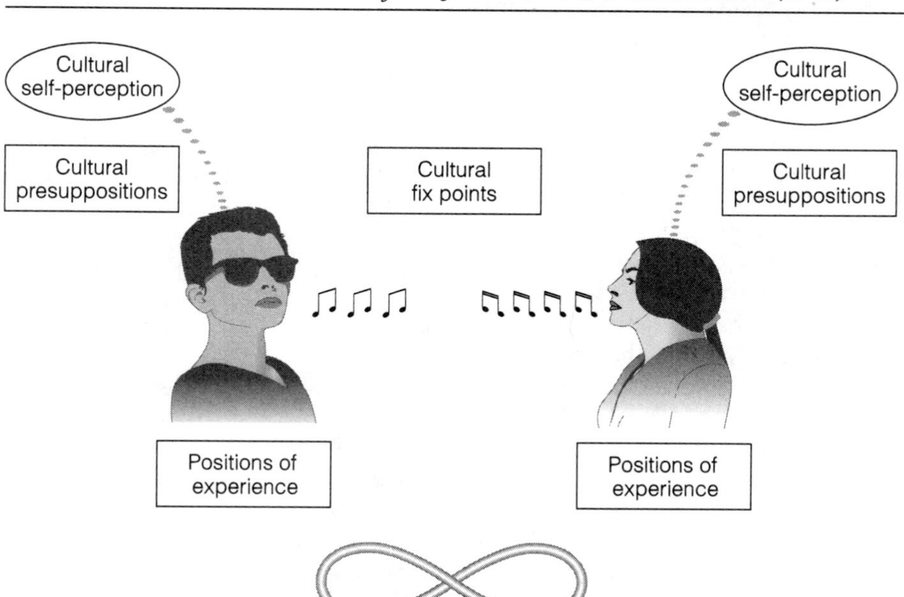

who are both addressers and addressees; (2) emphasizes the interconnectedness between the participants in the communication process; and (3) shows that the communication process is an infinite, ongoing process (Yoshikawa, 1987). The aim of the model is to let the practitioner or student think through an intercultural communication process and reflect upon it from a new perspective.

Positions of Experiences

The concept of *positions of experience* refers to the fact that all interpretations are bounded in individual experiences, but although the experiences are subjective, they are related to the person's social position.

From an everyday perspective, theoretically represented by Berger and Luckmann (1966), the term *experience* is central. In intercultural communication, we have to respect that our communication partner might have other experiences, and has been socialized to experience his or her world as real (Berger & Luckmann, 1966). It is impossible to ignore one's experiences. That is an important fact in intercultural communication. The philosopher Hans Georg Gadamer has been occupied with the meaning of understanding. Gadamer sees interpretations as being related to the experiences of the actor. The term *positions of experience* is inspired by Gadamer's (1989) term *horizon of experience:* "The Horizon is the range of vision that includes everything that can be seen from a particular vantage point" (p. 302).

Understanding is based upon experience. We understand the world on the basis of our own experiences, and our experience of the world is limited by our vantage point (Gadamer, 1989). In relation to intercultural communication, this means that we cannot see cultural differences as the only differentiation to interpretation, but we have to take the horizon into account. As I will argue later, the horizon may be limited by the social space of the actor. In that case, actors' experiences will be different, not only related to their different cultures, but also related to their social position in society.

The concept *positions of experience* is also inspired by awareness of the concept of *positioning*. The social constructionists Davies and Harré (1990) describe positioning as follows:

> Positioning, as we will use it, is the discursive process whereby selves are located in conversations as observably and subjectively coherent participants in jointly produced story lines. There can be interactive positioning in which what one person says positions another, and there can be reflexive positioning in which one positions oneself. However it would be a mistake to assume that, in either case, positioning is necessarily intentional. One lives one's life in terms of one's ongoing produced self, whoever might be responsible for its production. (p. 40)

Positioning between ethnic majority and ethnic minorities is often produced along national and ethnic differences. The minorities often have a hard time getting another positioning from the majority, not only in the media but also in the everyday position they are given (Hussain, Yilmaz, & O'Connor et al., 1997; Jensen, 2000).

Seen as an analytical tool, positions of experience first gives an awareness of how people's different positions are crucial to the interpretation of the communication. Second, positions of experience reflect that people in intercultural communication always have different opportunities to give different positions of themselves. Essential to a critical intercultural communication perspective is that social positions and experiences are not floating in space, but are created in social structures. Experiences and positionings are made in the social space on the given conditions of the individual. This point of view resembles Bourdieu's term *habitus* (Bourdieu, 1986; Bourdieu & Wacquant, 1992/1996).

Third, although the tool focuses on the individual differences, it is interconnected with structural differences. In the case of intercultural communication, ethnic background is always a part of a person's experience, but the actual role played in the communication is negotiated with other relations.

If we use positions of experience as an analytical tool, the following questions are relevant to ask:

Where and how in the communication does the actor tell about his/her primary experiences?[3]

How do different subject positions influence the actor's way of positioning him/herself in relation to culture?

In which ways does the actor's social position influence the actor's experiences and his or her interpretation of the communication process?

Cultural Presuppositions

Cultural presuppositions refers to knowledge, experience, feelings, and opinions we have toward categories of people that we do not regard as members of the cultural communities with which we identify ourselves.

The concept of cultural presuppositions is also inspired by Gadamer's work. The aim of this analytical tool originates from my interest in finding a term for "understanding across cultural communities." I found a piece of the answer in Gadamer's simplified doctrine: "All understanding is a matter of presuppositions" (Bukhdal, 1967). No matter what kind of knowledge we have about other groups, no matter how lacking and prejudiced it is, this knowledge is the basis for the interpretations we make.

The cultural presuppositions of an actor will always be part of available discourses in society.

> A discourse is a particular type of representation. A discourse is a group of statements, which provide a language for talking about, i.e., a way of representing a particular kind of knowledge about a topic. When statements about a topic are made within a particular discourse, the discourse makes it possible to construct the topic in a certain way. It also limits the other ways in which the topic can be constructed. (Hall, 1997, p. 201)

The intention of the concept of cultural presuppositions is to create awareness about the ordinary process whereby people outside our own social community are often characterized (negatively) on the basis of our own values. This explains why "they" (very often) are described as "the inadequate others" while our own culture is idealized. Whereas the actors' understandings are constructed on the basis of discourses in society, cultural presuppositions could be described as the actors' actual use of discourses in society. In an analysis of, for example, an intercultural interview and an interview with a topic of intercultural issue, it is also possible to find discursive formations.

> Whenever one can describe, between a number of statements, such a system of dispersion, whenever . . . one can define a regularity . . . we will say . . . that we are dealing with a discursive formation. (Foucault, in Hall, 1997, p. 202)

Cultural presuppositions are a very simple but practical tool to increase awareness of the discourses and discursive formations in everyday life. At the everyday level, it is helpful to be aware of how, for example, a client is categorizing "others."

In general, you can find the cultural presuppositions in communication or texts by asking:

How are "the others" described?[4]
How do the description and interpretation of the others tell something about our own values?[5]

Cultural Self-Perception

Cultural self-perception is the ways in which an actor expresses a cultural community as the one he or she identifies with.

Cultural self-perception is strongly connected with cultural presuppositions, as it is through the construction of "the others" that we construct narratives about ourselves. Cultural self-perception can point out the idealization that often occurs when the debating partners represent different values or different cultural communities. Cultural presuppositions and cultural self-perception will also be tools to grab ethnocentrism, as ethnocentrism is seeing your own culture as the natural center and comparing others' cultures with your own sovereignty.

The analytical goal of this tool is to gain access to the ways in which the actors understand their own cultural communities. Cultural self-perception can describe social communities, such as national, ethnic, or gender-contingent communities. In this connection, it is primarily used in relation to national cultures. Depending on which cultural community is emphasized, it can be linked to different identities. Cultural self-perception is often hidden as "the right way" to organize life. In practice this tool enables the researcher to ask:

What cultural communities does the actor identify with?
Does the actor identify him- or herself as distinct from other cultural communities?
Does the actor idealize his or her own cultural community?

Cultural Fix Points

Cultural fix points are the focal points that arise in the communication between two actors who both feel they represent a certain topic. For a topic to be seen as a cultural fix point, it requires that both actors identify with this topic, and that they position themselves in a discussion. Cultural fix points are not entirely arbitrary, but they relate to societal structures. Intercultural communication is normally related to misunderstanding and conflicts—although most intercultural communication is without any problems (Jandt, 1995). To be able to focus more upon the exception, I see fix points as a way to sharpen our views.

In relation to intercultural communication, the aim of the concept of cultural fix points is to identify some patterns in the conflicts that are characteristic of given periods. In Denmark in the 1990s, for example, we could point to gender roles, arranged marriages, education of children, and scarfs. It is impossible to predict whether these aspects will have significance, but we can investigate whether they are significant in the actual situations, because cultural fix points demand that both actors identify with a topic. In practice, a researcher can ask: What topics provoke emotional statements? In practice, the researcher listens for or reads for a deviation from the opponent's rhythm, speech turns, interruptions, vocal pitch, word constructions, slip of the tongue, eagerness, uncompleted sentences, argumentation pattern, and the like. Is it possible to identify a point of disagreement?

With these four tools for analysis—positions of experience, cultural presuppositions, self-perception, and fix points—the researcher can encircle how the actors interpret each other's expressions in everyday life. The tools for analysis offer a systematic work method in general analyses of what is going on in intercultural communication processes. I see the analytical tools as a possible way for practitioners to get a vocabulary of "the others" that makes them reflect upon their own everyday reaction to their clients or patients. However, fix points are also closely linked to the construction of identity in relation to "others." Cultural identity is, as I have argued earlier in the article, a very important part of intercultural communication.

CULTURAL IDENTITY IN INTERCULTURAL COMMUNICATION

I have always wondered why intercultural communications have always called forth so many emotions. With the concept of cultural identity, I think we get closer to at least a part of an explanation for that phenomenon.

Stuart Hall shows in his work that the game of identity is played everywhere in society, which is why we have to include the major significance of identity within intercultural communication (Hall, Held, & McGrew, 1992; Hall & du Gay, 1996). In relation to cultural identity, the work of Arjun Appadurai is interesting. Appadurai (1991) argues that within the global we have developed a number of "scapes" with a larger structural and identity-caring significance than the national communities. Appadurai mentions the following "scapes": (1) ethno-scapes, which are about integration; (2) media-scapes, dominated by mass media; (3) techno-scapes, referring to global technological development; (4) finance-scapes, which draw attention to the autonomous cycle of finances; and (5) ideo-scapes, which illustrate how ideologies are developed across national borders (pp. 192–193). With his "scapes," Appadurai points to a new form of imagined communities (Anderson, 1983) that could take over from the imagined communities of the nation.

Different Meanings

Like the term *culture,* the term *cultural identity* has many different meanings. And just as with "culture," different paradigms prefer certain meanings of the term. Thus we can point at a functionalist-based understanding of cultural identity where the goal is to find a national mind, a particular characteristic identity of the population as a whole (Røgilds, 1995). Within the humanities, the term *cultural identity* also exists, but with another meaning—a form of identity created by a uniform use of texts and exchange of and use of symbols as parts of identities (Fornäs, 1995, p. 240). From this perspective one might investigate, for example, how young people use and read symbols in fashion magazines. Within the constructivist perspective, it is a general understanding that cultural identity is a form of social identity constructed in relation to other people in a given period of time.

> Cultural identity is a core aspect of this welter of phenomena that confront us. The term refers to a social identity that is based on a specific cultural configuration of a conscious nature. History, language and race are all possible bases for cultural identity and they are all socially constructed realities. (Friedman, 1994, p. 238)

Friedman argues that cultural identity is a social identity based on specific cultural forms that are all socially constructed. One of the most characteristic features of cultural identity today is the meaning of politics. We have moved from broader politics based on universality such as Marxism to politics where gender, ethnicity, and local identity have been given central significance. This has created new social categories, new identities, and new political groups (Friedman, 1994).

Stuart Hall, who has been working with cultural identity from a cultural study tradition, agrees only in very general terms with Jonathan Friedman. Like Friedman, Hall also regards cultural identity as social identity, and he also agrees that it has to do with nation and race. Hall defines cultural identity as follows:

> Cultural identities—those aspects of our identities which arise from our "belonging" to distinctive ethnic, racial, linguistic, religious and, above all, national cultures. (Hall et al., 1992, p. 274)

Contrary to Friedman, Stuart Hall works with a decentralized subject or multiple identities. Identity, Hall argues, is historically rather than biologically defined. The self is fragmented and does not contain one identity but several, often contradictory identities. The subject's identity is not given, but the subject occupies different identities at different points of time (Hall et al., 1992; Gergen 1985, 1991).

> Identity becomes a "moveable" feast formed and transformed continuously in relation to the ways we are represented or addressed in the cultural systems which surrounds us. . . . Within us are contradictory identities pulling in different directions, so that our identifications are continuously being shifted about. (Hall et al., 1992, p. 277)

According to Hall et al., the reason why we see ourselves as coherent persons is the narratives we construct about ourselves. "If we feel we have a unified identity from birth to death, it is only because we construct a comforting story or 'narrative of the self' about ourselves" (p. 277).

In continuation of Collier and Thomas's (1988) use of cultural identity, Hall's use of the term is very interesting for the development of intercultural communication in complex societies. By working with multiple identities, we develop skills for pinpointing the identities that, for example, young people who live in diaspora express. These young people do not express that they are torn *between* two worlds, but that they live *in* two worlds. The idea of multiple identities is also relevant in relation to intercultural communication because it provides us with an explanation for why certain topics create heated discussions (fix points). If certain topics actualize different identities, the communication will have connotations that the participants might not be prepared for.

When identity is formed in relation to others, it also gets a political twist (Gergen, 1991). This happens, for example, when the majority fixes the minority in the idea that "they" are different because they practice another religion or lack national linguistic qualifications; this is part of the social process of "othering," in which the majority constructs and normalizes distances to other groups (Kelly 1998, Razack 1998). For example, a Turkish-Danish girl is constructed as traditionally Turkish by Danish girls and seen as inauthentic or confused if she chooses to position herself with more features in common with Danish girls (Jensen, 1998). The girl can choose between being in the group by positioning herself as Turkish, as the ethnically Danish girls expect, or otherwise having a lower status in the group. In both cases, the Danish girls are the defining group; through their construction, they maintain the right to include or exclude the Turkish-Danish girl. In everyday life's intercultural conversations, this means that ethnic minorities have to invalidate the majority's simplified understandings of them.

Cultural Identity As an Analytical Tool

Although Hall's definition of cultural identity is interesting, it does have an important weakness in relation to intercultural communication: It assumes that national identity will always be the primary identity. This means that we have not dissociated ourselves from intercultural research's underlying reducing way of seeing national culture as the most important explanation in a communication situation (Jensen, 1998, 16–19). To solve this problem, I suggest that the actualized identity depends on the topic—what the participants are talking about. Some conversations will actualize national identity, whereas other conversations will not concern national ideas at all. However, the conversation still has to be seen in an intercultural context.

Thus, I propose that we use an understanding of cultural identity that is not delimited by race, ethnicity, or nation, but as a figure that holds different kinds of identity such as gender, work, or hobby. By doing this, we do not create a hierarchic structure, and we avoid having one particular identity as the determining one. Figuratively speaking, we can see cultural identity as a yellow dandelion. Every little yellow petal symbolizes a fragment of our identities. In practice, all identities are in the flower all the time. It is only analytically that we can distinguish and fix the floating identities. Only in a short moment it is possible to point out specific fragments of identities (Jensen, 2001).

In practice, the concept of cultural identity can be used in two ways:

1. As training for professional practitioners to see users as more than ethnic minorities. Focusing, for example, on age or gender gives the social worker a possibility to be conscious of her or his cultural presuppositions toward the client.
2. To be conscious of one's own cultural identity. When does the nurse actualize her gender identity? When does she use her professional identity?

In relation to professional practitioners, their professional identity is of particular interest. In the Nordic countries, it is my guess that most education is national and not multiethnic in its basis. An everyday consequence of this fact is that it takes a lot of reflection and discussion for professional practitioners to find a multiethnic professionalism.

The Professional Cultural Meeting

I have argued that the global changes have made it important to work explicitly with intercultural communication in relation to professional practitioners in multiethnic societies. After a short presentation of my theoretical perspectives, I have shown how I see intercultural communication in everyday life. In presenting a model of intercultural communication, I have also discussed four different analytical tools, which are all part of the model. The last very important part of intercultural communication for practitioners is the concept of cultural identity. By operationalizing it, one can become more aware of one's own national or other identity.

To be a professional in multiethnic societies involves different degrees of intercultural awareness. To have intercultural competence as a practitioner is to have a professional knowledge about, for example, the analytical tools in intercultural communication I have presented and concepts such as globalization, culture, language, and intercultural communication cultural identity—and to work with antidiscrimination and equal ethnic rights as the basic assumption.

Notes

1. From 1972 to 1995, functionalist communication research monopolized the practice of education in intercultural communication in the United States and in almost all other Western countries through the highly influential textbook by Samovar and Porter, *Intercultural Communication: A Reader,* which is now in its 11th edition.
2. To be correct, it is a Möbius band, which can be illustrated by cutting a rubber band, twisting it around once, and putting it together in a shape like a sign of infinity. By following this shape, you change sides over and over again.
3. All primary experiences are registrated, even if they do not relate directly to culture. The intent of this collection is that the researcher can validate interpretations later on by comparing them with how the actors argue about other topics.
4. Where in the text do we find descriptions of groups in the plural? Where is the word "they" used? What do "they" do? Are there patterns for what "they" do? What words are used in the descriptions? Do the words have positive or negative connotations?
5. Is something seen as obviously right? Is an explicit value expressed? Is it taken for granted that some actions are rational?

References

Anderson, Benedict. (1983). *Imagined communities: Reflections on the origin and spread of nationalism.* London: Verso.

Appadurai, Arjun. (1991). Global ethnoscapes: Notes and queries for a transnational anthropology. In Richard G. Fox (Ed.), *Recapturing anthropology: Working in the present.* Santa Fe, NM: School of American Research Press.

Applegate, James, & Sypher, Howard. (1983). A constructivist outline. In William B. Gudykunst (Ed.), *International and Intercultural Communication Annual: Vol. 7. Intercultural communication theory: Current perspectives.* Beverly Hills, CA: Sage.

Applegate, James, & Sypher, Howard. (1988). A constructivist theory of communication and culture. In Young Y. Kim & William B. Gudykunst (Eds.), *International and Intercultural Communication Annual: Vol. 12. Theories in intercultural communication.* Newbury Park, CA: Sage.

Asante, Molefi K., & Gudykunst, William B. (Eds.). (1989). *Handbook of international and intercultural communication.* Newbury Park, CA: Sage.

Bauman, Zygmunt. (1999). *Globalisering: De menneskelige konsekvenser.* København: Hans Reitzels forlag.

Berger, Peter, & Luckmann, Thomas. (1966). *The social construction of reality: A treatise in the sociology of knowledge.* London: Penguin Books.

Bourdieu, Pierre. (1986). *Distinction: A social critique of judgements of taste.* London: Routledge and Kegan Paul.

Bourdieu, Pierre, & Wacquant, Loïc. (1992/1996). *Refleksiv sociologi: Mål og midler.* København: Hans Reitzel.

Brislin, Richard, et al. (Eds.). (1986). *Intercultural interactions: A practical guide.* Beverly Hills, CA: Sage.

Bukhdahl, Jørgen K. (1967). En filosofisk hermeneutik: En introduktion til Hans-Georg Gadamers "Sandhed og Metode." *Kritik,* nr. 4.

Collier, Mary Jane, & Thomas, Milt. (1988). Cultural identity: An interpretive perspective. In Young Y. Kim & William B. Gudykunst (Eds.), *International and Intercultural Communication Annual: Vol. 12. Theories in intercultural communication.* Newbury Park, CA: Sage.

Davies, Bronwyn, & Harré, Rom. (1990). Positioning: The discursive production of selves. *Journal for the Theory of Social Behaviour, 20*(1).

Featherstone, Mike. (1990). Global culture: An introduction. *Theory, Culture and Society, 7,* 1–14.

Fornäs, Johan. (1995). Youth, culture and modernity. In Johan Fornäs & Göran Bolin (Eds.), *Youth culture in late modernity.* London: Sage.

Friedman, Jonathan. (1994). *Cultural Identity and global process.* London: Sage.

Gadamer, Hans-Georg. (1989). *Truth and method* (2nd ed.). London: Sheed & Ward.

Gergen, Kenneth J. (1985). The social constructionist movement in modern psychology. *American Psychologist, 40*(3).

Gergen, Kenneth J. (1991). *The saturated self:. Dilemmas of identity in contemporary life.* New York: Basic Books.

Gertsen, Martine C. (1990). *Fjernt fra Danmark: Interkulturel kompetence i teori og praksis.* København: Samfundslitteratur.

González, Alberto, & Tanno, Dolores. (1999). *International and Intercultural Communication Annual: Vol. 22. Rhetoric in intercultural contexts.* Beverly Hills, CA: Sage.

Gudykunst, William B. (Ed.). (1983). *International and Intercultural Communication Annual: Vol. 7. Intercultural communication theory: Current perspectives.* Beverly Hills, CA: Sage.

Gudykunst, William B. (1994). *Bridging differences* (2nd ed.). Thousand Oaks, CA: Sage.

Gudykunst, William B. (1995). Anxiety/uncertainty management (AUM) theory: Current status. In Richard L. Wiseman (Ed.), *International and Intercultural Communication Annual: Vol. 19. Intercultural communication theory.* Thousand Oaks, CA: Sage.

Gudykunst, William B., & Kim, Young Yun. (1984). *Communication with strangers. An approach to intercultural communication.* New York: Random House.

Hall, Edward. (1959). *The silent language.* Greenwich, CT: Fawcett.

Hall, Stuart, & du Gay, Paul (Ed.). (1996). *Questions of cultural identity.* London: Sage.

Hall, Stuart, Held, David, & McGrew, Tony (Eds.). (1992). *Modernity and its futures.* London: Polity Press, Open University.

Hannerz, Ulf. (1992). *Cultural complexity: Studies in the social organization of meaning.* New York: Columbia University Press.

Hofstede, Geert. (1980). *Culture's consequences: International differences in work-related values.* London: Sage.

Hussain, Mustafa, Yilmaz, Ferruh, & O'Connor, Tim. (1997). *Medierne, minoriteterne og majoriteten: En undersøgelse af nyhedsmedier og den folkelige diskurs i Danmark.* København: Nævnet for Etnisk Ligestilling.

Hylland Eriksen, Thomas. (1993). Fleretniske paradokser: En kritisk analyse av multikulturalismen. *Grus,* nr. 41, Århus.

Jandt, Fred. (1995). *Intercultural communication: An introduction.* Thousand Oaks, CA: Sage.

Jandt, Fred, & Tanno, Dolores. (1994). Redefining the "other" in multicultural research. *Howard Journal of Communications, 5* (1–2).

Jandt, Fred, & Tanno, Dolores. (1996). *The "other" in multicultural research: An update and expansion.* Paper presented at the IAMCR 20th General Assembly and Scientific Conference, Sydney.

Jensen, Iben. (1998/2001). *Interkulturel kommunikation i komplekse samfund.* København: Roskilde Universitetsforlag.

Jensen, Iben. (2000). *Hvornår er man lige kvalificeret? Etniske minoriteters professionelle adgang til etablerede danske medier.* Købanhavn: Nævnet for Etnisk Ligestilling.

Jensen, Iben. (2001). Når den faglige identitet er national. *Psyke og Logos. 22*(1).

Kelly, Jennifer. (1998). *Under the gaze: Learning to be black in white society.* Halifax, NS: Fernwood.

Kincaid, Lawrence (Ed.). (1987). *Communication theory: Eastern and Western perspectives.* London: Academic Press/Harcourt Brace Jovanovich.

Martin, Judith, & Nakayama, Thomas. (2000). *Intercultural Communication in Contexts.* Mountain View, CA: Mayfield.

Okabe, Roichi. (1983). Cultural assumptions of East and West: Japan and the United States. In William B. Gudykunst (Ed.), *International and Intercultural Communication Annual: Vol. 7. Intercultural communication theory: Current perspectives.* Beverly Hills, CA: Sage.

Prosser, Michel. (1978). *The cultural dialogue: An introduction to intercultural communication.* Boston: Houghton Mifflin.

Razack, Sherene H. (1998). *Looking white people in the eye: Gender, race and culture in courtrooms and classrooms.* Toronto: University of Toronto Press.

Røgilds, Flemming. (1995). *Stemmer i et grænseland.* København: Politisk Revy.

Samovar, Larry A., & Porter, Richard E. (Eds.). (1991). *Intercultural communication: A reader* (6th ed.). Belmont, CA: Wadsworth.

Samovar, Larry A., Porter, Richard E., & Jain, N. (1981): *Understanding intercultural communication.* Belmont, CA: Wadsworth.

Sarbaugh, L. E. (1979). *Intercultural communication.* Rochelle Park, NJ: Hayden.

Søderberg, Anne Marie. (1994). Interkulturel kompetence: Hvad er det, og hvordan udvikler man det? In *Sprog og kulturmøde: Vol. 6. Kulturmøde og interkulturel kompetence.* Aalborg: Aalborg Universitet, Center for sprog og interkulturelle studier.

Yoshikawa, Muneo. (1987). The double-swing model of intercultural communication between the East and the West. In Lawrence Kincaid (Ed.), *Communication theory: Eastern and Western perspectives.* London: Academic Press/Harcourt Brace Jovanovich.

Concepts and Questions

1. How has globalization affected the study of intercultural communication?
2. Why does Jensen believe that a poststructuralist approach is the best way to understand culture in multiethnic societies?
3. What are the implications of Ulf Hannerz's position that talking about different national cultures is no longer appropriate?
4. What does Jensen claim to be an important difference between intercultural communication and other forms of communication as it applies to multiethnic societies?
5. What are the differences between the functionalist approach and the poststructuralist approach to the study of intercultural communication?
6. What are positions of experience, and how do they affect intercultural communication?
7. How does Jensen define cultual fix points? Why are they important to understanding the dynamics of intercultural communication?
8. How does Jensen use the notion of "scapes" to explain cultural identity?
9. Discuss the concept of cultural identity. What are its components? How does it influence intercultural communication?

Cultural Identity: Issues of Belonging

2

i am a door . . .
i am caught between two rooms
swinging from one to another.
grasping moments as the wind
sways me from the first to the next.
living loving, caressing life in each
taking a little from one
and giving to the other, and back.

i hear the strains of my mother's voice
over the aroma of the eggplant curry
wafting over my father's intense study
of the Indian Express*—his favorite newspaper*
the aunts and uncles came in droves
to my sister's wedding to eat
and gossip during the ceremony,
and through the night.
glimpses of life . . .very Indian.

in the other room, the surround sound
heard Simon and Garfunkel over troubled waters
while Pink Floyd cried about the walls in our lives
Simpsons and Butterfinger were definitely in
as Gore and Quayle babbled using innocuous verbiage.
the computer was never shut off
as reams of paper saw term papers

discuss new ways to communicate
glimpses of live . . . very American.

between these two worlds
i am happy, confused, angry
and in pain—all at the same time.
for i am a door caught between two rooms:
i see and feel both of them
but i don't seem to belong to either.

NAGESH RAO

We live an era of dynamic social transformation. The forces of globalization are exerting enormous pressures on the established nation-state geopolitical order. Institutions have created an environment in which electronic labor, capital, and media content flow nearly seamlessly across national borders. Waves of immigrants are leaving their homelands in search of greater opportunities in other countries and regions. International political and economic integration in the form of alliances and trade agreements are becoming common necessities. Collectively, these conditions represent powerful agents of social change and create a forceful milieu affecting the formation and maintenance of self-identity. Indeed, a frequent critique of globalization is that other nations and cultures will ultimately become homogenized representations of Western capitalism, losing much of the uniqueness inherent in the formation of their cultural identity. As a result of these evolving contemporary social conditions, it becomes important to understand the role of identity and how culture forms and preserves identity.

Perhaps the most central function of identity is to provide meaning by serving as a source of self-definition. In other words, we organize meaning around our self-identity (Castells, 1997). Identities serve as a foundation for meaning in part because of their origins, which can stem from a variety of influences, such as geography, history, fantasies, religion, and many, many more. Identity also takes various time- and scenario-dependent forms, to include nation, state, region, religion, ethnic, gender, socioeconomic status, profession, and others.

A common trait influencing identity formation and maintenance is culture. Identities are socially constructed through a cultural lens, employing the medium of communication. We identify with our initial cultural in-group as a function of enculturation, and later expand to other cultural groups or social institutions as a product of interaction (Castells, 1997). This results in a culturally bound concept of what type of identity is socially appropriate. For example, in the individualistic culture of the United States, army recruits are urged to be an "Army of One," which emphasizes the importance of self-determination, independence, and individual achievement. This emphasis is quite different from that of a collectivistic culture, where identity is strongly connected to, and dependent on, in-group membership. This conflict of identity is eloquently envisioned and voiced in the preceding verse by Professor Nagesh Rao.

In a world in which multicultural interactions are increasingly unavoidable and where sojourners often live and work for extended periods in other cultures, the influence of, and effects on, identity must be understood. For this reason, we offer five essays dealing with different aspects of culture and identity. We begin with an overview of culture identity, focusing on how people come to identify themselves with their various general and specific culture membership groups. In an article titled "Cultural Identity and Intercultural Communication," Mary Jane Collier examines the idea of culture by considering symbols and meanings, cultural norms, cultural history, and types of culture based on national and ethnic considerations as well as gender, profession, geographic location, organizations, and physical ability or disability. She relates how each of these factors contributes to the identification of culture along a general–specific dimension. After demonstrating the range of cultures available to individuals, Collier discusses cultural identification, revealing the diverse mechanisms by which individuals come to the particular cultural identification they hold.

When asked to specify their cultural identity, Euro-American students frequently respond "I'm just white, a white American" but then struggle to explain the heritage behind this self-applied designation. In the next essay, "Finding My Whiteness: A Narrative of Cultural Identification," Robert Krizek provides insight into the cultural identification of whiteness. Krizek explores whiteness using a narrative of how he began life with a cultural identification as a white person but, through the process of maturation, saw much of that identification slip away. Krizek then relates the experiences that moved him away from his identity and then back through a course of rediscovery. He concludes that through the process of narration it is possible for a person, regardless of ethnic, racial, or social background, to discover and examine his or her cultural identity.

To assist you in understanding this course of action, Krizek begins with a brief review of what has been and is being written about whiteness. He then proceeds with his own narrative of cultural identification, relating how he came to study whiteness as well as revealing the various aspects of that whiteness. He indicates how his original concept of himself as a white male led him to feel protected and grounded. Krizek points out that somewhere he lost his connections and then relates how those connections were rediscovered and recovered.

Frequently, the development of cultural identify is affected by conflict and historical circumstances. These dynamics are important in the next essay, in which Jolanta A. Drzewiecka and Nancy Draznin relate the experience of a Polish Jewish American's search for cultural identity. In their essay, "A Polish Jewish American Story: Collective Memories and Intergroup Relations," Drzewiecka and Draznin use a narrative format to relate the story of Nancy's Polish grandfather, who was raised in an environment of anti-Semitic prejudice and discrimination. The stories of his life became part of the fabric of Nancy's life. Although her experiences have not included the hurt or anger experienced by her grandfather, this background has had a profound effect upon Nancy in her search for her own unique cultural identity.

To help you understand the significance of family history in the development of cultural identity, the authors discuss the influence of collective memory on identity development. They demonstrate how the notion of collective memories can presume conflicting accounts of the past and how different communities may contest each other's memories. This conflict sometimes frustrates the development of one's own cultural identity.

Gender is another influential factor in the construction of identity. At first glance, it might seem rather simple. If you are born a boy, you develop a male identity; if born a girl, you develop a female identity. But when one's internal feelings of gender conflict with one's body's external manifestations, the world is suddenly not so simple. To help you understand this dynamic in the development of cultural identity, A. L. Zimmerman and Patricia Geist-Martin present a narrative essay about Amber, titled "The Hybrid Identities of Gender Queer: Claiming Neither/Nor, Both/And," which addresses the issues of how gender can affect the development of cultural identity. In Amber's case, you follow the identity construction of a person born into a female body but who identifies more with being male. By age seven, her tastes in dress were definitely those of a boy. By age eight, she knew that people often assumed she was male. By age ten, she was sometimes an embarrassment to her family because people would ask questions such as "What is your son's name?" As Amber grew older, she continued to encounter social situations in which her gender preferences brought frequent negative reactions.

Following Amber's story, the authors discuss hybridity, the coming together of two or more cultural identities and the resulting opportunity for development of a third identity. However, the ability to communicate about this alternative identity is inhibited because it lies outside the common language. The concept of hybridity applied to gender produces what the authors call "queer gender." This, they claim, disrupts the binary of being either all male or all female. The authors then continue Amber's narrative, detailing how she adapts to her queer gender identity and finally finds peace in claiming the identity of "both/and" while also claiming to be "neither/nor."

Our final essay, written before the events of 9/11, is concerned with the identity of Arab Americans. Nadine Naber's article, "Ambiguous Insiders: An Investigation of Arab American Invisibility," examines Arab American invisibility as a product of external and internal Arab American community influences. The essay begins with an overview of the history and evolution of the U.S. majority's categorization of Arab Americans. Naber explains that Arab American as an identity is a product of "anti-Arab" racism that developed after 1960. She considers "Arab American" to be a political term that tends to erase national, ethnic, religious, and other cultural differences among people linked only by a common language.

The U.S. media, according to Nader, have homogenized the inherent diversity of Arab Americans and created a stereotype identity for all people from the Middle East. She further contends that the media have largely ignored the existence of Middle Eastern women, except to portray them as suppressed and abused second-class citizens. The essay concludes with a discussion of how Arab Americans voice their presence in everyday life to make themselves heard or seen.

Reference

Castells, M. (1997). *The power of identity*. Malden, MA: Blackwell.

Cultural Identity and Intercultural Communication

MARY JANE COLLIER

Several useful approaches that can help you understand and improve the quality of your intercultural communication encounters are included in this book. One option you have for understanding why you and others behave in particular ways and learning what you can do to increase the appropriateness and effectiveness of your communication is to view communication from the perspective of cultural identity enactment.

This article presents an approach to culture that focuses on how individuals enact or take on one or more cultural identities. Questions that are answered here include the following: (1) What is a cultural identity? (2) How are multiple cultural identities created and negotiated with others? (3) How can knowledge of the cultural identity approach help you become more competent when dealing with persons who are taking on an identity different from yours? (4) What are the benefits of such an approach to intercultural communication for research, training, and practice?

CULTURE

We approach culture here in a very specific way. Culture is defined as a historically transmitted system of symbols, meanings, and norms (Collier & Thomas, 1988; Geertz, 1983; Schneider, 1976). Notice the emphasis placed on the communication process in the definition. Notice also, that culture is *systemic,* meaning it comprises many complex components that are interdependent and related; they form a type of permeable boundary.

This original essay first appeared in an earlier edition of the book. Mary Jane Collier teaches at the University of Denver.

Symbols and Meanings

The components of the system are patterned symbols such as verbal messages, nonverbal cues, emblems, and icons, as well as their interpretations or assigned meanings. Culture is what groups of people say and do and think and feel. Culture is not the people but the communication that links them together. Culture is not only speaking a language and using symbols but interpreting those symbols consistently; for example, traffic lights in South Africa are called "robots" and in England elevators are called "lifts." In urban areas, gang members change the items of clothing that denote gang membership periodically so that only in-group members know who is "in" and who is "out."

Norms

Another major component of the system of culture is normative conduct. Norms are patterns of appropriate ways of communicating. It is important not only to speak with symbols that are understood and to use nonverbal gestures or modes of dress so that the cues will be understood consistently, but also to use the symbols at acceptable times, with the appropriate people, with the fitting intensity. Japanese Americans may send their children to Japanese school and speak Japanese at home, but they may speak English at work and use direct and assertive forms of communication in business or educational settings. Malay women may wear traditional Muslim dress and show respectful silence to elders in the family, but they may be assertive and use a louder tone of voice among women in social settings.

History

The cultural system of communication is historically transmitted and handed down to new members of the group. Groups with histories include corporations, support groups, national groups, and civil rights groups. History is handed down when new employees are trained, "ground rules" are explained to new members of groups such as Alcoholics Anonymous, or dominant beliefs and the value of democracy are taught to U.S. American children in school.

We learn to become members of groups by learning about past members of the group, heroes, important precepts, rituals, values, and expectations for conduct. We are taught how to follow the norms of the group. In this way we perpetuate the cultural system. When a person becomes a college professor and joins a particular academic institution, she or he is taught about the mission of the institution, past academic heroes (faculty who have won awards, published prestigious works), the importance of "publish or perish" versus the importance placed on effective instruction, the role of sports or liberal arts in the institution, commitment to multiculturalism, and so on. The symbols and norms change over the life of the system, but there is enough consistency in what is handed down to be able to define the boundaries between systems (universities) and distinguish cultural members of one system from members of another.

Types of Cultures

Many groups (though not all) form cultural systems. Examples of many types of groups have already been included. In some cases, shared history or geography provides commonality of worldview or lifestyle, which helps create and reinforce a cultural system of communication.

To create a culture, groups must first define themselves as a group. This definition may be made on the basis of nationality, ethnicity, gender, profession, geography, organization, physical ability or disability, community, type of relationship, or other factors. We will discuss many of these groups later.

Once the group defines itself as a unit, a cultural system may develop. For instance, U.S. Americans define themselves as a group based on the use of English as a shared code; reinforcement of democracy through political discussion and action; individual rights and freedoms of speech, press, religion, and assembly as explicitly described in the Bill of Rights and enforced in the courts; and so forth. Attorneys or sales clerks or homemakers may be linked by similarities in daily activities and standard of living. Friends may see their group as including persons who like the same activities and support one another.

National and Ethnic Cultures. To better understand the many different types of cultures, we can categorize them from the more general and more common to those that are more specific. National and ethnic cultures are fairly general. These kinds of groups base membership on heritage and history that has been handed down through several generations. Their history is based on traditions, rituals, codes of language, and norms.

Persons who share the same nationality were born in a particular country and spent a significant number of years and a period of socialization in that country. Such socialization promotes and reinforces particular values, beliefs, and norms. Because many people contribute to the creation of a national culture's symbols, meanings, and norms, "national culture" is fairly abstract, so predictions about language use and what symbols mean can only be generalized. Japanese national culture, for instance, has been described as collectivistic, high context, high on power distance, and other-face oriented (Gudykunst & Ting-Toomey, 1988). Yet not all Japanese people follow these norms in every situation. But if we compare Japanese to Germans, the Japanese, as a group, are more group oriented and emphasize status hierarchies more than do Germans as an overall group (Hofstede, 1980).

Ethnicity is a bit different: Ethnic groups share a sense of heritage, history, and origin from an area outside of or preceding the creation of their present nation-state of residence (Banks, 1984). Ethnic groups, in most but not all cases, share racial characteristics, and many have a specific history of having experienced discrimination. In the United States, ethnic group members include African Americans, Asian Americans (Japanese Americans, Chinese Americans, Vietnamese Americans, Korean Americans, and so on), Mexican Americans, Polish Americans, Irish Americans, Native American Indians, and Jewish Americans, just to name a few examples.

Remember that national and ethnic cultures are the *communication systems* that are created by persons who share the same nationality or ethnicity. From this perspective, culture is the process of creating a perceived commonality and community of thought and action. Culture is based on what people say and do and think and feel *as a result* of their common history and origins.

Gender. Many subcategories of gender cultures exist. Groups create, reinforce, and teach what is interpreted as feminine or masculine. Groups also reinforce what is appropriate or inappropriate for a good husband, wife, feminist, chauvinist, heterosexual, gay, or lesbian. Mothers and fathers, religious leaders, teachers, and the media all provide information about how to be a member of a particular gender culture.

Profession. Politicians, physicians, field workers, sales personnel, maintenance crews, bankers, and consultants share common ways of spending time, earning money, communicating with others, and learning norms about how to be a member of their profession. Health care professionals probably share a commitment to health, to helping others, and to improving others' quality of life. They also share educational background, knowledge about their aspect of health care, and standards for practicing their profession.

Geographical Area. Geographical area sometimes acts as a boundary, contributing to the formulation of a cultural group. In South Africa, the area surrounding Cape Town has its own version of spoken Afrikaans, has a higher population of Coloreds (people of mixed race), and is viewed by many as the most cosmopolitan area in South Africa. The South in the United States has its own traditions, historical orientation, and southern drawl. Rural communities sometimes differ from urban communities in political views, values, lifestyles, and norms.

Organization. Large corporations such as IBM, Nike, or Xerox create the most common type of organizational culture. In this culture, members are taught the corporate symbols, myths, heroes, and legends, and what it means to be an employee. The proper chain of command, procedures and policies, and schedules are also taught. Finally, they learn the norms in the corporation—whom to talk to, about what, at which particular moment. Some corporations value "team players" while others value "individual initiative." Some corporations have mottos like "Never say no to an assignment" or "Never be afraid to speak up if you don't have what you need."

Support groups have their own version of organizational culture. Alcoholics Anonymous, Overeaters Anonymous, and therapy and support groups, among others, form their own sets of symbols, interpretations, and norms. "Let go and let God" is an important requirement in the Anonymous groups; relinquishing individual control to a higher power is a tool in managing one's addictions. Social living groups, such as sororities and fraternities, international dormitories, and the like, often create their own cultures as well.

Physical Ability or Disability. Groups form a culture based upon shared physical ability or disability. Professional athletic teams teach rookies how to behave and what to do to be an accepted member of the team. Persons who have physical disabilities share critical life experiences, and groups teach them how to accept and overcome their disability, as well as how to communicate more effectively with those who do not have the disability (Braithwaite, 1991).

CULTURAL IDENTIFICATION AS A PROCESS

Each individual, then, has a range of cultures to which she or he belongs in a constantly changing environment. Everyone may concurrently or simultaneously participate in several different cultural systems each day, week, and year. All cultures that are created are influenced by a host of social, psychological, and environmental factors as well as institutions and context.

Consider African Americans in the United States. In the past 40 years, myriad factors have affected what it means to be an African American in the United States, including civil rights marches, leaders such as Martin Luther King, Jr., affirmative action, racism, the resurgence of the Ku Klux Klan, television shows such as *Roots* and *Cosby,* films by Spike Lee, Anita Hill's testimony in the Senate confirmation hearings on Supreme Court nominee Clarence Thomas, and the riots among African Americans and Hispanics in South Central Los Angeles following the Rodney King verdict.

Cultures are affected not only by changing socioeconomic and environmental conditions, but by other cultures as well. A person who is a member of a support group for single mothers in her community is influenced by other cultural groups such as feminists, conservative religious groups, or the Republican party members who made family values and two-parent families an important issue in the 1992 presidential campaign. The important questions from a cultural identity approach may be things like "What does it mean to be a single mother who is Euro-American, Catholic, out of work, and living in a large city in the Midwest? How does that identity come to be, and how is it communicated to others? How does it change across different contexts and relationships?"

CULTURAL IDENTITY

Diverse groups can create a cultural system of symbols used, meanings assigned to the symbols, and ideas of what is considered appropriate and inappropriate. When the groups also have a history and begin to hand down the symbols and norms to new members, then the groups take on a *cultural identity.* **Cultural identity** is the particular character of the group communication system that emerges in the particular situation.

A Communication Perspective

Cultural identities are negotiated, co-created, reinforced, and challenged through communication; therefore, we approach identity from a communication perspective. *Social psychological perspectives* view identity as a characteristic of the person and personality, and self as centered in social roles and social practices. A *communication perspective* views identity as something that emerges when messages are exchanged between persons. Thus, identity is defined as an enactment of cultural communication (Hecht, Collier, & Ribeau, 1993).

Identities are *emergent;* they come to be in communication contexts. Because you are being asked to emphasize a communication perspective, what you study and try to describe and explain are identity patterns as they occur among persons in contact with one another. Although we have noted that such factors as media, literature, and art influence identity, our focus is directed at the interaction between people. Identities are co-created in relationship to others. Who we are and how we are differ and emerge depending on whom we are with, the cultural identities that are important to us and others, the context, the topic of conversation, and our interpretations and attributions.

Properties of Cultural Identity

As students and researchers in intercultural communication, we can apply our knowledge about how cultural identities are enacted and developed in order to explain and improve our understanding of others' conduct. We outline the properties or characteristics of cultural identities and then compare the properties across different cultural groups. These comparisons ultimately help us build theories of cultural and intercultural identity communication.

The first property we outline is self-perception; this addresses both avowal by the individual and ascription by others. Second, we note modes of expressing identity. Identities are expressed through core symbols, labels, and norms. The third property focuses on the scope of the identity, and whether the identity takes an individual, a relational, or a communal form. A fourth property examines the enduring, yet dynamic, quality of cultural identity. Fifth, affective, cognitive, and behavioral components of identity provide us with a means of contrasting what groups think, feel, say, and do. Sixth, we describe the content and relationship levels of interpretation in messages revealing cultural identity. Content and relationship interpretations allow us to understand when power and control issues contribute to conflict or when friendships and trust can be developed. Seventh, salience and variations in intensities characterize useful identity in new or unusual settings. Being the one who stands out in an otherwise homogeneous group causes us to be conscious of and perhaps alter the intensity with which we claim our identity.

Avowal and Ascription Processes. Each individual may enact various cultural identities over the course of a lifetime as well as over the course of a day. Identities are enacted in interpersonal contexts through avowal and ascription processes. **Avowal** is the self an individual portrays, analogous to the image she or he shows to others. Avowal is the individual saying, "This is who I am."

Ascription is the process by which others attribute identities to an individual. Stereotypes and attributions are examples of ascriptions. In part, identity is shaped by others' communicated views of us. For example, a black Zulu female's cultural identities in South Africa are shaped not only by her definition and image of what it means to be a black Zulu female but also by the white Afrikaners for whom she works, her Zulu family and relatives, the township in which she lives in poverty, her white teachers who speak Afrikaans and English, and so forth.

Another way of thinking about this is to say that cultural identities have both subjective and ascribed meanings. In Japan, a philosophy and practice known as *amae* is common. ***Amae*** signifies an other-orientation or group orientation, and a sense of obligation to the group. An individual is expected to sacrifice individual needs and give to others; others are expected to reciprocate, thereby maintaining the harmony and cohesiveness of the group (Doi, 1989; Goldman, 1992). *Amae* represents the interdependence of subjective and ascribed meanings in relationships. The meanings may not be shared across cultural groups, however. To many Japanese, such a complex, long-term, obligatory relationship with members of in-groups is a functional and revered system of relational maintenance. To U.S. Americans, such rules and obligations to others may appear to be unnecessary, threaten individuality and choice, and therefore be unacceptable.

Information about avowal and ascription can be useful in understanding the role others play in developing your own cultural identities. If a particular group has low self-esteem or a high need for status, those aspects of identity may be influenced by the stereotypes or conceptions held and communicated by other groups.

Modes of Expression: Core Symbols, Labels, and Norms. Cultural identities are expressed in core symbols, labels, and norms. Core symbols tell us about the definitions, premises, and propositions regarding the universe, and the place of humans in the universe, that are held by members of the cultural group. They are expressions of cultural beliefs about the management of nature and technology and such institutions as marriage, education, and politics. The symbols point us to the central ideas, concepts, and everyday behaviors that characterize membership in that cultural group. Sometimes these core symbols can be summarized into a set of fundamental beliefs; sometimes a particular mode of dress, gesture, or phrase captures the essence of a cultural identity. Carbaugh (1989) analyzed transcripts of the popular television talk show *Donahue*. After doing a content analysis of the comments made by audience members, he proposed *self-expression* as a core symbol of mainstream U.S. identity.

Authenticity, powerlessness, and expressiveness were identified as three core symbols among African Americans (Hecht, Ribeau, & Alberts, 1989; Hecht, Larkey, Johnson, & Reinard, 1991). These core symbols were posited after African Americans were asked to describe recent satisfying and unsatisfying conversations with other African Americans and with Euro-Americans, and to describe strategies for conversational improvement. African Americans talked about the need for persons to be authentic, honest, and real, described the negative impact of feeling powerless, and outlined a need to be expressive in their conduct.

Labels are a category of core symbols. The same label may vary widely in its interpretation. The term *American* is perceived as acceptable and common by many residents of the United States, as ethnocentric and self-centered by residents of Central America and Canada, and is associated with a group that is privileged, wealthy, and powerful by some countries that are not industrialized. *Hispanic* is a general term that many social scientists use to describe "persons of Mexican, Puerto Rican, Cuban, Central or South American, or other Spanish culture of origin, regardless of race" (Marin & Marin, 1991, p. 23). Persons may choose to describe their own ethnicity with a much more specific label such as *Mexican American* or *Chicano* or *Chicana*. Chicano and Chicana individuals may have their own ideas about what it means to be a member of that culture. Whether the label was created by members of the group or members of another group provides useful information about what the label means and how it is interpreted.

Cultural groups create and reinforce standards for "performing the culture" appropriately and effectively. Norms for conduct are based upon core symbols and *how they are interpreted*. Defining who you are tells you what you should be doing. Norms of appropriate and acceptable behavior, moral standards, expectations for conduct, and criteria to decide to what degree another is behaving in a competent manner form the prescriptive or evaluative aspect of cultural identity. An individual is successful at enacting identity when he or she is accepted as a competent member of the group. Immigrants, for example, are judged to be competent and accepted by members of the U.S. American culture when they speak English, use appropriate greetings, demonstrate respect for the individual rights of their neighbors to privacy, and so forth.

Attention to the property of shared norms gives us the ability to determine what is appropriate from the point of view of the group members. Comparing norms of conduct across groups and identifying norms in intercultural conversations are helpful in figuring out how to improve our own individual effectiveness as communicators. Finally, identification of norms in this way provides valid information for trainers, teachers, and practitioners as they develop their training programs.

Individual, Relational, and Communal Forms of Identity

Identities have individual, relational, and communal properties. As researchers of culture, we can study culture from the point of view of individuals. Each person has individual interpretations of what it means to be U.S. American or Austrian or Indian, and each person enacts his or her cultural identities slightly differently. If we want to understand why an individual behaves in a particular way, we can ask him or her to talk about that cultural identity and experience as a group member.

When we study culture from a relational point of view, we observe the interactions between people, friends, coworkers, or family members who identify themselves as members of the same or different groups. Then we can identify the themes in their talk, such as trust or power. Collier (1989) found that Mexican American friends emphasized the importance of their relationship by meeting frequently and spending a significant portion of time together. They also described the most important characteristics of friendship as support, trust, intimacy, and commitment to the relationship. In contrast, when Mexican Americans and Anglo-Americans talked about their friendships with one another, they described common activities, goals, and respect for family.

When we study culture in terms of its communal properties, we observe the public communication contexts and activities in communities and neighborhoods that establish cultural identity. Rituals, rites of passage, and holiday celebrations are other sources of information about how persons use cultural membership to establish community with one another.

Enduring and Changing Property of Identity

Cultural identities are both enduring and changing. As already mentioned, cultures have a history that is transmitted to new members over time. Cultural identities change because of economic, political, social, psychological, and contextual factors, not to mention the influence of other cultural identities. Enacting the cultural identity of being gay or lesbian in the 2000s has certain things in common with being gay in the 1990s and 1980s. Individuals who "come out of the closet" encounter similar stereotypes and ascriptions to those in earlier decades. However, the political climate in some areas of the country, in which ballot initiatives were proposed to limit the rights of gays or link gays with other groups such as sadomasochists, affect the cultural identity of the group. Sometimes context changes how one manifests identity and how intensely one avows an identity. Announcing your affiliation and pride as a member of the Right to Life anti-abortion coalition at a rally of pro-choice supporters is different from attending a Right to Life meeting and avowing your identity in that context.

Affective, Cognitive, and Behavioral Components of Identity

Identities have affective, cognitive, and behavioral components. Persons have emotions and feelings attached to identities. Such emotions change depending upon the situation. Sometimes, a particularly strong or violent avowal of an identity is a signal of the importance of that identity and the degree to which it is perceived to be threatened. Perhaps this knowledge can help us interpret why rioting occurred in South Central Los Angeles after the Rodney King verdict. The cognitive component of identity relates to the beliefs we have about that identity. Persons hold a range of beliefs about each culture group to which they belong, but certain similarities in beliefs become evident when you ask people to talk about what it means to be U.S. American or Thai or a member of Earth First!, an environmentalist group. Members of Earth First! share a belief in the value of ancient forests, a distrust of executives who run logging companies and politicians who support the lumber industry, and the view that spiking trees and sabotaging logging equipment is sometimes necessary as a form of protest. Such beliefs can be summarized into a core symbol—here, the name of the organization, *Earth First!*

The behavioral component of cultural identity focuses on the verbal and nonverbal actions taken by group members. We come to be members of a group through our actions with one another and our reactions to one another. These verbal and nonverbal actions can be studied, and patterns described. The dimensions of cultural variability described by Hofstede (1980), such as collectivism and individualism, are patterns of communicative conduct evident when particular cultural identities are enacted. Comparing what groups say and do allows us as researchers to begin to understand why some groups experience frequent misunderstandings or conflict.

Content and Relationship

Identities comprise both content and relationship levels of interpretation. When persons communicate with each other, messages carry information as well as implications for who is in control, how close the conversational partners feel to each other, or conversely how hostile they feel toward each other, how much they trust each other, or the degree of inclusion or exclusion they feel.

Sometimes persons use their in-group language to reinforce their in-group status and establish distance from the out-group (Giles, Coupland, & Coupland, 1991). At other times they may use the language of the out-group in order to adapt to and align with the out-group. Mexican Americans may speak Spanish when in neighborhood communities to preserve their history and roots and to reinforce their identification and bond as a people. The same persons may speak English at school or at work because the supervisor and executives of the company demand it.

Salience and Intensity Differences

Identities differ in their salience in particular contexts, and identities are enacted with different intensities at different times. The intensities provide markers of strong involvement and investment in the identity. As a white U.S. American female professor visiting South Africa, there were times when I was most aware of being a white minority among the black majority, times when I was aware of being a U.S. American who was stereotyped somewhat negatively, and times when I was most aware of being a college professor. But when I learned that female employees in South Africa do not receive maternity leave and receive a lower housing allowance than males, my feminist identity became more salient, causing me to adopt a stronger tone and assert my views about equal pay for equal work in a more direct manner when talking with male executives in corporations.

CULTURAL IDENTITY AND COMMUNICATION COMPETENCE

Using cultural identity as an approach can help us better analyze others' conduct and decide how to do what is mutually competent. Spitzberg and Cupach (1984) point out that communication competence requires motivation and knowledge, as well as skills, to demonstrate what behavior is appropriate and effective.

Cultural competence is the demonstrated ability to enact a cultural identity in a mutually appropriate and effective manner. Intercultural competence becomes a bit more complex. **Intercultural competence** is the reinforcement of culturally different identities that are salient in the particular situation. Intercultural competence occurs when the avowed identity matches the identity ascribed. For example, if you avow the identity of an assertive, outspoken U.S. American and your conversational partner avows himself or herself to be a respectful, nonassertive Vietnamese, then each must ascribe the corresponding identity to the conversational partner. You must jointly negotiate what kind of relationship will be mutually satisfying. Some degree of adjustment and accommodation is usually necessary.

A common problem in intercultural communication occurs when persons who describe themselves as the same nationality or ethnicity do not share ideas about how to enact their identity and disagree about the norms for interaction. Chicanos in the United States may differ from second- and third-generation Mexican Americans about the need to speak Spanish or call attention to their heritage. Nonetheless, understanding the identity being avowed and ascribed, and noting the intensity with which the identity is avowed, enables us to understand why a particular cultural identity emerges as salient in particular situations and therefore what contextual, social, or psychological factors are operating in the situation.

Some benefits of the cultural identity approach in intercultural communication situations include the following: We can acknowledge that all individuals have many potential cultural identities which may emerge in a particular situation. Remembering that identities change from situation to situation can be helpful in overcoming the tendency to treat others as stereotypical representatives of a particular group. Asking for information about what is appropriate for their cultural identity is an effective tool in becoming interculturally competent. Explaining what your own cultural identity norms are and why you behaved in a particular way can also be a useful way to increase the other person's understanding and can help develop relational trust.

Researchers, trainers, and practitioners can utilize the cultural identity approach to identify similarities and differences in behaviors, in interpretations, or in norms. It is possible to begin to explain why group members behave as they do or feel as they do in their conduct with others from the same and different groups. Trainers and teachers can compare group symbols, interpretations, and norms as well as teach others to develop analytical skills to use in their own situations.

Cultural identity as an approach to the study of culture and intercultural communication is only one of many approaches. Ongoing research, critique, and application will test the merit of the approach. Hopefully, the approach has sparked the beginning of a dialogue that will continue throughout all of our lifetimes.

References

Banks, J. (1984). *Teaching strategies for ethnic studies* (3rd ed.). Boston: Allyn & Bacon.

Braithwaite, D. (1991). "Just how much did that wheelchair cost?" Management of privacy boundaries by persons with disabilities. *Western Journal of Speech Communication, 55,* 54–274.

Carbaugh, D. (1989). *Talking American: Cultural discourses on* Donahue. Norwood, NJ: Ablex.

Collier, M. J. (1989). Cultural and intercultural communication competence: Current approaches and directions for future research. *International Journal of Intercultural Relations, 13,* 287–302.

Collier, M. J., & Thomas, M. (1988). Cultural identity: An interpretive perspective. In Y. Y. Kim & W. Gudykunst (Eds.), *Theories in intercultural communication* (pp. 99–122). Newbury Park, CA: Sage.

Doi, T. (1989). *The anatomy of dependence.* Tokyo: Kodansha.

Geertz, C. (1983). *Local knowledge.* New York: Basic Books.

Giles, H., Coupland, N., & Coupland, J. (1991). Accommodation theory: Communication, contexts and consequences. In H. Giles, N. Coupland, & J. Coupland (Eds.), *Contexts of accommodation: Developments in applied sociolinguistics.* Cambridge, England: Cambridge University Press.

Goldman, A. (1992). *The centrality of "ningensei" to Japanese negotiating and interpersonal relationships: Implications for U.S.–Japanese communication.* Paper presented at the Speech Communication Association Conference, Chicago.

Gudykunst, W., & Ting-Toomey, S. (1988). *Culture and interpersonal communication.* Newbury Park, CA: Sage.

Hecht, M., Collier, M. J., & Ribeau, S. (1993). *African-American communication.* Newbury Park, CA: Sage.

Hecht, M., Larkey, L. K., Johnson, J. N., & Reinard, J. C. (1991). *A model of interethnic effectiveness.* Paper presented at the International Communication Association Conference, Chicago.

Hecht, M., Ribeau, S., & Alberts, J .K. (1989). An Afro-American perspective on interethnic communication. *Communication Monographs, 56,* 385–410.

Hofstede, G. (1980). *Culture's consequences.* Newbury Park, CA: Sage.

Marin, G., & Marin, B. V. (1991). *Research with Hispanic populations.* Newbury Park, CA: Sage.

Schneider, D. (1976). Notes toward a theory of culture. In K. Basso & H. Selby (Eds.), *Meaning in anthropology.* Albuquerque: University of New Mexico Press.

Spitzberg, B. H., & Cupach, W. R. (1984). *Interpersonal communication competence.* Newbury Park, CA: Sage.

Concepts and Questions

1. How does viewing intercultural communication from a cultural identity perspective increase your competence as a communicator?
2. In what ways may the adherence to cultural norms vary depending upon one's immediate cultural identity?
3. Collier discusses types of cultures. Using her discussion as a basis for consideration, list the names of various cultural groups with which you identify. Do you find conflict between any of these identities?
4. How is cultural identify formed?
5. How does ascription contribute to the formation of cultural identity?
6. What are core symbols, and how do they contribute to the formation of cultural identity? List several core symbols that relate to your cultural identity.
7. What does Collier mean when she asserts that cultural identities are both enduring and changing?
8. How does cultural identity relate to communication competence?
9. What are some of the benefits of using the cultural identity approach to intercultural communication situations?

Finding My Whiteness: A Narrative of Cultural Identification

ROBERT KRIZEK

It has been more than 10 years since Tom Nakayama and I first began discussing and then writing about whiteness (see Nakayama & Krizek, 1995). In our article, we examined the discursive space of "white" as a normative and strategic rhetoric with various cultural and political implications. In our best postmodern language, Tom and I stated that we wanted to "map the terrain" and challenge the "uninterrogated" territory of whiteness. At the time these were necessary, perhaps even noble, goals. In retrospect, however, I must admit that those goals were, at best, only tangential for me. My purpose was far less noble and much more personal. I chose to explore the topic of whiteness because I wanted to regain perspective. I had hoped that by critically examining whiteness at the conceptual level, I would be able to somehow gain both the ability to articulate and the insight to appreciate a few of the specifics of my life, aspects of my identities as a white male that slowly but most certainly had vanished from my consciousness over the temporal stretch of my life. They had vanished, I realized, in part because I hadn't "interrogated" (read: reflected upon and written/talked about) the practices of my whiteness, my maleness, or my many other "nesses." In short, through my neglect I had lost my narratives, and I wanted to regain them.

In part because the 1995 article did not manage to address many of these personal issues, I continued to reflect upon, examine, and write about my various cultural identifications. This article affords me the opportunity to go beyond that 1995 article, therefore, and present my reasons for and my feelings about engaging my various identities, identities that had been lumped together and "lost" under the rhetorical banner of whiteness. As the product of a decade-long process, this article borrows ideas and language from a number of places. It contains a few of the phrases that managed to get into the Nakayama and Krizek piece (and many more lines our reviewers asked us to edit out). It also contains ideas and language from an unpublished coauthored conference paper (Gonzalez & Krizek, 1994), some bits of narrative from my dissertation (Krizek, 1995), and passages straight from my personal journal written as part of an ethnographic immersion on the Pine Ridge Indian reservation.

My purpose in writing this essay now—I haven't explicitly written about whiteness since the mid- to late '90s—is twofold. First, I would like to provide some local understanding of my identifications as a white male, just as others (Stage, 1999; Moon, 1999) have provided us with a glimpse of their whiteness. I believe that if we are to de-normalize whiteness, we need to not only expose its power (a critical as well as a conceptual/rhetorical endeavor) but also provide insight into its everyday cultural manifestations (an approach grounded in the examination of everyday practice). In sum, beyond the critical discussion of whiteness, there needs to be a dedication by white social researchers and, more specifically, ethnographers to examine their communities, their practices, and their lives beyond objectifying the "other" and/or looking at "deviant" lifestyles—theirs or others'—and to speak openly and honestly about what they find. Second, in this essay I also am attempting to encourage readers of all ethnic, racial, and social backgrounds to excavate (discover and examine) their own narratives of cultural identity by telling you about my journey. Social researchers, especially those of the interpretive ilk, should turn to the practices, both meaningful and mundane, of their own lives for inspiration for broader, more systematic cultural research. Understanding oneself (yes) and one's cultural identifications is, I would think, a necessary condition for becoming a proficient interpretive researcher/ethnographer.

As I write this essay, I imagine that it is very different from other authors' contributions to this volume. This supposition is based in large part on my reading of previous editions of this text. Although my broad topic is cultural identity, I engage a narrative approach to examining cultural identifications of whiteness, or better yet, I present a narrative about finding my whiteness. If I succeed in this endeavor, I will have convinced you that there is more to whiteness than normative

 Robert Krizek teaches at Saint Louis University.

and strategic rhetoric. There is individual experience and performance of whiteness as well. Before I begin with my narrative, in an effort to maintain some coherence with the rest of this volume, I provide a brief introduction to the literature about whiteness. I focus on those articles emanating from, or of particular interest to, the discipline of Communication.

WHAT'S BEING WRITTEN ABOUT WHITENESS

Although it is beyond the scope of my project to extensively "review" the literature on whiteness, I should at least introduce the reader to others who have examined the subject. There has been, after all, a great deal written about whiteness over the past 10 to 15 years. One of the most comprehensive and multifaceted discussions of whiteness, at least within the Communication discipline, is the volume edited by Nakayama and Martin (1999). This book contains a number of excellent and informative chapters, but perhaps more significant than any individual chapter, the book as a whole provides a remarkable resource regarding the subject of whiteness. For example, Johnson (1999) ends his chapter "Reflections on Critical White(ness) Studies" with not only the usual list of references to works cited in his article but also a "Selected Bibliography of Books on the Social Construction of Whiteness." As another example, Wander, Martin, and Nakayama (1999) discuss the sociohistorical foundations of racial categories in general and, more specifically, the racial ideology of whiteness. In doing so, these authors also provide an interesting list of works centering on racial classification and race theory. For more references on the subject of race classification, with a specific emphasis on the legal construction of race and whiteness, I suggest Tehranian (2000). Finally, in their chapter, Martin, Krizek, Nakayama, and Bradford (1999), expanding on their earlier article (Martin, Krizek, Nakayama, & Bradford, 1996), explore issues of self-labeling by white Americans. In this chapter, the authors provide yet another amalgamation of the whiteness literature mixed with a sprinkling of literature on labeling theory, identity, and ethnic labels. For a different and more recent perspective on the label "whiteness," I suggest Bahk and Jandt's (2004) article, in which they looked at both whites and nonwhites' perspectives on the privileged positionality of whiteness.

Although it may not be true of all of the literature cited above, much of the literature on whiteness in the '90s, including various chapters from the Nakayama and Martin (1999) text, adopted a critical perspective to explore the social and contextual factors that influence the discursive formation of whiteness. For example, our chapter (Nakayama & Krizek, 1999) takes a decidedly critical stance, as do, among others, chapters by Supriya (1999), by DeLuca (1999), and by Projansky and Ono (1999). All provide thorough discussions of critical and/or feminist scholarship relevant to the topic of whiteness in their reviews of the literature. This critical tradition continues in this decade as well. In her article, Shome (2000) raises the question of not whether whiteness should be studied but rather "how whiteness should be studied and for what political and reflexive end" (p. 370), providing a slightly different entrée into the whiteness literature. In the organizational realm, Grimes (2001, 2002) provides us with discussions of how the invisible nature of whiteness affects organizational life and the diversity management literature, and, in doing so, creates for the reader a reference list centering on race and whiteness with a decidedly organizational flavor. Others, such as Martin and Davis (2001) and Hytten and Adkins (2002), venture into discussions of pedagogy and whiteness, thereby providing us with still another variation of the critical scholarship on whiteness.

Other relatively recent publications have emanated from the pages of our discipline's journals with, to some lesser or greater degree, a critical framework focusing on whiteness as well. Jackson and Heckman (2002) discuss whiteness as revealed in the reactions of white students to racial hate mail circulated to minority students. Liera-Schwichentenberg (2000) briefly examines the difficult journey of those who have sought to pass from another racial identity into whiteness, and Rockler (2002) looks at syndicated comic strips, concluding, in part, that whiteness is a terministic screen that "informs media interpretation and promotes racial inequality" (p. 416). All of these articles provide reference lists full of the literature central to critical whiteness scholarship as well as contributing assorted articles, chapters, and books to the community of whiteness scholarship unique to their own topics and interests. A reader would do well to review these articles as well as the others I've mentioned above.

Over the past decade, however, there have been articles, perhaps somewhat critical in nature, but perhaps not, dedicated more to understanding the individual performance of whiteness. For example, on the more critical end of the continuum, Warren (2001) offers performance ethnography as a way to show "how whiteness gets accomplished through embodied actions and spoken interaction" (p. 185). For Warren, it is not enough to critically examine how whiteness operates at the conceptual or rhetorical level; he advocates using performance data gathered ethnographically to demonstrate whiteness in action. Also from a decidedly critical perspective, Moon (1999) explores "some of the white cultural communication practices by which 'whiteness' is made" (p. 195). She, like Warren, moves away from a conceptual examination of whiteness to an exploration of how whiteness gets played out in everyday practices. Another scholar who examines whiteness through a look at everyday practices of whites is Stage (1999). She employs an indigenous perspective (Gonzalez & Krizek, 1994) to "texturize" whiteness. Her intent was to provide voice and, thereby, bring into focus a rural community at the invisible center of white American culture. Her ultimate goal was to "gain some insight into how this segment of the white population, in general, views its position in society" (p. 79).

As with all of the articles cited in this brief introduction to the whiteness literature, these three articles—Warren, Moon, and Stage—both contribute to our understanding of whiteness and, through their reviews of literature, provide a source for other scholars to search when they too choose to interrogate whiteness. What follows in this chapter is consistent with the desire of these articles to examine performances of whiteness. It is, perhaps, most consistent with Stage's (1999) use of indigenous ethnography to texturize whiteness. It is a narrative of how I came to study whiteness as well as a narrative of aspects of my whiteness. At yet another, more implicit level, it is a call for social researchers to study what is meaningful and important in their lives.

A NARRATIVE OF CULTURAL IDENTIFICATION

Until a few weeks prior to my seventh birthday, my family lived above Gerber's Hardware Store in a modest second-floor apartment overlooking Oak Park Avenue. Our windows faced the marquee of the old Southern Theater across the street. Directly to the south of us, to the south of Gerber's, sat Johnson's Drug Store. It occupied the corner where the busy Oak Park Avenue met the not-as-busy Harrison Street. Around the corner, on the Harrison Street side of Johnson's, stood the swirling barber's pole that marked the entrance to Carl's Barber Shop. Those three—Gerber's, Johnson's, and Carl's—comprised most of the ground floor of our three-story gray slate building. They were the places of my childhood.

I miss those places. Some days, like today, I find myself wandering through fairly detailed remembrances of our apartment, that building, and its stores; yet, for the most part, the images and sounds of Oak Park and Harrison have lost their crispness, their certainty. They've faded. Even in my most vivid wanderings, some things now seem distant, almost foreign. But I know I felt comfortable living there—except, of course, for the dentist's office that shared a wall with our kitchen. I dreaded the sounds that passed from that office through our wall. I had been over there, on the other side, and knew what those sounds meant.

At night, much to my relief, the whirring noises ended. So did the faint smell of the drill working, burning. Our apartment filled instead with the reddish glow of the neon signs that buzzed, flickered, and hummed their advertisements for the stores below and the movie house opposite our windows. Somehow the light from those signs managed to elude the pale yellow venetian blinds covering our front room windows and even slide under the door to the bedroom I shared with my sister. It entered our room, however, not as separate startling beams but rather as a soothing sheet of illumination that wrapped itself around me like the wings of my guardian angel. The ever-so-faint glow of the neon kept the hidden yet certain dangers of darkness away and helped make the hours between dusk and dawn a little less fearful for a small boy. I know I felt safe there. Protected.

During the day, when the neon signs were silent and the sounds of torture from next door took over, I would venture down the back stairs to the world below. At times I went to escape those sounds, but always to find adventure. I spent hours exploring the aisles at Gerber's, looking at the miracles stacked floor to ceiling on the shelves before me—saws and sprinklers, rakes and wood rasps, paints and plungers, water faucets and window fans, even GE toasters and

Philco radios. To this day, hardware stores still hold that promise of adventure for me. For my parents, however, the triangle of Gerber's, Johnson's, and Carl's provided a '50s version of day care. The store owners and their employees knew me, most tolerated me, some even looked after me. After all, it was a time when parents could trust their kids to neighbors and friends, perhaps even strangers.

And then there was Johnson's, with its jars of candy, cigar boxes in glass display cases, racks of magazines, and stacks of daily newspapers. It had two phone booths with accordion doors and a window in back where we went to get our medicine. It housed, all at the same time, the inviting fragrances of sweet perfumes, the threatening smells of iodine-like antiseptics, and the sharp attractive aroma of cured tobacco. But, more important for me, Johnson's had a soda fountain. From there, as I sipped free charged water from a Coke glass, I could watch the adults buying their cough drops and cigarettes. Sometimes, when someone offered, I would gulp down a cherry Coke or diligently spoon my way through a root beer float. Those were times of nearly uncontrollable delight.

At Johnson's I idled away endless mornings and countless afternoons. Between sips and spoonfuls, I would spin round and round on backless emerald-colored stools that tottered on chrome cylindrical bases bolted to the once-white tile floor. Back and forth I would swivel, feet dangling, holding on, and expending seemingly boundless amounts of energy and enthusiasm. I listened and laughed, never really looking people in the eye. It was the early '50s, and people laughed a lot. Kids kept quiet, and we didn't challenge adults with our eyes. Despite all the commotion and constant movement, I felt secure. Grounded.

But Carl's Barber Shop—well, Carl's was where I had my special place. Ollie, the Negro man (it was 1953) who worked the shoe shine stand at the rear of the shop, would lift me up and set me atop the high-backed black leather bench where his customers sat. The leather squeaked against my hands when I slid to the far side of his four-person bench, out of the way of the men who paid Ollie to make their shoes sparkle. That was our deal, Ollie's and mine. I would sit there, out of the way, quiet. I remember straining to reach the nickel-plated footrests that jutted up from the marble block anchoring his bench. I stretched my blue Keds about as far as I possibly could and still remain seated on my lofty perch. Finally my toes would come to rest on the heels of the supports. Ollie always nodded his assurance. In the summer, a fan would rumble in a window below me. There, balanced between the bench and the footrests, I felt included, sort of grown-up. There, as the sugary scents of hair tonic and talcum powder filled my nostrils, I listened to the men talk about sports, politics, their work, their families, their lives. Often they told very personal stories, ones of failure but mostly ones of joy, stories of what they had seen and what they had done. I was the most comfortable there. More than in the reddish glow of my bedroom. More than in the mysterious and wondrous aisles of Gerber's. And even more than in Johnson's with its spinning stools, ice cream, and magazines. I liked the feel and smell of Carl's, and I especially liked hearing the stories. More than anything else about Oak Park and Harrison, I enjoyed listening to those stories.

Somewhere I lost contact with my connections. I lost my appreciation of the places and events that belonged to me, my family, our friends, and the heritage we share. I lost the feelings I had sitting atop Ollie's stand. The "misplacing" occurred over time and without much recognition or remorse on my part. The security, the sense of "feeling a part of" I had at Oak Park and Harrison vanished without my realizing it had ever been there. There's no one I can think of to blame, nowhere to lay responsibility; it just happened. Perhaps it was simply a cost of being white and being a male introduced to life by the monologue of the '50s, yet having to live in the dialogue of the '80s, the '90s, and now the new millennium.

A few years back in the *Los Angeles Times* (Njeri, 1989) I read that to varying degrees all of us who live in the United States give up something. Whether we are Chicano or Czech, male or female, whether we walk the streets of Teamsterville or the halls of the Robert Taylor Holmes projects, we have all been coerced into assimilating. The American agenda of assimilation extracts a heavy toll: a loss of perspective regarding many of the fundamental aspects of our identities. For most African, Asian, Hispanic, and Native American peoples in the United States, this agenda very nearly resulted in the eradication of their racial and ethnic identities under the guise of cultural normalization. Certainly they have paid a price that far exceeds anything asked of most of white America, especially males. I know they have paid and will continue to pay much more than has been asked of me.

Yet assimilation has had a normalizing effect on white Americans as well. I have come to believe that they—we, for I am white and American—pay a hidden price for being the dominant group in a society that has denigrated differences while demanding cultural homogeneity. As a consequence of the "white" assumption that "our experience is a universal experience," we have unwittingly engineered a social reality devoid of places and events that belong to any one of us. Although the particulars of my life and the lives of other white Americans have not been ripped from our consciousness as they have been from others, we have surrendered those particulars nonetheless. Rosaldo (1989) claims that "One achieves full citizenship in the nation-state by becoming a culturally blank slate" (p. 201). Many of us have lost what Lillian Rose (see Njeri, 1989) has called the "handles" of our culture—a distinct language, music, food, and unique traditions. Being "everything" for some may have resulted in being nothing.

As part of our losing the grip on our culture, we also have suffered a gradual erosion of the narratives depicting our cultural identities. Stories describing what is meaningful to or important about white Americans as individuals and as a cultural group have all but disappeared. Our stories, like the ones of Carl's Barber Shop, have evaporated in the everythingness of assimilation. Our narratives no longer reflect our identities as individuals, as sons, neighbors, or workers. Instead they have been commodified by the current mass mediated version of assimilation that shapes our identities into consumers and publics. The particulars, my particulars, like the experiences of Oak Park and Harrison, have faded from the narrative field of our lives. The process of self-definition has been handed over to the editors of magazines, the image makers and sound byte technicians of television, and the social scientists as purveyors of generalizations.

I confess that I have realized for quite some time that my life lacked certain cultural connections—a deep appreciation of family traditions, a sense of place, or a strong feeling of belonging. Long before my return to education in the mid 1980s, I had felt the inner tensions of such a void. It is possible, therefore, that my return may have been prompted by the frustration of not being able to identify a course of action capable of satisfying that void. It was only during the final two or three years of my graduate education, however, that I acquired an explicit awareness of matters involving cultural deficits and eroding narratives. It has been a gradual process from that point, one in which I have begun to comprehend the significance of my eroding narratives.

My introduction to these matters unfolded in graduate seminars as I witnessed a variety of historically marginalized and displaced individuals, mostly women, struggling to forge a space for their identities in the discourse of academia. Some were angry. As for the rest, there was an air of commitment and certainty, a cultural assuredness about them that I didn't recognize in myself. Some spoke of a devaluing of women's narratives and bodily experiences; others critiqued the sanitizing nature of Western history, science, and art dominated by white males. They pressed not only to have "their" stories heard but also to have them honored as legitimate, not alternative, forms of experience. While the angry ones made me uncomfortable with their pointing and blaming, I admired the others for their sense of purpose and willingness to share responsibility.

Although I caught only brief fragments of stories that provided me with even briefer glimpses of their cultural experiences, the discourse *about* their cultural connections seemed genuine nonetheless. They sounded sincere. I became convinced that the majority of these women and men possessed a firm grasp of their traditions as well as an appreciation of the events and places that made them, as individuals and cultural members, unique. They were grounded, like the men in Carl's Barber Shop. I felt a longing within me, realizing that such a grasp was presently beyond me. The irony did not escape me. I was culturally displaced, not them.

As I listened and recorded my thoughts, as all disciplined ethnographers do—even ethnographers-in-training, as I was back then—I noted that these classmates of mine somehow had maintained an awareness, some more complete than others of course, but all had maintained some vision of their primary identities. They had preserved this vision in their narratives despite the denigration, and in spite of the absence of legitimation confronting them in the American agenda of assimilation. Maybe it was in their struggle, in the opposition and resistance, that their narratives accrued personal and cultural currency. Whatever the reasons, it seemed to me that many of them enjoyed a meaningful, profound relationship with the stories that situated them as individuals within their cultural heritage.

My sense of disconnection ultimately regressed into a feeling of cultural invisibility. I had lost my cultural handles, my stories, my places. Consequently, I began to feel culturally transparent. However, the emotions and perceptions I had experienced in those classes, although unsettling, remained unconfronted and unexplored—that is, until I encountered the Lakota.

One summer in the early 1990s, I journeyed to the Pine Ridge Reservation near Porcupine, South Dakota, to participate in a seminar centering on self-reflexivity and fieldwork. Eight of us went as guests of the Pesla Oyate band of the Lakota people to their annual Brotherhood Gathering. While there, contrary to the precepts of traditional fieldwork, we cast our ethnographic gaze on ourselves not on the "other," the Lakota, or their ways. I arrived with a firm conviction implanted by my professor and intellectual guide for this journey that unless we, as social researchers, understand ourselves and our traditions, we will never be capable of understanding others. I left with that conviction more deeply entrenched than when I came, and today that conviction is stronger than ever. It is why I have written this essay.

At the Gathering I participated in a variety of ceremonies and everyday rituals of the Lakota. Each day I ventured forth from the dampness of my rented tent into the dampness of morning to celebrate the dawn with the smoke and water of the water of life ceremony. At night I collapsed into a surprisingly sound sleep, accompanied by the rhythmic beat of the Brotherhood drum. I looked forward to the celebration of both the beginning and the end of each day. While there, I danced an honor dance on the ceremonial grounds commemorating the death of a young Lakota man. Unexpectedly, the movements seemed natural. While there, in the threatening heat of a 13-by-13 sweat lodge, I prayed aloud for my mother's health as my body cleansed itself of unwanted toxins. I breathed through cracked pieces of sage to cool the air each breath eased into my lungs, determined to remain inside the small enclosure for the entire ritual. I remember sensing a physical bond with the 21 strangers who suffered along with me.

During my time at the Gathering, I came to value these and the other Lakota rituals. But something else happened in South Dakota. While immersed in the Lakota ceremonies and cultural places, I reacquired my perspective on the places and events that, at various times, have constituted my life. Distance and difference somehow encouraged access. The longing that had materialized in the classrooms of my education suddenly dissipated in the classroom of the field, replaced by a subtle mixture of resentment and confusion. But that combination also gave way, quickly succeeded by a determination to rekindle an appreciation of the events and places, past and present, that define my life. On a ridge in South Dakota, I found my whiteness.

Resentment is often a manifestation of jealousy, a bitter emotion that reflects an illness of the soul. The disaffection I experienced in South Dakota was not a symptom of this illness. Although I found them refreshingly appealing and self-enlightening, I did not covet the Lakota traditions, nor did I begrudge them their rituals. To the contrary, I respected my Lakota hosts for the deep affection they exhibited for their places and their rituals. It was the actions and words of the non–Native American guests of the Lakota that ignited my resentment.

Many of those in attendance at the Gathering, including a majority of the white Americans and most of my fellow graduate students, accorded the Lakota rituals and ceremonial settings a level of admiration that approached adoration. The reverence with which they treated the Lakota sweat lodge and ceremonial grounds far surpassed, it seemed, the respect they invested in their own cultural places and events. Perhaps they came to South Dakota simply to borrow and steal to replace the cultural emptiness of their lives. They sought symbols, not meaning or self-reflective understanding.

Along with my resentment, and perhaps indistinguishable from it, came confusion. By day two or three of my stay, I already had perceived a symmetry between the smoke and water of the morning ceremony and the incense and holy water of the Catholic services of my altar boy youth. By day four, the spectacle of the ceremonial grounds had conjured up in me images of stadiums and sporting contests, while the cadence of the nightly drums reminded me of the holiday parades that snaked down Oak Park Avenue. Everywhere in the differences I saw similarities. Therein resided my confusion. Why hadn't the others recognized the same similarities? Why were they all so willing to inflate the importance of the Lakota ceremonies, rituals, and events, yet ignore the significance of similar activities in their own everyday lives? And why, although operating completely outside the physical limits of my comfort zone, did I feel such a strong inner connection to the Lakota places?

My feelings of resentment and confusion evaporated in the heat and activity of the sweat lodge. While my male ego was busy demonstrating its determination to withstand the suffocating heat, my mind at some point drifted to the images (or was it a vision?) and sounds of a locker room. As the men around me jokingly taunted the newcomers among them, I recalled the hours I had spent in the caverns beneath ballparks and gymnasiums engaged in the same "needling" banter. Not everyone joked. Some in the lodge told stories, especially during the times the blanket over the door was peeled back to let in air or let out those among us who couldn't survive the heat. The storytelling made me think back to Carl's barbershop.

What bizarre yet, for me, extraordinarily balanced images: the memory traces of a locker room and a barbershop transposed onto the physical reality of a Lakota sweat lodge. All three had a "public" nature, certainly different from those "private" places that bind us to our jobs and family. All three places encouraged animated interaction, camaraderie, and storytelling against the backdrop of some other activity. All three were strongholds of male interaction. And all were places where I experienced that feeling of connection.

I realized, lying there in the sweat lodge with my mouth probing the ground trying to capture a wisp of cool air, that it was the conversation, the storytelling, the tempo and beat, along with a distinct yet undefinable "maleness" of the Lakota places that seemed so familiar and appealing. But these were *their* places, and I needed to regain my cultural visibility by reclaiming *my* places. I left South Dakota with a firm resolve to rediscover the places and practices that have been and continue to be a part of who I am. I took with me a determination to learn more about the relationship between identity and place, both on a personal and an academic level. I became determined to (re)discover the stories of my identities.

Quite a bit has happened to me since my days with the Lakota. Last year my mother passed away after a six-year battle with Alzheimer's. A little over nine days after my mom left me, my sister also died—suddenly, unexpectedly, and without the joy of relief I experienced with my mother. I bought a house with venetian blinds on some of the windows, refinished my Davy Crockett lunchbox from 1954, and found a real barber shop (not a hair salon). The shop sits right next to the railroad station turned preschool in the Old Webster section of downtown Webster Groves, a few blocks from where I live. Of course other things have happened to me along the way, but at the moment none seem more important than these.

The shop is called Nick's—like Carl's, a great name for a barbershop. A solid, no frills name that fits the image of a real barbershop, just as "Roadmaster" suits a big, heavy car or "The Corner Tap" seems an altogether suitable moniker for any neighborhood tavern that occupies a nearby street corner. Simple, straightforward, Nick's Barber Shop. I picked Nick's out of the local business directory the clerk gave me when I went to City Hall to sign up to have my water turned on (I think they wanted to see my "whiteness"). I picked it because of the name. Straightforward, simple.

Having gone there now for almost 10 years, one of the things I like best about the place, besides the name and the $10 haircuts, is the shoe shine stand positioned in the back corner of the shop, the farthest spot from the entrance. I can tell by marks on the floor that it once sat closer to the front, by the window opposite the first barber's chair—it once had a position of prominence. Now, however, it looks forgotten, worn around the edges, its black leather seat cracked and split, a piece of duct tape covering the worst of the damage, footrests scratched and tarnished from neglect. It's on the downward side of its better days.

From its appearance I'd guess the stand hasn't been in operation for quite some time, maybe years. It remains only as a remnant of the past, just another reminder of what once was, like the shop's two extra barber's chairs that now sit empty and ignored. Only Nick works his shop these days, even the busy ones. Someone has tried to make the old shoe shine stand look less conspicuous, not as useless, by placing three medium-sized plants and a stack of crumpled old magazines and torn G-men comics around the three sets of nickel-plated footrests that stretch up from its marble base. No order or plan to them, just there to help disguise the stand's uselessness. And yet the whole picture—leather seat, footrests, plants, comics—all still looks so worn out, tired. Sort of used up.

I began going to Nick's at the times I know that it'll be the most crowded. I enjoy waiting, sometimes an hour or more, just sitting and listening to the other people talk, joining in whenever the topic turns my way. I began going there on the days that I had nowhere special to be, when I was in no hurry, so I could enjoy the experience as I did during those carefree days of my youth at Oak Park and Harrison. I come for the conversation more than the haircuts. And if a haircut and a friendly round of storytelling isn't enough, for no additional charge Nick never fails to douse you with that sweet-smelling pale amber liquid when the time for the haircut and conversation ends. This is one of the rituals of a real barbershop, and Nick has got the ritual perfected. He splashes a few drops into his left hand, slaps his hands together, for a moment rubs his palms briskly in a tight circular motion, then half pats half massages your neck and ears. You tingle for a moment, but that's the fun of it. I've never known if it's hair tonic or aftershave, maybe a little of both, but I know I like the smell and feel. Finally, he applies the talcum powder with a few quick sweeps of the brush and, all too soon for me, removes the cape with the skill of a matador. None of this happens in a unisex hair salon, including conversations like the men had at Carl's. And in a hair salon, everything carries an extra charge. I come for the ritual as well.

One afternoon, as I sat in one of the chairs along Nick's wall listening to one fellow's replay of his week while awaiting my turn in Nick's chair, something just came over me. I saw that old forgotten stand over in the corner and couldn't resist. I think I knew, from the very first time I peered through the window of Nick's, that sooner or later this was going to happen. I got up, walked over to it, shoved a plant or two aside, grabbed the August 1989 *National Geographic,* and hoisted myself on up. There was no squeak left in the leather, but I could tell from the feel it once had one. The four other customers, and one young boy's mother, watched me in the mirror. All were careful to avoid directly looking me in the eye, but I could sense their expressions of surprise nonetheless. But no one commented. Nick looked right at me, but he didn't say a word either. He almost looked happy as I sat up there, my feet on one of the pairs of footrests, as if he remembered something good. When it was my turn for a haircut, I didn't budge, just stayed in my seat instead, deferring to the next customer in line. I let two, maybe three, people go ahead of me. I simply sat, listened, and talked. We told personal stories, some about failure, but mostly ones of joy. I felt a part of something sitting up there. I felt connected. Following that day, that experience, I began a three-and-one-half year study of 10 barbershops.

Somewhere I had lost that feeling of being a part of something, the one I had back in Oak Park sitting atop Ollie's shoe shine stand. And somewhere, by studying aspects of my primary identities and, in turn, by listening to the personal narratives of others, I regained it. I now have a newfound awareness, through journaling and my contact with the lifeworlds of others, of the places and practices that are special to me—ones that have fed and nurtured my identities. Until I began this work of exploring aspects of my primary identities, I never understood how important it is for all of us to tell the stories that we live, the ones that remind us who we are. To stop and reflect upon the pre-reflective experiences of our own lives and give meaning to it all, and then share that meaning with others so that they also have a sense of who we are, all this encourages connections—connections with our past and connections with others.

My work as an ethnographer remains focused in a personal desire to regain my cultural identity and places, and my work has brought me back to where I wanted to be. I've needed to sit in a barbershop, atop a shoe shine stand, listen to others talk about their successes and failures, and tell them about mine. This is how culture is passed on and self is realized. I had been looking for my cultural identity outside of myself, expecting something or someone to confer it upon me, instead of realizing that I had it inside of me the entire time, unarticulated. Connections are in the personal narratives we perform for self and others. As a social researcher, I want to position myself to hear those narratives and to assist myself and others in making those connections. This is the story, or some version of it, that I wanted to tell when I entered into studying whiteness with Tom Nakayama.

AND MY POINT IS? THE MORAL OF THE STORY

I saw a movie on the 5th of July this year—*America's Heart and Soul.* Its Web site (http://disney.go.com/disneypictures/heartandsoul/) proudly touts the movie as "the incredible story of America told one person at a time, a nation of individuals. No two alike." That's why I went—to hear the stories. Once there, the movie's narrator, presumably providing us viewers with the thoughts of the film's creator, filmmaker Louis Schwartzberg, claimed that what people need to do is discover (and we are left to assume this is what he has uncovered in his interviews with people from across America) that which is unique and remarkable about themselves. I disagreed.

Shortly after seeing Schwartzberg's movie, I read a book by William Zinsser (2004) titled *Writing About Your Life*. Zinsser's mission is to provide the reader with a template for writing about the people, places, and events that have been important to them in their lives. He tells us that "to write well about your life you only have to be true to yourself. If you make an honest transaction with your remembered experiences and emotions you'll reach the readers you want to reach" (p. 8). I had no idea when I selected Zinsser's book that it would help me realize why I had disagreed with the narrator's words. Unlike Schwartzberg, who advises us to look for the remarkable and unique, Zinsser asks the reader to look only for what has been meaningful and to talk about it as honestly as you can. I agree with Zinsser. If we spend our time trying to find the unique and remarkable aspects of our lives, we will wind up like my colleagues in South Dakota looking for their identities in the rituals of the Lakota—borrowing meaning from others. And are we really the best judge of what is unique and remarkable about our own lives?

Whiteness is a socially constructed racial classification. As such it has rhetorical, cultural, and political power. Our discourses have constructed it that way. It can exclude and dominate. Beyond its rhetorical nature and political power, whiteness is also present in everyday practices. In order to expose and denormalize whiteness, we must examine it both critically and experientially. Those of us who, through accidents of our biographies, have been cast in the center of this invisible whiteness need to be active in both the critical and the experiential unmasking; some of us are just better equipped to do one more than the other. Those of us in latter group, of which I consider myself a part, need to look at the meaningful and important aspects of our lives, our mundane and everyday lives, not constantly search for the remarkable and unique. We should take what we find and talk about it. Then, as social researchers, we should view our experiences as cultural manifestations, not simply as autobiographical details, and use them to provide inspiration for our research. I study barbershops. I study baseball. Both are aspects of my cultural identity(ies) and as such have meaning and importance.

I would hope that social researchers of all ethnic, racial, and social backgrounds excavate (discover and examine) their own narratives of cultural identity as I have. But because of the power of whiteness, it is particularly important for those of us at the center of the center, white males, to expose, name, and narrate how we experience the center.

References

Bahk, C. M., & Jandt, F. E. (2004). Being white in America: Development of a scale. *Howard Journal of Communications, 15*, 57–68.

DeLuca, K. (1999). In the shadow of whiteness: The consequences of constructions of nature in environmental politics. In T. K. Nakayama & J. N. Martin (Eds.), *Whiteness: The communication of social identity* (pp. 217–246). Thousand Oaks, CA: Sage.

Gonzalez, M. C., & Krizek, R. L. (1994). *Indigenous ethnography*. Paper presented at the annual Western Speech Communication Association Convention, San Jose, CA.

Grimes, D. S. (2001). Putting our own house in order: Whiteness, change, and organization studies. *Journal of Organizational Change Management, 14*, 132–143.

Grimes, D. S. (2002). Challenging the status quo? *Management of Communication Quarterly, 15*, 381–409.

Hytten, K., & Adkins, A. (2002). Thinking through a pedagogy of whiteness. *Educational Theory, 51*, 433–450.

Jackson, R. L., & Heckman, S. M. (2002). Perceptions of white identity and white liability: An analysis of white student responses to a college campus racial hate crime. *Journal of Communication, 52*, 434–450.

Johnson, P. C. (1999). Reflections on critical white(ness) studies. In T. K. Nakayama & J. N. Martin (Eds.), *Whiteness: The communication of social identity* (pp. 1–9). Thousand Oaks, CA: Sage.

Krizek, R. L. (1995). *The ethnography of events: A narrative analysis of non-routine public events*. Unpublished dissertation.

Liera-Schwichentenberg, R. (2000). Passing or whiteness on the edge of town. *Critical Studies in Media Communication, 17*, 371–374.

Martin, J. N., & Davis, O. I. (2001). Conceptual foundations for teaching about whiteness in intercultural communication courses. *Communication Education, 50*, 298–313.

Martin, J. N., Krizek, R. L., Nakayama, T. K., & Bradford, L. (1996). A study of self-labels for white Americans. *Communication Quarterly, 44*, 125–144.

Martin, J. N., Krizek, R. L., Nakayama, T. K., & Bradford, L. (1999). What do white people want to be called? A study of self-labels for white Americans. In T. K. Nakayama &

J. N. Martin (Eds.), *Whiteness: The communication of social identity* (pp. 27–50). Thousand Oaks, CA: Sage.

Moon, D. (1999). White enculturation and bourgeois ideology. In T. K. Nakayama & J. N. Martin (Eds.), *Whiteness: The communication of social identity* (pp. 177–197). Thousand Oaks, CA: Sage.

Nakayama, T. K., & Krizek, R. L. (1995). Whiteness: A strategic rhetoric. *Quarterly Journal of Speech, 18,* 291–309.

Nakayama, T. K., & Krizek, R. L. (1999). Whiteness as a strategic rhetoric. In T. K. Nakayama & J. N. Martin (Eds.), *Whiteness: The communication of social identity* (pp. 87–106). Thousand Oaks, CA: Sage.

Nakayama, T. K., & Martin, J. N. (Eds.). (1999). *Whiteness: The communication of social identity*. Thousand Oaks, CA: Sage.

Njeri, I. (1989, December 28). Facing up to being white. *Los Angeles Times*, pp. E1, E6.

Projansky, S., & Ono, K. A. (1999). Strategic whiteness as cinematic racial politics. In T. K. Nakayama & J. N. Martin (Eds.), *Whiteness: The communication of social identity* (pp. 149–174). Thousand Oaks, CA: Sage.

Rockler, N. R. (2002). Race, whiteness, "lightness," and relevance: African American and European American interpretations of *Jump Start* and *The Boondocks*. *Critical Studies in Media Communication, 19*, 398–418.

Rosaldo, R. (1989). *Culture and truth: The remaking of social analysis*. Boston: Beacon Press.

Shome, R. (2000). Outing whiteness. *Critical Studies in Media Communication, 17*, 366–371.

Stage, C. W. (1999). We celebrate 100 years: An "indigenous" analysis of the metaphors that shape the cultural identity of small town, U.S.A. In T. K. Nakayama & J. N. Martin (Eds.), *Whiteness: The communication of social identity* (pp. 69–84). Thousand Oaks, CA: Sage.

Supriya, K. E. (1999). White difference: Cultural construction of white identity. In T. K. Nakayama & J. N. Martin (Eds.), *Whiteness: The communication of social identity* (pp. 129–148). Thousand Oaks, CA: Sage.

Tehranian, J. (2000). Performing whiteness: Naturalization litigation and the construction of racial identity in America. *Yale Journal of Law, 109*, 817–848.

Wander, P. C., Martin, J. N., & Nakayama, T. K. (1999). Whiteness and beyond: Sociohistorical foundations of whiteness and contemporary challenges. In T. K. Nakayama & J. N. Martin (Eds.), *Whiteness: The communication of social identity* (pp. 13–26). Thousand Oaks, CA: Sage.

Warren, J. T. (2001). The social drama of a "Rice Burner": A (Re)construction of whiteness. *Western Journal of Communication, 65*, 184–205.

Zinsser, W. (2004). *Writing about your life.* New York: Marlowe.

Concepts and Questions

1. With what is the study of whiteness concerned?
2. What social dynamics are unique to whiteness as a cultural identity?
3. In his self-narrative about whiteness, Krizek refers to "protected" and "grounded." How do these concepts contribute to the development of an identity of whiteness?
4. What does Krizek mean when he refers to assimilation as having a normalizing effect on white Americans as well as people of color?
5. How does narrative play a role in the development of cultural identity?
6. What does Krizek mean by a sense of disconnection? What may result from such a sense of disconnection?
7. What is meant by the statement that whiteness is considered to be a socially constructed racial classification?

A Polish Jewish American Story: Collective Memories and Intergroup Relations

JOLANTA A. DRZEWIECKA
NANCY DRAZNIN

Our collective past continually exerts influence over us and our relations with others. As individuals, we might be tempted to disavow the collective historical baggage and start fresh, asserting our individual relationship with the world. But this relationship is already partially shaped by the time we are born. We can deny it, repress it, or ignore it, but we cannot erase it. It will sneak up on us when we least expect it, as it did on me one July Sunday evening at a dinner party at a friend's house. It was a warm, pleasant evening. There were quite a few people I enjoyed meeting for the first time as we mingled on the deck. That's how I met Nancy. When she found out that I was from Poland, she told me about her grandfather who emigrated from the eastern part of Poland, escaping hardships and anti-Semitism. A phrase from the story that stood out for me was, "He did not have anything good to say about the Poles." During my 15 years in the United States, I have met many people with ancestral ties to Poland. Usually, the conversations include vague but positive references to places of origin, language, names, or food. This one, however, tore right into one of the most painful parts of the Polish past, thrusting it into the present. Nancy was very friendly, and I did not detect any hostility or resentment; she simply summed up her grandfather's stories. The future, how we would communicate with each other, depended on how we understood the collective past.

When I met Nancy, I had been studying Polish American and Jewish Polish American relations in the United States for several years. My interest was in how these relations were shaped by memories of the past. Although the common past, in particular World War II, might seem distant to outsiders, I found that it continued to pulsate with significance. Its vitality was demonstrated by responses to *Neighbors*, a book written by NYU Professor Jan Gross and published in Poland and the United States in 2002. The book attributed a World War II pogrom against the Jewish population of a small Polish town, Jedwabne, to its Polish gentile neighbors acting under Nazi orchestration. This book evoked very strong reactions from Poles and Polish Americans who were concerned that its publication in the United States would reinforce the image of Poland as an anti-Semitic country and believed that any such charges were false. Other Polish Americans and Poles argued that it was necessary to acknowledge anti-Semitism, as well as the Polish tradition of religious tolerance, and declared their commitment to Catholic–Jewish dialogue. These responses demonstrated the continuing importance of collective memory of past events to current identities and intergroup relations. Who we are in the present is shaped by how we understand who we were collectively in the past.

I met Nancy again. The tinge of defensiveness I had felt when she talked about the anti-Semitism her grandfather had experienced prompted me to ask her if she would be willing to contribute the story to this chapter as a starting point for my discussion of the importance of history and collective memory to intercultural communication. In addition to Nancy's story of her grandfather's life in Poland and migration to the United States, I discuss the notion of collective memory and how it has influenced my understanding of Jewish–gentile relations in Poland. I also include a necessarily brief description of the historical context of gentile–Jewish relations in Poland. My discussion will focus on how, as individuals, we are historically situated and how we grapple with collective memories and history in our communication with others.

NANCY'S STORY

My grandfather, Herschel (Abraham) Zeigman, was born on March 23, 1902, in Mezeritch, Poland. The town was given to the Jews in the 16th century, and it became a center of commerce and Jewish culture. The chief industry was manufacturing brushes from swine bristles.

Although Mezeritch was a Jewish town, some 15 percent of the population was Polish Catholic, and there

---

This original essay appears here in print for the first time. Jolanta A. Drzewiecka teaches at Washington State University.

were two or three churches in the town. Poles would come in from the countryside to attend Mass, so my grandfather had contact with them on a regular basis.

My great-grandfather, Herschel's father, died of pneumonia before Herschel was born, or so he was told. Herschel was sent to live with his grandparents so that his mother could have the opportunity to look for another husband. The grandparents owned a store, and they sent Herschel to Cheder, or Hebrew school, when he was five or six. Because she was so busy, his grandmother would forget to send him a lunch, so Herschel would go hungry all day, after having only milk for breakfast. School ended at 5 P.M.

Herschel was small as a result of genetics and malnutrition. He described himself as "unfit for physical work." He grew up in a country that was so anti-Semitic that even in a majority Jewish town, a Pole could push him off the sidewalk as if the sidewalk did not belong to the Jews and they did not belong on the sidewalk. Although he did not relate other stories of anti-Semitism, there clearly were anti-Semitic feelings among the Poles, which erupted when the Nazis occupied Poland in 1939 and began to round up Jews for the death camps. Those Jews who were not shot by the Nazis were often shot by Poles. A few Poles were able to help a few Jews at great risk, but the majority did the opposite, whether out of fear or hatred. Though many of our relatives died during the Holocaust, Herschel had been in the United States for several years by that time.

Herschel made it clear that he hated the Poles: He hated to speak Polish although he was fluent, usually he spoke of his life in Poland only reluctantly, he made a clear distinction between being Polish and being Jewish, and he made an expression of disgust whenever he spoke of "Polacks."

When he came of age, Herschel was drafted into the Polish army, but feeling no loyalty to the Poles, he attempted to escape by attaching himself to the retreating Russian army. Once inside Russia, he was homeless and penniless. He began to make his way back to Mezeritch, working as he went. He caught typhus crossing a contaminated stream, but by what he would later call a godsend he made it back to Mezeritch, where his mother found him at the hospital. After he recovered, Herschel was now an army deserter. He fled to Danzig, which was a free city. He would be safe there, though utterly destitute. His uncle, who was living in America, sent him money for passage to the United States in 1924. It seems that he used a fake passport because there have always been questions about his name (legally Abraham, but everyone called him Herschel), his age, and his actual birthday. He received a letter from the president congratulating him for turning 100 on his 97th birthday, and though he always said his birthday was March 23, 1902, his gravestone reads April 23, 1899.

Grandpa made money peddling umbrellas in America. His uncle invested Herschel's first $1,000 badly and it was lost. Nevertheless, grandpa lived frugally, worked hard, invested wisely, and saved a nice nest egg. He married and had only one child, my mother. His wife died at the age of 44, leaving him widowed for 50 years.

The stories of my grandfather's experience are part of the fabric of my life. Like most contemporary Jews, I have suffered little overt anti-Semitism and no violent anti-Semitism, but the recent history of horrific crimes against Jews is never far from the surface of my consciousness. I keep a copy of my grandfather's story in my files and a picture of him as a boy in Poland with his extended family on my wall. Whenever I look at it, I'm reminded that his aunts were killed by the Nazis.

Having grown up in safety and prosperity, I don't feel any of Grandpa's hurt or anger. I'm more interested in healing and communication. This writing project came about because I wanted to reach out to a Polish woman I met at a party, find common ground, and ask her if she had heard of Mezeritch. Whenever I have an opportunity to communicate with someone who is from a society that has had conflict with Jews, I try to reach out. The result has been that I have had good conversations with Germans and Palestinians as well. I feel that this kind of individual conversation helps to bring about healing and peace in a small way. I loved my grandfather with all his understandable prejudices, but I can't feel the same way. The world is a different place now, much more dangerous in some ways and vastly safer in others. I hope that continued communication will eventually bring healing to all.

HISTORY AND COLLECTIVE MEMORY

History can be defined as a reconstruction and a representation of the past. Although it is not objective, in the sense that the historical record can only be represented from a particular point of view, it is focused on uncovering and (re)interpreting past events. Collective memory, conversely, is an ongoing process of public and collective engagement with the past. Collective memory can be defined as "a set of ideas, images, and feelings about the past" that results from a collective process of interpretation of "public offerings" consisting of presences and absences (Irwin-Zarecka, 1994, p. 4). Memories that we share with our social groups are constructed through a public process of representing information about particular events—"the presences."

Only a few of us might read history books on a regular basis. Most of us, however, have an idea and a feeling about past events that come from stories passed down to us by family members and teachers, articles in newspapers, historical fiction books, fictional and semi-factual movies, and documentaries. Nancy's story is an example of memories passed down from generation to generation. Such memories are crucial to our sense of identity and connection to the world, as her grandfather's memories are important to Nancy. She cherishes and respects her grandfather's history, but she also presents it in a way that allows for coexistence with other stories. That is, she does not claim that her grandfather's experiences entirely define gentile–Jewish relations in Poland. Instead, she simply presents his experiences and feelings as rightfully his. It is such straightforwardness that disarms possible defensiveness driven by a desire to protect one's identity by protecting the collective identity. Even after learning, teaching, and writing about intercultural communication for many years, I can detect such impulses in my own reactions. Sometimes, such impulses can overtake and turn collective memories into an ideological struggle that overshadows the wider picture and the complexity of different experiences and perspectives. This happens when we totalize our own experiences or those of our family members as definitive.

Further, the concept of collective memory suggests that information that is not available in books and popular media—the absences—is just as important to understanding our relationship to the past as information that is repeated. This is particularly problematic when the stories are not only partial but also fictionalized, yet they are interpreted as if they were the truth. Thus, the movie *Schindler's List* (Spielberg, Molen, & Lustig, 1993), although based on factual events, was a very partial and selective representation of the Holocaust. Yet it gripped the popular imagination so strongly that suggestions were made at the time of its release that it should be used in schools as a teaching tool.

In collective memories, the past is selectively made to matter to satisfy particular goals, needs, and emotions that groups have in the present (Hasian & Carlson, 2000; Irwin-Zarecka, 1994; Zelizer, 1998). Thus, no major Hollywood motion picture has been made about the U.S. government's refusal to recognize that the Holocaust was taking place or the turning away from U.S. shores of Jewish refugees, many of whom ended up later perishing in Auschwitz. Although this information is certainly available from many sources, it is not engaged in popular media in the same way, perhaps because it does not provide U.S. Americans with positive identities. Collective memory is a rhetorical bridge built from the present to the past, "an evoking of a past to frame a present but also to conform that past to the present" (Gronbeck, 1998, p. 58).

As a whole, collective memory is a creative and purposeful process that "allow[s] for the fabrication, rearrangement, elaboration, and omission of details about the past, often pushing aside accuracy and authenticity so as to accommodate broader issues of identity formation, power and authority, and political affiliation" (Zelizer, 1998, p. 3). From this perspective, the very notion of collective memories presumes "multiple conflicting accounts of the past" (Zelizer, 1998, p. 217). Different communities of memory sharing a past may contest each other's memories and struggle to impose one interpretation on others. My own experiences as well as the larger historical context of gentile–Jewish relations in Poland inform and frame my communication with Polish Jewish Americans. What matters in this process is how we engage with the historical accounts—how we build the bridge. This is the task that each individual has to undertake on his or her own.

I am Polish and gentile. I grew up in post–World War II Poland, where real Jewish individuals were mostly absent but the ideas and memories of Jews were not far from the surface of cultural consciousness. One of my earliest memories of realizing Jewish difference/presence is that when I was a child, a Jewish cemetery, situated right next door to a Catholic cemetery, was pointed out to me with a sense that it was a "different" place. The precise nature of the difference was vague and mysterious, but later it became clear to me that there was a stigma associated with the word "Jew" in Polish. Individuals or activities that were questionable in some way could be called "a Jew" or "Jewish." One could also be suspected or exposed to be Jewish. Zygmunt Bauman, a sociologist, explains that "the Jew" functions as a significant Other, a conceptually empty category that can be filled with any meaning necessary or convenient at the moment to mark a difference from the in-group and establish positive self-identity (Bauman, 1989). "The Jew" (in quotation marks) does not refer to real, concrete Jewish individuals or even to specific characteristics but to a collection of contradictory stereotypes that are circulated in social discourse to affirm the self through the contrast to the Other, represented as different, foreign, and negative. Then these stereotypes of the Other are reversed, as in a mirror, to affirm the self—the identity of the in-group (Hall, 1992). The negative characteristics of the Other portrayed in stereotypes imply, by contrast, positive characteristics in the self; that is, if they are bad, dishonest, or lazy, that implies that we are good, honest, or hardworking. The affirmation of the gentile/Catholic self in language is just one of the ways in which Jews were a very significant Other in Poland. The contributions of real Jewish individuals to Polish cultural, scientific, and social thought have been enormous.

Jews began migrating to Poland in the eighth century to escape religious persecution elsewhere (Wrobel, 2001). Their migration was often encouraged, and they were often able to negotiate special protections and rights with local authorities. Those benefits were often followed by anti-Semitism, resulting in restrictions, expulsions, and pogroms. In spite of these adversities, Jews built in Poland the largest Jewish community in the pre–World War II world. The Polish Jewish community's multiple relations with the pre–World War II Polish gentile/Catholic society ranged from separatists and separated to integrated, converted, and/or Polonized (Checinski, 1982; Hertz, 1961; Irwin-Zarecka, 1990; Schatz, 1991). According to historians and sociologists, the Catholic Church played a significant role in shaping these relationships as it often scapegoated and vilified, and sometimes praised, Jews (Bauman, 1989; Tomaszewski, 2001). The majority of the Polish population was Catholic, and the difference from the "Jewish Other" was fundamental to the "Polish" identity for much of the Polish population. Consequently, although Jews were Polish citizens and culturally Polish, discourse retained the sharp and telling distinction between "Poles" (Catholic Poles) and "Jews" (Jewish Poles), implying that Jews were not Polish. This distinction is active in Nancy's grandfather's language. I assume that he turned the word *Polak,* which means a Polish male person in the Polish language, into a plural by using English grammar and spelling—Polacks. Most U.S. Americans are familiar with the anglicized offensive term *Polacks,* coined in the context of hostile immigrant relations in the United States.

The town where I grew up, Bedzin, was a predominantly Jewish town before World War II, but most of its Jewish inhabitants perished in the Holocaust and many others left after the war. Although I learned that Jews were one of the primary targets and victims during World War II, the ongoing collective memory process focused on national patriotism, heroism, and suffering. Even though I was born more than 20 years after the war, I remember watching lots of documentary, semi-documentary, and fictional World War II films on TV, reading books, and listening to presentations by survivors of concentration camps at school. The memory of World War II is one of the most important elements forming Polish national identity, not least because World War II and its aftermath changed Polish borders and the Polish political system, situating Poland under the influence of the Soviet Union. Further, the memory of World War II heroism and suffering connects to the memory of other preceding historical events in which Poland lost its territories, for more than 100 years ceasing to exist as a political unit, its people imprisoned, exiled, or subjected to nationalization by Russian, Prussian, and Austrian regimes. The memory of national survival, focusing on the strength of the Polish culture, language, and Catholic religion, is part of the national ethos that excludes Jewish Poles who were active in that survival. This history facilitated an emergence of national myths in which the whole Polish nation stood bravely against the Nazi aggressor and then suffered collectively (Swida-Ziemba, 2000). Although many did, the complete picture was much more complex.

World War II victimized both groups, and the Holocaust created a Jewish graveyard in Poland, reducing the country's population of 3 million Polish Jews to between 350,000 and 500,000 (Tomaszewski, 2001).

After the initial postwar period of honoring Jewish martyrdom, gradually the official historiography turned Polish Jews into "Poles," ostensibly on the principle of avoiding distinctions that had led to the Holocaust (Irwin-Zarecka, 1990). However, this erased the specificity of the Jewish World War II experience, including Polish anti-Semitism. Further, when Jews were acknowledged, Polish efforts to save Jews became the dominant memory of World War II gentile–Jewish relations in Poland. To this day, World War II, the Holocaust, and relations between Jewish and gentile Poles during the war are a difficult, although very important, subject. Although Nancy's grandfather was already in the United States during the war, these issues are present in his story. Polish anti-Semitism, how many gentile Poles helped Jews, and whether they could have done more are still thorny issues. Hoffman (1997) attempts to capture the complexities, in part, by describing her own family history:

> My parents lived throughout that period in a region of Ukraine that belonged to Poland before the war and became Soviet immediately thereafter. On several occasions they had to escape hostile local peasants who might have given them away to the Nazi authorities. But my parents were also repeatedly helped by people who gave them food and temporary shelter, and by a peasant who hid them for nearly two years, with the full knowledge that he was thereby risking death for himself and his sons. The other awful aspect of my family story was that two relatives died because of an act of betrayal committed by a fellow Jew—a man who, in the hope of ensuring his own survival, led the Germans to a hiding place. (pp. 5–6)

In general, many gentile Poles prefer to remember that Poland was religiously tolerant through the centuries, making it possible for Jews to escape religious persecution in other countries and thrive in Poland. With regard to World War II, many gentile Poles remember that many gentiles risked their lives hiding Jews or helping them in other ways. As a child, I learned very little about Polish anti-Semitism at school and was very surprised by Polish anti-Semitism represented in the World War II documentary *Shoah* (Lanzmann, 1999). Many gentile Poles were very defensive about the film and argued that it represented only the worst part of Poland as if it applied to the whole. It is indeed a common reaction for members of dominant groups to demand that they not all be lumped together when their groups' prejudice is considered. However, this can only lead us further in the cycle of denial and mutual accusations. The most effective strategy in eradicating prejudice it to acknowledge one's group's domination and let go of the desire to set oneself apart. That does not mean that we have to plead guilty personally. Rather, we need to be able to open up a space for dialogue and understanding of what divides us. That's the rhetorical bridge I chose when dealing with issues surrounding Polish anti-Semitism because only this road enables me to establish relations with people. However, this requires that we examine the position of our own group and analyze not only personal but larger collective memories that position us to communicate with others in particular ways.

References

Bauman, Z. (1989). *Modernity and the Holocaust*. Ithaca, NY: Cornell University Press.

Checinski, M. (1982). *Poland: Communism, nationalism, anti-Semitism*. New York: Karz-Cohl.

Gronbeck, B. (1998). The rhetorics of the past: History, argument and collective memory. In K. J. Turner (Ed.), *Doing rhetorical history: Concepts and cases* (pp. 47–60). Tuscaloosa: University of Alabama Press.

Gross, J. (2002). Neighbors: *The destruction of the Jewish community in Jedwabne, Poland*. New York: Penguin Books.

Hall, S. (1992). The West and the rest: Discourse and power. In S. Hall & B. Gieben (Eds.), *Formations of modernity* (pp. 275–330). Cambridge, England: Polity Press/Open University.

Hasian, M. A., Jr., & Carlson, A. C. (2000). Revisionism and collective memory: The struggle for meaning in the *Amistad* affair. *Communication Monographs, 67*, 42–62.

Hertz, A. (1961). *Zydzi w kulturze polskiej* [Jews in Polish culture]. Paris: Instytut Literacki.

Hoffman, E. (1997). *Shtetl: The life and death of a small town and the world of Polish Jews*. New York: Houghton Mifflin.

Irwin-Zarecka, I. (1990). *Neutralizing memory: The Jew in contemporary Poland*. New Brunswick, NJ: Transaction.

Irwin-Zarecka, I. (1994). *Frames of remembrance: The dynamics of collective memory*. New Brunswick, NJ: Transaction.

Lanzmann, C. (Director). (1999). *Shoah* [Videorecording]. Les Films Aleph and Historia Films, with the assistance of the French Ministry of Culture. New York: New Yorker Films.

Schatz, J. (1991). *The generation: The rise and fall of the Jewish Communists of Poland.* Los Angeles: University of California Press.

Spielberg, S. (Director/Producer), Molen, G. R., & Lustig, B. (Producers). (1993). *Schindler's list* [Motion picture]. United States: Universal Studios.

Swida-Ziemba, H. (2000). *Rozbrajac wlasne mity* [Disarming our own myths]. *Znak, 541,* 41–48.

Tomaszewski, J. (2001). Historia [History]. In J. Tomaszeski & A. Zbikowski (Eds.), *Zydzi w Polsce* [Jews in Poland] (pp. 133–171). Warsaw: Wydawnictwo Cyklady.

Wrobel, P. (2001). Migracje [Migrations]. In J. Tomaszeski & A. Zbikowski (Eds.), *Zydzi w Polsce* [Jews in Poland] (pp. 330–353). Warsaw: Wydawnictwo Cyklady.

Zelizer, B. (1998). *Remembering to forget: Holocaust memory through the camera's eye.* Chicago: University of Chicago Press.

Concepts and Questions

1. In what ways might the collective pasts of people engaged in intercultural communication affect the communication process?
2. What is collective memory? How does collective memory contribute to the construction of a cultural identity?
3. What are some of the dangers of relying on collective memory as a source for defining cultural identity?
4. What do the authors mean when they refer to collective memory as a rhetorical bridge built from the present to the past?
5. In what ways do collective memories contribute to the building of stereotypes?
6. In your opinion, what role should collective memories have in the social construction of cultural identity?
7. The authors focus extensively on the role of religious differences in the social relations of the Poles. How do these differences contribute to the development of cultural identities?
8. What steps should people take to avoid the pitfalls of collective memories and yet use those memories in a useful manner to help construct their cultural identity?

The Hybrid Identities of Gender Queer: Claiming Neither/Nor, Both/And

A. L. Zimmerman

Patricia Geist-Martin

I'm seven years old and I know what I want. I want my hair short. I want to buy blue corduroys in the boys' clothing department. I want to wear boys' sneakers. And I definitely do not care about the grass stains on my knees from playing ball with the boys at recess. I don't understand why my mother keeps asking me to "wear a dress" and care about how I look. I sit on my panda bear comforter as she stands in my doorway, we go around and around in an endless discussion about my wardrobe. She pleads with great desire. I indignantly resist. I'm perplexed by her troubled response to my choice of what feels comfortable. She leaves defeated.

I win the discussion. Content, I lay out my clothing choice on my small bed; a pair of purple corduroys, a long-sleeved white-buttoned oxford, brown loafers, and the best piece of all, a black clip-on bow tie. Article by article I put on the clothing, feeling victorious, feeling happy. As I finger the bow tie and carefully clip it to both sides of the collar, I feel myself becoming something more, a little bit bigger perhaps. I already know that people look at me and think I'm strange. I don't know why, but I just can't bring myself to wear a dress.

At eight years old I know that people assume I'm a boy. I know this as I contemplate walking into a bathroom with large letters MEN on the door. I'm at an amusement park with my family and I can't find the women's bathroom. I hesitate at the entrance as carnival music fills my ears. I wonder, if I go in, will men scream at me to get out? Will someone come up to me and tell me that I'm a bad girl? Will it be obvious that I don't have a penis? I look around to make sure my family doesn't see me and walk in past the men

---

 A. L. Zimmerman teaches at Southern Illinois University and Patrician Geist-Martin teaches at San Diego State University.

standing at urinals to a bathroom stall. I'm afraid to sit down, believing I'll be found out if I do so. I stand in front of the toilet bowl trying to think of a way to urinate standing up without making a mess. I decide to sit down and go as fast as I can. Finished, I open the stall door. I stare at the floor as I walk, and then at my hands as I wash them. A few steps outside of the bathroom I remember to breathe again.

At 10 years old, I look like the picture perfect Midwestern boy on the sidewalk waiting for a parade to start. I sit next to my dad in a pair of multicolored boys' swim trunks and a plain green T-shirt. A man he knows comes up to the two of us and starts talking. After a while he asks my dad, "What's your son's name?" My dad chuckles a response, "This is my daughter, Amber." Slightly embarrassed, I hug my knees. The man, trying to recover from what he believes is a wrong assessment, quickly adds, "Well, that won't happen once she gets breasts!" My body gets hot and I want to disappear.

It's four years later and I have breasts. Now, at 14, I am standing in a small, hot, and sweat-filled locker room with 20 other girls. The walls are covered in red, matching the color of our faces as we recover from the basketball game our teams just played against one another. I stand next to my teammates, across the room from the opposing team. As I take off my shorts, revealing a pair of spandex, I hear laughing from across the room. A girl with long dark curly hair scrunches up her face and throws her words at me, "Are those boxers? What are you? Some kind of girl boy?" The other team members continue laughing as I hurriedly grab clothing to cover up. One of my teammates shouts back, "Shut up. She's more of a girl than you'll ever be." Silence fills the room except for the shuffling of clothes and their whispers.

At 17, I stand in line with 70 other female soldiers waiting for a seamstress to measure my body for a dress uniform. Just yesterday we marched more than 12 miles in the early morning summer humidity of Missouri, weapons in hand and packs on our backs. Our line stretches around old office cubicle dividers, a strange kind of maze housed in an old warehouse with no windows. Fans big enough to fill up a double doorway, placed strategically around the maze, ease the scorch of the midday sun. The line moves slowly as we all stand in our bras and underwear waiting our turn. Pockets of women chatter around me as I stand silently, patiently, waiting for my measurements. From a pocket next to me, a woman breaks out of her conversation, suspiciously glancing at my stomach and inquires, "Are you sure you're not a man?" I manage a fatigued shrug, "Yes." The other women around her follow her gaze to my midsection. Baffled, they stand assessing me. I stand confused by the question. I look down at my stomach, marked by ridges of tightly carved muscle, a result of thousands of basic training sit-ups and push-ups. I look up and then around me at the many women in line. Softer, rounder bodies stand next to my leaner, harder body. The line moves slightly as I continue to mull over myself as aberration.

At 22, my dark auburn hair hangs slightly above my shoulders and my closet is filled with more feminine clothing. I lie in bed with the shades drawn, fearful of the morning light. I consider my four-month depression resulting from my transition to a new city and a new academic graduate program. I want to break free and find my voice. So far, I'm still in the closet in this new place, along with the clothing that I wear in an attempt to "pass" as a "normal," heterosexual, "gender-appropriate" female. I run my fingers through the hair that continually bothers me, the hair that feels so apart from me. I want to cut it all off, be free of the strands that mask my queer movement. I know that if I cut it, the questions will come, and the looks will come. I also know if I cut it, I'll clean out my closet; it will be a kind of cleaning that brings me back to my body and my voice. I decide the time has come. I quickly dress in the dark. I drive to the nearest hair salon and nervously put down my name for a haircut. As I sit waiting, I waver in my decision. Maybe I'm being rash? Maybe I should reconsider? No. I need to cut it off.

A short woman with glasses and a thick Spanish accent calls my name, "Aumbear." I stand and hesitantly walk over to the swiveling seat. She casually asks, "Well, what are we doing today?" I puff up my chest and blurt, "Cutting it all off." With that I sit down, hoping that she does it without question, without trepidation. I can see in her face that she is concerned. After draping me with the hair cape, she selects a scissors from her drawer and worriedly asks me, "How much is cutting it all off?" Gaining steam in my decision, I assert, "All of it." She winces behind her glasses and turns to a woman cutting hair next to her, "She wants to cut it all off." Losing patience, I want to scream, "Just cut it!" Instead we find middle ground.

She is more comfortable cutting my hair little by little, checking in with me periodically about the length.

We start this game, and over and over I affirm, "Yes, shorter." She continues to cut nervously. I can feel myself gaining more and more confidence. I muse, contrary to the story about Sampson in the Bible, in which a man that derives strength from his hair, I gain strength as the hair falls. I do feel more strength as I exit the hair salon. I feel bare, clean to the world and to myself.

* * * * *

These narrative moments chronicle the journey of my gender queer body. It is a journey that offers insight into questions surrounding culture, communication, and identity. I focus my journey around three unfolding layers. First, I relate my gender queer experience to the concept of hybridity. Second, I offer two stories, highlighting my own questioning of identity, and how others question my identity. Lastly, I provide a final reflection on my journey of gender and hybridity.

DISCOVERING THE HYBRIDITY OF GENDER

As the world becomes increasingly globalized, identity becomes an increasingly complex site for understanding communicative interaction. It is in communication that identity is negotiated. Coover and Murphy (2000) find communication as "integral to the ongoing negotiation of self, a process during which individuals are defined by others as they, in turn, define and redefine themselves" (p. 125). When communicating identity, people make choices based on experiences of the body and how their bodies move in social environments (Eisenberg, 2001). Scholars like Bhabha (1994) and Hall (1990) indicate that identity crosses many borders and binaries. Shome and Hegde (2002) suggest that identity is "above all a performative expression of transnational change, an area of imminent concern to communication scholars" (p. 266). They write about the powerful possibilities of understanding the relationship between the hybrid of individual and collective identities.

The concept of hybridity is a fertile site to begin questioning identity. Kraidy (2002) describes the hybrid as "a communicative practice constitutive of, and constituted by, sociopolitical and economic arrangements" (p. 317). These arrangements are often written in and on the body within systems of hegemony. This writing in and on the body discursively situates bodies that exceed binary structures as the "other." It is within this "otherness" that the hybrid is most often explored. This is demonstrated throughout the previous stories: When people are unable to apply a gender language to the body of the person with whom they are communicating, they mark the person with the "other" label.

Hybridity is the coming together of two or more cultural identities and, in this process, offers a third or alternate identity that is often outside of language in that there is no prescriptive way to communicate about an alternate identity. Anzaldua (1987) writes about her experience of hybridity or mestiza, viewing her identity as one that breaks down the subject/object of the flesh, cultivating agency by moving away from dualisms. Bhabha (1994) also marks the hybrid identity as one that moves in a "third space," or beyond sociocultural dualisms. In the third space, hybrid identity "exceeds the frame of the image, it eludes the eye, evacuates the self as a site of identity and autonomy and—most important—leaves a resistant trace, a stain of the subject, a sign of resistance" (p. 49). The hybrid body enacts resistance by remaining fluid, by challenging the fixity of prescribed identity roles. It is this image of the body that opens up possibilities for revolutionary self-assertiveness of identity (Dash, 1995). For example, in that moment of need when the men's restroom was the only one I could find, I enacted a tentative resistance that carried with it an ever-present feeling of surveillance. Yet I know now what I questioned then: My self-assertiveness to move into spaces limited to only the "appropriate" gender was a mini-revolution aimed at trying on one of my hybrid identities.

In our attempt to understand this idea of revolutionary self-assertiveness, we turn to examining the gender queer, materially marked female body. We extend this examination by locating a gender queer body as a form of hybrid body. Gender queer is a matter of passing through different identities. Bornstein (1998) views gender queering as "when all the mechanical or automatic ways I've developed for dealing with people simply fall aside, or reveal themselves as the bag of tricks I use to grease the social machinery of my interactions" (p. 179). Hybridity functions in a similar way; it is a meshing of identities that demands new ways of communicating about identity, resulting in a transformation of culture and communication. As with the women in the stomach story, when a body does not fit culturally, it is difficult to communicate about it, and offers a fissure in the act of normalizing.

A queer gender body, then, disrupts this binary of all male or all female, creating a dialectical tension that offers a space to explore the temporality of Bhabha's (1994) proposed third space. The tension is created in communicative interactions when assumed gender roles are fragmented or broken. If the queer body or hybrid body cannot be categorized or fixed, it also cannot be regulated. This elusory action, although problematic for many queer bodies, does function as resistance. As Kanneh (1995) points out, "Not only, then, does the representation of the body characteristically oscillate between, and confuse, natural and cultural attributes in discussions of race, but feminine and masculine—or feminist and non-feminist—agency becomes an issue" (p. 348). The story about being able to identify gender by markings such as breasts introduces interesting questions about the identities given to women based on biology, and the ways in which is it acceptable to talk about women's body in our culture.

Another reason for focusing on this kind of queer body is to highlight the beneficial relationship between queer theory and the concept of hybridity. Both theories are concerned with the in-between and resistance; both are concerned with giving voice to muted identities. Yep (2003) situates queer as a world-making, an "opening and creation of spaces without a map, the invention and proliferation of ideas without an unchanging and predetermined goal, and the expansion of individual freedom and collective possibilities without the constraints of suffocating identities and restrictive membership" (p. 35). The hybrid identity functions in much the same way within and across cultures.

It is important to recognize that writing about "the queer body" is a different matter from writing about "a queer body" (Gingrich-Philbrook, 2001). In other words, each body discursively moves in and through the world with its own understanding in relation to the larger sociocultural context. One way to enter the relationship of self and culture in communication is expressing the hybrid body through personal narrative. Personal narratives, according to Langellier (1989), "participate in the ongoing rhythm of people's lives as a reflection of their social organization and cultural values" (p. 261). Engaging in personal narrative highlights the rhythm of stories, a rhythm that forms us, a rhythm we can embody to create new forms. Ellis and Bochner (2000) capture the role of narrative by suggesting that lived experience "both anticipates telling and draws meaning from it. Narrative is both about living and part of it" (p. 746). Personal narrative is a method of inquiry akin to hybridity as it seeks to illuminate the meanings found in the in-between spaces.

* * * * *

The personal narrative I share in this piece is my hybrid body, an experience of female gender queer movement in and through culture. In claiming hybrid status, I make a risky decision. I am a white, American, Western academic, identities that carry privilege in our current cultural structures. I am also a white, American, Western academic who is queer, inhabiting a space that continually works to deconstruct the oppression of my body, in terms of both gender and sexual identity. I desire to contribute to the dialogue surrounding culture, identity, and communication; speaking from my queer body is how I know to participate from an honest and reflective space. My personal queer narrative is how I come to understand the larger sociocultural phenomenon of hybrid identity, culture, and communication.

GENDER QUEER TRACING

I stare into my small bathroom mirror with a pair of hair clippers in my hand. The night beyond my windows is dark, icy, and silent. Inside, the vapid glow of a bare bulb casts shadows across my reflected image—an image that is no longer familiar to me, an image that often appears unfamiliar to me. As I grip the clippers, I wrestle with the decision to shave off my hair. The length of my hair is already considered short, so shaving it wouldn't be drastic, or would it? I look over at the clock. It reads 2:36 A.M. I take a deep breath and reason that my urge to shave my head must be connected to some late night delirium. I think about putting the clippers away and fading into the dark of my apartment to sleep peacefully with a full head of hair.

Yet, even as my mind ponders this movement, my fingers clench tighter around the electric silver teeth. I take a step toward the mirror, trying to get a closer look at the self this mirror is presenting. My eyes, the pictures of sunflowers floating in pools of sea green, my face, light etchings of worn stories, and my hair, a lifeless brown stringed mop—images I don't recognize of a person I'm not quite sure actually exists. I push up on the power button with my thumb. An electric hum fills the small bathroom. I raise the clippers to my head and allow the teeth to chew my hair in methodical rows. Clumps of hair fall onto my shoulders, trail down my shirt, and collect in a garden of locks at my feet. I run the clippers across my head over and over again with fervent intensity. I can't bear to leave behind a stray hair to tell the story of the past—a past I am trying to shave away with each stroke. I want to take this person I don't recognize and start over. I want to strip myself down to zero and add from there. I want to make my own meaning of self, so I can recognize the image in the mirror.

The image confuses me because when my body moves in the world, I am often perceived as that which I am not. Biologically, I was born the female sex. Culturally, I was socialized with the norms of female gender. Coupled together, these two realities provide a script for my body to act according to the expectations of a heterosexual woman. In claiming my own identity, I don't exactly fit either of these categories. In relation to others, I am perceived in many different ways. Sometimes my identity is perceived as young gay man. Sometimes it is heterosexual man. Sometimes it is dyke woman. Sometimes it is heterosexual woman. Sometimes people can't decide. Sometimes I can't decide. Why is it so important to decide?

* * * * *

It is a Friday night, warm and inviting, and I am walking with three friends to the local queer dance bar. It is a special night of drag performance to raise money for breast cancer awareness. We enter the double doors, shuffle to the cash register, pay the cover charge, and step into the bar. To the left is a dance floor that leads to a small stage. To the right is multitier seating to watch the drag show, play pool, or sit at the bar. We select a small table near the dance floor.

The air is thick with smoke and chatter as we wait for the performance to begin. I notice both men and women watching our table. I am keenly aware that both men and women are watching me. I wonder: Am I being perceived as queer boy or queer girl? As I contemplate, the show begins and beautiful drag queens fill the stage performing Madonna, the Pointer Sisters, Christina Aguilera, and Britney Spears. After the show, I flirt with a woman near the dance stage who acknowledges me as a woman (what did she communicate that told me this?). I also talk with a gay man who thought I was a cute queer boy (what did he communicate that told me this?). Part of me enjoys the gender bending, but part of me is exhausted by the many questions I am asked by others. Did you know that you look like a cute boy? Did you know that I wasn't sure if you were a boy or a girl?

I am also exhausted by the many awkward interactions I have in public spaces. Early one morning I wait in line to order a beverage at a coffee house. I stare up at the menu on the wall, trying to decide among the many options. As I approach the counter for service, I'm asked by the cashier, "How can I help you, sir?" I respond with my order, letting the label "sir" sit in the air between us. As I wait for my cup of hot coffee, I secretly hope that the cashier doesn't look at me more closely and then, with embarrassment, apologize for calling me sir. But this is what happens. Flustered, the cashier looks away, ending our communication. I want to tell the cashier that I don't care, that it doesn't matter to me how I'm labeled as long as I'm not feared. But I don't say anything. I take my coffee and sit down at a small circular table under a colorful painting of fish dancing. As I take my first sip of the steaming liquid, I overhear the cashier talking about me, feeling embarrassed, still uncomfortable with the uncertainty. I want to scream, "*Let it go, I don't care!* What I care about is your inability to handle ambiguity."

I care when good friends tell me that they never view me as anything but a woman. As I drive up a curvy wooded road, my friend Sam stares out the window angrily recounting a moment when a server has again referred to me as a man. She can't understand the gender misappropriation. It makes her feel uncomfortable. She wants to clearly mark my body as female. I stare at the passing row of trees and try to make an argument for discontinuity. She's still angry.

In another moment, my friend Roy is perplexed. We are walking around a lake on a balmy spring day, and he crinkles his nose as he tries to understand that some people mark me as male. He's always seen me as feminine. I share stories with him about the gender confusion I create. He is quiet, only the rhythm of our feet marking time while the wind fills the silent space between us.

My friend Ashley tells me that I'm good at being a woman. We lie next to one another sharing intimate stories. I look at her closely, and confess I that I disagree with her assessment. In a more forceful voice, she reiterates my excellent performance of woman. Inside I cringe, but do not tell her that it makes me feel extremely uncomfortable for her to fix that identity to my body.

* * * * *

The labels "man" and "woman" both feel foreign to my ears. Claiming either identity makes me feel uncomfortable. In one moment I champion a female body for the cause of reproductive rights of choice. In another moment I glean the privilege of male masculinity so that I'll be taken more seriously. When I do make a choice in these moments, am I reifying binary gender? Does living in a hybrid space mean I can choose to "pass" as either gender when it serves my best interest?

In the American culture in which I live, I'm well aware of how "my body" is associated with "the body" of female. I see the objectification of the female body for others' desires on flashy billboards, in glossy magazines, on dramatic television, and in blockbuster movies. I hear objectification through slang language of female body parts deployed to denigrate. Over and over I've been told that the worth of the female body is directly associated with its reproductive ability and consumable beauty. I am to wear long flowing hair, tastefully applied makeup, and worry about my weight. So when my body moves in the world, it communicates a resistance to the male gaze and ignores socially constructed gender imperatives. I leave a trail. The ambiguous hybrid I embrace leaves a resistive trail, challenging assumptions about the markings of gender.

For both hybrid and queer subjectivities, disruption, or marking of the third space, is indispensable in our efforts to illuminate the damage of oppressed bodies. By examining the issue of hybridity through my lens of lived experience, I have demonstrated the value of communicating hybrid identity across and through cultural experience. I hope that the sharing of my story offers a bridge toward understanding that all of our bodies carry stories that enhance our culture when we express them, and that these stories connect us.

I look into the mirror at my reflection. The image remains elusive to my understanding. My identity is fluid, exceeding the frame of the mirror. I rub my hands across the stubble on my head. I feel comforted by the neutral gender marking of a shaved head. I feel close to my body as in-between site. In this moment, I like not knowing, I like feeling lost in the gender continuum. Even if others view me as purely female or in the moment as male, I feel peace in claiming the identity of both/and while also claiming neither/nor.

References

Anzaldua, G. (1987). *Borderlands: The new mestiza—la frontera.* San Francisco: Spinsters/Aunt Lute.

Bhabha, H. K. (1994). *Location of culture.* London: Routledge.

Bornstein, K. (1998). *My gender workbook.* New York: Routledge.

Coover, G. E., & Murphy S. T. (2000). The communicated self: Exploring the interaction between self and social context. *Human Communication Research, 26,* 125–147.

Dash, M. (1995). In search of the lost body: Redefining the subject in Caribbean literature. In B. Ashcroft, G. Griffiths, & H. Tiffin (Eds.), *The postcolonial studies reader* (pp. 332–335). London: Routledge.

Eisenberg, E. M. (2001). Building a mystery: Toward a new theory of communication and identity. *Journal of Communication, 51,* 534–552.

Ellis, C., & Bochner, A. P. (2000). Autoethnography, personal narrative, reflexivity: Researcher as subject. In N. K. Denzin & Y. S. Lincoln (Eds.), *Handbook of qualitative research* (2nd ed., pp. 733–768). Thousand Oaks, CA: Sage.

Gingrich-Philbrook, C. (2001). Bite your tongue: Four songs of body and language. In L. C. Miller & R. J. Pelias (Eds.), *The green window: Proceedings of the Giant City Conference on performative writing* (pp. 1–7). Carbondale: Southern Illinois University.

Hall, S. (1990). Cultural identity and diaspora. In J. Rutherford (Ed.), *Identity: Community, culture, difference* (pp. 222–237). London: Lawrence & Wishart.

Kanneh, K. (1995). Feminism and the colonial body. In B. Ashcroft, G. Griffiths, & H. Tifflin (Eds.), *The postcolonial studies reader* (pp. 346–348). New York: Routledge.

Kraidy, M. M. (2002). Hybridity in cultural globalization. *Communication Theory, 123,* 316–339.

Langellier, K. M. (1989). Personal narratives: Perspectives on theory and research. *Text and Performance Quarterly, 9,* 243–276.

Loomba, A. (1998). *Colonialism/postcolonialism.* London: Routledge.

Shome, R., & Hedge, R. S. (2002). Postcolonial approaches to communication: Charting the terrain, engaging the intersections. *Communication Theory, 123,* 249–270.

Yep, G. A. (2003). The violence of heteronormativity in communication studies: Notes on injury, healing, and queer world-making. In G. A. Yep, K. E. Lovaas, & J. P.

Elia (Eds.), *Queer theory and communication: From disciplining queers to queering the discipline(s)* (pp. 11–60). New York: Harrington.

Concepts and Questions

1. How might the experience of growing up in a "hybrid" body affect the process of establishing one's cultural identity?
2. Reflect on the feelings a youth in a hybrid existence would experience while interacting with others in a variety of social situations.
3. What is meant by the idea of negotiating a "self," and how does communication enter into that process?
4. Hybridity is defined as the coming together of two or more cultural identities. Specify a number of situations beyond gender where hybridity enters into the definition of cultural identity.
5. The authors state that a queer gender body disrupts the binary of being all male or all female. How might this disruption affect the intercultural communication process?
6. How can people learn to communicate more effectively with people who possess queer gender hybrid identities?
7. What lessons can be learned about effective intercultural communication from having read this essay?

Ambiguous Insiders: An Investigation of Arab American Invisibility

NADINE NABER

I am invisible, understand, simply because people refuse to see me. Like the bodiless heads you see sometimes in circus sideshows, it is as though I have been surrounded by mirrors of hard, distorting glass. When they approach me they see only my surroundings, themselves, or figments of their imagination—indeed, everything and anything except me.

ELLISON, 1947/1972, p. 3

INTRODUCTION

Scholars, writers, and activists have labeled Arab Americans the "invisible" racial/ethnic group.[1] As writer Joanna Kadi states, "It's tough to name a group when most people aren't aware the group exists . . . that's why I coined this phrase for our community: The Most Invisible of the Invisibles" (Kadi, 1994, p. xix).

This article addresses Arab American "invisibility" as a product of factors both external and internal to the Arab American community. In Part One, I address "invisibility" as a central theme in the historical narrative of Arab immigrants and their descendants in North America. Government officials who have classified Arabs and their descendants according to multiple and conflicting categories have, in part, externally structured the social and historical invisibility of Arab Americans. Moreover, the Arab American community's diverse and constantly shifting makeup, as well as the fact that Arab Americans themselves have identified according to multiple, conflicting labels, shapes the internal difficulties associated with classifying this population.

In Part Two, I explore "invisibility" in terms of Arab Americans' paradoxical positioning within the U.S.

From *Ethnic and Racial Studies*, Vol. 23, No. 1, 2000, pp. 37–61.

racial/ethnic classification system and highlight strategies of Arab American individuals and communities seeking "visibility" on their own terms. In Part Three, I explore the mechanisms by which Arab Americans gain visibility by making themselves seen and heard by adopting the strategies prevalent in the general American culture.

PART ONE: INVISIBILITY, A HISTORICAL NARRATIVE[2]

Although most Arabs are Muslim, the Arabs who immigrated to the United States during the first period (1880–1945) were predominantly Christians of the Eastern rite sects of Greater Syria.[3] The majority were from Mount Lebanon (Naff, 1985, p. 3). The early immigrants' central motive for immigration was economic opportunity (Suleiman & Abu-Laban, 1989; Samhan, 1994). Although they pursued occupations such as millwork, garment making, and shop keeping, pack peddling was their most common trade (Naif, 1985; Shakir, 1997).[4]

Although most early immigrants intended to acquire wealth and return to their country of origin, the majority eventually became permanent U.S. residents (Suleiman, 1989; Abraham, 1995). No accurate records exist, but by 1916 it is estimated that 100,000 Arabs had immigrated to the United States (Naff, 1985, p. 2) and by 1924 the Arab population in the U.S. had reached 200,000. Scholars approximate that 195,000 were Christians and 5,000 were divided between Muslims and Druze; of the Christian population, the Maronites claimed 90,000, the Greek Orthodox 85,000, Greek Catholics 10,000; Protestants 5,000, and 5,000 were unaccounted (Hitti, cited in Ansara, 1958, p. 12).

However, the categories of identity that Arab immigrants used to identify themselves did not always correspond with the categories of identity recognized in U.S. society. The early immigrants primarily identified themselves according to family, kinship, village affiliation, and/or religious sect. However, in 1882, because they migrated from an Ottoman province (Syria), U.S. officials classified them as Turks. As a result, accurate statistical data on this new racial/ethnic group did not exist because Greeks, Albanians, Armenians, and other Eastern groups were all categorized under the Turkish appellative by state and local authorities (Halaby, 1980).

In 1899, immigration officials began to classify the early immigrants as a separate "Syrian" ethnic group (Halaby, 1980). But even among U.S. officials, inconsistencies over "Syrian" identity prevailed. Although in 1899 the Bureau of Immigration distinguished them from other Turkish subjects, the census of 1910 continued to include "Syrians" under the category "Turkey in Asia." Newspapers and magazines of this period indicate that writers were also in conflict about "Syrian" identity. They addressed the "Syrians" as Arabians, Armenians, Assyrians, and/or Turks, and often conflated these categories with the category "Syrian" (Halaby). Yet although early immigrants were classified according to a "foreign" national category by U.S. officials, most did not hold a concept of either "Syrian" or "Arab" nationalism. Most early immigrants were nationally committed to their new home, the United States, even though they remained culturally and socially attached to their homeland (Suleiman & Abu-Laban, 1989).

A 1914 debate on the racial status of "Syrians" exemplifies the complex nature of Arab identity in the United States during this early period. In 1914, a South Carolina judge ruled that "while Syrians may be Caucasian, they were not 'that particular free white person to whom the Act of Congress [1790] had denoted the privilege of citizenship'"—a privilege that he ruled was intended for persons of European descent (Samhan, 1994, p. 3). Although federal courts questioned the Syrians' citizenship rights, North American nativists of the early 20th century did not perceive the "Syrians" to be a significant threat compared to other immigrants because they were small in number and dispersed, and because their involvement in peddling was not particularly threatening to whites who resented the competition of immigrant labor (Samhan).

But even though the 1914 court decision was reversed in 1923, and even though Syrians were not perceived as a national threat, cases of discrimination against Syrians as nonwhites, Catholics, and foreigners were reported[5] (Samhan, 1994), particularly between 1914 and 1930, a period of much anti-immigrant sentiment. Dr. A. J. McLaughlin, for example, the United States health officer at Marine Hospital, who feared race degeneracy as a result of the new influx of immigrants, ended a report on immigration by referring to the Syrians as "parasites in their peddling habits" (Halaby, 1980, p. 6). Edward Corsi, the U.S. Commissioner of Immigration and Naturalization for the New York district, in an account of his experience at Ellis Island, *In the Shadow of Liberty,* stated that the Syrian is a "doubtful element" of "Mongolian plasma" attempting to contaminate the pure American stock (Halaby). Thus, from early on, the "Syrians" occupied a precarious social position within the U.S. racial system, which contributed to what came to be referred to as "invisibility." On the one hand, the Syrians' non-European origin received national attention; on the other hand, they were not targeted by racism and discrimination to the same extent as other communities that were more distinctly categorized as nonwhite, such as the Chinese, blacks, Jews, or Italians.

Significant shifts gradually transpired in the political and demographic makeup of Arab immigration and settlement among the second wave immigrants (post-1945) that complicated Arab immigrants' "Americanization" process. On the one hand, by mid-century Arab Americans were one of the best acculturated ethnic groups in America (Naff, 1985). A majority of Arab Americans identified as white/Caucasian, anglicized their names, replaced Arabic with English, and restricted their ethnic identity to the private sphere (Suleiman & Abu-Laban, 1989; Samhan, 1994), thereby participating in the process of cultural or ethnic erasure. On the other hand, after World War II, when Arab nations achieved a certain level of political autonomy from Western rule, Arab immigrants brought new and specific forms of Arab nationalism to the United States and began to self-identify according to the classification "Arab" more than the previous immigrant wave (Suleiman & Abu-Laban, 1989). The second wave immigrants also differed from the first wave immigrants in including a larger number of Muslims (Abraham, 1995, p. 86) and women (Naif, 1985, p. 117). Moreover, this group included refugees displaced by the 1948 Palestine War, others driven by particular political events, and many professionals and university students, unlike the previous immigrants.

Scholars characterize the third immigration period (post-1960s) by relaxed immigration laws, resulting in a rapid influx of Arab immigrants to the United States.[6] Heightened war and upheaval in the Arab world also contributed to the increase in Arab immigration and the altered immigration patterns during the third period. Overall, the post-1965 immigrants are more religiously and geographically diverse than previous groups and include more Muslims than Christians, as well as students, professionals, refugees, and entrepreneurs from every Arabic-speaking country and representing every religious sect in the Arab world (Suleiman & Abu- Laban, 1989). But it is their stronger sense of Arab nationalism, their heightened criticism of U.S. policy, and their weaker civic identification that distinguishes this wave from their predecessors (Samhan, 1994). "The importance of retaining the cultural and religious traditions of their homeland further juxtaposed the new immigrants from their American-born co-ethnics" (Samhan). The trend toward an intensified political consciousness among the third wave immigrants has been forged by the political stances opposing Western imperialism that they brought to the United States, ranging from pan-Arab sentiments to political Islam (Lin & Jamal, 1997), as well as the hostility and marginalization that Arab immigrants and Arab Americans encounter in North America.

The Arab–Israeli War of 1967 specifically initiated the shift toward a rising ethno-political consciousness among members of the Arab American community (Abraham, 1989; Suleiman & Abu-Laban, 1989). For many Arab Americans, the Arab–Israeli War signified the beginning of their social, political, and cultural marginalization. Not only did the war signify the confirmed alliance of the United States with Israel, but it gave Arab Americans their first taste of exclusion from a role in the political process (Suleiman, 1989). This period also saw the beginning of a war waged by the U.S. media against Arabs, at home and in the diaspora, that has distorted the meaning of the term *Arab* and further complicated Arab American identity. Following World War II and the declaration of Israel's independence, Arab Americans came to share in the experiences of other racialized U.S. communities that have been marked as being different from and inferior to whites/Caucasians. The media began to portray Arabs, Middle Easterners, and Muslims as a monolithic category and as one of the preeminent enemies of the West. This anti-Western, anti-American portrayal underlies the support of the American public for U.S. cultural and economic domination and military intervention in the Arab world.

Heightened awareness of political conflict between the United States and the Arab world, their experiences of social and political marginalization, and the 1960s ethos of ethnic revival in the United States (Zogby, 1990; Aswad & Bilge, 1996; Lin & Jamal, 1997) culminated in the development of a distinct

Arab American identity. After the Arab–Israeli war, many Americans of Arab descent, who previously identified themselves according to their country of origin, their religious affiliation, or as generically "American," united under the label "Arab American" and established numerous pan-ethnic organizations, such as Arab-American University Graduates, the National Association of Arab Americans, the American Arab Anti-Discrimination Committee, and the Arab American Institute.[7]

The development of a pan-Arab American identity in the post-1960s period demonstrates that, whereas pre-1960s generations tended to lose their identity to "Americanization," growing numbers of the new generations are leaning toward an ethnically distinct identity. The post-1960s unification under the pan-ethnic label "Arab America" can be understood as a political response to the process by which the state and the media came to group such geographically, culturally, and religiously diverse persons according to a singular label, "Arab," while attaching to it mythological, derogatory meanings. By building a coalition around the label "Arab American," activists redefined the term *Arab* on their own terms and deployed their racial/ethnic identity as a political strategy for claiming their rights.

But as Arab Americans attempt to define their ethnic identity, opposing forces simultaneously erase Arab Americans from the racial/ethnic map by distorting the meaning of the term *Arab* and obstructing Arab American participation in the political process. Samhan names this form of exclusion "political racism," in which anti-Arab attitudes and behavior have their roots "not in the traditional motives of structurally excluding a group perceived as inferior, but in politics" (Samhan 1987, p. 11). What distinguishes this new racism based on politics from traditional forms of racism based on biology or phenotype is that Arab Americans who choose to be active in Palestinian or Arab issues or organizations may be subjected to political racism, whereas those who choose not to be politically active may not. Jabara agrees that "today we are seeing a totally new phenomenon . . . premeditated, calculated attacks, not aimed at individual Arab Americans but at the political activity of Arab Americans" (Jabara, cited in Hasso, 1987).

The development of the label "Arab American" as a form of resistance to anti-Arab racism in the post-1960s era has meant rising tensions between Arab Americans and the majority U.S. culture. "The confused identity thrust upon the first wave emerged in the later immigrants as a confused identity of another type: one that perceives the cultural, political and religious values of their homeland in tension with the majority culture of their adopted country" (Samhan, 1994, p. 4).

This confused identity, I have suggested, has developed in the context of a range of historical circumstances. The shift from predominantly Christian to predominantly Muslim immigrants is one of many factors that render the historical question of whether Arab Americans should be considered white/Caucasian or a nonwhite minority still unresolved. While Christians have more easily built communities around white American Christians, Muslims tend to be perceived as outsiders to the white American mainstream. Islam, religiously and culturally, generally conflicts with the white mainstream "American" culture more than Christianity does. Moreover, as political conflicts have risen between the United States and the Arab world since mid-century, the Arab American community has come to experience various social paradoxes that further complicate their racial/ethnic identity and exacerbate the problem of Arab American "invisibility."

PART TWO: THE PARADOXICAL IDENTITY OF ARAB AMERICANS

The First Paradox: "Arab"

Although Arabs belong to a multiplicity of religious affiliations and emigrate from diverse regions, the idea that *Arab* can be defined as a monolithic category persists in popular North American images (in TV shows, films, and the news media). When this paradox displays itself in Arab Americans' everyday lives, it comes to mean that violence, racism, and discrimination against Arab, Middle Eastern, and Muslim individuals are acceptable behaviors.

Suad Joseph (in press) explains that when she teaches courses on the Middle East, she starts by arguing that it is impossible to find any agreement on a definition of Arab. She writes,

> There are Lebanese, Syrians, Palestinians, Iraqis, Kuwaitis, Yemenis, Saudi Arabians, Bahreinis, Qataris, Dubains, Egyptians, Libyans, Tunisians, Moroccans, Algerians, Sudanese, Eritreans, Mauritanians; there are Maronites, Catholics, Protestants, Greek Orthodox,

Jews, Sunnis, Shi'a, Druz, Sufis, Alwaties, Nestorians, Assyrians, Copts, Chaldeans, Bahais; there are Berbers, Kurds, Armenians, bedu, gypsies and many others with different languages, religions, ethnic and national identifications and cultures who are all congealed as Arab in popular representation whether or not those people may identify as Arab.

Furthermore, the categories "Arab" and "Middle Eastern" are conflated in popular representations. As a result, linguistic, cultural, racial, and historical differences between non-Arab Middle Easterners, such as Turks and Persians, and Arab Middle Easterners are erased (Joseph, in press; Naber, in press). By conflating the categories "Middle Eastern" and "Muslim," popular images also erase the reality that the majority of Muslims are neither Arab nor Middle Eastern, but Indonesian, Malaysian, Filipino, Indian, and Chinese (Joseph, in press). Joseph argues that "these sets of conflations are glossed on to Arabs in America, again covering the historical fact that almost all Arabs in America were, until very recently, Christians" (Joseph).

Conflations of the categories Arab, Middle Eastern, and Muslim are not new, nor are they specific to U.S. images. Rather, they are rooted in a history of Western prejudice against Islam (Said, 1978). Prior to the rise of Islam, the Byzantines viewed Arabs as primitive and sexually immoral savages. The Byzantines' views of Arabs structured those of Western Europe and constituted part of the Western image of Arabs during the rise of Islam. The dark and evil picture of Islam originally painted by the Byzantines came to dominate the attitudes of Western Europeans and was later transposed to the Americas by European colonists (Suleiman, 1989, p. 257).

Moreover, conflations of the categories Arab, Middle Eastern, and Muslim are not random or irrational, nor are they based on ignorance. Rather, they are products of a systematic process that scholars refer to as neocolonialism (Shohat & Stam, 1994). Neocolonialism employs contemporary ideological (that is, media portrayals/popular narratives) or economic strategies to ignore, displace, unravel, justify, uphold, and explain racism, genocide, sexism, gender inequality, nationalism, colonialism, and imperialism, as needed (Buescher & Ono, 1996). Neocolonialist media images, for example, portray a dominated group as a homogeneous mass with no differences among them and then characterize them as inherently different from and inferior to the dominant group. As a result, these images serve to justify and maintain colonialist, imperialist, and/or racist practices against the dominated group. "Neocolonialism pretends to offer a kinder version of present global economics [politics] than past colonialism; hence, its presence may at times be quite subtle" (Buescher & Ono).

I use the term *neocolonialism* to name the process by which media images (1) erase differences among Arabs, Middle Easterners, and Muslims; (2) portray a fixed boundary of difference between the "Arab/Middle Eastern/Muslim" and the "white American"; (3) create an imaginary hierarchical relationship between the superior "white American" and the inferior "Arab/Middle Eastern/Muslim"; and (4) serve to justify U.S. intervention in Middle East affairs. I add gender to my analysis by arguing that imaginary portrayals of gender relations among both the dominated and the dominant group are used to further justify colonialist, imperialist, racist, and patriarchal practices.

To explore the process through which the term "Arab American" comes to be incomprehensible, I investigate media images that conflate the categories Arab, Middle Eastern, and Muslim. I argue that Arab Americans are primarily associated with three different types of media images. These media types reinforce the idea of an "Arab/Middle Eastern/Muslim" generic and inferior Other. The first media type portrays generic Arab/Middle Eastern/Muslim men as irrationally violent, particularly toward women. The second media type portrays generic Arab/Middle Eastern/Muslim women as a supra-oppressed group of women in comparison to white American women, who are idealized to represent equality, democracy, and justice. The third media type is that of the "absent Arab woman" (Saliba, 1994). This image juxtaposes Arab men with white women, with Arab women entirely absent from the scene.

The first media type can be seen in episodes of the TV shows *Alice* (1980s) and *Trapper John MD* (1980s), the documentary *Death of a Princess* (1980), the Disney movie *Aladdin* (1992), and *New York Times* articles on female genital mutilation (1993–1996). These representations portray Arab women as victims of either Muslim or Arab culture's imaginary sexually abusive patterns.[8] Repeated images of excessively oppressed Arab/Middle Eastern/Muslim women justify Western intervention in Middle East affairs on the ground that, according to these images, Arab/Middle Eastern/Muslim society is cruel and backward and therefore in need of Westernization/civilization.

The second media type portrays a supra-oppressed and inferior group of Arab women as compared with white American women, who are depicted as the most liberated and superior group of women on earth. Films such as *Protocol* (1984), *Harem* (1985), and *Not Without My Daughter* (1991) exemplify this media type. In these films, generic Arab/Middle Eastern/Muslim women are portrayed as a homogeneous mass, with no differences among them, whereas a singular white American heroine acts not only as an individual but as liberator. The Arab/Middle Eastern/Muslim women are oppressed; the white American heroine is liberated. The distinction between the mass of Arab/Middle Eastern/Muslim women and the singular white American woman renders Arabs inferior in comparison with what is portrayed to be white American superiority.

Saliba (1994) explains the "absent Arab woman," the third media type, in terms of popular images of the Gulf War. For example, she argues that most newspaper articles on the Gulf War portrayed white American women in the military in comparison with Arab and white American men, while Arab women were completely absent from the scene. I would add that the "absent Arab woman" (Saliba) can be seen in the films *The Sheik* (1921), *Raiders of the Lost Ark* (1983), *Sahara* (1983), *True Lies* (1994), and *GI Jane* (1998). In these portrayals, Arab men are depicted as barbaric terrorists as compared with civilized white American women and absent Arab women. Arab women's absence from male spaces creates the idea of Arab/Middle Eastern/Muslim women's secondary social status compared to white American women who transgress male spaces. This media type portrays women's oppression as rooted in an oppressive Islamic culture that controls women, in contrast to a white American culture that produces women who are in control of themselves.[9]

But anti-Arab media images that perpetuate the idea of a generic Arab/Middle Eastern/Muslim enemy are not isolated from lived experience. The premieres of anti-Arab TV shows and films systematically coincide with specific U.S. government interventions in the Middle East region. Just before the 1967 Arab–Israeli War, for example, the film *Harum Scarum* portrayed a rich, corrupt Arab sheik (Elvis Presley) tying a woman to a stake. Films such as *Harum Scarum* have reinforced the U.S. government's use of Arab "backwardness" as a justification for supporting Israel.

The anti-Arab imaging in *Alice, Trapper John MD,* and *Death of a Princess* on television and the films *Raiders of the Lost Ark, Sahara, Protocol,* and *Harem* similarly reinforced U.S. government interests in the Middle East during the 1980s—when the Iranian revolution devastated the U.S. government (1981), when the United States intervened in Lebanon (1982), when U.S. Arab oil wars continued, and when the United States bombed Libya (1986).

The 1990s brought the Gulf War, continued U.S. support of Israeli occupation of Palestine, Israel's "accidental" bombing of Lebanon (1996), the repeated U.S. bombing of Iraq, and the U.S. bombings of Sudan and Afghanistan (1998). The 1990s also brought movies that perpetuated anti-Arab images of an Arab/Middle Eastern/Muslim enemy and justified U.S. intervention in the Middle East, including *Not Without My Daughter* (1991), *Aladdin* (1992), *True Lies* (1994), and *G. I. Jane* (1998).

Recently, anti-Arab media images have taken a new turn, signified by 20th Century Fox's film *The Siege* (1998), in which the generic backward Arab/Middle Eastern/Muslim enacts violence in the United States rather than in his home country. By bringing the Arab/Middle Eastern/Muslim enemy into a North American setting, *The Siege* intensifies the idea that "Arabs" are a threat to U.S. security and that "Americans" need to protect themselves from the "Arab enemy." American Muslims and Arab Americans who have seen portions of the film fear *The Siege* will "feed suspicion and hatred of Arabs and Muslims in the United States" (Goodstein, 1998). Although the American Arab Anti-Discrimination Committee (ADC) made serious efforts to engage in constructive dialogue with 20th Century Fox and suggested several ways in which the perpetuation of anti-Arab stereotypes could have been avoided, Fox met this concern with disregard (Maksoud, 1998).

Hala Maksoud, ADC president, responded to Fox's disregard for the Arab American community's disquiet over *The Siege.* Her response represents a consensus among many Arab American activists that anti-Arab media images not only contribute to Arab American invisibility by erasing who Arabs, Middle Easterners, and Muslims are, as well as the differences between these categories, but also help to reinforce the standard that violence and discrimination against Arabs and

Arab Americans are acceptable practices. In Maksoud's letter to Fox, she stated:

> The film is insidious, dangerous and incendiary. It is bound to have a negative impact on the millions of Arab Americans and Muslims in this country. It incites hate which leads to harassment, intimidation, discrimination and even hate crimes against people of Arab descent. (Maksoud, 1998)

Members of the Arab American community expressed concern over *The Siege* because attacks against Arab American individuals and community organizations tend to occur in the context of U.S. crises in the Middle East and the media images that sensationalize them. After the 1985 TWA hijacking in Lebanon, members of the ADC's Roxbury, Massachusetts, branch found a pipe bomb in front of their office and the ADC's West Coast regional director, Alex Odeh, was assassinated (ADC, 1986a). After the Odeh murder, ADC closed its New York City office, whose director, Bonnie Rimawi, had been harassed and threatened for months. But "anti-Arab violence and harassment, are quickly forgotten or have gone largely unnoticed in the American mainstream" (Abraham, 1989, p. 20). The unresolved Alex Odeh murder, for example, "would have faded completely from memory had not Arab Americans and others continued to press the government to keep the investigation open" (Abraham, 1989).

Abdeen Jabara, who was elected president of ADC in 1986, notes that in the aftermath of Odeh's assassination, "the silence on the part of public opinion makers—politicians, celebrities, religious and labour leaders—was deafening." He adds that "Arab Americans strained to find any public outcry over this brutal murder" (ADC, 1986a). Jabara contends that the motivation for these attacks was to halt the development of Arab American political organization and to exclude Arab Americans from the larger political process by instilling fear in the one Arab American organization that strives toward the development of a mass-based membership organization operating within the larger American society. According to Jabara, the media and public officials' lack of concern reflected both the weakness of Arab American organizations and the indifference, ignorance, or malice of the media and the public officials (ADC, 1986a). The Alex Odeh murder is but one example of the push-pull effect in which Arab American individuals and community organizations strive for "visibility" while dominant groups mark their issues as insignificant and nonexistent, thereby rendering Arab Americans "invisible" by excluding them from the larger American society.

Like the Odeh murder, numerous attacks against Arab Americans have coincided with U.S. interests or involvement in a Middle East crisis. Attacks and beatings against Arab students in the United States and violations against Arab Americans were reported when the United States bombed Libya in 1986. The 1985–1986 period also included the al-Faruqi murders, in which a Palestinian American Islamic scholar, who was outspoken in his views regarding the Palestine question, and his wife were killed in their suburban Philadelphia home (ADC, 1986b); attacks against ADC offices in Boston and Washington, arson at the United Palestinian Appeal office in Washington, and numerous other cases of vandalism and attacks against local Arab community offices and businesses; violence against Arabs, Muslims, and other Middle Easterners in Dearborn (Michigan), Houston, Chicago, Syracuse, Philadelphia, and Brooklyn (Abraham, 1989, p. 20); and the bombing and destruction of a Houston mosque (ADC, 1986a). In 1985, FBI director William Webster stated that Arab Americans and those supportive of "Arab points of view" had entered a "zone of danger" (ADC, 1986a).

The reality of Webster's statement intensified, particularly for the "LA 8," the seven Palestinians and one Kenyan who were arrested in Los Angeles on 26 January 1987 and publicly labeled "a terrorist threat" even though they were engaged in legitimate activities protected by the First Amendment. Although the FBI dropped charges that they were terrorists, the FBI used section 241 of the McCarthy era McCarren–Walter Act to state that aliens can be deported for possession and distribution of literature that promotes world Communism (a section of the law that has never been used in its 35-year history) (McDonnell, 1987, p. 5). Initially, the LA 8 were suspected "terrorists" because they were connected to an organization that the U.S. government classifies as "terrorist," even though the LA 8 only supported the organization's humanitarian efforts (Eversley, 1998). An Arab American publication reports that common activities among the LA 8 are Palestinian folk dancing and attendance at Arab American community events. Nonetheless, the LA 8 were treated as a maximum security risk and held in prison. Khader Hamide was in solitary confinement for the first 36 hours, and all the detainees, confined two to a small cell, spent 23 days in maximum confinement, were shackled even when they were escorted under guard to talk to their attorneys, and were not allowed to see their relatives (McDonnell, 1987, p. 5).

Although the LA 8 were released from prison almost a month after their arrest and have successfully fought repeated deportation attempts by the federal government by claiming selective enforcement, the Justice Department continues to fight back (Eversley, 1998). The Supreme Court heard their case in November 1998 and responded to their claim that selective enforcement was being used against them by deciding that "an illegal alien has no right to protest selective prosecution" and that "the U.S. government has the right to target illegal aliens for any reason, even if only to harass the nation that they come from" (Nawash, 1999). As of July 1999, the case is still pending. It will be heard next in immigration court (no date has been set), even though immigration courts are not allowed to consider constitutional matters. This means that the court will only hear what the LA 8 were accused of, and the LA 8 will not be allowed to rely upon the First Amendment in their defense.

Whether the LA 8 are deported or not, this incident and a series of events that followed it represent the U.S. government's attempt to instill fear in Arab Americans and the general American population so that they will avoid participation in Arab and Arab American community affairs. On 24 February 1987, an anonymous phone caller told the American Civil Liberties Union that if attorney Paul Hoffman was representing the LA 8, then he should be careful before lifting the bonnet of his car because it might blow up in his face. Maxine Shehadeh, the wife of detainee Michel Shehadeh, was fired from her job as director of a child care center for a Dominguez Hills firm, which labeled her an unstable employee (McDonnell, 1987). In response to phone calls from Arab Americans who were concerned that they could be arrested for going to Arab dances and programs, Mark Rosenbaum, an ACLU attorney stated, "What the U.S. government is saying to Arabs is Shut Up or Get Out of This Country" (McDonnell, 1987, p. 7).[10]

Not only do the LA 8 court proceedings signify the denial of these eight individuals' civil rights, but they also represent "political racism" (Samhan, 1987) and discrimination practiced against Arabs as a generic category, who are perceived to be associated with the generic label Arab/Middle Eastern/Muslim enemy. ADC reports that a Justice Department contingency plan was revealed during the LA 8 court proceedings. It instilled fear in the Arab American community by providing a blueprint for the mass arrest of 10,000 Middle Eastern residents of the United States. The plan also included provisions for detention in camps in Louisiana and Florida and the possible deportation of Middle Eastern residents (Joseph, in press).

But it is the FBI's continuing harassment of Arab Americans, which began, in part, with Nixon's "Operation Boulder" (1972),[11] that particularly chills "Arab students, and Arab American community members, in the exercise of their constitutional rights, and is not related to the discovery and prosecution of criminal activity" (ADC, 1986c). FBI tactics include phone calls and visits to individuals—whether they are U.S. citizens, resident aliens of Arab descent, or non-Arab Americans sympathetic to Arab causes—as well as to their relatives, neighbors, friends, and employers. "Invariably, no criminal charge is involved and the individuals are being investigated because of their origin and/or political beliefs" (ADC, 1986c, p. 2). The harassment is primarily intended to obtain noncriminal information about pro-Arab political activities; to obstruct interaction and cooperation between Arab political activists and other segments of North American society; and to diminish support for Arab American causes by creating an atmosphere of fear, suspicion, and isolation (ADC, 1986a, p. 4). According to ADC, Arab Americans are regularly harassed for exercising their First Amendment rights, including voicing their political views, belonging to American Arab organizations, organizing or participating in demonstrations in support of imprisoned Arabs, and urging a more balanced U.S. role in the Middle East (ADC, 1986c, p. 4).

Since the United States and Iraq went to war on 16 January 1991, a dramatic increase in the number of attacks involving physical violence such as arson, bombings, and physical assaults against Arab Americans has taken place (Joseph, in press). Moreover, during the Gulf War era, a *Sacramento Bee* newspaper article reported that U.S. Representative Norman Mineta referred to the 1987 contingency plan that the FBI and the Immigration and Naturalization Service had drawn up to detain Arab Americans at a camp in Oakdale, Louisiana, in the event of war with certain Arab states. Mineta said that the plan could still be initiated to "round up" Arab Americans (*Sacramento Bee,*

24 January 1991, p. A9, cited in Joseph, in press). Around the country, Islamic mosques were broken into or bombed, shots were fired into the homes of known Arab Americans, a taxi driver in Forth Worth, Texas, was attacked and killed, some Muslim schools and Islamic societies were vandalized, and hate calls were received by Arab Americans throughout the Gulf War period (Joseph). Jamin Raskin, a writer for *Nation* magazine, argued in a February 1991 article that Arab Americans are the Japanese of 1991 (Raskin, 1991, p. 117), and ADC has reported that "Arab Americans proved to be the domestic casualties of the war."

In the late 1990s, violence and discrimination against individuals and community organizations in the United States that are perceived to fit the generic label "Arab/Middle Eastern/Muslim enemy" continues. A 1998 *New York Times* article reported that more than two dozen immigrants around the country were facing deportation or exclusion from the United States largely on secret evidence that they are not permitted to see and that comes from people who are unidentified. The federal government defends the use of secret evidence in such cases because they involve allegations of association with terrorists, but not actual charges of terrorism. The article added that all 25 men being accused in those cases were of Arab descent or were Muslims. The article quoted Hala Maksoud, president of the ADC, who stated that this had the smell of "human and civil rights somehow being suspended when it comes to Muslims" (Smothers, 1998).

The reports of violence and discrimination against Arab Americans demonstrate that the conflation of the categories Arab/Middle Eastern/Muslim, which obliterates who Arab Americans really are, often manifests itself in the forms of racism, discrimination, and violence against Arab Americans in their everyday lives. When the United States attacks an Arab country, anyone who may be identified as an Arab, Muslim, or Middle Easterner living in the United States may be targeted as a terrorist enemy. I argue that this first paradox, in which the diverse Arab American community is lumped together into a generic Arab/Middle Eastern/Muslim, contributes to the invisibility of the Arab American community. Anti-Arab imaging removes all trace of the diverse composition of the Arab American community. The resulting attacks against individuals and community organizations install fear in Arab Americans and lead many Arab Americans to conceal their ethnic identity and avoid participation in Arab American community organizations, thereby halting the community's political development and silencing its voice within the larger American society.

The Second Paradox: Race

The United States is a society that grants persons their citizenship and their rights primarily according to their position within the U.S. racial system.[12] Arab Americans are seen as racially white—but not quite. According to the U.S. Census Bureau, Arab Americans are defined as whites and/or Caucasians. However, in many social contexts they are perceived and defined as nonwhites. A heated issue being currently debated by Arab American scholars and activists is whether Arab Americans should seek minority nonwhite status or remain classified as whites/Caucasians. But the question of Arab Americans' racial/ethnic classification is no simple matter.

Although many Arab Americans phenotypically (in terms of hair texture or skin color) pass as white, some live racially marked lives. Others are racially marked by choice, because they consciously decide to self-identify as "nonwhites" or as "persons of color" to distinguish themselves from European American whites and to align themselves politically with other racially marked groups, such as blacks, Asian Americans, Native Americans, and/or Chicanos(as)/Mexicans. They use the label "nonwhite" or "people of color" as a political strategy for claiming their rights in the face of racial/ethnic or religious discrimination. Moreover, many Arab Americans differentiate their histories, cultures, and religions from those of European Americans and other racial/ethnic groups by identifying as specifically "Arab," "Arab American," "Middle Eastern," or "Muslim." These Arab Americans are engaged in a process of identity affirmation. That is, they are reclaiming and redefining the meaning of "Arab," "Arab American," "Middle Eastern," or "Muslim" on their own terms, in the face of the state's and the media's distortion of their identities. A few Arab Americans introduce themselves in terms of non-Arab racial/ethnic labels, such as Greek, Italian, Puerto Rican, or generically American, to avoid the stigmatization often associated with the label "Arab."

However, Arab Americans do not always possess the power to choose "to pass" or "not to pass" as white. North Americans who associate Arabs with media images of the Arab world, the Middle East, or Islam often perceive Arab Americans, whether phenotypically marked or not, as different from and inferior to what is considered "white." When an Arab American's ethnic or religious identity is made public, media-created myths of Arabs frequently cast a shadow over their lived experiences and their identities. Especially during a political crisis between the United States and the Arab world, the U.S. media (including newspapers, TV shows, TV news, and Hollywood films) tend to portray Arab men as terrorist enemies and Arab women as pathologically oppressed by their men, their society, their religion, and their culture. But when no allusion to an Arab or Muslim identity is made, those who can "pass" as whites return to their neutral yet privileged position as "white Americans."

While Arab Americans (like other racial/ethnic communities) have been forced into the binary classification "either white or nonwhite," differences within the population indicate that Arab Americans do not quite fit into the United States' either/or racial labeling system. Whereas some Arab Americans have blonde hair and blue eyes, others have crimpy hair and very dark skin. Some members of the Arab American community (like members of other communities), can be classified into two overlapping categories at one and the same time. Should a Moroccan, for example, be classified as Middle Eastern or African American? Although many social scientists writing before the 1940s argued that "race" as a biological formation exists, most contemporary scholars agree that "race" is not a biological but a social and political construction (Frankenburg, 1994; Omi & Winant, 1994; Harrison, 1995). Because Arab Americans, as a population, do not biologically fit into any one fixed racial category (as is the case with other racial/ethnic groups), the debate about whether Arab Americans should be classified as "white" or in a separate racial/ethnic category can then be assessed in terms of the community's social and political positioning rather than its biological makeup.

The Third Paradox: Religion

The third paradox can be summed up as "All Arab Americans are Muslims; therefore, all Arab Americans are racially inferior to whites."

For most racial/ethnic groups, the media associate backwardness and inferiority with phenotype. A racist viewpoint, for example, would refer to African Americans as inferior to whites because they have dark skin or crimpy hair. Although some Arab Americans experience racism based upon phenotype, they may also experience another, unique form of racism. Many media portrayals that depict Arabs as inferior to whites are based on what I refer to as "the racialization of religion." In other words, Arab Americans become racially marked on the assumption that all Arabs are Muslim and that Islam is a cruel, backward, and uncivilized religion.

The corrupt men in the films *Not Without My Daughter* and *Protocol,* for example, are portrayed as barbaric, primarily because they are Muslim. They make references to their Muslim identity as they enact uncivilized violence and victimize women. Throughout the films, the abusive treatment of women is sensationalized to the extreme and blamed on Islam. Hala Maksoud (ADC president), in her letter to 20th Century Fox regarding their film *The Siege,* states that a clear and direct link is made between Islamic religious practices and terrorism. Indeed, images of a Muslim man washing his hands before prayer, as millions of Muslims do every day, precede acts of terror in the film. This firmly reinforces fear of Muslims in the viewer's mind. Without enumerating them, the film is packed with stereotypes of Arabs and Muslims as violent, unscrupulous, and barbarous (ADC, 1998).

The media's use of Islam as a device to racialize Arabs as distinct from and inferior to white Americans can be explained in terms of liberal humanist perspectives on religious politics. Liberal humanist discussions of religious politics make the assumption that religion is in opposition to modern liberal political structures (Mahmood & Reynolds, 1995, p. iv). Non-Western religions (specifically Islam) are regarded as especially antagonistic to what is understood as modern (Asad, 1995). With the global ascendancy of the West, there came the institutionalization of secular spheres within European discourse. Islamic communities (or revival movements) that are not conditioned by the secular tradition have been defined as anti-modern and degenerate as compared to secular societies, which are defined as modern and progressive. Many liberal humanist writers, for example, have referred to religious movements in Iran and Egypt as pathological (Asad, 1995, p. 1). I would suggest that media images exploit this liberal humanist position as part of the process of rendering Islam as anti-modern and creating and maintaining an ideological hierarchy between white Americans and the entire Arab/Middle Eastern/Muslim world.

The use of Islam as a means of racializing Arab Americans further complicates and confuses Arab American identity. I contend that it is primarily the distorted use of Islam, rather than phenotype, that marks Arab Americans as nonwhite Others. Thus, an additional factor that shapes Arab American invisibility is that Arab Americans do not quite fit the U.S. media's racial scale because they are racialized primarily through religion rather than phenotype.

The Fourth Paradox: The Intersection of Religion and Race

The social structure that Arab immigrants bring to the United States creates yet another paradox in the development of Arab American identities. Many Arab immigrants bring a social structure to the United States that organizes differences between social groups according to religious categories (Lavie, 1995). In Arab countries, new acquaintances commonly ask one another, "Are you Muslim or Christian?" But in the United States, difference is primarily organized according to racial/ethnic categories. New acquaintances commonly ask one another, "What are you, white or a person of color?"

The social structure that upholds religion as the primary marker of social difference is rooted in the Ottoman period of Middle East history. During the Ottoman period, before the nation-state (roughly the 16th to the 18th centuries), Islam was a mediating force that created religious categories that transcended ethnicity and organized social difference (Rodrigue, 1995, p. 82). The Ottomans established the fundamental categories of Muslim and non-Muslim, and each category had multiple subgroups. Although other groups existed, the differences between a Muslim and a non-Muslim were the predominant categories that structured social arrangements. Each religious sect or rite was organized into "millets," and civil rights were assigned and administered by religious sect or rite (Younis, 1995, p. 11). Consequently, the most important public discourse was one that defined groups and identities in terms of religious categories (Rodrigue, 1995, pp. 84–87).

A focus on the pre-Ottoman and post-Ottoman periods is important to our understanding of contemporary Arab immigration because despite the emergence of the nation-state, structures that organize difference according to religion have not disappeared in the Middle East and continue to structure Middle Eastern societies. Middle Eastern immigrants bring these structures with them when they immigrate to the United States (Lavie, 1995).

Research on the early Arab immigrant experience (Hitti, 1924; Kayal & Kayal, 1975; Haddad, 1981; Naif, 1985; Suleiman & Abu-Laban, 1989) reveals that immigrants identified themselves more in terms of their religious sect (and their family and/or village of origin) than they did in terms of their ethnic, racial, or national attachments. Philip and Joseph Kayal, for example, in their detailed study of the Syrian-Lebanese in America, demonstrate that the Church has been the most important source of identity for Melkites and Maronites in the United States (Kayal & Kayal, cited in Suleiman, 1987). Likewise, research on Arab Muslim immigrants indicates that upon arrival, most of them, like Christians, tend to identify primarily according to religious sect or village rather than race or ethnicity (Naif, 1985, p. 248).

But for Arab immigrants, the organization of difference according to religious categories has conflicted with the U.S. social structure that organizes difference according to race/ethnicity. Although early immigrants, for example, defined themselves in terms of their religious sect, U.S. immigration officials defined them in terms of racial/ethnic labels, such as "Turks" or "Other Asians." I suggest that the categories of race/ethnicity and religion overlap in the identities of Arab Americans and contribute to confusion over their identity. Although many Arab immigrants upon arrival primarily identified according to religious sect, they have learned that some racial/ethnic identification has had to be made (Suleiman, 1987). But for Arab Americans, who have been labeled "Turks," "Other Asians," "Syrians," "Arabs," "Muslims," "Middle Easterners," "white/Caucasians," and/or "nonwhites," racial/ethnic identification is no simple matter.

I have argued that the paradoxes of Arab American identity are multiple, but the dilemma facing the Arab American community is clear. By occupying a confusing status within the U.S. racial/ethnic system, Arab Americans have been rendered "invisible." But if "visibility" requires that Arab Americans should occupy a more distinct place within the U.S. racial/ethnic system, what place should they occupy? Should Arab Americans seek status as a separate racial/ethnic group, or remain classified as white?

Each paradox of Arab American identity reinforces the dilemma of Arab Americans' racial/ethnic status.

In my discussion of the first paradox, I argued that the mass media's conflation of the categories Arab/Middle Eastern/Muslim distorts the meaning of "Arab." But in distorting who Arabs really are, they mark Arab Americans as different from and inferior to whites and justify racial attacks against Arab Americans. When I addressed the second paradox, I argued that the U.S. Census classifies Arab Americans as whites and that many Arab Americans identify and pass as whites. However, the media portray Arab Americans as nonwhites, and some Arab Americans either do not pass as whites or self-identify as nonwhites. Like the first paradox, then, the second involves a dilemma of racial/ethnic classification.

In my analysis of the third paradox, the question of Arab Americans' unique and therefore confusing racial/ethnic status was brought to light. I argued that Arab Americans are "racialized through religion" rather than phenotype. I suggested that when Arab Americans, whether they are Christian, Muslim, Druze, or Jewish, are associated with the media's image of a generic Islam, they are perceived as nonwhite Others. Finally, within the fourth paradox, in which categories of religion meet categories of race, Arab Americans also face a dilemma of racial/ethnic identification. After immigration to the United States, although they primarily identify according to religious sect (and family and/or village of origin), they realize that some sort of racial/ethnic identification has to be made. But the question of what that racial/ethnic identification should be remains heatedly debated among Arab Americans.

PART THREE: VISIBILITY/ COMING TO VOICE

Although U.S. social categories render Arab Americans invisible on a socio-structural level, in everyday life individual Arab American actors gain visibility by making themselves heard or seen on their own particular terms, between the contradictions that bind them. In developing an understanding of the factors that render persons or communities invisible and exclude them from participation in the larger society, many university students and community organizers find room for movement in the cracks of the social system. They choose speaking up over silence and demand recognition over erasure. They maintain their language and their Arabic names; they call for equal rights and justice; they educate non-Arabs about who Arabs really are; and they teach their children. They are not embarrassed or afraid to identify as Arabs in public spaces, nor are they afraid to post fliers on telegraph poles in broad daylight announcing future events relevant to Arab Americans. These Arab Americans make choices that "allow [them] a measure of resistance against the larger patterns that map [them], a measure of self-creation" (Majaj, 1994, p. 83).

Although the voices and actions of individuals and community groups that make Arab Americans more visible in everyday life contribute to Arab American visibility, some scholars and activists suggest that additional socio-structural changes must be made to address the problem of "invisibility." Because rights are granted according to racial/ethnic categories in the United States, and because the United States organizes social differences according to racial/ethnic categories, many Arab Americans contend that the issue of Arab American "invisibility" must be dealt with in terms of Arab Americans' status within the U.S. Census racial/ethnic classification system. As long as Arab Americans are classified as whites, many scholars argue that they will remain relatively invisible and vulnerable in American society (Arab American Institute, 1994). What is necessary, according to some Arab Americans, is for Arab Americans to obtain federal status as a separate, nonwhite racial/ethnic group. However, not all Arab Americans agree with obtaining a separate category, indicating that the Arab American community as a whole is still in the process of defining itself and reaching a consensus on who they are and how they should be defined.[13]

CONCLUSION

The U.S. racializing system, reinforced by the U.S. media, has racialized Arab Americans according to a unique and contradictory process, resulting in their white-but-not-quite racial/ethnic status. The Arab American community's internally diverse and constantly changing makeup contributes to the complexities of classifying this population.

In addition to these factors, ongoing change in the makeup of the Arab American community necessitates both new methods for conceptualizing the community and further research on Arab American identity. The growing number of Muslim immigrants, in a context where "Arab" is already associated with Islam, places Arab Christians, who were previously a majority, in a new and different position within their community. If the distortion of Arab identity is produced through the association of Arab with Islam, will a trend to disassociate themselves from the category "Arab" and associate more with the "white" classification develop among Arab Christians?

New economic factions within the community may alter Arab American individuals' identification with either the "white" or the separate Arab or Middle Eastern racial/ethnic classification. The theory that "class whitens" means that economically mobile members of a given community enact white cultural practices while denying their own more than do members of the working class. Many Arab Americans have built communities within white middle- and upper-class neighborhoods, but an increasing number are entering the working class (Aswad & Gray, 1996). History indicates that movement into the working class, particularly among U.S.-born children of immigrant parents, leads to heightened political consciousness and identification with the traditions of other racially and/or economically oppressed groups rather than with mainstream white middle-class traditions. The Arab American community has reached a level of settlement within larger U.S. cities, such as Detroit, where research can be conducted that explores whether the children of Arab immigrants tend to orbit around the traditions of whites or nonwhites. Arab Americans' identification with a white or nonwhite identity will be altered depending on which American traditions Arab Americans come to orbit around.

Moreover, Arab Americans' racial/ethnic associations could be affected by changes in population size. Will the Arab American community's population size increase so that it factionalizes across class and racial lines in ways that are similar within larger immigrant racial/ethnic communities (that is, Latino, Asian American), or will an increase in population size lead to increased social and political cohesion and identification among Arab Americans as a separate racial/ethnic group? If there are no major shifts in population size, will the Arab American community develop in ways that are similar to the small East Indian communities in which families remain tight and class distinctions hardly take shape?

Although research is needed to assess how these changes might manifest themselves over time, the pressing issue of civil rights violations against Arab immigrants and Americans already forms Arab Americans' relationship to the U.S. racial/ethnic classification system and proves that denying Arab Americans their political rights has become an acceptable U.S. practice. This clearly distinguishes Arab Americans from European American whites. Arab Americans have not (yet) been racially victimized to the same degree as other communities that have a history of racial oppression within the United States, by the United States government (Asian Americans, African Americans, Chicanos(as)/Mexicans, and Native Americans). But particularly since the Gulf War, violence, racism, and discrimination against Arab Americans have rapidly increased.

Consequently, the Arab American community faces pressing new challenges. Community members who pass as white or who avoid participation in Arab American issues or politics may not ever feel the effects of their new positioning as the "enemy Other." But how will the community grapple with the crisis that sectors of the community that identify with Arab causes or organizations are denied their political rights and taken advantage of politically? And how will Arab Americans deal with the problem of racial discrimination experienced by community members who do not pass as white because of their appearance or their association with Islam? Will Arab Americans come together as a whole to defend the rights of sections of their community? Or will Arab Americans continue to straddle the white/nonwhite boundary until *The Siege* becomes a reality and any persons of Middle Eastern descent can be placed in detention camps like the Japanese? What type of racial/ethnic label might position Arab Americans so that they can adequately address contemporary social and political challenges? Although it is up to Arab Americans themselves to map their future, solving the problem of "invisibility" must be approached with the U.S. structure for granting group rights in mind.

In the United States, the right to political participation is granted to members of identifiable/visible racial and ethnic communities. This organizing system has placed individuals who want to be recognized/visible but do not want to acquiesce to North American racial divisions between a paradox (Ono, 1998). However, diverse communities that have been racialized by the state and the media, silenced by the larger American society, and denied their political rights have acquiesced to racial divisions and identified according to a racial/ethnic label (that is, Asian American) for the purpose of claiming their rights, gaining recognition, and attaining a voice (Ono, 1998).

Arab Americans cannot adequately address the extent to which they should acquiesce to U.S. racial/ethnic divisions until a consensus is reached on how to label the community and who should be included as its members. Consensus requires conversation, cooperation, and action among community members, activists, and researchers. Then, by building coalitions around a comprehensible racial/ethnic label, Arab Americans can determine their strategy for positioning themselves within the U.S. racial/ethnic system and defending themselves against external forces despite their internal divisions/differences, in order to gain visibility, voice, and recognition on their own terms.

Notes

1. See Hentoff (1990), Awad (1981), and Ohanian (1986).
2. A significant portion of research for this paper was conducted at the NAFF Arab American Collection, Smithsonian Institution, National Museum of American History.
3. For more information on why more Christians immigrated than Muslims and the factors that led to early Arab immigration to the United States, see Dlin (1961), Saliba (1982), Abraham (1995), and Younis (1995).
4. For more information on pack peddling, see Naff (1985) and Zogby (1990).
5. See Suleiman (1987, pp. 41–46) for an assessment of race prejudice against early immigrants. See Conklin and Flaires (1987, pp. 74–49) for an analysis of racism against Alabama's Lebanese Catholics in the early 1900s.
6. For demographic information on the third immigration period, see El-Badry (1994).
7. For more information about each Arab American organization, see Suleiman (1987) and Zogby (1990).
8. See Shaheen (1983) and Scheinn (1993).
9. See Shohat and Stam (1994).
10. See McDonnell (1987), Anderson and Atta (1991), LaFraniere (1991), AAI (1994), Gordon (1993); Opatrany (1993), and Paddock (1993).
11. See AAI (1994).
12. For an extensive study of rights, citizenship, and race in the United States, see Bock and Bowen (1998).
13. See Arab American Institute (1994) for more information about the debate over racial/ethnic status within the Arab American community. See Office of Management and Budget (1997a, 1997b) for more information on the federal government's response to the idea of creating a new, separate racial/ethnic category for Arab Americans.

References

Abraham, Nabeel. (1989). Arab American marginality: Mythos and practice. In Michael Suleiman (Ed.), *Arab Americans: Continuity and change* (pp. 17–44). Washington, DC: Arab American University Graduates.

Abraham, Nabeel. (1995). Arab Americans. In Judy Galens, Anna Sheets, & Robyn Young (Eds.), *Gale encyclopedia of multicultural America* (pp. 84–94). New York: Gale Research.

American Arab Anti-Discrimination Committee (ADC). (1986a). *Report on Arab-Americans under attack: ADC fights back: Congressional hearings on anti-Arab violence: A milestone for Arab American rights.* Washington, DC: Author.

American Arab Anti-Discrimination Committee (ADC). (1986b). *Report on the At Faroqi murders.* Washington, DC: Author.

American Arab Anti-Discrimination Committee (ADC). (1986c). *Report on the FBI and the civil rights of Arab Americans.* Washington, DC: Author.

American Arab Anti-Discrimination Committee (ADC). (1993). *Report on surveillance and defamation: Arab American political rights in times of crisis,* Washington, DC: Author.

American Arab Anti-Discrimination Committee (ADC). (1998). Letter issued by ADC president, Halo Maksound, to 20th Century Fox.

Anderson, Jack, & Atta, Van. (1991, January 27). Arab Americans: Suspects without probable cause. *Washington Post,* p. C7.

Ansara, James. (1958). Syrian-Lebanese immigration to the United States. *National Herald, 5,* 12–13.

Arab American Institute. (1994). *Report on executive summary of forum and discussion groups on minority status: Is it right for Arab Americans?* Washington, DC: Author.

Asad, Talal. (1995). Modern power and the reconfiguration of religious traditions [Interview by Saba Mahmood]. *Stanford Humanities Review, 5*(1), 1–18.

Aswad, Barbara, & Bilge, Barbara. (Eds.). (1996). *Family and gender among American Muslims: Issues facing Middle Eastern immigrants and their descendants.* Philadelphia: Temple University Press.

Aswad, Barbara, & Gray, Nancy. (1996). Challenges to the Arab American family and access (Arab Community Center for Economic and Social Services). In Barbara Aswad and Barbara Bilge (Eds.), *Family and gender among American Muslims* (pp. 223–241). Philadelphia: Temple University Press.

Awad, Gary. (1981, March). The Arab Americans: An invisible minority awakens. *News Circle,* pp. 10–15.

Beuscher, Derek, & Ono, Kent. (1996). Civilized colonialism: Pocahontas as neocolonial rhetoric. *Women's Studies in Communication, 19*(1), 127–153.

Bock, Derek, & Bowen, William. (1998). *Shape of the river: Long term consequences of considering race.* Princeton, NJ: Princeton University Press.

Conklin, Nancy, & Flaires, Nora. (1987). "Colored" and Catholic: The Lebanese in Birmingham, Alabama. In Eric Hooglund (Ed.), *Crossing the waters: Arabic-speaking immigrants to the United States before 1940* (pp. 69–84). Washington, DC: Smithsonian Institution Press.

Dlin, Norman. (1961). Some cultural and geographic aspects of the Christian Lebanese in metropolitan Los Angeles. Unpublished master's thesis, Geography Department, University of California, Los Angeles.

El Badry, Samia. (1994). The Arab American market. *American Demographics, 16*(1), 22–30.

Ellison, Ralph. (1972). *The invisible man.* New York: Vantage Books. (Original work published 1947).

Eversly, Melanie. (1998, October 22). Supreme Court to decide rights of immigrants: Arab Americans sue over First Amendment freedoms. *Detroit Free Press.*

Frankenberg, Ruth. (1994). *The social construction of whiteness: White women, race matters.* Minneapolis: Regents of the University of Minnesota.

Goodstein, Laurie. (1998, August 6). Film feeds hate, Arab groups say. *Sun-Sentinel,* p. E3.

Gordon, Rachel. (1993, January 27). Call for grand jury investigation of former SFPD cop. *San Francisco Examiner,* p. C5.

Haddad, Yvonne. (1981). The Lebanese community in Hartford. *Arab Perspectives, 2,* 9–16.

Halaby. (1980). *The newspaper debate between the Syrian immigrant nativists and Americanists: Its causes, effects and personalities.* Paper submitted to the NAFF Arab American Collection, National Museum of American History, Smithsonian Institution.

Harrison, Faye. (1995). The persistent power of "race" in the cultural and political economy of racism. *Annual Review of Anthropology, 24,* 47–74.

Hasso, Frances. (1987, February/March). Conspiracy of silence against Arab Americans. *News Circle,* pp. 14–18.

Hentoff, Nat. (1990, March/April). The "invisible" Arab Americans. *Issues,* pp. 6–7.

Hitti, Phillip. (1924). *The Syrians in America.* New York: George Doran.

Joseph, Suad. (in press). Against the grain of the nation: The Arab. In Michael Suleiman (Ed.), *Issues in Arab America.* Philadelphia: Temple University Press.

Kadi, Joanna. (1994). Introduction. In Joanna Kadi (Ed.), *Food for our grandmothers: Writings by Arab American and Arab Canadian feminists* (pp. viii–xx). Boston: South End Press.

Kayal, Philip, & Kayal, Joseph. (1975). *The Syrian-Lebanese in America: A study in religion and assimilation.* Boston: Twayne.

Lafraniere, Sharon. (1991, January 9). FBI starts interviewing Arab American leaders. *Washington Post,* p. A14.

Lavie, Smadar. (1995). Personal communication.

Lin, Ann Chih, & Jamal, Amaney. (1997, August). *Navigating a new world: The political assimilation of Arab immigrants.* Paper presented at the annual meeting of the American Political Science Association.

Mahmood, Saba, & Reynolds, Nancy. (1995). Introduction. *Stanford Humanities Review, 5*(1), iii–xi.

Majaj, Lisa. (1994). Boundaries: Arab/American. In Joanna Kadi (Ed.), *Food for our grandmothers: Writings by Arab American and Arab Canadian feminists* (pp. 65–86). Boston: South End Press.

Maksoud, Hala. (1998). *Letter to Fox.* E-mail letter distributed to American Arab Anti-Discrimination Committee Members, American Arab Anti-Discrimination Committee, Washington, DC.

McDonnell, Pat. (1987, February/March). Mass arrest of eight Palestinians and a Kenyan wife shocked and angered Arab Americans. *News Circle,* pp. 12–15.

Naber, Nadine. (in press). Race, religion and kitchen resistance: Examining the paradoxical existence of Arab American women. In Lenora Forestell (Ed.), *Women in the media.*

Naff, Alixa. (1985). *Becoming American: The Early Arab immigrant experience.* Carbondale and Edwardsville: Southern Illinois University Press.

Nawash, Kamal [ADC Legal Director]. (1999). Personal communication.

Office of Management and Budget. (1997a). *Recommendations from the Interagency Committee for the Review of the Racial and Ethnic Standards to the Office of Management and Budget concerning changes to the standards for the classification of federal data on race and ethnicity.* Washington, DC: United States Federal Register.

Office of Management and Budget. (1997b). *Revisions to the standards for the classification of federal data on race and ethnicity.* Washington, DC: United States Federal Register.

Ohanian, Bernard. (1986, June). The misunderstood minority. *San Francisco Focus,* pp. 40–51.

Omi, Michael, & Winant, Howard. (1994). *Racial formation in the United States.* London: Routledge.

Ono, Kent. (1998). Personal communication.

Opatrany, Dennis. (1993, April 8). Court documents say B'nai B'rith unit paid Gerard associate to snoop for nearly 40 years. *San Francisco Examiner.*

Paddock, Richard. (1993, April 9). Evidence of ADL spy operation seized by police. *Los Angeles Times.*

Raskin, Jamin. (1991, February 4). Remember Korematsu: A precedent for Arab Americans? *Nation.*

Rodrigue, Aaron. (1995). Difference and tolerance in the Ottoman Empire: Interview by Nancy Reynolds. *Stanford Humanities Review, 5*(1), 81–92.

Sald, Edward. (1978). *Orientalism.* New York: Vintage Books.

Saliba, Najib. (1982). Emigration from Syria. *The Word, 26*(3), 7–12.

Saliba, Therese. (1994). Military presences and absences. In Joanna Kadi (Ed.), *Food for our grandmothers: Writings by Arab American and Arab Canadian feminists* (pp. 125–132). Boston: South End Press.

Samhan, Helen. (1987). Politics and exclusion: The Arab American experience. *Journal of Palestine Studies, 16*(2), 20–28.

Samhan, Helen. (1994, April). *An assessment of the federal standard for race and ethnicity classification.* A handout distributed at the Center for Arab Studies Conference on Arab Americans, Georgetown University, Washington, DC.

Scheinn, Richard. (1993, January 10). Angry over "Aladdin": Arabs decry film's stereotypes. *Washington Post,* p. G1.

Shaheen. Jack. (1983). *The TV Arab.* Bowling Green, OH: Bowling Green State University Press.

Shakir, Evelyn. (1997). *Bint Arab: Arab and Arab American women in the U.S.* Westport, CT: Praeger.

Shohat, Ella, & Stam, Robert. (1994). *Unthinking Eurocentrism: Multiculturalism and the media.* New York: Routledge.

Smothers, Ronald. (1998, August 15). Secret evidence standing in way of new life for some immigrants. *New York Times,* p. A11.

Suleiman, Michael. (1987). Early Arab-Americans: The search for identity. In Eric Hooglund (Ed.), *Crossing the waters: Arabic-speaking immigrants to the United States before 1940* (pp. 37–55). Washington DC: Smithsonian Institution Press.

Suleiman, Michael. (1989). America and the Arabs: Negative images and the feasibility of dialogue. In Michael Suleiman (Ed.), *Arab Americans: Continuity and change* (pp. 251–272). Washington, DC: Arab American University Graduates.

Suleiman, Michael, & Abu-Laban, Baha. (1989). Introduction. In Michael Suleiman (Ed.), *Arab Americans: Continuity and change* (pp. 1–16). Washington, DC: Arab American University Graduates.

Younis, Adele. (1995). *The coming of the Arabic peoples to the United States.* New York: Center for Migration Studies.

Zogby, John. (1990). *Arab American today: A demographic profile of Arab Americans.* Washington, DC: Arab American Institute.

Concepts and Questions

1. List and discuss some of the social issues that work against the recognition and acceptance of Arab Americans as fully recognized members of U.S. society.
2. In what manner did European American stereotypes of Middle Eastern peoples affect the recognition of Arab American identity?
3. What does Naber mean when she speaks of Arab invisibility?
4. What post-1960s world events have influenced the recognition of Arab Americans?
5. Why does the paradox of Arabs' being defined as a monolithic category persist in the minds of many Americans?
6. In what way have popular media influenced American perceptions of immigrant Arabs?
7. How does the affiliation of many Arab Americans with the Islamic religion affect their identity in the United States?
8. What does Naber mean when she refers to Arabs as being "white, but not quite white"?
9. Explain how the various social factors such as racialization affect the individual development of an American Arab identity.

3 International Cultures: Understanding Diversity

All persons are puzzles until at last we find in some word or act the key to the man, to the woman: straightway all their past works and actions lie in light before us.

RALPH WALDO EMERSON

One of the most obvious yet often overlooked dynamics of human interaction is that your past experiences affect your behavior during communication. It is common knowledge that each of you acts according to the personal pattern of social perception that you bring to a communication event. Think for a moment about some of those situations in which you and some friends shared what you believed to be the same experience, yet later when you discussed the event you soon discovered there were differences in your perceptions of that event. For example, if you and your friends were out hiking and came upon a rattlesnake, the response (perception) of that event would be contingent upon each person's prior exposure to rattlesnakes. You might have had a reptile as a child and, therefore, found the experience of the snake very exciting. One of your friends, however, might have been bitten by a snake and would, therefore, have a very different reaction to the event you all were now facing. Although our example seems apparent, it nevertheless calls your attention to the fundamental truism that the messages you received were the same; yet because everyone has a unique personality and experiential background, each of you experienced a variety of feelings, sensations, and responses. Each of you brought your own unique background to the event, and as a result, each attributed different meanings to the shared experience. In short, the event meant what it did to you because of your unique past history.

Individual past personal histories take on added significance when the dimension of culture is introduced because each of you is a product of both your individual experiences and your culture—a culture you share with other people. As we indicated earlier, *culture* refers to those cumulative deposits of knowledge, beliefs, views, values, and behaviors that are acquired by a large group of people and passed on from one generation to the next. In this sense, culture affects you both consciously and unconsciously; it not only teaches you how and what to think but also dictates such values as what is attractive and what is ugly, what is good and what is evil, and what is appropriate and what is not. In short, your culture helps develop your unique pattern of social perception and tells you how to see and interpret your world. Furthermore, culture teaches you such things as how close to stand to strangers, how to greet friends, when to speak and when to remain silent, and even how to display your anger properly. When you are interacting with others and become disturbed by their actions, you can, for instance, cry, become physically violent, shout, or remain silent. The behaviors you display are a manifestation of what you have learned, and they are strongly influenced by your culture.

These cultural influences affect your ways of perceiving and acting; they contain the societal experiences and values that are passed from generation to generation. Because these behaviors are so much a part of your persona, there is a danger that you might forget that behaviors are culturally engendered and vary among cultures. This is why someone from Japan, for example, might remain silent if disturbed by another's actions, whereas an Israeli or an Italian would more likely verbalize their displeasure vigorously. Whatever the culture, you can better understand your behavior and the reactions of others if you realize that what you are hearing and seeing is a reflection of the other's culture. As you might predict, cultural understanding comes more easily when your cultural experiences are similar to those of the people with whom you are interacting. Conversely, when different and diverse backgrounds are brought to a communication encounter, it is often difficult to share internal states and feelings. In this chapter, we will focus on these difficulties by examining some of the experiences and perceptual backgrounds found among a sampling of international cultures.

We begin with this question: How do you learn to interact with and understand people who come from very different areas of the global village? This answer is not simple, yet it is at the core of this book. The need for such understanding is obvious. If you look around the world at any particular moment, you will find diverse cultures in constant interaction with one another. The nightly news makes it abundantly clear that all cultures, including those that are quite different from yours, are linked together in the global community. Events that happen in one part of the world can and do influence events all over the world. Whether it be concerns about the global economy, concerns about food, water, or energy, or major differences in sociopolitical philosophies, no culture can remain isolated from or unaffected by the rest of the world.

Two things are crucial if you are to relate effectively with people from diverse international cultures: (1) you must have knowledge about the people from other cultures; and (2) you must have respect for their diversity. This chapter offers five essays to assist you with both of those assignments. Through these essays, you will explore the rich diversity found in several international cultures. Although these cultures represent only a small portion of the countless cultures found throughout the world, they are somewhat representative and should enable you to discover how people in other cultures develop their view of the world. A culture's worldview—to a great extent—determines how its members perceive themselves, each other, and their place in the universe; it serves as an underlying pattern for interaction within a culture. We begin with a glimpse of worldview diversity by detailing the inherent differences between cultures holding an individualistic orientation and those that exhibit a collectivistic bent.

Of the many social psychological variables that describe cultures, one of the most significant is the individualism–collectivism continuum. People who live primarily in northern Europe, the present and former British Commonwealth, and the United

States tend toward individualism. In most Asian cultures, and particularly in East Asia, however, a social prejudice against individuality is common. In "Living Together vs. Going It Alone," Richard E. Nisbett discusses these cultural characteristics and the impact they have on individual and collective behavior. Members of independence-oriented cultures tend to value personal distinctiveness, whereas Asians are more likely to value sameness and blending in with others. Individual choices and personal preferences are characteristic of individualistic cultures, whereas in dependent societies available choices favor the group rather than the individual. In the same vein, individual-oriented persons tend to seek goals of personal accomplishment, whereas dependent-oriented individuals seek group accomplishment. Feelings of self-worth in independent cultures derive from individual success. In dependent cultures, these feelings are usually aligned with feelings of being in harmony with one's group.

Nisbett focuses on the independent versus the interdependent aspects of Western and Asian cultures. He shows, for example, that training for independence or interdependence begins very early. For Westerners, it is common for children to sleep in their own beds—quite often in separate rooms—promoting independence. Among Asians, it is much more common for children to sleep in the same bed as their parents—and perhaps other siblings—fostering an interdependent relationship. As children mature, the nature of their family and peer interactions fosters the development of independence or interdependence. Thus, independent and interdependent orientations become ingrained in children's personalities at a very early age. Independent orientations lead to insistence on freedom of individual action, desires for distinctiveness, a preference for egalitarianism and achieved status, and a belief in universal rules of proper behavior. For the interdependent personality, orientations include a preference for collective action, a preference for blending harmoniously with the group, acceptance of hierarchy and ascribed status, and variable rules of behavior that take into account the context and the nature of the relationships involved.

Nisbett ends his essay with a discussion of the Japanese notions of *erabi* and *awase:* the styles of conflict reduction and negotiation favored by independent and interdependent personalities. The Western *erabi* orientation involves a belief that the environment can be manipulated for individual goals and accomplishment. Debate is a major form of communicative behavior leading to the resolution of conflict. The Asian *awase* style assumes that the environment cannot be manipulated and that people must adjust themselves to it. Negotiations do not involve debate but are based on mutual trust and cooperation, which leads to a mutually satisfying outcome for all.

The importance of China as a leading player on the world stage cannot be overstated. China is currently the world's most populous nation, with its population approaching 1.3 billion. As China's participation in the world's economic arena continues to increase, the level of interpersonal contact between Americans and Chinese will also grow. Interactions, ranging from simple tourism to the negotiation of complex contracts and agreements covering trade, investment, and political alliances, have become commonplace. Business relationships and joint ventures will increase, and the influence of nongovernmental persons and agencies will become more evident. In fact, a recent novel offers a fictional account of what future relations with China may hold by describing how a nuclear confrontation between the United States and China is averted not by the diplomatic efforts of both governments but by a Boeing Company vice president who points out to the business interests in China the negative economic consequences of permitting the confrontation to persist. Needless to say, your ability to interact successfully with others from China in any of these arenas will require that you comprehend many of the deep underlying value dynamics of Chinese culture.

One such dynamic found in China—as well as in many other Asian cultures—is "face," which is intimately tied to how the Chinese feel and communicate with one another. In his article "The *Wei* (Positioning)–*Ming* (Naming)–*Lianmian* (Face) Continuum in Contemporary Chinese Culture," Wenshan Jia relates the importance of face within the Chinese culture and shows how it extends far beyond the idea of mere personal embarrassment and incorporates emotional, communicative, hierarchal, and personhood dimensions that govern interaction among the Chinese. He first defines the Chinese concepts of *wei, ming,* and *lianmian* and then shows how they function as a continuum where *wei* and *ming* converge to construct or create *lianmian* (face).

In his discussion, Jia shows how *wei* is a philosophical construct reflecting Chinese concepts of ontology and axiology. Jia sees *ming* as a linguistic/rhetorical construct that relates to the role of language as a means of understanding and interpreting reality. *Lianmian* is perceived largely as a sociopsychological construct that reflects a uniquely Chinese way of social interaction, communication, thinking, and feeling. From an emotive perspective, affect and human feelings are fundamental aspects of face. From a communicative view, face is a dynamic and fluid aspect that requires management throughout interaction. When viewed from a personhood perspective, face is a sacred object to be seen by the community.

Jia suggests that understanding Chinese face concepts and practices can generate important discoveries about the Chinese people and Chinese culture. In order to illustrate how *wei, ming,* and *lianmian* function in practice, Jia relates two case analyses of events within China that demonstrate how these three constructs exert their influence over events and help to maintain the hierarchy of the society.

Although countless dimensions define each culture, frequently a particular characteristic helps distinguish one culture from another. For example, in the United States, a heightened sense of individualism distinguishes it from most other cultures. In India, as Martin J. Gannon points out in the next essay, religion (Hinduism) forms the central theme of that culture. So strong is the pull of religion in India that it leads Gannon to believe that "Indian culture and society cannot be understood without reference to that tradition." Hence, our next selection, titled "India: The Dance of Shiva," offers us that reference.

Among Hindus, dancing is recognized as the most ancient and important of the arts. Gannon, therefore, uses the metaphor of dance as a means of describing and explaining Hindu culture. Hindus see life as a series of cycles, and Gannon believes that the best way to understand this Indian culture is by looking at the five most important cycles of Hinduism as a form of dance. These cycles are philosophy, life, family, social interaction, and work and recreation (rejuvenation). Gannon provides an in-depth description of each cycle and links each directly to the cultural life of India. As Gannon points out, "Hindu philosophy is the key to understanding India." Consequently, an awareness of the cyclic nature of Hindu philosophy, and the perceptions of the world it produces, is essential for you to communication effectively with people from the Indian culture.

Sub-Saharan Africa is a vast geographic area that is home to more than 35 countries, more than 100 tribal groups, and a multitude of cultures. To try and describe the cultures of Africa is way beyond the scope of this book. Yet, because sub-Saharan Africa compromises a major portion of the earth, it must not be ignored. Although there is a great deal of diversity among cultures, there is also some significant similarity.

In his article "Personality and Person Perception in Africa," Karl Peltzer draws on this similarity to construct a model of African socialization and personhood. Peltzer sees sub-Saharan Africa as a region of similar cultures that differ from other regions in the world because of a high illiteracy rate, subsistence-oriented economies, and highly permissive child-rearing practices. He emphasizes the risk of succumbing to stereotypes and glossing over the heterogeneity and complexity of African cultures by being mindful of the large degree of diversity found among African cultures. Yet Peltzer has identified three distinctive components of sub-Saharan African people: *traditional, transitional*, and *modern* individuals. Traditional people are those who still live within tribal village societies and are little affected by modernization. Transitional persons live in and shuttle between the traditional and modern cultures in their daily round of activities. Modern individuals participate fully in the activities of the contemporary industrial or postindustrial world. Peltzer uses the dimensions of *authority, group,* and *body-mind/environment* to analyze the socialization of traditional and transitional persons in order to illustrate the development of their personalities and social perceptional faculties.

In tracing this development, Peltzer makes frequent references to the differences in socialization found in sub-Saharan Africa and in Western cultures. These references are useful from a communicative perspective because they provide an understanding of the worldview and experiential background of traditional and transitional persons that can facilitate effective communicative interaction.

North of the Sahara in Africa lies a whole different cultural milieu. The countries that border the southern Mediterranean are predominately Islamic and are tied much more to the Middle East and Arabian culture. In order to sample part of the Arabic world, we will explore the ancient and fascinating culture of Egypt. In an essay titled "Communication with Egyptians," Polly Begley isolates those cultural elements that she believes are most crucial to foster interaction with Egyptians. She holds that three elements must be considered. The first is Egyptian worldview and religion. The Egyptian worldview comprises a culmination of various African civilizations and beliefs. Parts of the worldview are ancient, dating to Pharaonic-era beliefs. Other dimensions are derived from Islam, the predominant religion of Egypt. Egyptian values of tradition, social relationships, and hierarchical structure are a second major element of Egyptian culture. Because Egyptian culture is 4,000 to 5,000 years old, tradition is an important value. Social relationships are very important to the Egyptian because a part of the culture is a fear of loneliness. For the Egyptian, hierarchies according to age, gender, and experience are crucial. Ancient traditions outline the proper place and behavior of each person in Egyptian society. For Egyptians, the Arabic language is the third key element. Egyptians, like many other Arabic cultures, see language as a powerful tool. It promotes unity for Egyptians and permits them to construct their national identity. Using these three crucial elements as a structure, Begley provides numerous examples of how interaction between Egyptians and non-Egyptians can be improved by a knowledge of how these elements affect Egyptian interpersonal relationships.

Living Together vs. Going It Alone

Richard E. Nisbett

Most Westerners, or at any rate most Americans, are confident that the following generalizations apply to pretty much everyone:

- Each individual has a set of characteristic, distinctive attributes. Moreover, people *want* to be distinctive—different from other individuals in important ways.
- People are largely in control of their own behavior; they feel better when they are in situations in which choice and personal preference determine outcomes.
- People are oriented toward personal goals of success and achievement; they find that relationships and group memberships sometimes get in the way of attaining these goals.
- People strive to feel good about themselves; personal successes and assurances that they have positive qualities are important to their sense of well-being.
- People prefer equality in personal relations, or when relationships are hierarchical, they prefer a superior position.
- People believe the same rules should apply to everyone. Individuals should not be singled out for special treatment because of their personal attributes or connections to important people. Justice should be blind.

There are indeed hundreds of millions of such people, but they are to be found primarily in Europe, especially northern Europe, and in the present and former nations of the British Commonwealth, including the United States. The social-psychological characteristics of most of the rest of the world's people, especially those of East Asia, tend to be different to one degree or another (see Fiske, Kitayama, Markus, & Nisbett, 1998; Hsu, 1983; Markus & Kitayama, 1991b; Triandis, 1995).

Reprinted with permission of The Free Press, a Division of Simon & Schuster Adult Publishing Group, from *The Geography of Thought* by Richard Nisbett. Richard Nisbett teaches at the University of Michigan.

THE NON-WESTERN SELF

There is an Asian expression that reflects a cultural prejudice against individuality: "The peg that stands out is pounded down." In general, East Asians are supposed to be less concerned with personal goals or self-aggrandizement than are Westerners. Group goals and coordinated action are more often the concerns. Maintaining harmonious social relations is likely to take precedence over achieving personal success. Success is often sought as a group goal rather than as a personal badge of merit. Individual distinctiveness is not particularly desirable. For Asians, feeling good about themselves is likely to be tied to the sense that they are in harmony with the wishes of the groups to which they belong and are meeting the group's expectations. Equality of treatment is not assumed, nor is it necessarily regarded as desirable.

The rules that apply to relationships in East Asia are presumed to be local, particular, and well specified by roles rather than universals. An Asian friend told me the most remarkable thing about visiting American households is that everyone is always thanking everyone else: "Thank you for setting the table"; "Thank you for getting the car washed." In her country, everyone has clear obligations in a given context, and you don't thank people for carrying out their obligations. Choice is not a high priority for most of the world's people. (An East Asian friend once asked me why Americans found it necessary to have a choice among 40 breakfast cereals in the supermarket.) And Asians do not necessarily feel that their competence as a decision maker is on the line when they do have to make a choice.

Most Americans over a certain age well remember their primer, called *Dick and Jane*. Dick and Jane and their dog, Spot, were quite the active individualists. The first page of an early edition from the 1930s (the primer was widely used until the 1960s) depicts a little boy running across a lawn. The first sentences are "See Dick run. See Dick play. See Dick run and play." This would seem the most natural sort of basic information to convey about kids—to the Western mentality. But the first page of the Chinese primer of the same era shows a little boy sitting on the shoulders of a bigger boy. "Big brother takes care of little brother. Big brother loves little brother. Little brother loves big brother." It is not individual action but relationships between people that seem important to convey in a child's first encounter with the printed word.

Indeed, the Western-style self is virtually a figment of the imagination to the East Asian. As philosopher Hu Shih writes, "In the Confucian human-centered philosophy man cannot exist alone; all action must be in the form of interaction between man and man" (Shiu, 1919, p. 116, cited in King, 1991). The person always exists within particular situations where there are particular people with whom one has relationships of a particular kind—and the notion that there can be attributes or actions that are not conditioned on social circumstances is foreign to the Asian mentality. Anthropologist Edward T. Hall introduced the notion of "low-context" versus "high-context" societies to capture differences in self-understanding (Hall, 1976). To the Westerner, it makes sense to speak of a person as having attributes that are independent of circumstances or particular personal relations. This self—this bounded, impermeable free agent—can move from group to group and setting without significant alteration. But for the Easterner (and for many other peoples, to one degree or another), the person is connected, fluid, and conditional. As philosopher Donald Munro (1985) put it, "East Asians understand themselves in terms of their relation to the whole, such as the family, society, *Tao* Principle, or Pure Consciousness." The person participates in a set of relationships that make it possible to act; purely independent behavior is usually not possible or really even desirable.

Since all action is in concert with others, or at the very least affects others, harmony in relationships becomes a chief goal of social life. I have presented a schematic illustration intended to capture the different types of sense of self in relation to in-group, or close circle of friends and family; the illustration also conveys relative distance between in-group and out-group, or people who are mere acquaintances at most (Iyengar, Lepper, & Ross, 1999). Easterners feel embedded in their in-groups and distant from their out-groups. They tend to feel they are very similar to in-group members, and they are much more trusting of them than of out-group members. Westerners feel relatively detached from their in-groups and tend not to make as great distinctions between in-group and out-group.

Some linguistic facts illustrate the social-psychological gap between East and West. In Chinese, there is no word for "individualism." The closest one can come is the word for "selfishness." The Chinese character *jen*—benevolence—means two men. In Japanese, the word "I"—meaning the trans-situational, unconditional, generalized self with all its attributes, goals, abilities, and preferences—is not often used in conversation. Instead, Japanese has many words for "I," depending on audience and context. When a Japanese woman gives an official speech, she customarily uses *Watashi,* which is the closest Japanese comes to the trans-situational "I." When a man refers to himself in relation to his college chums, he might say *Boku* or *Ore.* When a father talks to his child, he says *Otosan* (Dad). A young girl might refer to herself by her nickname when talking to a family member: "Tomo is going to school today." The Japanese often call themselves *Jibun,* the etymology of which leads to a term meaning "my portion."

Figure 1 *Eastern and Western Views of the Relations Among Self, In-Group, and Out-Group*

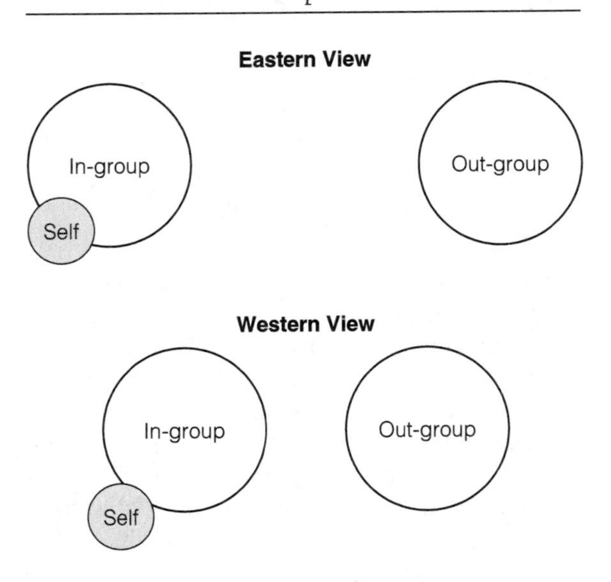

In Korean, the sentence "Could you come to dinner?" requires different words for "you," which is common in many languages, but also for "dinner," depending on whether one is inviting a student or a professor. Such practices reflect not mere politeness or self-effacement, but rather the Eastern conviction that one is a different person when interacting with different people.[1]

"Tell me about yourself" seems a straightforward enough question to ask of someone, but the kind of answer you get very much depends on what society you ask it in. North Americans will tell you about their personality traits ("friendly, hardworking"), role categories ("teacher," "I work for a company that makes microchips"), and activities ("I go camping a lot"). Americans don't condition their self-descriptions much on context (Holmberg, Markus, Herzog, & Franks, 1997). The Chinese, Japanese, and Korean self, on the other hand, very much depends on context ("I am serious at work," "I am fun-loving with my friends"). A study asking Japanese and Americans to describe themselves either in particular contexts or without specifying a particular kind of situation showed that Japanese found it very difficult to describe themselves without specifying a particular kind of situation—for example, at work, at home, or with friends (Cousins, 1989). Americans, in contrast, tended to be stumped when the investigator specified a context— "I am what I am." When describing themselves, Asians make reference to social roles ("I am Joan's friend") to a much greater extent than Americans do (Ip & Bond, 1995). Another study (Markus & Kitayama, 1991b) found that twice as many Japanese as American self-descriptions referred to other people ("I cook dinner with my sister").

When North Americans are surveyed about their attributes and preferences, they characteristically overestimate their distinctiveness. On question after question, North Americans report themselves to be more unique than they really are, whereas Asians are much less likely to make this error (Markus & Kitayama, 1991b). Westerners also prefer uniqueness in the environment and in their possessions. Social psychologists Heejung Kim and Hazel Markus asked Koreans and Americans to choose which object in a pictured array of objects they preferred. Americans chose the rarest object, whereas Koreans chose the most common object (Kim & Markus, 1999). Asked to choose a pen as a gift, Americans chose the least common color offered and East Asians the most common.

It's revealing that the word for "self-esteem" in Japanese is *serufu esutiimu*. There is no indigenous term that captures the concept of feeling good about oneself. Westerners are more concerned with enhancing themselves in their own and others' eyes than are Easterners. Americans are much more likely to make spontaneous favorable comments about themselves than are Japanese (Holmberg, Markus, Herzog, & Franks, 1997). When self-appraisal measures are administered to Americans and Canadians, it turns out that, like the children of Lake Wobegon, they are pretty much all above average. Asians rate themselves much lower on most dimensions, not only endorsing fewer positive statements but being more likely to insist that they have negative qualities (Kitayama, Markus, and Lieberman, 1995). It's not likely that the Asian ratings merely reflect a requirement for greater modesty than exists for North Americans. Asians are in fact under greater compunction to appear modest, but the difference in self-ratings exists even when participants think their answers are completely anonymous.

It isn't that Asians feel bad about their own attributes. Rather, there is no strong cultural obligation to feel that they are special or unusually talented. The goal for the self in relation to society is not so much to establish superiority or uniqueness, but to achieve harmony within a network of supportive social relationships and to play one's part in achieving collective ends. These goals require a certain amount of self-criticism—the opposite of tooting one's own horn. If I am to fit in with the group, I must root out those aspects of myself that annoy others or make their tasks more difficult. In contrast to the Asian practice of teaching children to blend harmoniously with others, some American children go to schools in which each child gets to be a "VIP" for a day.

Japanese schoolchildren are taught how to practice self-criticism, both to improve their relations with others and to become more skilled in solving problems. This stance of perfectionism through self-criticism continues throughout life. Sushi chefs and math teachers are not regarded as coming into their own until they've been at their jobs for a decade. Throughout their careers, in fact, Japanese teachers are observed and helped by their peers to become better at their jobs. Contrast this with the American practice of putting teachers' college graduates into the classroom after a few months of training and then leaving them alone to succeed or not, to the good or ill fortune of a generation of students (see Heine, Lehman, Markus, & Kitayama, 1999).

An experiment by Steven Heine and his colleagues captures the difference between the Western push to feel good about the self and the Asian drive for self-improvement (Heine, Kitayama, Lehman, Takata, Ide, & Leung, 2001). The experimenters asked Canadian and Japanese students to take a bogus "creativity" test and then gave the students "feedback" indicating that they had done very well or very badly. The experimenters then secretly observed how long the participants worked on a similar task. The Canadians worked longer on the task if they had succeeded; the Japanese worked longer if they failed. The Japanese weren't being masochistic. They simply saw an opportunity for self-improvement and took it. The study has intriguing implications for skill development in both the East and West. Westerners are likely to get very good at a "few things they start out doing well to begin with. Easterners seem more likely to become Jacks and Jills" of all trades.

Independence vs. Interdependence

Training for independence or interdependence starts quite literally in the crib. Whereas it is common for American babies to sleep in a bed separate from their parents, or even in a separate room, this is rare for East Asian babies—and, for that matter, babies pretty much everywhere else. Instead, sleeping in the same bed is far more common (Shweder, Balle-Jensen, & Goldstein, 1995). The differences are intensified in waking life. Adoring adults from several generations often surround the Chinese baby (even before the one-child policy began producing "little emperors"). The Japanese baby is almost always with its mother. The close association with mother is a condition that some Japanese apparently would like to continue indefinitely. Investigators at the University of Michigan's Institute for Social Research recently conducted a study requiring creation of a scale comparing the degree to which adult Japanese and American respondents want to be with their mothers. The task proved very difficult, because the Japanese investigators insisted that a reasonable endpoint on the scale would be "I want to be with my mother almost all the time." The Americans, of course, insisted that this would be uproariously funny to American respondents and would cause them to cease taking the interview seriously.

Independence for Western children is often encouraged in rather explicit ways. Western parents constantly require their children to do things on their own and ask them to make their own choices. "Would you like to go to bed now or would you like to have a snack first?" The Asian parent makes the decision for the child on the assumption that the parent knows best what is good for the child.

An emphasis on relationships encourages a concern with the feelings of others. When American mothers play with their toddlers, they tend to ask questions about objects and supply information about them. But when Japanese mothers play with their toddlers, their questions are more likely to concern feelings. Japanese mothers are particularly likely to use feeling-related words when their children misbehave: "The farmer feels bad if you did not eat everything your mom cooked for you." "The toy is crying because you threw it." "The wall says 'ouch'" (Azuma, 1994; Fernald & Morikawa, 1993). Concentrating attention on objects, as American parents tend to do, helps to prepare children for a world in which they are expected to act independently. Focusing on feelings and social relations, as Asian parents tend to do, helps children to anticipate the reactions of other people with whom they will have to coordinate their behavior.

The consequences of this differential focus on the emotional states of others can be seen in adulthood. There is evidence that Asians are more accurately aware of the feelings and attitudes of others than are Westerners. For example, Jeffrey Sanchez-Burks and his colleagues (2002) showed to Koreans and Americans evaluations that employers had made on rating scales. The Koreans were better able to infer from the ratings just what the employers felt about their employees than were the Americans, who tended to simply take the ratings at face value. This focus on others' emotions extends even to perceptions of the animal world. Taka Masuda and I showed underwater video scenes to Japanese and American students and asked them to report what they saw. The Japanese students reported "seeing" more feelings and motivations on the part of fish than did Americans; for example, "The red fish must be angry because its scales were hurt" (Masuda & Nisbett, 2001). Similarly, Kaiping Peng and Phoebe Ellsworth (2002) showed Chinese and American students animated pictures of fish moving in various patterns in relation to one another. For example, a group might appear to chase an individual fish or to scoot away when the individual fish approached. The investigators asked the students what both the individual fish and the groups of fish were feeling. The Chinese readily complied with the requests. The Americans had difficulty with both tasks and were literally baffled when asked to report what the group emotions might be.

The relative degree of sensitivity to others' emotions is reflected in tacit assumptions about the nature of communication. Westerners teach their children to communicate their ideas clearly and to adopt a "transmitter" orientation; that is, the speaker is responsible for uttering sentences that can be clearly understood by the hearer—and understood, in fact, more or less independently of the context. It's the speaker's fault if there is a miscommunication. Asians, in contrast, teach their children a "receiver" orientation, meaning that it is the hearer's responsibility to understand what is being said. If a child's loud singing annoys an American parent, the parent would be likely just to tell the kid to pipe down. No ambiguity there. The Asian parent would be more likely to say, "How well you sing a song." At first the child might feel pleased, but it would likely dawn on the child that something else might have been meant, and the child would try being quieter or not singing at all (Kojima, 1984).

Westerners—and perhaps especially Americans—are apt to find Asians hard to read because Asians are likely to assume that their point has been made indirectly and with finesse. Meanwhile, the Westerner is in fact very much in the dark. Asians, in turn, are apt to find Westerners—perhaps especially Americans—direct to the point of condescension or even rudeness.

There are many ways of parsing the distinction between relatively independent and relatively interdependent societies (see Doi, 1971/1981; Hampden-Turner & Trompenaars, 1993; Hofstede, 1980; Hsu, 1983; Markus & Kitayama, 1991a; Triandis, 1994, 1995), but in illustrating these it may be helpful to focus on four related but somewhat distinct dimensions:

- Insistence on freedom of individual action versus a preference for collective action
- Desire for individual distinctiveness versus a preference for blending harmoniously with the group
- A preference for egalitarianism and achieved status versus acceptance of hierarchy and ascribed status
- A belief that the rules governing proper behavior should be universal versus a preference for particularistic approaches that take into account the context and the nature of the relationships involved

These dimensions are correlated with one another, but it is possible, for example, for a given society to be quite independent in terms of some dimensions and much less so in terms of others. Social scientists have attempted to measure each of these dimensions, and other associated ones, in a variety of ways, including value surveys, studies of archived material, and experiments.

To examine the value of individual distinction versus harmonious relations with the group, Hampden-Turner and Trompenaars (1993) asked managers to indicate which of the following types of job they preferred: (a) jobs in which personal initiatives are encouraged and individual initiatives are achieved, or (b) jobs in which no one is singled out for personal honor but in which everyone works together.

More than 90 percent of American, Canadian, Australian, British, Dutch, and Swedish respondents endorsed the first choice—the individual freedom alternative—compared with fewer than 50 percent of Japanese and Singaporeans. Preferences of the Germans, Italians, Belgians, and French were intermediate.

The United States is sometimes described as a place where, if you claim to amount to much, you should be able to show that you change your area code every five years or so. (This was before the phone company started changing people's area codes without waiting for them to move.) In some other countries, the relationship with the corporation where one is employed and the connection with one's colleagues there are more highly valued than in the United States, and are presumed to be more or less permanent. To assess this difference among cultures, Hampden-Turner and Trompenaars asked their participants to choose between the following expectations: If I apply for a job in a company, (a) I will almost certainly work there for the rest of my life, or (b) I am almost sure the relationship will have a limited duration.

More than 90 percent of Americans, Canadians, Australians, British, and Dutch thought a limited job duration was likely. This was true for only about 40 percent of Japanese (though it would doubtless be substantially higher today after "downsizing" has come even to Japan). The French, Germans, Italians, and Belgians were again intermediate, though closer to the other Europeans than to the Asians.

To examine the relative value placed on achieved versus ascribed status, Hampden-Turner and Trompenaars asked their participants whether or not they shared the following view: Becoming successful and respected is a matter of hard work. It is important for a manager to be older than his subordinates. Older people should be more respected than younger people.

More than 60 percent of American, Canadian, Australian, Swedish, and British respondents rejected the idea of status being based in any way on age. About 60 percent of Japanese, Korean, and Singapore respondents accepted hierarchy based in part on age. French, Italians, Germans, and Belgians were again intermediate, though closer to the other Europeans than to the Asians.

Needless to say, there is great potential for conflict when people from cultures having different orientations must deal with one another. This is particularly true when people who value universal rules deal with people who think each particular situation should be examined on its merits and that different rules might be appropriate for different people. Westerners prefer to live by abstract principles and like to believe these principles are applicable to everyone. To set aside universal rules in order to accommodate particular cases seems immoral to the Westerner. To insist on the same rules for every case can seem at best obtuse and rigid, and at worst cruel, to the Easterner. Many of Hampden-Turner and Trompenaars's questions reveal what a marked difference exists among cultures in their preference for universally applicable rules versus special consideration of cases based on their distinctive aspects. One of their questions deals with how to handle the case of an employee whose work for a company, though excellent for 15 years, has been unsatisfactory for a year. If there is no reason to expect that performance will improve, (a) should the employee be dismissed on the grounds that job performance should remain the grounds for dismissal, regardless of the age of the person and his previous record; or (b) is it wrong to disregard the 15 years the employee has been working for the company, and does one have to take into account the company's responsibility for his life?

More than 75 percent of Americans and Canadians felt the employee should be let go. About 20 percent of Koreans and Singaporeans agreed with that view. About 30 percent of Japanese, French, Italians, and Germans agreed, and about 40 percent of British, Australians, Dutch, and Belgians agreed. (Atypically, on this question, the British and the Australians were closer to the continental Europeans than to the North Americans.)

As these results show, Westerners' commitment to universally applied rules influences their understanding of the nature of agreements between individuals and between corporations. By extension, in the Western view, once a contract has been agreed to, it is binding regardless of circumstances that might make the arrangement much less attractive to one of the parties than it was initially. But to people from interdependent, high-context cultures, changing circumstances dictate alterations in the agreement.

An important business implication of the differences between independent and interdependent societies is that advertising needs to be modified for particular cultural audiences. Marketing experts Sang-pil Han and Sharon Shavitt (1994) analyzed American and Korean advertisements in popular news magazines and women's magazines. They found that American advertisements emphasize individual benefits and preferences ("Make your way through the crowd"; "Alive with pleasure"), whereas Korean advertisements are more likely to emphasize collective ones ("We have a way of bringing people closer together"; "Ringing out the news of business friendships that really work"). When Han and Shavitt performed experiments, showing people different kinds of advertisements, they found that the individualist advertisements were more effective with Americans and the collectivist ones with Koreans.

Independence versus interdependence is of course not an either/or matter. Every society—and every individual—is a blend of both. It turns out that it is remarkably easy to bring one or another orientation to the fore. Psychologists Wendi Gardner, Shira Gabriel, and Angela Lee (1999) "primed" American college students to think either independently or interdependently. They did this in two different ways. In one experiment, participants were asked to read a story about a general who had to choose a warrior to send to the king. In an "independent" version, the king had to choose the best individual for the job. In an "interdependent" version, the general wanted to make a choice that would benefit his family (Trafimow, Triandis, & Goto, 1991). In another priming method, participants were asked to search for words in a paragraph describing a trip to a city. The words were either independent in nature (e.g., "I," "mine") or independent (e.g., "we," "ours").

After reading the story or searching for words in the paragraph, participants were asked to fill out a value survey that assessed the importance they placed on individualist values (such as freedom and living a varied life) and collectivist values (such as belongingness and respect for elders). They also read a story in which "Lisa" refused to give her friend "Amy" directions to an art store because she was engrossed in reading a book; they were then asked whether Lisa's behavior was inappropriately selfish. Students who had been exposed to an independence prime rated individualist values higher and collectivist values lower than did students exposed to an interdependence prime. The independence-primed participants were also more forgiving of the book-engrossed Lisa. Gardner and her colleagues repeated their study adding Hong Kong students to their American sample and also added an unprimed control condition. American students rated individualist values higher than collectivist values—unless they had been exposed to an interdependence prime. Hong Kong students rated collectivist values higher than individualist values—unless they had been exposed to an independence prime.

Of course, Easterners are constantly being "primed" with interdependence cues and Westerners with independence cues. This raises the possibility that even if their upbringing had not made them inclined in one direction or another, the cues that surround them should make people living in interdependent societies behave in generally interdependent ways and those living in independent societies behave in generally independent ways. In fact, this is a common report of people who live in the "other" culture for a while. My favorite example concerns a young Canadian psychologist who lived for several years in Japan. He then applied for jobs at North American universities. His adviser was horrified to discover that his letter began with apologies about his unworthiness for the jobs in question. Other evidence shows that self-esteem is highly malleable (Heine & Lehman, 1997). Japanese who live in the West for a while show a notable increase in self-esteem, probably because the situations they encounter are in general more esteem-enhancing than those typical in Japan (Kitayama, Markus, Matsumoto, & Norasakkunit, 1997). The social psychological characteristics of people raised in very different cultures are far from completely immutable.

Variants of Viewpoint

The work of Hampden-Turner and Trompenarrs makes clear that the West is no monolith concerning issues of independence versus interdependence. There are also substantial regularities to the differences found in Western countries. In general, the Mediterranean countries plus Belgium and Germany are intermediate between the East Asian countries, on the one hand, and the countries most heavily influenced by Protestant, Anglo-Saxon culture, on the other. There is more regularity even than that. Someone has said, "The Idea moves west," meaning that the values of individuality, freedom, rationality, and universalism became progressively more dominant and articulated as civilization moved westward from its origins in the Fertile Crescent. The Babylonians codified and universalized the law. The Israelites emphasized individual distinctiveness. The Greeks valued individuality even more and added a commitment to personal freedom, the spirit of debate, and formal logic. The Romans brought a gift for rational organization and something resembling the Chinese genius for technological achievement, and—after a trough lasting almost a millennium—their successors, the Italians, rediscovered these values and built on the accomplishments of the Greek and Roman eras. The Protestant Reformation, beginning in Germany and Switzerland and largely bypassing France and Belgium, added individual responsibility and a definition of work as a sacred activity. The Reformation also brought a weakened commitment to the family and other in-groups coupled with a greater willingness to trust out-groups and have dealings with their members. These values were all intensified in the Calvinist subcultures of Britain, including the Puritans and Presbyterians, whose egalitarian ideology laid the groundwork for the government of the United States. (Thomas Jefferson was merely paraphrasing the Puritan sympathizer John Locke when he wrote, "We hold these truths to be self-evident, that all men are created equal . . . with certain inalienable rights, that among these are life, liberty . . .")

There are also major differences among Eastern cultures in all sorts of important social behavior and values, some of which are related to independence versus interdependence.

I was in China in 1982 at the tail end of the Cultural Revolution. The country seemed extremely exotic—in both its traditional aspects and its Communist-imposed aspects. (This was well before a Starbucks was installed in the Forbidden City!) The first Western play to be performed in Beijing since the revolution was mounted while I was there. It was Arthur Miller's *Death of a Salesman.* The choice seemed very strange. I regarded the play as being not merely highly Western in character but distinctly American. Its central figure is a salesman, "a man way out there in the blue riding on a smile and a shoeshine." To my astonishment, the play was a tremendous success. But Arthur Miller, who had come to China to collaborate on production of the play, provided a satisfactory reason for its reception. "The play is about family," he said, "and the Chinese invented family." He might have added that the play is also about *face,* or the need to have the respect of the community, and the Chinese also invented face.

The Japanese have perhaps as much concern with face as do the Chinese, but probably less involvement with the immediate family and more commitment to the corporation. There are other marked differences between the Japanese and Chinese. The sociologist Robert Bellah, the philosopher Hajime Nakamura, the psychologist Dora Dien, and the social philosopher Lin Yutang, among many others, have detailed some of these differences (Bellah, 1957/1985; Dien, 1997, 1999; Lin, 1936; Nakamura, 1964/1985). Though social constraints are in general greater on both Chinese and Japanese than on Westerners, the constraints come primarily from authorities in the case of the Chinese and chiefly from peers in the case of the Japanese. Control in Chinese classrooms, for example, is achieved by the teacher, but by classmates in Japan. Dora Dien has written that the "Chinese emphasize particular dyadic [two-person] relationships while retaining their individuality, whereas the Japanese tend to submerge themselves in the group" (Dien, 1999, p. 377). Though both Chinese and Japanese are required to conform to move smoothly through their daily lives, the Chinese are said to chafe under the requirements and the Japanese actually to enjoy them. The Japanese are held to share with the Germans and the Dutch a need for order in all spheres of their lives; the Chinese share with Mediterraneans a more relaxed approach to life.

It is sometimes argued that one particular type of social relationship is unique to the Japanese. This is *amae,* a concept discussed at length by the Japanese psychoanalyst Takeo Doi (1971/1981, 1974). *Amae* describes a relationship in which an inferior, a child or employee, for example, is allowed to engage in inappropriate behavior—to ask for an expensive toy or to request a promotion at a time not justified by company policy—as an expression of confidence that the relationship is sufficiently close that the superior will be indulgent. *Amae* facilitates the relationship, enhancing trust between the two parties and cementing bonds, though these results come at some cost to the autonomy of the inferior.

The very real differences among Eastern cultures and among Western cultures, however, shouldn't blind us to the fact that the East and West are in general quite different from each other with respect to a great many centrally important values and social-psychological attributes.

AWASE AND *ERABI*: STYLES OF CONFLICT AND NEGOTIATION

Debate is almost as uncommon in modern Asia as in ancient China. In fact, the whole rhetoric of argumentation that is second nature to Westerners is largely absent in Asia. North Americans begin to express opinions and justify them as early as the show-and-tell sessions of nursery school ("This is my robot; he's fun to play with because . . ."). In contrast, there is not much argumentation or trafficking in opinions in Asian life. A Japanese friend has told me that the concept of a "lively discussion" does not exist in Japan—because of the risk to group harmony. It is this fact that likely undermined an attempt he once made to have an American-style dinner party in Japan, inviting only Japanese guests who expressed a fondness for the institution—from the martinis through the steak to the apple pie. The effort fell flat for want of opinions and people willing to defend them.

The absence of a tradition of debate has particularly dramatic implications for the conduct of political life. Very recently, South Korea installed its first democratic government. Prior to that, it had been illegal to discuss North Korea. Westerners find this hard to comprehend, inasmuch as South Korea has performed one of the world's most impressive economic miracles of the past 40 years and North Korea is a failed state in every respect. But because of the absence of a tradition of debate, Koreans have no faith that correct ideas will win in the marketplace of ideas, and previous governments "protected" their citizens by preventing discussion of Communist ideas and North Korean practices.

The tradition of debate goes hand in hand with a certain style of rhetoric in the law and in science. The rhetoric of scientific papers consists of an overview of the ideas to be considered, a description of the relevant basic theories, a specific hypothesis, a statement of the methods and justification of them, a presentation of the evidence produced by the methods, an argument as to why the evidence supports the hypothesis, a refutation of possible counterarguments, a reference back to the basic theory, and a comment on the larger territory of which the article is a part. For Americans, this rhetoric is constructed bit by bit from nursery school through college. By the time they are graduate students, it is second nature. But for the most part, the rhetoric is new to the Asian student, and learning it can be a slow and painful process. It is not uncommon for American science professors to be impressed by their hardworking, highly selected Asian students and then to be disappointed by their first major paper—not because of their incomplete command of English, but because of their lack of mastery of the rhetoric common in the professor's field. In my experience, it is also not uncommon for professors to fail to recognize that it is the lack of the Western rhetoric style they are objecting to, rather than some deeper lack of comprehension of the enterprise they're engaged in.

The combative, rhetorical form is also absent from Asian law. In Asia the law does not consist, as it does in the West for the most part, of a contest between opponents. More typically, the disputants take their case to a middleman whose goal is not fairness but animosity reduction—by seeking a Middle Way through the claims of the opponents (Leung, 1987). There is no attempt to derive a resolution to a legal conflict from a universal principle. On the contrary, Asians are likely to consider justice in the abstract, by-the-book Western sense to be rigid and unfeeling.

Negotiation also has a different character in the high-context societies of the East than in the low-context societies of the West (see Cohen, 1997). Political scientist Mushakoji Kinhide characterizes the Western *erabi* (active, agentic) style as being grounded in the belief that "man can freely manipulate his environment for his own purposes. This view implies a behavioral sequence whereby a person sets his objective, develops a plan designed to reach that objective, and then acts to change the environment in accordance with that plan" (Kinhide, 1976, pp. 45–46, cited in Cohen, 1997). To a person having such a style, there's not much point in concentrating on relationships. It's the results that count. Proposals and decisions tend to be of the either/or variety because the Westerner knows what he wants and has a clear idea what it is appropriate to give and to take in order to have an acceptable deal. Negotiations should be short and to the point, so as not to waste time reaching the goal.

The Japanese *awase* (harmonious, fitting-in) style, "rejects the idea that man can manipulate the environment and assumes instead that he adjusts himself to it" (Kinhide, 1976, p. 40, cited in Cohen, 1997). Negotiations are not thought of as "ballistic," one-shot efforts never to be revisited, and relationships are presumed to be long-term. Either/or choices are avoided. There is a belief that "short-term wisdom may be long-term folly" (Cohen, 1997, p. 37). A Japanese negotiator may yield more in negotiations for a first deal than a similarly placed Westerner might, expecting that this will lay the groundwork for future trust and cooperation. Issues are presumed to be complex, subjective, and intertwined, unlike the simplicity, objectivity, and "fragmentability" that the American with the *erabi* style assumes.

So, there are very dramatic social-psychological differences between East Asians as a group and people of European culture as a group. East Asians live in an interdependent world in which the self is part of a larger whole; Westerners live in a world in which the self is a unitary free agent. Easterners value success and achievement in good part because they reflect well on the groups they belong to; Westerners value these things because they are badges of personal merit. Easterners value fitting in and engage in self-criticism to make sure that they do so; Westerners value individuality and strive to make themselves look good. Easterners are highly attuned to the feelings of others and strive for interpersonal harmony; Westerners are more concerned with knowing themselves and are prepared to sacrifice harmony for fairness. Easterners are accepting of hierarchy and group control; Westerners are more likely to prefer equality and scope for personal action. Asians avoid controversy and debate; Westerners have faith in the rhetoric of argumentation in arenas from the law to politics to science.

None of these generalizations applies to all members of their respective groups, of course. Every society has individuals who more nearly resemble those of other, quite different societies than they do those of their own society; and every individual within a given society moves quite a bit between the independent and interdependent poles over the course of a lifetime—over the course of a day, in fact. But the variations between and within societies, as well as within individuals, should not blind us to the fact that there are very real differences, substantial on the average, between East Asians and people of European culture.

As nearly as we can tell, these social differences are much the same as the differences that characterized the ancient Chinese and Greeks. And if it was the social circumstances that produced the cognitive differences between ancient Chinese and Greeks, then we might expect to find cognitive differences between modern East Asians and Westerners that map onto the differences between the ancient Chinese and Greeks.[2]

Notes

1. The generic "I" is commonly used in China today, but this is a recent development following the Sun Yat-sen revolution in the early 20th century.
2. This is not to imply that marked differences have been present continuously. For example, no one would say that the 11th-century European peasant was much of an individualist, and both China and Japan have passed through periods in which individualism was highly valued, at least for artists and intellectuals.

References

Azuma, H. (1994). *Education and socialization in Japan*. Tokyo: University of Tokyo Press.

Bellah, R. (1985). *Tokagawa religion: The cultural roots of modern Japan*. New York: Free Press. (Original work published 1957)

Cohen, R. (1997). *Negotiating across cultures: International communication in an interdependent world.* Washington, DC: United States Institute of Peace Press.

Cousins, S. D. (1989). Culture and self-perception in Japan and the United States. *Journal of Personality and Social Psychology, 56,* 124–131.

Dien, D. S.-f. (1997). *Confucianism and cultural psychology: Comparing the Chinese and the Japanese.* Hayward: California State University.

Dien, D. S.-f. (1999). Chinese authority-directed orientation and Japanese peer-group orientation: Questioning the notion of collectivism. *Review of General Psychology, 3,* 372–385.

Doi, L. T. (1974). *Amae*: A key concept for understanding Japanese personality structure. In R. J. Smith & R. K. Beardsley (Eds.), *Japanese culture: Its development and characteristics*. Chicago: Aldine.

Doi, L. T. (1981). *The anatomy of dependence* (2nd ed.). Tokyo: Kodansha. (Original work published 1971)

Fernald, A., & Morikawa, H. (1993). Common themes and cultural variations in Japanese and American mothers' speech to infants. *Child Development, 64,* 637–656.

Fiske, A. P., Kitayama, S., Markus, H. R., & Nisbett, R. E. (1998). The cultural matrix of social psychology. In D. T. Gilbert, S. T. Fiske, & G. Lindzey (Eds.), *Handbook of social psychology* (4th ed., pp. 915–981). Boston: McGraw-Hill.

Gardner, W. L., Gabriel, S., & Lee, A. Y. (1999). "I" value freedom, but "we" value relationships: Self-construal priming mirrors cultural differences in judgment. *Psychological Science, 10,* 321–326.

Hall, E. T. (1976). *Beyond culture.* New York: Anchor Books.

Hampden-Turner, C., & Trompenaars, A. (1993). *The seven cultures of capitalism: Value systems for creating wealth in the United States, Japan, Germany, France, Britain, Sweden, and the Netherlands.* New York: Doubleday.

Han, S., & Shavitt, S. (1994). Persuasion and culture: Advertising appeals in individualistic and collective societies. *Journal of Experimental Social Psychology, 30,* 326–350.

Heine, S. J., Kitayama, S., Lehman, D. R., Takata, T., Ide, E., Leung, C., & Matsumoto, H. (2001). Divergent consequences of success and failure in Japan and North America: An investigation of self-improving motivation. *Journal of Personality and Social Psychology, 81,* 599–615.

Heine, S. J., & Lehman, D. R. (1997). *Acculturation and self-esteem change: Evidence for a Western cultural foundation in the construct of self-esteem.* Paper presented at the second meeting of the Asian Association of Social Psychology, Kyoto, Japan.

Heine, S. J., Lehman, D. R., Markus, H. R., & Kitayama, S. (1999). Is there a universal need for positive self-regard? *Psychological Review, 106,* 766–794.

Hofstede, G. (1980). *Culture's consequences.* Beverly Hills, CA: Sage.

Holmberg, D., Markus, H., Herzog, A. R., & Franks, M. (1997). *Self-making in American adults: Content, structure and function.* Unpublished manuscript, University of Michigan, Ann Arbor.

Hsu, F. L. K. (1983). The self in cross-cultural perspective. In A. J. Marsella, B. D. Vos, & F. L. K. Hsu (Eds.), *Culture and self* (pp. 24–55). London: Tavistock.

Ip, G. W. M., & Bond, M. H. (1995). Culture, values, and the spontaneous self-concept. *Asian Journal of Psychology, 1,* 29–35.

Iyengar, S. S., Lepper, M. R., & Ross, L. (1999). Independence from whom? Interdependence from whom? Cultural perspectives on ingroups versus outgroups. In D. A. Prentice & D. T. Miller (Eds.), *Cultural divides: Understanding and overcoming group conflict.* New York: Russell Sage Foundation.

Kim, H., & Markus, H. R. (1999). Deviance or uniqueness, harmony or conformity? A cultural analysis. *Journal of Personality and Social Psychology, 77,* 785–800.

King, A. Y.-c. (1991). Kuan-his and network building: A sociological interpretation. *Daedalus, 120,* 60–84.

Kinhide, M. (1976). The cultural premises of Japanese diplomacy. In J. C. f. I. Exchange (Ed.), *The silent power: Japan's identity and world role.* Tokyo: Simul Press.

Kitayama, S., Markus, H. R., & Lieberman, C. (1995). The collective construction of self-esteem: Implications for culture, self, and emotion. In J. Russell, J. Fernandez-Dols, T. Manstead, & J. Wellenkamp (Eds.), *Everyday conceptions of emotion: An introduction to the psychology, anthropology, and linguistics of emotion*. Dordrecht: Kluwer.

Kitayama, S., Markus, H. R., Matsumoto, H., & Norasakkunit, V. (1997). Individual and collective processes in the construction of the self: Self-enhancement in the United States and self-depreciation in Japan. *Journal of Personality and Social Psychology, 72,* 1245–1267.

Kojima, H. (1984). A significant stride toward the comparative study of control. *American Psychologist, 39,* 972–973.

Leung, K. (1987). Some determinants of reactions to procedural models for conflict resolution: A cross-national study. *Journal of Personality and Social Psychology, 53,* 898–908.

Lin, Y. (1936). *My country and my people*. London: Heinemann.

Markus, H., & Kitayama, S. (1991a). Cultural variation in the self-concept. In J. Strauss & G. R. Goethals (Eds.), *The self: Interdisciplinary approaches*. New York: Springer-Verlag.

Markus., H., & Kitayama, S. (1991b). Culture and the self: Implications for cognition, emotion, and motivation. *Psychological Review, 98,* 224–253.

Masuda, T., & Nisbett, R. E. (2001). Attending holistically vs. analytically: Comparing the context sensitivity of Japanese and Americans. *Journal of Personality and Social Psychology, 81,* 922–934.

Munro, D. J. (1985). *The concept of man in early China*. Stanford, CA: Stanford University Press.

Nakammura, H. (1985). *Ways of thinking of Eastern peoples*. Honolulu: University of Hawaii Press. (Original work published 1964)

Sanchez-Burks, J., Lee, F., Choi, I., Nisbett, R. E., Zhao, S., & Koo, J. (2002). *Conversing across cultural ideologies: East–West communication styles in work and non-work contexts*. Unpublished manuscript, University of Southern California.

Shiu, H. (1919). *Chung-kuo che-hsueh shi ta-kang* [An outline of the history of Chinese philosophy]. Shanghai: Commercial Press.

Shweder, R., Balle-Jensen, L., & Goldstein, W. (1995). Who sleeps by whom revisited: A method for extracting the moral goods implicit in praxis. In P. J. Miller, J. J. Goodnow, & F. Kessell (Eds.), *Cultural practices as contexts for development*. San Francisco: Jossey-Bass.

Trafimow, D., Triandis, H. C., & Goto, S. G. (1991). Some tests of the distinction between the private self and the collective self. *Journal of Personality and Social Psychology, 60,* 649–655.

Triandis, H. C. (1994). *Culture and social behavior*. New York: McGraw-Hill.

Triandis, H. C. (1995). *Individualism and collectivism*. Boulder, CO: Westview Press.

Concepts and Questions

1. Compare and contrast the beliefs and values of independent and interdependent persons.
2. What are some of the child-rearing dynamics that lead to the development of the interdependent person? The independent person?
3. Why is harmony a chief goal among interdependent people?
4. How do schools contribute to the development of an independent person? An interdependent person?
5. How do independent and interdependent people differ in their degree of sensitivity to others' emotional states?
6. How might American and Asian managers describe the kind of jobs they prefer?
7. How is product advertising affected when the target audience is composed of independent people? Of interdependent people?
8. Describe the *awase* and *erabi* forms or styles of conflict and negotiation.
9. What kinds of problems might arise during a contract negotiation if one team of negotiators subscribed to an *awase* style of negotiation and the other team subscribed to an *erabi* style?
10. How do time frames affect negotiations between Asians and Westerners?

The *Wei* (Positioning)–*Ming* (Naming)–*Lianmian* (Face) Continuum in Contemporary Chinese Culture

WENSHAN JIA

INTRODUCTION

In an attempt to describe communication dynamics in contemporary Chinese culture, I have identified a cluster of native terms that constitute a lens for gaining insights. These terms are *wei, ming,* and *lianmian*. I define *wei* as a position or "a positioning in the primary ontocosmology which should underlie any other constructed or developed system, for it is most fundamental and has everything to do with the very existence of a thing and its worth. In this sense *wei* can be said to define the worth and 'raison d'être' of anything, particularly those of the human person" (Cheng, 1996, p. 149). I define *ming* as a rhetorical instrument to bring about the exercise of *wei* and to translate *wei* into *lianmian*. I define *lianmian* as a practical social-moral construct of the Confucianist personhood which stands for the very worth defined by *wei*. The more worth is attached to a thing, particularly a person, the more power, influence, access to truth and the right to rule, which includes the rights to think, speak, reward, and punish, and access to wealth and privilege the person can have. In other words, *lianmian* is generated by *wei* via *ming*. While *wei* is the hub, *lianmian* functions as a set of spokes with *ming* as the spin. As a result, the culture is structured hierarchically, with different members of the society voluntarily or involuntarily occupying different positions, and the culture is maintained as a culture of authoritative-relational communication. In this paper, I argue that *wei, ming,* and *lianmian* conjointly construct and maintain contemporary Chinese culture as a culture of hierarchical-relational communication despite the fact that Western-style economic reform and social change preferring the equal-rational communication style have taken place in the past few decades.

In the following, I will first conduct a critical review of the relevant scholarly literature on *wei, ming* and *lianmian*. Then I will expound the *wei–ming–lianmian* interpretive framework on the basis of the review and with the application of examples.

REVIEW OF SCHOLARLY LITERATURE

Many prominent studies on Chinese face practices (Ho, 1976; Smith, 1894; Hwang, 1987; Chen, 1990; Ting-Toomey, 2003; Kipnis, 1995), seem to have ignored or downplayed the hierarchical nature of *lianmian* dynamics in Chinese culture thanks to some modern Western-style analytical lenses of equality. The theories used, such as the social exchange theory (Hwang), the Coordinated Management of Meaning (Chen), and face negotiation (Ting-Toomey), all tend to share an underlying assumption of modern Western culture that human beings are equal and individualistic. Such theories also do not take morality into consideration. These theories are primarily descriptive, with the suggestion that humans are inherently free and have choices. These ideas run counter to the Chinese Confucian, normative view of humans as beings with inherent moral responsibility to cultivate oneself into a gentle person (*junzi*) or a sage (*shengren*) who is morally superior only because she or he takes care of the issues of the community as a priority. The ideas are also opposite to the deeply held assumption of the Chinese that humans are unavoidably placed in different positions of moral and social hierarchies—that humans are as unequal as human fingers are not of equal length, as a Chinese folk saying goes.

The *Wei–Ming–Lianmian* Continuum

Wei. *Wei* is the starting point of the continuum. *Wei* is synonymous with *diwei, jibie* (grade or level

 Wenshan Jia teaches at Chapman University in Orange, California.

differentiation, status), and in extension, *dengji* (class or caste). *Wei* is such a pervasive construct in Chinese culture that Chung-Ying Cheng, a scholar of Chinese philosophy, has systematically articulated a Chinese philosophical view of both *lianmian* (1986) and *wei* (1996). Although the author does not cross-reference the two articles, his article on *wei* has extended and deepened my understanding of the *wei–ming–lianmian* (positioning–naming–moral/social face) continuum (1986, p. 342).

Reading the two articles in close relation to each other, one is likely to conclude that *wei,* as the process of standing up of a human being (*li*) or establishing himself or herself in the society by accomplishing a virtue (Cheng, 1996, p. 151), is the most fundamental process of accruing *lianmian* resources. *Wei* is omnipresent, because every "situation in which a thing finds itself is both a position and a stage which constitutes and confines and defines the thing" (p. 157). *Wei,* a central theme in *Zhouyi,* an ancient Chinese classic, reflects the Chinese view of the world as one made up of positions and life as a constant process of finding one's position and repositioning oneself in the world. This view of *wei* also translates the love of *wei* into a fundamental value of Chinese culture. Sense of *wei,* or status consciousness, has understandably become a prominent part of the Chinese cultural psyche. Contrary to the modern Western view of humans largely as free and equal individuals, the concept of *wei* suggests that the worth, dignity, power, influence, and access to resources of each and every human being should vary according to varying *wei*s or positions different human beings occupy. Because of this value, Chinese culture has acquired a fundamental belief that humans are of *wei,* by *wei,* and for *wei.*

The concept of *wei* has two implications. First, it implies that humans always live in a hierarchy of social and moral positions and thus are "naturally" unequal. The other implication is that *wei* is a dynamic process of transformation as well as a static entity. A person can "overcome the limitations of one's given position" (Cheng, 1996, p. 157) and transform oneself into a position higher than the current one by achieving more virtues or degenerate oneself down into a lower position than the current one by discarding the current virtues.

Confucianism is significantly built upon the onto-cosmology of *wei.* In Confucianism, both the hierarchy of moral positions and the hierarchy of social positions are established. In the moral hierarchy, there are three positions: *shengren* (sagehood) as the highest moral ideal, *junzi* (gentle personhood) as the typical moral ideal, and the mean personhood (*xiaoren*) as a status to be recycled. The values for self-cultivation are *ren* (benevolence or cohumanity), *yi* (loyalty), *li* (etiquette or ritual), *zhi* (wisdom), *xin* (trust), and *ti* (piety). A folk discourse of social hierarchy also operates in daily interaction. One hears the Chinese use idiomatic phrases such as *"zuo ren shang ren"* ("to become a person above all other persons"), *"chu ren tou di"* ("to stand out among people"), *"yi jing huan xiang"* ("to go back to one's hometown from rags to riches") and *"zhuo wan ren zhi shang yi ren zhi xia"* ("to become the person only next to the most important one and above all the rest"). All these are examples of the everyday Chinese discourse of *wei,* which stresses the value of *wei* in Chinese societies.

Examples of love of *wei* abound in contemporary scenes of China. One often reads stories of bribery and corruption in Chinese official or semi-official newspapers—that one would bribe officials higher up with about 10,000–20,000 Chinese dollars to become a vice-mayor of a rural township, 30,000–50,000 Chinese dollars for the position of mayor of a rural township, 100,000–200,000 Chinese dollars for the position of vice-county head, and so on. There is basically a hidden market price for each position; *wei* can be bought. For the bribers, this is a wise investment, for the positions they get with their bribes would garner them much greater symbolic and material resources, such as freedom, privilege, power, and loyalty from people below them, than the investment. It is a *ming-li shuangshou* (a double harvest in both reputation/status and privileges) because they have become *"ren shang ren"* (people above other people). However, by having done so, the bribers have denigrated themselves into a lower moral status, which constitutes a loss of *lian,* especially when such bribery gets reported and penalized. The amounts of money would be several years' salary for each position bought. But their love of position is more than their love of money because the positions they bought would make them more respected than the money they had. In other words, their status made them become people above other people (*ren shang ren*), but the money alone would not have been able to garner so much respect and power for them. These bribers are truly people of *wei*, by *wei,* and for *wei.*

Ming. *Ming* is between *wei* and *lianmian,* connecting the two. *Ming* is a Chinese word for language/rhetoric/communication. One can hardly tell one *wei* from another *wei* without each *wei* being labeled differently. Proper naming is expected to bring about the very birth of *wei* or the accurate representation of *wei*. It also goes hand in hand with *wei,* or positioning. Without naming, *wei* could not display its existence. Naming can be said to be the form of *wei*—the content or substance behind the name. Sometimes, naming is *wei* itself, or at least appearing so. Most important of all, proper naming should be discriminating and differentiating. The hierarchy of *wei* depends on an appropriate hierarchy of names. This means that each *wei* should have a distinct name. The varying amounts of humanity attached to varying *wei*s should be denoted clearly and accurately by each different naming and proper communication. For example, in the market-driven urban China nowadays, when asking for directions on the street, one is expected to call an adult male stranger "*laoban*" (boss) or "*laozong*" (CEO) to get genuine help, for these are the most respectful and most face-enhancing titles. The use of "*dashu*" (great uncle) or "*daye*" (great grandpa) would have less impact because they are regarded as old-fashioned; and the use of "*xianshen*" (literally meaning "the person who is born before me," or sir) might induce a cold shoulder or cold face from the adult male stranger because he might view it as too foreign. Indeed, as the above example shows, *ming* is so important that it can not only represent *wei* but also create a *wei* out of virtually nothing.

Lianmian. *Lianmian* functions at the very end of the continuum. This means that *lianmian* is the closest to the lifeworld, or the central, intangible, yet palpable, dynamics of the lifeworld. *Lianmian* work refers to the social display or revelation (both active and passive) and loaning (both active and passive) of one's *wei* and its import (social capital such as resources, influence, power, privileges, and care) to one's counterpart to outshine or empower him or her in social interaction. Such smooth interaction is taken for granted on condition that the interactants share experience and wisdom of the Confucian ethics and norms for proper human relations in a social world of hierarchy. *Lianmian* was and still is one of the central indigenous communication constructs of Chinese culture. As early as 1894, Arthur Smith insightfully pointed out: "Once rightly apprehended, 'face' will be found in itself a key to the combination lock of many of the most important characteristics of the Chinese" (p. 17). To Chung-Ying Cheng, *lianmian* plays as important a function in Chinese societies as law does in modern Western societies (1986, p. 340). To Xuewei Zai, *lianmian* plays an even more comprehensive role in Chinese societies. He concludes after a field study that *lianmian* "has been always exercising a tremendous influence on and even playing a decisive role in the politics, economy, education, physical training, military arts and all aspects of Chinese everyday life" (1995, p. 1997).

Many studies (Chang & Holt, 1994; Cheng, 1986; Scollon & Scollon, 1994; Ting-Toomey, 1988) emphasize the relational nature of *lianmian* in critique of Goffman's concept of face (1967) as instrumental and Brown and Levinson's facework (1987) as rationalist. However, the literature masks or ignores the hierarchical nature of the relational dimension of *lianmian*. In *lianmian* practice, hierarchy and relationality are almost inseparable. A person of a higher *wei* is supposed to provide a person of a lower *wei* sufficient safety and security. To reciprocate, the latter is expected to give and save as much face as possible to/for the former by being loyal and obedient. The relationship between the two can be described as mutually trustworthy and relational. However, this relationality occurs in the context of inequality and hierarchy from a modern Western point of view. The person of a lower *wei* may never be able to move to a higher *wei* so long as s/he stays in the hierarchical-relational loop. In reality, this relationality could often be used as a rhetorical device by persons of higher *wei*s to mask, legitimize, or humanize inequality and hierarchy, from a typical American view. Inequality and hierarchy embedded in *lianmian* have been unmasked by quite a few self-reflective and self-critical Chinese scholars: Yutang Lin (1935) argues that *lianmian* could be undemocratic because it renders all the rules, regulations, and laws ineffective. Zhongtian Lu (1996) points out that *lianmian,* together with *renqing,* constitutes a form of political governance laced in kindness which gives the people of higher *wei*s extreme flexibility to deal with subordinates and gives subordinates a sense of extreme uncertainty and insecurity. More recently, Jia (2001) finds that *lianmian,* "this very conflict-preventive and harmony-building mechanism" (p. 50), simultaneously "masks and reinforces the social hierarchy and in-groupness, which may breed inequality, injustice, and close-mindedness"

(p. 50), maintain the status quo, and block innovation and social mobility because *wei* and *ming*-based *lianmian,* if held sacredly, discourage change and challenge open competition. However, the opposite could be said about pure reason or intellect emphasized in the Western modernity discourse, which strives for equality and justice at the cost of failure to meet human needs for mutual trust, mutual dependability, and mutual relationship. How both could be combined creatively without hierarchy is a challenging practical question, as well as a challenging intellectual question, in East–West intercultural communication that remains to be answered.

Decoupling of *Lian* and *Mian*

The hierarchy of moral positions helps construct the concept of *lian,* whereas the hierarchy of social positions helps construct the concept of *mian*. Together, they cultivate a strong status or *wei* consciousness in the Chinese mind. *Lian,* to the Chinese, is the very stuff that secures minimum humanity. A popular Chinese saying testifies to the significance of *lian* in Chinese life: A person lives by his or her *lian* just as a tree lives by its bark (*Ren huo lian; shu huo pi*). The interchangeable use of "loss of *lian*" (*dioulian*) and "loss of personhood" (*diouren*), or loss of one's right to be a human being (as defined by the Chinese, of course), is often heard in daily interactions in a typical Chinese community. This means that to the Chinese, one's basic loyalty to the Confucian moral principles, such as *ren, yi, li, zhi, xin,* and *xiao,* would maintain his or her basic humanity, and loss of such loyalty would mean that this person has degenerated himself or herself into a brute or beast. *Mian* is social recognition through properly named titles or *weis,* not necessarily based on achievements. Sometimes, one strives for *mian* so much that the person becomes heartless, secretly drops *lian,* or sheds the human mask. Though *lian* and *mian* go hand in hand in name, in reality, relentless striving for *mian* is often found to have alienated *lian*. In the Chinese Communist era between 1949 and 1978, one would witness *lian* often abandoned by some people to gain *mian* or reputation as a Maoist. An example comes from one of my former English teachers. When she was in college during the 1960s, the era of the Chinese Cultural Revolution, she betrayed her parents and reported about her parents' anti-Maoist behavior to the government and gained trust and reputation among the Maoist Red Guards. From the Confucian perspective, she violated the moral principle of piety toward her parents and lost her *lian* or her Confucian persona, but she gained her *mian* or her high political status among the Red Guards. During the era of emerging capitalism since 1978, one has witnessed some people break into physical fights with neighbors and relatives for money, a violation of *ren* (benevolence), another Confucian moral principle. These deeds are typically regarded as *lian*-losing deeds, which also mean the loss of Confucian persona, while the high-end products and services they enjoy with the money help mark off their higher social status. Although a majority of the Chinese population still adheres to the *lianmian* ideal in daily interaction, both among themselves and with people of other countries, this traditional ideal and cultural pattern has been significantly challenged by both Communism and capitalism in China. How these two can be redefined and recoupled to creatively integrate the Confucian interpersonal ethics and the democratic-capitalist ethics constitutes an urgent practical problem to be solved intelligently.

The Tripartite Relationship

In the *wei–ming–lianmian* continuum, *wei* is a philosophical construct that reflects the Chinese way of knowing about reality (ontology), the Chinese way of interpreting reality (phenomenology), and the Chinese values about co-humanity (axiology). *Ming* is a linguistic/rhetorical construct that reflects the Chinese constructionist view of the role of language in our attempt to understand and interpret reality and in our attempt to ethically cultivate and transform humanity from mean personhood to gentle personhood or sagehood. *Lianmian* is largely a sociopsychological construct that reflects a uniquely Chinese way of social interaction, communication, thinking, emoting, and feeling—hierarchical, yet relationship-centered; practical, yet held as a sacred social object; instrumental, yet irrational at times, as the pages above illustrate.

If *wei* is said to be the origin of hierarchy, *ming* (naming) could be described as the process of articulation and symbolic construction of hierarchy, and *lianmian* is the dynamic process of communication, realization, and perpetuation of this hierarchy. *Wei* seems to be the ultimate source of *lianmian,* whereas naming connects *wei* and *lianmian* as the channel. On the other hand, *lianmian* dynamics or facework is the open-ended and concrete enactment of the *wei* structure in the lifeworld via proper naming. However, if facework does not accurately enact the *wei* structure and/or is misrepresented through improper naming, the *wei* structure could be altered. The three, at different levels or positions, constitute a coherent system of communication that further creates a unique culture.

CASE ANALYSES

Case of Government

The Chinese Communist Party Committee Office and the Mayor's Office of Ankang City, Shaanxi Province, in Northwest China issued a public announcement on June 25, 2003, on how to standardize the management of name plates by the gates of the buildings of each of the CCP agencies, government organs, and the people's bodies and other related organizations of all levels of and under the jurisdiction of the city. The following is a translation of the announcement, which was downloaded on July 11, 2003, at www.ankang.gov.cn/news/zwxx/20030525132935.mtml:

> To All County/District Chinese Communist Party Committees, All County/District People's Governments, the Chinese Communist Party Ankang City Committees and City Mayoral Departments, and All the People's Bodies:
>
> The name plates hanging on the gate of every building of all CCP agencies, administrations, and the people's bodies and their affiliates at all levels are important symbols of the scopes of the powers and natures. In recent years, with the changes of the structure of the administration and its subsequent changes of the agencies in Ankang, the name plates used by these agencies are not standardized in shape, size, and type of character used, hanging position, the order of the different name plates on the shared gates, and so on. In order to strengthen the management of the name plates of all these agencies/bodies, the following rules are to be followed:
>
> 1. In accordance with "The Approach to the Management of the City of Ankang's Agency Structuration," after the agencies are established, merged, or disbanded, registration is to be done in the agency structure office at the appropriate level in order to make, use, or destroy a name plate.
> 2. The name plates of the CCP agencies at city, county, and township levels are elongated stripe-shaped, painted in white, with the characters written in red from top to bottom, and are hung vertically. The name plates of the administrations, people's bodies, and other agencies at all levels, plus the second-tier agencies, are elongated stripe-shaped, painted in white, with the characters written in black from top to bottom, and are hung vertically. The name plates of the offices within these agencies are elongated stripe-shaped, painted in blue, with characters written in white from left to right, and are hung horizontally. The name plates of the second-tier agencies can be hung side by side with those of the administration offices on condition that the name plates of the former must be smaller in size. The offices within the administrative agencies must not hang their name plates parallel to the name plates of the administrative agencies. Ad hoc organizations must not hang their name plates. Agencies that have not been approved for operation by the agency structure offices must not hang name plates. Name plates must be hung in highly visible positions, and must look solemn, serious, with no decorations.
> 3. Name plates of the county/district party, administrative agencies, and the departments of the City Party Committee and City Administration must be 240 centimeters in length and 40 centimeters in width. The name plates of the second-tier agencies must be 230 centimeters in length and 38 centimeters in width. The name plates of the township Party committee, people's government, and the departments of the county/district Party committee and people's government and the people's bodies at this level are 220 centimeters in length and 36 centimeters in width. The name plates of the second-tier agencies at the township level are 215 centimeters in length and 34 in width. The name plates of the liaison offices of the city, county/district, township, and neighborhood are 30 centimeters in length and 12 centimeters in width. All the agencies at all the levels within the city must follow the above standards.
> 4. Name plates must bear legalized names. If the names have too many characters to be on a proper plate, they can be simplified consistent with the word name simplification standards and the approval of the appropriate office of agency

structuration. Name plates must use the simplified Chinese characters released by the State Council. The calligraphic style must be Sung style. The paint used to write names can be picked on the basis of need by the appropriate office of agency structuration.

Issued by the Office of the Chinese Communist Party Ankang Committee, Office of the People's Government of City of Ankang

The printout indicates that the document was issued online at www.ankang.gov.cn on June 25, 2003, at 1:29 P.M. China time.

In the above case, all the artifacts such as name plates, their different sizes and different colors, their hanging positions, different colors of Chinese characters, the order and directions of the flow of the characters, and so on are all translated into symbolic building blocks constituting and displaying the city's hierarchy of power and authority. This document also dictates occupants of different *wei*s within this hierarchy to communicate with one another in the ways consistent with the different *wei*s. The document also expects people within and outside the city to communicate with the different occupants of these *wei*s in the ways consistent with their *wei*s. People who hold the highest *wei*s, such as the Party Secretary of the Chinese Communist Party City Committee (an example of naming), who is assigned the most power, and the mayor (an example of naming), who is assigned the most power in the city only next to the Party Secretary, are expected to communicate (display their *lianmian*) dominantly in both business and social contexts with the rest of the officials and people, who are expected to give face to these two officials. In front of the provincial officials, these two most powerful city officials in the city are expected to communicate submissively (to give face to their higher-ups). On the other hand, the officials who have less power than these two and the people in the city are expected to communicate with the two submissively. If such rules are violated, either realistically or perceptually, the violators will be either overtly or covertly penalized by the more powerful.

The above discussion illustrates that how much face/social capital one displays or activates hinges upon the position or status one holds. This position or status is brought into social visibility and action by a given symbol or a proper name.

Case of Education

In recent years, there has been a growing trend for universities in China, especially flagship universities such as Peking University and Tsinghua University, to hire high-profile government officials to be affiliated professors as part of the education reform effort. Peking University's School of Journalism and Communication, for example, has hired about a dozen government officials from the Department of Culture, the Department of Propaganda, and others, to be affiliated professors. Tsinghua University's School of Journalism and Communication has hired Wang Daohan, the former boss of Jiang Zemin in Shanghai, as a professor. Zhu Rongji, the former premier, was Dean of School of Management of Tsinghua University. Qian Qisheng is still Dean of the College of International Relations of Peking University, and Li Zhaoxin, Foreign Minister, is a professor in the English Department of Peking University. Overseas Chinese scholars and students, lower in rank than those, are ignored or neglected, even though they are more knowledgeable in their respective fields as researchers and educators than the above-mentioned government officials. The underlying assumption of this practice is that authority or a high *wei* is not only the source of power and influence, but is also regarded as the major source of knowledge by these institutions of higher learning. This kind of practice seems to suggest that what is truth is determined by one's *wei* more than one's academic training or specialization; the higher one's *wei* is, the more truth and knowledge one is assumed to possess. The purpose of education in this context seems to be to legitimize and hallow authority, rather than remain skeptical of and challenge authority. Intended as an instrument to reform education and make it more innovative, this effort may end up with an opposite result. It seems to have strongly affirmed the value of authority in Chinese culture and may be making Chinese higher education less competitive and innovative rather than more competitive and innovative. What the universities got in exchange, with these big *wei*s and big names, was in all likelihood access to the means to curry favors such as more funding from higher-ups and more expansive *lianmian,* which do not directly translate into competitive edge in teaching and research.

In many of China's job advertisements published in *People's Daily* (Overseas Edition) aimed at luring overseas Chinese students and scholars to go back and work in China, one can read the different guidelines for male and female applicants. For male applicants, the age limit is 45 years old and below. But for females, the age limit is 40 years and below. For applicants who are Ph.D. advisers, the retirement age is 65 years old; but for those who are not Ph.D. advisers and male, the retirement age is 60 years old. For those who are not Ph.D. advisers and are female, the retirement age is 55. This means that the higher your current position is, on condition that you are male, the more years you are permitted to work; the lower your current position is, on condition that you are female, the fewer years you are allowed to work. This personnel policy, from the contemporary Western perspective, perpetuates the age hierarchy and the gender hierarchy that have been in practice for thousands of years in China. To a typical person of Western culture, this is a policy of double discrimination: age discrimination and gender discrimination.

The Returned Overseas Chinese students and scholars are urged by the Chinese press to communicate in their workplaces back in China in the Chinese way instead of the Western way in order to survive and flourish in the contemporary Chinese society or *jiaoji bentuhua*. At the same time, however, the Chinese official discourse calls for China's further globalization (*yu guoji jieguei*). This means that overseas Chinese students and scholars who have returned to China need to communicate according to the norms, rules, and rituals of the culture of relational authority instead of using the norms, rules, and rituals of the Western culture of equality and individuality. What is the use of spending money and time studying Western culture if these students and scholars are expected to readapt to the *wei–ming–lianmian* culture instead of acting as mediators between the two conflicting cultures and as agents of change for both the cultures? Again the question: How can these students and scholars remain bicultural in communicating with Westerners while in the West and with Chinese coworkers when they are back in China?

Comparison with the West

The formal discourse of hierarchy in the West is marginal. The legal, political, and social discourse of equality, freedom, and liberty dominates the society, which either helps reduce equality or masks inequality and hierarchy existent in reality. In education, the private corporate world, and the U.S. military, for example, hierarchy is a given, but law and procedure make sure that equality prevails. Social equality, such as first-name basis, informal and open social interaction, and casual style of dress, may mask deep economic inequality and hierarchy, such as disparities in housing, transportation, pay, bank savings and investments, and so on. However, in front of law, everyone does enjoy equality in most cases. It was reported that Hillary Rodham Clinton violated the rule of a janitor in Lincoln Center before the press conference by then President Clinton and then Chairman Jiang Zeming in 1998. Hillary walked across the sign set up by the janitor. The janitor saw her and ordered her to get out of the area, which was being cleaned in Lincoln Center. The journalist asked him if he knew that the lady he had yelled at was the First Lady. The janitor replied, "Of course I know!!!" It was also reported by the *Boston Globe* in 1997 that then Governor Weld of Massachusetts was issued a speeding ticket by his own city police. It was reported in 2002 that the mayor of a small city in Colorado was arrested by his own city police following an emergency domestic violence report by his wife. Such reports are rarely heard in China because very few would dare to punish those who are in power according to law. Many chauffeurs of government officials in China violate traffic rules, but very few police dare catch them; they use sirens anytime they want to make the traffic give way for the government officials' cars or motorcades. On the streets in a typical Chinese city, one may hear the sirens of cars carrying government officials, at the level of or equivalent to department directors within a provincial government or higher, much more often than those of police vehicles and fire squads. In a typical American city, the scenario is most likely to be the opposite. This illustrates the significance of government officials in the *wei–ming–lianmian* culture and the significance of civic matters in a culture of public accountability and professionalism.

Signs of Change in Chinese Culture

In the field of technology industry in China today, most of the CEOs are young people. This represents a major change in respect for age in Chinese culture in the past 10 years. In this sector in China, as in the

United States, youth is respected as a symbol of innovation and competition. In the Chinese cyberspace showcased by www.omnitalk.com, walls of political, social, and economic hierarchy are crumbling for the first time in Chinese history. Chinese citizens are enjoying equality in expressing themselves, to be read and valued as never before. The value of competition is also entering into educational administration. Peking University's current effort to institute the Western type of tenure system is revolutionizing Chinese organizational behavior. These are growing cracks of change in the culture of authority. These cracks will hopefully contribute to a pervasive transformation of Chinese culture of authority into a hybrid of sufficient equality and constructive authority—a new culture of *wei–ming–lianmian*–equality.

CONCLUSION

From the historical perspective, the aura of authority in Chinese culture has been becoming thinner and thinner. The practice of authority has become less formalized, less overt, and more covert, compared with the past. For example, the practice of bound feet is no longer. *Koutou* is no longer. However, the above case analyses show that the *wei–ming–lianmian* practice is affirmed and accented in many areas of contemporary Chinese society, such as government and education. It is my hypothesis that such a communication practice is carried over to many other sectors of Chinese society, such as the social, organizational, and international spheres. The *wei–ming–lianmian* framework delineated above will hopefully provide a much-needed sense of direction for international persons who have little experience in dealing with the Chinese in making sense of, and selectively adapting to, their Chinese counterparts' communication behavior. For the Chinese immersed in the *wei–ming–lianmian* culture to better deal with both legitimate and illegitimate challenges to authority lodged by Western counterparts (some Western scholars and politicians argue for the need to restore and protect legitimate authority from being endangered), perhaps the freedom/rights/equality/justice–persuasion–change framework, detailed in various dimensions such as theological, philosophical, philological/rhetorical/legal, and social/cultural/psychological, could help.

References

Brown, P., & Levinson, S. (1987). *Politeness*. Cambridge, England: Cambridge University Press.

Chang, H., & Holt, R. (1994). A Chinese perspective on face as inter-relational concern. In S. Ting-Toomey (Ed.), *The challenges of facework* (pp. 95–132). Albany, NY: SUNY Press.

Chen, V. (1990). Mien tze at the Chinese dinner table: A study of the interactional accomplishment of face. *Research on Language and Social Interaction, 24,* 109–140.

Cheng, C. (1986). The concept of face and its Confucian roots. *Journal of Chinese Philosophy, 13,* 329–348.

Cheng, C. (1996). *Zhouyi* and philosophy of *wei* (positions). *Extreme-Orient, Extreme-Occident, 18,* 150–175.

Goffman, E. (1967). On face-work. In E. Goffman, *Interaction ritual* (pp. 5–45). New York: Pantheon.

Ho, D. Y. (1976). On the concept of face. *American Journal of Sociology, 81,* 867–884.

Jia, W. (2001). *The remaking of the Chinese character and identity in the 21st century: The Chinese practices*. Westport, CT: Ablex.

Kipnis, A. (1995). "Face": An adaptable discourse of social surfaces. *Positions, 1*(3), 119–147.

Lin, Y. (1935). *My country and my people*. New York: Reynal & Hitchcock.

Lu, Z. (1996). Insights into the worldly affairs constitute knowledge and experience in dealing with issues concerning human feelings is as good as ability to write good articles *(shishi dongming jie xuewen, renqing lianda ji wenzhang)*: On the psychology of *renqing* and *mianzi*. In Z. Lu, *Zhongguoren de chuantong xintai* [The social psychology of Chinese tradition] (pp. 141–152). Hongzhou, Zhejiang, China: Zhejiang People's Press.

Office of Chinese Communist Party Angkang City Committee and Office of the Ankang People's Government. (2003, June). Zhonggun Ankang Shiwei Bangongshi, Ankangshi Renmin Zenfu Bangongshi Guanyu Gueifan Geji Dang de Jigou, Guojia Xengzheng Jiguan, Renmin Tuanti Jiqisuoshu Shiyedanwei Biaopai Guanli de Tongzhi [The announcement on the management of the name plates of the agencies of all levels of the Chinese Communist Party, government, people's bodies, and their affiliates by the Office of the Chinese Communist Party Ankang Committee and Office of Ankang City Government]. Retrieved on July 11, 2003, at http://www.ankang.gov.cn.

Scollon, R., & Scollon, S. (1994). Face parameters in East–West discourse. In S. Ting-Toomey (Ed.), *The challenges of facework* (pp. 133–158). Albany, NY: SUNY Press.

Smith, A. (1894). *The Chinese characteristics*. New York: Fleming H. Revell.

Ting-Toomey, S. (2003). Managing intercultural conflicts effectively. In L. A. Samovar & R. E. Porter (Eds.), *Intercultural communication: A reader* (10th ed., pp. 373–384). Belmont, CA: Wadsworth.
Ting-Toomey, S. (1988). Intercultural conflict styles. In Y. Y. Kim & W. B. Gudykunst (Eds.), *Theories of intercultural communication* (pp. 213–238). Newbury Park, CA: Sage.
Zai, X. (1995). *Zhongguoren de lianmian guan* [The Chinese perspective on *lianmian*]. Taipei, Taiwan: Guiguan Press.

Concepts and Questions

1. Describe the concept of face as a dynamic of Chinese culture.
2. How do the constructs of *wei* and *ming* interact to construct *lianmian*, or face, in contemporary Chinese culture?
3. What are the relationships between high moral positions and the development of *lianmian*?
4. In what manner does face serve to manage self-focused emotions?
5. What sort of connection is there between face and self-concept in Chinese culture?
6. What does Jia mean when he refers to *ming* as a linguistic/rhetorical construct?
7. In interpersonal communication, how does face help mediate interaction between people?
8. It appears that for the Chinese, face is somewhat akin to a commodity in that it can be accumulated or lost. This being the case, how might the desire to accrue face affect interaction?
9. How does age relate to employment guidelines for male and female applicants in China?
10. How would an understanding of face facilitate communication between you and a Chinese citizen?

India: The Dance of Shiva

MARTIN J. GANNON

Sex may drive the soap operas in America. But in India what really moves the dishwashing liquids are serials based on ancient myths of Indian gods.

KARP AND WILLIAMS (1998), p. A1

India is a country bursting with diversity—virtually every writer describes it as one of the most culturally and geographically diverse nations in existence. It is the second largest country in the world, with a population of 950 million, and it is about one third the size of the United States.

Religious diversity is a major feature of India, and it is fitting that our image of, and cultural metaphor for, this country should be based on religion. As Swami Vivekananda so succinctly stated: "Each nation has a theme in life. In India religious life forms the central theme, the keynote of the whole music of the nation."

For 2,000 years of its history, India was almost completely Hindu. But for the past millennium or more, Indian culture has been a synthesis of different racial, religious, and linguistic influences; Hinduism itself has undergone many changes owing to the impact of other faiths. Therefore, it is incorrect to contend that Indian culture is solely a Hindu culture. However, to begin to understand India, we must start with Hindu traditions. The overwhelming majority of Indians are still tradition oriented, and changes in their culture and society cannot be understood without reference to that tradition.

There are numerous deities or gods in the Hindu religion, each being different manifestations of one Supreme Being. The most important gods are Brahma (the Creator), Vishnu (the Preserver), and Shiva (the Destroyer). Among the greatest names and appearances of Shiva is Nataraja, Lord of the Dancers. The Dance of Shiva has been described as the "clearest image of the activity of God which any art or religion can boast of" (Coomaraswamy, 1924/1969, p. 56),

From Martin J. Gannon, *Global Cultures,* 3rd. ed. Thousand Oaks, CA: Sage Publications, 2001, pp. 47–65. Reprinted by permission of Sage Publications.

and it also reflects the cyclical nature of Hindu philosophy. Through this metaphor, we will begin to explore Indian culture and society.

Among Hindus, dancing is regarded as the most ancient and important of the arts. Legend attributes to it even the creation of the world: Brahma's three steps created earth, space, and sky. Every aspect of nature—man, bird, beast, insect, trees, wind, waves, stars—displays a dance pattern, collectively called the Daily Dance *(dainic nrtya)*. But nature is inert and cannot dance until Shiva wills it; he holds the sacred drum, the *damaru*, whose soundings set the rhythms that beat throughout the universe. Shiva is like a master conductor, and the Daily Dance is the response of all creation to his rhythmic force.

Shiva is seen as the first dancer, a deity who dances simply as an expression of his exuberant personality (Banerji, 1983, p. 43). His dance cannot be performed by anyone else, because Shiva dances out the creation and existence of the world. But just as the mortal dancer gets tired, so, too, does Shiva lapse periodically into inactivity. The cosmos becomes chaos, and destruction follows the period of creation. This concept of the Dance of Shiva is innate in the Eastern ideas of movement and history—it is continuous and both constructive and destructive at the same time (Gopal & Dadachanji, 1951).

The Dance of Shiva represents both the conception of the world processes as a supreme being's pastime or amusement *(lila)*, and the very nature of that blessed one, which is beyond the realm of purpose or understanding (Coomaraswamy, 1924/1969). The dance symbolizes the five main activities of the Supreme Being: creation and development *(srishti)*; preservation and support *(sthiti)*; change and destruction *(samhara)*; shrouding, symbolism, illusion, and giving rest *(tirobhava)*; and release, salvation, and grace *(anugraha)*.

India's history reflects the cycles of chaos and harmony epitomized by the Dance of Shiva. Time after time, India has recovered from episodes that would have ended the existence of any other nation. In fact, Shiva's son, Ganesh, is the symbol of good arising from adversity. According to the legend, Parvati, the consort of Shiva, would spend hours bathing, dressing, and adorning herself. This often meant that Shiva was kept waiting, so Parvati set their son Ganesh on guard to prevent Shiva's bursting in on her unannounced and catching her in a state of unreadiness. One day, Shiva was so frustrated by Ganesh's actions that he cut off the child's head. Distraught, Parvati completely withdrew from her lord, and Shiva realized he would have to restore the child to her if he was to win her back. He resolved to use the first available head he could find, which happened to be that of a baby elephant. The boy regained his life and now had the added advantage of the elephant's wisdom. Similarly, India's past and present contributions to art, science, and the spiritual world of the unknown are immense, despite periods of turmoil and apparent anarchy.

CYCLICAL HINDU PHILOSOPHY

The Indian perspective on life tends to differ most sharply from that of Europe and the United States in the value that it accords to the discipline of philosophy (Coomaraswamy, 1924/1969, p. 2). In Europe and America, the study of philosophy tends to be regarded as an end in itself—some kind of mental gymnastic—and as such, it seems of little importance to the ordinary man or woman. In India, philosophy tends to overlap with religion, and it is regarded as the key to life itself, clarifying its essential meaning and the way to attain spiritual goals. Elsewhere, philosophy and religion pursued distinct and different paths that may have crossed but never merged (Munshi, 1965, p. 133). In India, it is not always possible to differentiate between the two.

In Hindu philosophy, the world is considered illusory, like a dream, the result of God's *lila*. According to one interpretation, *Bharata Varsha*, the ancient name of India, literally means "land of the actors" (Lannoy, 1971, p. 286). In an illusionary world, people cannot achieve true happiness through the mere physical enjoyment of wealth or material possessions. The only happiness worth seeking is permanent spiritual happiness as distinguished from these fleeting pleasures. Absolute happiness can result only from liberation from worldly involvement through spiritual enlightenment. Life is a journey in search of salvation *(mukti)*, and the seeker, if he or she withstands all of the perils of the road, is rewarded by exultation beyond human experience or perception *(moksha)*. In the same way that the Dance of Shiva leads the cosmos through a journey, Hindu philosophy directs each individual along a path.

There are basically four paths or ways that lead to the ideal state: intense devotion or love of God *(bhakti yoga)*, selfless work or service *(karma yoga)*, philosophy or knowledge of self *(nana yoga)*, and meditation or psychological exercise *(raja yoga)*. The four ways are not exclusive, and an individual may choose or combine them according to the dictates of temperament and circumstance. Whatever path is followed, every Hindu is aware of the difficulty of reaching the ideal state in a single lifetime. This is the point at which the concept of reincarnation, or the cycle of lives, becomes important.

Individual souls *(jivas)* enter the world mysteriously—by God's power, certainly, but how and for what purpose is not fully explainable (Smith, 1958, p. 100). They begin as the souls of the simplest forms of life, but they do not vanish with the death of their original bodies. Rather, they simply move to a new body or form. The transmigration of souls takes an individual *jiva* through a series of complex bodies until a human one is achieved. At this point, the ascent of physical forms ends, and the soul begins its path to *mukti*. This gives an abiding sense of purpose to the Hindu life—a God to be sought actively and awaited patiently through the cycles of many lives.

The doctrine of reincarnation corresponds to a fact that everyone should have noticed: the varying age of the souls of people, irrespective of the age of the body ("an old head on young shoulders"). Some people remain irresponsible, self-assertive, uncontrolled, and inept to their last days; others are serious, friendly, self-controlled, and talented from their youth onward. According to Hindu philosophy, each person comes equipped with a highly personalized unconsciousness, characterized by a particular mix of three fundamental qualities: *sattva* (clarity, light); *rajas* (passion, desire); and *tamas* (dullness, darkness). Relative strength differs from one person to another, but in the Hindu idea of destiny, the unconscious has an innate tendency to strive toward clarity and light (Kakar, 1978).

The birth of a person into a particular niche in life and the relative mix of the three fundamental qualities in an individual are determined by the balance of the right and wrong actions of his or her soul through its previous cycles. The rate of progress of the soul through this endless cycle of birth, life, and death—the soul's karma—depends on the deeds and decisions made in each lifetime. One way of mapping the probable karma of an individual is to consult astrological charts at the time of his or her birth, and this is an important tradition in Indian society.

The Dance of Shiva portrays the world's endless cycle of creation, existence, destruction, and recreation, and Hindu philosophy depicts the endless cycle of the soul through birth, life, death, and reincarnation. We will now turn to examining the cycle of individual life within that greater series of lifetimes.

THE CYCLE OF LIFE

According to Hindu philosophy, a person passes through four stages of life, the first of which is that of a student. The prime responsibility in life during this stage is to learn. Besides knowledge, the student is supposed to develop a strong character and good habits, and emerge equipped to produce a good and effective life.

The second stage, beginning with marriage, is that of a householder. Here, human energy turns outward and is expressed on three fronts: family, vocation, and community. The wants of pleasure are satisfied through the family, wants of duty through exercising the social responsibilities of citizenship, and the wants of success through employment.

The third stage of life is retirement, signifying withdrawal from social obligations. This is the time for a person to begin his or her true education—to discover who one is, and what life is all about. It is a time to read, think, ponder over life's meaning, and to discover and live by a philosophy. At this stage, a person needs to transcend the senses and dwell in harmony with the timeless reality that underlies the dream of life in this natural world.

The Hindu concept of retirement is exemplified in a story told by a traveler in India (Arden, 1990, p. 132). The traveler saw a white-bearded man seated on a blanket, writing in a notebook. The man looked up and smiled as the traveler walked past. "Are you a Buddhist?" the traveler asked, to which the man shook his head. "A Hindu? A Muslim?" Again, he shook his head, and replied, "Does it matter? I am a man." The traveler asked what the man was writing. "The truth," he said, "only the truth."

The final stage is one of *sannyasin*, defined by the *Bhagavad-Gita* as "one who neither hates nor loves anything." In this stage, the person achieves *mukti* and is living only because the time to make the final ascent has not come. When he or she finally departs from this world, freedom from the cycle of life and death is attained.

A person can pass through the four stages of life in a single lifetime or stay at each stage for many lifetimes. Even Buddha is reputed to have passed through several hundred lives. Progress is determined in light of the activities and inclination of the person at each stage of life. For example, Indian religion is replete with rituals, the primary purpose of which is to receive the blessings of God. Each ceremony involves the singing of religious songs *(bhajans)* and discourses by priests and other religious people *(satsang)*. The sincerity with which people indulge in these activities and apply the tenets of the philosophy in their practical life determines their progress through the cycle of life and death. A person may expound philosophy at great length, go to the temple every day, and offer alms to saints and the poor, yet indulge in all sorts of vices. These contradictions in life are resolved on death by karma, which dictates that upon reincarnation, each person will receive rewards or punishment for his or her accumulated good and bad deeds.

The Hindu desire for positive outcomes of daily activities, resulting in positive karma, leads us to a brief discussion of the importance of astrology. With so much at stake, almost everyone in India consults the stars, if not on a daily basis, then at least on important occasions. Matching the horoscopes of a bride and groom is as much a part of planning a marriage as choosing the flower arrangements. It is routine for Indians to consult the stars about the best day to close on a house or sign an important contract. When it was revealed that an astrologer helped former President Ronald Reagan's wife, Nancy, set her schedule, Americans hooted with derision. In contrast, no one in India batted an eye when India's former prime minister, Narasimha Rao, delayed naming his cabinet because an astrologer warned that the intended day was not auspicious enough.

Like Hindu philosophy, the Indian concept of time is cyclical, characterized by origination, duration, and disappearance ad infinitum. This is reflected in the dramatic structure of a traditional Sanskrit play. These plays are typically based on the themes of separation and reunion, and they tend to end as they begin. Various devices are used—the dream, the trance, the premonition, and the flashback—to disrupt the linearity of time and make the action recoil upon itself (Lannoy, 1971, p. 54). Similarly, the Dance of Shiva is a repetitive cycle of creation, existence, and destruction—constant change within a period of time, but ultimately, time itself is irrelevant.

In an attempt to neutralize the anguish of impermanence and change, the carved religious images that every village home possesses are made of permanent materials, such as clay or metal. This also reveals the functional role of the image in a materially restricted environment. The practice of religion at home is one of the main reasons Hinduism was able to survive the invasion of foreign powers over the centuries. And just as religion is important to the family, so, too, the family plays a dominant factor in Indian society.

THE FAMILY CYCLE

Most Indians grow up in an extended family, a form of family organization in which brothers remain together after marriage and bring their wives into their parental household or compound of homes. Recent migration to cities and towns in search of economic opportunities has contributed to the weakening of many traditions, including that of extended families. In this section, we describe family traditions that exist most strongly in the India of about 400 million people that continues to be affected marginally by industrialization. While weakened in some parts of society, many aspects of the family cycle are still important to all.

The preference for a son when a child is born is as old as Indian society. A son guarantees the continuation of the generations, and he will perform the last rites after his parents' death. This ensures a peaceful departure of the soul to its next existence in the ongoing cycle of life. The word *putra,* or son, literally means "he who protects from going to hell." In contrast, a daughter has negligible ritual significance. She is normally an unmitigated expense—someone who will never contribute to the family income and who, upon marriage, will take away a considerable part of her family's fortune as her dowry. Although formally abolished, the institution of dowry is still widespread in India, but it is becoming increasingly fashionable among educated Indians not to indulge in the practice.

A striking reflection of this gender preference is the continued masculinization of the Indian population, particularly in the north. There are 108 males to 100 females. The main reasons for this outcome are the higher mortality rate of female children and the tendency to limit family size once there is a sufficient number of sons. Also, the recent availability of sex determination tests has allowed women to ensure that their firstborn is a boy, because they can abort unwanted female children.

Just as the Dance of Shiva represents preservation, overlooking, and support, parents tend to nurture their children with great care. A Hindu child grows up in the security of the extended family and has few contacts with other groups until it is time for school. Although the mother is chiefly responsible for the care of the child, there is also close contact with other females and mother-surrogates, and this continues for much longer than in many other cultures. A child is usually breastfed for at least two years (although significantly less in the case of a female child) and will be fed any time that it cries. Consequently, most infants are virtually never left alone. The strong ties of home life do not conflict with the Hindu belief in the liberty of the soul removed from worldly concerns. Love of family is not merely a purpose in itself but a way to the final goal of life. Love will not yield the rewards of *mukti* when it remains self-centered; that is why Hindus try to diffuse their love over sons, daughters, guests, and neighbors (Munshi, 1965, p. 115).

Children in India are considered sacred, a manifestation of God, but if the Hindu ideal is a very high degree of infant indulgence, reality is somewhat different in the poorer areas of India. Here, there are typically many young children under one roof, and 1 in 10 will die in infancy, so babies are not regarded as extraordinary creatures. Except for the firstborn son, they tend to be taken for granted. This is reinforced by the belief in rebirth; because an individual is not born once and once only, he or she cannot be regarded as a unique event. The mother has probably witnessed the birth of several babies and may have seen them die, too. When her child cries, falls sick, or is accidentally hurt, she is not beset with feelings of intense guilt. A mother's work may be long and hard, both in the home and in the fields, so she is unable to give her child undivided attention.

Even as the Dance of Shiva leads the world through the joys of existence, an element of chaos is inherent in the world's Daily Dance. Similarly, nature in India has been full of threats to a child's safety—famine, disease, and chronic civil disorder. As a rule, until modern times, more than half of all deaths befell children in their first year of life. But as the nation got a grip on its affairs, and as campaigns against diseases such as malaria and smallpox took hold, mortality rates fell. By 1981, nearly three out of four newborns could expect to survive to age 20 (Narayana & Kantner, 1992, p. 26). The cultural importance of children is derived from the need to carry on the cycle of life. This continued importance is reflected in statistics that show that although death rates have fallen since 1921, birth rates have declined much more slowly.

Government attempts to regulate the birth rate have become synonymous with its sterilization programs. Resentment against coerced sterilization in India helped defeat Indira Gandhi's government in 1977. As a result of the political fallout, birth control was set back as a popular cause. Middle-class Indians, influenced by education and the desire for an improved standard of living, are increasingly adopting family planning methods. But when the formidable psychic barrier of traditional Hindu beliefs in the life cycle is considered, it seems clear that rapid population growth will continue in the poorer, rural areas.

An Indian father is frequently remote, aloof, and a much-feared disciplinary figure, just as Shiva is distant from the world he nurtures. But there are also special bonds between father and son, and the relationship is one of mutual dependence. A son must obey his father unquestioningly, pay him respect, and offer complete support in every need both in life and after death. The father owes his son support, a good education, the best possible marital arrangement, and inheritance of property. One Indian proverb reads: "A son should be treated as a prince for five years; as a slave for ten years; but from his sixteenth birthday, as a friend."

The son learns very early in life that women are lower in status than men. The position of any woman in this hierarchical society means that she must constantly be making demands and pleading with superiors for one thing or another. The son soon develops an attitude of superiority. A female's authority can seldom be absolute, except for the unchallengeable position that the senior grandmother may inherit. A son finds out that anger may be productive; violent outbursts of anger are often effective if directed against someone of uncertain status. Similarly, the destructive powers of the Dance of Shiva are effective in creating new opportunities and patterns.

The relative position of men and women is clear in Indian society, and the question of competitive equality is not customarily considered. The Hindu marriage emphasizes identity, not equality. Generally, women are thought to have younger souls, and therefore, they are nearer to the world than men and inferior to them. Girls are trained to be submissive and docile, and to fulfill culturally designated feminine roles. The ideal of womanhood in Indian tradition is one of chastity, purity, gentle tenderness, self-effacement, self-sacrifice, and singular faithfulness. Throughout history, Indian women have had dual status—as a wife, she seduces her husband away from his work and spiritual duties, but as a mother, she is revered.

Among the crosses women have had to bear in Indian society are female infanticide, child marriage, *purdah* (feminine modesty and seclusion), marital mistreatment, and the low status of widows. Until the mid-19th century, the voluntary immolation of the widow on her husband's funeral pyre *(sati)* was not uncommon; the widow believed her act would cleanse her family of the sins of the three generations. Poor families are more likely to be fearful of not being able to scrape together enough money to find their daughters husbands and may resort to killing infant girls. Generally speaking, however, the lower down the economic hierarchy, the more equal are the relations between the sexes. Of course, many factors can bring about or alleviate hostile feelings toward women, but they often view the various forms of mistreatment suffered by women as part of their destiny as a woman. The Dance of Shiva is not destined to lead to joy throughout the world, and if the corresponding experience of humankind includes some unhappiness for women in society, that is simply the way things are.

A man's worth and recognition of his identity are bound up intimately in the reputation of his family. Lifestyle and actions are rarely seen as the product of individual effort, but are interpreted in the light of family circumstance and reputation in the wider society. Individual identity and merit are enhanced if the person has the good fortune to belong to a large, harmonious, and closely knit family, which helps safeguard a child's upbringing and advance a person in life. The family contributes to decisions that affect an individual's future, maximizes the number of connections necessary to secure a job or other favors, comes to aid in times of crisis, and generally mediates an individual's experience with the outside world. For these reasons, the character of the respective families weighs heavily in the consideration of marriage proposals.

Arranged marriage is still the norm in India. Advertisements regularly appear in European and American newspapers to identify potential candidates. The Western concept of romantic love arises from the Western concept of personality and, ultimately, from the un-Indian concept of equality of the sexes. Still, the concept of life as an illusion makes the idea of loveless marriage easier to understand.

Marriages are usually for a lifetime, because divorce is considered socially disgraceful. The average age for Indian women to marry is 18 to 19, whereas only about 13% of U.S. women of this age are married. The percentage of Indian women aged 15 to 19 who are married ranges from 14% in states where a high value is put on female education, to more than 60% in less developed states (Narayana & Kantner, 1992, p. 31). In the case of child marriage, the girl lives at her parents' home until she is about 15 or 16 years of age, after which she moves to the home of her husband's family. A newly arrived daughter-in-law is sometimes subject to varying forms of humiliation until she becomes pregnant. This treatment originated historically from the urgent need to ensure the early birth of a son in times of low life expectancy. Also, the size of the dowry that a girl brings with her can also determine how she is treated or mistreated in her husband's home. The husband's family may keep making demands on her for additional support from her family, and if it is not forthcoming, she may be tortured or even burned alive, although the outcry against such treatment seemingly has diminished such illegal practices.

The restricted life of women in the conservative atmosphere of India does not prevent them from developing a strong sense of self-respect. Their ultimate role is to preserve unity and continuity in the chain of life, and there is pride and dignity in their sense of identity with the family and their role as wife and mother. Indian society seems to have given women, rather than men, resilience and vitality under the difficult circumstances of life in that country. But ultimately, all respond to the Dance of Shiva, and whether that brings great joy or unhappiness to the current life is irrelevant compared to the ongoing search for salvation, or *mukti*.

Since the beginning of time, dancing has been a rite performed by both men and women; Shiva and his wife, Parvati, are often depicted in ancient sculptures as one composite figure, half male and half female. Typical figurines of Shiva are four-armed, with broad masculine shoulders and curving womanly hips. Similarly, there is a place for both genders to contribute to Indian society today. In this century, Indian women have undergone a social revolution more far-reaching and radical than that of men. While this process has been going on, women have attained positions of distinction in public and professional life. The political dominance of Indira Gandhi is one example of how women can be held in high esteem by all Indians.

In summary, it can be seen that the extended family unit is still a strong feature of Indian society. Just as the Dance of Shiva wills all nature to respond to its rhythm, so, too, each member of the family fulfills a role dictated by family tradition.

THE CYCLE OF SOCIAL INTERACTION

A sense of duty *(dharma)* is the social cement in India; it holds the individual and society together. Dharma is a concept that is wider than the Western idea of duty, because it includes the totality of social, ethical, and spiritual harmony (Lannoy, 1971, p. 217). Dharma consists of three categories: universal principles of harmony *(sanatana dharma),* relative ethical systems varying by social class *(varnashrama dharma),* and personal moral conduct *(svadharma)*. Among the prime traditional virtues are leading a generous and selfless life, truthfulness, restraint from greed, and respect for one's elders. These principles are consistent with a virtually global idea of righteousness. Hinduism has progressed through India's moments of crisis by lifting repeatedly the banner of the highest ideals. The image of the Dance of Shiva is strongly evoked by the following passage from the *Bhagavad-Gita:*

> Whenever the dharma decays, and when that which is not dharma prevails, then I manifest myself. For the protection of the good, for the destruction of the evil, for the firm establishment of the national righteousness, I am born again and again. (Deutsch, 1968, p. 31)

The oldest source of ethical ideas is the *Mahabharata,* or Great Epic (of Bharata), the first version of which appeared between the seventh and sixth centuries B.C. It is a huge composite poem of 90,000 couplets, in 18 books, that traces the rivalry between two families involved in an unrelenting war. The story is interrupted by numerous episodes, fables, moral tales, and long political and ethical discourses, all of which illustrate the illusory nature of the world and encourage the reader to strive for God. This sacred book, a repository of Hindu beliefs and customs, is based on the assumption that dharma is paramount in the affairs of society. The epics took at least 1,000 years to compose and are still the most widely read and respected religious books of the Hindus. The most popular and influential part of the epics is the *Bhagavad-Gita* ("Song of the Blessed One"), a book Gandhi once said "described the duel that perpetually went on in the hearts of mankind."

A recent European traveler in India gave this illustration of the power of dharma. Sitting precariously among local people on top of a bus during a long journey, the traveler was astounded when a sudden shower of money fell into the dusty road behind them. An Indian alongside the traveler began shouting and pounding on the roof of the bus for the driver to stop. At some distance down the road, the bus pulled over and the man rushed away. All of the passengers disembarked and waited for the Indian to return, laughing at his comic misfortune and manic disappearance. Eventually the man reappeared, clutching a big handful of notes, including Western money. It was then that the traveler realized his own wallet was gone from his back pocket; it had come loose and blown away from the top of the bus, scattering the equivalent of a year's income for the average native (about $350). The Indian, a total stranger, had run back and convinced the poverty-stricken locals to hand over the money they were gathering ecstatically from their fields. The traveler began to thank his new friend for his troubles, but with the comment "It was my duty," the Indian declined to take any reward.

It is generally believed that social conflict, oppression, and unrest do not stem from social organizations, but originate in the nonadherence to dharma by those in positions of power. Their actions have created the cycle of disharmony. Hindus see a quarrel as a drama with three actors—two contestants and a peacemaker—and not one of the protagonists but the peacemaker is seen as the victor in the dispute, because he or she has restored harmony (Lannoy, 1971, p. 198). Individuals who head institutions are believed to be the sole repositories of the virtues and vices of the institution. Traditionally, social reform movements focused not so much on abolishing the hierarchical organizations or rejecting the values on which they are based, but on removing or changing the individuals holding positions of authority in them (Kakar, 1978). For example, during the declining years of both the Mughal and British Indian empires, the ruling classes enjoyed lives of luxury and extravagance in India. Conspicuous consumption by the aristocratic elites at the expense of the productive classes still exists in the India of the early 21st century. The identity may have changed, but the attitude remains.

The issues behind the social and political ferment in India today are not rooted primarily in economic deprivation and frustration, although these make the mix more volatile (Narayana & Kantner, 1992, p. 2). Rather, it is the widespread feeling that the institutions on which the society was founded no longer work. In a reflective piece written shortly after the assassination of Rajiv Gandhi, the New Delhi correspondent of *The Economist* ("Death Among the Blossoms," 1991) wrote:

> The state is seen as corrupt and callous, incapable of delivering justice or prosperity to the people. . . . The police and civil servants are seen as oppressors and terrorists. The law courts are venal and can take decades to decide a case. The rule of law does not seem to be working in settling people's grievances. What seems to work is violence and money, and all political parties are engaged in a mad race to maximize the use of both. . . . Amid this moral decay, religious, ethnic and caste crusades have a growing appeal. People find a purity in them which they do not find in secular, national parties. And an increasing number of people are willing to kill in the name of causes that they find holier than the discredited law of the land. (p. 40)

The tragic recourse to mob violence by religious followers at different times in the country's history is a contradiction that astounds casual observers of India. How can such terrible things happen in a country where everyone believes in harmony and awaits the ultimate consequences of good and bad deeds in reincarnation? Hindus believe that *sila,* character or behavior, has its roots in the depths of the mind rather than in the heat of the action (Lannoy, 1971, p. 295). Because all worldly acts are transient, part of the illusion of life, they can have no decisive moral significance. Within the Dance of Shiva, destruction exists as strongly as creation and preservation; so it is with India.

This is not to say that violence is condoned by the Hindu faith; just the opposite applies. However, Hindus avoid the theological use of the terms "good" and "evil," and they prefer to speak of "knowledge" and "ignorance"—*vidya* and *avidya.* Destructive acts done by people who are ignorant are not regarded as sins, but those acts committed by people aware of their responsibilities are counted against them in their seeking of *mukti.*

Bathing in the holy water of the Ganges is believed to wash away all the sins of the person, and it is required of every Hindu at least once in his or her life. Indians tend to synthesize or integrate with nature because they assume that this is the natural relationship of human beings with the world, unlike Westerners, who tend to exploit the physical environment for their own purposes. But the belief in the spiritual purity of the Ganges is so strong that government attempts to clean up the badly polluted waters have little chance of being effective. Many people simply do not accept that anything can spoil the Ganges's perfection. As a consequence, rotting carcasses of both animals and partly cremated people are a common sight along the riverbanks. The image of death among life, decomposition next to creation, and pollution mixed with purity is evocative of the Dance of Shiva.

Another pervasive social dimension in India is the caste system *(verna),* which is now officially outlawed but is still a source of constant tension. Following the assumed natural law that an individual soul is born into its own befitting environment, Hindus assume that an individual belongs to a caste by birth. There are four main castes, each of which contributes to society in specific ways: (1) Brahmans, seers or religious people; (2) administrators; (3) producers such as skilled craftspeople and farmers; and (4) followers or unskilled laborers. Each of these natural classes has its appropriate honor and duties, but as privilege has entered the scale, with top castes profiting at the expense of those lower down, the whole system has begun to disintegrate. Below the system is a fifth group, the untouchables, who lie outside of the major activities of society. Its members are engaged in work that is considered socially undesirable and unclean. Untouchability, as it exists today, is often described as a perversion of the original caste system.

Within each caste or group, there are numerous subcastes, or *jati,* that influence the immediacy of all daily social relations, including work. About 3,000 *jati* exist, and they are further divisible into about 30,000 sub-*jati,* with unwritten codes governing the relationships between *jatis.* Friendships with members of the same *jati* tend to be closer and more informal than those with members of other *jatis.* As a general rule, a person's name provides information not only about his or her own *jati* but also about the region of the country from which the person's family originated. For example, Gupta is a family name from the trading class, although many have gone into teaching. Most Guptas come from the North Indian states of Haryana, Uttar Pradesh, and West Bengal.

The *jati's* values, beliefs, and prejudices become part of each individual's psyche or conscience. The internalized *jati* norms define the right actions, or dharma, for an individual—he or she feels good or loved when living up to these rules, and guilty when transgressing them.

When society was divided strictly by caste, there was no attempt to realize a competitive equality, and within each caste, all interests were regarded as identical. But that also meant that equality of opportunity existed for all within the caste—every individual was allowed to develop the experience and skills that he or she needed to succeed at the caste's defined role. The castes were self-governing, which ensured that each person was tried and judged by his peers. Central authorities viewed crimes committed by upper-caste members more severely than those of the lower caste. Because it was simply not possible to move outside of the caste, all possibility of social ambition, with its accompanying tension, was avoided. This suits the Hindu belief in harmony. The comprehensiveness of the caste system, together with holistic dharma, contributed to the stability that prevailed among the vast mass of people for much of India's history. Preservation of order, interspaced with disorder, is a characteristic of the Dance of Shiva.

The worst facet of the caste system falls on the untouchables. This caste has come to be the symbol of India's own brand of human injustice, victims of a system that kept people alive in squalor. Of course, social hierarchy is universal, found not only among the Hindus but also among the Muslims, Christians, Sikhs, Jains, and Jews (Srinivas, 1980). There is also a prevalence of pollution taboos in all civilizations, including the most advanced and modern; eliminating dirt is an attempt to introduce order into the environment (Lannoy, 1971, p. 146). But Hindu society pays exceptional attention to the idea of purity and pollution, and historically, this has resulted in the virtual ostracism of the untouchables from the rest of society.

By way of historical explanation, Hindus believed that proximity to the contaminating factor constitutes a permanent pollution that is both collective and hereditary. Therefore, they had a dread of being polluted by members of society who were specialists in the elimination of impurity. Hindu society was more conscious of grading social groups according to their degree of purity than of a precise division of castes into occupations. The untouchables—traditionally, society's cleaners, butchers, and the like—were at the bottom of the Hindu hierarchy because they were considered irrevocably unclean. A similar caste system was developed in Japan, and it, too, has been outlawed, although its effects are still being felt.

Although India's traditional social structure was based on institutionalized inequality, today the government, and supposedly the nation, too, is committed to social equality. Beginning with Mahatma Gandhi, public figures have tried to reform the attitudes of Indian society toward the untouchables. Gandhi named them *Harijan,* literally, "Children of God." The entire caste system was declared illegal by the Constitution, and today, untouchables are guaranteed 22.5% of government jobs as compensation for traditional disfavor. These policies have met with some success, but such a deep-rooted prejudice cannot be eliminated by a mere stroke of the pen.

The ambiguity of caste in occupational terms is another wedge by which the lower castes push their way upward on the scale. However, ambiguity is not so great as to render the system inoperative. Violations of caste norms, such as inter-caste marriage, still evoke responses of barbaric ferocity. Educated Indians look upon such incidents as throwbacks to the inhumanity of feudal times that must be dealt with sternly by the authorities. But efforts to create greater equality of opportunity for members of the traditionally disadvantaged castes meet stiff resistance from these same ranks (Narayana & Kantner, 1992, p. 5).

Additional reforms remain problematical, as recent history suggests. In 1990, the government introduced policies reserving 27% of central and state jobs for these castes and Christian and Muslim groups that were socially backward. In protest, dozens of upper-caste students burned themselves to death. The upper-caste Brahmans, a mere 5.5% of the population, have traditionally run government departments, but the struggle for jobs in India is so intense that the students saw themselves as victims of injustice, not historical oppressors. The prime minister at the time, V. P. Singh, was forced to resign when the government's coalition partner withdrew its support of the government, mainly over caste reform issues.

The Harijan quickly realized their ability to assert their democratic rights as equal citizens through organized political activity. The effect of politicization of caste in modern times has made it clear that power is becoming ascendant over status. Modern education also acts as a solvent of caste barriers. These factors hold out the best hope for the disappearance of caste over the longer term.

The hierarchical principle of social organization has been central to the conservatism of Indian tradition. Among the criteria for ordering are age and gender. Elders have more formal authority than younger people, and, as we have already related, men have greater authority than women. Many times, women are not involved in social functions or conversations and are required to cover their heads in front of elders or mature guests. Most relationships are hierarchical in structure, characterized by almost maternal nurturing on the part of the superior, and by filial respect and compliance on the part of the subordinate. The ordering of social behavior extends to every institution in Indian life, including the workplace, which we will examine shortly.

It is clear that the traditional social structure of India is undergoing change and reform. This is consistent with the evolutionary aspects of the Dance of Shiva. But any change requires the destruction of old ways, and pressure is beginning to build within the old system. It may be that before those changes are complete, Shiva will rest, and chaos will rule for a time. Or perhaps a new rhythm is beginning for the dance of the 21st century, and the Daily Dance of Indian society will quietly adjust in response.

THE WORK AND RECREATION (REJUVENATION) CYCLE

There are several different perspectives on the importance of work: to earn a living; to satisfy the worldly interests of accomplishments, power, and status; and to fulfill the desire to create and care for the family. An aspect considered more important in India is that work enables, prepares, and progresses the individual through the cycle of life toward the ultimate aim of achieving *mukti*. The Indian approach to work is best defined by the *Bhagavad-Gita:* "Both renunciation and practice of work lead to the highest bliss. Of these two, the practice of work is better than its renunciation" (Deutsch, 1968, p. 60).

Work was prescribed originally as duty (dharma) without any concern for material outcomes. Castes were occupational clusters, each discharging their roles and, in turn, being maintained by the overall system. But meeting the obligations to one's relatives, friends, and even strangers, as well as maintaining relationships, constituted the ethos of the system. Even with the rapid expansion of industrial activity in the 20th century, requiring large-scale importation of Western technology and work forms, Indians have internalized Western work values only partially. Today, with government-mandated affirmative action, it is not unlikely that someone from a higher caste may work for someone from a lower caste. Many Indians have developed a state of mind that allows them to put aside caste prejudice in the workplace but, on returning home, to conduct all of their social activities strictly according to caste norms.

We have already seen how family life develops an acute sense of dependence in the individual that serves to fortify the participative and collective nature of society. Similarly, most Indian organizations have numerous overlapping in-groups, with highly personalized relationships between the members of each group. They cooperate, make sacrifices for the common good, and generally protect each other's interests. But in-groups often interfere with the functioning of formally designated sections, departments, and divisions, and they can lead to factionalism and intense power plays within an organization. Just as disorder within order is a characteristic of the Dance of Shiva, so, too, is incompetence often overlooked because work performance is more relationship oriented than contractual in nature. A competent person may be respected but not included in a group unless he or she possesses the group characteristics.

Family, relatives, caste members, and people speaking the same language or belonging to the same religion may form in-groups. Typically, there are regionally oriented subgroups, formed on the basis of states, districts, towns, and villages from which people's families originated. Within the group, Indians are informal and friendly.

Geert Hofstede's (1980) attitudinal survey of the cultural differences among some 53 countries is especially helpful in the case of India, which tends to cluster with those countries where there is a high degree of uncertainty avoidance. Indians tend to work with lifelong friends and colleagues and minimize risk-taking behavior. This orientation is consistent with the Hindu philosophy of life as an illusion, Indians' preoccupation with astrology, and their resignation to karma. India also falls with those countries characterized by large power distances. However, India ranks 21st of the 53 nations on individualism. Although we might expect a more collectivistic orientation, this ranking may reflect the influence of British rule. Finally, India has a high score on masculinity, which is consistent with the emphasis on male domination in Hinduism. Generally, the values described by Hofstede reflect a historical continuity and resilience of the Indian social system, despite the onslaught of foreign invasions, colonial rulers, and economic dislocations.

The hierarchical principle continues to be a source of stagnation in modern Indian institutions. Younger people have a limited, or no, say in decision making. Persistent critical questioning or confrontations on issues necessary to effect change simply do not occur. Any conflict between intellectual conviction and developmental fate manifests itself in a vague sense of helplessness and impotent rage. Gradually, the younger workers resign themselves to waiting until they become seniors in their own right, free to enjoy the delayed gratification that age brings with it in Indian society. The apparent lack of control and ambition displayed by the participants at work is similar to the resignation of the world to the will of Shiva. The world responds to Shiva's rhythm, captive of its pace, and is unable to influence it.

The importance of honoring family and *jati* bonds leads to nepotism, dishonesty, and corruption in the commercial world. These are irrelevant abstract concepts; guilt and anxiety are aroused only when individual actions go against the principle of primacy of relationships, not when foreign standards of ethics and efficiency are breached. This creates legendary tales of corrupt officials that are shared widely among travelers and businesspeople who have spent time in India.

Indian organizations have been shaped by colonial experiences that have bureaucratized them and polarized the positions of the rulers (managers) and the ruled (workers). As a consequence, the role of the manager tends to be viewed as that of an order-giver or autocrat. In "Going International" (1983), a popular management training videotape, there is a telling vignette involving an American manager and one of his Indian subordinate managers. As a general rule, American managers perceive their role to be that of a problem solver or facilitator and attempt to involve subordinates in routine decisions (Adler, 1997). The American manager in this videotape attempted to use this style with his Indian subordinate, who wondered about his superior's competence and held him in some contempt for not being autocratic. The clear implication is that American managers must act more authoritatively in India than in the United States.

In the areas of rejuvenation and recreation, one of their sources for the Indian people is participation in the many religious festivals held throughout the year. These festivals are usually associated with agricultural cycles or the rich mythology of India's past. In some regions, community festivals involve the active participation of not only Hindus, but also members of other religions. Family bonds are emphasized and strengthened repeatedly through the joint celebration of religious festivals. The Indian sense of fun and play is given free rein during the festivities, which often include riddles, contests of strength, role reversals, and rebellious acts. Just as the Dance of Shiva is an expression of his joy and exuberance, festivals give Hindus an opportunity to express their feelings of devotion and happiness.

Religious raptures, possessions, and trances are common during Indian seasonal festivals. This is a structured and, in some cases, highly formalized phenomenon that enriches the consciousness of the individual and the group. There are also the attendant dangers of degeneration into hysterical mob psychology, which Indian history has witnessed many times. Festivals allow the discharge of intense emotion that is otherwise submerged in a network of reciprocity and caste relations, but they also can be used to reestablish order. In this sense, festivals mirror the activity, relapse, and reordering of the cosmos that is the result of the Dance of Shiva. But just as the dancer cannot help dancing, the celebrant is not always capable of restraining his or her religious fervor.

Memorials to the grand line of India's "modern gods"—Mahatma Gandhi, Jawaharlal Nehru, and now Indira Gandhi—are as much the objects of pilgrimages as any temple or festival. Indira Gandhi was killed by her own trusted Sikh bodyguards just five months after she ordered the storming of the Golden Temple at Amritsar by the Indian army to dislodge Sikh rebels. Her home in New Delhi is now a museum and shrine visited by thousands daily. The spot in her garden where she was gunned down is bracketed by two soldiers; her bullet-ridden *sari* (dress) is on display inside. Crowds gather before these, many weeping.

Another Indian example is that of N. T. Rama Rao, a former movie star and chief minister of the state of Andhra Pradesh from 1983 to 1989. Rama Rao acted in leading roles in more than 320 films with mythical, historical, and folklore themes. Among the masses, Raffia Rao was associated with the qualities of the gods he played, and when he gave up his movie career to establish a new political party, he was voted into office immediately. The fact that his party's radical Hindu fundamentalist policies sometimes caused strife within society is not inconsistent with the concurrently constructive and destructive nature of the Dance of Shiva.

The favorite pastime of Indians is watching movies, either at movie theaters or through renting videos from the shops that have sprung up all over the country, and today, India's "Hollywood" is the second largest producer of films in the world. Movies that draw on images and symbols from traditional themes are dominant in popular Indian culture. They incorporate but go beyond the familiar repertoire of plots from traditional theater. Films appeal to an audience so diverse that they transcend social and spatial categories. The language and values from popular movies have begun to influence Indian ideas of the good life and the ideology of social, family, and romantic relationships. Robert Stoller's definition of fantasy, "[the] protector from reality, concealer of truth, restorer of tranquility, enemy of fear and sadness, and cleanser of the soul" (1975, p. 55), includes terms that are equally attributable to the illusory nature of the Dance of Shiva, and it is easy to understand why films play such a major role in Indian recreation and rejuvenation.

CONCLUSION

India is the heart of Asia, and Hinduism is a convenient name for the nexus of Indian thought. It has taken 1,000 to 1,500 years to describe a single rhythm of its great pulsation, as described by the *Mahabharata*, or Great Epic. By invoking the image and meaning of the Dance of Shiva, and drawing parallels between this legendary act of a Hindu deity and many of the main influences of traditional Indian life, we have attempted to communicate the essence of India's society in this paper.

It is not always possible to identify a nicely logical or easily understandable basis for many of the contradictions that exist in Indian society, just as it is difficult to explain the existence of racism, sexism, and other forms of intolerance and injustice in Western countries. In India, the philosophy of life and the mental structure of its people come not from a study of books but from tradition (Munshi, 1965, p. 148). However much foreign civilization and new aspirations might have affected the people of India, the spiritual nutrient of Hindu philosophy has not dried up or decayed (Munshi, 1965, p. 148); within this tradition, the role of the Dance of Shiva, described as follows, is accepted by all Hindus (Coomaraswamy, 1924/1969):

> Shiva rises from his rapture and, dancing, sends through inert matter pulsing waves of awakening sound. Suddenly, matter also dances, appearing as a brilliance around him. Dancing, Shiva sustains the world's diverse phenomena, its creation and existence. And, in the fullness of time, still dancing, he destroys all forms—everything disintegrates, apparently into nothingness, and is given new rest. Then, out of the thin vapor, matter and life are created again. Shiva's dance scatters the darkness of illusion *(fila)*, burns the thread of causality *(karma)*, stamps out evil *(avidya)*, showers grace, and lovingly plunges the soul into the ocean of bliss *(ananda)*. (p. 66)

India will continue to experience the range of good and bad, happiness and despair, creation and destruction. Through it all, its people will continue their journey toward *moksha*, salvation from the worldly concerns of humankind. Hindu philosophy is the key to understanding India and how a nation of such diversity manages to bear its immense burdens while its people seem undeterred and filled with inner peace and religious devotion.

And through it all, Shiva dances on.

References

Adler, N. (1997). *International dimensions of organizational behavior* (3rd ed.). Cincinnati, OH: South-Western.

Arden, N. (1990, May). Searching for India along the great trunk road. *National Geographic, 186,* 177–185.

Banerji, P. (1983). *Erotica in Indian dance.* Atlantic Highlands, NJ: Humanities Press.

Coomaraswamy, A. (1969). *The dance of Shiva.* New York: Sunwise Turn. (Original work published 1924)

Death among the blossoms. (1991, May 25). *The Economist, 322,* 39–41.

Deutsch, E. (1968). *Bhagavad gita.* New York: Holt, Rinehart & Winston.

Going international: Part 2. Managing the overseas assignment [Videotape]. (1983). Available from Copeland Griggs Productions, San Francisco, 415/668-4200.

Gopal, R., & Dadachanji, S. (1951). *Indian dancing.* London: Phoenix House.

Hofstede, G. (1980). *Culture's consequences.* Beverly Hills, CA: Sage.

Kakar, S. (1978). *The inner world.* New York: Oxford University Press.

Karp, I., & Williams, M. (1998, April 22). Leave it to Vishnu: Gods of Indian TV are Hindu deities. *Wall Street Journal,* A1, A6.

Lannoy, R. (1971). *The speaking tree: A study of Indian culture and society.* New York: Oxford University Press.

Munshi, K. (1965). *Indian inheritance* (Vol. 1). Bombay: Bharatiya Vidya Bhavan.

Narayana, G., & Kantner, I. (1992). *Doing the needful.* Boulder, CO: Westview University Press.

Smith, H. (1958). *The religions of man.* San Francisco: Harper-Collins.

Srinivas, M. (1980). *India: Social structure.* Delhi: Hindustan.

Stoller, R. (1975). *Perversion: The erotic form of hatred.* New York: Pantheon.

Concepts and Questions

1. Why is dance an appropriate metaphor to help you understand Indian culture?
2. How does the "dance of Shiva" help define the deep structure of Indian culture?
3. How do European and American cultural perspectives of life in relation to the study of philosophy differ from that of Indian culture?
4. How might the Hindu concept of continual birth and rebirth contribute to intercultural misunderstandings?
5. Describe the structure of the Indian family. What roles and relationships exist between men and women? How do children fit into the structure of the Indian family?
6. Describe the Indian caste system and how it functions within contemporary Indian culture.
7. How does "institutionalized inequity" relate to the caste system?
8. How do the Hindu concepts of purity and pollution affect interpersonal relationships?
9. What problems might an American manager experience when working with an Indian workforce?
10. How do Indian cultural values toward work differ from those found in the United States?

Personality and Person Perception in Africa

KARL PELTZER

This paper describes the construction of an African socialization and personhood model, drawing from research on child-rearing practices and cultural concepts of personhood in African societies as well as clinical psychological practice with African patients (Jahoda, 1982; Morakinyo & Akiwowo, 1981; Nsamenang, 1992; Peltzer, 1995). Psychoanalytically oriented material from West Africa (Collomb & Valentin, 1970; Parin, Morgenthaler, & Parin-Mattley, 1971) and contributions from anthropology (see Riesman, 1985) were also applied in the development of the model. Here the term *personhood* will be used in considering relational and contextual aspects of African concepts of personality as opposed to the Western concept, which separates the individual from the social context and emphasizes a pronounced self (Riesman, 1985; Shweder & Bourne, 1984; Sökefeld, 1999).

In geographical terms, this study is restricted to sub-Saharan Africa. Africa is a vast continent and consists of many different cultures; consequently, some of the findings can be applied only to particular groups in specific geographic regions. If the term "African" is still used in different contexts, it should be kept in mind that the findings are limited to the particular group under study. In line with Okeke, Draguns, Sheku, and Allen (1999, p. 140), it is possible to identify some promising and convergent trends that have emerged from several decades of personality-oriented research in Africa.

Care has been taken to avoid the risk of succumbing to stereotypes and glossing over the heterogeneity and complexity of psychological phenomena in Africa, by being mindful (1) of the great diversity among African cultures (no generalization applies to all of them and allowances must be explicitly made for multiplicity of trends, atypical features, and exceptional instances); (2) that within any culture the general expectation is for a multimodal distribution of all—or most—personality characteristics; and (3) that within a specific individual, provision is made for the coexistence of several, sometimes apparently incompatible or even mutually exclusive, trends.

The geographic region "Africa South of the Sahara" is seen here as a region of similar cultures which differs from other regions in the world due, for example, to a high illiteracy rate, subsistence-oriented economies, and highly permissive child-rearing practices. Okeke et al. (1999, p. 150) summarized six essential socialization experiences common in African societies as follows: (1) close bodily contact with the mother during infancy and prompt relief of hunger and physical discomfort during this state of development; (2) mothering by several adults during infancy and early childhood; (3) systematic inculcation of respect and obedience toward parents, elders, and other adults beginning shortly after weaning and continuing through early and middle childhood; (4) rather relaxed and unpressured training toward bodily self-control; (5) providing a rather wide scope for exploration of the physical and social environment early in life and tolerating, if not actively encouraging, a great deal of independence as soon as the child becomes fully mobile; and (6) peer groups of children of the same age and gender assuming importance as agents of socialization, providers of security and acceptance, and sources of self-esteem.

There are, however, variations in contemporary African populations. Peltzer (1995, p. 25) has identified the following three distinctive components of the people inhabiting present-day sub-Saharan Africa: (1) *traditional* persons who are yet little affected by modernization and who are functioning within the established and seemingly timeless framework of their culture; (2) *transitional* persons, often living in, and shuttling between, the two cultures in the course of their daily round of activities—for example, between work and home or between the temporary urban-living dwelling and the ancestral traditional village where their extended family continues to reside; and (3) *modern* individuals, participating fully in the activities of the contemporary, industrial or postindustrial world. This trichotomy is relevant to personal experience and functioning, and it serves as an integral dimension in the model of sub-Saharan personality development.

From *Social Behavior and Personality,* 2002, *30*(1), pp. 83–94. Reprinted by permission of the Society for Personality Research, Inc. Karl Peltzer teaches at the University of the North, Sovenga (Pieetersburg), South Africa.

The socialization of traditional and transitional persons can be illustrated in the form of a model in three dimensions: (1) the *authority* dimension (vertical, diachronic, historic); (2) the *group* dimension (horizontal, synchronic, social); and (3) the *body-mind/environment* dimension.

THE AUTHORITY DIMENSION

Traditional Personhood

The traditional person in African societies is socialized from birth to death into the authority dimension, which is based on the principles of age and seniority and which consists of the mother, elder siblings, father, elders, ancestors, and God. The child acquires knowledge and behavior patterns which focus mainly on its conduct in the presence of elders (Parin et al., 1971, p. 505). Younger persons are expected to show respect to the senior in the context of greetings, rituals of thanksgiving, and control of aggression. In return, the senior is responsible for protecting and advising any junior when asked to do so. Children learn, through education and through imitation of respected persons, how to behave toward other people in the framework of this hierarchy (Staewen & Schönberg, 1980, p. 188).

The first phase of personhood is from birth to weaning (about 18–24 months). Here the infant usually experiences an extremely positive attitude, immediate gratification of every desire, and permanent unshadowed affection, without any form of frustration or sibling rivalry. As a result of this symbiotic relationship between the mother and the infant during the first phase, the infant does not internalize the external authorities, norms, values, and rules until it is weaned (Parin, 1972, p. 254).

During the second phase, from weaning to adolescence, the child develops identifications with its aggressors. The first identification with an aggressor is with the mother who weaned it. The frustration and aggression originating from this are coped with by forming "ideal-parents-images" in which the child can take part (participative projection). Through incorporating and participating in the omnipotent qualities of the object (mother), which the subject projects onto the object, the child can compensate for the frustration and powerlessness of experiences after weaning (Parin et al., 1971, p. 501). The child transfers the power of the mother to satisfy all needs onto other authorities such as elder siblings, the father, and supernatural projective systems like ancestors and God (Burton & Reis, 1981, p. 679).

The development of traditional personhood is seen by Sow (1980, p. 126) "not as a 'completed' system . . . it is perpetually 'in the making.'" The life cycle—birth, adulthood, old age, death, and their associated rites of passage—is seen as the process by which the person passes from the present to the past. The ancestor is symbolically the source of the power and fertility of his descendants. Birth signifies the return of a dead person, following a cycle alternating between the poles of death, mother, and child, in which the child's ambiguous identity places the mother in a cycle of her own descent: the child is linked to a uterine ancestor beyond the begetter father (Ortigues, Ortigues, & Zempléni, 1989). This means that the outlook of the traditional time concept is cyclic and death is not regarded as final, in contrast to the linear concepts in Western societies. Given the importance attached to social rather than technical values, delayed gratification and future orientation are less necessary. Indeed, the short life span, subsistence mode of production, and slow pace of change in traditional societies may contribute to a cyclic time concept which does not emphasize future, past, or present.

The status of a full person is really acquired only with old age, which takes on an ancestral quality (Sow, 1980, p. 126). The dynamic character of the formation of the traditional person does not focus on early childhood in the past. There is no particular fixation on early childhood and no defense is internalized since almost no frustrating experiences occurred. Having little or no internal defiance for protection, the individual regresses easily and massively (Collomb & Valentin, 1970, p. 365). In conclusion, one may say that the traditional African person views himself in the here and now with an outlook which is diffuse and oriented toward different stages in the past and which is not fixated on one stage.

Transitional Personhood

The transitional person is no longer so potently ruled by the authority and diachrony described above. The continuity of socialization has been broken and the gulf between the generations has become apparent. Traditional authority and advice in general, which serves as communication links as well as frames of reference, are losing their hold and are no longer listened to. Schools impose other masters besides the father, an authority other than that of the ancestor. The nuclear family, which is not based on the authority of the elder family members, is becoming the standard model. The father and mother become proprietors of the child as an object, bearer of hopes and new values (Collomb & Valentin, 1970, p. 382). Being affected by this transitional socialization process, the transitional African may, particularly in times of crisis, return to the traditional authority which was once part of his culture.

THE GROUP DIMENSION

Traditional Personhood

After weaning, the traditional person is socialized into the group dimension, which is based on associations with those of the some age and sex and with school— or work—mates. The authority and omnipotence of the mother and father are transferred to siblings and age-mates, preferably of the same sex (Parin, 1978). The mother-as-support is widely diffused to many mothers and fathers, in a system of multilateral possibilities of identification including brothers, peers, older companions, father, and ancestors (Zempléni-Rabain, 1973, p. 333). Through the projective identification of the "ideal-parents-image" onto group-mates the child can compensate for lost omnipotence (Parin et al., 1971, p. 501). Thus Africans are able to identify themselves with relations who evoke a wide range of feelings and a wide range of possible gratifications.

With increasing age, a mechanism for self-regulation evolves in the fraternal group due to the power inherent in the world of the adult, whose direct intervention is no longer needed. The informal teaching of sharing and exchange norms passes more and more into the hands of the siblings and age-mates themselves (Zempléni-Rabain, 1973, p. 233). Learning is focused on self-responsible observations and practical participation in knowledge-constituting activities with multiple attentional orientations. The resulting knowledge contributes to, or broadens, the competencies of the family or the primary group as a whole, where role conformity is especially valued. Knowledge is considered as representing a "shared" property of the family. The concept of interpersonal competence is being regarded as the capability of cooperation with others in order to reach goals of the group (Keller, 1998). With regard to the possession of the means of production, Parin et al. (1971, p. 533) have found in studying the Agni in West Africa that the means of production are owned only in a theoretical and symbolic way, since anyone can share in the yields. The only property which counts emotionally and brings security and satisfaction is the property of the clan in terms of children or human beings.

The person becomes socially integrated into the family, the group, and the community as well as becoming integrated into circles of intense sociality like initiation societies, age-grade associations, or their functional equivalents (Edwards, 1992, p. 285). Munroe and Munroe (1997, p. 299) note than the male and female gender roles are sharply contrasted throughout most of traditional Africa. Here, the female on the one hand and the male on the other receive equal education with high acceptance of weak members of the group. The females are socialized into female secrets and the males into male secrets, which will increase the attraction between the two sexes (UNICEF, n.d.). As he or she advances in age with his or her set, a whole solidarity-competition complex as well as a sense of a community develops.

The individual is taken over by the group. His or her basic value resides in fusion with the group (Riesman, 1985). Rabain (1979, pp. 42–43) notes:

> To the mother it is said: "Your child is not your possession, your thing, it is a relative, it is our child." To the child it is said: "You do not own your mother, you cannot have her to yourself, she and you are subject to our law."

The individual has no intrinsic value outside the network of kinship and social status, but remains dependent upon the group and its values, norms, and ideals (Collomb & Valentin, 1970, p. 367). The behavior of Africans is a manifestation of the collective virtues of the family and the group. There is no necessity for him or her to internalize group norms since he or she is part of the group and its collective consciousness, which provides little room for guiding principles within him- or herself (Forssen, 1979, p. 148). The traditional person identifies with the group in such a way that group actions or responses are experienced as his own (Riesman, 1985). In the person, the collective selves of the community are experiences (Ogbonnaya, 1994, p. 75). Eaton and Louw (2000, p. 210) found among African-language speakers more interdependent self-construal than among English speakers in South Africa. In order to maintain his or her relationships, he or she must have a definite status and comply with the norms of his or her group. The concept of locus of control in African societies generally tends to focus on external rather than interval attributions (Okeke et al., 1999, p. 151).

Transitional Personhood

The transitional person is no longer so much a "group person" as the traditional person because he or she has undergone a process of individuation through emphasis on competence, competition, and the desire to excel. Rites of passage are becoming empty forms that can no longer fulfill their reassuring and integrating roles. Age and sex groups are disappearing. By the time they reach adolescence, transitional Africans realize that they are individuals, concerned mainly with themselves and for themselves, responsible for their own destiny and in opposition to others. The community, which was a natural extension of the family, is gradually losing its function and meaning as organizer of the individual's social life and provider of the frame of reference for individual actions. The human continuity, which up to now provided unity and solidarity, has been broken. The relationship with the group is losing its strength and is being replaced by more egoistic investments (Collomb & Valentin, 1970, p. 389). Investment in social values in terms of relationships with children, relatives, and other people is being exchanged for retentive expropriation (Parin, 1978, p. 125). The child becomes the property of the reproductive couple and not the collective property of the two families and kinships. The breakdown of the "group superego" results in an increase in guilt feelings, since people can no longer project onto others so easily the responsibility for bad events (Murphy, 1978, p. 239). Socialization now takes place at least partly outside the family. In addition to schools, the mass media and the peer group have become important programming institutions.

THE BODY-MIND/ENVIRONMENT DIMENSION

The body-mind can be seen as a micro cosmos and the environment as a macro cosmos. Socialization into the microcosm is affected by people in the authority and group dimensions, whereas socialization into the macro cosmos is affected by the nonhuman objects in the environment. Natural elements, components of the body, and states of mind are perceived to be interrelated as part of a whole, as micro cosmos to macro cosmos, and to be in continuous interaction in such a way that energies are exchanged in both spheres (White & Marsella, 1984, p. 16).

Traditional Personhood

The socialization of the traditional person in the micro cosmos or body-mind dimension is based on a body-mind unity. Since the traditional person is less socialized into the macro cosmos owing to the greater emphasis placed on human beings than on the physical environment, unity between body and mind exists to a greater degree in the micro cosmic sphere of the traditional person. "The body is the mind and the mind is the body" (Morakinyo & Akiwowo, 1981, p. 26). Within the micro cosmic sphere the body is not neglected, as it is in Western societies, so body-mind unity can be maintained.

Traditional African mother–infant interaction emphasizes bodily contact in the form of holding, breast-feeding, carrying on the back, caressing massage (UNICEF, n.d.), fondling, and sleeping close together. The activities of the infant remain closely bound to bodily sensations longer than in the Western setting. The mother and infant have a private language which passes through the child's body (UNICEF, n.d.). This means that the infant concentrates more on bodily gratifications like sucking and biting than on the exploration of the external environment (Parin et al., 1971, p. 533). The body-image is shaped by massaging and by encouraging the infant to touch the breast with hand and mouth (Dores & Renandin, 1979, p. 113). Even when the mother starts giving the infant porridge, the aim is not to encourage exposure to objects (i.e., food) or to substitute food for breast milk, but for the more psychosocial purpose of amusing or calming the infant (UNICEF, n.d.). As a result, the child learns to use the body as a means of communication and develops kinesthetic empathy. Rabain (1979, p. 275) suggests that corporal care and rhythmic and rocking movements are illustrative of a collative investment in the body. The importance of such contact is demonstrated not only in infancy but also in daily exchanges throughout adulthood. It is through these exchanges that people's needs to touch each other and to remain close appear as social regulators of mood. Keller and Eckensberger (1998, p. 75) describe infant care as coactive care settings in African cultures, where the prevalent mode of interaction seems to be body contact ("back and hip cultures" versus "crib and cradle cultures"); for example, U.S. American babies are held only half as much as Guaii babies (Whiting, 1981, p. 160). Carrying and body contact thus provide the infant with tactile and vestibular stimulation which creates the interactional experience of emotional warmth. The study of early mother–child interactional situations leads to the distinction between the experience of contiguity and warmth as two separate parenting components. Especially parental contiguity in terms of prompt reactiveness toward the infant's signals (latency span beyond one second) fosters experiences of causality, predictability, and controllability. The interactional context of body contact provides the infant with the experiences of warmth and positive attunement. Warmth can be regarded as fostering feelings of relatedness, empathy, and compliance (Keller, 1998).

The child shares all the mother's movements, accompanying her as she works or dances. Frequently the child is involved in rhythm, dance, music, and singing. Igaga and Versey (1978, p. 61) found that Ugandan subjects showed better rhythmic performance abilities than did English subjects, since there are many types of rhythm that accompany social and ceremonial occasions and encourage different activities such as work. Imitation, which plays an important role in traditional socialization, is determined by reciprocal interaction with the mother and usually involves bodily movement. When children imitate adult activities, they see this as identical with play and games, which means that socio-technical or technical activity is more psychosocially organized and perceived (UNICEF, n.d.). Even after weaning, the child is incorporated into new, more collective relationships with his or her peers and others and in the extended family, in which body contact continues to play a prominent role. As a result, the traditional person is more inclined to use the body as a means of expressing and communication himself/herself to others than is the Western person, who is more dependent on purely verbal means of communication (Parin et al., 1971, p. 545).

The traditional person is socialized primarily by people, while the Western person is socialized primarily by objects (Agiobu-Kemmer, 1984, p. 189). By being exposed to people, the traditional person will develop more social intelligence than technological intelligence. The qualities encouraged are respect, obedience, and conformity at the expense of curiosity, exploration, originality, and individualized constructive play related to objects. Primary conceptual domains arising from this emphasis on social or micro cosmic development concern relationships between people—for example, kinship systems and supernatural theories of illness and misfortune—leading to the framing of accounts of causation in a personal or social context rather than in the material terms of Western culture. In contrast to the traditional person's concerns with people and social processes, Western intelligence seems to favor an object orientation, with a strong and aggressive concern for control and exploitation of the environment (Mundy-Castle, 1985). Serpell (1984, p. 111) found that rural African communities evaluated a social-cooperative disposition as an internal component of intelligence. Okeke et al. (1999, p. 154) state that the positive consequences of this social orientation are readily apparent. They include a high level of social sophistication in interacting with others, usually within one's in-group; personal sensitivity; ease of social interaction, at least within one's familiar social milieu; and freedom from disruptive social anxiety or social inhibition—for example, in the form of shyness. Furthermore, Okeke et al. (1999, p. 153) note that the cognitive style prevalent in Africa is oriented toward synthesis rather than analysis. Africans are less disposed toward extricating a component or an element from a pattern of stimuli into which it is embedded. Thus, global, holistic, intuitive, and expressive cognitive operations prevail over fragmentary, isolated, or detail-oriented mental activities.

Transitional Personhood

In the transitional person, bodily forms of expression have been systematically reduced through the introduction of formal education, changes in child-rearing practices (involving less body contact and earlier weaning), and a shift in the economy from subsistence to market production. The rhythmical oscillation of the subsistence mode of production is synchronized with the time-calculating machines such as the clock and with quantitative criteria to measure productivity (Bastide, 1973, p. 104); hence a dichotomy of work and leisure has come into being. Body and mind are no longer a unity, and the mind is more highly valued than the body. This has been demonstrated, for instance, by Ndetei and Muhangi (1979, p. 272) in Kenya, where the head, as representative of the mind and indicating technological intelligence, has become more important to transitional Kenyans than the abdomen, as representative of the body and indicating social intelligence. The emphasis on the superiority of the mind has led systematically to more body and affect control in transitional Africans.

Relations between parents and children have become closer, as a consequence of the creation of the nuclear family, and a new moral solicitude for the transitional child's well-being has come into existence. Thus, internalization is encouraged and the individual superego is created. The internal locus of control becomes more relevant than it used to be, while the external locus of control becomes less relevant. As a result, the transitional person's emotions and actions become his own responsibility to a greater degree. Undesirable feelings of anger and hostility that were previously projected onto supernatural objects and that elicited cohesive support within the family may now be attributed by the transitional youth to parental control and may call for confrontation and challenge.

In conclusion, it can be reasonably argued that the two divisions of *authority, group,* and *body-mind/environment* and *traditional, transitional,* and *modern personhoods* provide a basic framework for understanding the development of personality and personhood in sub-Saharan Africa.

References

Agiobu-Kemmer, I. (1984). Cognitive aspects of infant development. In H. Curran (Ed.), *Nigerian children: Developmental perspectives* (pp. 174–117). London: Routledge and Kegan Paul.

Bastide, R. (1973). Techniques of rest and relaxation: A transcultural study. *Transactional Psychiatric Research Review, 10,* 103–107.

Burton, R. V., & Reis, J. (1981). Internalization. In R. H. Munroe, R. L. Munroe, & B. B. Whiting (Eds.), *Handbook of cross-cultural human development* (pp. 675–688). New York: Garland.

Collomb, H., & Valentin, S. (1970). The black African family. In H. J. Anthony & C. Kompernik (Eds.), *The child and his family: The international yearbook for child psychiatry and allied disciplines* (Vol. 1, pp. 359–388). New York: Wiley-Interscience.

Dores, M., & Renandin, N. (1979). African childhood. *Etudes Psychotherapiques, 10,* 111–115.

Eaton, L., & Louw, J. (2000). Culture and self in South Africa: Individualism–collectivism predictions. *Journal of Social Psychology, 140,* 210–217.

Edwards, C. P. (1992). Cross-cultural perspectives on family–peer relations. In R. D. Parks & G. W. Ladd (Eds.), *Family–peer relationships: Models of linkage* (pp. 285–316). Hillsdale, NJ: Erlbaum.

Forssen, A. (1979). *Roots of traditional personality development among the Zaramo in Coastal Tanzania.* Helsinki: Scandinavian Institute of African Studies.

Igaga, J. M., & Versey, J. (1978). Cultural differences in rhythmic performances. *Psychology of Music, 6,* 61–64.

Jahoda, G. (1982). *Psychology and anthropology.* London: Academic Press.

Keller, H. (1998, July). *Different socialization pathways to adolescence.* Paper presented at the Fourth Africa Regional Conference of the International Society for the Study of Behavioural Development, Windhock/Namibin.

Keller, H., & Eckensberger, H. L. (1998). Kultur und Entwicklung. In H. Keller (Ed.), *Lehrbuch Entwicklungspsychologie* (pp. 57–96). Bern: Huber.

Morakinyo, O., & Akiwowo, A. (1981). The Yoruba ontology of personality and motivation: A multidisciplinary approach. *Journal of Biological Structure, 4,* 19–38.

Mundy-Castle, A. (1985, April). *Human behaviour and national development: Conceptual and theoretical perspectives.* Paper presented at the National Conference on Human Behavior and the Challenges of National Development in Nigeria, University of Ife, Ile-Ife.

Munroe, R. L., & Munroe, R. H. (1997). Logoli childhood and the cultural reproduction of sex differentiation. In T. S. Weisner & C. Bradley (Eds.), *African families and the crisis of social change* (pp. 299–314). Westport, CT: Bergin & Garvey/Greenwood.

Murphy, H. B. M. (1978). The advent of guilt feelings as a common depressive symptom: A historical comparison on two continents. *Psychiatry, 41,* 229–242.

Ndetei, D. M., & Muhangi, J. (1979). The prevalence and clinical presentation of psychiatric illness in a rural setting in Kenya. *British Journal of Psychiatry, 135,* 269–272.

Nsamenang, A. B. (1992). *Human development in cultural context: A third world perspective.* Newbury Park, CA: Sage.

Ogbonnaya, A. O. (1994). Person as community: An African understanding of the person as an intrapsychic community. *Journal of Black Psychology, 20,* 75–87.

Okeke, B. L., Draguns, J. G., Sheku, B., & Allen, W. (1999). Culture, self, and personality in Africa. In Y. T. Lee, R. C. McCauley, & J. G. Draguns (Eds.), *Personality and person perception across cultures* (pp. 139–162). Mahwah, NJ: Erlbaum.

Ortigues, M. C., Ortigues, H., & Zempléni, A. (1989). Clinical psychology and anthropology. In K. Peltzer & P. O. Ebigbo (Eds.), *Clinical psychology in Africa* (pp. 228–239). Frankfurt/Main: IKO Verlag.

Parin, P. (1972). A contribution of ethnopsychoanalytic investigation to the theory of aggression. *International Journal of Psycho-Analysis, 53,* 251–257.

Parin, P. (1978). Ethnopsychoanalyse: Ein Studium des Menschen in senier Gesellschaft. In H. Wulff (Ed.), *Ethhnopsychiatrie.* Wiesbaden: Akademische.

Parin, P., Morgenthaler, E., & Parin-Mattley, G. (1971). *Filrchte deinen nilchsten wie dich selbst: Psychoanalyse und Gesellschaft am Modell der Agni in West Afrika.* Frankfurt/Main: Suhrkamp.

Peltzer, K. (1995). *Psychology and health in African cultures: Examples of ethnopsychotherapeutic practice.* Frankfurt/Main: KIO Verlag.

Rabain, J. (1979). L'investissement collectif du corps de l'enfant: Exemples africains. *Neuropsychiatrie de l'Enfance et de l'Adolescence, 39,* 274–276.

Riesman, P. (1985, November). *The person and the life cycle in African social life and thought.* Paper presented at the 28th Annual Meeting of the African Studies Association, New Orleans.

Serpell, R. (1984). Research on cognitive development in sub-Saharan Africa. *International Journal of Behavioural Development, 7,* 111–127.

Shweder, R. A., & Bourne, E. J. (1984). Does the concept of the person vary cross-culturally? In A. J. Marsella & G. M. White (Eds.), *Cultural conceptions of mental health and therapy* (pp. 97–140). Dordecht: A. Reidel.

Sökefeld, M. (1999). Debating self, identity, and culture in anthropology. *Current Anthropology, 40,* 417–431.

Sow, I. (1980). *Anthropological structures of madness in Black Africa.* New York: International Universities.

Stilwen, C., & Schönberg, F. (1980). *Kulturwandel and Angstentwicklung bei den Yoruba West Afrikas.* München: Seltforum.

UNICEF. (n.d.). *Cradle of humanity: Child rearing, mothercraft (Africa)* [Film]. Co-produced with French Television (ORTF).

White, G. M., & Marsella, A. J. (1984). Cultural conceptions in mental health research. In A. J. Marsella & G. M. White (Eds.), *Cultural conceptions of mental health and therapy* (pp. 3–38). Dordecht: A. Reidel.

Whiting, J. W. M. (1981). Environmental constraints on infant care practices. In R. H. Munroe, R. L. Munroe, & G. B. Whiting (Eds.), *Handbook of cross-cultural human development* (pp. 155–179). New York: Garland.

Zempléni-Rabain, J. (1973). Food and the strategy involved in learning fraternal exchange among Wolof children. In P. Alexandre (Ed.), *French perspectives in African studies.* London: Oxford University Press.

Concepts and Questions

1. Describe how the six "essential socialization experiences common in African societies" listed by Peltzer can be used to understand the socialization of African children.
2. Describe the differences between traditional, transitional, and modern individual as outlined by Peltzer.
3. Explain how these three categories might be used to understand social psychological development in other parts of the world. Would they apply to indigenous people in Central or South America? If yes, why; if no, why not?
4. How do children raised in the traditional mode differ from children in the transitional mode with regard to their values and attitudes toward authority?
5. How might the upbringing of children with an integrated sense of dance and rhythm affect their ability to communicate interculturally with Westerners?
6. How does the group orientation manifest itself in the persona of African children?
7. Why might the group orientation of traditional and transitional Africans be a problem in intercultural communication?
8. What does Peltzer mean by the body-mind/environment dimension?
9. Peltzer uses the term *personhood.* What does he mean by this term?
10. How does the developed personhood of traditional children and transitional children differ?

Communication with Egyptians

Polly A. Begley

Cairo made my eyeballs ache. It is a city of coloured splendour, alive and moving, with a hundred gay pigments astir in the sunshine, and every thoroughfare stuffed full, as it seems, of processioning and pageantry.

Arthur Edward Copping, 1910

As the sun rises above the ancient land of Pharaohs, the *Muezzin* calls faithful Muslims to prayer over the city's loudspeakers. Egypt, claiming more than 4,000 years of history, is a country of extremes: an ancient center of learning and mystery, overwhelming poverty next to grand architectural wonders, sandstorms and sunshine mingling with smog, and the fertile Nile Valley surrounded by desert. The 6,671 kilometers of the Nile River is lifeblood for Egyptian civilization. The Nile is known as a "precious gift yet a perilous master" (Crawford, 1996, p. 39). The unpredictable river gives life through its waters while periodically destroying canals, houses, or entire towns.

People have long been intrigued by Egyptian culture—mysterious pyramids, sacred temples hewn from rocky cliffs, enigmatic hieroglyphs, and centuries-old traditions. The Greek historian Herodotus, born around 484 B.C., was one of the first scholar-tourists to extol the wonders of Egypt to the rest of the world. Modern architecture, philosophy, mathematics, literature, and science have all been influenced by Egyptian wisdom. Specifically, Socrates, Aristotle, and Pythagoras all learned from the Egyptians. Even our alphabet may have evolved from ancient hieroglyphs (Crawford, 1996). Modern Egyptologists still wonder at the near-perfect preservation of writings on 3,000- to 4000-year-old stones and temples. In villages along the Nile today, the *Fellahin,* or peasants, employ the same tools and agricultural methods from Pharaonic periods. Government experts sent to these communities are told that modern irrigation ideas are unnecessary because "we have done it this way for thousands of years." Clearly, one must know a great deal about Egypt's history, customs, and traditions before she or he is prepared to appreciate the rich tapestry of its culture.

We cannot presume that this brief essay can comprehensively cover thousands of years of history and tradition. Scholars who focus on cultural studies know that learning is a continual process. Even a lifetime of study and experience, however, would not be enough to unravel the secrets of Egyptian civilization. The purpose of the review, then, is to seek an understanding of interactions among Egyptians and non-Egyptians by examining relevant cultural characteristics. Specifically, the primary emphasis will be on aspects of culture that influence intercultural communication. To this end, we will discuss the three important aspects of culture: (1) worldview and religion, (2) values, and (3) language.

EGYPTIAN WORLDVIEW AND RELIGION

Worldview represents common perception among the members of a cultural group. Samovar and Porter (2000) define *worldview* as "a culture's orientation toward such things as God, nature, life, death, the universe, and other philosophical issues that are concerned with the meaning of life and with 'being'" (p. 11). A religion or philosophy essentially attempts to explain the unexplainable for the people of a particular community.

The Egyptian worldview began as a culmination of various African civilizations and beliefs. The name *Egypt* came from the Greek name *Aegyptos,* but before that it was *Kemet,* Blackland, to the native peoples (Crawford, 1996). When the Sahara dried up and became a desert, several African groups migrated to the Nile Valley. The harsh famine and flood cycles of life near the Nile forced the people to become organized and ever vigilant. Religion was an important part of this orderly existence, and as many as 2,000 deities were part of Kemetic beliefs. The lack of distinction between science, art, and religious philosophy is reflected in the belief that each action in everyday life was the earthly symbol of a divine activity.

Kemet developed into a great civilization because of divine leadership and geography. The Pharaohs

 Polly Begley teaches at Fresno City College, Fresno, California.

were incarnations of the Universal God, Horus, and they ruled with absolute and divine power in early Kemet. The first monarch, Menes, established his dynasty around 3150 B.C. when he united upper and lower Kemet. The nation had an advantage geographically during the early dynastic period because vast scorching deserts protected the population from invaders on most sides (Brega, 1998). Herodotus wrote of a mighty army of 50,000 soldiers that was literally swallowed by the sands about 2,500 years ago. Archaeologists recently discovered remains deep in the desert that may prove the tale of this lost army (Stowe, 2000). Essentially, ancient Kemet people could focus on nation building, art, science, and philosophy because they were spared from the threat of external attack.

Today, Pharaonic-era beliefs are confined to museums and tourist sites, but traces of Kemet could never be completely erased from the Nile, sands, and people of this ancient land. In A.D. 619, nomadic Arabs invaded Egypt, and eventually Islam replaced other religious beliefs to become the prevailing worldview in modern Egypt. Ancient Egyptian history is considered to be anti-Islamic and has been replaced with Islamic history in Egyptian schools (Gershoni & Jankowski, 1995). Christianity is the only other religious minority and has dwindled to less than 13% of the population. A small enclave of Christians lives in central Egypt, but violence plagues their relations with their Muslim neighbors. Egyptian Muslims find solace in the religious beliefs of Islam and answer questions of existence through the sacred words of the Islamic holy book (Koran). An examination of Islamic history, principles, contemporary practices, and the role of religious beliefs within politics can provide insight into the behavioral and communicative patterns of its adherents.

Islamic History

The historical roots of Islamic beliefs are important to intercultural communication because religion influences every part of everyday life in Egyptian Muslim communities. Islam began with Mohammed, who was the last of God's prophets. God spoke to Mohammed through the angel Gabriel about A.D. 610, and the messages were recorded in the Koran. The Koran, the book of Islam, is the only miracle claimed by Mohammed and is considered to be the exact words of God. This holy book contains 114 chapters (or *suras*) and outlines the will of God for the loyal followers of Islam (Waines, 1995).

Although descriptions of Mohammed range from praising to condemning, no one can argue that he did not have a vast influence on all of Arabia, including Egypt. Historically, the Middle East was turbulent. Vast areas, harsh deserts, tribes, and a precarious value placed on human life contributed to turmoil in the region. Although numerous leaders had previously attempted to create a consolidated empire, Mohammed and his followers were able to unite Arabia under their control. When Islam was first introduced to Egyptians, an established set of ancient beliefs dated back thousands of years. These beliefs included countless deities and complicated rituals for Egyptians. In contrast, Islamic beliefs were easy to understand and to follow for the common people.

Islamic beliefs dominate every moment from birth to death and beyond. Almost 85% to 90% of Egypt's population, and more than 1 billion people worldwide, are followers of Islam. Muslims seek Islam to find "the peace that comes when one's life is surrendered to God" (Smith, 1991, p. 222). This worldview reflects one of the youngest and fastest growing major religions in the world. Some of the reasons why this religion is appealing to a large number of people can be understood by examining the principles of Islam such as tenets, pillars, and universal allure.

Islamic Principles

Four tenets are central to understanding Islam: (1) It is a monotheistic religion. (2) God created the world. (3) Humans are fundamentally good from birth because they are God's creations and without "original sin." Muslims believe in the innate goodness of humanity, but contemporary societies "forget" their divine origins. (4) For each Muslim there will be a day of judgment when God decides whether each person will go to heaven or be condemned to hell (Smith, 1991).

Islam outlines five pillars for Muslims. First, *shahada* (creed) is the confession of faith: "*La ilaha illa'llah,*" translated as "There is no God but God, and Muhammad is his prophet" (Smith, 1991, p. 244). Second, *salat* (prayer) is an important part of everyday life. Muslims are required to stop for prayer five times a day, facing in the direction of the holy city of Mecca. Murphy (1993) described the call to prayer in Cairo, Egypt: "'God is great,' the muezzins proclaim, their words furiously amplified to rock concert proportions through the city's narrow and winding streets, a celebration of holiness at 70 decibels" (p. 1). Third, *zakat* (giving alms) to the poor is expected of each person. Fourth, *sawm* (fasting) during the month of Ramadan is required. This fast prompts Muslims to be disciplined and reminds them to be more charitable to the hungry and the poor within their societies. Finally, the *hajj* (pilgrimage) to Mecca is a requisite trip for those who are able to make the journey (Nigosian, 1987).

Islam possesses a universal allure, which appeals to Egyptians. This allure comes about, first, because Islam is a religion of action, not of contemplation. Second, Muslims from all cultural and ethnic groups are recognized as equal members within the religion. Believers are thus united in an international fraternity of Islam. Mohammed's words are clear on this issue: "A Muslim is the brother of a Muslim; he neither oppresses him nor does he fail him, he neither lies to him nor does he hold him in contempt" (Lippman, 1995, p. 185). Third, Islam does not require complicated rituals or sacrifices. If one repeats the shahada creed, then he or she is a Muslim. Good Muslims follow the five pillars. The accepting simplicity of Islam unites and strengthens the people of Egypt.

Islam and Politics

Egyptian government has long recognized the power of Islam within the general populace. Each political group publicly supports the *Shari-a* (religious laws), advocates that religious principles should be taught in schools, and allows family concerns to be decided by Islamic ideologies. The constitution also declares Islam the state religion. Government support of Shari-a, however, has not prevented a rising number of secular laws. An ongoing Egyptian dilemma stems from trying to balance Islamic religious laws with attempts to bring modernization to industry and business. The introduction of new technology, as well as Western influences, has promoted lenient secular laws that are often contrary to traditional religious standards.

An increasing number of secular laws, technological advance, outside influence, a population explosion, and rising unemployment have created factions of religious fundamentalism. Some Egyptians believe that problems in their country are the result of society, especially the government, ignoring the principles of Islam. Religious beliefs offer the hopes of stability and orderliness during times of agitation and change. This Islamic fundamentalism has caused increased demands for a return to Shari-a (Sisk, 1992), which has resulted in increasing numbers of Egyptians following the Islamic pillars and practicing segregation by gender; more women in recent years have adopted full or partial veils in public places, and sporadic protests of foreign intrusion have occurred in Egyptian cities.

Sojourners should be aware of Islamic religious beliefs while conducting business or traveling in Egypt. The Koran exhorts everyone, especially women, to cover themselves modestly. Egyptians wear less revealing clothing and feel more comfortable communicating with others who adopt conservative attire. Egyptians also feel that it is their responsibility to help others in need. There is a long tradition of Egyptians taking anyone into their tent for sustenance or shelter from the harsh desert. Sojourners who receive help while in Egypt are told that "God wills it," as explanation for Egyptian hospitality. Travelers or business executives who display knowledge of and respect for Islamic beliefs are more likely to establish friendships and profitable business relations in Egypt. Although religious beliefs are an important part of Egyptian culture, they are only one part of understanding communication with Egyptians. In the next section, we will consider Egyptian cultural values that are relevant to intercultural communication.

EGYPTIAN VALUES

Cultural values are vital areas of study for intercultural communication scholars. Samovar and Porter (2000) state:

> Cultural values define what is worth dying for, what is worth protecting, what frightens people, what are proper subjects for study and for ridicule, and what types of events create group solidarity. Most important, cultural values guide both perception and behavior. (p. 11)

If we can discover why people act a certain way, their fears, and their passions, then we can begin to understand how to improve communication among people of diverse cultures. Three fundamental values in Egyptian culture are tradition, relationships, and hierarchical devotion.

Tradition

World histories reveal that the groups of people who have had the richest traditions have also had long-lived societies. Weick (1995) points out that cultures characterized by a "tradition of conduct" or that have a "well-developed folklore of action should survive longer than those that do not" (p. 126). These traditions of conduct serve to pass expertise and experience to the next generations. An Egyptian proverb points out the worth of past knowledge: "Lost is the person who forgets his or her past." Because Egyptian culture is 4,000 to 5,000 years old, it is not surprising that tradition is an important value.

This importance within the Egyptian population is reflected in several different ways. Egypt has a tradition of being a rural nation. The peasant farmers along the Nile are proud of their farming heritage and are often resistant to change. Ancient paintings depict types of donkey-powered waterwheels that are still in use today. Egyptians have survived countless epidemics, floods, droughts, and conquerors. The population has "a centuries-old capacity for letting life flow by, a little like the Nile, . . . and it is as though the present generations had inherited a seen-it-all-before attitude from their forbears" (Wayne & Simonis, 1994, p. 33). Their unity in pleasure and suffering, while holding onto their traditions, contributes to the endurance of Egyptian culture for thousands of years.

Religions traditions, as previously mentioned, are an important part of life in Egypt. Ancient Egyptians thought that "every action, no matter how mundane, was in some sense a religious act: plowing, sowing, reaping, brewing, building ships, waging wars, playing games—all were viewed as earthly symbols for divine activities" (West, 1995, p. 46). Contemporary Egyptians also maintain that their religious beliefs play a pivotal role in family, politics, business, and education.

Egyptians may express polite interest in the traditions and ancestors of guests in their country. Higher regard is attributed to the person who can recite details about his or her family members from the past four to five hundred years. This strong value placed on traditions serves to pass on knowledge, but can also inhibit rapid changes. Visitors to Egypt should never underestimate the amount of time that it will take to establish relationships, new contacts, or introduce technological innovations.

Relationships

Egyptians have the capability to endure, but there is still something that frightens them. The people of Egypt fear loneliness, and they wish to always be surrounded by a network of relatives and friends (Hopwood, 1982). They combat loneliness by placing great value on relationships. The importance of relational harmony developed from the time Menes united upper and lower Kemet in 3150 B.C. Nile Valley inhabitants found that collectivism was the most effective way for a diverse group of people with limited resources to live in peace.

In Egyptian collectivism, family, social, and business are all relationships that are taken seriously and give Egyptians great pleasure. The crucial events of a person's lifetime are birth, marriage, and death. These principal daily concerns of everyday life emphasize the interconnectedness of the individual with the family. Each person represents a social collective and sacrifices his or her needs for the greater good of that group.

Reassurance and warmth from familial relations are feelings replicated in other relationships. Kinship terms are used in various situations to reinforce positive connections among people. For example, "Egyptian politicians, from the President on down, emphasize their position as 'father figures' to the masses" (Inborn, 1996, p. 159). The family is the basic building block of society and is a model for interactions throughout society.

The first questions that Egyptians ask guests in a conversation concern group affiliations. "Where is your family?" "Where is your father?" "Where are your classmates or coworkers?" Egyptians assume that people prefer group travel or activities. Tourists commonly report that locals never give oral directions, but always insist on accompanying them directly to their destination—no matter how far away.

A relational focus is also reflected in the blurred boundary lines between social and business interactions. Officials constantly maintain open-door policies and engage in friendly discussions with several people at one time. Building and maintaining good relations take priority over other activities in society. Egyptians often conduct lengthy business meetings without ever touching on business matters. A sojourner in Egypt realizes the power of relations after waiting at an Egyptian Embassy for five hours to get a visa. Even then, there is no guarantee the paperwork will be processed before closing time. On the other hand, if good relations have been established with the family who runs the hotel, then its members may realize that one of their son's classmates works in the embassy. The visa would be delivered within half an hour to the door of the hotel after a single phone call. Relationships are a source of pleasure and are also a way to get things done in a rigidly structured society.

Hierarchical Structure

Hierarchies according to age, gender, and experience are crucial in Egyptian society. Ancient traditions outline the proper place and behavior of each person in society. Interpersonal relationships are characterized by "a worldview professing the existence of a cosmic hierarchical order: The sound order of things is a descending scale of superiors and subordinates" (Yadlin, 1995, p. 151). The cosmic order begins with the major religions of Egypt. Pharaohs were considered to be god-rulers who were divine mediators for the people. The Nile civilization may have been one of the first matriarchal civilizations because ancient Pharaohs inherited the bloodline (Crawford, 1996). In this agrarian society, male and female deities ruled from the heavens, and both men and women were responsible for the collective security of the family.

In Islam as well, humans submit to God's will in all matters. God is the ultimate creator, authority, and judge for all people. The first words that sojourners will learn upon arrival in Egypt are *Insha' allah*. The translation is, "If God wills it." Explanations such as "God decides" or "It's when God wants it" reflect the accepted order of life. Muslims do not question their fate, because God alone knows their destiny. A part of that destiny for Egyptians is fulfilling their roles in the overall social structure of society.

In Muslim families, the oldest male in the family wields authority and power. This patriarch is responsible for the safety and well-being of his family members. Sons and daughters consider carefully how their public behavior influences their family. The oldest son may conduct business or interactions, but the father makes final decisions. Muslims regard these roles and practices as a natural part of life, and women and men are staunch advocates and devotees of the traditional hierarchical order. Hierarchies are produced and reinforced through the language of family and societal communication.

EGYPTIAN LANGUAGE AND CULTURE

Language is a powerful tool. Our manner of speech can have a significant influence on another's behavior. The words that we choose can reflect the way that we look at the world and perceive others. For centuries, Arabs have recognized the power of language and have used Arabic to convey unity, worldview, and artistic impressions. Arabic is one of the oldest living languages in the world. It is the beautiful and flamboyant language spoken by Egyptians and other people of the Middle East.

If you venture into an Egyptian city, you will hear the rhythmic Arab verses of the Koran chanted aloud during daily prayers. Walls of Egyptian mosques are not painted with pictures or scenes—they are covered with decorative Arabic calligraphy. A sojourner who learns a few words of Arabic will quickly gain friends in this region. Egyptians are also willing to share their knowledge of Arabic with others. On many occasions, a well-timed response of *Mish muskmlla* (No problem) or *Insha' allah* (If God wills it) will elicit approval and improve relations with Egyptians.

Arabic and Unity

What we say, how we say it, and why we say it are all related to our culture. Egyptians use their language to construct appropriate national identities and unity within the population. For example, Egyptians did not consider themselves Arabs until the seventh century, when Arabic became the predominant way to communicate in the region (Lippman, 1995). Today, Egyptian children learn only in Arabic and are taught to memorize and proudly recite lengthy verses of the Koran. The Middle East consists of various countries and cultural and ethnic groups, but Egyptians will readily proclaim, "But we are all Arabs!"

Arabic helps promote unity within a region just as different linguistic styles can cause disunity. For example, bargaining in Egypt is considered to be an enjoyable way to pass time and build relationships. Historically, Egyptians expect and love haggling, but for Israelis, "trading was not a pleasurable pastime, but part of a struggle for survival in a hostile environment. Thus, where bargaining has positive connotations for the Arab, for the Israeli it is reminiscent of a rejected and despised way of life" (Cohen, 1990, p. 139).

Negotiations between Israel and Egypt have been taking place since 1948, and their different linguistic styles have caused more than one impasse during talks.

Arabic and Worldview

Arabic is used to convey the Islamic worldview. Classical Arabic (which is also the written language) is sacred because it is the dialect of the Koran (Hall, 1977, p. 31). The importance of the Koran within Islamic societies actually preserved the integrity of the classical tongue. Other major languages branched out into various dialects or became obsolete, but classical Arabic is still widely spoken among Muslims of every region. Public prayers and ceremonies worldwide are conducted in Arabic even if the Muslim adherents are not Middle Eastern Arabs.

Second, *jihad* is an Arabic word from the Koran that has often been incorrectly translated as "holy war." The mere mention of an Islamic *jihad* has been depicted within Western literature as religious fanatics on a killing rampage, and terrorist attacks are automatically attributed to Islamic fundamentalists (Hopfe, 1976). "Literally the word [*jihad*] means 'utmost effort' in promotion and defense of Islam, which might or might not include armed conflict with unbelievers" (Lippman, 1995, p. 113). Although there are some violent fundamentalist groups, these factions cannot realistically represent the whole of Islamic followers.

Finally, Western readers of Koranic translations have reported that the holy book is repetitive, confusing, and lacks compelling features (Nigosian, 1987). Muslims maintain that these translations do not reflect the astounding beauty and rhythmic qualities of the original Arabic verses. The linguistic style of Koranic writings serves as a model for literature and speech throughout Islamic societies.

Writing as Art

Ancient hieroglyphs used the same word to signify both writing and art. Ancient Kemetic texts focused on "medicine, science, religion, social and cosmic organization, and the life cycle" (Crawford, 1996, p. 9). Arabic is now used as an art form in Egypt. One of the foremost sights in every Egyptian city is the mosque decorated inside from top to bottom with Arabic calligraphy. Egyptian homes commonly have a scroll depicting the 99 names of God in exquisite script. The mastery of spoken and written classical Arabic is indicative of education and rank in Egypt. Arabic is a language that pleases the eyes, ears, and spirits of the people. Sojourners who learn Arabic or adopt a descriptive and elegant style of speaking in another language will attain a higher level of credibility while in Egypt.

CONCLUSION

This article reviews aspects of the Islamic worldview, cultural values, and language that influence communication with Egyptians. Visitors to Egypt find that travel or business ventures are more rewarding experiences if they take the time to learn about specific cultural characteristics. If its 5,000 years of history and tradition can provide a rich cultural heritage and wisdom for Egyptians, then other cultures can also learn from one of the oldest civilizations in the world.

References

Brega, I. (1998). *Egypt: Past and present.* New York: Barnes & Noble.

Cohen, R. (1990). Deadlock: Israel and Egypt negotiate. In F. Korzenny & S. Ting-Toomey (Eds.), *Communicating for peace: Diplomacy and negotiation* (pp. 136–153). Newbury Park, CA: Sage.

Crawford, C. (1996). *Recasting ancient Egypt in the African context: Toward a model curriculum using art and language.* Trenton, NJ: Africa World.

Gershoni, I., & Jankowski, J. P. (1995). *Redefining the Egyptian nation,* 1930–1945. New York: Cambridge University Press.

Hall, E. T. (1977). *Beyond culture.* Garden City, NY: Anchor Books.

Hopfe, L. M. (1976). *Religions of the world.* Beverly Hills, CA: Glencoe.

Hopwood, D. (1982). *Egypt: Politics and society, 1945–1981.* London: Allen and Unwin.

Inhorn, M. C. (1996). *Infertility and patriarchy: The cultural politics of gender and family life in Egypt.* Philadelphia: University of Pennsylvania Press.

Lippman, T. W. (1995). *Understanding Islam: An introduction to the Muslim world* (2nd ed.). New York: Meridian.

Murphy, K. (1993, April 6). World report special edition: A new vision for Mohammed's faith. *Los Angeles Times*, p. 1.

Nigosian, S. (1987). *Islam: The way of submission.* Great Britain: Crucible.

Samovar, L. A., & Porter, R. E. (2000). Understanding intercultural communication: An introduction and overview. In L. A. Samovar & R. E. Porter (Eds.), *Intercultural communication: A reader* (9th ed., pp. 5–16). Belmont, CA: Wadsworth.

Sisk, T. D. (1992). *Islam and democracy: Religion, politics, and power in the Middle East.* Washington, DC: United States Institute of Peace Press.

Smith, H. (1991). *The world's religions: Our great wisdom traditions.* San Francisco: HarperCollins.

Stowe, M. A. (2000, August 28). Swallowed by the sands: Archaeologists hope to solve the mystery of Persia's lost army of Egypt. *Discovering Archaeology: Scientific American* [Internet]. www.discoveringarchaeology.com/articles.082800-sands.shtml

Waines, D. (1995). *An introduction to Islam.* Cambridge, England: Cambridge University Press.

Wayne, S., & Simonis, D. (1994). *Egypt and the Sudan* (3rd ed.). Hawthorn, Australia: Lonely Planet.

Weick, K. (1995). *Sensemaking in organizations.* Thousand Oaks, CA: Sage.

West, J. A. (1995). *The traveler's key to ancient Egypt: A guide to the sacred places of ancient Egypt.* Wheaton, IL: Quest Books.

Yadlin, R. (1995). The seeming duality: Patterns of interpersonal relations in a changing environment. In S. Shamir (Ed.), *Egypt from monarchy to republic: A reassessment of revolution and change* (p. 151).

Concepts and Questions

1. Why does Begley say it is hard to "think like an Egyptian"?
2. What aspects of Islamic history offer insights into the Egyptian culture? What aspects of your own culture's history would offer valuable insights for someone wanting to study your culture?
3. Why does Begley assert that "Islamic beliefs dominate every moment from birth to death and beyond"?
4. Begley offers four tenants central to understanding Islam. What are they? Does your worldview have similar or dissimilar tenants?
5. What does Begley mean when she writes "Islam is a religion of action, not contemplation"? Is your religion one of action or contemplation?
6. Why is the Arabic language so very important to the Egyptians? What aspects of their language make it unique?
7. What does Begley imply when she talks about Arabic as an art?
8. What communication patterns within your culture might present problems when communicating with someone from Egyptian culture?

Co-Cultures: Living in Two Cultures

4

All people have the right to be equal and the equal right to be different.

SHIMON PEREZ

In Chapter 3, we focused on international cultures—cultures that exist outside the immediate borders of the United States. In this chapter, we turn our attention to some of the multicultural dynamics found among diverse cultural groups residing in the United States. In most instances, members of these groups hold dual or multiple cultural memberships, hence the term *co-cultures*. Members of these co-cultures may share a number of similar characteristics such as religion, economic status, ethnic background, age, gender, sexual preference, or race. These co-cultures frequently also have many of the defining characteristics found in any culture—a specialized language system, shared values, a collective worldview, and common communication patterns. These diverse co-cultures, however, have the potential to bring new experiences and ways of interacting to a communication encounter. Their communicative behaviors are sometimes confusing and baffling to members of the dominant culture. Anyone who is not aware of and does not understand the unique experiences of these co-cultures is open to a range of communication problems.

The United States, in many respects, is a pluralistic and multicultural society. Consequently, there is a vital need for effective communication between the dominant culture and the numerous co-cultures as well as between the co-cultures themselves. You cannot communicate effectively with members of co-cultures until you reduce any prejudices and stereotypes and learn to appreciate the uniqueness of co-cultures. Ignorance, prejudices, and stereotypes often lead to false assumptions about members of co-cultures that are incorrect, hurtful, and even insulting.

Any look at contemporary American society will reveal an abundance of co-cultures. As an obvious consequence, we are not able to include every co-culture in this chapter. Our selection was based on three considerations: (1) we needed to make efficient use of limited space; (2) we wanted to include some social communities that are often in conflict with the dominant culture; and (3) we wanted to emphasize the co-cultures with which you are most likely to interact. To this end, we selected a representation of the major co-cultures found in the United States. We should add, however, that additional co-cultures will be examined in subsequent chapters as we explore the verbal and nonverbal dimensions of intercultural communication.

We begin this chapter with an essay by Young Yun Kim that provides an ideological position from which intercultural communication among co-cultures can proceed. Central to this ideology, Kim proclaims, is the theme of individualism. In her essay, "*Unum* and *Pluribus*: Ideological Underpinnings of Interethnic Communication in the United States," Kim examines the historical development of American social institutions that were based on such liberal themes as equal rights and equal opportunity and enshrined in the Declaration of Independence, the Constitution, and the Bill of Rights.

Even with all of these traditional beliefs, Kim is quick to point out, however, that "Americans today are far from being of a same mind about various social issues" such as interethnic or interracial relations. As she notes, "interethnic relations have become a perpetual sore spot in the American consciousness in which many Americans are galvanized into an "us-against-them" posture in the form of "identity politics" which leads to a "politics-of-difference" and a "politics-of-recognition."

Having established the current social dilemma, Kim goes on to analyze the issues of race, ethnicity, and interethnic relations. Her analysis reveals four types of interethnic communication messages: *assimilation, pluralism, reconciliation,* and *extremism,* all of which she describes in detail. This discussion is followed by a synthesis that leads to the conclusion that the future of interethnic relations is not yet clear. Americans will continue to struggle with competing visions of *Unum* and *Pluribus*—visions of what it means to be American. She notes, however, "that interethnic issues continue to engage American passion is itself an affirmation, and a hallmark, of the American liberal tradition. . . . [which] contributes to the stability of the American democracy."

Worldview is a primary contributor to the deep structure of a culture, and cultural diversity in worldview strongly affects interaction between people during intercultural communication. Among the U.S. population, the Native American co-culture numbers more than 2.3 million. The Native American worldview differs significantly from that of the traditional European American culture. In order to help you understand the uniqueness of the Native American worldview, we include the next essay, "Does the Worm Live in the Ground? Reflections on Native American Spirituality," by Michael Tlanusta Garrett and Michael P. Wilbur. These authors introduce the fundamental aspects of Native American spirituality: walking in step, medicine, harmony, relation, and vision.

Walking in step refers to coming together or connecting with the essence of Native American spirituality. It is described as a feeling of connection with traditional Native American spiritual beliefs. For the Native American, medicine is more than a pill you take to cure illness. Medicine is everywhere; it is the very essence of one's inner being—a power that connects everyone to every living being through the heart. Living in harmony and balance with the natural environment is central to Native American beliefs because life is seen as a gift from the Creator—a gift to be treated with the utmost care and respect. The aspect of relation refers to all things' being connected—a total way of existing in the world. Thus, the concept of family extends to brothers and sisters in the animal world, the plant world, and the mineral world, as well as Mother Earth and Father Sky. Finally, vision involves knowing what to do with the gift of life—an inner knowledge of your purpose in the greater meaning of life.

From these aspects of Native American culture come an understanding of the basis for the unique worldview shared by many Native Americans. Knowledge of these dynamics will help facilitate intercultural communication with the Native American co-culture.

The number of biracial marriages in the United States has been on the increase since 1967, when anti-miscegenation laws were found to be unconstitutional. Even though biracial marriages remain socially unacceptable to some segments of society, the number of such marriages doubled between 1970 and 1990. Changing demographics in the United States have provided the opportunity for diverse people to meet each other in their neighborhoods, schools, workplaces, and churches, creating the opportunity for people to meet and establish biracial relationships. These relationships may be taxed not only by the problems inherent in any couple relationship but also by the dynamics of cultural diversity. To help you gain insight into the problems of biracial relationships, Donna M. Stringer, in her article "Let Me Count the Ways: African-American/European-American Marriages," explores these relationships and the cultural dynamics that can cause conflict and misunderstanding. As she outlines the areas in which misperceptions or cultural conflicts can occur, she suggests ways to improve communication and reduce the potential for misunderstandings.

Stringer asserts that any life partnership or marriage is challenged by differing values, communication styles, conflict styles, and nonverbal behaviors, which have the potential to dissolve the relationship. When the relationship is biracial, however, additional challenges are present because of diverse cultural backgrounds. If the couple is able to understand and explore their differences using an intercultural communication model, Stringer believes the relationship is more likely to benefit and intimacy to grow deeper.

In her article, Stringer reviews cultural values and explores the differences between terminal and instrumental values. She posits that terminal values are goals, whereas instrumental values are exhibited as behaviors used to obtain the goal. She then looks at values through a series of value continua or dimensions that describe opposite poles, such as individualism–collectivism. She believes that it is necessary for partners to identify both terminal and instrumental values as well as to identify values along critical dimensions in order to reduce misperceptions and conflict.

Next, Stringer examines both verbal and nonverbal communication styles as they apply to African-American/European-American relationships. She discusses the differences between direct and indirect communication styles, high- and low-context systems, and detached versus attached communication. From a nonverbal perspective, she discusses eye contact and time orientations as they apply in these relationships. Stringer believes that through the open exploration of cultural backgrounds, values, and communication styles, partners in biracial relationships can both avoid conflict and resolve it when it does occur.

In the past two decades, attention has been focused on a social community previously taken for granted by many segments of American society—women. Because women are so much a part of everyone's perceptual field and daily life, very few scholars, until recently, studied this group as a co-culture. Yet the experiences of females, regardless of the culture, often produce unique ways of perceiving the world and interacting in that world. Such events as successful campaigns for local, state, and national political office by women in unprecedented numbers and the advancement of women to top-level management and CEO status in major business settings have confirmed that the co-culture of women does indeed exist, and that society must give serious consideration to understanding how this feminine co-culture differs from the masculine culture.

One major difference between the feminine and masculine communities is their communicative behaviors. In their article "Gendered Communication Styles," Julia T. Wood and Nina M. Reich assert that these behaviors can complicate interactions and relationships. The authors begin by making the important distinction between sex (determined by genetic codes that program biological features) and gender (often thought of as the cultural meaning of sex). Their position is that "sex is innate, whereas gender is learned and, therefore, changeable."

Wood and Reich believe that people—both men and women—become gendered through the influence of many factors. They hold that two of the most important of these factors are (1) social expectations for males and females and (2) interaction in sex-segregated children's play in groups. Through peer interactions, children learn two very different sets of rules regarding communication. Girls learn to be cooperative, not to criticize, and to pay attention. Boys, on the other hand, are taught to be assertive, to focus on outcomes, and to be competitive. These behaviors produce different communication styles that are manifest in what Wood and Reich refer to as feminine and masculine communication communities. Within these communities, members embrace similar understanding and learn how to use talk and the purposes it serves. It is through this form of interaction that you learn what masculine and feminine mean in society and how you are expected to think, talk, feel, and act.

Wood and Reich continue their essay by analyzing several situations in which communication has gone awry and showing how common misunderstandings occur in gendered communication. They conclude their essay by suggesting six ways for improving communication between males and females.

The next co-culture we present is that of the disabled. In recent years, disabled persons have been recognized as a co-culture in our society. Although there are approximately 14 million disabled Americans between the ages of 16 and 64, they often find themselves either cut off from or misunderstood by the dominant nondisabled culture. Dawn O. Braithwaite and Charles A. Braithwaite look at some of the reasons for this isolation in "'Which Is My Good Leg?': Cultural Communication of Persons with Disabilities." They specifically examine how disabled persons view their communication relationships with nondisabled persons. Reviewing research consisting of more than 100 in-depth interviews with physically disabled adults, the Braithwaites have discovered that these disabled people go through a process of redefinition that involves three steps: (1) redefining the self as part of a "new" culture, (2) redefining disability, and (3) redefining disability for the dominant culture. By becoming familiar with these steps, you can learn to improve your communication with members of the disabled co-culture.

Our last essay in this chapter will introduce you to the communication patterns and dynamics associated with the gay and lesbian culture. In his article "In Plain Sight: Gay and Lesbian Communication and Culture," William F. Eadie recognizes that there are a variety of mindsets, ranging from hostile to accepting, regarding the gay and lesbian culture. Nevertheless, he challenges you to acquaint yourself with the unique cultural characteristics and communication styles of the gay and lesbian members of society.

In his approach to the issue, Eadie specifies three general statements about lesbian and gay culture: (1) being open about sexual orientation is a political statement; (2) lesbian and gay culture exists by dealing with tensions about how open to be about one's sexuality; and (3) although lesbian and gay culture is driven by sexual attraction and desire, being lesbian or gay is not only about sex. Each of these concepts is discussed in detail, revealing the social proscriptions and dynamics that affect lesbian and gay culture and communication.

Unum and *Pluribus*: Ideological Underpinnings of Interethnic Communication in the United States

YOUNG YUN KIM

The United States was founded as a construction organized by the ideology of classical liberalism in the Enlightenment tradition—a tradition rooted in the theories of European and Anglo-American philosophers such as John Locke, Adam Smith, and John Dewey. Central to this ideology is the theme of *individualism,* "the social priority of the individual vis-à-vis the State, the established Church, social classes . . . or other social groups" (Abercrombie, 1980, p. 56). While recognizing the existence of infinite individual differences, classical liberalism also stresses *universalism* that sees human nature presupposing and transcending social group categories such as ethnicity and race. As Michael Billig and associates (1988) have noted, "The assertions 'We are all human' and 'We are all individuals' are both equally and self-evidently 'true'" (p. 124). The liberal themes of individualism and universalism are further linked to the theme of *procedural equality*—that is, "equal rights" and "equal opportunities" afforded to all individuals in the form of "human rights," the basic requisite of a free and democratic society. Enshrined in the Declaration of Independence, the Constitution, the Bill of Rights, and democratic and capitalistic institutions, these and related liberal principles constitute the core of the American cultural ethos, projecting a vision of American society that seeks to transcend a monolithic tribal ancestral and territorial condition. Essayist Henry Grunwald captured this liberal tradition in a bicentennial essay (*Time,* July 5, 1976):

> The U.S. was not born in a tribal conflict, like so many other nations, but in a conflict over principles. Those principles were thought to be universal, which was part of the reason for the unprecedented policy of throwing the new country open to all comers. (p. 35)

Given these traditional ideals, however, Americans today are far from being of a same mind about various social issues. In fact, the opposite is true when it comes to "interethnic" (or "interracial") relations. Ever since the Reconstruction era of the late 19th century when "civil rights" debates began (cf. Wilson, 1998), American society has experienced an extraordinary degree of unease, conflict, self-criticism, and mutual criticism as it struggled to reconcile the ideals of individualism, universalism, and procedural equality with the reality of inequality, real or perceived, along particular ethnic/racial group lines. In recent decades, the traditional primacy of the individual has been increasingly challenged by the claims of the primacy of ethnic group identity over individual identity, particularistic group grievances that are historically and institutionally rooted, and the necessity to redress such grievances so as to achieve equal group status.

This American dilemma continues to stir heated public debates. Indeed, interethnic relations have become a perpetual sore spot in the American consciousness. They galvanize Americans into "us-against-them" posturing in the form of "identity politics"—also described as "politics of difference" and "politics of recognition." Essayist Russell Baker (*New York Times,* May 5, 1994) laments this situation in an essay titled "Gone with the Unum":

> I have always been an "*E Pluribus Unum*" person myself, but the future does not look bright for an "*E Pluribus Unum*" America. The melting pot in which the Pluribus were to be combined into the Unum was not the success its advertisers had promised. . . . What is new these days is the passion with which we now pursue our tribal identities. . . .
>
> O, Unum, what misery we courted when we forsook thee for Pluribus. (p. A15)

This original essay is a revision of an earlier essay that first appeared in the tenth edition. This essay is a modified version of an article of the same title that was published in *International Journal of Intercultural Relations* (Kim, 1999). Young Yun Kim teaches at the University of Oklahoma.

ANALYSIS

This author has sought to better understand and appreciate the often contentious political landscape of the contemporary United States with respect to issues of race, ethnicity, and interethnic relations. To this end, differing views and opinions of American people have been scrutinized against the backdrop of the classical liberal ideological tradition.

Guiding this analysis is a systemic, interactive theoretical conception of interethnic communication (Kim, 1997). In this model, an individual's communication behavior influences, and is influenced by, multiple layers of contextual factors, including the ideological milieu of the society at large. On the one hand, societal ideology serves as a "common sense" for everyday thinking of ordinary individuals—an intellectual "frame" that they do not themselves invent but that has a history (Billig, 1991, p. 1). What individual Americans think, say, or do about ethnicity, race, and interethnic relations is at least partly a reflection of, or a response to, the liberal ideological tradition of the society at large. In turn, the contents of everyday opinions communicated are themselves potential seeds for continuing evolution of the societal ideological tradition. The reciprocal nature of the ideology and communication behavior is a "stimulus-and-response" rather than a one-directional causal relationship. In turn, communication messages are not merely expressions of speakers' passive thoughts; to say something is very often to "fight"—in the sense that messages serve as strategy and tactics for advocating one's own version of the ideology in the broader society so as to affect the ideological milieu itself.

Ideology, in this sense, refers to "lived ideology"—"a latent consciousness or philosophy," "a society's way of life," or "what passes for common sense within a society" (Billig, 1991, pp. 27–29). Ideology is seen as a set of social forces that stimulates, substantiates, and constrains the intellectual beliefs and expressions of thinking individuals. Individuals do not blindly follow the dictates of the mental schema within the ideology, but formulate and express their opinions by invoking socially shared beliefs *as their own.* Even in making remarks that are self-serving or internally contradictory, communicators are assumed to consider their argument "reasonable" or even "persuasive" in the eyes of a "rational" audience. In Billig's (1991) words:

> To maximize their chances of being persuasive, speakers should make appeal to the *sensus comunis,* which they share with their audience. Particularly useful are commonplaces, or the sort of moral maxims which are laden with clichéd appeals to values. Thus, orators' discourse, which seeks to create new movements of opinion towards a position not commonly shared, will rehearse old commonly shared stereotypes. (p. 21)

Based on the fundamental linkage between an individual's communication behavior and the societal ideology, a variety of data have been analyzed to identify multiple ways the traditional ideology of classical liberalism plays out in contemporary American interethnic communication messages. Among the data examined in the present analysis are messages of political and civic leaders, activists, academicians, and ordinary citizens. All of the data have been found in public sources such as published books and journals, articles in newspapers and newsmagazines, and interviews broadcast on radio and television. Some of them are captured in naturally occurring events, whereas others were expressed in the form of personal reflections and testimonials. The data have been analyzed through a qualitative-interpretive exercise to surface the ideological themes underlying the publicly communicated messages.

The analysis has revealed four types of interethnic communication messages: (1) assimilationism, (2) pluralism, (3) reconciliation, and (4) extremism. Each of these message types is described in the following discussion. Commonly rooted in the ideology of classical liberalism, these message types nonetheless illuminate the differing sets of beliefs and moral visions being voiced by Americans today. Together, they constitute a full spectrum of ongoing debates and arguments about what American society is, should be, and should be doing, with respect to issues of ethnicity, race, and interethnic relations.

MESSAGES OF ASSIMILATIONISM

Three core principles of classical liberalism—individualism, universalism, and procedural equality—continue to directly and powerfully underpin the mainstream thinking of Americans about interethnic relations. These liberal ideals shape the arguments commonly referred to as *assimilationism.* Employing such metaphors as "melting pot" and "color-blind society," assimilationist messages project a societal vision in which immigrants and indigenous ethnic minorities are mainstreamed into the normative culture and institutions. In this vision, the government is responsible for universally applying societal rules to all its citizens irrespective of skin color and religious creed. Immigrants and ethnic minorities, in turn, are expected to assimilate themselves socially and culturally, so as to become fully functional in the American society.

Assimilationist messages celebrate personal achievement and self-reliance. These messages place individual identity over and above group identity and question the validity and morality of categorical thought. Although each person is unique, all humans are also endowed with the same set of universal human needs, rights, and responsibilities. Prejudice directed for or against individuals simply based on group membership is morally wrong, not only because it is irrational but also because its focus on social categories contravenes the intellectual or moral prescription to value the unique qualities of every individual. The primacy of the individual over the group hinges on the value of equality as it pertains to the premise of common human nature and basic human rights that call for equal application of laws and rules to all people regardless of their group categories. A fair society is one in which all individuals, regardless of their backgrounds, are granted equal rights and equal opportunity.

Equality in this view means "fair play"—a notion rooted in a biopsychological (or naturalistic) worldview and the notion of "equity." This view accepts and appreciates differential individual merits in the allocation of resources and status based on the presumption that "there is a natural distribution of human talent, ranging from the few individuals of genius and talent to the defective and delinquent" (Rossides, 1976, p. 9). Each person, and each person alone, is seen as ultimately responsible for his or her own achievement of status. Everyone is expected to "play by the rules." Insistence on group-based policies such as affirmative action in college admissions and employment practices is "un-American"—one that endangers the larger fraternity of all Americans and obscures differential individual merits that must be *earned* individually. Emphasis on group identity over individual identity is deemed wrong because it renders itself to what essayist Pico Iyer (1990) calls "state-sponsored favoritism" that mandates racial or ethnic "preferences" or "quotas" and "reverse discrimination." Iyer (1990), himself an Indian-born immigrant and world traveler, expresses his objection to such practices as follows:

> As an alien from India, I choose to live in America precisely because it is a place where aliens from India are, in principle, treated no better (and no worse) than anyone else. . . . The problem with people who keep raising the cry of "racism" is that they would have us see everything in terms of race. They treat minorities as emblems, and everyone as typecast. . . . As an Asian minority myself, I know of nothing more demeaning than being chosen for a job, or even a role, on the basis of my race. Nor is the accompanying assumption—that I need a helping hand because my ancestors were born outside Europe—very comforting. . . . Are we, in fact, to cling to a state of childlike dependency? (p. 86)

The assimilationist emphasis on individualism, universalism, and procedural equality has been repeatedly promoted in presidential inauguration addresses. Presidents, regardless of their party affiliations, have exalted the assimilationist values as the very heart of the American identity—a common identity constituted by individual identities and one that transcends category-based distinctions. President Clinton, for example, spoke of American citizens' "primary allegiance to the values America stands for and values we really live by" and stated, "Long before we were so diverse, our nation's motto was E Pluribus Unum—out of many, we are one. We must be one—as neighbors; as fellow citizens; not separate camps, but family" (*Weekly Compilation of Presidential Documents, 31,* October 23, 1996, p. 851). The universal principles of individual identity and procedural equality are amply echoed in remarks of many other Americans. A newspaper reader wrote to the editor of the *New York Times Magazine* (April 29, 1992), objecting to an earlier article "Cultural Baggage" on the significance of ethnic group identity:

> I've been fighting ethnic labels since I was 12 or 13, and decided that only I had a right to define myself. . . . I am not almost WASP. I am African-American. I'm also part Cherokee from both sides of my family. But so what? . . . I've taken risks with my life that only I am responsible for, and I have reaped

> substantial rewards for daring to be myself and not just different. (p. 10)

Stanley Crouch, an African American essayist, speaks to the common humanity of all races in arguing against racial politics in his book *Always in Pursuit* (1998): "We . . . observe ourselves functioning in almost every capacity and exhibiting every inclination from the grand to the gaudy, from the idealistic to the shallow ethnic con" (p. 268). Likewise, Richard Lacayo, in an essay titled "Whose Peers?" in a special issue of *Time* magazine (Fall 1993), objects to those who have argued for a guarantee of minority representation in jury composition in courtroom trials:

> [Some] advocates argue that just such a guarantee of minority representation should be part of the law. . . . If that is so, is the only solution an outright racial-quota system? And how finely would the jury need to be divided? Could Latinos in general judge other Latinos? Or would Cuban Americans be needed for the trial of Cuban Americans, Mexican Americans for other Mexican Americans and so on? If the goal is better justice and greater legitimacy, American juries certainly need to be more representative. But in a just society, the process of creating a true assembly of peers need not be reduced to a systematic gathering of the tribes. (p. 61)

Perhaps one of the most compelling articulations of the traditional liberal ideals and of disapproval of identity politics is offered by Glenn C. Loury (1993), a prominent economic theorist and a public intellectual, who reflects on his own social identity as an African American and his individual identity as a human being:

> The most important challenges and opportunities that confront me derive not from my racial condition, but rather from my human condition. I am a husband, a father, a son, a teacher, an intellectual, a Christian, a citizen. In none of these roles is my race irrelevant, but neither can racial identity alone provide much guidance for my quest to adequately discharge these responsibilities. . . . The expression of my individual personality is to be found in the blueprint that I employ to guide this project of construction. The problem of devising such a plan for one's life is a universal problem, which confronts all people, whatever their race, class, or ethnicity. (pp. 7–10)

MESSAGES OF PLURALISM

Directly challenging the aforementioned assimilationist messages are the messages of *pluralism* or "multiculturalism." Prominent in pluralist messages is the idea of the sanctity of the group. This notion is traceable to the experiences of unequal treatment, perceived or real, of certain individuals along ethnic lines. To varying degrees, pluralist messages replace the old "melting pot" metaphor with newer ones such as "mosaic," "quilt," and "salad bowl" that emphasize the distinctiveness of ethnic groups. As such, pluralist messages uphold *group identity* as a vital, if not primary, construct of personhood, highlighting that we are different "types" of persons defined by social categories such as race, ethnicity, language, culture, and national origin. Rooted in the worldview of *relativism* that classifies humanity into categories of distinct qualities, pluralist messages emphasize in-group sameness and point to the existence of a "natural attitude" (cf. Garfinkel, 1967) for their moral and intellectual claims for group distinctiveness.

Pluralist messages are predicated on the persistent reality of racial and ethnic prejudice—a reality in which the old liberal ideal of procedural equality is seen as not working well when it comes to serving the needs of certain minority groups. The sense of systematic mistreatment along ethnic and racial lines has given way to a new demand for a new politics of resentment and victimization. Instead of defining equality procedurally in terms of fairness of rules, pluralist messages advocate the contrary belief in *status equality* (in place of procedural equality)—a demand for equal results in the interest of "emancipation" of specific groups that are historically oppressed or presently in need of institutional support through remedial laws and public policies. This outcome-based conception of equality is opposed to the procedure-based, universalistic view of equality, in that it allows for differential procedural treatments relative to different groups. Along this line, arguments have been made for a redistribution of power and resources to overcome racial inequalities (Hacker, 1992). Some pluralists advocate such an action as a remedy for status inequalities between and among ethnic and racial groups.

This pluralist position rejects the biopsychological explanation of inequality and replaces it with a sociocultural (or structural) explanation. That is, human beings are inherently equal in their original states, but their original natures become distorted and corrupted in the process of interaction with others in society and through the development of institutions such as language, culture, property, law, and social stratification among people (Tsuda, 1986, pp. 62–63). The traditional liberal notions of individual identity, universalistic application of laws, rules, rights, and responsibilities to everyone, and procedural equality without respect to equal outcomes are deemed a false ideology in that it serves only the end of legitimizing the capitalist system of "winners" and "losers" in society. In seeking group identity, relativism, and status equality, pluralist messages present race and ethnicity not merely as a basis for claiming cultural and social distinctiveness, but also as a central rallying point, a focal means to combat unjust practices such as "institutional racism." Prominent in these messages, accordingly, are terms such as ethnic "empowerment," "pride," "dignity," and "justice." Debunking the important liberal values of American life such as "intellectual freedom" and "free speech," pluralist messages demand suppression of "hate speech," loosely defined as words that a minority group finds offensive.

Specifically, schools and universities have sought to bring about a greater diversity of the university curriculum by replacing it with one "that would focus on the achievements of marginalized peoples and on the sins of the nation's founders" (Traub, 1998, p. 25). In San Francisco, for instance, the school board is reported to be developing a plan to require every high school student in the district to read works by authors of color (*New York Times,* March 11, 1998, p. A21). Many university campuses have rejected the idea of an immutable canon of indispensable Western classics in favor of recognizing the reality of ethnic diversity in the United States. Curriculum changes like these have become commonplace, reflecting the emergence of pluralism in national consciousness at the end of the 1980s advocating the normative rights of minority groups. Some advocates of pluralism have even attempted to extend the pluralist messages to arguing for a guarantee of minority representation as part of the law. Believing that race influences not only prominent cases such as the Rodney King trial but also most cases involving minority defendants, Sheri Lynn Johnson, a law professor, believes defendants should be guaranteed three members of their own racial group on a 12-member jury (cited in Lacayo, 1993, p. 61).

The pluralist themes underlie a remark made by a Native American civilian worker at a military station:

> I don't feel too good about White people. They seem like they treat Indians as lower. I dislike the treatment . . . they kind of look down on me because I am an Indian. . . . I fit in the Indian world more than the White world. There is a lot of difference between the Indian [world] and the White world. (cited in Kim, Lujan, & Dixon, 1998, p. 259)

Also expressing the pluralist themes is the following reaction to the recent court decision on the role of race-based affirmative action programs in admission decisions at the University of Michigan (*New York Times,* Editorials/Letters, March 30, 2001):

> Even with affirmative action in place, law school classes here at the University of Michigan are overwhelmingly dominated by white men. The compelling interest in maintaining such programs applies not just to minority students, but to all students who will now see even fewer nonwhite faces and even fewer nonwhite faces as law school classes become even more homogeneous. Our legal system has produced yet another significantly disappointing decision, and many of us here fear that America is on the verge of taking one giant leap backward. (p. A22)

Molefi K. Asante, a distinguished scholar of African American studies, offers an eloquent argument against the "old" assimilationist ideals. In its place, Asante advocates the pluralist counter-ideals of group identity and status equality based on a particularistic view of human nature. In an essay titled "Racism, Consciousness, and Afrocentricity," Asante (1993) reflects on his experience of growing up in a racist society and explains how he came to reject W. E. B. Du Bois' notion of "double consciousness" as a tragic outcome inescapable in the "Eurocentric" society. Asante proposes "Afrocentricity" as an alternative intellectual model based on which African Americans can claim an equal identity and status as a distinct people:

> The feeling that you are in quicksand is inescapable in the quagmire of a racist society. You think that you can make progress in the interpretation of what's happening now only to discover that every step you take sinks the possibility of escaping. You are a victim despite your best efforts to educate those around you to the obvious intellectual mud stuck in their minds. . . .

> Even from my young adult years I thought a precondition of my fullness, a necessary and natural part of my maturity, was the commitment to be who I am, to be Afrocentric. . . . Afrocentricity is the active centering of the African in subject place in our historical landscape. This has always been my search; it has been a quest for sanity. (pp. 142–143)

MESSAGES OF RECONCILIATION

Straddled between the aforementioned ideological poles of assimilationism and pluralism are the voices of ideological reconciliation. These voices are what sociologist Alan Wolfe in *One Nation, After All* (1998) asserts as occupying "the vital center"—the "middle" America. Based on 200 in-depth interviews conducted in the Boston, Atlanta, Tulsa, and San Diego metropolitan areas, Wolfe (1998) found "little support for the notion that middle-class Americans are engaged in bitter cultural conflict with one another" (p. 278). Instead, according to Wolfe, they are "struggling to find ways in which their core beliefs can be reconciled with experiences that seem to contradict them" (p. 281), while insisting on a set of values "capacious enough to be inclusive but demanding enough to uphold standards of personal responsibility" (p. 322).

The messages of reconciliation reflect the struggle of Americans seeking moderation, tolerance, accommodation, integration, and balance. At the same time, reconciliation messages indicate a great deal of ambivalence and even contradiction in the way many Americans think about the issues of race, ethnicity, and interethnic relations. They may, for example, support bilingual programs, but only if they are short-lived and not used as a political goal or instrument of power demanded by every group for its own separate slice of the political pie. They may support multiculturalism, but only to the extent that ethnic identity is subsumed under the common "American identity" that emphasizes individualism. Or they may support affirmative action programs based on group identity, but consider "quota" systems as unfair, divisive, and ultimately counterproductive.

Messages of reconciliation such as these can be traced to the mainstream, integrationist civil rights movement led by Martin Luther King, Jr. In this movement, the traditional liberal ideals of individualism and procedural equality have been largely upheld in the struggle to eliminate systematic discrimination against African Americans as a group. Such a position of integration and reconciliation is eloquently expressed in the widely quoted "I Have a Dream" speech King delivered before the Lincoln Memorial on August 28, 1963:

> So I say to you, my friends, that even though we must face the difficulties of today and tomorrow, I still have a dream. It is a dream deeply rooted in the American dream that one day this nation will rise up and live out the true meaning of its creed—we hold these truths to be self-evident, that all men are created equal. . . . I have a dream my four little children will one day live in a nation where they will not be judged by the color of their skin but by the content of their character. I have a dream today. (in C. S. King, 1993, p. 101)

An attempt at ideological reconciliation was voiced in a remark former President Clinton made during a roundtable discussion on race televised on PBS (Public Broadcasting System) on July 9, 1998: "I believe there is an independent value to having young people learn in an environment where they're with people of many different racial and ethnic backgrounds. And the question is, How can you balance that with our devotion to merit?" (*New York Times*, July 9, 1998, p. A21). A similar stance of reconciliation has been voiced by Hugh Price, president of the National Urban League. In his keynote address at the League's 1998 annual conference, Price shared his belief that the current conditions in the United States offer blacks the "best shot we have ever had to shove ourselves the rest of the way into the American mainstream" (*New York Times*, August 13, 1998). Racial discrimination still exists, Hughes pointed out, but African American parents must take greater responsibility for the education of their children:

> With unemployment so low, employers are gobbling up almost every willing and able worker with a pulse. Shame on us if we don't seize this historic opening in the economy. . . . I think we are moving rapidly toward the day when if you've got something to put on the table, employers aren't going to care what color you are. (p. A23)

Likewise, on Columbus Day in 1992, Niles Bird Runningwater, then president of the Indian Student

Association at the University of Oklahoma, communicates a message of reconciliation:

> We don't choose to protest this fallacy of American history, but rather to celebrate the survival and continuance of Indian peoples. . . . By doing this we can fully acknowledge 500 years of coexistence of Indian and non-Indian peoples in America. . . . We're trying to do our part in togetherness and participation by eliciting communication and excitement concerning the respect of others' cultures. (*Oklahoma Daily,* March 24, 1992, p. 3)

Moderate voices such as these often escape media attention or get lost in the midst of loud and conspicuous voices of committed ideologues from the left and the right. Yet messages of reconciliation are all around us when we look for them. In his autobiography, *Walking with the Wind* (1998), John Lewis, a leader of the civil rights movement since the 1960s and currently a Democratic congressman from Georgia, articulates his abiding faith in the "Beloved Community," a vision of what society could become were people of all class and ethnic backgrounds to reach across the barriers that divide them. Richard Rorty, in his book *Achieving Our Country* (1998), argues for ideological moderation and objects to intransigent "leftists" and "conservatives." In *Someone Else's House* (1998), Tamar Jacoby professes her faith in interethnic integration and calls for realism that appreciates the real progress between blacks and whites that has taken place in American society and insists on the need for both blacks and whites to stay on the long and slow course of integration. An ideological reconciliation is also sought by Gerald Graff in *Beyond the Culture Wars* (1992) and by Alan Ryan in *Liberal Anxieties and Liberal Education* (1998). Both authors support the principles of multiculturalism and other pluralistic theories, while insisting that category-based ideas of cultural diversity in the academe must be moderated and put in dialogue with traditional courses to avoid continuation of a disconnected curriculum and mutual resentment.

MESSAGES OF EXTREMISM

The full spectrum of American public discourse on interethnic relations further includes the marginal voices of separatism, often characterized as "extremist" views. Whereas the aforementioned messages of assimilationism, pluralism, and reconciliation commonly adhere to the societal goal of interethnic *integration* (while disagreeing on specific visions as to how to achieve this goal), extremist messages often express a preference for maximum in-group/out-group *separation.* Some of the most unambiguous separatist messages come from those identified with "extreme right" groups including the Ku Klux Klan, neo-Nazis, Skinheads, and the so-called Patriot movements. Members of such groups are known for their commitment to racial purism, the supremacy of the white race, and in some cases, even arms training and preparation for a race war (Southern Poverty Law Center, 1998). George Burdi, who is reported to be working to revitalize the neo-Nazi movement through a newly powerful network, the Internet, states his separatist view toward blacks:

> To put black men and women in American society, which is traditionally and essentially established on European traditions, and to say, "Here you go, you're an equal, now compete," is just as ridiculous as assuming that you could move white people to the Congo and have them effectively compete. . . . the progeny of slaves cannot live in harmony with the progeny of slavemasters. (*New York Times Magazine,* February 25, 1996, pp. 40–41)

Of course, separatist messages come from the "extreme left" as well, including such contemporary ethnic nationalist groups as the New Black Panthers and the Nation of Islam. Among such messages are Leonard Jefferies' description of white Americans as "ice people" and Louis Farrakhan's call for black nationalism and economic reparations, his assertion of black racial superiority, and his condemnation of Jews as "bloodsuckers," which have been widely reported (e.g., *Time,* February 28, 1994, pp. 21–25). Farrakhan is also reported to have called the United States "the Great Satan" during a visit in 1996 to Iran and proclaimed, "You can quote me: God will destroy America at the hands of the Muslims" (*Time,* February 26, 1996, p. 12; *Washington Post,* February 26, 1996, pp. A1, A6). Farrakhan explains his separatist view in an interview featured in *Time* (February 28, 1994, pp. 21–25) as follows:

> My ultimate aim is the liberation of our people. So if we are to be liberated, it's good to see the hands that are holding us. And we need to sever those hands

> from holding us that we may be a free people, that we may enter into a better relationship with them than what we presently have. (p. 25)

Extreme separatist messages are heard even from those who are unaffiliated with a recognized extremist group. Although not always explicit, separatist views can be easily inferred from the inflammatory rhetorical devices employed to condemn or scapegoat an out-group or position the in-group as "victims." Among such messages is the phrase "culture war" Patrick Buchanan used in a speech he delivered during the 1992 Republican convention, connoting an unmistakable line drawn to "defend" what is believed to be the authentic American culture. Indeed, separatist messages appear to be becoming increasingly louder: Robert Kimball (1990) characterizes black studies in universities as "this war against Western culture" (p. xi); minority student protesters at Stanford University chant "Down with racism, Western culture's got to go" (*New York Times,* October 25, 1995, pp. A1, B8); a black student leader at Northwestern University insists that no black people can be racists "because racism is a function of power" (*New York Times,* October 25, 1995, p. B8); a group of Hispanic students at Cornell University occupy a building to demand separate Hispanic housing (*New York Times,* April 20, 1994, p. B8).

Thus, *the extremes meet.* As dramatically as the separatist messages of the extreme right and the extreme left differ in their respective claims, they converge in rigid in-group/out-group distinction, characterization of the in-group as "victims," full-blown confrontational rhetorical posturing, and fortification of mutually intransigent moral claims. Separatist messages of both kinds violate the rationality and civility normally expected by most Americans in public discourse. As such, extremist messages are deemed to be beyond the realm of what most Americans consider "reasonable." As Billig et al. (1988) observe, "the extreme bigot is free to play consistently and unambiguously in an area which is beyond reality but which taunts reality. There is no need to hedge and qualify statements in order not to pass a seemingly unreasonable judgment" (p. 118). It is not surprising, then, that separatist arguments do not resonate with the American public at large and, instead, are usually met with messages of rejection of one kind or another.

Even though mainstream Americans diverge in their views on the *locus* of American life (individual vs. group identity); the nature, rights, and responsibilities of humans (universalism vs. relativism); and the meaning of equality (procedural equality vs. status equality), they are largely united in their objection to the separatist vision of the United States and in their shared condemnation of "hate" messages as fundamentally "un-American."

Exemplifying such common reactions to separatist messages are the responses of several readers to a *Time* magazine cover story featuring Farrakhan, entitled "Pride and Prejudice" (February 28, 1994, pp. 21–34). Their letters to the editor characterize Farrakhan in such unflattering terms as a "wild, hate-mongering preacher," "the Minister of Rage," "streetwise hipster who shrewdly plays to the emotions of the most miserable and hopeless of his own people." One reader admonishes the editor for even featuring the story in the magazine:

> As an African American, I find it very upsetting that every time Farrakhan speaks the media give him a microphone and an amplifier. . . . We should stop pointing fingers and making excuses that seem to confuse and anger more than unite our community. We can't continue at this level. We just can't.

Others have responded to Farrakhan's separatist messages by warning against putting group identity over individual identity. Shelby Steel, an African American professor at San Jose State University, points to the danger of excessive claims of group identity in an opinion column in the *New York Times* (March 13, 1994, p. E17):

> Louis Farrakhan personifies a specific territory in the collective imagination of black America. (Only this place in the imagination explains the vast disparity between his prominence and his rather small following.) It is the territory where the group ceases to be a mere identity or culture and becomes a value in itself. Here the group becomes synonymous with truth, and no longer needs approval from others. . . . It is precisely their break from universal truths—tolerance, brotherhood, fair-mindedness—that enables them to assert the supremacy of their group.

SYNTHESIS

The present analysis has revealed varied renditions of the liberal ideological tradition. Classical liberalism is reproduced by individual Americans not so much in terms of a set of universally commonsensical values, as in the form of often dilemmatic and sometimes embattled conflicting values. Communication messages addressing issues of race, ethnicity, and interethnic relations do not automatically mirror the traditional liberal themes of individualism, universalism, and procedural equality. Rather, they are dynamically challenged by the contrary themes of group identity, particularism, and equal group status.

This ideological dialectic undergirds messages of assimilationism and pluralism, along with messages of reconciliation and separatism. These themes and counter-themes of classical liberalism broadly help us understand the full spectrum of messages we hear today. The traditional individualistic and universalistic ideals and the principle of procedural equality are most closely aligned with messages of assimilationism, generally identified as the position of the mainstream political right. On the other hand, messages of pluralism, often associated with the mainstream political left, advocate the primacy of group identity, application of laws and public policies relative to historical and institutional conditions particular to a group, so as to close the existing unequal status between groups. Struggling between these two ideological views are the moderating, balancing, integrating, and often conflicted messages of reconciliation representing Middle America. In contrast, messages of extremism are commonly identified with the views of the extreme right and the extreme left—messages that emphasize in-group victimhood and moral superiority and maximum in-group/out-group separation.

Together, these four ideological positions constitute an *ideological circle,* illustrated in Figure 1. In this circle, the four positions are differentiated based on two bipolar dimensions: (1) the horizontal dimension of classical liberal and contrary themes, and (2) the vertical dimension of integrationist and separatist visions for the American society. The oppositional relationship between the assimilationist messages of liberal themes and pluralist messages of counter-themes is indicated by their respective positions of three o'clock and nine o'clock. Linking these two message types are the integrationist messages of reconciliation placed at the twelve o'clock position. The separatist messages of extremism (from both the extreme political right and the extreme political left) are merged into the six o'clock position, opposite from the position of the integrationist messages of reconciliation.

Figure 1 *Ideological Circle*

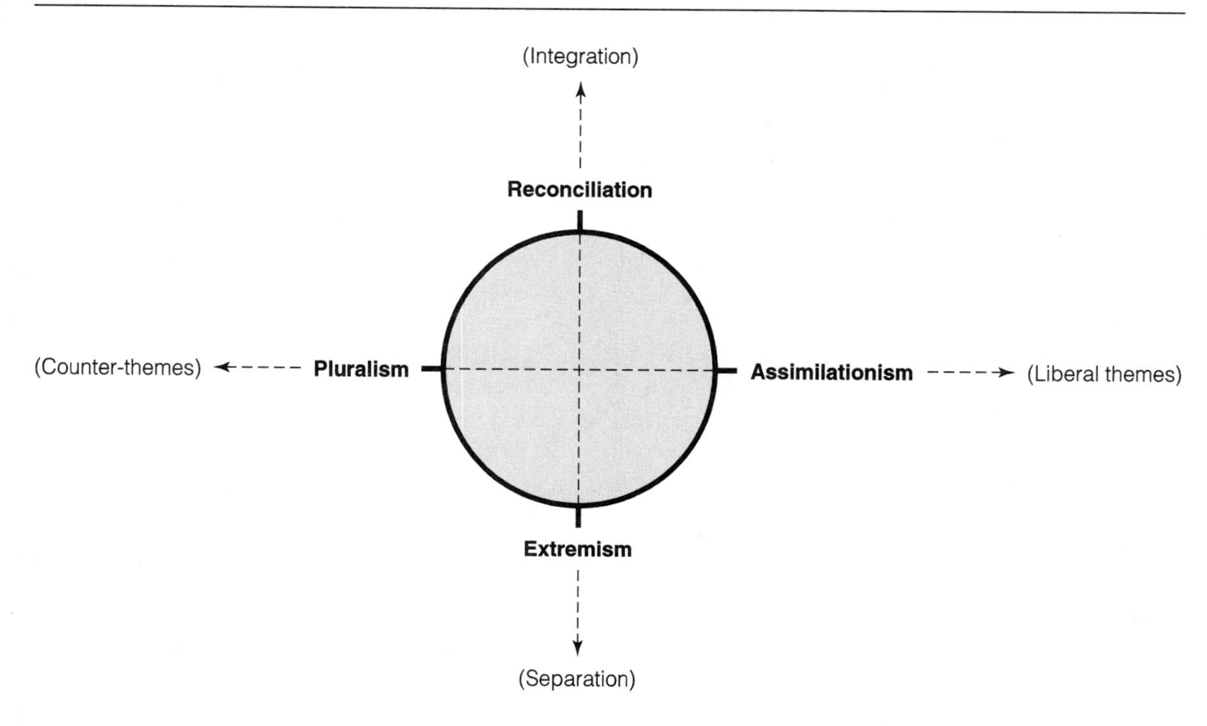

Even while being rigorously challenged by the voices advocating pluralism and extremism, the classical liberal ideals continue to occupy the mainstream of American consciousness on interethnic relations in the form of assimilationism and reconciliation. The liberal tradition contains its own contrary themes, unresolved tensions, a dialectic—an ideological push-and-pull that often gives rise to heated debates and, in some cases, even acts of violence. These debates are not confined to the level of intellectual analysis; both themes and counter-themes have arisen from, and passed into, everyday consciousness of Americans who reflect on, and speak to, various issues of ethnicity and race. Indeed, we do not blindly follow the dictates of classical liberalism. Rather, we exercise a degree of freedom in making our own individual interpretations and judgments within the constraints of the liberal ideological tradition.

This conclusion is largely supported by findings from public opinion polls. In a 1997 Time/CNN poll of more than 1,100 Americans, 96% of the respondents agreed with the assimilationist statement "It should be the duty of all immigrants to learn English if they plan to stay in this country." In response to the question "Which comes closest to your view on bilingual education in public schools?" only 11% agreed with the pluralist view that "children of immigrants should be taught in their native language indefinitely." This is in sharp contrast with the 48% of the respondents who indicated "children of immigrants should be taught in their native language only until they know enough English to join regular classes," and with the remaining 40% who said "all children should be taught in English" (Gray, 1993, p. 70). Similar sentiments underlie the decisive passage of "Proposition 227" in 1998 by California voters, thereby eliminating all bilingual education programs and replacing them with intensive English language instruction.

Likewise, when "Ebonics" ("Black English") was endorsed by the Oakland Unified School District Board of Education at the end of 1996 as a legitimate language program, many public leaders who often diverge ideologically with respect to interethnic relations converged in denouncing and rejecting it as an "extremist," "dangerous," and "divisive" idea. From the camp commonly known as the "political right," former Republican Senator Lauch Faircloth of North Carolina persisted in stating what had become the common view: "But I think Ebonics is absurd. This is a political correctness that has simply gone out of control." Similar voices were heard from the "political left" as well. Jesse Jackson stated, "I understand the attempt to reach out to these children, but this is an unacceptable surrender, bordering on disgrace" (cited in Lewis, 1998). Senior *Wall Street Journal* editor Joseph N. Boyce was even more indignant: "As a black person and father of four, I find such notions insulting and, yes, racist" (cited in Palmeri, 1997). Poet Maya Angelou was also quoted to have been "incensed" by the plan, while Oakland writer Ishmael Reed labeled it a "travesty" (cited in Palmeri, 1997). Relatedly, the results of Gallup polls taken over the recent decades (1972 through 1997) show a dramatic increase in the percentage of white Americans who are willing to vote for a black candidate for president (from 35% to 93%) and who approve of marriage between blacks and whites (25% to 61%) (*USA Today*, August 8, 1995, p. A11).

The continuing efficacy of liberal ideology transcending ethnic categories is also reflected in the fact that, roughly from the 1960s to the 1990s, the number of interracial marriages in the United States has escalated from 310,000 to more than 1.1 million and that the incidence of births of mixed-race babies has multiplied 26 times as fast as that of any other group. As of the early 1990s, 52% of Jewish Americans, 65% of Japanese Americans, and 70% of Native Americans are reported to have married out of their faith, race, or ethnic heritage (Smolowe, 1993, pp. 64–65). Increasingly, individuals of mixed racial and ethnic backgrounds add complexity to the ideological dialectic. Arvil Ward (1993), half Asian and half black, describes his identity experience as follows:

> I found myself in an argument on a flight from Washington D.C. to Memphis. . . . This time it was with a member of the Black Freedom Fighters Coalition, or so his jacket, which was covered in epigrams and names from black history, said. A few minutes into our flight, he noticed that I was reading Shelby Steele's *The Content of Our Character.* Since he asked, I started to tell him what I thought I understood of the conservative Steele's ideas. . . . "Why do you clutter up your mind with all that stuff" he asked, his voice dripping with drama like a preacher. . . . He asked me what right I had to say I was black. Yeah, I had black skin, he agreed, but I didn't sound black. . . . "You Filipino, right? . . . It is people like you that will sell us out when the

revolution comes," he said. . . . Could he have known that all my life, I struggled for black acceptance, many times at the expense of my Asian side? (pp. 111–112)

Exactly how the nature of American interethnic relations and the underlying forces of ideological beliefs will unfold in the future remains to be seen. Some observers (e.g., Suarez-Orozco & Paez, 2002) foresee a continuing trend of pluralism. In *The Latino Wave* (2004), Jorge Ramos, news anchor of Univision, speaks to this trend by highlighting the large and rapidly increasing numbers of Hispanic Americans who tend to maintain a strong allegiance to their countries of origin. Debates will doubtlessly continue as Americans struggle with competing visions of *Unum* and *Pluribus*—visions of what it means to be American. Free and public debates, indeed, are essential for American society to guard itself against stagnation, disintegration, and entropy. The very fact that interethnic issues continue to engage American passion is itself an affirmation, and a hallmark, of the American liberal tradition. This tradition contributes to the stability of the American democracy, one that most Americans recognize, cherish, and celebrate. In the essayist Grunwald's (1976) words:

> So one must love America, most of all and most deeply for its constant, difficult, confused, gallant and never finished struggle to make freedom possible. One loves America for its accomplishments as well as for its unfinished business—and especially for its knowledge that its business is indeed unfinished. . . . One ultimately loves America for not what it is, or what it does, but for what it promises. . . . we must deeply believe, and we must prove, that after 200 years the American promise is still only in its beginning. (p. 36)

References

Abercrombie, N. (1980). *Class, structure and knowledge.* Oxford: Basil Blackwell.

Asante, M. (1993). Racism, consciousness, and Afrocentricity. In G. Early (Ed.), *Lure and loathing: Essays on race, identity, and the ambivalence of assimilation* (pp. 127–148). New York: Penguin.

Baker, R. (1994, May 5). Gone with the Unum. *New York Times*, p. A15.

Billig, M. (1991). *Ideology and opinions: Studies in rhetorical psychology.* London: Sage.

Billig, M., Condor, S., Edwards, D., Gane, M., Middleton, D., & Radley, A. (1988). *Ideological dilemmas: A social psychology of everyday thinking.* London: Sage.

Crouch, S. (1998). *Always in pursuit: Fresh American perspectives, 1995–1997.* New York: Pantheon Books.

Garfinkel, H. (1967). *Studies in ethnomethodology.* Englewood Cliffs, NJ: Prentice-Hall.

Graff, G. (1992). *Beyond the culture wars: How teaching the conflicts can revitalize American education.* New York: Norton.

Gray, P. (1993, Fall). Teach your children well. *Time,* pp. 68–71.

Grunwald, H. (1976, July 5). Loving America. *Time,* pp. 35–36.

Hacker, A. (1992). *Two nations: Black and White, separate, hostile, unequal.* New York: Charles Scribner's Sons.

Iyer, P. (1990, September 3). The masks of minority terrorism. *Time,* p. 86.

Jacoby, T. (1998). *Someone else's house: America's unfinished struggle for integration.* New York: Free Press.

Kim, Y. Y. (1997). The behavior–context interface in interethnic communication. In J. Owen (Ed.), *Context and communication behavior* (pp. 261–291). Reno, NV: Context Press.

Kim, Y. Y., Lujan, P., & Dixon, L. (1998). "I can walk both ways": Identity integration of American Indians in Oklahoma. *Human Communication Research, 25*(2), 252–274.

Kimball, R. (1990). *Tenured radicals: How politics has corrupted higher education.* New York: Harper & Row.

King, C. S. (1993). *The Martin Luther King, Jr. companion: Quotations from the speeches, essays, and books of Martin Luther King, Jr.* (selected by Coretta Scott King). New York: St. Martin.

Lacayo, R. (1993, Fall). Whose peers? *Time* (Special Issue, *The New Faces of America*), pp. 60–61.

Lewis, J. (1998). *Walking with the wind: A memoir of the movement.* New York: Simon & Schuster.

Loury, G. (1993). Free at last? A personal perspective on race and identity in America. In G. Early (Ed.), *Lure and loathing: Essays on race, identity, and the ambivalence of assimilation* (pp. 1–12). New York: Allen Lane/Penguin.

Palmeri, A. (1997, October). *Ebonics and politics: A Burkian analysis.* Paper presented at the annual meeting of the National Communication Association, Chicago.

Ramos, J. (2004). *The Latino wave: How Hispanics will elect the next American president.* New York: Rayo.

Rorty, R. (1998). *Achieving our country: Leftist thought in twentieth-century America.* Cambridge, MA: Harvard University Press.

Rossides, D. (1976). *The American class system: An introduction to social stratification.* Washington, DC: University Press of America.

Ryan, A. (1998). *Liberal anxieties and liberal education.* New York: Hill & Wang.

Smolowe, J. (1993, Fall). Intermarried . . . with children. *Time* (Special Issue, *The New Faces of America),* pp. 64–65.

Southern Poverty Law Center. (1998, Spring). *Intelligence Report, 90.*

Suarez-Orozco, M., & Paez, M. (Eds.). (2002). *Latinos: Remaking America.* Berkeley: University of California Press.

Traub, J. (1998, June 28). Nathan Glazer changes his mind, again. *New York Times Magazine,* pp. 22–25.

Tsuda, Y. (1986). *Language inequality and distortion.* Philadelphia: John Benjamin.

Ward, A. (1993). Which side are you on? *Amerasia Journal, 19*(2), 109–112.

Wilson, K. (1998, May). The contested space of prudence in the 1874–1875 civil rights debate. *Quarterly Journal of Speech, 84*(2), 131–149.

Wolfe, A. (1998). *One nation, after all.* New York: Viking.

Concepts and Questions

1. Why has the *E Pluribus Unum* concept of a "melting pot" society failed to materialize in contemporary American society?
2. How do "tribal identities" contribute to interethnic conflict?
3. What characterizes messages of assimilation? From whom are messages of assimilation most likely to emerge?
4. Can or do messages of assimilation lend themselves to improved interethnic communication?
5. Give an example of a message of pluralism. How do messages of pluralism differ from messages of assimilation?
6. What are messages of reconciliation? How do they relate to messages of assimilation and messages of pluralism?
7. From whom are messages of reconciliation most likely to emanate?
8. What are messages of extremism? Which groups of American society are most likely to promulgate messages of extremism?
9. How can an understanding of the philosophical underpinnings of the messages of assimilation, plurality, reconciliation, and extremism lead to better interethnic communication?
10. How can the American struggle between *Unum* and *Pluribus* be resolved?

Does the Worm Live in the Ground? Reflections on Native American Spirituality

MICHAEL TLANUSTA GARRETT
MICHAEL P. WILBUR

Everyone knows that grandparents and grandchildren often have a very special bond that goes beyond words. Still, from time to time, the way grandchildren act can get on the nerves of grandparents (and, of course, the way grandparents act can get on children's nerves, too). Tsayoga was a good little boy—sensitive, quiet, inquisitive, but also very stubborn. He was a good boy, but he had to do things his own way, and he couldn't always understand why things weren't the way he thought they should be. "But why?" he might ask his grandfather—over and over and over. Sometimes, Grandfather would get a little frustrated with the boy who might be busy listening but not hearing. "Tsayoga," the old man would say abruptly sometimes, "does the worm live in the ground, or does the worm fly in the sky?" "Grandfather," the little boy would answer, "the worm lives in the ground." "Well, OK then," Grandfather would reply.

OVERVIEW

There seems to be a great deal of misunderstanding these days about what Native American spirituality actually means and what it involves (Matheson, 1996). This misunderstanding in mainstream American culture has developed for several reasons, including the historical exploitation of *Native* (term used interchangeably with *Native American* and *Indian*)

Reprinted from *Journal of Multicultural Counseling and Development,* 27, October 1999, pp. 193–201. Michael Tlanusta Garrett teaches at Western Carolina University, Cullowhee, North Carolina. Michael P. Wilbur teaches at the University of Connecticut, Storrs.

culture and the often stereotyped portrayal of Native Americans in the media as noble savages or hostile Indians bent on destruction. In addition, more recently, misunderstanding has developed as a result of non–Native Americans' attempting to interpret or conduct Indian ceremonies or spiritual practices without always having a true understanding of the meaning or power of those ceremonies or practices for the Indian nation from which it comes, or without being "qualified" to do so (i.e., being trained as a Medicine person).

For this and other historical reasons, many Native American traditionalists often share very little of the "true knowledge" of certain beliefs or ceremonies for fear that this knowledge will be misunderstood or misused as it has been historically (Deloria, 1994). Bear in mind, it has only been since 1978, with the passage of the American Indian Religious Freedom Act, that Native Americans have been able to legally practice their spirituality and traditional ways in this country. That is only 20 years . . . not a long time. For Native American traditionalists, protecting the sacred ways was and is a matter of survival, but it is also a matter of respect for the power that is involved in such ways. This power goes beyond any one individual and, according to the traditions, must be respected and treated with great care so as to do no harm.

So who are Native Americans, and what is this power to which we refer? Across the United States, there are more than 558 federally recognized and several hundred state-recognized Native American nations (Russell, 1998). Given the wide-ranging diversity of this population consisting of 2.3 million people, it is important to understand that the term *Native American spirituality* encompasses the vastness and essence of more than 500 different tribal traditions represented by these hundreds of Indian nations. Navajo, Catawba, Shoshone, Lumbee, Cheyenne, Cherokee, Apache, Lakota, Seminole, Comanche, Pequot, Cree, Tuscarora, Paiute, Creek, Pueblo, Shawnee, Hopi, Osage, Mohawk, Nez Perce, Seneca—these are but a handful of the hundreds of tribal nations that exist across the United States. Is it possible to grasp the essence of so many rich and diverse spiritual traditions? One wonders how Grandfather might respond.

To better understand some of the basic concepts relating to Native American spirituality, it is necessary to consider some of the underlying values that permeate a Native worldview and existence. Several authors have described common core values that characterize "traditionalism" across tribal nations (Heinrich, Corbine, & Thomas, 1990; Herring, 1990; Little Soldier, 1992; Peregoy, 1993; Thomason, 1991). Some of these values include the importance of community contribution, sharing, acceptance, cooperation, harmony and balance, noninterference, extended family, attention to nature, immediacy of time, awareness of the relationship, and a deep respect for elders (Dudley, 1992; Dufrene, 1990; J. T. Garrett & M. T. Garrett, 1994, 1996; M. T. Garrett, 1996, 1998; Heinrich et al., 1990; Herring, 1990, 1997; Lake, 1991; Plank, 1994; Red Horse, 1997). All in all, these traditional values show the importance of honoring through harmony and balance what is believed to be a very sacred connection with the energy of life; this is the basis for Native spirituality across tribal nations.

Different tribal languages have different words or ways of referring to this idea of honoring one's sense of connection, but the meaning is similar across nations in referring to the belief that human beings exist on Mother Earth to be helpers and protectors of life. In Native communities, it is not uncommon, as an example, to hear people use the term *caretaker.* Therefore, from the perspective of a traditionalist, to see one's purpose as that of caretaker is to accept responsibility for the gift of life by taking good care of that gift—the gift of life that others have received and the surrounding beauty of the world in which we live. The purpose of this article is to share some of the basic cultural elements contributing to what is known as Native American spirituality and to offer implications for counseling. Four concepts central to Native American spirituality will be discussed, including Medicine, Relation, Harmony, and Vision. To begin with, however, it is important to consider what it means from a traditional Native American perspective to "walk in step."

WALKING IN STEP

As you hear the sound of the drum rumbling low to the sharp, impassioned cries of the singers, the vibration moves through you like a storm that rises in the distance, building slowly in the azure sky, then unloading in a rhythmic yet gentle pounding of the soil. Anyone, Native or non-Native, who has ever had the opportunity to experience the colors, movement, sounds, tastes, and smells of the powwow (a pan-traditional, ceremonial giving of thanks), understands the feeling that passes through you. It is different for every person, but if you really experience the feeling, you know that it is connection. For some, it is a matter of seeing old friends or making new ones. For some, it is the image of the dancers moving in seemingly infinite poses of unity and airy smoothness to every flowing pound of the drum. For some, it is the laughter and exchange of words and gestures. For some, it is silent inner prayer giving thanks for another day of life. For some, it is the delicious taste of your second and third helping of that piping hot fry bread. Whatever it is, in the end, it is coming together on one level or another, and walking in step with the Greater Circle.

As one reads the aforementioned description of what it is like to experience a powwow, it becomes easier to relate to the experience of someone who might actually be there by paying attention to the senses and to the resulting emotional experience of the event. This is an important lesson in coming to understand how a Native person might experience the world from a traditional point of view. More or less, the essence of Native American spirituality is about "feeling." The feeling of connection is something that is available to all of us, although experienced in differing ways. It is important to note that the spiritual beliefs of Native Americans depend on several factors, including level of acculturation (traditional, marginal, bicultural, assimilated, pan-traditional); geographic region; family structure; religious influences; and tribally specific traditions. (For a further discussion of levels of acculturation, see J. T. Garrett & M. T. Garrett, 1994; M. T. Garrett, 2000.) It is possible, however, to generalize to some extent about several basic beliefs characterizing Native American traditionalism and spirituality across tribal nations. Adapted from Locust (1988), the following elaborates on some basic Native American spiritual and traditional beliefs:

1. There is a single higher power known as Creator, Great Creator, Great Spirit, or Great One, among other names (this being is sometimes referred to in gender form, but does not necessarily exist as one particular gender or another). There are also lesser beings known as spirit beings or spirit helpers.
2. Plants and animals, like humans, are part of the spirit world. The spirit world exists side by side with and intermingles with the physical world. Moreover, the spirit existed in the spirit world before it came into a physical body and will exist after the body dies.
3. Human beings are made up of a spirit, mind, and body. The mind, body, and spirit are all interconnected; therefore, illness affects the mind and spirit as well as the body.
4. Wellness is harmony in body, mind, and spirit; unwellness is disharmony in mind, body, and spirit.
5. Natural unwellness is caused by the violation of a sacred social or natural law of creation (e.g., participating in a sacred ceremony while under the influence of alcohol, drugs, or having had sex within four days of a ceremony).
6. Unnatural unwellness is caused by conjuring (witchcraft) from those with destructive intentions.
7. Each of us is responsible for our own wellness by keeping ourselves attuned to self, relations, environment, and universe. (pp. 317–318)

This list of beliefs in Native American spirituality crosses tribal boundaries but is by no means comprehensive. It does, however, provide a great deal of insight into some of the assumptions that may be held by a "traditional" native person. To better understand more generally what it means to "walk in step" according to Native American spirituality, it is important to discuss four basic cultural elements: Medicine, Harmony, Relation, and Vision.

MEDICINE: EVERYTHING IS ALIVE

Walk into any classroom of children these days and ask them playfully, "Have you had your Medicine today?" and many of them will tell you yes. If you ask them what kind of medicine, sadly, they will tell you Ritalin, or a painkiller, or some type of cold medicine, among other things. In native tradition, the concept of "Medicine" is starkly different from what medicine has become in mainstream American society. So what is Medicine? Crowfoot, a Blackfoot leader, spoke the following words in 1890 as he lay dying:

> What is life? It is the flash of a firefly in the night. It is the breath of a buffalo in the wintertime. It is the little shadow which runs across the grass and loses itself in the sunset.

In the preceding quote, once again, the importance of experiencing life through the senses and through one's emotional experience becomes apparent as a way of understanding Medicine. In the traditional way, Medicine can consist of physical remedies such as herbs, teas, and poultices for physical ailments, but Medicine is simultaneously something much more than a pill you take to cure illness, get rid of pain, or correct a physiological malfunction. Medicine is everywhere. It is the very essence of our inner being; it is that which gives us inner power. Medicine is in every tree, plant, rock, animal, and person. It is in the light, the soil, the water, and the wind. Medicine is something that happened 10 years ago that still makes you smile when you think about it. Medicine is that old friend who calls you up out of the blue just because he or she was thinking about you. There is Medicine in watching a small child play. Medicine is in the reassuring smile of an elder. There is Medicine in every event, memory, place, person, and movement. There is even Medicine in "empty space" if you know how to use it.

In many Native American traditions, every living being possesses this inner power called Medicine that connects us to all other living beings through the heart; however, if we fail to respect our relations (with all living beings, the Creator, Mother Earth, ourselves, and the Four Directions) and to keep ourselves in step with the universe, we invite illness by falling out of harmony and balance, much like a dancer failing to move in step with the rhythm of the drum. A person's Medicine is his or her power, and it can be used for creative purposes or destructive purposes—either contributing to or taking away from the Greater Circle of Life. Being in harmony means being "in step with the universe"; being in disharmony means being "out of step with the universe."

HARMONY: EVERYTHING HAS PURPOSE

Every living being has a reason for being. Traditional Native Americans look on life as a gift from the Creator. As a gift, it is to be treated with the utmost care out of respect for the giver. This means living in a humble way and giving thanks for all of the gifts that one receives every day, no matter how big or small. The importance of humility is illustrated in the following words spoken by Tecumseh, Shawnee leader, more than a century ago:

> When you arise in the morning, give thanks for the morning light, for your life and strength. Give thanks for your food and the joy of living. If you see no reason for giving thanks, the fault lies in yourself.

One of the reasons it is so important in the traditional way to maintain a humble stance is not for fear of punishment by the Creator, but rather to maintain a keen awareness of all the gifts that surround us and to keep our spirit open and receptive. In this way, we are able to be of service to others and much more able to walk the path of peace. The person who walks with their peace is very difficult to get off balance.

Acceptance is a very important part of living in harmony and balance in a worldview that emphasizes that everyone and everything has a reason for being. There is no such thing as a good experience or a bad experience because everything that happens is of value in offering us the opportunity to learn and "see more clearly" how to live in harmony (M. T. Garrett & J. E. Myers, 1996; Herring, 1994; Tafoya, 1997). Therefore, in the traditional way, trying to control things or people is considered a waste of energy because it is believed that everything is as it should be at any given point in time.

Native American spirituality often places great emphasis on the numbers four and seven. The number four represents the spirit of each of the directions—east, south, west, and north—usually depicted in a circle. The number seven represents the same four directions as well as the upper world (Sky), lower world (Earth), and center (often referring to the heart, or sacred fire) to symbolize universal harmony and balance (visualized as a sphere). In the traditional way, you seek to understand what lessons are offered to you by giving thanks to each of the four directions for the wisdom, guidance, strength, and clarity that you receive. Not every tribe practices the directions in this way, but almost all tribes have some representation of the four directions as a circular symbol of the harmony and balance of mind, body, and spirit with the natural environment (and spirit world).

It is interesting to note, however, that, unlike in other religious traditions, in Native American spirituality it is considered disrespectful—even arrogant—for a person to "ask" anything of the Creator. Rather, people give thanks for what they do have. It is assumed with the Creator as with people that if something is to be revealed to you, it will be revealed when it is time. This view emphasizes once again the values of respect and humility. Traditionalists seek help and guidance more directly from spirit helpers or spirit guides. The Creator is one to be honored and revered by walking the path of harmony and balance, respecting all one's relations.

RELATION: ALL THINGS ARE CONNECTED

Central to Native American spiritual traditions is the importance of "relation" as a total way of existing in the world. The concept of family extends to brothers and sisters in the animal world, the plant world, the mineral world, Mother Earth, Father Sky, and so on. The power of relation is symbolized by the Circle of Life (sometimes referred to as the Web of Life), so commonly represented throughout the customs, traditions, and art forms of Native people (Dufrene, 1990). This Circle of Life is believed, in many tribal traditions, to consist of the basic elements of life: fire/sunlight, earth, water, and wind. These four points also denote, in Cherokee tradition for instance, spirit, nature, body, and mind referred to as the Four Winds (or the Four Directions). The concept of relation is further illustrated by Black Elk, Oglala Lakota Medicine Man, in the following excerpt:

> You have noticed that everything an Indian does is in a circle, and that is because the Power of the World always works in circles, and everything tries to be round. . . . The sky is round, and I have heard that Earth is round like a ball, and so are all the stars. The wind, in its greatest power, whirls. Birds make their nests in circles, for theirs is the same religion as ours. . . . Even the seasons form a great circle in their changing, and always come back again to where they were. The life of a person is a circle from childhood to childhood, and so it is in everything where power moves (as cited in M. T. Garrett, 1998, p. 75).

The circle thus reflects not only the interrelationship of all living beings but the natural progression or growth of life itself. Harmony and balance are necessary for the survival of all life. Thus, living in "proper relations" and giving thanks to "all our relations" are common phrases in Indian country.

Respect for Medicine also means practicing respect for the interconnection that we share. Across tribal nations, certain natural or social laws must be observed out of respect for relation. These often point to restrictions on personal conduct regarding such things as death, incest, the female menstrual cycle, witchcraft, certain animals, certain natural phenomena, certain foods, and marrying into one's own clan and in strict observance of ceremonial protocol (Locust, 1988). In general, a rule of thumb in Native tradition is that you (1) never take more than you need, (2) give thanks for what you have or what you receive, (3) take great care to use all of what you do have, and (4) "give away" what you do not need (or what someone else may need more than you).

VISION: EMBRACE THE MEDICINE OF EVERY LIVING BEING AND YOUR VISION

Across tribal nations, many different ceremonies are used for healing, giving thanks, celebrating, clearing the way, and blessing (Lake, 1991). Among the various traditions, a few examples of ceremonies include sweat lodge, vision quest, clearing-way ceremony, blessing-way ceremony, pipe ceremony, sunrise ceremony, sun dance, and many, many others (Heinrich et al., 1990; Lake, 1991). One of the functions of ceremonial practice is to reaffirm one's connection with that which is sacred. In American mainstream ideology, the purpose of life consists of "life, liberty, and the pursuit of happiness." From a traditional Native perspective, a corollary would be "life, love, and learning." Once you understand and respect the Medicine, learn to live in harmony, and honor your relations, the final important step in the traditional way is knowing what to do with the gift of life with which you have been blessed:

> In a conversation with his aging grandfather, a, young Indian man asked, "Grandfather, what is the purpose of life?" After a long time in thought, the old man looked up and said, "Grandson, children are the purpose of life. We were once children and someone cared for us and now it is our time to care." (Brendtro, Brokenleg, & Van Bockem, 1990, p. 45)

Now, that is not to say that Native Americans believe that the purpose of everyone's life is to go and have children, but the deeper value of the relationship as an integral part of seeking purpose is evident. In the traditional way, one moves through the "life circle" from *being cared for* to *caring for* (Red Horse, 1980, 1997).

It is important throughout life to either seek your vision or continue honoring your vision. In Native tradition, vision is an inner knowledge of your own Medicine and purpose in the Greater Circle revealed to you through your spirit helpers. This means connecting with your inner power and opening yourself to the guidance of the spirits. This may happen in ceremony, or it may happen in other ways such as through dreams, particular signs, animal messengers, or certain experiences/events that come your way for a reason. Understanding one's vision is understanding the direction of one's path as a caretaker moving to the rhythm of the sacred heartbeat. As Black Elk, an Oglala Lakota Medicine man, put it: "The good road and the road of difficulties, you have made me cross: and where they cross, the place is holy."

CONCLUSION

One wonders, as we reflect on Native American spirituality, about the question that my great-grandfather posed to my father so many times when he was being a stubborn, inquisitive little boy: "Does the worm live in the ground, or does the worm fly in the sky?" This is a question we should ask ourselves when we interact with Native Americans. This is a question we should ask ourselves the next time a delicate, colorful butterfly wanders past us. Things are not always as they seem.

References

Brendtro, L. K., Brokenleg, M., & Van Bockem, S. (1990). *Reclaiming youth at risk: Our hope for the future.* Bloomington, IN: National Education Service.

Deloria, V., Jr. (1994). *God is red: A Native view of religion.* Golden, CO: Fulcrum.

Dudley, J. I. E. (1992). *Choteau Creek: A Sioux reminiscence.* Lincoln: University of Nebraska Press.

Dufrene, P. M. (1990). Exploring Native American symbolism. *Journal of Multicultural and Cross Cultural Research in Art Education, 8,* 38–50.

Garrett, J. T., & Garrett, M. T. (1994). The path of good medicine: Understanding and counseling Native Americans. *Journal of Multicultural Counseling and Cross-cultural Development, 22,* 134–144.

Garrett, J. T., & Garrett, M. T. (1996). *Medicine of the Cherokee: The way of right relationship.* Santa Fe, NM: Bear & Company.

Garrett, M. T. (1996). Reflection by the riverside: The traditional education of Native American children. *Journal of Humanistic Education and Development, 35,* 12–28.

Garrett, M. T. (1998). *Walking on the wind: Cherokee teachings for harmony and balance.* Santa Fe, NM: Bear & Company.

Garrett, M. T. (2000). Red as an apple: Native American acculturation and counseling with or without reservation. *Journal of Counseling and Development, 78,* 3–13.

Garrett, M. T., & Myers, J. E. (1996). The rule of opposites: A paradigm for counseling Native Americans. *Journal of Multicultural Counseling and Development, 24,* 89–104.

Heinrich, R. K., Corbine, J. L., & Thomas, K. R. (1990). Counseling Native Americans. *Journal of Counseling and Development, 69,* 128–133.

Herring, R. D. (1990). Understanding Native American values: Process and content concerns for counselors. *Counseling and Values, 34,* 134–137.

Herring, R. D. (1994). The clown or contrary figure as a counseling intervention strategy with Native American Indian clients. *Journal of Multicultural Counseling and Development, 22,* 153–164.

Herring, R. D. (1997). Counseling Native American youth. In C. C. Lee & B. L. Richardson (Eds.), *Multicultural issues in counseling: New approaches to diversity* (2nd ed., pp. 37–47). Alexandria, VA: American Counseling Association.

Lake, M. A. (1991). *Native healer: Initiation into an ancient art.* Wheaton, IL: Guest.

Little Soldier, L. (1992). Building optimum learning environments for Navajo students. *Childhood Education, 68,* 145–148.

Locust, C. (1988). Wounding the spirit: Discrimination and traditional American Indian belief systems. *Harvard Educational Review, 58,* 315–330.

Matheson, L. (1996). Valuing spirituality among Native American populations. *Counseling and Values, 41,* 51–58.

Peregoy, J. J. (1993). Transcultural counseling with American Indians and Alaska Natives: Contemporary issues for consideration. In J. McFadden (Ed.), *Transcultural counseling: Bilateral and international perspectives* (pp. 163–191). Alexandria, VA: American Counseling Association.

Plank, G. A. (1994). What silence means for educators of American Indian children. *Journal of American Indian Education, 34,* 3–19.

Red Horse, J. G. (1980). Indian elders: Unifiers of families. *Social Casework, 61,* 490–493.

Red Horse, J. G. (1997). Traditional American Indian family systems. *Families, Systems, and Health, 15,* 243–250.
Russell, G. (1998). *American Indian facts of life: A profile of today's tribes and reservations.* Phoenix, AZ: Russell.
Tafoya, T. (1997). Native gay and lesbian issues: The two-spirited. In B. Greene (Ed.), *Ethnic and cultural diversity among lesbians and gay men* (pp. 1–10). Thousand Oaks, CA: Sage.
Thomason, T. C. (1991). Counseling Native Americans: An introduction for non–Native American counselors. *Journal of Counseling and Development, 69,* 321–327.

Concepts and Questions

1. How do the authors define the concept of Native American spirituality?
2. Why do some Native Americans tend not to reveal the true knowledge of their spiritual ceremonies to non–Native Americans?
3. What is meant by a "sense of connection"? How does that sense direct Native American behavior?
4. What do Garrett and Wilbur refer to when they write about "walking in step"? What feelings would generally be associated with walking in step?
5. What seven generalizations do the authors draw regarding Native American spiritual and traditional beliefs? How might these beliefs affect intercultural communication?
6. What is the role of Native American Medicine in experiencing life? How does the concept of medicine apply to the individual?
7. How does the concept of harmony relate to purpose? How do the numbers four and seven relate to harmony?
8. Garrett and Wilbur assert that for Native Americans all things are connected. How does this sense of connectedness affect the concept of family?
9. What is the Circle of Life? How does it relate to the concept of relation?
10. What do the authors imply when they speak of "seeking your own vision"?

Let Me Count the Ways: African-American/European-American Marriages

DONNA M. STRINGER

INTRODUCTION

Biracial relationships have a long history in the United States. According to the U.S. Census Bureau (1993, cited in Orbe & Harris, 2001), biracial marriages have more than doubled each decade from 1970 to 1990. This is particularly significant given the fact that antimiscegenation laws did not become unconstitutional until 1967 and biracial marriages continued to be socially unacceptable until very recently (Gallup, 2003). The most recent census identified startling numbers of people who identify as biracial or multiracial and who are in biracial marriages (U.S. Census Bureau, 2001). As the demographics in the United States become increasingly diverse, people meet each other in their neighborhoods, schools, workplaces, and churches more than ever before in history. The end result of this diversity and greater integration will be an increasing number of biracial relationships between people who share experiences and values. Understanding both the benefits and the challenges experienced by couples in these relationships can help prepare those who are considering a biracial relationship for greater success. This article will outline specific areas in which Black/White heterosexual couples might experience misperceptions and/or cultural conflicts and suggest ways to reduce those potential misunderstandings.

The term *race* is socially constructed and has been used historically by groups in power to separate and

 Donna Stringer is President, Executive Diversity Services, and a faculty member of the Intercultural Communication Institute.

control "outsiders." It is also a term that is currently being challenged by DNA research (Graves, 2001). Because race is neither scientifically accurate nor socially positive, it is tempting to replace the term *race* with the term *ethnic* as a more accurate word, indicating shared systems of cultural beliefs, behaviors, and history. Orbe and Harris (2001) make a cogent argument that race continues to be one of the most important issues in the United States—separating people socially, economically, and politically. They argue that developing effective interracial communication is key to the future of this country and that eliminating the use of the word *race* from race relations will not facilitate this discussion. Consequently, although so-called race may not exist in a way that science can measure, it certainly does exist in the minds of both those who do and those who do not see race relations and biracial marriages in a positive light. As a result, we will be using the terms *race* and *ethnicity* interchangeably in this chapter.

Any life partnership or marriage (gay or straight, biracial or monoracial) is challenged by differences in values, communication styles, conflict styles, and nonverbal behaviors—often resulting in irresolvable conflicts leading to dissolution of the relationship. When the couple is able, however, to understand and explore their differences using a cross-cultural communication model, it is more likely that the relationship will benefit from the differences and intimacy will grow deeper as a result. How each of us communicates and perceives others is a combination of our personal history and our cultural learning. In a biracial heterosexual relationship, each person has his/her personal history, gender culture, and ethnic culture. Although each also brings other cultural leanings (education, occupation, religion, etc.) to the relationship, we will simplify the discussion by focusing on gender and ethnicity. We will also limit our discussion to African-American/European-American heterosexual relationships—not because we don't think homosexual and other ethnic/racial partnerships may share similarities with straight Black/White couples, but because we want to avoid the all-too-frequent error of overgeneralizing from one population to another. We are hopeful that both gay couples and other ethnic/racial mixes will find the general intercultural communication approach helpful, even though the specific cultural norms of Black/White may not apply to them.

GETTING STARTED: (MIS)PERCEPTIONS THAT BRING US TOGETHER

Orbe and Harris (2001) discuss six theories for why people do/don't engage in interracial marriages. The reasons people might engage in a biracial relationship include social and/or economic mobility, rebellion against society or family, sexual curiosity, and exhibitionism. Anti–race mixing and religious bias were found to be the major justifications for opposition to interracial marriages. What is noticeable about these six theories is the degree to which they are negatively motivated and/or based on socially encouraged stereotypes.

Stringer and Reynolds (2002) found a very different landscape in interviewing 40 people who are in biracial (African-American/European-American) couples that have been together for a minimum of seven years, confirming the structural theory of Kouri and Lasswell (1993, cited in Orbe & Harris, 2001) that demographics and mutual attraction lead to interracial marriages. These individuals virtually all pointed to common values: career, family, religious, or recreational commonalities as the initial source of their attraction to each other. That is, the opportunity to meet someone who was racially different from themselves with whom they shared common interests, experiences, and goals was a primary driver in the development of a marital relationship. In fact, these interviewees suggested that it was the negative theories cited by Orbe and Harris that created external pressure for them rather than being the source of their attraction to each other.

Early in most relationships, the two parties revel in their "likeness." They look for the ways in which they share values, behaviors, preferences, and life goals. It is the ways in which they are alike that lead them to believe they want to spend more time together in a marriage or life partnership. It is the ways in which they differ, however, that can enrich each other's lives if they are willing to explore those differences as a richness or resource. Typically, however, these differences are initially a source or irritation or conflict. It is by exploring and understanding the differences that couples can resolve conflicts and come to a deeper understanding and intimacy with each other. Remembering the initial attraction can assist couples in the process of exploring misperceptions, reducing conflicts, and maintaining a lifelong intimate relationship.

In a biracial, heterosexual relationship it is often difficult to identify whether any difference we experience is a result of gender or ethnicity. Exploring the differences using a cross-cultural communication and values approach can assist in sorting this out. On the one hand, when in conflict, whether the conflict is about gender or ethnic differences may not make any difference. On the other hand, understanding each partner's gender culture and ethnic culture can be helpful in developing a better understanding and appreciation for why each person believes and acts the way she or he does. This understanding can both reduce conflicts and facilitate resolution of conflicts when they do occur.

Perception and attribution are keys to any effective cross-cultural partnership (Singer, 1998). Each person learns a way to behave in the world and expects others to behave in similar ways. This works if both people have experienced the same cultural learning. When people cross cultures, however, there is a tendency to continue attributing meaning to behaviors that is consistent with each individual's cultural learning. For example, a European American female who has learned to communicate in a relatively indirect and "soft" way in order to maintain relationships is very likely to attribute anger to her African American male partner who communicates in a more direct, engaged, or passionate manner—because if *she* talked in a direct, engaged way, it would be because she was angry. Additionally, if she has internalized, even unconsciously, the stereotype of Black men as potentially dangerous, his anger may feel more threatening to her than if she thinks another female or a White male is angry. Understanding one's own cultural learning, then, is important because it helps to identify the attributions being made and is a place to begin exploration of differences in meaning.

Ironically, in cross-gender, Black/White relationships, different cultural learning can both detract from understanding, as in the paragraph above, and contribute to understanding. For example, both European American women and African Americans are inclined to use perpendicular nods to indicate they are listening or encouraging the other to talk, whereas the same nod for White men is generally intended to communicate agreement or understanding (Hughes & Baldwin, 2002; Tannen, 1990). Thus, such a nonverbal behavior, which could lead to misunderstanding in a monoracial couple, would tend to be interpreted the same by a biracial Black male/White female couple.

Foeman and Nance (1999) identify a four-stage model for development of healthy biracial relationships. In the first stage, the couple becomes *aware* of their cultural differences. Both partners must be aware of their own personal cultural beliefs, learn their partner's personal beliefs, understand their own cultural groups' norms, and learn their partner's cultural group norms. In other words, they see both themselves and their partner as individuals *and* as a member of a group. In the second stage, each partner develops the skills necessary to *cope* with the external pressures their relationship may experience. The third stage is when the couple's own *identity emerges*—they develop their own perspectives and expectations of the relationship. And finally, the couple figures out how to successfully *maintain* their relationship in light of their individual differences, group differences, and external pressures the relationship may experience.

There is a large body of data about cross-cultural values, communication styles, and nonverbal behaviors. This literature provides us with norms for women, men, African Americans, and European Americans. It must be recognized that cultural norms are just that—norms. It has been well documented that there is more variation within a group than there is between groups. Nonetheless, norms, if treated as a generalization and not a stereotype, can be useful as a way to begin cultural explorations. The reader is cautioned that these data will not apply to every individual or couple.

GETTING TO KNOW YOU: CULTURAL VALUES

Every culture teaches its members a set of core values as well as specific behaviors that are expected to demonstrate each core value. Sharing at least some core values is one of the keys to successful long-term relationships. When a couple mixes different cultural value systems (male/female, Black/White), there are many opportunities for misunderstanding the other's values, even if the values are the same. We will explore two value approaches and how they can impact a biracial relationship.

Milton Rokeach (1973) initially made a distinction between *terminal* and *instrumental values:* terminal values are the goals or core values; instrumental values are the behaviors used to get to the desired goal or core value. It is quite possible to share terminal values but exhibit different behaviors. It is also possible to have different terminal values but exhibit the same behaviors. For example, two people can share a terminal value of close family ties. One achieves this goal behaviorally by sharing a house with four generations of family; the other, by communicating with members of the family regularly, even though they are spread all over the world. The reverse is also true. Two people can share instrumental values (behaviors); for example, they may both work hard to earn as much money as possible. Their terminal values, however, may be quite different. For one person, the goal is the security of having a college fund for his or her children; the other person sees the goal as experiencing travel and material goods. If partners assume that they know the other's values based on behaviors, misperceptions and conflict can result.

A second way to look at values is through a series of *value continua* or *dimensions* that describe two opposite poles (e.g., individualism–collectivism) that represent a range of real-life value orientations for the same dimension (Kluckhohn, 1961). If one partner most values individualism and believes that the couple has the right and/or responsibility to take care of their own family while the other partner values collectivism and believes that they have a responsibility to their larger extended families' needs, a potential source of conflict exists.

Clearly identifying *both* terminal and instrumental goals for each partner *and* identifying values on some of the more critical dimensions before marriage or commitment can result in fewer misperceptions, misunderstandings, or conflicts.

Although there is a multitude of value continua that couples can explore as a method of better understanding each other and reducing misperceptions, we will focus on five that appear to create the greatest potential for misunderstanding in biracial relationships between African Americans and European Americans (Stringer & Reynolds, 2002). We also offer suggested ways to manage each difference with the benefit of developing a wider behavioral repertoire, which will be advantageous to the relationship as well as to the cultural competence of each individual.

1. **Terminal goal: completing a job or activity; instrumental behavior: task vs. relationship.** Both women and African Americans tend to be more relationship oriented, whereas men and European Americans tend to be more task oriented. Thus, this value issue is most likely to be a challenge for White male/Black female couples. If one partner begins a job by wanting to talk, develop a better understanding of the other's perspective, and behaving in ways that are relationship building and the other partner wants to jump right into the "doing," conflict can arise. The person with greater relationship orientation may perceive the task-oriented partner as cold, unfeeling, or controlling; the task-oriented person may see the relationship orientation as wasting time or being emotionally dependent or needy. A primary solution to this issue is to agree to spend a limited time talking about the job or activity before beginning; another approach is to take turns being "in charge" of tasks and approaching them in the way the person "in charge" prefers.
2. **Terminal goal: maintaining a harmonious relationship; instrumental behavior: avoiding vs. confronting issues.** Both women and European Americans tend to be more conflict avoidant, whereas African Americans and men tend toward confronting issues. This issue is complicated by communication styles, with African Americans being more engaged/passionate in their verbal style and European Americans more rational/detached in their style. Consequently, when an African American male is demonstrating his need to maintain a harmonious relationship with his European American wife by confronting an issue about which they disagree, she may see him as being aggressive or threatening because of his communication style. She may also want to confront the issue but would do so with such a different communication style (calm, quiet, linear) that he sees her as disengaged and not caring. In this case, they both have the same terminal goal of maintaining harmony, *and* the same instrumental behavior of confronting the issue, but the communication style with which they confront the issue is so different that misperception or misinterpretation of each other becomes a real possibility. One solution to this difference is to discuss—not during a conflict—how each person's communication style feels to the other and what the intent of his/her style is to each person. Understanding that the more detached

communicator *does care and is not ready to disengage and leave* and the attached communicator *is not about to implode/explode or leave the relationship* is an insight that allows both parties to continue discussions, allow their partner to use her/his own style, and listen to the content rather than react to the style (Hecht, Collier, & Ribeau, 1993).

3. **Terminal goal: achievement of success; instrumental behaviors: individualism vs. collectivism.** Both European Americans and men have a tendency to demonstrate individualism, whereas women and African Americans are more likely to lean toward collectivism. This can affect decisions about whose career takes priority and whether career is more important than family needs, especially extended family needs. If one partner makes decisions about his/her career that impacts the family, or ignores the extended family, it may not only affect the relationship but may also be attributed to race or gender rather than value differences. For example, a Black female (from a collectivism view) may believe her White husband (from an individualism point of view) insists on relocating not so much to benefit his career as to escape spending so much time in the Black community and/or with her family—*or* because he believes the man's career should always come first.
4. **Terminal goal: independence vs. dependence; instrumental behaviors: maintenance of rules for behavior vs. flexibility of behaviors.** This value shows up particularly in child-rearing practices, with the European American culture typically encouraging independence and flexible rules and the African American community more likely to teach children to be more dependent (this value is tied to the collectivism value cited above) with far less flexible rules for behavior. This is clearly tied to the historical issue of safety, especially for African American males, if they violated—or were perceived to violate—any "rules" for behavior. There is also a notable gender difference here, with girls typically given less flexibility in European American families but boys being given less flexibility in African American families. The potential conflict in a biracial partnership is the sense that the spouse "doesn't understand." That is, the Black male doesn't understand the danger for his white daughters, and the White mother doesn't understand the danger for her Black son. Understanding the history of violence against girls and Black boys can be helpful in resolving these differences.
5. **Terminal goal: respect for authority; instrumental behaviors: formality and strong power distance vs. informality and weak power distance.** Again, for historical reasons, the Black culture tends toward far more formality and power distance, whereas the White culture tends toward more informality and weaker power distance. Thus, the Black parent may want to enforce far stricter rules for behavior than the White parent. And the Black extended family may not approve of the parenting style or the informality of the White partner, experiencing it as disrespectful. The extended White family, on the other hand, may read the greater formality of their Black son- or daughter-in-law as standoffish or arrogant. Understanding the history of both African Americans and White immigrants in the United States can be helpful in understanding this potential value difference.

IT'S NOT WHAT YOU SAY: COMMUNICATION STYLES

The importance of communication cannot be overstated—and indeed has been stressed by many authors. Again, because of cultural learning, men and women have different communication style norms—as do Blacks and Whites. This is not true of every individual from those cultures, of course, but exploring what styles each partner has can be a way to avoid misperceptions. We will look at three different style differences that can affect biracial relationships.

Direct vs. Indirect

Both African American and European American cultures tend to communicate in a more direct manner (except in conflict, when European Americans tend to be far less direct). Women tend to be less direct in style than men, which can create tension in a partnership. Direct communicators will say what they want, need, or think very clearly. The value that underlies this style is one of time and task—to save time and achieve a task as quickly as possible, a direct communicator provides information as clearly and directly as possible. Indirect communicators, on the other hand, may "beat around the bush"—give a lot of extraneous information, tell a story, give an example, or even give information through a third party. The value underlying this style is one of relationship—communicating that something is important, but not at the risk of violating or damaging the relationship. This style is intended to build relationship and avoid any possible embarrassment, insults, or conflicts. It helps both parties save face. The challenge, of course, is that the direct style can be seen as rude or disrespectful to the indirect communicator. The indirect style can be seen as manipulative or disrespectful to the direct communicator. And, perhaps as important, a direct communicator often misses the message of the indirect communicator—simply does not hear the message.

As with most of the other style issues, a solution is for each partner to understand and genuinely value the other person's approach. A direct communicator can take a deep breath and be prepared to spend a few minutes listening and engaging with his/her partner—and appreciating that the indirect communicator is often the keeper of the relationship. The indirect communicator can practice summarizing the message and getting to the point a bit more quickly—and appreciating that the direct communicator may save time that can be used for relationship activities.

High Context vs. Low Context

Every culture and every family shares a high-context communication system—things that aren't fully explained because "everyone understands them." This is rarely intentional, or even conscious. The challenge, of course, is that those marrying into the family don't have the history or the cultural context for understanding high-context messages, which can lead to them feeling like outsiders. When the friends or family begin "reminiscing," the new family member may not feel included and may attribute their exclusion to their race or ethnicity. "You know, if I were White/Black, they would make a greater effort to include me." A solution to this is for each partner to be more intentional about providing a context or history for events or stories being shared.

Detached vs. Attached, or Rational Discussion vs. Sincere Argument

A detached communicator discusses issues calmly and "objectively." An attached communicator, on the other hand, discusses issues with patience, conveying his or her personal feelings. The detached style is normed more highly for both European Americans and men; the attached is normed for both African Americans and women. The detached communicator can be amused, frustrated, or irritated that the attached communicator is always "so emotional" and unable to talk about anything quietly and factually. The attached communicator wonders why the detached individual is so clinical and "doesn't care about anything."

These styles can become even more exaggerated during disagreement or conflict. And the styles, rather than the issue under discussion, can become the conflict. Henderson (1999) points out that in conflict, Whites tend to want to shut down the discussion as quickly as possible, perceiving the Black style as contentious, argumentative, or threatening. Blacks, on the other hand, "prefer emotion to avoidance, which they perceive as being hypocritical, devious or insincere."

Talking with each other about these styles can help partners conclude that the attached individual is not "dangerous or out of control emotionally" and the detached individual does, indeed, care. This can be a very useful place to begin. It can also be helpful for the detached communicator, if she or he is the European American in the partnership, to understand that in African American cultural communication patterns, volume of voice or words being used do not typically predict danger. The predictor of physical danger is typically signaled through physical movement, not words (Kochman, 1981).

A primary solution to these style differences is to identify each partner's styles, gain an understanding of what each person intends/means with his/her style, and look at the advantage/disadvantage of each style, thereby gaining the ability to interpret/perceive one's partner more accurately across these style differences.

HERE'S LOOKING AT YOU: NONVERBAL BEHAVIORS

Samovar and Porter (2003) point out that up to 90% of the social content of a message is transmitted nonverbally. Further, we both communicate and decode others' nonverbal messages unconsciously most of the time. The following nonverbal behaviors, therefore, are worth discussion between biracial partners as a means of making the attributions for behaviors more conscious and more accurate.

Eye Contact

Dominant U.S. culture trains and expects direct eye contact. Hughes and Baldwin (2002) point out that "Whites tend to look more while listening than . . . speaking; Blacks look more while speaking . . ." Many southern-raised African Americans and many women in the United States have learned that direct eye contact may be dangerous, and so many use it more carefully. Misperceptions can certainly occur if partners are using different eye contact rules—and don't consciously understand why they are reacting negatively to the other individual.

Smiles

White women are encouraged to smile far more often than are Black women (Samovar & Porter, 2003). The potential for misperceptions here is large: "Isn't she glum?—or angry!" or "How phony she is, smiling all the time!"

Monochronic/Polychronic

This refers to the use of time. Monochronic is the ability to track one thing at a time; polychronic is the ability to do multiple things at once. The polychronic individual may see the monochronic partner as not contributing or doing enough; the monochronic person may perceive the polychronic partner as being disorganized or scattered. The challenge here is to identify outcomes: What does each person actually contribute to the relationship? Typically, both contribute pretty equally, although in very different ways.

SUCCESSFULLY MANEUVERING THE MADNESS MAZE

Most biracial couples partner for the same reasons as any other couple: similar values and life dreams. And they have many of the same internal and external pressures as any other couple. Additionally, they often need to maneuver differences in cultural values (terminal and/or instrumental), communication styles, and nonverbal behaviors. Engaging in open exploration of how each partner's history, experience, and cultural learning affect how he/she behaves and how each interprets the other person's behaviors can be an enormous asset in avoiding conflict—and resolving it when it inevitably occurs.

This analysis of interracial intimacy is meant as both a hopeful and a cautionary tale.

> Individuals who cross the color line to marry, build families, and form identities show us that race need not be an insurmountable divide. . . . Imperiled though interracial intimacy may be, it holds out a seductive promise. We can undo race before it undoes us. (Moran, 2001, p. 196)

References

Foeman, A. K., & Nance, T. (1999). From miscegenation to multiculturalism: Perceptions and stages of interracial relationship development. *Journal of Black Studies, 29*(4), 540–557.

Gallup Organization Poll. (2003). *Civil rights and race relations.* Reported in the AARP Magazine, May/June 2004.

Graves, J. L. (2001). *The emperor's new clothes: Biological theories of race at the millennium.* Piscataway, NJ: Rutgers University Press.

Hecht, M. L., Collier, M. J., & Ribeau, S. A. (1993). *African American communication.* Newbury Park, CA: Sage.

Henderson, G. (1999). *Our souls to keep: Black/White relations in America.* Yarmouth, ME: Intercultural Press.

Hughes, P. C., & Baldwin, J. R. (2002). Black, White, and shades of gray: Communication predictors of "stereotypic impressions." *Southern Communication Journal, 68*(1), 40–56.

Kluckhohn, F. (1961). *Variations in value orientations.* Evanston, IL: Row, Peterson.

Kochman, T. (1981). *Black and White styles in conflict.* Chicago: University of Chicago Press.

Moran, R. F. (2001). *Interracial intimacy: The regulation of race and romance.* Chicago: University of Chicago Press.

Orbe, M. P., & Harris, T. M. (2001). *Interracial communication: Theory into practice.* Belmont, CA: Wadsworth.

Rokeach, M. (1973). *The nature of human values.* New York: Free Press.

Samovar, L. A., & Porter, R. E. (2003). *Intercultural communication: A reader* (10th ed.). Belmont, CA: Wadsworth.

Singer, M. R. (1998). *Perception and identity in intercultural communication.* Yarmouth, ME: Intercultural Press.

Stringer, D. M., & Reynolds, A. B. (2002). *Interviews with 20 Black/White biracial couples.* Unpublished manuscript.

Tannen, D. (1990). *You just don't understand: Women and men in conversation.* New York: William Morrow.

U.S. Census Bureau. (2001). www.census.gov

Concepts and Questions

1. What problem does Stringer see with using the term *race*?
2. Stringer suggests that any life partnership is challenged by differences. What are some of these differences, and how might they affect a relationship? How might these challenges apply to biracial marriages?
3. Aside from initial mutual interpersonal attraction, why might people choose to engage in interracial marriages?
4. What does Stringer mean when she asserts that perception and attribution are key to any effective cross-cultural partnership?
5. The sharing of at least some core values is considered to be one of the keys to successful long-term relationships. What do you believe to be the essential core values a couple must share to support a successful relationship?
6. Discuss ways in which an understanding of terminal goals can lead to the reduction of misperceptions in a biracial relationship.
7. What is meant by the term *terminal goal,* and how do these goals affect relationships?
8. How do communication styles affect biracial relationships?
9. How might inherent differences in nonverbal behaviors affect communication between biracial couples?

Gendered Communication Styles

JULIA T. WOOD
NINA M. REICH

Men Are from Mars, Women Are from Venus. This is the outrageous claim—and 1992 book title—that has made John Gray both very famous and very rich. His series of Mars and Venus books (*On a Date, In the Bedroom, Together Forever,* etc.) portray women and men as radically different due to innate and unchangeable factors. Years of research, however, indicate that most differences between the sexes are neither as unalterable nor as substantial as Gray claims. Rigorous study of gender differences shows that John Gray's claims are highly exaggerated and fuel stereotypes about women and men (Wood, 2002). Yet Gray's books have captured millions of readers because they emphasize something that we know from our own experiences: There are some differences between how most women and men communicate, and those differences can complicate interaction and relationships.

In this article, we'll discuss what those differences are and how they do—or don't—support the claim that women and men are so different, they are from different planets. Despite John Gray's book title, women and men are really from the same planet—Earth. Yet planet Earth includes many different social communities—ones defined by ethnicity, religion, sexual orientation, socioeconomic standing, (dis)abilities, age, gender, sex, and many others. People have a lot in common because they belong to the same species and live on the same planet. At the same time, there are some differences that reflect people's participation in different social communities.

After reading this article, you should understand how we learn gendered ways of communicating and why misunderstandings sometimes arise when masculine

---

 Julia T. Wood is the Lineberger Professor of Humanities and a Professor of Communication at the University of North Carolina at Chapel Hill. Nina Reich teaches at Loyola Marymount University in Los Angeles, California.

and feminine communication styles meet in conversation. Insight into gendered communication styles will enhance your ability to interact effectively with people who communicate in both masculine and feminine ways. In addition, you will be empowered to choose the style of communication you want to use in various situations.

THE SOCIAL CONSTRUCTION OF GENDER

Perhaps you have noticed that we use the terms *feminine* and *masculine* as well as the terms *women* and *men*. The former refer to gender and the latter to sex, which are distinct phenomena. *Women, men, male,* and *female* are words that specify sex, which biology determines. In contrast, *feminine* and *masculine* designate genders, which are meanings and expectations that society attaches to the sexes. Before we can understand gendered communication patterns, we need to clarify what gender is and how it differs from sex.

Sex

Sex is determined by genetic codes that program biological features. Of the 46 pairs of human chromosomes, one pair controls sex. Usually this unit has two chromosomes, one of which is always an X chromosome. If the second chromosome is a Y, the fetus is male; if it is an X, the fetus is female. (Other combinations have occurred: XYY, XXY, XO, and XXX.) During gestation, genetic codes direct the production of hormones so that fetuses develop genitalia and secondary sex characteristics consistent with their genetic makeup. (Again there are exceptions, usually caused by medical interventions. See Wood (2005), for a more thorough discussion.)

We rely on biological features to classify people as male and female: external genitalia (the clitoris and vagina for a female, the penis and testes for a male) and internal sex organs (the uterus and ovaries in females, the prostate in males). Hormones also control secondary sex characteristics such as percentage of body fat (females have more fat to protect the womb when a fetus is present), how much muscle exists, and amount of body hair. There are also differences in male and female brains. Females and males tend to specialize in different lobes of the brain. Usually females also have thicker, or better developed, corpus callosa, which are the bundles of nerves connecting the two brain lobes. This suggests women may be more able to cross between hemispheres than men (Hines, 1992).

Gender

Gender is considerably more complex than sex. For starters, you might think of gender as the cultural meaning of sex. A culture constructs gender by arbitrarily assigning certain qualities, activities, feelings, aptitudes, and roles to each sex. Society then weaves these assignments into the fabric of social life so that we see it as natural for women to stay home with babies and men to be competitive in careers. This means that we are not born with a gender, but we become gendered as we internalize and then embody society's views of femininity and masculinity. Because there is diversity among societies and each one changes over time, the meaning of gender is neither universal nor stable. Instead, femininity and masculinity reflect the beliefs and values of particular cultures in certain eras.

It should now be clear to you that gender and sex are not synonymous. Sex is biological, whereas gender is socially constructed. Sex is innate, whereas gender is learned and, therefore, changeable. Sex is established by genetics and biology, whereas gender is produced and reproduced by particular societies at particular times. Barring surgery, sex is permanent, whereas gender varies over time and across individuals' life spans. Whereas our sex stays the same across situations, we may choose to embody different genders in different situations. For instance, both women and men tend to be more nurturing with children than in work situations, and members of both sexes tend to be more competitive in atheletic contests than in social interactions.

BECOMING GENDERED

Let's now look more closely at how people become gendered. Many factors influence our gender development. Two of the most imporant are (1) the continuous communication of social expectations for males and females; and (2) interaction in sex-segregated children's play groups.

Communication of Social Expectations and Development of Gender

Cultural constructions of gender are communicated to individuals through a range of structures and practices that make up our everyday world. From birth on, individuals are besieged with communication that presents cultural prescriptions for gender. Beginning with the pink and blue blankets wrapped around newborns, gender socialization continues in interactions with parents, teachers, peers, and media. In magazines and on television, we are more likely to see women in the home and men in the boardroom; girls in soft colors and frilly fashions and boys in darker colors and rugged clothes; women needing help and men performing daring rescues; men driving cars and women riding in them. In cartoons and prime-time programming, we see male characters being more active (bold, dominant, aggressive) than female characters (more subdued, subordinate, and gentle). In kindergarten and elementary school, children are more likely to see women as teachers and men as principals, a difference that sends a clear message about the status society prescribes for each sex. In offices, virtually all secretaries and receptionists are female, sending the message that assisting others is part of feminine identity. When children visit toy stores, they see pink bicycles with delicate baskets for girls and blue or black bicycles with sturdy baskets for boys. As children participate in the many spheres of society, they receive continuous messages that reinforce social views of gender.

The pervasive messages about how boys and girls are "supposed to be" make gender roles seem natural, normal, and right. Since cultures systematically normalize arbitrary definitions of gender, we seldom reflect on how *unnatural* it is that half of humanity is assumed to be deferential, emotional, and interested in building relationships, whereas the other half is assumed to be ambitious, assertive, and self-sufficient. If we do reflect on social definitions of masculinity and femininity, they don't make a great deal of sense!

The intensity and pervasiveness of social prescriptions for gender ensure that most females will become predominantly feminine (nurturing, cooperative, sensitive to others) and most males will become predominantly masculine (assertive, competitive, independent). Notice that we stated *most* females and males will become *predominantly* feminine or masculine. Very few, if any, people are exclusively one gender. You can be masculine, feminine, or—like most of us—a combination of genders that allows you to be effective in diverse situations.

Peer Interaction's Impact on Development of Gender

A second significant influence on the development of gender is peer interaction among children. As children play together, they teach each other how to be boys and girls. Insight into the significance of play was pioneered by Daniel Maltz and Ruth Borker (1982), who studied children at play. The researchers noticed that recreation was usually sex segregated, and boys and girls tended to favor discrete kinds of games—the ones that are socially prescribed for each sex through media, advertising, toy manufacturers, parents, and others. Whereas girls were more likely to play house, play school, or jump rope, boys tended to play competitive team sports like football and baseball. Because different goals, strategies, and relationships characterize some girls' and boys' games, the children learned divergent rules for interaction. Engaging in play, Maltz and Borker concluded, contributes to socializing children into predominantly masculine and feminine identities (again, notice the word *predominantly*).

Maltz and Borker's classic study has been replicated by other researchers, who have shown that their findings continue to hold up in the present time. Psychologist Campbell Leaper (1994, 1998) reports that children still tend to prefer sex-segregaged play groups, a finding that is reinforced by other researchers (Clark, 1998; Harris, 1998; Moller & Serbin, 1998). Leaper and the other researchers also report that the sex-segregaged play groups engage in different kinds of games that, in turn, socialize them into different ways of communicating.

Girls' Games. Many games that girls typically play, such as house and school, require just two or three people, so they promote personal relationships. Further, these games don't have preset or fixed rules, roles, and objectives. Whereas touchdowns and home runs are goals in boys' games and roles such as pitcher, forward, and blocker are clearly defined, how to play house is open to negotiation. To make their games work, girls talk with each other and agree on rules, roles, and goals: "You be the mommy and I'll be the daddy, and we'll clean house." From unstructured, cooperative play, girls learn three basic rules for how to communicate:

1. Be cooperative, collaborative, inclusive. It's important that everyone feel involved and have a chance to play.
2. Don't criticize or outdo others. Cultivate egalitarian relationships so the group is cohesive and gratifying to all.
3. Pay attention to others' feelings and needs, and be sensitive in interpreting and responding to them.

In sum, games that are more likely to be played by girls emphasize relationships more than outcomes, sensitivity to others, and cooperative, inclusive interpersonal orientations.

Boys' Games. Unlike girls' games, some of the games that boys are more likely to play involve fairly large groups (for instance, baseball requires nine players plus extras to fill in) and proceed by rules and goals that are externally established and constant (there are nine innings, three strikes and you're out). Also, boys' games allow for individual stars—MVP, for instance—and, in fact, a boy's status depends largely on his rank relative to others. Boys' games teach three rules of interaction:

1. Assert yourself. Use talk and action to highlight your ideas and to establish your status and leadership.
2. Focus on outcomes. Use your talk and actions to make things happen, solve problems, and achieve goals.
3. Be competitive. Vie for the talk stage. Keep attention focused on you, outdo others, and make yourself stand out.

Some of the games more likely to be played by boys emphasize achievement—both for the team and the individual members. The goals are to win for the team and to be the top player on it. Interaction is more an arena for negotiating power and status than for building relationships with others, and competitiveness is customary in masculine communities.

Given the variation in typical games played by children, it's not surprising that most girls and boys learn some different ways of communicating. We use the qualifying word *most* to remind you that we are discussing general differences, not absolute ones. Some women sometimes act in ways that are considered masculine, and some women have a primarily masculine style. Some men sometimes act in ways that are considered feminine, and some men have a primarily feminine style. In the majority of situations, however, most females adopt a primarily feminine style of communicating, and most males adopt a predominantly masculine one.

In combination, messages woven into the fabric of society and peer interaction among children clarify how people become gendered.

FEMININE AND MASCULINE COMMUNICATION COMMUNITIES

Beginning in the 1970s, scholars noticed that some groups of people share communication practices not common to, or understood by, people outside of the groups. This led to the realization that there are distinctive speech communities, or communication communities. William Labov (1972) defined a speech community as existing when a set of norms regarding how to communicate is shared by a group of people. Within a communication community, members embrace similar understandings of how to use talk and what purposes it serves.

Once scholars realized that distinctive speech communities exist, they identified many, some of which are discussed in this book: African Americans, Native Americans, gay men, lesbians, people with disabilities. Members of each of these groups share perspectives that outsiders seldom have. By extension, the values, viewpoints, and experiences that are distinct to a particular group influence how members of that group communicate. That's why there are some gender differences in why, when, and how we communicate.

Feminine and masculine speech communities have been explored by a number of scholars (Aries, 1987; Beck, 1988; Coates & Cameron, 1989; Johnson, 1989; Kramarae, 1981; Spender, 1984; Tannen, 1990a, 1990b; Treichler & Kramarae, 1983; Wood, 1993a, 1993b, 1993c, 2005; Wood & Inman, 1993). Their research reveals that most girls and women operate from assumptions about communication and use rules for communicating that differ in some ways from those endorsed by most boys and men.

Table 1 *Differences Between Feminine and Masculine Communication Culture*

Feminine Talk	Masculine Talk
1. Use talk to build and sustain rapport with others.	1. Use talk to assert yourself and your ideas.
2. Share yourself and disclose to others.	2. Personal disclosures can make you vulnerable.
3. Use talk to create symmetry or equality between people.	3. Use talk to establish your status and power.
4. Matching experiences with others shows understanding and empathy ("I know how you feel").	4. Matching experiences is a competititve strategy to command attention. ("I can top that.")
5. To support others, express understanding of their feelings.	5. To support others, do something helpful—give advice or tell them how to solve a problem.
6. Include others in conversation by asking their opinions and encouraging them to elaborate. Wait your turn to speak so others can participate.	6. Don't share the talk stage with others; wrest it from them with communication. Interrupt others to make your own points.
7. Keep the conversation going by asking questions and showing interest in others' ideas.	7. Each person is on her or his own; it's not your job to help others join in.
8. Be responsive. Let others know you hear and care about what they say.	8. Use responses to make your own points and to outshine others.
9. Be tentative so that others feel free to add their ideas.	9. Be assertive so others perceive you as confident and in command.
10. Talking is a human relationship in which details and interesting side comments enhance depth of connection.	10. Talking is a linear sequence that should convey information and accomplish goals. Extraneous details get in the way and achieve nothing.

At the heart of the process by which we become gendered is human communication. It is through interaction with others that we learn what masculine and feminine mean in our society and how we are expected to think, talk, feel, and act. Communication is also the primary means by which we embody gender personally. When we conform to social prescriptions for gender, we reinforce prevailing social views of masculinity and femininity. Table 1 summarizes how these differences in gender communities may affect communication.

MEN AND WOMEN IN CONVERSATION: GENDERED PATTERNS AND MISUNDERSTANDINGS

Differences learned in childhood may be carried into adult interaction. Individuals who are exclusively feminine or masculine limit their effectiveness to those situations that call for the gendered style they can enact. On the other hand, individuals who refuse to be restricted to only a feminine or masculine style challenge and sometimes change social views of gender. In addition, they enhance their communication repertoire so they are likely to be competent in a wide range of situations. In the next section, we'll examine some examples of problems that can arise when people don't understand and know how to use both masculine and feminine styles of communication.

Gender Gaps in Communication

To illustrate the practical consequences of limiting yourself to only one gendered style of communication, let's consider some concrete cases of communication. As you read the following examples of common problems in communication between women and men, you'll probably find that several are familiar to you.

- **What counts as support?** Rita is really bummed out when she meets Mike for dinner. She explains that she's worried about a friend who has begun drinking heavily. When Mike advises her to get her friend into counseling, Rita repeats how worried she feels. Next, Mike tells Rita to make sure her friend doesn't drive after drinking. Rita explodes that she doesn't need advice. Irritated at her lack of appreciation for his help, Mike asks, "Then why did you ask for it?" In exasperation Rita responds, "Oh, never mind, I'll talk to Betsy. At least she cares how I feel."

- **Tricky feedback.** Roseann and Drew are colleagues in a marketing firm. One morning he drops into her office to run an advertising plan by her. As Drew discusses his ideas, Roseann nods and says "Um," "Uh huh," and "Yes." When he finishes, Roseann says, "I really don't think that plan will sell the product." Feeling misled, Drew demands, "Then why were you agreeing the whole time I presented my idea?" Completely confused, Roseann responds, "What makes you think I was agreeing with you?"
- **Expressing care.** Dedrick and Melita have been dating for two years and are very serious. To celebrate their anniversary, Melita wants to spend a quiet evening in her apartment where they can talk about the relationship and be with just each other. When Dedrick arrives, he's planned a dinner and concert. Melita feels hurt that he doesn't want to talk and be close.
- **I'd rather do it myself.** Chris is having difficulty writing a paper for a communication class, because the professor didn't give clear directions for the assignment. When Chris grumbles about this problem, Pat suggests Chris ask the professor or a classmate to clarify directions. Chris resists, and says rather sharply, "I can figure it out on my own."
- **Can we talk about us?** Anna asks her fiancé, Ben, "Can we talk about us?" Immediately Ben feels tense—another problem on the horizon. He prepares himself for an unpleasant conversation and reluctantly nods assent. Anna then thanks Ben for being so supportive during the last few months when she was under enormous pressure at her job. She tells him she feels closer than ever. Although Ben feels relieved there isn't any crisis, he's also baffled. If there isn't a problem, he doesn't see why people need to talk about the relationship. He thinks if it's working, you should let it be.

You've probably been involved in conversations like these. And you've probably been confused, frustrated, hurt, or even angry when a member of the other sex didn't give you what you wanted or didn't value your efforts to be supportive. If you're a woman, you may think Mike should be more sensitive to Rita's feelings and Dedrick should cherish time alone with Melita. If you're a man, it's likely that you empathize with Mike's frustration and feel Rita is giving him a hard time when he's trying to help. Likewise, you may think Melita is lucky to have a guy willing to shell out some bucks so they can do something fun together.

Who's right in these cases? Is Rita unreasonable? Is Melita ungrateful? Are Dedrick and Mike insensitive? Is Chris stubborn? Did Roseann mislead Drew? When we focus on questions like these, we fall prey to a central problem in gender communication: the tendency to judge. Because Western culture is hierarchical, we're taught to perceive differences as better and worse, not simply as different. Yet the inclination to judge one person as right and the other wrong whenever there's misunderstanding usually spells trouble for close relationships.

But judging is not the only way we *could* think about these interactions, and it's not the most constructive way if we want to build good relationships. More productive than judging is understanding and respecting different styles of communication. Once we recognize there are many styles of interacting, we can tune into perspectives other than our own and increase our personal communication repertoires.

Understanding Gendered Communication

Drawing upon earlier sections of this article, we can analyze the misunderstandings in these five dialogues and see how they grow out of the different interaction styles cultivated in feminine and masculine speech communities. Because there are some differences in how most men and women have learned to communicate, they may have different ways of showing support, interest, and caring. This also implies they may perceive the same communication in dissimilar ways.

In the first scenario, Rita's purpose in talking with Mike isn't just to tell him about her concern for her friend; she also sees communication as a way to connect with Mike (Aries, 1987; Riessman, 1990; Tannen, 1990b; Wood, 1993a). She wants him to respond to her feelings, because that will enhance her sense of closeness to him. Schooled in masculinity, however, Mike views communication as an instrument to do things, so he tries to help by giving advice. Rita feels he entirely disregards her feelings, so she doesn't feel close to Mike, which was her primary purpose in talking with him. Advice would be great, but only after Mike responds to her feelings.

In the second example, the problem arises when Drew translates Roseann's feedback according to masculine rules of interaction. Many women learn to give lots of response cues—verbal and nonverbal behaviors to indicate interest and involvement in conversation—because that's part of using communication to build relationships with others. Masculine communities, however, focus on outcomes more than processes, so many men use feedback to signal specific agreement and disagreement (Beck, 1988; Fishman, 1978; Tannen, 1990b; Wood, 1993b). When Drew hears Roseann's "ums," "uh huhs," and "yeses," he assumes she is agreeing. According to her community's rules, however, she is only showing interest and being responsive, not signaling agreement.

Dedrick and Melita also experience misunderstanding based on gendered communication styles. In feminine communities, talking is a way—probably the primary way—to express and expand closeness. This is why many women feel close when engaged in dialogue (Aries, 1987; Riessman, 1990; Wood, 1993a). Masculine socialization, in contrast, stresses doing things and shared activities as primary ways to create and express closeness (Cancian, 1987; Swain, 1989; Wood & Inman, 1993). Someone who is predominantly masculine is more likely to express caring for a friend by doing a concrete favor (washing a car, fixing an appliance) or doing something with the friend (skiing, going to a concert) than by talking explicitly about his or her feelings. Notice the pronouns we used in the last sentence. We stated *his or her* to remind you that gender is not the same thing as sex. A woman might have a predominantly masculine communication style, just as a man might have a predominatly feminine style. And both men and women might vary their communication styles to suit different situations.

Those men who are primarily masculine generally experience "closeness in doing" (Swain, 1989). By realizing that doing things is a valid way to be close, feminine individuals can avoid feeling hurt by partners who propose activities. In addition, feminine individuals who want to express care in ways that masculine people prefer might think about what they could do for or with others, rather than what they could say (Riessman, 1990). At the same time, verbal expressions of caring are likely to be preferred by individuals who are predominantly feminine.

Masculinity's emphasis on independence underlies Chris's unwillingness to ask others for help in understanding an assignment. What we've discussed about gender identity helps us understand this difference. Chris's refusal to ask others for help reflects masculine prescriptions that emphasize independence and self-sufficiency. Unless Pat realizes this difference between them, they will continue to frustrate each other.

In the final case, we see a very common misunderstanding in gender communication. Feminine communication communities prioritize the process of communicating, so many women find talking about relationships an ongoing source of interest and pleasure. In contrast, within masculine communication communities, talk tends to be perceived as an instrument for acomplishing things, such as solving problems, rather than a means to enhance closeness (Wood, 1993a, 1993b, 1993c). Given these disparate orientations, "talking about us" sometimes means very different things to most men and women. Anna's wish to discuss the relationship because it's so good makes no sense to Ben, and his lack of interest in a conversation about the relationship hurts Anna. Again, each person errs in relying on inappropriate rules to interpret the other's communication.

Many problems in communication between genders result from faulty translations. This happens when we interpret others according to our rules of communication. Just as we wouldn't assume Western rules apply to Asian people, so we'd be wise not to assume one gender's rules pertain to the other. When we understand gender communities and when we respect the logic of each one, we empower ourselves to communicate in ways that enhance our relationships.

COMMUNICATING EFFECTIVELY BETWEEN GENDERS

Whether it's a Northern American thinking someone who eats with the hands is "uncouth" or a woman assuming a man is "closed" because he doesn't disclose as much as she does, we're inclined to think that what differs from our ways of doing things is wrong. Ethnocentric judgments seldom improve communication or enhance relationships. Instead of debating whether feminine or masculine styles of communication are better, we should learn to see the value of both styles. The information we've covered, combined with this book's emphasis on understanding and appreciating diverse communication styles, can be distilled into six principles for effective communication between members of different social groups.

1. **Suspend judgment.** This is first and foremost. As long as we are judging differences as right or wrong, better or worse, we aren't respecting the distinct integrity of each style. When you find yourself confused in cross-gender conversations, resist the tendency to judge. Instead, explore constructively what is happening and how you and your partner might better understand each other.
2. **Recognize the validity of different communication styles.** We need to remind ourselves there is a logic and validity to both feminine and masculine communication styles. Feminine emphases on relationships, feelings, and responsiveness don't reflect an inability to adhere to masculine rules for competing, any more than masculine stress on instrumental outcomes is a failure to follow feminine rules for sensitivity to others. It is inappropriate to apply a single criterion—either masculine or feminine—to both genders' communication. Instead, we need to realize that different goals, priorities, and standards pertain to each.
3. **Provide translation cues.** Now that you realize men and women tend to learn different rules for interaction, it makes sense to think about helping the other gender translate your communication. For instance, in the first example, Rita might have said to Mike, "I appreciate your advice, but what I need first is for you to talk with me about my feelings." A comment such as this helps Mike interpret Rita's motives and needs. After all, there's no reason why he should automatically understand rules that weren't taught in his communication community.
4. **Seek translation cues.** We can also improve our interactions by seeking translation cues from others. If Rita didn't tell Mike how to translate her communication, he could have asked, "What would be helpful to you? I don't know whether you want to talk about how you're feeling or brainstorm ways to help your friend. Which would be better?" This message communicates clearly that Mike cares about Rita and wants to support her, if she'll just tell him how. Similarly, instead of assuming Rita had deliberately misled him, Drew might have taken a more constructive approach and said, "When you nodded your head while I was talking, I thought you agreed with my ideas. What did it mean?" This kind of response would allow Drew to learn something new.
5. **Enlarge your own communication style.** Studying communication that differs from our own teaches us not only about other cultures and speech communities, but also about ourselves and the communities to which we belong. If we're open to learning and growing, we can enlarge our own communication repertoire by incorporating skills more emphasized in other groups. Individuals socialized into masculinity could learn a great deal from feminine ways of supporting friends. Likewise, feminine people could expand the ways they experience intimacy by appreciating "closeness in the doing" that is a masculine specialty. There's little to risk and much to gain by incorporating additional skills into our communication repertoires.

   As human beings, we have the capacity to choose how to present ourselves at different moments and in diverse contexts. Enlarging your personal repertoire empowers you to be effective in a wide range of situations, regardless of whether they call for masculine, feminine, or blended communication styles. For example, a female or a male attorney is likely to be dominant and assertive in a courtroom, yet the same woman or man can be nurturing and supportive when interacting with children. Although you may be primarily feminine or primarily masculine, you do not have to behave consistently in all situations. Instead, you can be an agent who chooses how to present yourself in particular situations.
6. **Suspend judgment.** If you're thinking we already covered this principle, you're right. It's important enough, however, to merit repetition. Judgment is so thoroughly woven into Western culture that it's difficult not to evaluate others and not to defend our own positions. Yet as long as we're judging others and defending ourselves, we're probably making no headway in communicating more effectively. So, suspending judgment is the first and last principle of effective communication between women and men or between members of any communication communities.

SUMMARY

As women and men, most of us have been socialized into primary gender identities that reflect cultural constructions of femininity and masculinity. We become gendered as we interact with our families, childhood peers, and society as a whole—all of whom teach us what gender means and how we are expected to embody it in our attitudes, feelings, and interaction styles. This means that communication produces, reflects, and reproduces genders and imbues them with a taken-for-granted status that we seldom notice or question. Through an ongoing, cyclical process, communication, culture, and gender continuously recreate one another.

Because we all live within the overall culture, there is substantial overlap between men and women and between masculine and feminine communication. At the same time, there are some differences between most women's and most men's communication (notice the word *most*). When we fail to recognize that genders sometimes rely on some dissimilar rules for talk, we may misread each other's meanings and motives. To avoid the frustration, hurt, and misunderstandings that occur when we apply one gender's rules to the other gender's communication, we need to recognize and respect the distinctive validity and value of each style. Ideally, we also choose to learn how to use each style effectively.

Mars and Venus and Back to Earth

Let's return to John Gray's claims that differences between women's and men's communication are innate (inborn), absolute, and unchangeable. The research that we've discussed refutes Gray's claims. Our differences are not innate; rather, they are learned in speech communities and from society's communication of prescriptions for gender. The differences we've noted aren't absolute, because not all women communicate according to the rules of feminine communities all the time and not all men according to the rules of masculine communities all the time. And clearly our communication styles—because they are learned—are amenable to change. Men do not have to go to their "cave" as Gray suggests. Men can be, and at times are, expressive and nurturing. Likewise, women can choose to be, and oftentimes are, assertive and outcome oriented.

We can do a lot to minimize the occasional misunderstandings fostered by differences between masculine and feminine communication styles. The first step is to move beyond Gray's simplistic notions that sex determines how we communicate. When we abandon that unfounded idea, we realize that our gendered communication styles are not static. We can choose to adapt our ways of communicating to the demands of various situations. If we decide to enlarge our communication repertoires and choose how to express ourselves from situation to situation, both men and women can be effective in numerous interactions and in our interpersonal relationships.

What we've covered in this article provides a good foundation for the ongoing process of learning not just how to get along with people of both genders, but to appreciate and grow from valuing the different perspectives on interaction, identity, and relationships that masculine and feminine communities offer. And we don't have to make an interplanetary flight—or buy a book by John Gray—to learn these things.

References

Aries, E. (1987). Gender and communication. In P. Shaver (Ed.), *Sex and gender* (pp. 149–176). Newbury Park, CA: Sage.

Beck, A. (1988). *Love is never enough.* New York: Harper & Row.

Cancian, F. (1987). *Love in America.* Cambridge, England: Cambridge University Press.

Clark, R. (1998). A comparison of topics and objectives in a cross section of young men's and women's everyday conversations. In D. Canary & K. Dindia (Eds.), *Sex differences and similarities in communication* (pp. 303–319). Mahwah, NJ: Erlbaum.

Coates, J., & Cameron, D. (1989). *Women in their speech communities: New perspectives on language and sex.* London: Longman.

Fishman, P. M. (1978). Interaction: The work women do. *Social Problems, 25,* 397–406.

Gray, J. (1992). *Men are from Mars, women are from Venus.* New York: HarperCollins.

Harris, J. (1998). *The nurture assumption.* New York: Simon & Schuster/Free Press.

Hines, M. (1992, April 19). *Health Information Communication Network, 5,* 2.

Johnson, F. L. (1989). Women's culture and communication: An analytic perspective. In C. M. Lont & S. A. Friedley (Eds.), *Beyond boundaries: Sex and gender diversity in communication.* Fairfax, VA: George Mason University Press.

Kramarae, C. (1981). *Women and men speaking: Frameworks for analysis*. Rowley, MA: Newbury House.

Labov, W. (1972). *Sociolinguistic patterns*. Philadelphia: University of Pennsylvania Press.

Leaper, C. (1994). *Childhood gender segregation: Causes and consequences*. San Francisco: Jossey-Bass.

Leaper, C. (1998). The relationship of play activity and gender to parent and child sex-typed communication. *International Journal of Behavioral Development, 19*, 689–703.

Maltz, D. N., & Borker, R. (1982). A cultural approach to male–female miscommunication. In J. J. Gumpertz (Ed.), *Language and social identity* (pp. 196–216). Cambridge, England: Cambridge University Press.

Moller, L., & Serbin, L. (1998). Antecedents of toddler gender segregation: Cognitive consonance, gender-typed toy preferences and behavioral compatibility. *Sex Roles, 35*, 445–460.

Riessman, J. M. (1990). *Divorce talk: Women and men make sense of personal relationships*. New Brunswick, NJ: Rutgers University Press.

Spender, D. (1984). *Man made language*. London: Routledge and Kegan Paul.

Swain, S. (1989). Covert intimacy: Closeness in men's friendships. In B. J. Risman & P. Schwartz (Eds.), *Gender and intimate relaltionships* (pp. 71–86). Belmont, CA: Wadsworth.

Tannen, D. (1990a). Gender differences in conversational coherence: Physical alignment and topical cohesion. In B. Dorval (Ed.), *Conversational organization and its development: XXXVIII* (pp. 167–206). Norwood, NJ: Ablex.

Tannen, D. (1990b). *You just don't understand: Women and men in conversation*. New York: William Morrow.

Treichler, P. A., & Kramarae, C. (1983). Women's talk in the ivory tower. *Communication Quarterly, 31*, 118–132.

Wood, J. T. (1993a). Engendered identities: Shaping voice and mind through gender. In D. Vocate (Ed.), *Intrapersonal communication: Different voices, different minds*. Hillsdale, NJ: Erlbaum.

Wood, J. T. (1993b). Engendered relationships: Interaction, caring, power, and responsibility in close relationships. In S. Duck (Ed.), *Processes in close relationships: Vol. 3. Contexts of close relationships*. Beverly Hills, CA: Sage.

Wood, J. T. (1993c). *Who cares? Women, care, and culture*. Carbondale: Southern Illinois University Press.

Wood, J. T. (2002). A critical essay on John Gray's portrayals of men, women, and relationships. *Southern Communication Journal, 6*, 201–210.

Wood, J. T. (2005). *Gendered lives: Communication, gender, and culture* (6th ed.). Belmont, CA: Wadsworth.

Wood, J. T., & Inman, C. C. (1993). In a different mode: Masculine styles of communicating closeness. *Journal of Applied Communication Research, 21*, 279–295.

Concepts and Questions

1. What does this chapter suggest about girls who are socialized in masculine communities and who play traditionally masculine games and boys who are socialized in feminine communities and play traditionally feminine games? Which gender's rules of communication would they be likely to learn?
2. What is the difference between a person's sex and his or her gender?
3. Imagine a friend held up Gray's book *Men are from Mars, Women Are from Venus* and said to you, "This is a great book! It totally explains why men and women communicate differently." What would you say to your friend?
4. Wood and Reich encourage you to learn how to use both masculine and feminine styles of communicating. Why do they advocate this? What positive outcomes do they think result from learning multiple ways of communicating?
5. Based on your experiences, what are the most important differences between feminine and masculine styles of communication?
6. What methods do Wood and Reich suggest to help improve understanding in cross-gender communication? From your personal experiences, can you add to their list?
7. In the examples of miscommunication, one scenario featured a student named Chris who was unwilling to ask for help with an assignment. Did you assume Chris was male? Did you assume Chris's friend, Pat, was female? How would your views of Chris and Pat's interaction change if they were both male, they were both female, or Chris was female and Pat was male?

"Which Is My Good Leg?": Cultural Communication of Persons with Disabilities

Dawn O. Braithwaite
Charles A. Braithwaite

UNDERSTANDING COMMUNICATION OF PERSONS WITH DISABILITIES AS CULTURAL COMMUNICATION

Jonathan is an articulate, intelligent, 35-year-old professional man who has used a wheelchair since he became paraplegic when he was 20 years old. He recalls inviting a nondisabled woman out to dinner at a nice restaurant. When the waitperson came to take their order, she looked only at his date and asked, in a condescending tone, "And what would *he* like to eat for dinner?" At the end of the meal the waitperson presented Jonathan's date with the check and thanked her for her patronage.[1]

Kim describes her recent experience at the airport: "A lot of people always come up and ask can they push my wheelchair. And, I can do it myself. They were invading my space, concentration, doing what I wanted to do, which I enjoy doing; doing what I was doing *on my own*. . . . And each time I said, 'No, I'm doing fine!' People looked at me like I was strange, you know, crazy or something. One person started pushing my chair anyway. I said [in an angry tone], 'Don't touch the wheelchair.' And then she just looked at me like I'd slapped her in the face."

Jeff, a nondisabled student, was working on a group project for class that included Helen, who uses a wheelchair. He related an incident that really embarrassed him. "I wasn't thinking and I said to the group, 'Let's run over to the student union and get some coffee.' I was mortified when I looked over at Helen and remembered that she can't walk. I felt like a real jerk." Helen later described the incident with Jeff, recalling,

> At yesterday's meeting, Jeff said, "Let's run over to the union" and then he looked over at me and I thought he would die. It didn't bother me at all; in fact, I use that phrase myself. I felt bad that Jeff was so embarrassed, but I didn't know what to say. Later in the group meeting I made it a point to say, "I've got to be running along now." I hope that Jeff noticed and felt OK about what he said."

Although it may seem hard for some of us to believe, these scenarios represent common experiences for many people with physical disabilities and are indicative of what often happens when people with disabilities and nondisabled others communicate.

The passage of the Americans with Disabilities Act (ADA), a "bill of rights" for persons with disabilities, highlighted the fact that they are now a large, vocal, and dynamic group within the United States (Braithwaite & Labrecque, 1994; Braithwaite & Thompson, 2000). People with disabilities constitute a large segment of the American population that has increased over the years; estimates of how many people in the United States have disabilities run as high as one in five (Cunningham & Coombs, 1997; Pardek, 1998).

There are two reasons for increases in the numbers of persons with disabilities. First, as the American population ages and has a longer life expectancy, more people will live long enough to develop disabilities, some of them related to age. Second, advances in medical technologies now allow persons with disabilities to survive life-threatening illnesses and injuries where survival was not possible in earlier times. For example, when actor Christopher Reeve became quadriplegic after a horse-riding accident in May 1995, advances in medical technology allowed him to survive his injuries and to live with a severe disability.

In the past, most people with disabilities were sheltered, and many spent their lives at home or living in institutions; today, they are very much a part of the American mainstream. Each of us will have contact with people who have disabilities within our families, among our friends, or in the workplace. Some of us will develop disabilities ourselves. Marie, a college

 An earlier version of this article has appeared in earlier editions. Dawn O. Braithwaite is Director of International Studies at the University of Nebraska-Lincoln.

student who was paralyzed after diving into a swimming pool, remarked:

> I knew there were disabled people around, but I never thought this would happen to me. I never even *knew* a disabled person before *I* became one. If before this happened, I saw a person in a wheelchair, I would have been uncomfortable and not known what to say.

Marie's comment highlights the fact that many nondisabled people feel uncomfortable, some extremely so, interacting with people who are disabled. As people with disabilities continue to live, work, and study in American culture, there is a need for people with and without disabilities to know how to communicate effectively.

DISABILITY AND CULTURAL COMMUNICATION

Our goal in this chapter is to focus on communication between nondisabled persons and persons with disabilities as *intercultural communication* (Carbaugh, 1990). People with disabilities use a distinctive speech code that implies specific models of personhood, society, and strategic action that differ from those of nondisabled people. People with disabilities develop distinctive meanings, rules, and ways of speaking that act as a powerful resource for creating and reinforcing perceptions of cultural differences between people with and without disabilities. The distinctive verbal and nonverbal communication used by people with disabilities creates a sense of cultural identity that constitutes a unique social reality.

Several researchers have described the communication of disabled and nondisabled persons as intercultural communication (Braithwaite, 1990, 1996; Emry & Wiseman, 1987; Fox, Giles, Orbe & Bourhis, 2000; Padden & Humphries, 1988). That is, we recognize that people with disabilities develop certain unique communicative characteristics that are not shared by the majority of nondisabled individuals. In fact, except for individuals who are born with disabilities, becoming disabled is similar to assimilating from being a member of the nondisabled majority to being a member of a minority culture (Braithwaite, 1990, 1996). The onset of a physical disability requires learning new ways of thinking and talking about oneself, and developing new ways of communicating with others.

Adopting a cultural view of disability in this chapter, we start by introducing communication problems that can arise between persons in the nondisabled culture and those in the disabled culture. Second, we discuss some of the weaknesses of the earlier approaches researchers used to understand communication between nondisabled and disabled persons. Third, we discuss research findings from interviews with people who have physical disabilities that show them engaged in a process of redefinition; that is, they critique the prevailing stereotypes about disability, and they communicate in order to redefine what it means to be part of the disabled culture. Last, we talk about important contributions both scholars and students of intercultural communication can make to improve relations between people with and without disabilities.

Challenges for Communicators Who Are Disabled

As we adopt a cultural view and attempt to understand the communicative challenges faced by people with disabilities, it is useful to understand what a disability is. We start by distinguishing between "disability" and "handicap." Even though people often use these two terms interchangeably in everyday conversation, their meanings are quite different. The two terms imply different relationships between persons with disabilities and the larger society. The term *disability* describes those limitations that a person can overcome or compensate for by some means. Crewe and Athelstan (1985) identify five "key life functions" that may be affected by disability: (a) mobility, (b) employment, (c) self-care, (d) social relationships, and (e) communication. Many individuals are able to compensate for physical challenges associated with the first three key life functions through assistive devices (e.g., using a wheelchair or cane or using hand controls to drive a car), through training (e.g., physical therapy or training on how to take care of one's personal needs), through assistance (e.g., hiring a personal care assistant), or through occupational therapy to find suitable employment.

A disability becomes a *handicap* when the physical or social environment interacts with it to impede a person in some aspect of his or her life (Crewe & Athelstan, 1985). For example, a disabled individual with paraplegia can function well in the physical environment using a wheelchair, ramps, and curb cuts, but s/he is handicapped when buildings and/or public transportation are not accessible to wheelchair users. When a society is willing and/or able to create adaptations, people with disabilities are able to lead increasingly independent lives, which is very important to their self-esteem and health (Braithwaite & Harter, 2000; DeLoach & Greer, 1981). For people with disabilities, personal control and independence are vitally important, and "maintenance of identity and self-worth are tied to the perceived ability to control the illness, minimize its intrusiveness, and be independent" (Lyons, Sullivan, Ritvo, & Coyne, 1995, p. 134). This does not mean that people with disabilities deny their physical condition, but rather that they find ways to manage it, to obtain whatever help they need, and to lead their lives (Braithwaite & Eckstein, 2003).

It is important to realize that the practical and technological accommodations that are made to adapt the physical environment for people with disabilities are useful for nondisabled people as well. Most of us are unaware of just how handicapped we would be without these physical adaptations. For example, the authors' offices are located on the upper floors of our respective office buildings, and we often get to our office via elevator. We know that stairs take up a significant amount of space in a building. Space used for the stairwell on each level takes the place of at least one office per floor. The most space-efficient way to get people to the second floor would be a climbing rope, which would necessitate only a relatively small opening on each floor. However, how many of us could climb a rope to reach our offices? Clearly, we would be handicapped without stairs or elevators. When a student is walking with a heavy load of library books, automatic door openers, ramps, curb cuts, elevators, and larger doorways become important environmental adaptations that everyone can use and appreciate. Physical limitations become handicaps for all of us when the physical environment cannot be adapted to meet our shortcomings.

Challenges to Relationships of People with Disabilities

Although it is possible to identify and find accommodations for physical challenges associated with mobility, self-care, and employment, the two key life functions of social relationships and communication often present much more formidable challenges. It is often less difficult to detect and correct physical barriers than it is to deal with the insidious social barriers facing people with disabilities. Coleman and DePaulo (1991) label these social barriers as "psychological disabling," which is common in Western culture where "much value is placed on physical bodies and physical attractiveness" (p. 64).

When people with disabilities begin relationships with nondisabled people, the challenges associated with forming any new relationship are often greater. For nondisabled people, this may be due to lack of experience interacting with people who are disabled, which leads to high uncertainty about how to interact with a person who is disabled (Braithwaite & Labrecque, 1994). Nondisabled persons may be uncertain about what to say or how to act. They are afraid of saying or doing the wrong thing or of hurting the feelings of the person with the disability, much as Jeff was with his group member, Helen, in the example at the beginning of this chapter. As a result, nondisabled persons may feel overly self-conscious, and their actions may be constrained, self-controlled, and rigid because they feel uncomfortable and uncertain (Belgrave & Mills, 1981; Braithwaite 1990; Dahnke, 1983; Higgins, 1992). Their behaviors, in turn, will appear uninterested or unaccepting to the person who is disabled. The nondisabled person will need to figure out how to communicate appropriately. Higgins (1992) pointed out that sometimes these communication attempts are not successful: "Wishing to act in a way acceptable to those with disabilities, they may unknowingly act offensively, patronizing disabled people with unwanted sympathy" (Higgins, 1992, p. 105).

High levels of uncertainty can negatively affect interaction and relationship development between people. It becomes easier to avoid that person rather than deal with not knowing what to do or say. Interestingly, researchers have found that the type of disability a person possesses does not change the way nondisabled persons react to them (Fichten, Robillard, Tagalakis, & Amsel, 1991). Although uncertainty reduction theory can be overly simplistic, especially when applied to ongoing relationships, this theory is useful in understanding some of the initial discomfort nondisabled people may feel when interacting with a stranger or early acquaintance who is disabled. Understanding the effects of uncertainty, people with disabilities work to devise ways to help nondisabled others reduce their discomfort (Braithwaite, 1990, 1996; Braithwaite & Labrecque, 1994).

Even when a nondisabled person tries to "say the right thing" and wants to communicate acceptance to the person with the disability, his or her nonverbal behavior may communicate rejection and avoidance instead (Thompson, 1982). For example, people with disabilities have observed that many nondisabled persons may keep a greater physical distance, avoid eye contact, avoid mentioning the disability, or cut the conversation short (Braithwaite, 1990, 1991, 1996). These nondisabled persons may be doing their best not to show their discomfort or not crowd the person with the disability. However, the outcome may be that the person with the disability perceives they do not want to interact. In this case, a person's disability becomes a handicap in the social environment as it can block the development of a relationship with a nondisabled person, who finds the interaction too uncomfortable.

Complicating matters, many nondisabled people hold stereotypes of people from the disabled culture. Coleman and DePaulo (1991) discuss some of these stereotypes concerning disabled people:

> For example, they often perceive them as dependent, socially introverted, emotionally unstable, depressed, hypersensitive, and easily offended, especially with regard to their disability. In addition, disabled people are often presumed to differ from nondisabled people in moral character, social skills, and political orientation. (p. 69)

Stereotypes like these do nothing but raise the level of uncertainty and discomfort the nondisabled person is experiencing.

When nondisabled persons make the effort to overcome discomfort and stereotypes to interact with people from the disabled culture, they often find themselves with conflicting expectations. On the one hand, Americans are taught to "help the handicapped." At the same time, Americans conceptualize persons as "individuals" who "have rights" and "make their own choices" (Carbaugh, 1988) and thus are taught to treat all people equally. However, when nondisabled persons encounter a person with a disability, this model of personhood creates a real dilemma. How can you both help a person and treat that person equally? For example, should you help a person with a disability open a door or try to help him up if he falls? If you are working with a blind person, should you help her find a doorway or get her lunch at the cafeteria? These dilemmas often result in high uncertainty for nondisabled people, who often end up trying to give more help than people with disabilities want or need (Braithwaite & Eckstein, 2003). In the end, it may simply seem easier to avoid situations in which you might have to interact with a disabled person rather than face feelings of discomfort and uncertainty (this is how many people react to communicating with people from other cultures). However, avoidance is not a very good solution in the end, especially if this person is to be a member of your work group or family, for example.

It should not be surprising to learn that most people with disabilities are well aware of the feelings and fears many nondisabled persons have. In fact, in research interviews, people with disabilities tell us they believe they "can just tell" who is uncomfortable around them or not. They are able to provide a great amount of detail on both the verbal and nonverbal signals of discomfort and avoidance of nondisabled persons (Braithwaite, 1990, 1996; Braithwaite & Eckstein, 2003), and they develop communication strategies to help them interact in these situations. For example, people with disabilities tell us that when they meet nondisabled persons, they will communicate in ways designed to get the discomfort "out of the way." They want the nondisabled person to treat them as a "person like anyone else," rather than focus solely on their disability (Braithwaite, 1991, 1996). For example, they may talk about topics they believe they have in common with the nondisabled person, such as cooking, sports, or music.

People with disabilities develop strategies to help them handle situations in which they might need help from nondisabled others in order to help reduce the uncertainty and discomfort of the nondisabled person (Braithwaite & Eckstein, 2003). For example, two men who are wheelchair users who need help getting out of their van in parking lots described how they plan ahead to get the help they need:

> Well, I have a mobile phone. . . . I will call into the store and let the store manager or whoever know, "Hey, we're in a white minivan and if you look out your window, you can see us! We're two guys in wheelchairs, can you come out and help us get out of the van?"

These men plan ahead to avoid having to ask for help and putting nondisabled strangers in potentially uncomfortable communication situations. Other people described situations in which they might accept help that they did not need because they understood that refusing help might increase the discomfort and uncertainty of the nondisabled person.

CHANGING THE FOCUS OF RESEARCHERS

When we first began looking at the research on communication between nondisabled and disabled persons, three problems came clearly to the forefront (for a recent summary, see Thompson, 2000). First, very little was known about the communication behavior of disabled people. Although a few researchers have studied disabled persons' communication, most of them have studied nondisabled persons' *reactions* to disabled others. These studies on "attitudes toward disabled persons" are analogous to the many studies that look at majority members' attitudes toward other "minority groups." A look at the intercultural communication literature as a whole reveals few studies from the perspective of persons representing minority groups. Although there has been some improvement over the years, there is still relatively little information on communication from the perspective of people with disabilities.

A second, related problem is that many researchers talk *about* people with disabilities, not *with* them. People with disabilities have rarely been represented in survey data. Most often these studies consist of nondisabled people reporting their impressions of disabled people. In experimental studies, the disabled person is most often "played" by a nondisabled person using a wheelchair (and not surprisingly, most people can tell that this is not a disabled person!). There are still too few studies that give us a sense of how people with and without disabilities communication in actual conversations.

Third, and most significant, the research has most often taken the perspective of the nondisabled person; that is, researchers tend to focus on what people with disabilities should do to make nondisabled others feel more comfortable. Coming from this perspective, researchers do not consider the effects of communication on the person with the disability. For example, several studies have found that nondisabled persons are more comfortable when people with disabilities disclose about their disability, so the researchers suggest that disabled people should self-disclose to make nondisabled others more comfortable. Braithwaite (1991) points out that these researchers have forgotten to look at how self-disclosing might affect people who are disabled. Therefore, what we see coming from much of the nondisabled-oriented research is an *ethnocentric bias* that ignores the perspective of people from the disabled culture. Although there has been more research from the perspective of disabled interactants in recent years, there are still too few empirical studies, and we are left with a very incomplete picture of the communication of people who are disabled.

In the remainder of this chapter, we will present selected findings from ongoing studies conducted from the perspective of people with disabilities that help us understand the communication of people with and without disabilities from a cultural perspective. These research findings come from more than 100 in-depth interviews completed by the first author with adults who are physically disabled. All of these people have disabilities that are visible to an observer, and none of them has significant communication-related disabilities (e.g. blindness, deafness, speech impairments). The goal of the research has been to describe communication with nondisabled people from the frame of reference of people who are disabled. Doing research by talking *with* people who are disabled helps to bring out information important to them and allows people with disabilities to describe experiences from their own cultural framework.

PROCESS OF REDEFINITION

A central theme emerging from the interviews is what we call *redefinition;* that is, people who are disabled critique the prevailing stereotypes about being disabled, they create new ways of perceiving themselves and their disability, and they develop ways of communicating as a result. We were able to see three types of redefinition: (a) redefining the self as part of a "new" culture, (b) redefining the concept of disability, and (c) redefining disability for the dominant culture.

Redefining the Self as Part of the Disabled Culture

In research interviews, many people with disabilities talk about themselves as part of a minority group or a culture. For some of the interviewees, this definition crosses disability lines; that is, their definition of "disabled" includes all those who have disabilities. For others, the definition is not as broad; when they think of disability, they are thinking about others with the same type of disability they have. For example, some of the people with mobility-related disabilities also included blind and deaf people with the discussed disability, and others talked only about other wheelchair users. However narrowly or broadly they define it, however, many do see themselves as part of a minority culture. For example, one of the interviewees said that being disabled "is like *West Side Story.* Tony and Maria; white and Puerto Rican. They were afraid of each other; ignorant of each other's cultures. People are people." Another man explained his view:

> First of all, I belong to a subculture [of disability] because of the way I have to deal with things, being in the medical system, welfare. There is the subculture. . . . I keep one foot in the nondisabled culture and one foot in my own culture. One of the reasons I do that is so that I don't go nuts.

This man's description of the "balancing act" between cultures demonstrates that membership in the disabled culture has several similarities to the experiences of other American cultural groups. Many of the interviewees have likened their own experiences to those of other cultural groups, particularly to the experiences of American people of color. Interviewees describe the loss of status and power that comes from being disabled, and they perceive that many people are uncomfortable with them simply because they are different.

When taking a cultural view, it is important to recognize that not everyone comes to the culture the same way. Some people are born with disabilities, and others acquire them later. For those people who are not born with a disability, membership in the culture is a process that emerges over time. For some, the process is an incremental one, as in the case of a person with a degenerative disease such as multiple sclerosis that develops over many years. For a person who has a sudden-onset disability, such as breaking one's neck in an accident and "waking up a quadriplegic," moving from the majority (a "normal" person) to the minority (a person who is disabled) may happen in a matter of seconds. This sudden transition into the disabled culture presents many significant challenges of redefinition and readjustment in all facets of an individual's life (Braithwaite, 1990; 1996; Goffman, 1963).

If disability is a culture, when does one become part of that culture? Even though a person is physically disabled, how one redefines oneself, from "normal" or nondisabled to disabled, is a process that develops over time. It is important to understand that becoming physically disabled does not mean one immediately has an awareness of being part of the disabled culture (Braithwaite, 1990, 1996). In fact, for most people, adjusting to disability happens in a series of stages or phases (Braithwaite, 1990; DeLoach & Greer, 1981; Padden & Humphries, 1988). DeLoach and Greer (1981) describe three phases of an individual's adjustment to disability: (1) stigma isolation, (2) stigma recognition, and (3) stigma incorporation. Their model helps us understand what is occurring in the process of adjustment to disability as acculturation. During this process, persons with disabilities progress from the onset of their disability to membership in the disabled culture.

Imagine the experience of Mark, a college student majoring in physical education who has a car accident and wakes up to find he is paralyzed. Mark enters the first phase, *stigma isolation,* upon becoming disabled. At this point, he is focusing on rehabilitation and all of the physical changes and challenges he is experiencing. It is likely that Mark has not yet noticed the changes in his social relationships and communication with nondisabled others.

The second phase, *stigma recognition,* begins when Mark realizes that his life and relationships have changed dramatically and he will need to find ways to minimize the effects of his disability as much as possible. Mark may try to return to normal routines and old relationships; for example, he may return to college. This can be a frustrating phase, because often things have changed more than the person at first realizes. Mark may try to reestablish his old relationships, only to find that his friends are no longer comfortable with him or that they can no longer share activities they had in common. For example, Mark may find it hard to maintain relationships with his friends from his softball team. Mark's friends, who were visiting him around the clock in the hospital, may not know what to do or say around him and may even start to avoid him. It is at this point that persons who are disabled start to become aware that they are now interacting as members of a different culture than they were before, and they begin to assimilate the new culture into their identity and behavior (Braithwaite, 1990, 1996). Mark may notice how his friends are treating him, and he may not enjoy their company much at this point either.

This begins the third phase, what DeLoach and Greer (1981) call *stigma incorporation*. At this point, persons with a disability begin to integrate being disabled into their identity, their definition of self. The person begins to understand both the positive and negative aspects of being disabled and begins to develop ways to overcome and cope with the negative aspects of disability (DeLoach & Greer, 1981). In this stage of adjustment, people with disabilities develop ways of behaving and communicating so that they are able to function successfully in the nondisabled culture (Braithwaite, 1990, 1996). For example, after all he has experienced, Mark may find he now has an interest in psychology and sees more career opportunities there. When he switches his major, he finds he has a knack for statistics that he never knew he had, organizes a study group for his statistics class, and starts to make new friends.

Braithwaite (1996) argues that stigma incorporation represents what Morse and Johnson (1991) have labeled "regaining wellness," which occurs when individuals begin to take back control of their own lives and relationships, live as independently as possible, and adapt to new ways of doing things in their lives. Individuals develop ways of communicating with nondisabled others that help them live successfully as part of the disabled and nondisabled cultures simultaneously (Braithwaite, 1990, 1991, 1996; Braithwaite & Labrecque, 1994; Emry & Wiseman, 1987). This is what researchers call interability, intergroup communication (see Fox et al., 2000).

In this third phase, then, the person incorporates the role of disability into his or her identity and into his or her life. One man said, "You're the same person you were. You just don't do the same things you did before." Another put it this way: "If anyone refers to me as an amputee, that is guaranteed to get me madder than hell! I don't deny the leg amputation, but I am *me*. I am a whole person. *One*." It is during this phase that people can come to terms with both the negative and positive changes in their lives. One woman expressed it this way:

> I find myself telling people that this has been the worst thing that has happened to me. It has also been one of the best things. It forced me to examine what I felt about myself . . . my confidence is grounded in me, not in other people. As a woman, I am not as dependent on clothes, measurements, but what's inside me.

The late actor Christopher Reeve demonstrated the concept of stigma incorporation in an interview with Barbara Walters, four months after his devastating accident:

> You also gradually discover, as I'm discovering, that your body is not you. The mind and the spirit must take over. And that's the challenge as you move from obsessing about "Why me?" and "It's not fair" and move into "Well, what is the potential?" And, now, four months down the line I see opportunities and potential I wasn't capable of seeing back in Virginia in June . . . genuine joy and being alive means more. Every moment is more intense than it ever was.

One implication of this example is that stigma incorporation, becoming part of the disabled culture, is a process that develops over time.

Redefining Disability

A second type of redefinition discussed by interviewees is redefining the concept of disability. For example, one interviewee explained, "People will say, 'Thank God I'm not handicapped.' And I'll say, 'Let's see, how tall are you? Tell me how you get something off that shelf up there!'" His goal in this interchange is to force others to see disability as one of many *characteristics* of a person. From this perspective, everyone is handicapped in one way or another by our height, weight, sex, ethnicity, or physical attributes, and people must work to overcome those characteristics that are handicapping. Short people may need a stool to reach something on a high shelf, and people who are very tall may be stared at and certainly will not be able to drive small, economy-size cars. Most middle-aged professors cannot climb a rope to their office and need the accommodation of stairs. Similarly, people with disabilities must adapt to the physical and social challenges presented to them. One interviewee, who conducts workshops on disability awareness, talked about how he helps nondisabled people redefine disability:

> I will say to people, "How many of you made the clothes that you're wearing?" "How many of you grew the food that you ate yesterday?" "How many of you built the house that you live in?" Nobody raises their hand. Then after maybe five of those, I'll say, "And I bet you think you're independent." And I'll say, "I'll bet you, if we could measure how independent you feel in your life versus how independent I feel in mine, then I would rate just as high you do. And yet here I am 'depending' on people to get me dressed, undressed, on and off the john, etc. It's all in our heads, folks. Nobody is really independent." I can see them kind of go "Yeah, I never thought of it that way." And they begin to understand how it is that somebody living with this situation can feel independent. That independence really is a feeling and an attitude. It's not a physical reality.

It is also important to remember that, like any characteristic that we have, disability is context-specific. For example, a blind person will function better in a dark room than sighted persons, who will find themselves handicapped in that environment. The first author of this chapter spent several days at Gallaudet University in Washington, D. C. At Gallaudet, where most students are deaf, it was the *author* who was disabled, as she needed interpreters to talk with the students there. At Gallaudet, people talk about being part of Deaf culture, but not about being disabled.

Redefining disability can also be reflected through changing the language we use to talk about disability. One interviewee objected to the label "handicapped person," preferring the label "persons with a handicapping condition." He explained why: "You emphasize that person's identity and then you do something about the condition." The goal is to speak in ways that emphasize the *person,* rather than the disability. One interviewee, who had polio as a child, rejected the term "polio victim" and preferred to label herself as "a person whose arms and legs do not function very well." Talking with disability activists around the nation, we find many different approaches to language and labels about disability. One way we have found to accentuate the person is to talk about "*people* with disabilities" rather than "disabled people." The goal is to emphasize the person first, before introducing the disability, much like using the label "people of color." These are all forms of strategic action that help to create and maintain a sense of unique cultural identity among persons with disabilities (Braithwaite, 1996; Braithwaite & Thompson, 2000).

Redefining disability is also reflected in sensitizing oneself to commonly used labels for being disabled, such as being a "polio victim" or an "arthritis sufferer," or being confined to a wheelchair" or "wheelchair bound." When trying to redefine disability as a characteristic of the person, one can change these phrases to a "person with polio," a "person who has arthritis," or a "wheelchair user." Some researchers suggest that we avoid talking about the communication of disabled and nondisabled people and instead use the phrase "interability communication" (see Fox et al., 2000). At first glance, it may be tempting to think this is no more than an attempt at political correctness, but those who understand language and culture know how strongly the words we use influence our perception of others, and theirs of us. The way people with disabilities are labeled will affect how they are seen by others and how they perceive themselves.

One of the more humorous and, at the same time, powerful examples of language regarding disability is the use of "TABs" to refer to nondisabled people. "TAB" is short for "temporarily able-bodied." One interviewee joked, "Everyone is a TAB. . . . I just got mine earlier than you!" Being called a TAB serves to remind nondisabled persons that no one is immune from disability. From this perspective, everyone is becoming disabled! It certainly does challenge our perspective to think about that. To end our discussion of disability and language, whatever labels we choose to use, it is clear that the language both creates and reflects the view of people with disabilities and disabled culture.

In addition to redefining disability, the interviewees also redefined "assisting devices" such as wheelchairs or canes. For example, one man told the following story about redefining his prosthetic leg:

> Now there were two girls about eight playing and I was in my shorts. And I'll play games with them and say "Which is my good leg?" And that gets them to thinking. Well, this one [he pats his artificial leg] is not nearly as old as the other one!

Another interviewee redefined assisting devices this way: "Do you know what a cane is? It's a portable railing! The essence of a wheelchair is a seat and wheels.

Now, I don't know that a tricycle is not doing the exact same thing." Redefining assisting devices helps us see how they might mean different things to disabled and nondisabled persons. For example, several interviewees expressed frustration with people who played with their wheelchairs. One interviewee exclaimed, "This chair is not a toy, it is *part of me*. When you touch my chair, you are touching *me*." Another woman, a business executive, expanded on this by saying, "I don't know why people who push my chair feel compelled to make car sounds as they do it." In these examples, then, the problem is not the disability or the assisting device, but how one perceives the person using them.

Redefining Disability Within Nondisabled Culture

Last, as people with disabilities redefine themselves as members of a culture, they also define what it means to have a disabling condition. Our experience is that people with disabilities are concerned with changing the view of disability within the larger culture (Braithwaite, 1990, 1996). Most people with disabilities we have encountered view themselves as public educators on disability issues. People told stories about taking the time to educate children and adults on what it means to be disabled. They are actively working to change the view of themselves as helpless, as victims, or as ill, and the ensuing treatment such a view brings. One wheelchair user said:

> People do not consider you, they consider the chair first. I was in a store with my purchases on my lap and money on my lap. The clerk looked at my companion and not at me and said, "Cash or charge?"

This incident with the clerk represents a story we heard from *every* person in some form or another, just as it happened to Jonathan and his date at the beginning of this chapter. One woman, who has multiple sclerosis and uses a wheelchair, told of shopping for lingerie with her husband accompanying her. When they were in front of the lingerie counter, the clerk repeatedly talked only to her husband, saying, "And what size does she want?" The woman told her the size, and the clerk looked at the husband and said, "And what color does she want?"

Persons with disabilities recognize that nondisabled persons often see them as disabled first and as a person second (if at all). The most common theme expressed by people with disabilities in all of the interviews is that they want to be *seen and treated as a person first*. One man explained what he thought was important to remember: "A lot of people think that handicapped people are 'less than' and I find that it's not true at all. . . . Abling people, giving them their power back, empowering them." The interviewees rejected those situations or behaviors that would not lead them to be seen. A man with muscular dystrophy talked about the popular Labor Day telethon:

> I do not believe in those goddamned telethons . . . they're horrible, absolutely horrible. They get into the self-pity, you know, and disabled folk do not need that. Hit people in terms of their attitudes then try to deal with and process their feelings. And the telethons just go for the heart and leave it there.

One man suggested what he thought was a more useful approach:

> What I am concerned with is anything that can do away with the "us" versus "them" distinction. Well, you and I are anatomically different, but we're two human beings! And at the point, we can sit down and communicate eyeball to eyeball; the quicker you do that, the better!

Individually and collectively, people with disabilities do identify themselves as part of a culture. They are involved in a process of redefinition of themselves, and of disability. They desire to help nondisabled people understand and internalize a redefinition of people of the disabled culture as "persons first."

CONCLUSION

The research we have discussed highlights the usefulness of viewing disability from a cultural perspective. People with disabilities do recognize themselves as part of a culture, and understanding communication and relationships from this perspective sheds new light on the communication challenges that exist. Some time ago, Emry and Wiseman (1987) first argued for the usefulness of intercultural training about disability issues. They called for unfreezing old attitudes about disability and refreezing new ones. Our experience indicates that people with disabilities would agree with this goal.

We have asked people with disabilities whether they had training in communication during or after their rehabilitation. We anticipated that they would have received information and training to prepare them for changes in their communication and relationships after becoming disabled. We speculated that this education would be especially critical for those who experience sudden-onset disabilities because their self-concepts and all of their relationships would undergo such radical changes. Surprisingly, we found that less than 30% of the interviewees received disability-related communication training.

We believe intercultural communication scholars can help design research and training that could help make the transition from majority to minority an easier one (Braithwaite, 1990; Emry & Wiseman, 1987). We are encouraged by some advances that are taking place in educational and organizational settings (e.g., Colvert & Smith, 2000; Herold, 2000; Worley, 2000). We also see the need for research that expands to different types of disabilities—for example, for those with invisible disabilities (e.g., emphysema, diabetes) and socially stigmatized disabilities such as HIV. Overall, we see important contributions for communication scholars to make. When Braithwaite and Thompson (2000) published their *Handbook of Communication and People with Disabilities,* they were struck by how many researchers in communication studies are now studying disability communication and how many of these scholars are disabled. Clearly, the future does look brighter than when we began our work in disability and communication some years back. However, we still have a long way to go.

We do believe that students of intercultural communication should have an advantage in being able to better understand the perspective of people with disabilities, as presented in this chapter. We hope that you will be able to adapt and apply intercultural communication concepts and skills to interactions with persons in the disabled culture. We believe that people with disabilities themselves will better understand their own experience if they study intercultural communication and come to understand the cultural aspects of disability.

In closing, taking an intercultural perspective on communication and disability culture leads us to suggest the following practical proscriptions and prescriptions.

DON'T:

- *Avoid* communication with people who are disabled simply because you are uncomfortable or unsure.
- *Assume* that people with disabilities cannot speak for themselves or do things for themselves.
- *Force* your help on people with disabilities.
- *Use terms* such as "handicapped," "physically challenged," "crippled," "victim," and the like, unless requested to do so by people with disabilities.
- *Assume* that a disability defines who a person is.

DO:

- *Remember* that people with disabilities have experienced others' discomfort before and likely understand how you might be feeling.
- *Assume* that people with disabilities can do something unless they communicate otherwise.
- *Let people with disabilities tell you* if they want something, what they want, and when they want it. If a person with a disability refuses your help, don't go ahead and help anyway.
- *Use terms* such as "*people* with disabilities" rather than "disabled people." The goal is to stress the *person first,* before the disability.
- *Treat* people with disabilities as *persons first,* recognizing that you are not dealing with a disabled person but with a *person* who *has* a disability. This means actively seeking the humanity of the person with whom you are speaking, and focusing on individual characteristics instead of superficial physical appearance. Without diminishing the significance of a person's physical disability, make a real effort to focus on all the many other aspects of that person as you communicate.

Note

1. The quotes and anecdotes in this chapter come from in-depth interviews with people who have visible physical disabilities. The names of the participants in these interviews have been changed to protect their privacy.

References

Belgrave, F. Z., & Mills, J. (1981). Effect upon desire for social interaction with a physically disabled person of mentioning the disability in different contexts. *Journal of Applied Social Psychology, 11,* 44–57.

Braithwaite, D. O. (1990). From majority to minority: An analysis of cultural change from nondisabled to disabled. *International Journal of Intercultural Relations, 14,* 465–483.

Braithwaite, D. O. (1991). "Just how much did that wheelchair cost?": Management of privacy boundaries by persons with disabilities. *Western Journal of Speech Communication, 55,* 254–274.

Braithwaite, D. O. (1996). "Persons first": Expanding communicative choices by persons with disabilities. In E. B. Ray (Ed.), *Communication and disenfranchisement: Social health issues and implications* (pp. 449–464). Mahwah, NJ: Erlbaum.

Braithwaite, D. O., & Eckstein, N. (2003). Reconceptualizing supportive interactions: How persons with disabilities communicatively manage assistance. *Journal of Applied Communication Research, 31,* 1–26.

Braithwaite, D. O., & Harter, L. (2000). Communication and the management of dialectical tensions in the personal relationships of people with disabilities. In D. O. Braithwaite & T. L. Thompson (Eds.), *Handbook of communication and people with disabilities: Research and application* (pp. 17–36). Mahwah, NJ: Erlbaum.

Braithwaite, D. O., & Labrecque, D. (1994). Responding to the Americans with Disabilities Act: Contributions of interpersonal communication research and training. *Journal of Applied Communication Research, 22,* 287–294.

Braithwaite, D. O., & Thompson, T. L. (Eds.). (2000). *Handbook of communication and people with disabilities: Research and application.* Mahwah, NJ: Erlbaum.

Carbaugh, D. (1988). *Talking American.* Norwood, NJ: Ablex.

Carbaugh, D. (Ed.). (1990). *Cultural communication and intercultural contact.* Hillsdale, NJ: Erlbaum.

Coleman, L. M., & DePaulo, B. M. (1991). Uncovering the human spirit: Moving beyond disability and "missed" communications. In N. Coupland, H. Giles, & J. M. Wiemann (Eds.), *Miscommunication and problematic talk* (pp. 61–84). Newbury Park, CA: Sage.

Covert, A. L., & Smith, J. W. (2000). What is reasonable: Workplace communication and people who are disabled. In D. O. Braithwaite & T. L. Thompson (Eds.), *Handbook of communication and people with disabilities: Research and application* (pp. 141–158). Mahwah, NJ: Erlbaum.

Crewe, N., & Athelstan, G. (1985). *Social and psychological aspects of physical disability.* Minneapolis: University of Minnesota, Department of Independent Study and University Resources.

Cunningham, C., & Coombs, N. (1997). *Information access and adaptive technology.* Phoenix, AZ: Oryx Press.

Dahnke, G. L. (1983). Communication and handicapped and nonhandicapped persons: Toward a deductive theory. In M. Burgoon (Ed.), *Communication yearbook 6* (pp. 92–135). Beverly Hills, CA: Sage.

DeLoach, C., &, Greer, B. G. (1981). *Adjustment to severe physical disability: A metamorphosis.* New York: McGraw-Hill .

Emry, R., & Wiseman, R. L. (1987). An intercultural understanding of nondisabled and disabled persons' communication. *International Journal of Intercultural Relations, 11,* 7–27.

Fichten, C. S., Robillard, K., Tagalakis, V., & Amsel, R. (1991). Casual interaction between college students with various disabilities and their nondisabled peers: The internal dialogue. *Rehabilitation Psychology, 36,* 3–20.

Fox, S. A., Giles, H., Orbe, M., & Bourhis, R. (2000). Interability communication: Theoretical perspectives. In D. O. Braithwaite & T. L. Thompson (Eds.), *Handbook of communication and people with disabilities: Research and application* (pp. 193–222). Mahwah, NJ: Erlbaum.

Goffman, E. (1963). *Stigma: Notes on the management of spoiled identity.* New York: Simon & Schuster.

Herold, K. P. (2000). Communication strategies in employment interviews for applicants with disabilities. In D. O. Braithwaite & T. L. Thompson (Eds.), *Handbook of communication and people with disabilities: Research and application* (pp. 159–175). Mahwah, NJ: Erlbaum.

Higgins, P. C. (1992). *Making disability: Exploring the social transformation of human variation.* Springfield, IL: Charles C. Thomas.

Lyons, R. F., Sullivan, M. J. L., Ritvo, P. G., & Coyne, J. C. (1995). *Relationships in chronic illness and disability.* Thousand Oaks, CA: Sage.

Morse, J. M., & Johnson, J. L. (1991). *The illness experience: Dimensions of suffering.* Newbury Park, CA: Sage.

Padden, C., & Humphries, T. (1988). *Deaf in America: Voices from a culture.* Cambridge, MA: Harvard University Press.

Pardeck, J. T. (1998). *Social work after the Americans with Disabilities Act: New challenges and opportunities for social service professionals.* Westport, CT: Auburn House.

Thompson, T. L. (1982). Disclosure as a disability-management strategy: A review and conclusions. *Communication Quarterly, 30,* 196–202.

Thompson, T. L. (2000). A history of communication and disability research: The way we were. In D. O. Braithwaite & T. L. Thompson (Eds.), *Handbook of communication and people with disabilities: Research and application* (pp. 1–14). Mahwah, NJ: Erlbaum.

Worley, D. W. (2000). Communication and students with disabilities on college campuses. In D. O. Braithwaite & T. L. Thompson (Eds.), *Handbook of communication and people with disabilities: Research and application* (pp. 125–139). Mahwah, NJ: Erlbaum.

Concepts and Questions

1. In what ways does becoming disabled lead to changes in a person's communication patterns?

2. What are some of the cultural problems inherent in communication between nondisabled and disabled persons?
3. Why do Braithwaite and Braithwaite believe you should learn about the communication patterns of disabled persons? What purpose will be served by your knowing this information?
4. Give examples of what Braithwaite and Braithwaite mean when they say that "the distinctive verbal and nonverbal communication used by persons with disabilities creates a sense of cultural identity that constitutes a unique social reality"?
5. How would you distinguish between *disability* and *handicap*?
6. Why is nonverbal communication a factor when nondisabled persons and persons with disabilities engage in communication?
7. Enumerate the problems Braithwaite and Braithwaite describe relating to the current research being conducted on persons with disabilities.
8. What is meant by the term *redefinition*?
9. How would you answer the following question: If disability is a culture, then when does one become part of that culture?

In Plain Sight: Gay and Lesbian Communication and Culture

WILLIAM F. EADIE

Some of you will be eager to read this chapter, and others of you will want to avoid it. That's how strong people's feelings are about lesbian and gay culture in the United States today. Many college students see their lesbian and gay classmates as people who are too different, who rock the boat too much, or whose strange ways are simply threatening. Students committed to their religious beliefs may see their lesbian and gay classmates as people who need to be saved, to be rescued from their sinful ways. Some male students may see classmates they consider to be gay as easy targets for bullying or even abuse. Some students and their parents worry that lesbian and gay faculty members may attempt to "recruit" students who are in their classes. Students who know that they are lesbian or gay may find that this chapter reminds them too much of the feelings of being outcasts and "second class" that they have been working to overcome. Students who are questioning their sexuality may find that reading this chapter helps them, or they may find that it confuses them all the more.

There are so many different potential mindsets that readers will have when beginning this chapter that it will be impossible to address all of them. I will probably end up offending some of you at least some of the time.

That said, I'm going to present some viewpoints on lesbian and gay culture in the United States and discuss how communication is both distinctive and serves to create and re-create that culture. I use the term "viewpoints" because there is no precise way to define, measure, and track developments in lesbian and gay culture, so we have to rely on observers to analyze and present what they see. As mine is one of the major viewpoints in this chapter, it is only fair that you know something about the history and perspective I bring to writing the chapter.

 William F. Eadie is Professor and Director of the School of Communication, San Diego State University.

I am a gay man in my 50s. My youth was "pre-Stonewall"; that is, I was entering into adulthood as a group of drag queens, who were being hassled by undercover police officers for no other offense than being men dressed as women, began a demonstration in front of the Stonewall Bar in the Greenwich Village section of New York City on June 28, 1969. The demonstration attracted scores of gays and lesbians to the scene, and what came to be known as the Stonewall Riots began the Gay Liberation Movement. I was raised in a comfortable but conservative environment, and in elementary school I was branded a "sissy." As I was not terribly coordinated, I was among the last picked for teams on the playground, and I was more interested in the performing arts than I was in sports. My parents insisted, however, that I should be engaged in doing "boy" things, so I tried every imaginable sport, and I became a very active participant in Scouting (Cub Scouts, Boy Scouts, Explorers). Some gay men report feeling more affinity and comfort with women, but I was not one of those. I was happiest being with one best male friend, and I've always had a male best friend, and sometimes more than one close male friend, throughout my life.

In college, my best male friend was openly gay. Going to college had been a liberating experience for me, but I was still very emotionally tied to my parents, who on more than one occasion had said negative things about gays. Secretly, I was pleased to be able to rebel against my parents' authority by having a gay friend, though I never told them he was gay. For his part, my friend became convinced over the several years we were in school together, that I, too, was gay. He started taking me to gay bars, hoping I would take the hint, and when I didn't he decided to seduce me. I enjoyed the experience, but the thought of rebelling *that* much against my parents' hopes and dreams for me frightened me. I promptly declared that I wasn't gay and proceeded to stay in the closet for 20 more years.

After I finally did come out to myself and others, I looked back on those years. I realized that I knew all along that I was gay but wasn't willing to admit it to myself for fear that being open about my sexuality would ruin my life and my prospects for success. In retrospect, being honest probably would have made my life even better than I imagined at the time. I wasn't ready to come out before my father died. I came out to my mother, and she was not at all happy about it. Over time, though, she decided that I was still the son she knew and loved; only now she knew a little more about me.

Today, I am relatively comfortable with my sexuality. I don't mind if people know that I'm gay, but I don't make a big deal of it, either. If you met me, you probably wouldn't be surprised to learn that I was gay, but neither would you want to pin a huge "GAY" button on my shirt. I still love the performing arts, and I sing with two choruses, one of them a gay men's chorus. I'm still not very proficient at sports, but I enjoy noncompetitive activities such as bicycling and recreational skiing. I'm not nearly as uncomfortable being around women as I was when I was younger. And it pains me that Scouting, an organization from which I benefited a great deal, has chosen to discriminate openly against boys who are or who might be gay.

From my experience, I can make three general statements about lesbian and gay culture, which I'll elaborate in the following sections:

1. Being open about sexual orientation is a political statement, one that has ramifications for the sorts of relationships one can establish with others.
2. Lesbian and gay culture exists by dealing with tensions about how open to be about one's sexuality.
3. Lesbian and gay culture is driven by sexual attraction and desire, but ultimately being lesbian or gay is not only about sex.

MAKING A POLITICAL STATEMENT

More than other nonmajority groups, lesbians and gay men have a better chance of living undetected by individuals within mainstream society. Whereas ethnicity and national origin are relatively easy to discern by merely looking at an individual, sexual orientation is not readily apparent.

Of course, there are plenty of people who think that they can tell otherwise. When I was in high school, students called Thursday "Queersday" and passed around the story that those who wore green on Thursday would be saying to all that they were gay. A group of lesbian and gay college students later turned that kind of thinking on its head when they declared that all students who wore jeans to school on Thursday would be telling their classmates that they were gay.

Pranks aside, why would students focus on clothing as an indicator that a classmate is gay? Perhaps it is because children from an early age are made very aware of differences and by adolescence there is tremendous pressure to conform. A person who dresses differently enough to be beyond the boundaries of conformity communicates "outsider" status. So, a male who wears colors that are a bit too bright or gaudy or a female who dresses down all the time but who otherwise does not seem to be making another identity statement (such as being a "stoner" or a "skater") may be judged by others to be gay.

And gay youth feel their outsider status intensely. One of the most eloquently written descriptions of these feelings comes from Paul Monett's award-winning memoir, *Becoming a Man:*

> Everyone else had a childhood, for one thing—where they were coaxed and coached and taught all the shorthand. . . . And every year they leaped further ahead, leaving me in the dust with all my doors closed. . . . Until I was twenty-five, I was the only man I knew who had no story at all. . . . That's how the closet feels, once you've made your nest in it and learned to call it home. Self-pity becomes your oxygen. (Monette, 1992, p. 1)

Of course, what is in fashion changes rapidly and probably isn't a good indicator of sexuality over time. In urban areas, one can easily find male "metrosexuals" and gay men who dress alike. And the *New York Times* has reported that a lesbian style not only exists but influences the clothing choices of heterosexual women in a piece provocatively headlined "The Secret Power of Lesbian Style" (Trebay, 2004).

If clothing is becoming less and less of a giveaway, then what clues do people use to judge sexuality? In all likelihood, the first thing people will judge is any behavior that doesn't correspond with the individual's apparent gender. So, if men act "feminine" or women act "masculine," they are likely to be assumed to be gay. Indeed, gay men and lesbians may incorporate some aspects of opposite-gender behavior in order to be noticed by other gay men and lesbians. But the adoption of these behaviors doesn't necessarily mean that the individual would rather *be* the opposite gender. Most lesbians and gays are happy being women or men; they are simply emotionally and sexually attracted to members of the same gender.

Media portrayals of lesbians and gays have helped both to perpetuate stereotypes and, more recently, to promote tolerance and acceptance. According to Fejes and Petrich (1993), who reviewed a large number of studies on how lesbians and gays had been portrayed in films, on television, and in the news, gay characters in entertainment were often cast as farcical, weak, or menacing.

Smyth (2004), in a more recent study of gay male portrayals in newsmagazine stories, identified four classic stereotypes of gay men: (1) gay males are effeminate, (2) gay males are "sick" or mentally ill, (3) gay males are sexual predators, and (4) gay males are "violent, libido-driven monsters." Smyth studied stories that appeared in *Time* and *Newsweek* between 1946 and 2002, and he found that there were three distinct periods reflecting differences in how these periodicals covered gays. From 1946 to 1969, the newsmagazines portrayed gay men almost exclusively from a dark point of view, as sexually deviant, predatory, and sick. From 1969, following the Stonewall Riots, to 1980, coverage focused mostly on the emerging Gay Liberation movement, and reactions to that movement, mostly from religious or quasi-religious groups. Although the articles themselves often focused on an emerging gay male identity and political agenda, many of the articles still mentioned the old stereotypes. It was also during this period that the American Psychiatric Association removed homosexuality from its list of mental illnesses. From 1980 to 2002, the number of articles about gays surged dramatically. Portrayals of gay men as effeminate dropped sharply, though the newsmagazines were still interested in gay serial killers and unusual sexual practices. The prevalence of HIV and AIDS among gay men helped to perpetuate the "sick" stereotype, and coverage of the spread of AIDS perpetuated the stereotype of the sexual predator.

Even though these stereotypes have been dissipating in media coverage, they persist in many people's thinking. And, like all stereotypes, they have some basis in fact. There are certainly gay men who are effeminate, sick, predatory, or prone to sex-related criminal acts, but to characterize all or even most gay men as having one or more of these qualities would miss the mark completely. Some scholars would characterize these stereotypes as being products of *heterosexism;* that is, they arise from an assumption that behavior of heterosexual individuals is "normal" and behavior of homosexual individuals is "deviant," as opposed to merely "different." In terms of sheer numbers, there are probably more heterosexual men than gay men who are effeminate, sick, predatory, or prone to sex-related criminal acts, because same-sex orientation is statistically still very much the exception (independent estimates range anywhere from 2–5% of the population, though lesbian and gay activists claim that these estimates are low because people are motivated to hide their sexual orientation—these activists like to use a 10% figure).

One way that many people seem to have of letting go of their stereotypes is to meet someone who doesn't fit them. A survey of San Diegans conducted during the time when Massachusetts started to marry lesbian and gay couples legally found that respondents who claimed to know at least one lesbian or gay person held more favorable attitudes toward lesbians and gays generally than did those who claimed to know no lesbians or gays. Income seemed to be a factor in associating with known lesbians and gays, as the largest number of people who said they knew no gay individuals were those who made under $20,000 annually. And the more you know, the better. People with the most favorable attitudes knew the largest number of gay people, and vice versa. Other factors also influenced people's attitudes. Those with liberal political ideologies held the most favorable attitudes, though even those describing themselves as very conservative split about evenly in feeling positively and negatively about gay people generally. Those who were not regular churchgoers also held more favorable attitudes, though churchgoers, like conservatives, split about evenly in their attitudes. Women were more likely to hold favorable attitudes than men, and younger people's attitudes were far more favorable than those of older people. Overall, in this poll, 60% of respondents said that they viewed lesbians and gays favorably, 26% viewed these groups unfavorably, and 14% were unsure how they felt ("Poll Analysis," 2004). A study of viewers of the television show *Will and Grace,* which features gay characters in leading roles, found that they held more positive attitudes toward lesbians and gays than did people who did not watch the show (Schiappa, Gregg, & Hewes, 2003). Although one might expect that people seek out television programming that fits with their attitudes, positive attitudes toward lesbians and gays persisted even among those viewers who did not claim to have lesbian or gay friends.

Even though these numbers indicate that attitudes are changing, there is still danger associated with being openly lesbian or gay. This danger seems to affect people under 21 to the greatest degree. In a study published in the *American Journal of Public Health,* researchers reported on a survey of 1,248 gay and bisexual men aged 18–27 who lived in Austin, Texas, Albuquerque, New Mexico, or Phoenix, Arizona. Overall, 5% of those surveyed reported that they had been the victims of anti-gay violence, and 11% indicated that they had been discriminated against because they were gay. But of those under 21, the numbers jumped to 10% having experienced anti-gay violence, and half reported that they had been discriminated against because they were gay (Huebner, Rebchook, & Kegeles, 2004).

These data bring us back to the main point of this section—that being openly lesbian or gay is a political statement. When the odds are only 60–40 that others will have a favorable attitude toward you as a lesbian or gay man, and when the odds are even greater that your openness at a young age may result in negative, even violent, consequences, it's no wonder that many nonheterosexual individuals keep that information to themselves. They may date members of the opposite sex and may also marry and have families. Men especially, however, will often seek anonymous same-sex encounters outside of marriage, because the means for having such encounters are readily (though not always legally) available. These men may deny that they have any same-sex attraction and claim that these encounters are necessary for a variety of reasons (e.g., "I don't get enough sex at home," "My wife won't do things sexually for me that other men will do," "I get a thrill out of anonymous encounters"). Public health workers call these individuals MSMs (Men who have Sex with Men). People in the African American community call this practice "dl," or being "on the down low." This group, along with intravenous drug users, has the highest risk for contracting HIV/AIDS.

So, despite the potential for negative consequences, it is healthier for people to be open about their same-sex attraction. But getting to that point is not always easy. D'Augelli (1994) theorized that there are what he called "six interactive stages that non-heterosexual" individuals pass through as they develop an identity:

1. Recognizing that one's attractions and feelings are not heterosexual, as well as telling others that one is not heterosexual.
2. Summarizing self-concepts, emotions, and desires into a personal identity as gay/lesbian/bisexual.
3. Developing a nonheterosexual social identity.

4. Disclosing one's identity to parents and redefining familial relationships afterward.
5. Developing capabilities to have intimate gay/lesbian/bisexual relationships.
6. Becoming a member of a gay/lesbian/bisexual community.

It is possible that these stages can be passed through quickly, but it is equally as likely that these stages will progress slowly, if at all. Each stage requires some degree of change in how one talks, and each stage requires the ability to share with others what heretofore one considered to be private information. As people search for new ways of talking and for what they might consider to be the "right words" to say, they look to the examples of others. This process of learning to communicate differently helps lesbian and gay individuals assimilate into the lesbian/gay/bisexual community.

The fact that disclosure of information about one's sexuality may evoke responses ranging from "That's wonderful" to spews of hateful words makes such disclosure a political one. "Political" communication, in this case, is constituted by messages that have the potential for promoting controversy. "Political" also means that such a disclosure tends to carry with it an assumption that the speaker holds a set of attitudes and beliefs that may be at odds with those of the listener. Such assumptions may not be correct. For example, lesbians and gays may be seen as antagonistic to organized religion, but many consider themselves to be quite devout. Lesbians and gays may also be seen as holding liberal political views, but their views on most matters may be quite conservative.

D'Augelli's stages of identity formation are called "interactive" because they rely on communication with others to occur. As same-sex attraction is controversial information, lesbians and gays beginning on D'Augelli's stages need to find strategies for disclosing this information. These initial disclosures will usually be tentative and told to a confidant, often a trusted friend or adult who is not a parent (e.g., a teacher, counselor, adult neighbor, clergyperson, aunt or uncle). The initial messages may not be in the form "I am lesbian," but may be more general statements, such as "I'm having trouble with starting to date. My friends are dating, but I'm not," or even a statement such as "I'm not sure that people like me." The realization that one is attracted to members of the same sex may be present, but the individual may be choosing to hide that information behind what is often legitimate confusion. Depending on the response, individuals may finally say that they think they are more attracted to members of the same sex than to members of the opposite sex, or they may label themselves lesbian, gay, or bisexual. In many cases, the first formulation of sexual identity may be "I'm bisexual," because the speaker may believe that this statement is more socially acceptable than "I'm gay."

Once some form of admission that "I am different" is made, the gay or lesbian person will begin to look for information that will help him or her figure out what is going on. Sometimes this information search is confined to books, magazines, or informational Web sites. Other times the information may come from pornography or erotica or from seeking out places where gays or lesbians gather. Often these places will be where anonymous sex might be had. Males in particular will try to experiment with gay sex to see if they find it to be exciting. The fact that sex in public places is usually against the law may add to the thrill of the experience. In many cases, younger gay men will become involved with men older than they are in these environments. These older men (they may be as little as five or ten years older) will sometimes serve as role models as well as sex partners. Sometimes, however, the older men will only be interested in having sex with a younger partner.

As the lesbian or gay individual has contact with other lesbians and gays and compares her- or himself favorably to those other individuals, the idea that "I am different" should eventually become "I am gay." At that point, the dilemma becomes whether and how to let others know of one's sexual identity.

The process of "coming out of the closet" is actually described by all of D'Augelli's stages, taken collectively. The moments when lesbian or gay individuals actually tell the people closest to them of their sexual identity should ideally be (1) when the individual is ready and prepared to make the disclosure, and (2) when the family members are ready to hear what their child or sibling has to say. In many cases, however, these scenes are not nearly so clean and well planned. Parents may learn about their child's sexuality by catching them with same-sex pornography, by reading their diaries, or by discovering them with a same-sex partner. Or initial sexual experimentation may lead to trouble with the law or delinquency. Or the son or daughter may burst out with the information at an unplanned moment.

Reactions to this information will be varied. The ideal reaction, from the lesbian or gay person's point of view, is described on the Web site of the support organization Parents and Friends of Lesbians and Gays (PFLAG):

> Some people are able to take the news in stride. But many of us went through something similar to a grieving process with all the accompanying shock, denial, anger, guilt and sense of loss. So if those are the feelings with which you're dealing, they're understandable given our society's attitudes towards gays, lesbians and bisexuals.
>
> Don't condemn yourself for the emotions you feel. But, since you love your GLBT [gay, lesbian, bisexual, transgendered] friend or relative, you owe it to him or her—and to yourself—to move toward acceptance, understanding and support.
>
> While it may feel as if you have lost someone, you haven't. Your loved one is the same person he or she was yesterday. The only thing you have lost is your own image of that person and the understanding you thought you had. That loss can be very difficult, but that image can, happily, be replaced with a new and clearer understanding of your loved one. (http://www.pflag.org/support/family.html)

Still, there are many families in which parents and siblings do not process this news in nearly as supportive a manner. Some family members will immediately cut off contact with the lesbian or gay member. Some families will try to persuade the lesbian or gay person that "this is a phase" or that "you can change." In the larger community, coming out as lesbian or gay is grounds for excommunication in some religious denominations, and lesbian or gay individuals who work for religious organizations may well find themselves out of a job after their same-sex attraction becomes known. Disclosure of same-sex attraction is grounds for dismissal from the U.S. Armed Forces.

No wonder that individuals who are questioning their sexuality are reluctant to talk to others about it until they are sure of a lesbian or gay identity. And no wonder that some people stay in the closet for years, as I did. Many lesbian and gay individuals feel tensions in their relationships with family, work, and social and religious institutions. Lesbians and gays may resolve these tensions in a variety of ways. They may decide to create alternative support institutions, such as "families of choice," as opposed to "families of origin." They may strive to achieve at work or in an arena where they can gain recognition. They have formed alternative social and religious structures. They have also become politically active, seeking to root out and eliminate discrimination wherever they find it. In doing so, these groups may employ tactics ranging from traditional lobbying to attention-grabbing demonstrations such as same-sex "kiss-ins."

It is usually difficult for a lesbian or gay person to progress to D'Augelli's fifth stage, learning how to develop intimate same-sex relationships, without having completed at least some of the fourth stage, allowing the people who matter to them to know them as sexual beings. Intimacy, by its very nature, demands a degree of honesty that is usually suppressed by the need to hide a major portion of oneself. In addition, fear of being discovered, or fear of what others will think, or the very real fear of losing one's job can keep people in hiding and afraid of their own sexuality. But sometimes, finding another person to trust and love can help an individual to be more open about same-sex attraction. Of course, intimate relationships can and do happen between people who can't be open with others. Sometimes these relationships are described to others as "roommates" or "friends," which is how a neighbor of mine described his living arrangement with his partner of 17 years when I first met him. As soon as he realized that I was sympathetic to his situation, however, he began talking to me in much more open terms. The ability to be openly a part of an intimate relationship in the community at large is a test of not only how accepting the person has become of her or his own sexuality but how interactions with the community can create a climate in which the couple are accepted and included by those around them.

D'Augelli's final stage entails becoming a part of a lesbian/gay/bisexual community. This stage, too, does not necessarily wait for the other stages to finish, but can occur even while completing the earliest stages of the process. High school gay–straight alliance clubs can provide a supportive place to be different in an environment that puts a high premium on conformity. Universities often provide not only a means for lesbians and gays to gather but also private groups, typically run by a counseling center, where questioning students can explore their sexuality. Lesbian and gay community centers also provide "coming out" workshops and other social services designed to assist people in finding a community and feeling as though they belong there.

Having a community typically involves having a concentration of like-minded people with whom to interact on a daily basis. The 2000 U.S. Census was the first to allow individuals to identify themselves as same-sex couples, and Gates and Ost (2004) have compiled the Census data to learn about lesbian and gay living patterns. They found that gay male and lesbian female couples tend to live on the East or West Coast of the United States, though not necessarily in the same locales. The ten most popular spots for gay male couples to live were San Francisco, CA; Fort Lauderdale, FL; Santa Rosa, CA; Seattle–Bellevue–Everett, WA; New York, NY; Jersey City, NJ; Los Angeles–Long Beach, CA; Santa Fe, NM; Oakland, CA; and Miami, FL. Gay male couples tended to live in places that had higher concentrations of other gay couples, and they tended to live in more urban areas. For lesbian female couples, the most popular places were often more rural in character: Santa Rosa, CA; Santa Cruz–Watsonville, CA; Santa Fe, NM; San Francisco, CA; Oakland, CA; Burlington, VT; Portland, ME; Springfield, MA; Corvallis, OR; and Madison, WI. Gates and Ost also reported that 99% of U.S. counties had at least one same-sex couple living there, giving credence to activists' cries that "We are everywhere!"

Once in a community, gays and lesbians will often become involved in social organizations, such as square dancing or choral singing, business and networking groups such as a lesbian and gay Chamber of Commerce, and causes that benefit the community as a whole. Because lesbian and gay communities are controversial, however, these organizations will almost assuredly have political ramifications, if not be overtly political. Over time, gay men have been involved in prevention of HIV/AIDS transmission and in raising funds for research on this disease, which began in the gay community but now affects far more heterosexual people worldwide. Lesbians have been actively involved in raising awareness about breast cancer and in funding breast cancer research. Both groups have campaigned against laws that allow discrimination in hiring and housing or that criminalize private and consensual sexual practices commonly engaged in by lesbian and gay couples. These campaigns culminated in the U.S. Supreme Court's 2003 decision in *Lawrence v. Texas*, in which Justice Anthony Kennedy, writing for the Court majority, declared that two gay men could engage in consensual sexual activity in the privacy of one's home and "still retain their dignity as free persons." Most recently, the lesbian and gay community has been galvanized by a drive to legalize marriage for same-sex couples. This drive has created a fair amount of national debate, as well as spawning legal attempts to restrict the term "marriage" to recognizing relationships between opposite-sex couples. But the *New York Times'* decision to print announcements of the unions of same-sex couples in its wedding announcements pages did much to increase the social acceptability of those relationships.

DEALING WITH THE TENSIONS OF BEING OPEN ABOUT SEXUALITY

In U.S. culture, gays and lesbians needed to remain hidden yet visible for so long that they developed ways of signaling their sexual orientation to like-minded people that would remain oblique to society as a whole. Or they choose to be so flamboyant that their sexuality could not be ignored.

The author and playwright Oscar Wilde proved to be a masterful practitioner of hiding a gay subtext in his stories and plays, work that was acclaimed by mainstream critics and audiences alike. For example, in his novella *The Picture of Dorian Gray,* Wilde concocted a tale about a man who finds the secret to staying eternally beautiful and youthful. The secret is a portrait of himself that he has hidden in his attic. The portrait, not the man, is the one that ages. Ultimately, the story ends in horror and the man receives his comeuppance, but its central fantasy appealed to the soul of every gay man who read it. Wilde himself was married to a woman but had many dalliances with young men, including at least one long-term lover. Tried in court for being a homosexual, which was, at the time, against the law, Wilde defending himself by claiming that he merely enjoyed the company and energy of younger men. Wilde was convicted and jailed, however, and the experience left him sick and defeated, unable to produce the kind of tales that had once made him the toast of London.

Wilde has been credited as being the first practitioner of "camp." Camp has evolved into a central concept in understanding gay culture. In her famous 1964 essay "Notes on 'Camp,'" critic Susan Sontag defined camp as a "sensibility," as opposed to an idea or a thing. Sensibilities, according to Sontag, are difficult to describe, but she argued that camp is a sensibility that requires aesthetic appreciation, because it is a style or taste. Because styles and tastes change frequently, however, one must be nimble and not given to set ways of seeing the world. Indeed, camp often turns the world on its ear, relying on exaggeration and a tendency to see double meaning in words and acts. Camp is theatrical, an attempt to be and do extraordinary things. Camp is "fabulous" (Sontag, 1964).

In a later essay, Meyer (1994) extended Sontag's analysis to argue that camp encompasses how lesbians and gays perform their lives in front of others. Camp is the embodiment of how gay individuals manage the tensions of being open about their sexuality in a society that brands them as deviant. Rather than hide one's difference, camp helps the gay or lesbian person to find an alternative way of being in the world, a "queer" reality that doesn't have to rely on the norms of mainstream society—a reality that, in fact, often mocks those norms.

A good example of this alternate reality is the concept of drag. Drag not only bends the idea of gender by allowing men to dress up as women and women as men, but it requires that the "drag queen" or "drag king" play with the character in some way. Puns are a commonly used form of verbal play. For example, "Anita Mann" has undoubtedly been used more than once as a drag name.

Perhaps a good way of explaining drag would be to compare it to female impersonation. Let's say that both a drag queen and a female impersonator are portraying actress Carol Channing. The female impersonator will attempt to look and sound as much like Carol Channing as possible, to create the illusion of Carol Channing as a tribute to her talent. The drag queen, on the other hand, will portray an exaggerated version of Carol Channing, playing with her persona to distort it in humorous or ironic ways.

Drag also allows an individual to be "someone else," at least for a while. One acquaintance of mine confided to me, "When I go to a bar in drag, all of the cute boys want to talk to me. I have a quick mouth, and they love my comebacks. But out of drag, I'm a large, older man, and if I went into the same bar as that person, those boys wouldn't have anything to do with me. In drag, I'm fun and safe, but out of drag I'm someone to be avoided."

IT'S ABOUT SEX BUT NOT ONLY ABOUT SEX

Of course, the point of same-sex attraction is that gays and lesbians want to find someone of the same gender with whom to be physically, emotionally, and spiritually intimate. Recall, however, that although D'Augelli's (1994) stages of developing a nonheterosexual identity include the capacity to form and maintain intimate same-sex relationships, D'Augelli places this capacity down his list, after coming out to family and friends. Clearly, a lot of developing a lesbian and gay identity involves exploring one's same-sex attraction and learning to flirt with and meet people who might be candidates for intimate relationships. And many, if not most, lesbians and gays do not wait until they have found their "soul mate" before having sex. Gay men often talk about finding Mr. Right, as opposed to finding Mr. Right-Away. As you might imagine, the latter is much easier to locate.

Meeting other lesbian and gay people is not an easy task, however. If one is in a "safe" space, where everyone there is gay or accepting of same-sex attraction, then conversing openly is not a problem. Bars have traditionally filled this role, though to a greater extent for men than for women; San Diego, for example, supported more than 20 gay bars but only 2 lesbian bars at the time this essay was written. Coffeehouses and some community-based restaurants have also emerged as bar alternatives, especially for gay and lesbian youth who are not of legal drinking age, and for those who may want a less pressured atmosphere. Social and volunteer organizations also serve as safe spaces for lesbians and gays to meet.

Meeting someone outside of these spaces can be tricky, especially if one isn't sure that the other person shares one's same-sex attraction. Most lesbians and gay males develop some sense of who around them might also be lesbian or gay (this intuitive ability is referred to as "gay-dar"). In public places, contact is usually established by exchanging gazes, typically more than once. Holding another's gaze is generally interpreted as a sign that the other person might be interested. A conversation will often ensue, and an early task in that conversation will be to say something socially acceptable but that the other person can identify as a gay reference. Leap (1996), who has studied how gay men use English, provides an example of a conversation between a clothing sales clerk and a customer:

C: What are you asking for these? [*Points to one set of gray sweatshirts*]

S: Oh, I'm afraid they're not on sale today. But that colored shirt would look nice on you. [*Points to a pile of lavender sweatshirts, which are on sale*]

C: Yeah, I know. I own a few of them already. [*Grins*]

S: [*Grins back, no verbal comment*] (1996, p. 13)

Undoubtedly, both men walked away from this conversation with the knowledge that they were both gay. They understood that fact by (a) the reference to "lavender," a color generally associated with being gay; (b) the exaggerated response to the suggestion that the lavender shirt would look good on the customer; and (c) the fact that both men had exchanged mutual glances prior to beginning the conversation and that both grinned at the end of it. The conversational space was thus "safe," though still public, and if the two had been interested in pursuing each other's company further, they would have exchanged contact information.

The previous example involved two men who might have been interested in each other as potential friends or potential dates ("Mr. Right"). When gay men are looking for sex partners ("Mr. Right-Away"), however, they will tend to use mostly nonverbal signals to do so. What gay men call "cruising" typically starts with making eye contact with someone as the two pass each other. If one is interested, that person will typically slow down and look back. If the other person also looks back, one person may begin to follow the other person. The two might stop and begin a conversation, or they might silently look for a place to have sex. Generally, when men engage in an anonymous sexual encounter, the less they know about the other person the better. Of course, sex in public places is, for the most part, against the law, so some men cruise for sex and then take their "trick" to a private space. There is always some level of danger associated with anonymous sex, and for some men that level of danger may be a part of the reason that cruising is exciting. Part of the reason that HIV/AIDS was transmitted so quickly between gay men in the 1980s was that cruising did not have to be so carefully hidden and peer pressure to have a lot of anonymous sex was strong. One of the principal obstacles that had to be overcome in safer-sex campaigns within the gay community was to encourage gay men to avoid risky behaviors in an environment in which talking was discouraged. Early HIV prevention campaigns focused on talking to your partner about your HIV status, which was, and still is, a good idea for couples who were dating or in a relationship. The solution seemed to be to teach gay men to regard every sex partner as being HIV-positive until proven otherwise.

Most lesbians and gay men put a high premium on dating and forming intimate relationships, however. In this way, they are quite a bit like the rest of the populace, and their courtship communication patterns in many ways resemble those of their heterosexual counterparts in similar age groups. Lesbian and gay couples do have unique issues to negotiate on their way to achieving intimacy at all of the physical, emotional, and spiritual levels, however. For one thing, the issue of "who does what" in the relationship has to be worked out bit by bit. In heterosexual relationships, societal expectations for the roles that men and women play can either be followed or they can be reversed by the couple's decision. In lesbian and gay relationships, couples generally reject the notion that one of them plays the "man" and the other plays the "woman." So, each physical or emotional task has to be worked out, either consciously or by one person's taking on that task and having it become part of who that person is in the relationship. Many lesbians and gay men also reject that their relationships should have to conform to the normative expectations of the heterosexual community. These issues often revolve around setting rules for how much physical, emotional, or spiritual attraction is allowed to each member of the couple outside of the relationship. This work is hard, and if it becomes too hard or leads to major conflict before the couple has committed to each other, there will be a tendency to break off the relationship rather than to work through the conflicts.

The fact that same-sex couples have no legal standing in most geographical locations also means that couples either have to keep their finances and other matters separate, or they have to draft legal documents spelling out their agreements, knowing that the validity of those documents may be challenged successfully, perhaps by members of an individual's family, at some future date. Although some lesbians and gay men may reject the idea of "marriage" as a religious institution, the legal institution of "marriage" provides a shortcut for allocating benefits and privileges to one's partner that a legal contract is hard-pressed to provide. And the emotional and ceremonial institution of "marriage" as a public commitment of two people to each other would surely help couples to cement their partnerships. No wonder so many lesbians and gays have been energized to work for ways of providing legal marriage for same-sex couples.

SOME CLOSING THOUGHTS

In writing this essay, the readers I was keeping in mind were traditionally aged university sophomores and juniors. So, I have tried to select and emphasize material that I thought might be most relevant to both the intellectual and emotional journeys of 19- or 20-year-olds. Clearly, not every second- or third-year college student is 19 or 20 years old, and if you fall into a different category, my examples may not fit where you are in your life so well.

I have also tried to emphasize material that might be common to both lesbians and gay men. Because I am a gay man, doing so probably means that I have shorted lesbians in important ways. So, if you'd like to read more about lesbians in particular, I refer you to several works that I have listed in the references (Allen, 1990; Coyle & Kitzinger, 2002; Dunne, 1997; Jay, 1995; Stein, 1997).

I have also ignored almost completely the "BT" part of the LGBT formulation—bisexuals and transgendered. Both of these groups are more hidden, even within the gay community. I have heard gay men say that bisexual men are actually gay men in denial and that men who call themselves bisexual are really interested in sex and nothing more. I have heard lesbians become angry when a woman who was with another woman starts dating a man instead. But I've also heard that bisexuals are different from lesbians and gay men, as well as claims that most people are probably at least somewhat bisexual (Woody Allen once famously remarked that "bisexuality immediately doubles your chances of having a date on Saturday night"). I also wrote earlier that exhibiting the behavior of the other gender doesn't necessarily identify one as a lesbian woman or gay man, and I commented that many, if not most, of us were quite happy being men or women. Transgendered individuals, on the other hand, do sense that they ought to be the opposite gender from what they are, physically. Much of the research on transgendered individuals is new, so checking an advocacy Web site, such as that of the National Transgender Advocacy Coalition (http://www.ntac.org/research/), should provide up-to-date information on this topic.

Finally, I have avoided writing about many of the political issues about which many lesbians and gay men care deeply, as well as about several of the tensions that exist within the gay community. These tensions include poverty and homelessness among lesbians and gays, racism and sexism among gay men and lesbian women, concerns about how to foster healthy communication among lesbians and gay men of different ages (see, for example, Hajek & Giles, 2002), and worries that lesbian and gay culture is becoming too mainstream, resulting in the possible loss of the community's identity (Hattersley, 2004; McNamara, 2004).

Despite these shortcomings, I hope that I have provided you with some insight about communication among gay men and lesbians and how that communication manifests itself in the United States as a "culture." It used to be said that the members of the lesbian and gay community were "hiding in plain sight." Now that so many of us are no longer hiding, I hope that this information will help you to understand the ways in which members of this community may be different and the ways we are the same.

References

Allen, J., Ed. (1990). *Lesbian philosophies and cultures*. Albany: State University of New York Press.

Coyle, A., & Kitzinger, C. (Eds.). (2002). *Lesbian and gay psychology: New perspectives*. Oxford: Blackwell.

D'Augelli, A. R. (1994). Identity development and sexual orientation: Toward a model of lesbian, gay, and bisexual development. In E. J. Trickett, R. J. Watts, & D. Birmans (Eds.), *Human diversity: Perspectives on people in context* (pp. 312–333). New York: Oxford University Press.

Dunne, G. A. (1997). *Lesbian lifestyles: Women's work and the politics of sexuality*. Toronto: University of Toronto Press.

Fejes, F., & Petrich, K. (1993). Invisibility, homophobia and heterosexism: Lesbians, gays and the media. *Critical Studies in Mass Communication, 10,* 395–422.

Gates, G. J., & Ost, J. (2004). *The gay and lesbian atlas*. Washington, DC: Urban Institute Press.

Hajek, C., & Giles, H. (2002). The old man out: An intergroup analysis of intergenerational communication among gay men. *Journal of Communication, 30,* 698–714.

Hattersley, M. (2004, January–February). Will success spoil gay culture? *Gay and Lesbian Review Worldwide, 11,* 33–34.

Huebner, D. M., Rebchook, G. M., & Kegeles, S. M. (2004). Experiences of harassment, discrimination, and physical violence among young gay and bisexual men. *American Journal of Public Health, 94*(7), 1200–1203.

Jay, K., Ed. (1995). *Dyke life: A celebration of the lesbian experience*. New York: Basic Books.

Leap, W. L. (1996). *Word's out: Gay men's English*. Minneapolis: University of Minnesota Press.

McNamara, M. (2004, April 25). When gay lost its outré. *Los Angeles Times*. Online at http://www.latimes.com/features/lifestyle/la-ca-mcnamara25apr25,1,6298374.story

Meyer, M., Ed. (1994). *The politics and poetics of camp*. London: Routledge.

Monette, P. (1992). *Becoming a man: Half a life story*. New York: Harcourt Brace Jovanovich.

Poll analysis. (2004). Online at http://www.kpbs.org/Other/DynPage.php?id=1108.

Schiappa, E., Gregg, P., & Hewes, D. (2003, November). *Can one TV show make a difference? Will & Grace and the parasocial contact hypothesis*. Paper presented to the National Communication Association, Miami Beach, FL.

Smyth, M. (2004, May). *(Mis-)Shaping gay, lesbian and bisexual representation in popular discourse: Historical analyses*. Paper presented to the International Communication Association, New Orleans.

Sontag, S. (1964, Autumn). On "camp." *Partisan Review, 30.*

Stein, A. (1997). *Sex and sensibility: Stories of a lesbian generation*. Berkeley: University of California Press.

Trebay, G. (2004, June 27). The secret power of lesbian style. *New York Times*, sect. 9, p. 1.

Concepts and Questions

1. Why would some readers be eager to read Eadie's article while others would prefer to avoid it?
2. How does Eadie's personal history affect your attitudes toward the lesbian and gay culture?
3. How does revealing one's lesbian or gay sexuality become a political statement? What specific behaviors might be interpreted as a political statement?
4. How does dressing normally associated with the lesbian and gay lifestyle influence straight fashions?
5. How do media portrayals of lesbians and gays perpetuate stereotypes? And how do the media foster positive images toward gays and lesbians?
6. What are the six interactive stages through which nonheterosexual individuals pass as they develop their identity?
7. How does Eadie describe the process by which gays and lesbians deal with the tensions associated with being open about sexuality?
8. What does Eadie mean when he refers to being in a "safe" space when meeting other lesbian and gay people?
9. What are some of the unique communication patterns Eadie has discussed? How do these forms of communicating serve the lesbian and gay culture?

5 Intercultural Messages: Verbal and Nonverbal Communication

The sum of human wisdom is not contained in any one language, for not a single language is capable of expressing all forms and degrees of human comprehension.

EZRA POUND

As a member of the human species, one of your distinguishing features is your ability to use language (i.e., to receive, store, retrieve, manipulate, and generate linguistic symbols). All 6.5 billion plus of you acknowledge the past, take part in the present, and prepare for the future. By simply making certain sounds, marks on paper, and movements, you can relate to and interact with others. Hence, at first blush, verbal and nonverbal language appears rather simple. Yet, as you know from personal experience, accurately sharing your ideas and feelings is not a simple matter. In short, communication is a complex activity. The series of readings in this chapter seeks to explain some of those complexities—especially as they apply to culture.

This chapter contends that a culture's use of verbal and nonverbal symbols involves much more than sounds and meanings. It also involves forms of reasoning, how discourse is carried out, specialized linguistic devices such as analogies and idioms, the use of time and space, unique ways of moving, and behaviors that display emotions. Hence, understanding the verbal and nonverbal language of any culture means viewing language from this larger perspective. This eclectic outlook toward language will help you understand the interaction patterns of cultures and co-cultures that are different from your own.

All of the selections in this chapter are predicated on the following truism: *Verbal and nonverbal meanings are learned and reside within people*. These meaning-evoking symbols consist of both verbal and nonverbal behaviors. Further, for each culture, there is a very elaborate set of symbols to which people within that culture have learned to attach meaning. Although we consider these forms of symbolic interaction separately for convenience, we hasten to point out their interrelatedness. As nonverbal behavior accompanies verbal behavior, it becomes an integral part of the total symbolic interaction. Verbal messages often rely on their nonverbal accompaniment for cues that aid the receiver in decoding the verbal symbols. Nonverbal behaviors not only serve to amplify and clarify verbal messages but can also serve as forms of symbolic interaction without verbal counterparts.

When you communicate verbally or nonverbally with other members of your own culture, you do so with seeming ease. Your experiential backgrounds are similar enough that you share basically the same meanings for most of the words and actions used in everyday communication. But even within your culture, you sometimes disagree about the meanings of many of the verbal and nonverbal symbols being used. As words and actions move further from the reality of sensory data and become more abstract, there is far less agreement about appropriate meanings. In the use of words, for example, what do highly abstract words such as *love, freedom, equality, democracy, terrorism,* and *civil rights* mean to you? Do they mean the same things to everyone? If you are in doubt, ask some friends; take a poll. You will surely find that people have different notions of these concepts and consequently different meanings for these words. Their experiences have been different, and they hold different beliefs, attitudes, values, concepts, and expectations. Yet all, or perhaps most, of these people are from the same culture. Their backgrounds, experiences, and concepts of the universe are quite uniform. When cultural diversity is added to the process of decoding words, much larger differences in meanings and usage are found. A very simple yet vivid example can be seen in the unadorned word *dog.* To Americans, the word represents a furry, friendly, domesticated pet—for some, even a member of the family. Yet for many Muslims the meaning is very different. Dogs are perceived as unclean, and calling someone a dog is often used as a curse word.

What is true of the often ambiguous nature of words can also be seen in our use of nonverbal actions. Think for a moment of all the different interpretations that can be attached to touch, gaze, attire, movement, space, and the like when you send and receive messages. It is indeed true to say that you communicate not only with your words but also with your actions. Successful intercultural communication therefore requires that you recognize and understand culture's influence on both verbal and nonverbal interaction.

Having briefly highlighted some of the important characteristics of verbal language, let us pause and do the same for nonverbal symbols. Nonverbal behavior is largely unconscious. You use nonverbal symbols spontaneously, without thinking about what posture, what gesture, or what interpersonal distance is appropriate to the situation. Nonverbal behavior is critically important in intercultural communication because, as with other aspects of the communication process, these behaviors reflect cultural diversity. In other words, culture largely determines which posture, which gesture, or which interpersonal distance is appropriate in a host of social situations.

In studying nonverbal communication, we need to keep in mind two perspectives. First, culture tends to determine the specific nonverbal behaviors that represent specific thoughts, feelings, or states of the communicator. Thus, what might be a sign of greeting in one culture might very well be an obscene gesture in another. Or what is considered a symbol of affirmation in one culture could be meaningless or even signify negation in another. Second, culture determines when it is appropriate to display or communicate various thoughts, feelings, or internal states; this is particularly evident in the display of emotions. Although there seems to be little cross-cultural difference in the nonverbal behaviors that represent emotional states, there can be significant cultural differences in the specification of which emotions may be displayed, the degree to which they may be displayed, who may display them, and when or where they may be displayed.

To this point we have stressed the idea that the symbols you use, be they verbal or nonverbal, are directly tied your culture. The first essay, "The Nexus of Language, Communication, and Culture" by Mary Fong, introduces you to this fundamental idea. Fong begins with a brief review of the Sapir–Whorf hypothesis, which proposed linguistic relativity and was one of the first modern observations of the relationship between language and culture. She then traces later developments in this area that have led to ethnographic research approaches to the study of language and culture. Applying these techniques in two studies of Chinese language use, Fong shows not only the ways in which ethnographic approaches are employed, but also the rich linguistic practices of the Chinese.

Our second essay, by Helen Kelly-Holmes, not only highlights the link between language and culture, it also discusses how language is a vehicle for talking about culture. Kelly-Homes believes that although there is no such "thing as a completely homogenous linguistic group," specific languages nevertheless give people a shared identity. In her essay, "German Language: Whose Language, Whose Culture?", Kelly-Holmes begins by reminding you that meanings are found not in words, but in the meanings that cultures attach to them. And while her essay "attempts to estimate the role of the German language in contemporary culture," the basic elements of her chapter, such as assigning meaning, cultural identity, the role of accents and dialects, the position of gender, and the Anglicizing of German (making German words out of English words) apply to nearly all cultures.

The essay further describes how cultural differences in the perception and use of language can help you understand gender distinctions within the German culture. For example, Kelly-Holmes points out that because of the way Germans employ masculine and feminine nouns, the German language often excludes women.

With the growth and impact of global economics and the widespread increase in worldwide technology, cultures are finding it increasingly difficult to maintain the purity of their languages. Hence, throughout the world, pride in one's language is being tested as people from Cairo to Hong Kong are finding their languages peppered with Anglicisms. Understanding how Germans, and indeed other cultures, deal with verbal ethnocentrism can offer you valuable insights into the problems associated with this new phenomenon.

Conflict in the Middle East between Israeli Jews and Palestinians has a long and bloody history. Antecedents of today's conflicts extend over thousands of years. Traditional discord notwithstanding, there might be ways in which the negative stereotypes, mutual delimitation, and severe miscommunication that highlight today's relationships could be managed through an understanding of transformative dialogues. In their essay "Dialogue and Cultural Communication Codes Between Israeli Jews and Palestinians," Donald G. Ellis and Ifat Maoz analyze cultural communication codes in order to establish dialogue between the opposing sides.

Ellis and Maoz posit that the Israeli-Jewish and Arab cultures have emerged from the special circumstances of their history, resulting in different norms of communication. These different histories are manifest in diverse speech codes that reflect nearly opposite cultural differences. Ellis and Maoz suggest that Arab language employs speech codes that seek to "accommodate" or "go along with," which orients speakers toward harmonious relationships. On the other hand, they assert that the Israeli-Jewish speech code is direct, pragmatic, assertive, explicit, and clear. These speech code differences are essentially the opposite of one another and, according to Ellis and Maoz, are partially responsible for the failure of dialogue to resolve the conflict surrounding the two cultures. The authors believe that by studying speech codes, you can better understand the linguistic bases of cultural conflict and be better prepared to help mediate that conflict.

One of the major premises of this chapter is the idea that culture affects nearly every aspect of how people use language. Our next selection maintains that the reach of culture even affects public speaking. That is to say, the common components of public speaking, such as organization, evidence, credibility, and argumentation, have a culture dimension attached to them. In "Public Speaking Patterns in Kenya," Ann Neville Miller is concerned with how the culture in the East African nation of Kenya perceives and uses public speaking. Miller begins with a brief summary of the major cultural dimensions advanced by Geert Hofstede (individualism–collectivism, power distance) and Edward T. Hall (monochromic and polychromic time, high- and low-context communication). With these two theoretical perspectives as a backdrop, she then moves to a comparison of U.S. and Kenyan public speaking patterns as they apply to (1) speaking purposes, (2) supporting material, (3) credibility, and (4) speech structure.

In the United States, most public speaking situations call for an informative or persuasive speech. Such is not the case in Kenya. As Miller notes, the average Kenyan, in contrast, makes abundant use of ceremonial speeches. The popularity of these speeches over those preferred by Americans is a reflection of cultural values. For example, in the United States, with its long history of argumentation and debate, persuading others to one's point of view is commonplace. In Kenya, where community, proper protocol, formal greetings, and tribute are important, the ceremonial speech is widely used.

In the area of supporting material, people trained in public speaking in the United States learn to use evidence such as statistics to try to persuade an audience. However, Miller suggests, "The most convincing type of supporting material for a Kenyan public speech is a narrative." Part of employing narratives also has Kenyan speakers choosing proverbs over statistics.

Miller makes comparisons between the United States and Kenya with regard to organizational patterns. In the United States, successful speakers are those who organize their speeches in a highly structured, logical, linear pattern. For many Kenyan speakers, the pattern is best seen as a bicycle wheel with the spokes wandering out to the rim. Miller adds, "The speaker gives illustrations, proverbs, and tells stories and then returns back to the thesis at the center, though not exactly at the place from which they departed." Again, when compared to the organization used by a Western speaker, such a pattern would appear to be aimless and without a logical configuration. All of Miller's examples and comparisons make it clear that people who give speeches call on their culture when selecting the rhetorical devices they deem most appropriate and effective.

Possibly one of the most important areas of intercultural communication—both internationally and domestically—is between U.S. Americans and Mexicans. The June 11, 2001, issue of *Time* magazine was devoted to a special issue called "Welcome to Amexica," which detailed the unique culture that is developing along both sides of the U.S.–Mexican border. Here a hybrid culture is emerging that is a combination of European American, native Mexican, and Spanish-influenced Mexican backgrounds. To help you better understand the nature of this culture and the Mexican values that contribute to it, our next essay, "Mexican *Dichos*: Lessons Through Language" by Carolyn Roy, explores Mexican values as expressed by *dichos*. *Dichos* are popular proverbs, adages, and sayings that pass on many of the values that are important to Mexicans. The proverbs and adages shine a light on what the particular culture deems important. For example, Roy discusses how key values such as the cheerful acceptance of the "will of God," the need to place trust in others with great care, the significance of appearances, the necessity to guard one's privacy and not breach the privacy of others, prescribed gender roles; a communal spirit, and the importance of family are expressed and reinforced through use of Mexican *dichos*.

As noted in the introduction to this chapter, nonverbal message are also culture bound. That is to say, your perception and use of nonverbal symbols are linked directly to your culture. Peter A. Andersen and Hua Wang, in their essay "Unraveling Cultural Cues: Dimensions of Nonverbal Communication Across Cultures," make the same point in the following manner: "Culture shapes the display rules of when, how, what, and with whom certain nonverbal expressions should be revealed or suppressed and dictates which displays are appropriate in which specific situations." To help us appreciate and understand these codes, Andersen and Wang begin by summarizing briefly the basic codes of nonverbal communication: physical appearance (attire), proxemics (space and distance), chronemics (time), kinesics (facial expressions, movements, gestures), haptics (touch), oculesics (eye contact and gaze), vocalics (paralanguage), and olfactics (smell). After a discussion of these basic codes, the authors move to an analysis of how these codes can differ from one culture to another. Andersen and Wang organize their comparative study around the six key intercultural dimensions of high and low context, identity, power distance, gender, uncertainty, and immediacy.

Our final essay moves us from a discussion of cultural diversity in nonverbal communication in general to an analysis of a specific culture. Edwin R. McDaniel, in his piece "Japanese Nonverbal Communication: A Reflection of Cultural Themes," examines some nonverbal communication patterns found in the Japanese culture. As a means of demonstrating the link between culture and communication, McDaniel examines the communication behaviors of the Japanese culture and traces the reasons for these behaviors. By presenting what he refers to as "cultural themes," McDaniel explains how Japan's social organizations, historical experiences, and religious orientations are directly connected to Japanese nonverbal behavior. In a propositional survey, McDaniel presents a series of 11 propositions that tie various cultural themes to how the Japanese perceive and use kinesics (movement), oculesics (eye contact), facial expressions, proxemics, touch, personal appearance, space, time, vocalics or paralanguage, silence, and olfactics (smell).

The Nexus of Language, Communication, and Culture

Mary Fong

Throughout the centuries, scholars around the world have been interested in both oral and written languages and the role they serve in contributing to cultural societies. Confucius observed that proper human conduct maintains a civil society, and cautioned: "If language not be in accordance with the truth of things, affairs cannot be carried on to success." Saint-Exupery's comment that "to grasp the meaning of the world of today we use a language created to express the world of yesterday," and the biblical injunction "may the words of my mouth and the meditation of my heart be acceptable in thy sight, oh Lord" also reflect this concern. In the current era, anthropologists, linguists, psychologists, philosophers, and communication scholars continue to try to fathom the role of language and communication in human activity and its nexus to culture.

In this essay, I first define language, communication, and culture. Then, I examine briefly some basic perspectives about the relationship between language, communication, and culture. In the course of this analysis, I begin with a description of the Sapir–Whorf hypothesis and then review the more current directions of language, communication, and culture research. Finally, in order to demonstrate some of the relationships between language, communication, and culture using qualitative methodologies, I draw from research on the Chinese culture to demonstrate the nexus of language, communication, and culture in examples from both cultural and intercultural interactions.

This original essay first appeared in the 10th edition. Mary Fong teaches at California State University, San Bernardino.

INTERRELATIONSHIP OF LANGUAGE, COMMUNICATION, AND CULTURE

Language, communication, and culture are intricately intertwined with one another. Language is a symbolic system in which meaning is shared among people who identify with one another. Both verbal and nonverbal aspects of language exist. In the study of language and culture, the verbal aspect of both written and spoken communications has been the predominant focus of research.

Spoken language is a vehicle for people to communicate in social interaction by expressing their experience and creating experience. Words reflect the sender's attitude, beliefs, and points of view. Language expresses, symbolizes, and embodies cultural reality (Kramsch, 1998). Communication cannot exist without language, and language needs the process of communication to engage people in social interaction.

Both language and communication reflect culture. For Sherzer (1987), culture is the organization of individuals who share rules for production and interpretation of behavior. Language and communication represent an individual's symbolic organization of the world. Language is a medium that reflects and expresses an individual's group membership and relationships with others. Both written and oral languages are shaped by culture, and in turn, these languages shape culture. As Kramsch points out:

> Culture both liberates and constrains. It liberates by investing the randomness of nature with meaning, order, and rationality and by providing safeguards against chaos; it constrains by imposing a structure on nature and by limiting the range of possible meanings created by the individual. (1998, p. 10)

With this same tenor, language and communication both liberate and constrain. Language and communication enable people to express themselves, while simultaneously constraining them to conform to shared cultural standards. Culture is a social system in which members share common standards of communication, behaving, and evaluating in everyday life.

PERSPECTIVES ON LANGUAGE AND CULTURE

A major proponent of linguistic relativity and one of the first modern observations of the relationship between language and culture is the Sapir–Whorf hypothesis. This notion proposes a deterministic view that language structure is necessary in order to produce thought. In other words, language and its categories—grammar, syntax, and vocabulary—are the only categories by which we can experience the world. Simply stated, language influences and shapes how people perceive their world, their culture. This vision dominated scholarly thinking as a point of discussion, research, and controversy for more than five decades.

The Sapir–Whorf hypothesis also holds that language and thought co-vary. That is, diversity in language categories and structure lead to cultural differences in thought and perceptions of the world. This position is known as *linguistic relativity.* Sapir (1951) believes that the "real world" is largely built on the unconscious language habits of the group. Benjamin Whorf was a student of Edward Sapir at Yale University from about 1931 (Carroll, 1992). Initial publications of Whorf's (1956) views about language and culture were printed in a series of articles in 1940–1941. He writes:

> We cut nature up, organize it into concepts, and ascribe significances as we do, largely because we are parties to an agreement to organize it in this way—an agreement that holds throughout our speech community and is codified in the patterns of our language. (p. 213)

Sapir and Whorf's ideas have been understood to mean that people who speak different languages segment their world differently. Thus, any language such as Russian, Chinese, or German structures a "Russian," "Chinese," or "German" reality by framing and screening what these cultural members pay attention to. If there is a word for "it" in their language, then cultural members know that "it" exists, and if not, "it" is nonexistent to them.

For instance, when I was five years old, I remember my mother asked me to stick out my tongue so that she could look at it. She looked at it briefly and said in Chinese Cantonese, *"Ni yao yi hay,"* meaning "You have heat." My mother observed the texture, color, and coating of my tongue and lips. In the Chinese culture, it is common knowledge that an aspect of our physical health is viewed in terms of *yi hay* (heat) or *leung* (cool), which are extreme conditions that may be balanced through various types of foods and herbs. It is not the actual temperature of the food, but rather the *nature* of the food that produces a cool or warm effect on your body. If a person eats too many fried and baked foods and not enough cool foods such as particular fruits, vegetables, and liquids, then the person will eventually have a condition of too much heat in the body. If a person has a cool condition, one way to increase the heat in one's body is to lessen the consumption of cool foods and to increase one's diet of warm nature foods. This is one way that the Chinese strive to maintain a healthy physical balance.

This is an example of a "Chinese" reality of framing and screening what these cultural members pay attention to. On the other hand, the "American" reality promotes eating a well-balanced diet from the four main food groups: fruits and vegetables, meat and poultry, breads and grains, and dairy products. The American reality does not typically categorize food as warm or cold in nature in understanding and maintaining a balanced diet to increase one's health.

The system of labeling food, drink, medicines, herbs, illnesses, and medical procedures as either cold or hot is based on a system originating with the ancient Greeks and spreading to Central Asia (Dresser, 1996). For instance, as perceived in many Asian cultures, after a major surgery or childbirth, the body loses blood, energy, and heat. Therefore, the heat must be replenished, and avoidance of drinking cold water, eating cool foods, or taking showers is recommended. Middle Eastern and Latin American peoples also have a system of classifying foods, medicines, and procedures, but all cultural groups may differ in varying degrees depending on their principles (Dresser, 1996).

The situation of my mother observing my physical condition and the examples of foods, medicines, and procedures provide instances of how various cultural people segment their world and reality in varying ways. Furthermore, this natural cultural process of thinking and perceiving influences how members may communicate by accepting or rejecting particular foods, medicines, and procedures in certain circumstances. A person who is not familiar with another person's cultural ways will be likely to misinterpret the person's actions.

Another scholar, Brown (1958), in part disagreed with the Sapir–Whorf hypothesis and argued that a cultural member's worldview is not determined by language. He held, rather, that people categorize their world by attaching labels to what is out there. People use language to do what they need it to do. According to Brown, people will label an object, an idea, a process, and so forth based on the importance and utilization it has for them. For example, CDs, DVDs, cell phones, and the Internet are relatively new inventions that need labeling through language so that people can communicate their ideas about them. Because antiquated technology such as a record player, a rotary phone, or a slide rule is no longer important or used by people, the once common labels for these objects are now archived in museums and hardly referred to in conversation. Brown's position, however, supports the idea of linguistic relativity because the perceptual categories that are frequently used receive labels, whereas unused or insignificant categories may not be labeled.

Several research studies on color terms and color perception tested the Sapir–Whorf hypothesis (Berlin & Kay, 1967; Bruner, Oliver, & Greenfield, 1966; Greenfield & Bruner, 1966; Kay & Kempton, 1984). Eastman (1990) reviewed these studies that supported the idea of linguistic relativity and stated, "It appears to be the case that world view is a matter more of linguistic relativity than linguistic determinism" (p. 109).

Other researchers have found it difficult to test how strongly the structure of a language influences the worldview of people because reliable methods for assessing the worldview of a cultural people independently of the language they speak are needed (Brown, 1976; Carroll, 1967; Kay & Kempton, 1984). The deterministic view of the Sapir–Whorf hypothesis is not taken seriously (Kramsch, 1998). Carroll (1992) believes that researchers and theorists generally regard Sapir–Whorf as either unconfirmable or incorrect because the evidence offered in its support is viewed as being flawed. He further contends that if the hypothesis can be sustained, it would only suggest a weak influence of language structure on thought.

The linguistic-relativity view of the Sapir–Whorf hypothesis is its strength and contribution in understanding an aspect of the differences in language and culture. It is not so much if languages can be translated into one another, which they can, for the most part, if two speakers are of different languages; but rather, the two speakers coming from different cultures are operating under different language and communication systems that are designed differently, which influences their perceptions and interpretation of an event. As Kramsch (1998) suggests, speakers from different cultures define reality or categorize experience in different ways. Achieving understanding across languages is dependent on common conceptual systems rather than on structural equivalences. They may differ in terms of the meaning and value of a concept.

CURRENT RESEARCH TRENDS AND DIRECTIONS

In 1974, Hymes described the development of linguistic research in the first half of the 20th century, which was distinguished by a drive for the autonomy of language as an object of study and a focus on description of [grammatical] structure, and in the second half of the century, which was distinguished by a concern for the integration of language in sociocultural context and a focus on the analysis of function (p. 208).

Hymes's description was accurate because the second half of the 20th century was marked by several research methods, such as discourse analysis, pragmatics, ethnography of communication, rhetorical analysis, and quantitative analysis, as ways to investigate the linkages among language, communication, and culture. Examples of themes of interest to researchers are the relationship between language and context, the relationship between language and identities (i.e., personal identity, social role identity, and cultural ethnolinguistic identity), and multiple functions and meanings of language and communication in relationship to culture (Ting-Toomey, 1989).

Current approaches to the study of language, communication, and culture are developmental, interactional, and social psychological. The *developmental* approach focuses on language acquisition and cultural communication practices simultaneously in the language development stages of a child. Developmental theorists are interested in understanding the connection between language and cognitive processing in a culture (Ting-Toomey, 1989). The *interactional* approach investigates what people are doing with speech as they interact face to face in a particular interactional context. Interactional theorists are interested in identifying appropriate communication styles and norms in various cultures (Ting-Toomey, 1989). The *social psychological* approach explores the underlying factors that influence language choices in multilingual communication contexts. For example, group comparison factors, identity salience factors, and attitudinal and motivational factors have significant association to the language accommodations process in intergroup communication situations. Social psychological theorists are interested in delineating specific social psychological conditions that account for first-language or second-language usage in majority and minority groups in cultural communities globally (Ting-Toomey, 1989).

For some researchers, the controversy over whether language determines or reflects thought or thought determines or reflects language is not the primary concern. According to Sherzer (1987), what is at issue is the analysis of discourse as the "embodiment of the essence of culture and as constitutive of what language and culture relationship is all about." Sherzer (1987) also views discourse as the intersection where language and culture interrelate: "It is discourse that creates, recreates, focuses, modifies, and transmits both culture and language and their intersection" (p. 295).

For Sherzer (1987), culture is the organization of individuals who share rules for production and interpretation of behavior. Language represents an individual's symbolic organization of the world. Language is a medium that reflects and expresses an individual's group membership and relationships with others. Discourse analysis derives from pragmatics and speech act theory (Saville-Troike, 1989). *Pragmatics* or *speech act theory* refers to the study of the connotative (inner) and denotative (outer) meanings of "expressions when used in a conversation or a written work" (Paul, 1987, p. 101). According to Silverstein (1976), pragmatics is "the study of the meaning of linguistic signs relative to their communicative functions" (p. 20). Pragmatics also entails cultural members applying their knowledge of the world to the interpretation of what is said and done in interaction (Fromkin & Rodman, 1983; Gumperz, 1982).

The ethnography of communication provides the researcher with a framework of observation and interviewing techniques to facilitate capturing the interlocutors' meanings in various communicative acts both culturally and interculturally. The ethnographer endeavors to describe the communicative choices that interlocutors make. This involves describing and accounting for the interpretive systems and practices through which members construct actions and deal with behaviors.

Hymes (1962), the originator of the ethnography of communication, states that the "study of speech as a factor in cognitive and expressive behavior leads to concern with the ethnographic patterning of the uses of speech in a community" (p. 102). Investigating language, communication, and culture is discovering not only linguistic structural regularities, but also regularities of usage that have motives, emotions, desires, knowledge, attitudes, and values attached to them. An essential aim of studies on language, communication, and culture using the ethnography of communication approach is to make implicit cultural beliefs, attitudes, values, norms of interpretation, rules of speaking, norms of interaction, and so forth explicit in order to understand and to practice communication competence within a particular culture, and eventually in intercultural interactions.

LANGUAGE STUDIES

Some of the sample findings in the cultural and intercultural studies that follow are illustrations of language and culture analysis. The qualitative methods—discourse analysis, pragmatics, and ethnography of communication—jointly provide tools and perspectives to make possible an in-depth examination of the communicative phenomena.

A Cultural Study

An ethnographic study of the Chinese New Year celebration in Hong Kong (Fong, 2000) provides one instance of the manner in which the Chinese employ language to reverse bad luck. By examining a speaking pattern that is used when someone makes a negative comment during the Chinese New Year, it is possible to understand how Chinese people are prepared to avoid arguments and negative talk during the Chinese New Year. It is possible to understand how Chinese are prepared to handle a rule violation.

Chinese people engage in positive talk and try to avoid arguments and negative talk during the Chinese New Year. Spoken words are carefully watched to avoid saying words that signify death, sickness, poverty, or anything else unlucky. All of the participants in this cultural study agreed with the same ideas as the following participant, who explains why negative comments during the New Year celebrations are avoided:

> Of course you don't say unlucky things. Always be positive. Chinese New Year is supposed to be a happy occasion. Try not to say something unlucky, like mentioning death or misfortune. Say it after the New Year. Perhaps some people may even think that

saying those things during Chinese New Year will bring bad luck in the coming year. Those things may happen.

If someone accidentally talks about something unfortunate or utters a negative comment during this holiday, the rule of positive speaking is violated in this context. The hearer of the message may say:

/tou^{3} hæu^{2} sæy^{2} dzɔi^{3} gɔŋ^{2} gwɔ^{3}/*
("Spit out your saliva; speak once more.")

Another expression that participants in the study reported is:

/tsɔi^{1}/ or /tsɔu^{1}, dai^{6} gæt^{7} lei^{6} si^{6}/
("lucky" or "very lucky, auspicious")

These expressions are said in order to reverse the bad luck that has been invited into good luck.

To understand what linguistic devices the Chinese employ, it is necessary to understand a few rules of behavior and speaking. Shimanoff (1980) proposes an "If . . . then . . ." method of concisely stating a rule of behavior. To develop Shimanoff's method of stating behavioral rules, I will add a "because . . . meaning . . ." sequence in order to add a meaning component to a formulation of a communication rule.

In this situation, the sequential rule statement begins with the initial linguistic "If . . ." slot that provides information on the particular context, condition, or situation, such as a speech event, speech act, or genre. It is followed by the "then . . ." slot, which refers to the speaking and/or behavioral interaction pattern discovered from the researcher's ethnographic data analysis.

The third linguistic device, the "because . . ." slot, provides a concise rationale for why people of a particular culture behave the way they do. Here, an underlying belief, value system, or cultural principle may be revealed to provide an explanation for a people's way of communicating. The final linguistic device, the "meaning . . ." slot, serves the same function as Hymes's component norm of interpretation of a symbol, the speaking and/or behavioral interaction pattern, a particular speech act, speech event, scene, and so forth.

These sequential rules statement provide the following formula:

If . . . (context, condition, or situation, such as a speech event, speech act, or genre),
then . . . (speaking and/or interaction pattern),
because . . . (belief, value system, or cultural principle),
meaning . . . (norm of interpretation of a symbol, speaking pattern, interaction pattern, a particular speech act, speech event, scent, etc.).

Applying these sequential rules to the Chinese custom of reversing the negative comments can be expressed in a concise rule statement using the following formula:

If a person makes a negative comment on Chinese New Year Day,
then a Hong Kong Chinese person who hears it should say:
/tsɔi^{1}/ or /tsɔi^{1}, dai^{6} gæt^{7} lei^{6} si^{6}/
("lucky" or "very lucky, auspicious")
/tou^{3} hæu^{2} sæy^{2} dzɔi^{3} gɔŋ^{2} gwɔ^{3}/
("Spit out your saliva; speak once more.")
because this is believed to counteract the bad luck and create good luck,
meaning that the negative comments will not come true in the coming new year.

An Intercultural Study

An intercultural study on compliment interactions between Chinese immigrants and European Americans from the perspective of Chinese immigrants (Fong, 1998) found that the two cultural groups have differing ways of speaking in compliment interactions (Chen, 1993; Chiang & Pochtrager, 1993; Fong, 1998). European Americans on the West Coast and in the Midwest generally accept a compliment (Chen, 1993; Chiang & Pochtrager, 1993; Fong, 1998).

On the other hand, the literature reports that Chinese have the tendency to deny compliments in order to give an impression of modesty (Chen, 1993; Chiang & Pochtrager, 1993; Gao, 1984; Zhang, 1988). In one study (Fong, 1998), an informant from Mainland China explained the primary difference and the internal similarity between two cultural groups:

> On the surface I say "no, no, no." . . . But inside I accept it. I feel really excited. In western culture, they say "yes" means accept the compliment. But in China, people say "no," but really, really accept the compliment. Different [speaking] way, but the feeling is the same. (p. 257)

Four adaptations by Chinese immigrant participants (CIPs) to European American compliments were found. An orientation is a state or condition that is changeable from one interaction to another depending on one's adaptation to intercultural communication differences. Four orientations in which the CIP can be located are (1) intercultural shock state, (2) intercultural resistance state, (3) intercultural accommodation state, and (4) bicultural competence state. For the purpose of this essay, we will capture a glimpse of one of the orientations, the intercultural shock state, in order to have a sense of Chinese immigrants' thinking and speaking patterns.

Affectively, CIPs reported feeling uncomfortable, unnatural, uneasy, nervous, stressed, embarrassed, surprised, shocked, or afraid when a European American complimented them. The situational outcome of the intercultural compliment interaction for CIPs, however, was an appreciation in receiving praise because they felt accepted, liked, and welcomed by European Americans. CIPs reported that compliments helped them reduce some of their stress as a newcomer to the United States.

Cognitively, CIPs in the intercultural shock state have minimum knowledge of the intercultural communication differences in compliment interactions with European Americans. Before coming to the United States, CIPs reported that they were not familiar with the European Americans' generosity in giving (1) compliments, (2) compliments containing strong positive adjectives, (3) compliments intended to encourage a person after an unsatisfactory performance, and (4) compliments on a wide variety of topics; and they were unfamiliar with (5) accepting compliments and (6) face-to-face compliments in all types of relationships.

Behaviorally, five speaking patterns were found; two examples are provided here. One type of compliment response that Chinese immigrants used was the Direct Denial + Verbal Corrective/Prescriptive response. Following is a reported intercultural compliment interaction:

(American) Boyfriend: You're the most beautiful person that I've seen.

(Hong kong) Girlfriend: Oh gaaa. Oohh. Please don't say that.

Because Chinese immigrants value indirectness and modesty, the compliment was interpreted as being direct (e.g., face-to-face, expressing openly with positive adjectives on the complimentee's appearance), which is contrary to the reported Chinese way of compliment interactions. The response was made to avoid self-praise and to suggest to the complimenter not to make such a direct compliment.

CIPs who were in the intercultural shock state were also found to use the Silence response. The following intercultural compliment interaction is reported to have occurred at work:

(American Female) Boss: I want to thank you for doing a wonderful job. You're very, very nice.

(Chinese Female) Worker: [silence]

Chinese immigrant interlocutors value modesty highly, but they are also aware of one of the American values of directly accepting and appreciating compliments. The compliment was interpreted as direct (i.e., face-to-face, expressing openly their positive thoughts with positive adjectives), which is contrary to the reported Chinese way of compliment interactions. The response was made because Chinese immigrant recipients reported that they felt ambivalent about which cultural response to use; thus the Chinese immigrant recipient remained silent.

CONCLUSION

The excerpt from the cultural study (Fong, 2000) illustrates the Chinese way of thinking and speaking. When a negative comment is made during the Chinese New Year holiday, the Chinese way of thinking is interpreting the incident as forthcoming bad luck in the coming new year. Through speech, however, the perceived bad luck is reversed to good luck.

The intercultural compliment interaction study (Fong, 1994) sheds light on the way Chinese immigrants in the intercultural shock state reveal patterns of thinking and speaking. The denial response is a pattern of speaking that is commonly used in the intercultural shock state. CIPs in this orientation essentially perceive European Americans as being generous in giving compliments with relatively strong positive adjectives, and in accepting compliments.

Current ethnographic methods hold that the best way to capture a view of language, communication, and culture is to observe the communicative phenomenon in a naturalistic setting and to have cultural members identify and classify the interaction or event as being culturally significant. The crossroads of language, communication, and culture is found in the culturally shared meaning of ideas and behaviors that are voiced as symbolic utterances, expressions, dialogue, and conversations in such various contexts as interpersonal and group interactions, research interviews, and public speaking forums.

In the two qualitative studies described in this essay, the ways of speaking and thinking were the two primary interrelated foci that reveal and reflect the outer and inner shared substances of communications that primarily make up a speech community. To examine a speech community's patterns of speaking without also discovering the norms of interpretation or the shared sociocultural knowledge of cultural members is to silence their cultural humanness as a speech community. To study only the shared sociocultural knowledge of cultural members and not attend to how it is relevant to their way of speaking is to lose an opportunity to understand more about different cultural communication styles. In accomplishing this goal, potential sources at borderlines and intersections of cultural differences are able to richly understand and resolve intercultural conflicts.

Both examples of findings from the mentioned qualitative studies illuminate, in part, what Hymes (1974) has suggested:

> It has often been said that language is an index to or reflection of culture. But language is not simply passive or automatic in its relation to culture. . . . Speaking is itself a form of cultural behavior, and language, like any other part of culture, partly shapes the whole; and its expression of the rest of culture is partial, selective. That selective relation, indeed, is what should be interesting to us. Why do some features of a community's life come to be named—overtly expressible in discourse—while others are not? (p. 127)

Note

*The International Phonetic System was used in transcribing this and other Chinese dialogue.

References

Berlin, B., & Kay, P. (1967). *Universality and evolution of basic color terms.* Working Paper #1, Laboratory for Language Behavior Research, University of California, Berkeley.

Brown, R. (1958). *Words and things.* New York: Free Press.

Brown, R. (1976). In Memorial Tribute to Eric Lennenberg. *Cognition, 4,* 125–153.

Bruner, J., Oliver, R. R., & Greenfield, P. M. (1966). *Studies in cognitive growth.* New York: Wiley.

Carroll, J. B. (1967). Bibliography of the Southwest Project in Comparative Psycholinguistics. In D. Hymes (Ed.), *Studies in southwestern ethnolinguistics* (pp. 452–454). The Hague: Mouton.

Carroll, J. B. (1992). Anthropological linguistics: An overview. In W. Bright (Ed.), *International encyclopedia of linguistics.* New York: Oxford University Press.

Chen, R. (1993). Responding to compliments: A contrastive study of politeness strategies between American English and Chinese speakers. *Journal of Pragmatics, 20,* 49–75.

Chiang, F., & Pochtrager, B. (1993). A pilot study of compliment responses of American-born English speakers and Chinese-born English speakers. (Available in Microfiche only, ED 356649)

Dresser, N. (1996). *Multicultural manners.* New York: Wiley.

Eastman, C. M. (1990). *Aspects of language and culture* (2nd ed.). Novato, CA: Chandler & Sharp.

Fong, M. (1994). Patterns of occurrence of compliment response types. In *Chinese immigrants' interpretations of their intercultural compliment interactions with European-Americans.* Unpublished doctoral dissertation, University of Washington, Seattle.

Fong, M. (1998). Chinese immigrants' perceptions of semantic dimensions of direct/indirect communication in intercultural compliment interactions with North Americans. *Howard Journal of Communications, 9*(3), 245–262.

Fong, M. (2000). "Luck talk" in celebrating the Chinese New Year. *Journal of Pragmatics, 32,* 219–237.

Fromkin, V., & Rodman, R. (1983). *An introduction to language* (3rd ed.). New York: CBS Publishing and Holt, Rinehart, & Winston.

Gao, W. (1984). Compliment and its reaction in Chinese and English cultures. *Working papers in discourse in English and Chinese* (pp. 32–37). Canberra: Canberra College of Advanced Education.

Greenfield, P. M., & Bruner, J. S. (1966). Culture and cognitive growth. *International Journal of Psychology, 1,* 89–107.

Gumperz, J. J. (1982). *Discourse strategies.* New York: Cambridge University Press.

Hymes, D. (1962). The ethnography of speaking. In T. Gladwin & W. Sturtevant (Eds.), *Anthropology and human behavior* (pp. 99–137). Washington, DC: Anthropological Society of Washington.

Hymes, D. (1964). Toward ethnographies of communication: The analysis of communicative events. *American Anthropologist, 66,* 21–41.

Hymes, D. (1974). *Foundations in sociolinguistics: An ethnographic approach.* Philadelphia: University of Pennsylvania Press.

Kay, P., & Kempton, W. (1984). What is the Sapir–Whorf Hypothesis? *American Anthropologist, 86,* 65–79.

Kramsch, C. (1998). *Language and culture.* London: Oxford University Press.

Paul, A. (1987, July 15). Review of Joseph H. Greenberg, *Language in the Americas. Chronicle of Higher Education,* 6.

Sapir, E. (1951). The status of linguistics as a science. In D. Mandelbaum (Ed.), *Selected writings* (pp. 160–166). Berkeley: University of California Press.

Saville-Troike, M. (1989). *The ethnography of communication* (2nd ed.). New York: Basil Blackwell.

Sherzer, J. (1987). A discourse-centered approach to language and culture. *American Anthropologist, 89,* 295–309.

Shimanoff, S. B. (1980). *Communication rules: Theory and research.* Beverly Hills, CA: Sage.

Silverstein, M. (1976). Shifters, linguistics categories, and cultural description. In K. H. Basso & H. A. Selby (Eds.), *Meaning in anthropology* (pp. 11–56). Albuquerque: University of New Mexico Press.

Ting-Toomey, S. (1989). Language, communication, and culture. In S. Ting-Toomey & F. Korzenny (Eds.), *Language, communication, and culture* (pp. 9–15). Newbury Park, CA: Sage.

Whorf, B. L. (1956). *Language, thought, and reality: Selected writings of Benjamin Lee Whorf* (J. B. Carroll, Ed.). Cambridge, MA: MIT Press. (Original work published 1940)

Zhang, Z. (1988). A discussion of communicative culture. *Journal of Chinese Language Teacher Association, 23,* 107–112.

Concepts and Questions

1. What does Fong imply when she suggests that language and thought vary with one another? Do you agree?
2. Can you think of specific examples that illustrate the link between culture and language?
3. Can you explain what Fong means when she states that language influences and shapes how people perceive their world and their culture?
4. What is meant by the following statement: "People who speak different languages segment their world differently"?
5. How do Chinese immigrants and Americans differ in their ways of compliment interactions?
6. When referring to Sherzer, what does Fong means when she writes "Culture is the organization of individuals who share rules for production and interpretation of behavior"?
7. How do the Chinese use language to reverse bad luck?
8. In what ways do the Chinese and the Americans express themselves differently?

German Language: Whose Language, Whose Culture?

HELEN KELLY-HOLMES

The encounter with the German language happens in manifold ways. It may be an intercultural encounter that takes place in a multinational company or on a tourist visit to Germany, Austria, or Switzerland; it may be random, a fleeting word or phrase overheard in the news headlines; it may occur in the most unexpected place—for instance, the menu of a restaurant in a Spanish holiday resort where the German version is, disarmingly, placed before the English. The more intensive encounter with German often takes place in the classroom; here too there are many possibilities. It may be motivated by the desire to maintain some link with the country of one's forebears, as in the case of the heritage learner in Australia or Argentina; it may take place in the German for Foreigners classroom in any German-speaking country, where the encounter with German is a necessary hurdle for the immigrant or asylum seeker; or it may take place in one of the many foreign language classrooms of the English-speaking world in which German is being taught. It is just such an encounter I would like to relate, before beginning our discussion of language and contemporary culture.

One day, in a translation class I was teaching, our deliberations on Peter Schneider's (1990) witty and thought-provoking study of German culture following unification in 1990 led to an insightful discussion on the dimensions of national culture. In the particular chapter we were translating, he uses the analogy of identical twins (i.e., East and West Germany) separated at birth to explore whether or not there is some sort of overarching, primordial "German" culture that could have survived political and economic upheavals, ideological polarization, and 40 years of isolation and separation. He further extends his hypothesizing to consider whether or not German-speaking Switzerland and Austria might not also share this "original" culture. We decided to explore what this German culture might be, and the white board at the top of the class was very quickly covered in suggestions: music, a literary canon, political experiences, folk and fairy tales, geographical space, a governmental system, shared history, economic practices, ideologies, religion. Finally, the German exchange student at the back of the class got the chance to intervene: "I think you've forgotten the most important thing. For me, it would have to be the language." "Ah, yes, of course," the British students, all studying German, nodded in agreement. "That's obvious. Why didn't we think of it?"

This story, I think, illustrates some fundamental differences between the role played by language in culture in German-speaking countries, on the one hand, and Anglophone or English-speaking countries—even Great Britain, the "home" of the English language—on the other. Language may not be something that automatically counts as part of culture and identity in the Anglophone world, whereas I think this claim could be made with a good degree of confidence for the German-speaking world. This chapter is an attempt to estimate the role of the German language in contemporary culture. Language, like culture, is something lived, shared, cumulative, multifaceted, and contradictory. It is imperfect, mongrelized; at one and the same time, both natural and manipulated. It is not something we can put in a test tube in order to carry out experiments. It is instead something that is constantly changing—it is alive. And it only lives through its speakers. Words themselves have no inherent meanings. Meanings are instead attached to them by members of a speech community, a culture. Thus, just like our random and not-so-random encounters with German, describing and discussing the language means taking a snapshot, different from one we could have taken yesterday, different from the one we might take tomorrow.

The chapter begins with a general discussion of the link between language, culture, and identity before going on to look at the facts and figures of the German language. The second part of this chapter attempts to provide a brief outline of the recent historical context of the German language, then goes on to look at linguistic diversity in German-speaking countries and how this both reflects and is reflected in cultural diversity. The third section looks at who "owns" the German

From *Contemporary German Cultural Studies* (London: Hodder Arnold, 2002), pp. 40–60. Helen Kelly-Holmes teaches at Aston University, Birmingham, UK.

language and discusses the cultural impetus for and reactions against standardization and "foreign" words. The final section addresses the issue of how the German language is experienced and perceived from outside of Germany and how these experiences and perceptions contribute to the understanding of German culture and identity beyond the German-speaking world.

LANGUAGE AND CULTURE

The first thing we need to understand about the association between language and culture is that it is not a simple, one-way, cause-and-effect relationship. We should think of it instead as something two-way or circular or even multilayered. We cannot say that language contributes to culture without acknowledging at the same time that culture contributes in turn to language. In order for a cultural or social group to exist, there must be a common language; in order for a common language to come into existence, a social or cultural group needs to create it. Likewise, the main vehicle we have for talking about and expressing culture is language. Through using this language, our links are strengthened, we become a more coherent cultural group, we learn more about ourselves, we evolve cultural practices, and our common identity as members of that group may be reinforced. We can find examples of this in almost every minute of our daily lives. Television news, for example, is addressed to a national or local audience (a cultural group whose members identify to a greater or lesser extent with each other). Because of this, the presenter can take for granted that certain concepts and words do not need to be explained and that a certain level of common knowledge can be assumed because she/he is speaking to people who share some sort of culture and identity. They would have been through the same educational system, they experience a similar type of press in the newspapers they read, they may share the same or a related religion and have similar values and mores, they may have read some of the same books and seen many of the same films, they are talked to by the same politicians on the radio or television, they shop in the same shops where they buy the same brands, they see the same advertisements every day, they watch the same television programs, and so on. Similarly, as a result of watching this news program every day, the national or local group has even more in common. They will discuss the events reported on with friends, family, and workmates. They will bring new words and concepts that they hear on the news program into their everyday conversation. Their culture and identity are reinforced by watching this program.

This is, of course, a very great generalization. What about age differences, gender differences, ethnic differences, educational differences, religious differences, political differences, class differences, linguistic differences? It goes without saying that all of these occur within national frontiers. There is no such thing as a completely homogeneous linguistic and cultural group. However, despite this, we can still claim that sharing the German language and living in a country in which that is the language through which people go about their daily business—being part of what in German is called a *Kommunikationsgemeinschaft,* or speech and communication community—does give people some sort of shared culture and identity. An important point here is that this "membership" in a nation or country does not preclude membership in other cultural, identity, and linguistic groups. For instance, we may speak a language other than the official or dominant one at home, making us part of a regional or ethnic minority speech community. If we are members of a football team, we share the language and experiences with other members of that team to a very great extent, and with members of other football teams in other parts of the country and even across the world too, to a greater or lesser extent, making up a kind sub–speech community and culture.

Another concept we need to acknowledge here is that language is not simply a code—anyone who has ever attempted anything but the most basic translation will already realize this. Because languages are inextricably linked to cultures, they invariably reflect this in their vocabulary, structures, rules about politeness, and so on. A good example here is the difference between American English and British English. If a language were simply a set of scientifically derived and defined units of meaning, unaffected by the people who use them and the situations in which they are used, then there would be no differences in vocabulary, spelling, or usage between the United States and Great Britain. As it is, the many variations show how languages are the result of political, economic, historical, social, ideological, and cultural processes. To take a fairly banal example, there is no Federal Reserve in England because England, unlike the United States, is not a federal country; the equivalent institution is called the Bank of England. Likewise, the name of the "equivalent" German institution, the *Bundesbank*, is the result of a number of important aspects of recent and not so recent German history—for example, the fact that Germany has only been a unified group of *Länder* or states since 1871 and the fact that the Americans fitted some aspects of their federalism to German social, economic, and political life during the postwar occupation and denazification. Something as basic as this—the way in which a country is governed and organized economically, politically, and administratively—may seem to have little to do with its language. But when we look closely, we see that all of these processes naturally take place through the language and inevitably mould and develop it. An experience from another translation class may serve to illustrate this. In the text we were discussing, the German *"Innenminister"* was mentioned. The student who was presenting his translation to the group had translated this as "Home Secretary." He argued that this was the British "equivalent" and, as such, was the appropriate choice. There followed a lengthy discussion, at the end of which the student opted instead for the generic "Minister of the Interior." He had a point, to a certain extent, in that the British Home Secretary does indeed have some functions in common with the German *Innenminister;* however, while the former also has responsibility for Justice, his German counterpart does not, this task being allocated to a specific Minister for Justice (*Justizminister*) in Germany. Thus, the difference between these two terms reflects different ways of organizing matters of state—something that is both a product of and an ingredient in culture. Another argument against using the "British" term was the fact that it would mean little to readers in English-speaking countries outside the United Kingdom, all of which have their own particular term for this office. Again, if language were indeed a code, like computer programming languages, then why would there be all these different words for what is a more or less similar function?

LINGUISTIC DIVERSITY, CULTURAL DIVERSITY

On my first trip to Germany as a teenager, I stayed with a family in Jülich (near Düsseldorf) who spoke German that was very familiar to me from my school lessons, books, and tapes, and I had few problems understanding them. One day we went to visit relatives who lived in the countryside about 50 miles away. Instantaneously, the father, a lawyer who spoke *Hochdeutsch* (or standard German), suddenly switched to what sounded like a completely different language when he greeted his cousins. He then proceeded to translate for me as I tried to get accustomed to their language, their version of the German language—alive and well and less than an hour away from where I thought I was learning to speak that language!

Although we have regional varieties of English in Anglophone countries, it is fair to say that they tend to manifest themselves mainly in terms of different accents. People may unconsciously modify this accent in certain conditions—for example, intensifying it when they return home to a region in order to feel a sense of belonging and be accepted, modifying it and attempting a more standard pronunciation when they are in a different part of the country or in a different social setting. German regional (and national in the cases of Austrian German and, even more so, Swiss German) variation encompasses far more than simply phonological changes relating to pronunciation and accent. Sentence structure, meanings, and vocabulary are all subject to change. These quite major differences are termed a dialect (as opposed to an accent), and there are many dialects found throughout German-speaking countries. There is of course an obvious question here—namely, what is the difference between a dialect and a language? One rather facetious but very telling answer that has been posited is that a language has a flag and an army or navy; this makes some sense when we consider, for instance, that Dutch is defined as a language, whereas *Bayrisch* (Bavarian) and *Sächsisch* (Saxon)—both of which are far removed from Standard or High German—are both classified as dialects. Dialects are often defined sociologically, politically, or economically rather than linguistically. Such dialects both reflect and reinforce a strong regional culture and identity; in the words of Schlosser (1983), they are "eine Grammatik der Erfahrungen und Gefühle"—a grammar of experiences and feelings. When asked, many Germans will often refer first to their region, rather than to their country, when defining their culture and identity. Knowledge of their dialect—the ability to speak a dialect and switch to and from it—is fundamental to identity and culture in many parts of Germany, and interestingly, in a country where few are prepared to profess a pride in their nation, many more feel comfortable expressing pride in a regional identity and culture.

It is important to remember, however, that the relationship with dialect is not the same throughout German-speaking countries. In some parts of Germany and Austria—for example, in urban areas—dialect may be viewed as the preserve of older people, being for mainstream culture little more than a *Reliktsprache* or heritage language; in other parts (such as Southern Germany), it is the main variety, used in all situations, and nonspeakers are forced to learn it in order to take part in the culture (Mattheier, 1980). It should also be pointed out that perceptions of the standard language can also vary in different German-speaking areas. For example, as Moosmuller (1995, p. 259) points out, the use of the standard in the electronic media in Austria is "widely perceived as artificial." It is important, therefore, to look at the relationship between dialects and standard varieties on a case-by-case level in order to gain a thorough understanding of how dialects impact on local, regional, and national culture.

Not only are dialects a means of expressing a lived, shared culture; their status also depends on their relationship—or perceived relationship—with culture. Braun (1998) claims that the evolution from dialect to *Kultursprache,* or language of culture (and presumably to official or national language), depends on the particular dialect's changing relationship with "high" culture. For many, dialect is concerned with "low culture" (for example, terms such as "vulgar speech" are often used to describe this way of speaking), and even though speakers may see the dialect in question in a positive way in terms of its social function—providing a means of convivial conversation—they and nonspeakers may still view its relationship with culture (and here we mean "high" culture) in a negative way. Unfortunately, research carried out by Bernstein (1971) in the late 1960s, which concluded that children who spoke dialect (what he termed "restricted code") rather than the standard language (in his words, "elaborated code") were disadvantaged in the education system and wider society, was used to discourage parents from passing on the local dialect to their children. The consequences of this for dialects, or *Plattdeutsch,* in poorer parts of Germany, such as *Ostfriesland,* where migration to other parts of Germany was a fact of life, were quite devastating.

The transition to a written form is a key point in the movement from dialect to *Kultursprache* because, by proving itself capable of expression of high forms of literature, such as original prose and poetry, the dialect shows that it is also worthy of being a vessel for containing and expressing culture. Once the dialect's credentials in the literary sphere have been established, it will then make inroads into other areas of public culture such as the media (television news), the administration, education, and government. We can observe this process taking place for Swiss German and Lëtzebuergesch, having come from a situation where many people in Luxembourg were ashamed to admit they spoke the language in the wake of the Second World War.[1] Traditionally dialect was the preserve of spoken language, written texts—particularly public, media and official—being formulated in Standard German. However, in recent years, this diglossic situation (where different and distinct varieties of languages are used for different and distinct purposes) has changed somewhat, and more and more dialect is found in public and media texts such as advertising and television. Interestingly, once the preserve of *Hochdeutsch* and a disseminator of the standard language, television has in recent years seen a relaxation in linguistic practice. It is now not uncommon to come across dialects and informal language in traditionally high-register domains such as news programs. For example, MDR *(Mitteldeutscher Rundfunk),* the regional channel for Sachsen, Thüringen, and Sachsen-Anhalt, has never tried to cover up its pride in its regional dialects (some of which are among the most maligned in Germany!) since it was set up following the post-unification reorganization of broadcasting in East Germany. In an advertisement for the East German *Glückauf* beer, the slogan "Wo mit Glückauf gegrüßt wird, wird auch Glückauf getrunken" (Where people greet each other with *Glückauf,* they also drink *Glückauf*) makes specific reference to mining dialect in the *Erzgebirge* region of Saxony—the dialect being seen as linked with the local beer as part of local pride and culture. In Alsace, an increasing number of children's books are available in written Alsatian. This mini-revolution in using dialects in written texts and in contexts in which they would not have been used before (such as television news or by politicians making speeches) reflects a situation in which regional cultures and identities are intensifying, and these linguistic varieties are seen as a way of expressing a culture and identity that are specific to a particular part of Germany or a German-speaking country.

Regional and national varieties and dialects are not the only ways of expressing identities and cultures, however. The use of slang, or *Umgangssprache,* is also an attempt to express an identity, usually tied up with being a member of a group, defined by age (teenagers, for example), occupation (for example, shop-floor workers), and so on. *Fachsprache,* or specialist language—what we might call jargon—also provides important varieties of German. In almost all professional, scientific, and occupational areas there is a body of more or less specialized vocabulary and expressions shared by people who work in that particular sector and which makes them feel part of a particular linguistic group and culture. This notion—and perhaps more important, awareness of and knowledge about it—is again, arguably, more developed in German-speaking than in English-speaking countries. When using this language, such groups create their own mini-cultures, which can serve to include those who "speak the language" and exclude those who do not.

A group that has often felt excluded by the German language is women; in fact, it has been claimed that they are often rendered invisible by its patriarchal grammar. An example of this, highlighted by Patrick Stevenson (1997), is that only the masculine form of nouns such as *Student* and *Lehrer* can be used when talking about a mixed group of males and females or when not wanting to specify a particular sex. An alternative to this, which has been promoted by proponents of nonsexist language in Germany and which is in use in a number of sectors of society, is the capital *I,* as in *StudentInnen* and *LehrerInnen.* However, this is not included in the revised Duden dictionary, published in 1996 to cover the spelling reforms.[2] Furthermore, as one of the foremost feminist linguists, Luise Pusch (1997b), points out, the decision makers in this process of spelling and language reform, the three countries commission and the commission of the Institut der Deutschen Sprache in Mannheim, although representing the major German-speaking countries in Europe, were exclusively male. Despite these shortcomings, Pusch still concludes that "the process of language change set in motion by women during the last twenty years is the most significant and far-reaching linguistic innovation of the century" (1997a, p. 323).[3]

If we were asked to think of a multilingual German-speaking country in Europe, Switzerland would perhaps be the first country to come to mind. However, even though Switzerland is officially a multilingual country, all the German-speaking countries are, in practice, multilingual to a greater or lesser extent. In certain regions of Germany, there are speakers of Frisian, Danish, and Sorbian. In addition, like all large economies, Germany has a substantial number of immigrants who have come to that country for a variety of motivations and have lived there for varying lengths of time. Consequently, there are significant numbers of speakers of other languages, including Turkish, Slavic languages (e.g., Serbo-Croat, Russian, Polish), Italian, Greek, Arabic, and many other European, Asian, and African languages. These groups of immigrants are collectively known as *Ausländer*[4]—the term itself is an interesting example, again, of how language reflects culture, legalities, and ideologies. The word is frequently translated as "foreigner." For the English speaker, a foreigner is someone who comes from another country for a brief period of time, a visit or a holiday; however, many of these "foreigners" were in fact born in Germany, the second or third generation of immigrants who came in the 1960s to fill Germany's need for *Gastarbeiter* (guest or migrant workers). Despite this fact, the term still continues to be used to describe people who have spent most or all of their lives in Germany, but who belong to a different ethnic group. The New Duden (1996) also gives the "equivalent" for *Ausländer* as "foreigner," "alien." We need to ask ourselves what the effect of using such a word has on the status of these individuals and groups within society. The most significant group of *Ausländer* comprises those individuals of Turkish origin, more than 1.8 million. Although not all of these individuals will necessarily have equal competence in speaking the Turkish language or will use it on an everyday basis or even transmit it to their children, they still constitute a very significant minority language group in Germany with their own linguistic culture. For example, the leading Turkish-language tabloid, *Hürriyet,* sells more than 400,000 copies in Germany (twice as many as *Die Welt,* for instance), and it is estimated that 86 percent of Turkish origin households receive Turkish language satellite television programs via TRT International (Ohlwein, Schellhase, & Wolf, 1997, p. 178).

What all these examples of linguistic and cultural variation show us is that we cannot consider Germany to be simply a linguistically and culturally homogeneous country. While at a national—and indeed an international level—there is the unifying cultural and identity marker of the German language, groups, localities, and regions all share various types of "German" and construct and reinforce a variety of complementary and competing cultures and subcultures, the sum of which equate to German language and culture.

WHOSE GERMAN? WHOSE CULTURE?

A subject like spelling might seem a long way removed from an exciting topic such as culture. However the debates about spelling reform in German that began in the late 1980s opened up a whole discussion of who owns the heart and soul of the German language.

It may seem absurd to the outsiders from the English-speaking world to have institutions and groups concerned with the defense and maintenance of their respective languages: institutions that discuss how new concepts can be described and translated (usually from English) into acceptable forms; bodies that are concerned with domesticating foreign words—by giving them a gender, for instance—and deciding when a foreign word has become part of the German language; linguists (and politicians) who are concerned with the "purity" of the language and who decide on spelling. Such issues may never have occurred to a monolingual English speaker. There would appear to be very little need to preserve or defend their language, because English is seen by French and German speakers, and in fact speakers of many other languages in the world, as the key culprit and triumphant conqueror here. The idea of a threat to Anglophone culture is as surreal as the actual threat to Francophone and Germanophone cultures is real. *Sprachkultur,* which Patrick Stevenson defines as "the conscious attempt to cultivate the knowledge and use of the language as the embodiment of the German cultural tradition" (1997, p. 186), is a very real topic in contemporary German-speaking culture.

The original codification and standardization of German spelling were seen as an important part of linguistic and ultimately national unification from 1871 on. Up to that time, the individual states had had their own separate rule books. Karl Duden published his first dictionary in 1880 for all of Germany, and in 1901 the rules that were in operation until recently were agreed. When proposals for reform and simplification of German spelling were unveiled in 1988, they "resulted in media uproar. Every commentator, feature writer, and talk-show host was suddenly an expert on orthography" (Glück & Sauer, 1995, p. 86). A modified version of these new norms is now being implemented on a gradual basis. However, spelling and language norms are not something removed from everyday culture. Spelling is not just the rules, but also how the rules are used in day-to-day communication—and the process is not simply one-way. As Glück and Sauer point out, there has been a good deal of relaxation in spelling norms, not least as a result of everyday use and experimentation with language in advertising and the media.

One thing that invariably strikes the visitor to Germany in particular—but this applies also to the other German-speaking countries—or the casual viewer/reader of German media is the number of English words and phrases. Advertising is an area in which the use of English is particularly prominent. Sometimes it may be a simple buzzword or slogan. In other cases, it will be a whole sentence or complex phrase that requires more than a surface knowledge of English. In a number of cases, English is used because the product or service being advertised is of British or American origin. For example, the British brand Rover uses the English slogan "You're welcome" when advertising its cars in Germany. However, the extent of English usage in all areas of the media in German-speaking countries has meaning, use, and significance independent of the countries in which it is spoken. Its use may be a symbol of globalism, of youth, of progress and modernity; at one and the same time, it can bear the properties of pan-Europeanness, Americanness, and internationalism. For example, an advertisement for Rolf Benz, a furniture manufacturer, contains a number of English vocabulary items, such as *"unser Showroom."* The text is set against a background graphic of a trendily dressed couple living in an apartment furnished with the most modern furniture. The atmosphere is sophisticated and worldly. The slogan sums this up: "Rolf Benz: Living at its Best." Conversely, advertisements for products aimed at an older audience tend to avoid foreign words in favor of their German counterparts in an attempt to appeal to a sense of traditional culture.

There are many reasons for the preponderance of anglicisms or English words in German, particularly in the media. One was the economic aid given to

Germany by the United States through the Marshall Plan. This not only contributed to the *Wirtschaftswunder* or economic miracle of the postwar period, but also helped to cement German–American relations. Because of the Cold War and East Germany's allegiance to the Soviet Union, it became inevitable that West Germany would follow a Western orientation in its politics and economics, and in the second half of the 20th century, this sphere was dominated by the United States. Probably the most significant factor accounting for the quantity of anglicisms today is the omnipresence of American and Anglophone international culture and the status of English as a global lingua franca.

Attitudes towards these anglicisms and their impact on German-speaking culture vary greatly depending on age, education, linguistic ability, and experience. For every person who feels that he/she accommodates international communication and openness to other cultures, there is someone else who feels that such people are the harbingers of *Denglisch*—the dreaded hybrid of Deutsch and English spoken by a generation who will master neither language adequately. The Internet and its vocabulary appear for many to have consolidated the position of the English language in German linguistic culture and exemplify the German language's easy access policy regarding foreign words. As Dieter Zimmer (1997) points out, the Germans have only translated 57% of IT and Internet vocabulary into German, far less than the Spanish (80%), the Polish (82%), the French (86%) and the Finnish (93%), despite the fact that German is one of the major European languages. The heated debates that take place on the Internet about these issues illustrate that the topic is hotly contested in Germanophone culture. The following sample contributions about whether or not to translate the word "site" speak for themselves:

> *Die Fachleute verbinden mit den englischen Begriffen inzwischen klare Vorstellungen, waehrend eine deutsche Uebersetzung zunaechst einmal etabliert werden mueßte.* (Experts working in the IT area know exactly what is meant by the English words, whereas a German translation would first of all have to become established and accepted.)
>
> *Die deutschen Sprachen sind also die Sprachen des Volkes und vielleicht sollte man dem Volk auch die Hoheit ueber die deutschen Sprachen ueberlassen. Oft ist das "Volk" im Umgang mit neuen Kulturen und Woertern viel unverkrampfter als viele Intellektuelle und Sprachpuristen.* (The Germanic languages are, after all, the languages of the people and perhaps the people should be given control over these languages. Ordinary people are often much less inhibited than many intellectuals and language purists when it comes to new cultures and words.)
>
> *Es [kann] gar nicht so schwer sein, deutsche Begriffe fuer den Informatikbereich zu finden. Ich glaube, dass es oft einfach Faulheit ist, wenn wir die englischen Begriffe uebernehmen. Ein(e)(?) web-site waere schlicht und einfach eine Internet-Adresse.* (It cannot really be that difficult to find German expressions for the IT sector. I think that it is often due to sheer laziness that English terms are used. A web-site is an *"Internet-Adresse,"* plain and simple.)
>
> *Projekte, die amerikanisch geprägte und international etablierte Fachsprache der Informationstechnologie zu regionalisieren, kann man mit dem gleichen Humor betrachten, als wollten einige Germanisten den Medizinern das Lateinische und Griechische verbieten. Gegen die so entwickelten Sprachkraempfe schlage ich als Therapie freundliches Laecheln vor, solange man uns nicht mit der Kraft des Gesetzes dazu bewegen will, uns daran zu halten.* (Attempts to localize the internationally established language of IT which has been moulded by American English is as crazy as Germanists trying to ban medics from using Latin and Greek. Laughter is the best medicine for these linguistic spasms, just so long as no one is going to try to make us all abide by some rule about this.) (http://www.dafnett.com.br/diskuss/site001.htm)

LANGUAGE, CULTURE AND EXTERNAL PERCEPTIONS

A few years ago, following a number of unpleasant incidents, the German School in London decided to issue guidelines to its pupils. One recommendation was to avoid acting provocatively in public by, for instance, speaking German with each other. It is depressing to think that speaking German in a non-German-speaking country could be perceived as provocative, but it is perhaps not surprising when we consider external attitudes to the German language, particularly among people who have never learned the language and who have had only limited encounters with it. Many will comment on what a "hard" language it is (presumably as opposed to a "soft" language such as French or an "easy" language such as English). Mark Twain's famous quotations about the impossibility of the German language (it would, he claimed, take 30 years to master the language, as opposed to 30 hours for English, and 30 days for French), and his conclusion that many German compounds were not words but alphabetic processions, seem to ring true for many who have no knowledge of the German language.

Value judgments about languages and the people who speak them are part of our own culture too. After all, how could we feel part of a particular culture if it did not exclude some other people? What would make it special? Many of these stereotypes are formed and fed by our own language via our media. It is hardly surprising that many people have a negative attitude toward German, thinking of it as an "aggressive language," because their first encounter with the language often takes place through films about the Second World War in which very nasty-looking German soldiers are played by Anglophone actors with a German accent! It may seem rather absurd that such images and encounters inform attitudes toward the German language, but we have only to consider the effect of inserting a German word (or an English word with a "German" accent) into a sentence. Why does a speaker do this? What effect is s/he trying to achieve? For example, a very negative review of a German restaurant in London that appeared in the *Sunday Times* included vocabulary such as *"Herr," "la, la,"* and *"ubernationale* cuisine." The inclusion of these words certainly added to the bilious tone of the review. In a television report about a *Star Trek* convention, one participant, when asked how to impersonate the fearsome Klingon race, advised that the best thing was probably to look very angry and shout something in German! People are all too familiar with the tabloid headlines in the United Kingdom that deliberately use German words such as *"Achtung"* and *"Herr"* to conjure up negative feelings and associations.

On the other hand, a positive association which the German language appears to have for non-German-speakers internationally and which impacts on their perception of German culture is that of technology. Not surprisingly, this is an association German manufacturers have been keen to exploit when selling their products. As a result, we regularly come across German words in automobile advertisements. The best example of this is Audi's well-known slogan *"Vorsprung durch Technik,"* a rather strange slogan which roughly means jumping ahead through technology. The decision was taken not to translate this for advertising in non-German-speaking countries, and this clearly paid off for Audi, as it is now one of the best known and recognized advertising slogans and a standard "German" phrase of the non-German-speaking Anglophone.

All of these examples may seem fairly harmless, but for someone who has little or no contact with German speakers and whose only exposure to the language is through such channels, these very minor encounters with the German language take on a very great significance, summing up for that person and whole groups of people, in a metonymic way, what German culture is. And, because of the history of the first half of the 20th century, German is often a "misunderstood" and misrepresented language. The very substantial financial and human resources allocated to cultural and linguistic institutions such as the Goethe Institute are intended to go some way toward improving knowledge and understanding of the German language and, by extension, German culture internationally. In conclusion, to come back to the translation class mentioned at the beginning of the chapter, it is important to remember that the apparent coincidence of language, culture, nation, and identity is not something that has existed in perpetuity. We should never make the mistake of assuming a sacred and ancient link between language, culture, and identity. Once we start digging beneath what appears to be a prototypical nation-state, we will inevitably unearth the hand of someone—politician, preacher, entrepreneur—who has manipulated this combination with some goal in sight, be it ideological, political, religious, or economic. Language may not always be the cause, but instead the effect, of national culture. As with all languages, encountering German, learning the language, and studying the culture are not really about seeking out the "true" German language and culture; instead, they involve opening up to the contradictions and inconsistencies that are the lived linguistic culture.

Notes

1. For a comprehensive history of Lëtzebuergesch, see Newton (1996). Hogan-Brün (2000) also contains a chapter on the German language in Luxembourg.
2. The spelling reform is discussed in more detail below.

3. An important point to make here is that there is a danger when considering the important issue of sexist language in assuming that male or masculine language is the norm. A challenging and refreshing accompaniment to any exploration of feminist linguistics is *Masculinity and Language* (1997), edited by two Germanists, Sally Johnson and Ulrike Hanna Meinhof.
4. A number of immigrants, mainly from Russia and other states of the former Soviet Union but also from certain other countries in Eastern Europe, are afforded special status as *Aussiedler* or ethnic Germans. This is because they come from German-speaking minority groups in these countries.

References

Bernstein, B. (1971). *Social class, language and socialisation.* The Hague: Mouton.

Braun, P. (1998). *Tendenzen in der deutschen Gegenwartssprache—Sprachvarietäten* (4th ed.). Stuttgart: Kohlhammer.

Glück, H., & Sauer, W. W. (1995). Norms and reforms: Fixing the form of language. In P. Stevenson (Ed.), *The German language and the real world* (pp. 95–116). Oxford: Clarendon Press.

Hogan-Brün, G. (Ed.) (2000). *National varieties of German outside Germany.* Oxford: Peter Lang.

Johnson, S., & Meinhof, U. H. (Eds.). (1997). *Masculinity and language.* Oxford: Blackwell.

Mattheier, K. J. (1980). *Pragmatik und Soziologie der Dialekte: Einführung in die Kommunikative Dialektologie des Deutschen.* Heidelberg.

Moosmuller, S. (1995). Evaluation of language use in public discourse: Language attitudes in Austria. In P. Stevenson (Ed.), *The German language and the real world* (pp. 257–278). Oxford: Clarendon Press.

Nelde, P., & Darquennes, J. (2000). German in old and new Belgium. In G. Hogan-Brün (Ed.), *National varieties of German outside Germany* (pp. 121–138). Oxford: Peter Lang.

Newton, G. (Ed.). (1996). *Luxembourg and Lëtzebuergesch: Language and communication at the crossroads of Europe.* Oxford: Clarendon Press.

Ohlwein, M., Schellhase, R., & Wolf, B. (1997). Marketing and the marketplace. In N. B. R. Reeves & H. Kelly-Holmes (Eds.), *The European business environment—Germany* (pp. 160–211). London and Boston: International Thompson Business Press.

Pusch, L. (1997a). Language is publicity for men—but enough is enough! In P. Herminghouse & M. Mueller (Eds.), *Gender and Germanness: Cultural productions of nation* (pp. 323–326). Providence and Oxford: Berghahn.

Pusch, L. (1997b). The New Duden: Out of date already? In P. Herminghouse & M. Mueller (Eds.), *Gender and Germanness: Cultural productions of nation* (pp. 327–330). Providence and Oxford: Berghahn.

Schlosser, H. D. (1983). Die "Dialekrwelle"—eine Gefahr für die Hochsprache? *Der Sprachdienst, 1983*(3–4).

Schneider, P. (1990). *Extreme Mittellage—eine Reise durch das deutsche Nationalgefühl.* Reinbek bei Hamburg: Rowohlt.

Stevenson, P. (1997). *The German-speaking world.* London: Routledge.

Zimmer, D. (1997). *Deutsch und anders: Die Sprache im Modernisierungsfieber.* Reinbek: Rowohlt.

Concepts and Questions

1. What does Kelly-Holmes mean when she writes that "Words themselves have no inherent meanings? Meanings are instead attached to them by members of a speech community, a culture?"
2. Explain the following sentence: "We cannot say that language contributes to culture without acknowledging at the same time that culture contributes in turn to language."
3. Why does Kelly-Holmes say dialects are often defined sociologically, politically, or economically rather than linguistically?
4. Why in Germany do dialects often reflect status?
5. How does the German language exclude women through its grammar?
6. How do the German media contribute to the Anglicizing of the German language?

Dialogue and Cultural Communication Codes Between Israeli Jews and Palestinians

Donald G. Ellis
Ifat Maoz

Even a casual observer of contemporary political events knows that Israeli Jews and Palestinian Arabs are locked in severe conflict that often becomes violent. The origins of the conflict between Israeli Jews and Palestinian Arabs can be traced to the end of the 19th century with the appearance of political Zionism and the resulting waves of Jewish immigration to Palestine. Zionism sought to establish a Jewish state in Palestine. On the same land, however, lived Arabs, with a Palestinian national identity. This resulted in a clash between the Jewish and Palestinian communities over ownership of the land, the right of self-determination, and statehood. Violence between the two communities first erupted in the 1920s and has pervaded the relationship in various forms, and with varying degrees of intensity, since that time (Kelman, 1997; Rouhana & Bar-Tal, 1998).

The communal clash that characterized the first decades of the 20th century escalated into a war that involved the neighboring Arab states. This war erupted after the United Nations (UN) declared, in November 1947, the partition of Palestine into two states—one Arab and one Jewish. The Palestinians rejected the UN partition plan, and an independent Jewish state was established in 1948. Israel won the war, and most Palestinians who lived in the portion of Palestine on which Israel was now established were dispersed to the neighboring Arab countries, partly having fled war zones and partly having been expelled by Israeli forces (Maoz, 1999).

Other historical turning points in the relationship between Israelis and Palestinians include the 1967 war between Israel on one side, and Egypt, Jordan, and Syria on the other, which brought the remainder of Palestine under Israeli control. The first *intifada,* or uprising, was an uprising of the Palestinians in the West Bank and Gaza Strip territories, expressing resistance to the Israeli occupation of these territories. It began in 1987 and lasted until 1993 (Rouhana & Bar-Tal, 1998).

In 1993 peace accords were signed in Oslo, Norway, which signaled a breakthrough in the relations between Israelis and Palestinians. This dramatic agreement included an exchange of letters of mutual recognition between representatives of the two peoples, which was followed by a declaration of principles that stipulated the establishment of a Palestinian authority in Gaza and Jericho as a first step in Palestinian self-rule (Kelman, 1997). At this point, which indeed was historic, prospects for the success of the peace process seemed exceptionally good. There was hope that the peace accords would end violence and lead to reconciliation; however, a few years after signing the accords, it became clear that this optimism was premature.

A chain of violent incidents began in November 1995 with the assassination of the then prime minister of Israel and continued with several terrorist attacks in the first half of 1996. These events signaled a slowdown in the Israeli–Palestinian peace process. Increasingly, the adversaries presented obstacles and impediments to the peace process, posed problems for the implementation of the different stages of the agreements, and violated the agreements. In October 2000, the Al Aqsa *intifada* broke out, and the relationship between the Israelis and the Palestinians again took a violent turn.

Yet political leaders from both sides continue to try and return to peace making and peace building. Although the conflict centers on the issue of land, and who has legitimate rights to the land—an issue that has strong historical, religious, and emotional significance—it is also a cultural conflict, a conflict over identities and recognition. The political and cultural differences between Israeli Jews and Palestinians involve negative stereotypes, mutual delegitimization, and severe miscommunication. Dialogue and group encounters are one way to cope with these difficult problems. Dialogue sessions between Israeli Jews and Palestinians involve a process of transformative communication aimed at improving the relations between the sides (Maoz, 2000b).

This original essay first appeared in the 10th edition and has been revised for this edition. Donald G. Ellis teaches at the School of Communication at the University of Hartford, West Hartford, Connecticut. Ifat Maoz teaches in the Department of Communication at The Hebrew University, Mt. Scopus Campus, Jerusalem, Israel.

TRANSFORMATIVE COMMUNICATION BETWEEN GROUPS IN CONFLICT

Intergroup dialogues are useful venues for growth, change, and conflict management. Transformative dialogue between cultural groups in conflict helps reduce prejudice and hostility and foster mutual understanding (Gergen, 1999). Such dialogue experiences have been successful at helping groups cope with conflict in Northern Ireland, South Africa, and the Middle East.

The notion of transformative contact or dialogue, when used in the context of intergroup conflict, draws heavily from the contact hypothesis in social psychology. This theory was first presented by Allport (1954) and since has been the subject of numerous studies (Amir, 1976; Pettigrew, 1998). The *contact hypothesis* states that under certain conditions, contact between groups in conflict reduces prejudice and changes negative intergroup attitudes. The contact hypothesis is optimal under certain conditions:

1. The two groups should be of equal status, at least within the contact situation. Contact of unequal status, where the traditional status imbalance is maintained, can act to perpetuate existing negative stereotypes.
2. Successful contact should involve personal and sustained communication between individuals from the two groups.
3. Effective contact requires cooperative interdependence, where members of the two groups engage in cooperative activities and depend on one another in order to achieve mutual goals.
4. Social norms favoring equality must be the consensus among the relevant authorities.

TRANSFORMATIVE DIALOGUES BETWEEN ISRAELIS AND PALESTINIANS

The first attempts to address the dispute between Israelis and Palestinians by means of structured communication events were in interactive problem-solving workshops that were developed by Herbert Kelman from Harvard University in the early 1970s and have been conducted since then by him and his colleagues (Kelman, 1997). These workshops brought together politically active and influential Israelis and Palestinians for private, direct communication facilitated by unofficial third-party mediators (Kelman, 1995, 1997). Since the Oslo peace agreements in 1993, numerous Israeli–Palestinian dialogue events have been conducted each year, targeted at grassroots populations from both sides (Adwan & Bar-On, 2000). These dialogue events typically last two to three days and are aimed at building peace and reconciliation through processes of constructive communication (Maoz, 2000b). Both Israelis and Palestinians facilitate the dialogues. In some sessions all of the participants meet, and in others they are divided into smaller groups. There are also several uninational meetings in which participants meet only with members of their own group. Dialogues are conducted either in English or in Hebrew and Arabic with translation.

The concept of "dialogue" as discussed by scholars such as Martin Buber, Carl Rogers, and Mikhail Bakhtin is the general guiding principle of these groups. That is, the goal of the communication is to avoid "monologue," or the pressure of a single authoritative voice, and to strive for "dialogue," which emphasizes the interplay of different perspectives where something new and unique emerges. At its best, dialogue is a search for deep differences and shared concerns. It asks participants to inquire genuinely about the other person and avoid premature judgment, debate, and questions designed to expose flaws.

The process of change and transformation during dialogue is difficult, complex, and slow. Many issues enter the mix of politics, psychology, culture, and communication. In our work we have found that the communication process remains central. There is simply no possibility for reconciliation and peace without sustained interaction. Therefore, we direct our attention to the issues in culture and communication that characterize these groups. The remainder of this article is devoted to explaining the cultural communication codes that typify interactions between Israeli Jews and Palestinians and how these speech codes are expressed in actual dialogues when Israeli Jews and Palestinians are arguing.

SPEECH CODES

Whenever groups of people live in a culture, they have certain characteristics and behaviors in common. We know, for example, that people in cultures dress similarly, share tastes in food preparation, and have many common attitudes, but they also share orientations toward communication. Members of cultural communities share principles of language use and interpretation. This simply means that your use of language (word choice, slang, accents, syntax) and your tendencies to interpret and understand this language in a certain way depend on your cultural membership. For example, assume you overhead the following conversation (Ellis, 1992):

Jesse: Yea, I'm thinkin' 'bout getting some new ink.

Gene: Really, where you gonna put it?

Jesse: Oh, I don' know. I've still got some clean spots.

For the moment, this conversation is probably pretty confusing and odd. What does it mean to "get new ink"? Why is Gene concerned about where to put it? What do "clean spots" refer to? Who are these people, and what cultural functions is this conversation serving? Is Jesse thinking about buying a new bottle of ink for his fountain pen and Gene does not think there will be room for it on his messy desk?

This is a conversation between two tattoo enthusiasts who live and work among others in a tattoo culture that has developed norms of speaking. If you were a member of the culture and understood the "speech code," then you could participate in this conversation easily and competently. You would know that "new ink" refers to a "new tattoo" and that "clean spots" are places on the body that have no tattoos. You would understand the personal identity satisfaction that members of this culture gain from their unique code of communication.

Jesse and Gene are speaking in a cultural code, and you can only understand and participate in the conversation if you understand the code. The concept of speech codes has been studied by Bernstein (1971), Ellis (1992, 1994), and Philipsen (1997). Philipsen's treatment is most thorough in communication, and it is the perspective we rely on here. But first we describe two cultural communication codes termed *dugri* and *musayra* known to characterize Israeli Jews and Arabs, respectively. This discussion will be followed by an elaboration of the concept of speech codes and an explanation of their role in intercultural communication dialogues for peace.

Israeli-Jewish and Arab cultures have emerged from the special circumstances of their history, and different norms of communication emerge from this history. These contrasting speech codes can make for difficult and uncoordinated communication. Several researchers have described an Arab communication code called *musayra* (e.g., Feghali, 1997; Katriel, 1986). *Musayra* means "to accommodate" or "go along with." It is a way of communicating that orients the speaker toward a harmonious relationship with the other person. *Musayra* emerges from the core values of Arab culture that have to do with honor, hospitality, and collectivism. An Arab speaker who is engaging in the code of *musayra* is being polite, indirect, courteous, and nonconfrontive to the other member of a conversation.

More specifically, *musayra* is composed of four communication features. The first is *repetition,* in which the communication is characterized by repetitive statements that are formulaic in nature. Repetition is used primarily for complimenting and praising others, which is an important communication activity when you are trying to be gracious and accommodating. Repetition is also used as an argumentative style, in which repeated phrases rather than Western-style logic are used to influence beliefs. *Indirectness* is a second feature of the *musayra* code. This communication strategy reflects the cultural tendency to be interpersonally cautious and responsive to context. By being indirect, one can shift positions more easily to accommodate the other person. Indirectness also facilitates politeness and face saving. *Elaboration* is a third feature, which pertains to an expressive and encompassing style. It leads to a deeper connection between speakers and affirms relationships. The final characteristic is *affectiveness,* or an intuitive and emotional style. Again, this allows for identification with the other person and the maintenance of an engaged relationship.

The speech code of Israeli Jews is a sharp contrast to *musayra.* Israeli Jews employ a direct, pragmatic, and assertive style. This style has been termed *dugri* by Katriel (1986). *Dugri* means "straight talk" and is a well-documented code used by Israeli Jews. *Dugri* is the opposite of *musayra. Dugri* speech is "to the point," with the communication of understanding and information as the most important communicative goals. Emotional appeals and personal niceties are of secondary importance. In *musayra* it is important to maintain the face or positive image of the other speaker. In *dugri* speech the speaker is more concerned with maintaining his or her own image of clarity and directness.

Dugri and *musayra* are excellent examples of speech codes. Philipsen (1997) describes five main ideas that characterize cultural speech codes. We can see how these ideas are powerfully ingrained in the communication of cultural members and are often responsible for misunderstanding and problems in intercultural communication. We further elaborate on *dugri* and *musayra* by explaining them within the context of the five principles of speech codes.

Speech Codes Are Culturally Distinctive

Speech codes are identified with a specific people in a specific place. When you first listen to people speak, you often ask or wonder, "Where are they from?" Language is always identified with locations such as countries (e.g., American English, British English, or Australian English), regions (e.g., the South, East), or neighborhoods. Israeli *dugri* speech is associated with native-born Israelis of Jewish heritage in the land of Israel. The code is unique to Jews primarily of European heritage, and the code became crystallized in the pre-state period of the 1930s and 1940s (Katriel, 1986). *Musayra* is culturally distinct for speakers of Arabic and members of Arabic cultures; however, its geographic location is more complex than *dugri* because Arabic cultures are more geographically diverse. In both cases, however, when speakers of a code change geographic locations, they modify their code use.

Speech Codes Result from a Psychology and Sociology Unique to the Culture

Speech codes are intimately connected to the psychological qualities of a culture. They are related to how people see themselves. In other words, certain attitudes, values, and states of mind are more descriptive of one culture than another. For example, an Arab using a *musayra* code is maintaining consistency with his culture's expectations of honor. Honor is a controlling psychological value that legitimates a modesty code and the hospitality that one bestows. To use a *musayra* code—to be indirect, affective, and polite—is to maintain honor and express a distinct psychology of Arabs. Israeli Jews, on the other hand, use *dugri* to express their strong native identity. This identity is rooted in the pride and strength they feel with respect to the state of Israel. Historically, Jews were a dislocated and oppressed people, but the establishment of the state of Israel altered this historical condition. *Dugri* speech is a communicative expression of this pride.

The Meaning and Significance of Messages Fundamentally Depend on Codes

You may be familiar with the maxim that "meanings are in people, not words." This means that true understanding of a communication depends on the people speaking and the code they use. When people communicate, they are performing some type of action, and others interpret that action. The interpretation relies on the speech code. When an Arab speaker displays a *musayra* code and is polite, indirect, and courteous, a non–code user might interpret this speech as being weak, obsequious, or manipulative. This interpretation can lead to communication problems. Israeli Jews have a reputation for being rude and aggressive. The *dugric* code contains a directness of style that includes bluntness and forthrightness. It is not uncommon to hear Israeli Jews in a meeting say things like "you are wrong" or "not true." This kind of directness is considered rude by many people, but not if you understand the code. A listener who "speaks" the *dugri* code will not come to any hasty conclusions about the dispositions of the other speaker, because the same code is used to define the communicative act. In other words, bold utterances such as "you are wrong" are understood as normal ways of speaking rather than a rude way of speaking.

Speech Codes Are Located in the Language and Communication of Native Speakers

This simply means that speech codes are on display in the language of others. These codes are not inside the heads of others or contained in the generalities about culture. They are empirically observable in the communication of cultural members. Thus, when a native Israeli speaks directly and bluntly, the *dugri* code is very apparent. Speech codes are also found in the ritualized functions of communication. These are the known and repeated ways of organizing interaction, and they have code-specific symbolic forms. A greeting ritual is an example. An African American will greet another African American differently than he would a white person. These people might use certain vocabulary and body movements to signal a bond or friendship. The same is true for *dugri* and *musayra*. Both have symbolic forms that project and affirm an identity. By studying these symbolic forms and communication patterns, we can discover how the cultural world is orderly rather than chaotic.

Speech Codes Can Be Used to Understand, Predict, and Control Communication

The artful understanding and use of speech codes can be used to improve communication. People do not communicate like machines. Even if they are steeped in cultural codes, they often think reflectively about the code and alter typical patterns. This means there is potential for change and opportunities to avoid the more troublesome aspects of codes. An Israeli who is being very *dugri* can learn to recognize how others perceive him or her and perhaps alter certain patterns of communication. Moreover, situations can alter speech codes. In the next section of this essay, we explain how codes are influenced by particular communication situations.

ARGUMENT BETWEEN ISRAELI JEWS AND PALESTINIANS

Argument is a persistent characteristic of the relationship between Israeli Jews and Palestinians. In fact, argument is important to these groups because at least it is an acceptable mechanism of conflict resolution. We would rather these two groups argue than shoot at each other. We might expect from the previous discussion that *dugri* speech would be characteristic of Israeli Jews and the mode of speech preferred by them during argument, because Israeli Jews have a speech code that includes an argumentative style. *Musayra,* on the other hand, is not argument oriented at all. Interestingly, the little research that exists on Arab argument patterns is consistent with *musayra*. Hatim (1991), in a study devoted to this issue, found that argumentation in modern Arabic is related to politeness and saving face.

Group status is one of the problems for groups in dialogue situations. When cultural groups are different in status, the arguments produced by the high-status groups can carry more weight. Israeli Jews, given their military and economic advantages, carry considerably more status into dialogues. Moreover, their speech codes are more conducive to argument. But dialogue groups that work to promote open discussion and equal relations can help lessen status differences. They become a context that levels differences. Even though Arabs come from a cultural background where argument is considered disrespectful, there are situations in which this difference can be diminished.

In our studies (Ellis & Maoz, 2001), we found that the arguments during political dialogues between Israeli Jews and Palestinians were not necessarily consistent with expectations from cultural speech codes. In other words, the Israeli Jews do not necessarily use more assertive arguments, and the Arabs are not necessarily less overtly aggressive. It appears that the dialogue context of communication does alter speech codes and provides an environment for more equal status discussion. Palestinians are more assertive during these dialogues than speech code theory would suggest. They speak more and engage in more reasoning and elaboration. This means that they state propositions and then support them with evidence in the classic tradition of argument.

The Israeli Jews are somewhat consistent with the *dugri* code because they are quick to object to allegations and challenge assertions made by the Palestinians. Their experience with the *dugri* code makes it easy for them to sharply deny charges and demand justifications. But these dialogues do provide an environment for transformative communication because they afford the Palestinians an opportunity to accuse the Israeli Jews of historical injustices. This is why the Israeli Jews are typically on the defensive with objections and challenges to various statements. But, interestingly, the Israeli Jews are also more hesitant and submissive in these dialogues. They qualify their arguments, backtrack, and provide context. Again, they are being challenged and responding in an accommodating and yielding manner rather than in a style associated with *dugri*. The dialogue context, and its transformative qualities, is probably responsible for these changes because typical roles are altered.

This dialogue context may also strengthen the sense of unity for groups with minority status, and the communication patterns reflect this fact. The Palestinians argue in such a way that they elaborate and provide evidence for arguments in a manner much more akin to *dugri* than their own *musayra*. They clearly use the context to transform themselves into a power coalition. The Palestinians engage in a form of "tag-team" argument (Brashers & Meyers, 1989), in which the group engages in repetitive elaboration of a point to produce the perception of unity. Following is an example of a tag-team argument. The Palestinians are expressing their anger about being prevented from entering Jerusalem. The Israelis say it is because of security, but the Palestinians "gang up" on the Israelis, saying that the security measures—checkpoints that the Palestinians must pass through that are monitored by the Israeli military—do not work and it is just harassment.

PAL: If we go into Jerusalem not through the *Machsom* (Hebrew word for "checkpoint"), I can go in. They see me, and they don't care. It is that they want to make it difficult for me.

PAL: There are three ways to go from Bethlehem to Jerusalem.

PAL: If I want to go to Jerusalem, I am there in five minutes.

PAL: Sixty thousand Palestinians every day go to Israel without permission, every day; forty thousand with permission. So it's not security, it's politics. This is the information. I am not saying this to support.

The Palestinians are emboldened. The dialogue context helps transform the indigenous code of each group. This is an important matter with respect to the power relationship between the groups. It suggests that the speech codes are pliant and that situations and activities can be found that reduce the cultural strength of these codes and make change and growth more possible. Moreover, these communication experiences balance the relationship between hostile and unequal groups in order to promote egalitarianism and make future interactions more productive.

CONCLUSION

In this article we have explained and illustrated cultural communication patterns between Israeli Jews and Palestinians. These two groups are in bitter conflict and experiencing tremendous pressures and tensions for reconciliation and change. Clearly, national leaders and negotiators for peace need to solve the legal and legislative issues with respect to land, sovereignty, and other legal obligations. But true peace and prosperity "on the ground" will come only when these two groups learn to work together and improve communication. We have shown in this essay that each national group has evolved a different code and orientation to communication. These codes can be bridges or barriers to communication. Although communication codes are relatively firm, they are not unyielding. We have shown that there are contexts and situations in which codes do not predict communication behavior. But more important, a thorough understanding of codes is necessary for dialogue and negotiation. Even words that are translated the same from different languages carry additional cultural baggage that is lost in the translation. Words are not neutral. They acquire their meaning from a culturally charged set of symbols that make up a speech code. The task for the future is to continually explore the nature of speech codes and their role in dialogue and conflict management.

References

Adwan, S., & Bar-On, D. (2000). *The role of non-governmental organizations in peace building between Palestinians and Israelis*. Jerusalem: PRIME (Peace Research Institute in the Middle East), with the support of the World Bank.

Allport, G. (1954). *The nature of prejudice*. Reading, MA: Addison-Wesley.

Amir, Y. (1976). The role of intergroup contact in change of prejudice and ethnic relations. In P. Katz (Ed.), *Towards the elimination of racism* (pp. 245–308). New York: Pergamon.

Bernstein, B. (1971). *Class, codes and control* (Vol. 1). London: Routledge & Kegan Paul.

Brashers, D. E., & Meyers, R. A. (1989). Tag-team argument and group decision making: A preliminary investigation. In B. E. Gronbeck (Ed.), *Spheres of argument: Proceedings of the sixth SCA/AFA conference on argumentation* (pp. 542–550). Annandale, VA: Speech Communication Association.

Ellis, D. G. (1992). Syntactic and pragmatic codes in communication. *Communication Theory, 2*, 1–23.

Ellis, D. G. (1994). Codes and pragmatic comprehension. In S. A. Deetz (Ed.), *Communication yearbook 17* (pp. 333–343). Thousand Oaks, CA: Sage.

Feghali, E. (1997). Arab cultural communication patterns. *International Journal of Intercultural Relations, 21*, 345–378.

Gergen, K. (1999, May). *Toward transformative dialogue*. A paper presented to the 49th Annual Conference of the International Communication Association, San Francisco.

Hatim, B. (1991). The pragmatics of argumentation in Arabic: The rise and fall of a text type. *Text, 11,* 189–199.
Katriel, T. (1986). *Talking straight: Dugri speech in Israeli sabra culture.* London: Cambridge University Press.
Kelman, H. (1995). Contributions of an unofficial conflict resolution effort to the Israeli-Palestinian breakthrough. *Negotiation Journal, 52,* 19–27.
Kelman, H. (1997). Group processes in the resolution of international conflicts: Experiences from the Israeli-Palestinian case. *American Psychologist, 52,* 212–220.
Maoz, I. (2000a). An experiment in peace: Processes and effects in reconciliation aimed workshops of Israeli and Palestinian youth. *Journal of Peace Research, 37,* 721–736.
Maoz, I. (2000b). Multiple conflicts and competing agendas: A framework for conceptualizing structured encounters between groups in conflict—The case of a coexistence project between Jews and Palestinians in Israel. *Journal of Peace Psychology, 6,* 135–156.
Maoz, I., & Ellis, D. G. (2001). Going to ground: Argument in Israeli-Jewish and Palestinian encounter groups. *Research on Language and Social Interaction, 34,* 399–419.
Maoz, M. (1999). From conflict to peace? Israel's relations with Syria and the Palestinians. *Middle East Journal, 53,* 393–416.
Pettigrew, T. (1998). Intergroup contact theory. *Annual Review of Psychology, 49,* 65–85.
Philipsen, G. (1997). A theory of speech codes. In G. Philipsen & T. L. Albrecht (Eds.), *Developing communication theories* (pp. 119–156). Albany: State University of New York Press.
Rouhana, N., & Bar-Tal, D. (1998). Psychological dynamics of intractable ethnonational conflicts: The Israeli-Palestinian case. *American Psychologist, 53,* 761–770.

Concepts and Questions

1. What roles do land rights, religion, and cultural conflict play in defining the communicative dynamics of Israeli Jews and Palestinian Arabs?
2. What do Ellis and Maoz mean when they refer to "transformative communication"?
3. How does transformative communication help improve the communication between groups in conflict?
4. What conditions must be met between two groups in conflict before the contact hypothesis will help reduce prejudice and negative intergroup attitudes?
5. How does the concept of "dialogue" as discussed by Martin Buber, Carl Rogers, and Mikhail Bakhtin provide guiding principles for transformative dialogue?
6. How do cultural differences in speech codes affect communication between Israeli Jews and Palestinian Arabs? Provide some examples of differences in speech codes for each of these groups.
7. What have been the major circumstances that have led to the development of the unique speech codes among Israeli Jews and Palestinian Arabs?
8. *Musayra,* which means "to accommodate" or "to go along with," plays a major role in the speech codes of Palestinian Arabs. What are the four communicative features *of musayra?*
9. How do the speech codes of Israeli Jews differ from those of the Palestinian Arabs?
10. What do Ellis and Maoz mean when they assert that the meaning and significance of messages fundamentally depend on speech codes?

Public Speaking Patterns in Kenya

ANN NEVILLE MILLER

Culture affects every level of the public speaking process—from what constitutes a relevant example or offensive topic, to the different interpretations assigned to direct eye contact and specific gestures, to the variation in the types of evidence and argument that are most convincing to a particular audience. These differences and many others are best understood as patterns created by threads that run through the entire societal fabric. As Albert (1972) observed of Burundian speech, these practices make sense in the context of larger cultural values.

It is in the spirit of adding to knowledge about the variety of public speaking practice across the globe and to making sense of these differences in the light of overarching cultural orientations that this article examines characteristics of public speaking in the East African nation of Kenya. We will take as an organizing framework the two most frequently cited dimensions of cultural variability identified by Dutch sociologist Geert Hofstede, individualism–collectivism and power distance, as well as Edward T. Hall's concepts of monochronic and polychronic time and high- and low-context communication. But first a proviso: It is important to recognize that beyond the obvious impossibility of describing all significant influences on rhetorical practice in any single country, it is particularly difficult in Kenya (as in many other African nations) where each of the 40 to 50 indigenous cultural and linguistic groups has its own rules, values, and traditions. Some common themes that run throughout these numerous groups will be discussed here as "Kenyan culture," but any comments made must be recognized as generalizations about this diversity. The article will begin with a brief description of Kenyan value orientations and then move on to examine public speaking practices as outgrowths of these cultural patterns. Examples are based on the author's personal experience of living and working in Kenya for nine years, discussions with Kenyan colleagues and friends, and research conducted during that time on characteristics of Kenyan public speaking.

A BRIEF LOOK AT KENYAN VALUE ORIENTATIONS

Collectivism

Probably the construct most frequently used to explain similarities and differences between cultures is individualism versus collectivism (Gudykunst, 1998). African cultures as a group are considered to be collectivistic as opposed to individualistic (Hofstede, 1994; Kenyatta, 1965; Mbiti, 1970; Moemeka, 1997; Olaniran & Roach, 1994; Onwumechili, 1996). Some African scholars, in fact, have cited this as the defining quality of the African mindset (Gyekye, 1997). In collectivistic cultures, according to Hofstede (1991), "The 'we' group (or ingroup) is the major source of one's identity, and the only secure protection one has against the hardships of life. Therefore one owes lifelong loyalty to one's ingroup, and breaking this loyalty is one of the worst things a person can do" (p. 50). Kenyatta (1965), writing during the colonial era, observed regarding his own traditional Kikuyu culture in central Kenya, "The personal pronoun 'I' was used very rarely in public assemblies. The spirit of collectivism was [so] much ingrained in the mind of the people" (p. 188).

The collectivistic mindset affects every aspect of life. Responsibilities toward family in Kenya extend far down the genealogical line, and are financial as well as social. Families are frequently found housing or paying school costs for nephews, nieces, and cousins whom they may not know particularly well. Weddings, funerals, and other events, no matter how far away they take place geographically, must be attended, and usually span an entire day. In the workplace, collectivism may be manifested by the desire for job security and training over personal fulfillment (Hofstede, 1991). Employees at Kenyan businesses are rarely fired for incompetence, and as with family obligations, it is important to show solidarity with coworkers at significant times in their lives. For example, some time ago the author took part in a discussion about who would represent the university department at the

This original essay appears here in print for the first time. Ann Neville Miller is a Ph.D. candidate at the University of Georgia and teaches at Daystar University in Nairobi, Kenya.

funeral of a colleague's father. It was essential that the group be represented, even though the journey to and from the funeral would take three entire days.

Power Distance

Related to collectivism and also characterizing Kenyan culture is the orientation of high power distance. Power distance is defined as the extent to which less powerful members of society view the unequal distribution of power as a normal part of life (Hofstede, 1991); it is a description of the way a given society handles inequality. In low power distance societies such as the United States, egalitarianism is a primary value. People in these societies do not place much emphasis on titles, ceremony, and other outward displays of power. By contrast, most African societies are considered to be high power distance (Hofstede, 1991; Olaniran & Roach 1994), and consider such practices very important.

In the family, for instance, respect and deference to parents and older relatives is a lifelong obligation. Children are not expected to make their own decisions or contradict those of their elders. In Kenyan families, the power hierarchy is clearly delineated: the father is the supreme authority, followed by the mother and then frequently the oldest child. To directly question the word of the father in many families is unthinkable. When children begin school, their relationship to their teachers is similar to what they have with their parents. In Kenyan primary school classrooms, the teacher is an authoritative figure who displays less nurturing behavior than in a similar classroom situation in many Western nations (Maleche, 1997). In the workplace, a lower-level worker may feel uncomfortable ever directly addressing injustice by a superior unless there is a groundswell of popular dissent behind him/her. Even then the more likely method would be to approach the authority figure indirectly, either with hints or through an intermediary.

Monochronic and Polychronic Time

According to anthropologist Edward T. Hall, in cultures where the monochronic view of time predominates, people tend to run their lives by schedules in a linear fashion (Hall, 1983). They concentrate on only one thing at a time, compartmentalizing their lives—hence the term *mono*chronic. Time to such people is like a commodity; it can be bought, saved, wasted, or spent. Most Northern Europeans and North Americans operate on monochromic time. On the other hand, the prevailing view of time in Kenya is polychronic; what is important is not schedules and efficiency, but events and people. If a workshop, dedication ceremony, fundraiser, or other event takes longer than anticipated (which it often does if speeches run long and there are more speeches than originally planned), Kenyans believe it is more important to complete the event than to adhere to rigid schedules attendees might have for the rest of the day. Nor does being on time mean the same thing in Kenya as in the United States. It is not uncommon for weddings and other social events to begin hours late. Most people simply wait out the delays and take advantage of the opportunity to socialize. Because of increased globalization and the influence of Western media, some accommodation to the monochromic system has been made by urban Kenyans in recent years. For example, several large churches in Nairobi that are popular as wedding venues have begun to require that the ceremony begin within half an hour of the scheduled time, otherwise an extra fee is added. Overall, though, operating in monochromic time still appears to be an uncomfortable fit. The professionals who arrive at work in the morning with appointments for the day penciled in their diaries more often than not by afternoon have ordered their secretaries to make a string of calls postponing their meetings.

High- and Low-Context Communication

Although Hall's conception of high- and low-context elements in cultures is very encompassing, the focus here is on his application of these terms to interactions. According to Hall (1981), high-context communication features "pre-programmed information that is in the receiver and in the setting, with only minimal information in the transmitted message." Low-context transactions, he explains, are the opposite: "Most of the information must be in the transmitted message in order to make up for what is missing in the context" (p. 101). Because they accommodate change easily and rapidly, low-context messages are prevalent in technologically driven societies like the United States. High-context messages are the norm in most collectivistic societies. A great amount of information is held in common among members, and so less needs to be said explicitly. Kenyan traditional culture falls toward the high-context end of the continuum. One of the marks of wisdom in the elderly is the ability to convey messages indirectly through the use of proverbs and analogies, in public as well as in private settings. A child may not be told the error of her ways in so many words, but a carefully selected story related by the grandmother clearly communicates the correction.

PUBLIC SPEAKING PATTERNS AS OUTGROWTHS OF KENYAN VALUES

Having looked briefly at overarching Kenyan values, we now turn to examining the impact of these orientations on public speaking practice. Current research on the topic provides little guidance, as Africa is one of the least studied areas of the world in intercultural communication literature (Gudykunst, 1998; Shuter, 1997). Even in Kenya itself, there are no formal theories explaining why people speak in public today as they do. The closest approximation is descriptions in the fields of cultural anthropology and oral folklore of traditional ceremonies among specific groups. As Western-developed constructs, Hall and Hofstede's categorizations are necessarily limited in their capacity to portray communication from a truly African viewpoint, but they do provide a useful ground for comparison with more Eurocentric public speaking practice. Previous research by the author with Kenyan students and instructors of public speaking (Miller, 2002) has identified four areas of major areas of difference between mainstream U.S. and Kenyan public speaking patterns: speaking purposes, supporting material, credibility, and speech structure. These categories will be used as a framework for the present examination of Kenyan public speaking.

Speaking Purposes

Much public speaking in the United States is informative or persuasive in purpose; ceremonial occasions for public speaking are less common. This is due in part to the stress that mainstream U.S. culture places on informality. The average Kenyan, in contrast, will give far more ceremonial speeches in life than any other kind. These may be speeches of greeting, introduction, tribute, and thanks, among others. Life events both major and minor are marked by ceremonies, and ceremonies occasion multiple public speeches.

This means that unlike the majority of people in the United States, who report that they fear speaking in public, possibly even more than they fear death (Bruskin Report, 1973; McCroskey, 1993; Richmond & McCroskey, 1995), for most Kenyans public speaking is an unavoidable responsibility. For example, when a Kenyan attends a church service or other event away from home, s/he will often be asked to stand up and give an impromptu word of greeting to the assembly. In more remote areas, where literacy rates are low and there is little access to electronic media, this word of greeting can serve an informative purpose as well, because the one who has traveled often brings news of the outside world. The "harambee," a kind of community fundraising event peculiar to Kenya, is characterized by the presence not only of a guest of honor but also of various other dignitaries of a stature appropriate to the specific occasion, all of whom are likely at some point to address the gathering. Weddings and funerals overflow with ceremonial speeches, as virtually any relative, friend, or business associate of the newly married or deceased may give advice or pay tribute. Older members of the bride's family, for example, may remind her how important it is to feed her husband well, or warn the groom that in their family men are expected never to abuse their wives but to settle marital disputes with patience. Even the woman selected to cut the cake expects to give a brief word of exhortation before performing her duty. The free dispensing of advice, a hallmark of Kenyan wedding celebrations, would be out of place at most receptions in the United States, where the focus of speeches is normally more on remembrances and well-wishing.

In fact, when it comes to marriage, speech making begins long before the actual wedding day, at bridal negotiations where up to 40 or 50 people from the two families attempt to settle on a bride price. At these negotiations especially, but in other ceremonial speeches as well, "deep" language replete with proverbs and metaphors is expected. The family of the man may explain that their son has seen a beautiful flower, or a lovely she-goat, or some other item in the compound of the family of the young lady and that they would like to obtain it for their son. In a negotiation of this type that the author recently attended, the speaker for the bride's relatives explained that the family would require 20 goats as a major portion of the bride price. Since both parties were urban dwellers and would have no space to keep that many animals, the groom's family conferred with one another and determined that the bride's family really wanted cash. They settled on what they considered a reasonable price per goat, multiplied it by 20, and presented the total amount through their designated spokesperson to the representative of the bride. The original speaker looked at the money and observed dryly that goats in the groom's area were considerably thinner than those the bride's family was accustomed to![1] This type of indirect communication, the subtlety of which affords immense satisfaction and sometimes amusement to both speaker and listener, is a form of the high-context communication described by Hall. A full appreciation of the speech requires extensive knowledge of shared experiences and traditions.

Kenyan ceremonial speeches also display a formality that similar speeches in the United States may not. For example, it is very important at fundraisers, funerals, and other occasions for the master of ceremonies to be aware of any VIPs who are present and to ask them to give greetings in order of prominence. The unwritten rules for giving thanks at the end of such occasions are similar. The speaker must be careful to offer thanks to all persons present who have anything to do with the event. A member of parliament who speaks at many school fundraisers, for example, explained that he is careful to learn the history of the school and be sure to pay tribute to persons who have made substantial contributions to its success in the past. Even in small gatherings, a person of particular prominence should be allowed to make opening and closing remarks and be escorted from the room at the appropriate time.

The prevalence of ceremonial speeches and the importance placed on recognition of persons of status is clearly tied to the Kenyan value of high power distance. Because differences in power are considered natural in society, it is also natural that much of public speaking should be dedicated to affirming those distinctions. Titles must be carefully mentioned and due respect given by allowing the important person to speak. Omission of requisite recognition may not be taken lightly, as when one important politician walked late into an assembly, escaping the notice of the master of ceremonies. By the end of the event, someone had called the attention of the emcee to the presence of the politician, at which point he offered him an opportunity to address the group. The politician did so, but not without first making several pointed comments about not having been asked to speak earlier.

The joining together by the community to give and receive speeches of advice for newlyweds, congratulations of colleagues, and comfort for the bereaved is also an expression of the Kenyan value of collectivism. Although this value has been modified to a degree in urban areas by the influences of Western media and globalization, it is still true that marriage, widowhood, and other major life events are community experiences. As Mbiti (1970) observes, "Whatever happens to the individual happens to the whole group, and whatever happens to the whole group happens to the individual" (p. 141). It is not surprising, then, that ceremonial speeches, frequent and formal, are a central part of the lives of most Kenyans.

Supporting Material

Traditional Kenyan speeches are not normally based on extensive formal research. Whereas in the United States statistics are often used as evidence for the assertions made, in most Kenyan speech contexts facts and figures are not especially persuasive. Kenyans think more relationally. A Kenyan pastor once told the author a story to emphasize this point. One day he stopped along the road to give a ride to a stranger. His passenger explained that he was trying to get to the hospital because his brother had just been in a bus accident. "What do you think I asked him?" the pastor prodded rhetorically as he related the tale. "I didn't ask how many people were involved. I asked him *who*. Africans don't care about numbers, we care about the relationships."

The most convincing type of supporting material for a Kenyan public speech is a narrative, and the most convincing type of narrative is the personal story. "Subjectivity is the only sensible approach to the African mind," asserts one African professor of communication who studied in the United States. "In the West an overuse of personal stories might make the speaker appear not to be objective, but not with us. We believe you only really know about something if you've experienced it." Both speakers and audiences enjoy a good story, and the accomplished speaker will develop suspense, humor, and vivid characterizations in the telling. A listener from the United States may be surprised to find that once the narrative has unfolded, the speaker may not explicitly explain the connection of the story to the main point of the speech, but simply move on to other illustrations. What is happening in such cases, though, is understandable from the standpoint of high-context communication; audience members are being given the pleasure of inferring the underlying message for themselves. Scollon and Scollon (1981) view an evidently similar practice in Athabaskan oral narrative performance as a paying of respect by the narrator to the autonomy of the listener.

Beyond narratives, several other means of supporting one's point are common in Kenyan speeches. Proverbs, which like narratives teach lessons in a subtle way, are a sign of wisdom and experience; it is the old who are normally most familiar with proverbs and maxims. That is why an older person, such as the paternal uncle, is frequently in charge of conducting marriage negotiations. Such a person has the linguistic skill necessary to perform the intricate verbal dance required in pre-wedding speeches. In the urban environment, where audiences at most events are composed of people from several language groups, proverbs from the speaker's vernacular can still be used, but the speaker usually provides translation into Swahili or English. Songs can also be supporting material. A speaker may insert a song in the middle of the speech, singing ability or lack thereof being irrelevant. For example, in a graduation speech several years ago, the academic dean of a leading private Kenyan university, in an interesting synthesis of the traditional and contemporary, broke into strains of R. Kelly's "I Believe I Can Fly," then continued making his points.

Even audience response can be considered a type of supporting material. A speaker can leave the end of a sentence hanging and wait for the audience to fill in the blank, or lead the audience in chanting specific phrases. The latter practice has been used liberally by the nation's presidents. Founding president Jomo Kenyatta, for example, at Kenya's first independence day, led the audience in a crescendo of "Moto! Moto!" (Swahili for "Fire! Fire!") prior to commencing his speech. Many preachers drive home their points by allowing their audience to complete their sentences. At first glance these techniques might not appear to qualify as evidence, yet the function is exactly that of convincing the audience that the speaker's points are correct. As noted above, the use of narratives, proverbs, and songs is related to the Kenyan pattern of high-context communication, as they require shared experience for full understanding.

A close examination of these supporting materials also reveals a connection to the value of collectivism. Members of the audience at a public speech are not spectators. They are participants coming together to construct a shared communal meaning in the occasion. Audience response is part of that process; members are convinced that the speaker's assertions are true because they have participated in creating them. In a different way, willingness to sing during a speech is related to collectivism as well. In individualistic societies like the United States, where persons must strive to prove their own worth, singing in front of an audience is a risk unless one is sure of one's abilities. Speakers in the collectivistic Kenyan culture, however, are already assured of their worth as members of the group, so level of talent is not as much of a concern. The Luganda people in neighboring Uganda express this truth in their proverb "The one who doesn't sing well sings among his own."

Credibility

The need for speaker credibility is as essential in Kenya as it is in the United States. The factors that determine credibility, however, are different. Wealth, family status, age, and ethnicity—all demographic factors—are of highest importance. Wealth, whether in terms of herds, wives, children, or money, is a strong determinant of credibility. Its effect, however, is mitigated by the extent to which that wealth has been used to help other members of society. Marital and family status are also critical in a way that may be difficult for audiences in the United States to imagine. In many rural areas in Kenya, an unmarried man, or a married man with no sons or few children, cannot speak with authority. To participate in deliberative speaking about decisions affecting the village, he must have attained the status of elder, which often involves producing a certain number of sons or children. Traditionally, women could speak in public only on certain occasions, although in recent years this has changed. For example, a growing number of female politicians, including members of parliament, the former head of civil service, and one of the leading opposition voices in the most recent presidential election, have regularly addressed large gatherings both rural and urban. As in many collectivistic societies, age is less venerated in Kenya now than in the past. Nevertheless, even now, in certain situations the young cannot address the old in a public gathering (or in a private one either, for that matter), at least not without permission.

Finally, in a nation with 40 distinct cultural groups, ethnicity and language are important as well. Certain tribal groups have more credibility than others in addressing the nation as a whole. In culturally homogeneous gatherings, of course, to be from the same group and speak the same language is invaluable. However, language can be planned for particular effects in multiethnic gatherings as well. The immediate past president of the country, Daniel Moi, frequently divided his speeches into a more formal English section and a folksier second portion that he delivered in Swahili. It was in the second section, while using an African language, that he attempted to connect at a more emotional level with his constituents.

The Kenyan view of credibility appears to be closely tied to the value of high power distance. Similar to Albert's (1972) observations of speech behavior in Burundi, in Kenya persons with a particular status—whether due to age, wealth, or family—are automatically assured of a hearing in the public arena. Persons without these qualities understand that gaining credibility in a public speaking situation, unless they can borrow credibility through endorsement by someone who does possess these attributes, will be a challenge. In recent years, education has become an additional factor in speaker credibility, with advanced degrees mentioned in the introduction of a speaker automatically conferring a certain amount of respect. On this issue, Mbennah (1999) notes that although an elderly speaker would generally be considered more credible, in a case where technical expertise is required the audience would consider a young person possessing this knowledge to be more credible than an elderly person who did not.

Speech Structure

Various researchers, beginning with Kaplan (1966), have suggested that the logical and organizational patterns of rhetoric are determined by culture; they are not universal. Although it is generally recognized that most mainstream U.S. speeches are organized linearly, linear patterns do not represent the only logical systems available to public speakers. The organization of many Kenyan speeches could be represented as a bicycle wheel, or what Kearney and Plax (1996) call a web organizational pattern. The spokes wander out repeatedly to the rim as the speaker gives an illustration, mentions a proverb, or tells a story, and then return back to the thesis at the center, though usually not exactly at the place from which they departed. Often there is only one main point in such a speech, but it is developed by an abundance of supporting material. Westerners in the audience might feel bewildered and even bored because they are unable to follow the logic that ties all the points together, whereas Kenyan listeners would be absorbed in the stories and delighted with their subtle convergence back into the central theme.

It is difficult to convey this technique in print, but an introductory speech given at a large gathering at a Kenyan university recently may give an abbreviated idea of it. The master of ceremonies at the event welcomed the audience and then launched into a story about his childhood in a poor family in rural Kenya. He related that while still quite small he slept late one morning, much to his mother's irritation. Explaining this took some time as he made a number of humorous comments about how many children slept in one bed, how his mother normally disciplined him when she caught him misbehaving, how inclined he was to oversleeping at that stage of life, and so on. After the audience was thoroughly caught up in his description, the speaker brought the story to a climax. When he finally crawled out of bed, he said, his mother directed his attention outside to the garden where he was surprised to see that everything growing there had been completely flattened. "Now you see how when you are not alert you miss important things," she admonished him. "While you were sleeping, elephants were here and you never knew it." The speaker then addressed the audience directly: "We have elephants with us this morning." Amid general laughter, he invited the distinguished guests onto the stage. The implication of the story, of course, made through an amusing, much embellished personal anecdote, was that the audience should pay attention to the words of the very big people coming to address them. The point was made indirectly, and then only after the story was savored for its own sake. This might, in a Western setting, have seemed like a tangential sort of introduction, but within the Kenyan cultural environment it was extremely effective. The "bicycle wheel," or web, speech pattern that it exemplifies can be seen as an outgrowth of the collectivistic world view, depending as it does on extensive personal narratives into which the audience enters as co-participants, and incorporating the subtle connections characteristic of high-context communication.

Under the category of speech structure we will also include the use of time in public speeches. Unlike many speeches in the United States, the majority of Kenyan speeches are not time limited. A speaker may easily wax eloquent for an hour. Even speakers given the role of delivering preliminary speeches to the main guest may speak for half an hour or more, though admittedly to the secret chagrin of their audiences who most often would prefer to hear the guest of honor. Since programs often begin long after the stated hour, the end result is that of day-long celebrations for many large public events. Not uncommon is the experience of a Kenyan colleague who got lost on the way to a wedding and arrived a full two hours late. The church compound was full of milling people, and might have led an unaccustomed observer to assume that the wedding was already over. However, a quick check on the situation revealed that, in fact, the bride had not yet even arrived at the church. The tardy guest joined the rest of the crowd in waiting another 45 minutes until the bride came. Despite the late beginning, the wedding reception was allowed to run its full course of speeches, winding up many hours later. This situation is not unusual in Kenyan weddings, where last-minute haggling over the details of the marriage negotiations may take place when the groom's family comes on the wedding day to escort his fiancée from her homestead.

This aspect of public speaking is related to both the polychronic view of time and the value of collectivism that most Kenyans hold. What is important is that the significance of the event be fully acknowledged. If that means many speakers and long speeches, so be it. Because the group is valued more highly than individual interests, it is necessary to give every relevant person the opportunity to be heard at a given occasion. Harmony is more important than whether or not an individual makes it to his or her next appointment.

CONCLUSION

Much more could be said about Kenyan public speaking practices. Even this brief discussion suggests that although the basic categories that must be considered in presenting a speech are possibly universal (Clark, 1957), what makes for effective invention, arrangement, style, memory, and delivery varies across cultures. In an increasingly global society, it is important for public speakers and audiences to understand something of the variety of culturally defined expectations regarding the form of a public speech, and that many of these differences in practice are tied to deep-seated values and traits. In collectivistic cultures like Kenya, a public speech is more than a performance by a skilled actor; it is a shared experience. It drives home its message by allowing audience members to exert the mental effort to interpret and make connections for themselves, thereby creating an even stronger bond between speaker and audience through shared comprehension. It instantiates community ties by the ritual of recurring ceremony. And with a perspective that would sound postmodern had it not been established over hundreds of years of tradition, Kenyan listeners accept the subjective experiences of the speaker with the topic as the most telling evidence possible in a public speech. As a central feature in the lives of most Kenyans, public speaking is a distinct expression and shaper of cultural identity.

Note

1. Although it is outside of the purpose of this article to discuss the significance of the custom of African bride price, it should be noted that in most cultures the practice traditionally has not been seen as "buying" a wife, but as a means of bonding the two families together in mutual obligation and in that way strengthening the marriage of the two individuals. It also serves to show appreciation to the bride's family for the fine quality of upbringing they have given to the future daughter-in-law. The bride price is rarely paid at once, but through repeated meetings between the families that cement their relationship. Nor has it traditionally been funded solely by the parents of the groom, but rather pooled from various members of the extended family in yet another expression of collectivism.

References

Albert, E. (1972). Culture patterning of speech behavior in Burundi. In J. Gumperz & D. Hymes (Eds.), *Directions in sociolinguistics: The ethnography of communication* (pp. 72–105). New York: Holt, Rinehart and Winston.

Bruskin Report. (1973, July). *What are Americans afraid of?* (Research Rep. No. 53)

Clark, D. (1957). *Rhetoric in Greco-Roman education.* New York: Columbia University Press.

Gudykunst, W. (1998). Individualistic and collectivistic perspectives on communication: An introduction. *International Journal of Intercultural Relations, 22,* 107–134.

Gyekye, K. (1997). *Tradition and modernity: Philosophical reflections on the African experience.* New York: Doubleday.

Hall, E. (1981). *Beyond culture.* New York: Doubleday.

Hall, E. (1983). *The dance of life: The other dimension of time.* New York: Doubleday.

Hofstede, G. (1991). *Cultures and organizations: Software of the mind.* London: McGraw-Hill.

Kaplan, R. (1966). Cultural thought patterns in inter-cultural education. *Language Learning, 16,* 1–20.

Kearney, P., & Plax, T. (1996). *Public speaking in a diverse society.* Mountain View, CA: Mayfield.

Kenyatta, J. (1965). *Facing Mount Kenya.* New York: Vintage Books.

Maleche, H. (1997). *A comparison of teacher and student attitudes toward teacher behavior in Kenyan schools.* Unpublished master's thesis.

Mbennah, E. (1999). *The impact of audience world view on speaker credibility in persuasive speaking: The case of afrocentric and eurocentric audiences.* Unpublished doctoral dissertation.

Mbiti, J. (1970). *African religions and philosophy.* New York: Doubleday.

McCroskey, J. (1993). *An introduction to rhetorical communication* (6th ed.). Englewood Cliffs, NJ: Prentice Hall.

Miller, A. (2002). An exploration of Kenyan public speaking patterns with implications for the American introductory public speaking course. *Communication Education, 51,* 168–183.

Moemeka, A. (1997). Communalistic societies: Community and self-respect as African values. In C. G. Christians & M. Traber (Eds.), *Communication ethics and universal values* (pp. 170–193). London: Sage.

Olaniran, B., & Roach, D. (1994). Communication apprehension and classroom apprehension in Nigerian classrooms. *Communication Quarterly, 42,* 379–389.

Onwumechili, C. (1996). Organizational culture in Nigeria: An exploratory study. *Communication Research Reports, 13,* 239–249.

Richmond, V., & McCroskey, J. (1995). *Communication: Apprehension, avoidance, and effectiveness* (4th ed.). Scottsdale, AZ: Gorsuch Scarisbrick.

Scollon, R., & Scollon, S. (1981). *Narrative, literacy and face in interethnic communication.* Norwood, NJ: Ablex.

Shuter, R. (1997). Revisiting the centrality of culture. In J. N. Martin, T. K. Nakayama, & L. A. Flores (Eds.), *Readings in Cultural Contexts* (pp. 39–47). New York: Mayfield.

Concepts and Questions

1. Why is there more ceremonial than persuasive and informative speaking in Kenya?
2. What is a major difference between people in the United States and those in Kenya with regard to their fear of public speaking?
3. How would the formality or informality found in a culture influence the perception and use of public speaking techniques?
4. Why would the notion of power distance influence public speaking? In what ways might this influence be manifested?
5. How does the concept of collectivism exhibit itself in Kenya?
6. Why do Kenyans rely on the narrative for supporting material in the public speaking context, whereas in the United States people use statistics and testimony to help accomplish their speech purpose?
7. How does the bicycle organization pattern differ from the linear method used in the United States? Does it remind you of speech organizational schemes from other cultures?

Mexican *Dichos:* Lessons Through Language

Carolyn Roy

MEXICAN CULTURE AND ITS REFLECTED IMAGES

The late Octavio Paz, one of Mexico's most renowned writers, asserts in his classic *The Labyrinth of Solitude: Life and Thought in Mexico* that the Mexican's "face is a mask" (Paz, 1961, p. 29). Paz thereby implies that knowing *the* Mexican national character might be impossible. Carlos Fuentes, another of Mexico's most esteemed men of letters, employs the imagery of dark, ancient Aztec polished hematite mirrors reflecting the soul of Mexico when he writes: "Is not the mirror both a reflection of reality and a projection of the imagination?" (Fuentes, 1992, p. 11). Despite the self-confessed inscrutable nature of Mexican national character, *dichos*—popular sayings including, but not limited to, *proverbios*/ proverbs, *adagios*/adages, and *refranes*/ refrains—open an avenue for exploring the attributes most esteemed and salient in Mexican popular culture. Using Fuentes' metaphor, however, our understanding of Mexican culture remains a darkly reflected image. Our understanding is further obscured by the difficulty of precise idiomatic translation of the complex Mexican language that hybridizes the Spanish brought from Europe with the intricately nuanced indigenous languages, predominantly Nahuatl, of Mexico's native peoples. Nevertheless, popular sayings heard from the northern reaches of the Chihuahuan desert to the highlands of southern Chiapas do provide insight into some commonly held values in Mexican culture.

Such popular sayings transmit "what a culture deems significant" (Samovar & Porter, 2001, p. 36). Examination of these orally transmitted traditional values offers an excellent means of learning about another culture because these oft-repeated sayings fuse past, present, and future. These sayings focus our attention on basic principles accepted within the culture. The premise of this present exercise is that we can learn much about Mexican values through scrutiny of these distilled lessons of life transmitted through their language.

Although some of these popular sayings are uniquely Mexican, many more of them were brought to Mexico by Spaniards after 1519; therefore, they reflect the fusion of cultures, especially Castilian and Muslim, found in recently "reconquered" and unified early-16th-century Spain. Because many values are universally human, similar sayings may be found just as often in cultures around the globe. For example, most cultures attribute some responsibility for a child's character or nature to the parents; hence, in the United States one might hear "like father, like son" or "a chip off the old block" while in Mexico the close approximation is *de tal palo, tal astilla* (from such a stick, such a splinter). But the proverb *Al nopal nomás lo van a ver cuando tiene tunas* (One only goes to see the cactus when it has prickly pear fruit) derives specifically from the Mexican milieu. However, one might readily overhear a parent in the United States complaining to an adult child, "You only come to see me when you want something." So the principle of the saying is universal, but the expression relates uniquely to its culture. Although some sayings are culturally unique, and others universal, our purpose here is to focus on specific Mexican sayings that reflect some of the values of that culture.

MEXICAN *DICHOS*

Popular sayings—*dichos*—reflect many of the basic values of contemporary Mexican society, although the roots of these expressions of popular culture extend far back into both European and pre-Columbian Native American civilizations. Although many of these expressions demonstrate the universality of proverbs generally, many uniquely mirror Mexican reality. Yolanda Nava writes about Latin American culture in general, but her observation applies equally well to Mexican sayings in particular. She notes, "Dichos feel good on the tongue . . . they are, after all, a verbal shorthand which . . . elders used countless times to remind [one] . . . to behave wisely" (2000, p. 35). *Dichos* may be pithy condensations of wisdom gained through centuries

This original essay first appeared in the 10th edition. Carolyn Roy teaches in the Department of History at San Diego State University, California.

of experience. They are one form of transmitting folk wisdom. The sayings selected here might be heard in any Mexican household.

Many of the proverbs in the following sections may be readily consulted in Sellers (1994), but caution must be exercised in reviewing Sellers' interpretations of these *dichos.* One must always maintain cognizance of the cultural context. Although a Mexican might playfully jest, saying *No hagas hoy lo que puedas hacer mañana* (Don't do today what you can put off until tomorrow), such should not be taken literally (as Sellers apparently does, p. 26). This inverted *dicho* merely jocularly reminds the listener that one should *No dejar para mañana lo que se puede hacer hoy* (Not put off until tomorrow what can be done today), a well-known adage in many cultures.

The Mexican tradition of playfulness with words, as in the previous example, or the use of double meaning (*doble sentido,* often with obscured sexual undertones—most frequently heard with such apparently innocuous words as *huevos*/eggs, *aguacates*/avocados, and so on, used as anatomical designations), or using a word for its exact opposite, has ancient roots in pre-Columbian Mexican linguistic practices. Among the Aztecs, it was proper practice to refer to an older person as "my dear young one," much as a Mexican mother today may call her toddler "my dear father" (*mi papito*). Those expressions chosen for discussion here reflect some of the values central to Mexican popular culture. These values include cheerful acceptance of the "will of God," the need to place trust with great care, the significance of appearances, the necessity to guard one's privacy and not breach that of others, prescribed gender roles, a communal spirit, and the importance of family.

Acceptance of "God's Will"

No hay mal que por bien no venga. (There is no bad that good does not accompany.) Mexicans have often been characterized as fatalistic, but their nature seems more than merely accepting of the inevitable. Much of Mexican folk wisdom relates to acceptance of poverty and even laughing at it. Mexican folk seem to relish the challenge of finding happiness in the face of adversity. Some of the most frequently heard proverbs reflect that optimism. This proverb might be equated to "It's an ill wind that brings nobody good," but that does not carry the same positive outlook that the Spanish phrase indicates. Closer to the Mexican concept might be "Every cloud has a silver lining."

Mejor reír que llorar. (Better to laugh than to cry.) If one laughs at adversity, whether a simple upset of plans or that which is most inevitable—death—then there is nothing that can disturb one's happiness. Much of Mexican art reflects the duality of life and death, as can be seen in art from pre-Columbian times to the present. The very popular woodcuts of José Guadalupe Posada depicting skeletons in scenes that range from the mundane to the hilariously outrageous clearly demonstrate the Mexican's friendly attitude toward death. If one can laugh, then there is no need for lament.

El hombre propone y Dios dispone. (Man proposes and God disposes.) Few Mexican women would dare to make plans, whether it be meeting for lunch tomorrow or making plans for a child's future, without adding before concluding those plans, *Si Dios quiere* (If God wills). It would be presuming much to think that one could control the future which is viewed as in God's hands alone. In the South of the United States, one hears a similar expression made popular by Southern folklorists: "If the Lord's willing and the creek don't rise," but this seems less an attitude of fatalistic acceptance than an almost humorous excuse in the event of inclement weather in the backwoods. Whereas *Si Dios quiere* is an expression used almost exclusively by Mexican women, "If the Lord's willing" may be used by males or females.

No por mucho madrugar amanece más temprano. (No matter how early one rises, the sun will not come up any sooner.) One must simply accept what one cannot change. Nothing is accomplished by unnecessary effort. Only the foolish will attempt to defy the forces of nature.

Cuando el pobre tiene para carne sea vigilia. (When the poor have [money] to buy meat, it must be Lent.) The poor must accept that when they have the good fortune to have money, then it will be a time of fasting (not eating meat). The poor must accept that they will not have good luck. This is an instance of making fun of—of laughing at—adversity. If I am poor, I should expect to eat beans and tortillas, not meat.

Quien canta su mal espanta. (He who sings frightens away his grief.) By singing, the individual can dispel sadness and drive away gloom. Singing and other forms of music accompany most private Mexican gatherings, but can also be heard in the Metro stations and on street corners of metropolitan centers.

Sparing Bestowal of Trust

En confianza está el peligro. (There is danger in trust.) For the Mexican to place trust in another, particularly anyone who is not a blood relative, indicates that person is held in very high esteem. But when one does bestow trust, then the greatest harm possible would be to betray that trust. It is a great risk to have faith in another; therefore, trust must never be granted lightly.

La confianza también mata. (Trust also kills.) Betrayal of trust kills the spirit as surely as a bullet might kill the body. And the betrayal of trust would be the gravest ill that one friend could commit against another. Another *dicho* conveys the gravity of betrayal of trust: *Ni te fíes de amigo reconciliado, ni de manjar dos veces guisados.* (Do not trust a reconciled friend nor a dish twice cooked.) If a trust has been betrayed, the lost trust can never be recovered.

Del dicho al hecho hay mucho trecho. (From said to done, there is a great gap.) One should not trust that promises will be fulfilled. Even with the best of intentions, circumstances intervene; thus one should always be prepared to accept less than is promised, thereby avoiding disappointment.

Músico pagado foca mal son. (The musician who has been paid plays bad music.) The most foolish act that an employer could commit would be to pay the worker before the task is completed. Such an employer would not be viewed as kind or generous, merely foolish. If a worker is paid in advance, then the foolish employer deserves to be treated with contempt. One of the first lessons to be learned when interacting within Mexican culture is that easy trust is not valued. Trust/*confianza* must be given sparingly and only after being earned. Reserving payment until the work is completed is viewed as prudent. The lesson of the saying is that paying for a job before it is completed produces bad results.

The Importance of Appearances

Dime con quien andas y te diré quien eres. (Tell me with whom you associate [walk, travel], and I will tell you who you are.) Whom you choose as your companions and associates reflects your quality. If you associate with "common people," then you will be judged common. It follows that one always seeks to associate with people of higher status in order to improve on one's station in life. In English one hears "Birds of a feather flock together," but that does not fully convey the idea that one can rise in status by associating with a better class of people.

Quien anda con lobos a aullar se aprenda. (One who goes around with wolves learns to howl.) In this same vein is the biblical principle in English "Evil companions corrupt good morals." If you run with the wolves, you will learn their wild ways; therefore, one should avoid such savages and associate with cultured society. One must choose associates with great care. They not only reflect one's position, but they also influence one's character.

El que es buen gallo dondequiera canta. (A good rooster can crow anywhere.) Despite the previous admonitions, quality is quality no matter the circumstance. A person of true character will show that character in all circumstances, but a person of poor character will not be able to measure up in difficult circumstances.

Respect for Privacy

Agua que no has de beber, déjala correr. (Water that you do not have to drink, leave it to flow.) Aranda (1977) translates this as "Don't meddle in others' affairs; don't start trouble." If you stir up the water, then it will be undrinkable for anyone. So let everyone tend to their own problems and thus avoid spreading them to others.

Bueno aconsejar, mejor remediar. (It is good to give advice, but it is better to solve the problem.) When there is a problem, it is good to give advice when it is sought, but it would be better to solve the problem. If you cannot solve the problem, then refrain from giving advice. And there are even times when the truth is better left unsaid, as attested by the proverb *Si dices la verdad no pecas, pero no sabes los males que suscitas* (If you tell the truth you do not sin, but you don't know the troubles you cause, so keep your own counsel).

En boca cerrada no entran moscas. (Flies do not enter a closed mouth.) If you keep your mouth shut, then you will not have to worry about "putting your foot in it." Be careful of what you say, because *Un resbalón de lengua es peor que el de los pies* (A slip of the tongue is worse than a slip of the foot). The foot will heal, but damage done by words will not. Also, *Rezarle solo a su santo* (Pray only to your saint); that is, only someone who can help you should know of your problems.

Mejor quedarse para vestir los santos que tener que desvestir un borracho. (It is better to remain single than to have to undress a drunk.) Women who do not marry are often said to "dress the saints"; that is, they spend their lives caring for the images of saints, which often involves making new garments for the images or painting and refurbishing them. Thus, single women often justify their unmarried state by suggesting that they prefer dressing the saints' images to having to undress a drunken husband.

Más vale solo que mal acompañado. (It is better to remain single than to be disagreeably accompanied.) In a society in which women are viewed as weak and vulnerable, single women must justify their unmarried state, so that women most often cite the refrain that it is better to be single than to be married to an unbearable spouse.

A la mujer ni todo el amor ni todo el dinero. (To a woman neither all your love nor all your money.) A real Mexican male must maintain control of himself and his money. Men make a certain portion of their income available to women for maintaining the household, but the rest of their earnings belong to them. One of the great enigmas of Mexican culture is the *machismo* (strong, dominant male) versus *marianismo* (long-suffering, submissive female). This concept is most readily seen in the fact that *cantinas*/bars are exclusively for males (and women of ill repute).

Triste está la casa donde la gallina canta y el gallo calla. (Sad is the house where the chicken crows and the rooster is quiet.) The proper role for a man is as the master of his house, and the woman should be silent. It is a reversal of proper roles for the Mexican woman to make the decisions and the man to allow her to do so. In English a similar refrain is "A whistling girl and a crowing hen always come to some sad end." Women are assigned their proper roles and men theirs. A sad state results when these roles are reversed.

Communalism

Mucha ayuda, poco trabajo. (Much help, little work.) When many work together, it is little work for any of them. When work is shared, it goes quickly and is not much effort for anyone. The tradition of communal work precedes European contact with the New World. Among the Aztecs, taking turns at doing community service was widely practiced.

Vida sin amigos, muerte sin testigos. (Life without friends; death without witnesses. Life without friends, no mourners when it ends.) If one does not live so as to have many friends, then death will come with no one there to mourn that death. In Mexican culture, it is extremely important that there be mourners to accompany the deceased. It has long been common practice to pay mourners so that the dead will be accompanied to the cemetery. Again, this reflects the importance of one's public persona, one's appearance to the rest of the world, even in death.

Family

¿A dónde vas que valgas más? (Where are you going that you are worth more?) Where would you be valued more than at home? The Mexican family is extended, but still very close. When an individual needs help, the family is expected to supply it. The understanding is that you are always better off at home.

Amor de padre o madre, lo demás es aire. (The love of mother or father, everything else is air.) Compared to a mother or father's love, there is nothing else of importance. Father and mother will love their children when everyone and everything else fails. It is not unusual to encounter adult children living in the home of their parents and even rearing their own children in that same home. At times this is done out of economic necessity, but just as often it is the extended family. Grandparents become the caregivers for the offspring and take a hand in their upbringing.

SUMMARY

Popular sayings reflect basic cultural values. They do not even require literacy because they transmit the values orally to all who hear them. They metaphorically condense timeless lessons into readily recalled phrases. Through *dichos* we are reminded that our experiences are not unique; others have experienced the same things in other times and other places and left us messages to guide us. By reviewing a selection of Mexican *dichos,* one readily perceives some of that culture's more significant values: cheerful acceptance of one's lot in life, the need to exercise caution, the importance of appearances, the sanctity of privacy, proper gender roles, communalism, and family.

References

Aranda, C. (1977). *Dichos: Proverbs and sayings from the Spanish.* Santa Fe, NM: Swanstone Press.

Fuentes, C. (1992). *The buried mirror: Reflections on Spain and the New World.* New York: Houghton Mifflin.

Nava, Y. (2000). *It's all in the frijoles: 100 famous Latinos share real-life stories, time-tested dichos, favorite folktales, and inspiring words of wisdom.* New York: Fireside.

Paz, O. (1961). *The labyrinth of solitude: Life and thought in Mexico.* New York: Grove Press.

Samovar, L. A., & Porter, R. E. (2001). *Communication between cultures* (4th ed.). Belmont, CA: Wadsworth.

Sellers, I. M. (1994). *Folk wisdom of Mexico.* San Francisco: Chronicle Books.

Concepts and Questions

1. How does the study of familiar sayings help us understand some of the important values of a particular culture?
2. Which Mexican sayings discussed by Roy are heard in other cultures?
3. Can you think of some sayings from your own culture and relate the specific values they represent?
4. What are your favorite familiar sayings? Why have you selected these?
5. What sayings in the United States stress the value of individualism?
6. What Mexican sayings reflect the underlying religious philosophy of the culture?

Unraveling Cultural Cues: Dimensions of Nonverbal Communication Across Cultures

PETER A. ANDERSEN
HUA WANG

"We would never forget the first meeting with our Japanese in-laws. We were embarrassed when Naomi's 60-year-old father bowed to us, and her parents were astonished to see us open our arms and ready to jump on and give them a huge American welcome hug." Intercultural encounters like this one between a Japanese and an American family are becoming increasingly common and the source of considerable confusion. Immigration, travel, and intercultural marriages are more common than ever before, and it is more important than ever to unravel the cues of culture, particularly unspoken ones.

With the advances in communication technologies, people today have a wide variety of ways to connect with each other. Some scholars have claimed that given a greater number of communication channels, the impact of geographic distance is diminishing, and the world is getting smaller and smaller (Blieszner & Adams, 1992; Wood, 1995). This ongoing technological revolution "will blur national boundaries and it will transform the nation state in a way humans have not witnessed for a millennium" (Andersen, 1999b, p. 540). With dramatically increasing numbers of people pursuing higher education, traveling for business and pleasure, and immigrating to another country, the probability of communicating with people from other cultures is greater than ever before (Brown, Kane, & Roodman, 1994; Stafford, 1988).

 Peter A. Andersen teaches at San Diego State University. Hua Wang is affiliated with San Diego State University.

However, as the opening vignette showed, oftentimes interactions between people from different cultures, especially in early stages of communication, are confusing and frustrating. The situation gets more complicated when linguistic barriers in many intercultural transactions are compounded by differences in nonverbal behavior. In comparison to verbal communication, nonverbal messages are frequently more ambiguous as they are being simultaneously signaled and interpreted through multiple channels (e.g., facial expressions, bodily gestures, tones of voice, spatial relationships, and physical environment). In addition, although nonverbal communication can take place both intentionally and unintentionally, it often operates at a lower level of awareness than language does. People are not very conscious of their own nonverbal behavior, which is enacted mindlessly, spontaneously, and unconsciously (Andersen, 1999a; Burgoon, 1985; Samovar & Porter, 1985). Overall, nonverbal communication is a pervasive and powerful form of human behavior that involves a subtle, nonlinguistic, multidimensional, and spontaneous process (Andersen, 1999a).

Culture is "the manifold ways of perceiving and organizing the world that are held in common by a group of people and passed on interpersonally and intergenerationally" (Hecht, Andersen, & Ribeau, 1989, p. 163). Culture is mainly an implicit nonverbal phenomenon because most aspects of one's culture are learned through observation and imitation rather than by explicit verbal instruction or expression. The primary level of culture is communicated implicitly, without awareness, and chiefly by nonverbal means (Andersen, 1999a; Hall, 1984; Sapir, 1928). Nonverbal communication has both biologically determined and culture-specific aspects. Some factors are innate and genetic, producing cross-cultural similarities in nonverbal behavior (Brown, 1991; Ekman, 1972), but abundant differences also exist, creating miscommunication and intercultural friction and confusion.

Nonverbal messages serve a variety of functions in intercultural communication (Ting-Toomey, 1999). People rely on nonverbal cues as their identity badges through which they place themselves and others into categories (Burgoon, Buller, & Woodall, 1996). From artifacts such as clothing, jewelry, cosmetics, and accessories to use of vocalic cues such as pitch, volume, articulation, and tempo, individuals in different cultures present, enhance, and/or assert a sense of self via various nonverbal behaviors (Ting-Toomey, 1999). Not only do nonverbal messages reflect strong personal identity, they also carry and infer powerful feelings, emotions, and attitudes, typically through facial, bodily, and gestural movement and use of voice (Ting-Toomey, 1999). Culture shapes the display rules of when, how, what, and with whom certain nonverbal expressions should be revealed or suppressed (Ekman & Friesen, 1975; Ekman & Oster, 1979) and dictates which displays are appropriate in which specific situations.

Prior research on intercultural communication in general, and nonverbal communication in particular, has provided many useful and interesting anecdotes. This chapter attempts to connect all these fragmented accounts and proposes a theoretical perspective that helps to explain and understand thousands of differences in nonverbal communication across cultures. The article will first briefly review research in cross-cultural differences that lie along eight nonverbal codes—*physical appearance, proxemics, chronemics, kinesics, haptics, oculesics, vocalics*, and *olfactics*—and then focus on six primary dimensions of cultural variation in nonverbal behavior based on the seminal work of Hall (1966b, 1976, 1984) and Hofstede (1980, 1991, 1998, 2001; Hofstede, Pedersen, & Hofstede, 2003), as well as many follow-up scholarly efforts in the field (Andersen, 1988, 2000; Fernandez, Carlson, Stepina, & Nicholson, 1997; Gudykunst & Nishida, 1986; Hecht, Andersen, & Ribeau, 1989; Merritt, 2000; Shackleton & Ali, 1990). The six dimensions of intercultural nonverbal communication are *context, identity, power distance, gender, uncertainty,* and *immediacy*.

NONVERBAL CODES

Nonverbal messages provide what verbal messages cannot express, and usually generate more trust than verbal messages (Andersen, 1999a; Ting-Toomey, 1999). A smile, a wink, a scowl, a squeaky voice, prolonged eye contact, fingers drumming on a tabletop—all these mannerisms reveal inner feelings. Nonverbal communication runs the gamut from easily readable threatening gestures to attitudes expressed by body posture or hidden beneath the surface of spoken words (Sheridan, 1978). The hidden differences in these various areas and masked meanings of specific nonverbal messages interweave in any intercultural encounter. Given that most discussions of nonverbal communication across cultures have been anecdotal and atheoretical, with numerous examples of intercultural differences for each nonverbal code discussed in detail, we will discuss the basic codes of nonverbal communication only briefly.

Physical Appearance

Physical appearance, the most externally obvious nonverbal code, includes relatively stable physical features of human beings such as gender, height, weight, color of skin, and body shape, as well as the artifacts associated with physical appearance such clothes, jewelry, makeup, and accessories. All of these elements play an important role during initial encounters. Cultural attire is obvious and leads to ethnic stereotypes. During a field study conducted at an international airport, the senior author witnessed Tongans in multicolored ceremonial gowns, Sikhs in white turbans, Hasidic Jews in blue yarmulkes, and Africans in white dashikis—all alongside Californians in running shorts and halter tops (Andersen, 1999a). Little formal research has been conducted on the impact of physical appearance on intercultural communication. Discussions of intercultural differences in appearance are provided by Scheflen (1974) and Samovar, Porter, and Stefani (1998). Although blue jeans and business suits have become increasingly accepted attire internationally, local attire still abounds. Preoccupation with physical appearance is hardly a new phenomenon. Since the dawn of culture, humans from the upper Paleolithic period (40,000 years ago) to the present have adorned their bodies in great variety of ways (Samovar et al., 1998).

Proxemics

Nonverbal communication differences can be traced back to a culture's perception of the most fundamental elements—space and time. *Proxemics* generally examines communication via interpersonal space and distance. Research has documented that cultures differ substantially in their use of personal space, their regard for territory, and the meanings they assign to proxemic behavior (Gudykunst & Kim, 1992; Hall, 1959, 1966a, 1966b, 1976; Scheflen, 1974). For example, people from Mediterranean and Latin cultures maintain close distance, whereas people from northern European and Northeast Asian cultures maintain greater distances. But this behavior is also highly contextual. At rush hour in Tokyo, the normally respectful, distant Japanese are literally jammed into subways and trains.

Chronemics

The study of meanings, usage, and communication of time is probably the most discussed and well-researched nonverbal code in the intercultural literature (Bruneau, 1979; Gudykunst & Kim, 1992; Hall, 1959, 1976, 1984). Some cultures follow monochronic time schedules and use time in linear ways, whereas people in polychronic cultures tend to engage in multiple activities simultaneously (Hall & Hall, 1987). The perceptions of time vary dramatically from culture to culture. In the United States, time is viewed as a commodity that can be wasted, spent, saved, and used wisely (Andersen, 1999a). In Arab and Latin American cultures, bringing in a historical time perspective is very important before addressing the current issue (Cushner & Brislin, 1996). To many Asians, time is more of a relational issue than clock time issue (Tung, 1994). And in some less developed countries, life moves to the rhythms of nature—the day, the seasons, the year; such human inventions as seconds, minutes, hours, and weeks have no real meaning.

Kinesics

Kinesic behavior studies include some aspects of people's facial expressions, body movements, gestures, and conversational regulators (Gudykunst & Kim, 1992; Hall, 1976; Samovar et al., 1998; Scheflen, 1974). Research shows that facial expressions can be harder to interpret than most people realize. A recent study reported subtle differences in the appearance of facial expressions of emotion across cultures; these facial expressions of emotion can contain nonverbal "accents" that identify the expresser's nationality or culture (Marsh, Elfenbein, & Ambady, 2003). Gestures differ dramatically in meaning, extensiveness, and intensity. Stories abound in the intercultural literature of gestures that signal endearment or warmth in one culture but may be obscene or insulting in another. Scholars specifically focusing on spontaneous gestures accompanying speech claim that both the types and timing of gestures can vary with the language spoken (Goldin-Meadow, 2003).

Haptics

Tactile communication, called *haptics,* also shows considerable intercultural variation (Jourard, 1966; Andersen & Leibowitz, 1978; Ford & Graves, 1977;

McDaniel & Andersen, 1998; Samovar et al., 1998). Research has shown vast differences in international and intercultural touch in amount, location, type, and public or private manifestation (Jones, 1994; McDaniel & Andersen, 1998). Italians and Greeks are more "touchy" people than the English, French, and Dutch. Touching is less common and more embarrassing and discomforting among Chinese and Japanese. And to touch an Arab Muslim with the left hand, which is reserved for toilet use, is considered a social insult (Samovar & Mills, 1998).

Oculesics

One important code of nonverbal communication that has attracted considerably less intercultural research attention is *oculesics,* the study of messages sent by the eyes—including eye contact, blinks, eye movements, and pupil dilation (Gudykunst & Kim, 1992; Samovar et al., 1998). Because eye contact has been called an "invitation to communicate," its variation cross-culturally is an important communication topic. In North America and Western Europe direct eye contact communicates interest and respect, whereas Japanese people may look away from another's eyes almost completely to be polite (Samovar & Mills, 1998).

Vocalics

Vocalics, or *paralanguage,* includes all the nonverbal elements involved in using the voice. Not surprisingly, culture affects the use of vocalics (Gudykunst & Kim, 1992; LaBarre, 1985; Samovar et al., 1998; Scheflen, 1974). Members of cultures with strong oral traditions, such as African Americans and Jews, tend to speak with more passion; Italians and Greeks talk much more and more loudly than Asians, who appreciate silence as a way of showing politeness (Samovar & Mills, 1998). However, music and singing, universal forms of aesthetic communication, have been almost completely overlooked in intercultural research, except for an excellent series of studies (Lomax, 1968) that identified several groups of worldwide cultures through differences and similarities in their folk songs.

Olfactics

Finally, *olfactics,* the study of interpersonal communication via smell, has been virtually ignored in intercultural research despite its importance (Samovar et al., 1998). Americans are the most smell-aversive culture in the world (Andersen, 1998). Most of the world's people emit natural body smells, but the cultures in the most developed parts of the world use an array of cosmetics to eliminate body odor or to replace it with natural smells.

DIMENSIONS OF INTERCULTURAL NONVERBAL COMMUNICATION

Research has shown that cultures can be located along dimensions that help explain why people act in different ways. Most cultural differences in nonverbal behavior are a result of variations along the dimensions discussed in the following sections (see Table 1).

Context

The first cultural dimension of communication proposed decades ago is *context*—the degree to which communication is explicit and verbal or implicit and nonverbal. Hall (1976, 1984) has described high-context cultures in considerable detail: "A high context (HC) communication or message is one in which most of the information is either in the physical context or

Table 1 *Dimensions of Intercultural Nonverbal Communication*

Dimension	One Extreme	The Other Extreme
Context	Low Context	High Context
Identity	Individualism	Collectivism
Power Distance	Low Power Distance	High Power Distance
Gender	Femininity	Masculinity
Uncertainty	Uncertainty Avoidance	Uncertainty Tolerance
Immediacy	Low Contact	High Contact

internalized in the person, while very little is in the coded, explicit, transmitted parts of the message" (Hall, 1976, p. 91). "In a high-context culture such as that of Japan, meanings are internalized and there is a large emphasis on nonverbal codes" (Lustig & Koester, 1999, p. 108). Married couples or old friends skillfully use HC or implicit messages that are nearly impossible for an outsider to understand. The situation, a smile, or a glance provides implicit meaning that does not need to be articulated. In HC cultures, information integrated from the environment, the context, the situation, and nonverbal cues gives the message meaning that is not available in explicit verbal utterance.

Low-context (LC) messages are the opposite of HC messages; most are communicated through explicit code, usually via verbal communication (Andersen, 1999a; Hall, 1976). LC messages must be detailed, unmistakably communicated, and highly specific. Unlike personal relationships, which are high-context message systems, institutions such as courts of law and formal systems such as mathematics and computer languages require explicit LC systems because nothing can be taken for granted (Hall, 1984).

There are huge cultural variations in the degree of context used in communication. Research suggests that the lowest-context cultures are Swiss, German, North American, and Scandinavian (Gudykunst & Kim, 1992; Hall, 1976, 1984). LC cultures are logical, analytical, linear, and action oriented, and people tend to stress clearly articulated spoken or written messages (Hall, 1984). Cultures that have some characteristics of both HC and LC systems would include the French, English, and Italian (Gudykunst & Kim, 1992), which are less explicit than northern European cultures.

The highest HC cultures are found in Asia, especially China, Japan, and Korea (Elliott, Scott, Jensen, & McDonough, 1982; Hall, 1976, 1984; Lustig & Koester, 1999). Although most languages are explicit, LC communication systems, in China even the language is an implicit, high-context system. To use a Chinese dictionary, one must understand thousands of characters that change meaning in combination with other characters along with the context. Zen Buddhism, a major influence in Asia, places a high value on silence, lack of emotional expression, and the unspoken, nonverbal parts of communication (McDaniel & Andersen, 1998). Americans often complain that the Japanese never "get to the point," but they fail to recognize that HC culture must provide a context and setting and let the point evolve (Hall, 1984). In a study of airport farewell episodes, McDaniel and Andersen (1998) found Asians to be the least tactile of any cultural group on earth. American Indian cultures with ancestral migratory roots in East Asia are remarkably like contemporary Asian culture in several ways, especially in their need for high context (Hall, 1984). Latin American cultures—a fusion of Iberian (Portuguese–Spanish) and Asian traditions—are also high-context cultures. Likewise, southern and eastern Mediterranean people and people from the Persian Gulf, including Persians, Arabs, Greeks, and Turks, are HC cultures as well.

Communication is used very differently in HC and LC cultures. Andersen, Hecht, Hoobler, and Smallwood (2002) suggest that these differences between HC and LC communication can be explained by four principles.

1. *Verbal communication and other explicit codes are more prevalent in low-context cultures such as the United States and northern Europe.* People from LC cultures are often perceived as excessively talkative, belaboring of the obvious, and redundant. People from HC cultures may be perceived as nondisclosive, sneaky, and mysterious.
2. *HC cultures do not value verbal communication the same way that LC cultures do.* Elliot et al. (1982) found that more verbal people were perceived as more attractive in the United States, but less verbal people were perceived as more attractive in Korea, which is an HC culture.
3. *HC cultures are more reliant on and tuned in to nonverbal communication.* In LC cultures, most people, particularly men, fail to perceive as much nonverbal communication as do members of HC cultures. Nonverbal communication provides the context for all communication (Watzlawick, Beavin, & Jackson, 1967), but people from HC cultures are particularly affected by these contextual cues. Thus, facial expressions, tensions, movements, speed of interaction, location of the interaction, and other subtle forms of nonverbal communication are likely to be more easily perceived by and have more meaning for people from HC cultures.
4. *In HC cultures, interactants expect more than in LC cultures* (Hall, 1976). People in HC cultures anticipate that communicators will understand unspoken

Table 2 *Summary of Context Dimension*

Dimension 1. Context	One Extreme: Low Context	The Other Extreme: High Context
The degree to which communication is explicit and verbal or implicit and nonverbal.		
Core Value	Freedom of speech, directness	Silence, indirectness
Nonverbal Traits	Literal meaning, specific details, and precise time schedules	Information in the physical context, or internalized in the person
Typical Cultures	Switzerland, Germany, North America	China, Japan, Korea

feelings, implicit gestures, and environmental clues that people from LC cultures do not process. Given that both cultural extremes fail to recognize these basic communication differences, intercultural attributions about behavior are often incorrect.

In conclusion, HC cultures rely more on nonverbal communication and less on verbal communication (see Table 2). Generally, HC cultures are also somewhat more collectivistic and less individualistic than LC cultures (Gudykunst et al., 1996; Andersen et al., 2002). Given this association, it is appropriate that the next dimension of culture to be examined is cultural identity: individualism–collectivism.

Individualism–Collectivism

A culture's degree of *individualism versus collectivism* is one of the most extensively researched dimensions of culture. Individualistic cultures emphasize I-identity and value personal rights and freedom, whereas collectivistic cultures advocate we-identity and are more group oriented. Individualism–collectivism determines how people live together—alone, in families, or in tribes (Hofstede, 1980)—their values, and how they communicate. Americans are extreme individualists, take individualism for granted, and are blind to its impact until travel brings them into contact with less individualistic, more collectivistic cultures.

Individualism has been applauded as a blessing and has been elevated to the status of a national religion in the United States. Indeed, the best and worst in our culture can be attributed to individualism. Proponents of individualism have argued that it is the basis of liberty, democracy, freedom, and economic incentive and serves as protection against tyranny. Conversely, individualism has been blamed for our alienation from one another, loneliness, selfishness, and narcissism. Indeed, Hall (1976) has claimed that as an extreme individualist, "Western man has created chaos by denying that part of his self that integrates while enshrining the part that fragments experience" (p. 9). There can be little doubt that individualism is one of the fundamental dimensions that distinguishes cultures. Western culture is individualistic, so people rely on personal judgments to a greater degree than group decisions. Eastern cultures emphasize harmony among people, between people and nature, and value collective judgments (Andersen et al., 2002). Tomkins (1984) demonstrated that an individual's psychological makeup is the result of this cultural dimension. Western civilization has tended toward self-celebration, positive or negative. In Asian culture, another alternative is represented, that of harmony among people and between people and nature.

In a landmark intercultural study of individualism in 40 noncommunist countries, Hofstede (1980) reported that the 10 most individualistic nations (starting with the most) were the United States, Australia, Great Britain, Canada, the Netherlands, New Zealand, Italy, Belgium, Denmark, and Sweden, all of which primarily derive from European cultures. The least individualistic nations (starting with the least) were Venezuela, Colombia, Pakistan, Peru, Taiwan, Thailand, Singapore, Chile, and Hong Kong, all of which are Asian or South American cultures. Likewise, Sitaram and Codgell (1976) reported that individuality is a primary value in Western cultures, of secondary importance in African cultures, and of little importance in Eastern and Muslim cultures.

Even though the United States is the most individualistic country on earth (Andersen, 1999a;

Hofstede, 1980), some of its regions and ethnic groups diverge in their degree of individualism. Elazar (1972) found that the central Midwest and the Mid-Atlantic states have the most individualistic political culture, whereas the Southeast is the most traditional and least individualistic; however, this relationship is all relative and, by world standards, even Alabama is an individualistic culture. As Bellah, Madsen, Sullivan, Swidler, and Tipton (1985) stated, "Individualism lies at the very core of American culture. . . . Anything that would violate our right to think for ourselves, judge for ourselves, make our own decisions, live our lives as we see fit, is not only morally wrong, it is sacrilegious" (p. 142). Likewise, different ethnic groups may vary within a culture. African Americans, for example, greatly emphasize individualism (Hecht, Collier, & Ribeau, 1983), whereas Mexican Americans emphasize group and relational solidarity more (Andersen et al., in press). Americans' extreme individualism makes it difficult for them to interact with and understand people from other cultures. America is unique; all other cultures are less individualistic. As Condon and Yousef (1983) stated, "The fusion of individualism and equality is so valued and so basic that many Americans find it most difficult to relate to contrasting values in other cultures where interdependence greatly determines a person's sense of self" (p. 65).

The degree to which a culture is individualistic or collectivistic affects the nonverbal behavior of that culture in every way (see Table 3). First, people from individualistic cultures are more remote and distant proximally. Collectivistic cultures are interdependent; as a result, the members work, play, live, and sleep in proximity to one another. One recent study reports that people in individualistic cultures are more distant proximally than collectivists (Gudykunst et al., 1996). Hofstede (1980) cites research suggesting that, as hunters and gatherers, people lived apart in individualistic, nuclear families. When humans became agricultural, the interdependent extended family began living in proximity in large families or tribal units. Urban industrial societies returned to a norm of individualism, nuclear families, and a lack of proximity to one's neighbors, friends, and coworkers.

Culture also sets up the way people use time. In a study of doing business with Japanese, researchers discovered that the Japanese are slow to reach a decision, whereas Americans prefer to take immediate actions (Hall & Hall, 1987). The greatest distinction between the two cultures lies in the Japanese's strong dependence on groups. They base their individual identities on the groups they belong to and seek dependent relationships from larger entities, especially employers. However, such dependency would be considered a negative trait in the United States because Americans value independence.

Kinesic behavior tends to be more coordinated in collectivistic cultures, where people match one another's facial expressions, and body movements are in sync with each other. Where families work collectively, movements, schedules, and actions need to be highly coordinated (Argyle, 1975). In urban cultures, family members often do their "own thing," coming and going, working and playing, eating and sleeping on different schedules. People in individualistic cultures also smile more than do people in normatively oriented cultures (Tomkins, 1984). Individualists are responsible for their relationships and their own happiness, whereas

Table 3 *Summary of Identity Dimension*

Dimension 2. Individualism–collectivism	**One Extreme: Individualism**	**The Other Extreme: Collectivism**
The degree the society reinforces individual or collective achievement and interpersonal relationships.		
Core Value	Individual freedom	Group harmony
Nonverbal Traits	Proximally distant, different schedules, expressive of emotions	Proximally close, coordinated facial expressions and body movements
Typical Cultures	United States, Australia, Great Britain	Venezuela, Colombia, Pakistan

normatively or collectively oriented people regard compliance with norms as a primary value and personal or interpersonal happiness as a secondary value (Andersen, 1999a). Matsumoto (1991) reports that "collective cultures will foster emotional displays of their members that maintain and facilitate group cohesion, harmony, or cooperation, to a greater degree than individualistic cultures" (p. 132). Porter and Samovar (1998) report that people in individualistic cultures display a wider range of emotions, particularly to outgroups, than are displayed by collectivists, who are discouraged from showing a range of positive and/or negative emotions outside of the immediate in-group.

Similarly, Lustig and Koester (1999) maintain that "people from individualistic cultures are more likely than those from collectivistic cultures to use confrontational strategies when dealing with interpersonal problems; those with a collectivist orientation are likely to use avoidance, third-party intermediaries, or other face-saving techniques" (p. 123). In collectivistic cultures, people suppress both positive and negative emotional displays that are contrary to the mood of the group, because maintaining the group is a primary value (Andersen, 1999a). Bond (1993) found the Chinese culture to be lower in frequency, intensity, and duration of emotional expression than other cultures. Bond asserts that "the expression of emotion is carefully regulated out of a concern for its capacity to disrupt group harmony and status hierarchies" (p. 245).

People in individualistic cultures are encouraged to express emotions because individual freedom is a paramount value. Research suggests that people in individualistic cultures are more nonverbally affiliative. Intuitively, the reason for this is not obvious because individualism does not require affiliation; however, Hofstede (1982) explained:

> In less individualistic countries where traditional social ties, like those with extended family members, continue to exist, people have less of a need to make specific friendships. One's friends are predetermined by the social relationships into which one is born. In the more individualistic countries, however, affective relationships are not socially predetermined but must be acquired by each individual personally. (p. 163)

In individualistic countries such as the United States, affiliativeness, dating, flirting, small talk, smiling, and initial acquaintance are more important than in collectivistic countries where the social network is more fixed and less reliant on individual initiative. Bellah et al. (1985) maintain that for centuries in the individualistic and mobile North American society, people could meet more easily and their communication was more open; however, their relationships were usually more casual and transient than those found in more collectivistic cultures.

In an impressive study of dozens of cultures, Lomax (1968) found that a country's song and dance styles were related to its level of social cohesion and collectivism. Collectivistic cultures are higher in "groupiness" and show both more cohesiveness in singing and more synchrony in their dance style (Lomax, 1968). It isn't surprising that rock dancing, which emphasizes separateness and "doing your own thing," evolved in individualistic cultures such as England and the United States. These dances may serve as a metaphor for the whole U.S. culture, where individuality is more prevalent than in any other place (Andersen, 1998).

Power Distance

Another basic dimension of intercultural communication is *power distance*—the degree to which power, prestige, and wealth are unequally distributed in a culture. Power distance has been measured in many cultures using Hofstede's (1980) Power Distance Index (PDI). Like individualism, power distance varies greatly among cultures. Cultures with high PDI scores have power concentrated in the hands of a few rather than more equally distributed throughout the population. Condon and Yousef (1983) distinguish among three cultural patterns: democratic, authority-centered, and authoritarian. The PDI is highly correlated (.80) with authoritarianism, as measured by the Facism or authoritarianism scale (Hofstede, 1980).

High-PDI countries, from highest to lowest, are the Philippines, Mexico, Venezuela, India, Singapore, Brazil, Hong Kong, France, and Colombia (Hofstede, 1982), all of which, except for France, are southern countries located near the equator. Likewise, Gudykunst and Kim (1992) report that both African and Asian cultures generally maintain hierarchical role relationships characteristic of high power distance. Asian students are expected to be modest and deferent nonverbally in the presence of their instructors. Likewise, Vietnamese people consider employers to be their mentors and will not question orders.

The lowest PDI countries are, respectively, Austria, Israel, Denmark, New Zealand, Ireland, Sweden, Norway, Finland, Switzerland, and Great Britain (Hofstede, 1980), all of which are European or of European origin, middle-class, democratic, and located at high latitudes. The United States is slightly lower than the median in power distance, indicating smaller status differentials than in many other countries. Cultures differ in terms of how status is acquired. In many countries, such as India, class or caste determines one's status. In the United States, power and status are typically determined by money and conspicuous material displays (Andersen & Bowman, 1999).

As suggested above, the latitude of a country is an important force in the determination of power distance. Hofstede (1980) claims that latitude and climate are the major forces shaping a culture. He maintains that the key intervening variable is that technology is needed for survival in a colder climate, which produces a chain of events in which children are less dependent on authority and learn from people other than authority figures. Hofstede (1980) reports a high, .65 correlation between PDI and latitude. In a study conducted at 40 universities throughout the United States, Andersen, Lustig, and Andersen (1990) report a –.47 correlation between latitude and intolerance for ambiguity, and a –.45 correlation between latitude and authoritarianism. This suggests that residents of the northern United States are less authoritarian and more tolerant of ambiguity. Northern cultures may have to be more tolerant and less autocratic to ensure cooperation and survival in harsher climates.

It is obvious that power distance would affect a culture's nonverbal behavior (see Table 4). In high-PDI cultures, such as India, a rigid caste system may severely limit interaction, as in the case of India's "untouchables." More than 20% of India's population are untouchables, who lie at the bottom of India's five-caste system (Chinoy, 1967). Any contact with untouchables by members of other castes is forbidden and considered "polluting." Certainly, tactile communication among people of different castes is greatly curtailed in Indian culture. High-PDI countries with less rigid stratification than India may still prohibit free interclass dating, marriage, and contact, all of which are taken for granted in low-PDI countries. In a recent study on status-related behavior, although a similar gap was found between perceptions of behavior of lower- and higher-status people in Japan and the United States, greater differences were discovered in the hierarchical Japanese culture than in a more egalitarian U.S. culture (Kowner & Wiseman, 2003).

Social systems with large power discrepancies also produce unique kinesic behavior. Cultures with high power distance encourage emotions and expressions that reveal status differences. For instance, in high-power-distance cultures, people are expected to show only positive emotions to high-status others and only negative emotions to low-status others (Matsumoto, 1991). According to Andersen and Bowman (1999), subordinates' bodily tension is more obvious in power-discrepant relationships. Similarly, Andersen and Bowman (1999) report that in power-discrepant circumstances, subordinates smile more in an effort to appease superiors and appear polite. The continuous smiles of many Asians are a culturally inculcated effort to appease superiors and smooth social relations—behaviors that are appropriate to a high-PDI culture.

The power distance of a culture also affects vocalic and paralinguistic cues. Citizens of low-PDI cultures

Table 4 *Summary of Power Distance Dimension*

Dimension 3. Power Distance	**One Extreme: Low Power Distance**	**The Other Extreme: High Power Distance**
The degree of equality or inequality between people in the country or society.		
Core Value	People's equality	Respect for status
Nonverbal Traits	Located at high latitudes, more tactile, relaxing and clear vocalic cues	Located near the equator, untouchable, regulated nonverbal displays
Typical Cultures	Austria, Israel, Denmark	Philippines, Mexico, Venezuela

Table 5 *Summary of Gender Dimension*

Dimension 4. Gender	One Extreme: Femininity	The Other Extreme: Masculinity
The degree of traditional gender role of achievement, control, and power.		
Core Value	Caring for others	Material success
Nonverbal Traits	Relaxed and coordinated vocal patterns, nurturing	High level of stress, loud, aggressive
Typical Cultures	Sweden, Norway, the Netherlands	Japan, Austria, Venezuela

are generally less aware that vocal loudness may be offensive to others. American vocal tones are often perceived as noisy, exaggerated, and childlike (Condon & Yousef, 1983). Lomax (1968) has shown that in countries where political authority is highly centralized, singing voices are tighter and the voice box is more closed, whereas more permissive societies produce more relaxed, open, and clear sounds.

Gender

Perhaps the most researched issue in social science during recent decades is gender. Nations and cultures, like humans, can be viewed as masculine or feminine. The gender orientation of culture has an impact on many aspects of nonverbal behavior (see Table 5). These include the nonverbal expressions permitted by each sex, occupational status, nonverbal aspects of power, the ability to interact with strangers or acquaintances of the opposite sex, and all aspects of interpersonal relationships between men and women. *Gender,* as discussed in this article, refers to the rigidity of gender rules. In masculine cultures, gender rules are more rigid and traits such as strength, assertiveness, competitiveness, and ambitiousness are valued. In more feminine or androgynous cultures, attributes such as affection, compassion, nurturance, and emotionality are valued (Bem, 1974; Hofstede, 1980). In less rigid cultures, both men and women can express more diverse, less stereotyped sex-role behaviors.

Cross-cultural research shows that girls are expected to be more nurturant than boys, although there is considerable variation from country to country (Hall, 1984). Hofstede (1980) has measured the degree to which people of both sexes in a culture endorse masculine or feminine goals. Masculine cultures regard competition and assertiveness as important, whereas feminine cultures place more importance on nurturance and compassion. Not surprisingly, the masculinity of a culture is negatively correlated with the percentage of women in technical and professional jobs and positively correlated with segregation of the sexes in higher education (Hofstede, 1980).

Countries with the 10 highest masculinity index scores, according to Hofstede (1980), are Japan, Austria, Venezuela, Italy, Switzerland, Mexico, Ireland, Great Britain, Germany, and the Philippines. The 10 countries with the lowest masculinity scores are Sweden, Norway, the Netherlands, Denmark, Finland, Chile, Spain, Portugal, Thailand, and Peru. Not surprisingly, high-masculinity countries have fewer women in the labor force, have only recently afforded voting privileges to women, and are less likely to consider wife rape a crime than are low-masculinity countries (Seager & Olson, 1986).

Not surprisingly, the Scandinavian countries, with their long history of equal rights for women, are at the top of the list of feminine countries. But why would South American cultures be less masculine and not manifest the Latin pattern of machismo? Iberian countries, Spain and Portugal, have relatively feminine cultures, as do their South American cultural descendents such as Chile and Peru. Hofstede (1980) suggests that machismo is more present in the Caribbean region than in the remainder of South America. In fact, South America, as compared to Central America, has a much higher percentage of working women, much higher school attendance by girls, and more women in higher education (Seager & Olson, 1986).

A significant amount of research suggests that androgynous patterns of behavior (that is, both feminine and masculine) result in more self-esteem, social competence, success, and intellectual development for both males and females (Andersen, 1999a).

Nonverbal styles where both men and women are free to express both masculine traits (such as dominance and anger) and feminine traits (such as warmth and emotionality) are likely to be both healthier and more effective. Buck (1984) has demonstrated that males may harm their health by internalizing emotions rather than externalizing them as women usually do. Internalized emotions that are not expressed result in more stress and higher blood pressure. Not surprisingly, more masculine countries show higher levels of stress (Hofstede, 1980).

Considerable research has demonstrated significant vocal differences between egalitarian and nonegalitarian countries. Countries in which women are economically important and where sexual standards for women are permissive show more relaxed vocal patterns than do other countries (Lomax, 1968). Moreover, those egalitarian countries show less tension between the sexes, more vocal solidarity and coordination in their songs, and more synchrony in their movement (Lomax, 1968).

The United States tends to be a masculine country, according to Hofstede (1980), although it is not among the most masculine. Intercultural communicators should keep in mind that other countries may be either more or less sexually egalitarian than the United States. Most countries are more feminine than the United States (that is, nurturing and compassionate), so Americans of both sexes seem loud and aggressive by world standards. Likewise, Americans' attitude toward women may seem sexist in extremely feminine locations such as Scandinavia.

Most important, in relatively more feminine countries, both men and women can engage in either masculine or feminine nonverbal behaviors. In masculine countries, the nonverbal behavior of men and women is carefully proscribed and must adhere to a narrower sexual script. So, for example, in feminine countries like Sweden and Norway, women can engage in more powerful speaking styles, wear masculine clothing, and be more vocally assertive. Similarly, men in feminine countries can show emotions such as sadness or fear and engage in more nurturing and less dominant behaviors.

Uncertainty

Some cultures value change and ambiguity, whereas others value stability and certainty. *Uncertainty* is a cultural predisposition to value risk and ambiguity (Andersen et al., 2002; Hofstede, 1980). At the individual level, this quality is called tolerance for ambiguity (Martin & Westie, 1959). People with intolerance of ambiguity have high levels of uncertainty avoidance and seek clear, black-and-white answers. People with tolerance of ambiguity have low levels of uncertainty avoidance and tend to be more tolerant, to accept ambiguous answers, and to see many shades of gray. Similarly, Hofstede (1980) reports that a country's neuroticism or anxiety scores are strongly correlated with uncertainty avoidance. High uncertainty avoidance is negatively correlated with risk taking and positively correlated with fear of failure.

Countries vary greatly in their tolerance for uncertainty. In some cultures, freedom leads to uncertainty, which leads to stress and anxiety. Hofstede (1980) maintained that intolerance of ambiguity and dogmatism are primarily a function of the uncertainty-avoidance dimension rather than the power-distance dimension. The 10 countries with the highest levels of uncertainty avoidance are Greece, Portugal, Belgium, Japan, Peru, France, Chile, Spain, Argentina, and Turkey (Hofstede, 1980). Countries whose culture originated in the Mediterranean region, especially southern European and South American countries, dominate the list. The 10 countries lowest in uncertainty avoidance and highest in tolerance are Singapore, Denmark, Sweden, Hong Kong, Ireland, Great Britain, India, the Philippines, the United States, and Canada. This list is dominated by northern European and South Asian cultures; many of these countries were originally part of the British Empire. Not surprisingly, these low-uncertainty-avoidant countries have a long history of democratic rule that is likely to be the cause and an effect of low uncertainty avoidance. Catholic and Islamic countries are higher in uncertainty avoidance, whereas Protestant, Hindu, and Buddhist countries tend to be more accepting of uncertainty (Hofstede, 1980). Eastern religions and Protestantism tend to be less "absolute," whereas Catholicism and Islam are more "absolute" and certain religions. Andersen, Lustig, and Andersen (1990) report that intolerance for ambiguity is much higher in the American South than in the northern states, tending to reflect the international pattern of latitude and tolerance.

Few studies have examined nonverbal behavior associated with uncertainty. Hofstede (1980) maintains that countries high in uncertainty avoidance tend to display emotions more than do countries that are low

Table 6 *Summary of Uncertainty Dimension*

Dimension 5. Uncertainty	One Extreme: Uncertainty Avoidance	The Other Extreme: Uncertainty Tolerance
The degree of avoidance or tolerance for uncertainty and ambiguity within the society.		
Core Value	Certainty, what is different is dangerous	Exploration, what is different causes curiosity
Nonverbal Traits	More emotional displays, higher level of anxiety	More positive and friendly to strangers
Typical Cultures	Greece, Portugal, Belgium	Singapore, Denmark, Sweden

in uncertainty avoidance. Furthermore, he reports that the emotional displays of young people are tolerated less in countries with high uncertainty avoidance. Certainly, disagreement and nonconformity are not appreciated if uncertainty avoidance is high. Nonverbal behavior is more likely to be codified and rule-governed in countries with high uncertainty avoidance. This seems to fit a country such as Japan, but the hypothesis remains to be tested. Hofstede (1980) found that nations high in uncertainty avoidance report more stylized and ritual behavior, so we should expect that nonverbal behavior is more prescribed in these cultures. When people from the United States communicate with people from a country such as Japan or France (both high in uncertainty avoidance), the Americans may seem unruly and unconventional, whereas their Japanese or French counterparts might seem too controlled and rigid to the Americans (Lustig & Koester, 1999).

Research on uncertainty reduction and avoidance has been extended from interpersonal communication to the study of intercultural communication (Berger & Gudykunst, 1991; Gao & Gudykunst, 1990; Gudykunst, 1993, 1995; Gudykunst & Hammer, 1988), resulting in Gudykunst's Anxiety/Uncertainty Management Theory. The theory seeks to explain attitudes and behaviors toward strangers and members of other cultures (Gudykunst, 1995). Interacting with people outside of our group induces physiological arousal that is experienced as anxiety. This is consistent with the work of Hofstede (1980), who has shown that people in uncertainty-avoidant countries experience and show more anxiety than in other countries. The theory suggests that more secure, uncertainty-tolerant groups are more accepting toward people from another group or culture. Of course, much of this takes place at subtle nonverbal levels. People from cultures that embrace uncertainty are much more likely to treat strangers with positive nonverbal behaviors such as smiles and other indications of immediacy and warmth (see Table 6).

Immediacy

Immediacy behaviors and interpersonal warmth are actions that signal closeness, intimacy, and availability for communication rather than avoidance and greater psychological distance (Andersen, 1985, 1998). Examples of immediacy behaviors are smiling, touching, eye contact, closer distances, and more vocal animation. Some scholars have labeled these behaviors as "expressive" (Patterson, 1983). Cultures that display considerable interpersonal closeness or immediacy have been labeled "contact cultures" because people in these countries stand closer together and touch more (Hall, 1966a). People in low-contact cultures tend to stand apart and touch less. According to Patterson (1983):

> These habitual patterns of relating to the world permeate all aspects of everyday life, but their effects on social behavior define the manner in which people relate to one another. In the case of contact cultures, this general tendency is manifested in closer approaches so that tactile and olfactory information may be gained easily. (p. 145)

Interestingly, high-contact cultures are generally located in warmer countries nearer the equator and low-contact cultures are found in cooler climates father from the equator. Explanations for these latitudinal variations have included energy level, climate, and metabolism (Hofstede, 1980; Andersen et al., 1990). Evidently, cultures in cooler climates tend to be more task-oriented and interpersonally "cool," whereas cultures in warmer climates tend to be more interpersonally oriented and interpersonally "warm." Even within the United States, the warmer latitudes tend to be higher-contact cultures. Andersen et al. (1990) report a .31 correlation between latitude of students' university and touch avoidance. These data indicate that students at universities located in the so-called Sunbelt are more touch oriented. Pennebaker, Rimé, and Sproul (1994) found a correlation between latitude and expressiveness within dozens of countries. Northerners are more expressive than southerners, according to their data, in Belgium, Croatia, France, Germany, Italy, Japan, Serbia, Spain, Switzerland, and the United States, with an overall difference within the entire Northern Hemisphere. Pennebaker et al. (1994) conclude:

> Logically, climate must profoundly affect social processes. People living in cold climates devote more time to dressing, to providing warmth, to planning ahead for food provisions during the winter months. . . . In warm climates, people are more likely to see, hear, and interact with neighbors year around. Emotional expressiveness then would be more of a requirement. (pp. 15–16)

Similarly, Andersen et al. (1990) conclude:

> In Northern latitudes societies must be more structured, more ordered, more constrained, and more organized if the individuals are to survive harsh weather forces. . . . In contrast, Southern latitudes may attract or produce a culture characterized by social extravagance and flamboyance that has no strong inclination to constrain or order their world. (p. 307)

Traditionally, research has shown that high-contact cultures comprise most Arab countries, including North Africa; the Mediterranean region, including France, Greece, Italy, Portugal, and Spain; Jews from both Europe and the Middle East; Eastern Europeans and Russians; and virtually all of Latin America (Condon & Yousef, 1983; Jones, 1994; Jones & Remland, 1982; Mehrabian, 1971; Patterson, 1983; Samovar, Porter, & Jain, 1981; Scheflen, 1972). Australians are moderate in their cultural contact level, as are North Americans (Patterson, 1983). Research generally found that low-contact cultures comprise most of northern Europe, including Scandinavia, Germany, and England; British Americans; white Anglo-Saxons (the primary culture of the United States); and virtually every Asian country, including Burma, China, Indonesia, Japan, Korea, the Philippines, Thailand, and Vietnam (Andersen, Andersen, & Lustig, 1987; Heslin & Alper, 1983; Jones, 1994; Jones & Remland, 1982; McDaniel & Andersen, 1998; Mehrabian, 1971; Patterson, 1983; Remland, 2000; Samovar, Porter, & Jain, 1981; Scheflen, 1972). Recent research reported by Remland (2000) indicates that people do touch significantly more in southern Europe than in northern Europe.

Other recent studies suggest that the biggest differences in immediacy are not between North America and Europe, both of which are probably moderate- to high-contact cultures. Compared to the rest of the world, Asia is an extreme noncontact culture (McDaniel & Andersen, 1998; Remland et al., 1991). These two studies question whether Hall's (1966) original designation of some cultures as "low contact" is an oversimplification. Whether a generational shift or internationalization may have produced this change is unclear, but much of the Western world, including the

Table 7 *Summary of Immediacy Dimension*

Dimension 6. Immediacy	One Extreme: Low Contact	The Other Extreme: High Contact
The degree of closeness, intimacy, and availability for communication.		
Core Value	Public and body contacts are not comfortable	Body contacts are signals for friendliness and communication
Nonverbal Traits	Located in cooler climates, stand apart and touch less, stay "cool"	Located in warmer countries nearer the equator, stand closer together and touch more, expressive
Typical Cultures	Japan, China, Korea	North Africa, France, Brazil

United States, appears to be a contact culture. Indeed, McDaniel and Andersen's (1998) study of public touch suggests that the biggest difference is between Asians, who rarely touch in public, and virtually every other culture, which all manifest higher degrees of public touching. These findings are consistent with other research suggesting that China and Japan are distinctly nontactile cultures (Barnland, 1978; Jones, 1994).

Without a doubt, cultures differ in their immediacy (see Table 7). Generally, people living in northern countries, northern parts of individual countries, in traditional cultures, and in Asia are the least immediate and expressive. Conversely, people living in the south, modern countries, and non-Asian cultures are the most expressive and immediate. Obviously, these findings are painted with a fairly broad brush and will await a more detailed cultural portrait.

CONCLUSIONS

These six dimensions of intercultural nonverbal communication aim at providing a theoretical framework that helps move studies on nonverbal communication across cultures from detailed descriptions to the realm of meanings, functions, outcomes, and relationships behind the screen. This list is neither exhaustive nor discrete. However, scholars and culture practitioners have increasingly utilized the conceptual scaffold outlined in this chapter to better understand and further explain the underlying basis of thousands of cultural differences in nonverbal behavior.

Although studying these six dimensions cannot ensure competence in intercultural communication, combining cognitive knowledge from intercultural readings and courses with actual encounters with people from other cultures will definitely help boost one's intercultural communication competence. More important, these six dimensions of cultural variation in nonverbal communication have pointed out directions for future studies. As Andersen, Hecht, Hoobler, and Smallwood (2002) have suggested, the rich interplay among the six dimensions, the interactions among people who differ along the same dimensions, the phenomenon that some members of a society do not seem to fully manifest the general tendencies of a particular culture, and group behavior investigated in well-situated cultural context are of great research value and potential.

References

Andersen, J. F., Andersen, P. A., & Lustig, M. W. (1987). Opposite-sex touch avoidance: A national replication and extension. *Journal of Nonverbal Behavior, 11*, 89–109.

Andersen, P. A. (1985). Nonverbal immediacy in interpersonal communication. In A. W. Siegman & S. Feldstein (Eds.), *Multichannel integrations of nonverbal behavior* (pp. 1–36). Hillsdale, NJ: Erlbaum.

Andersen, P. A. (1988). Explaining intercultural differences in nonverbal communication. In L. A. Samovar & R. E. Porter (Eds.), *Intercultural communication: A reader* (5th ed., pp. 272–282). Belmont, CA: Wadsworth.

Andersen, P. A. (1998). The cognitive valence theory of intimate communication. In M. T. Palmer & G. A. Barnett (Eds.), *Progress in communication sciences: Vol. 14. Mutual influence in interpersonal communication: Theory and research in cognition, affect, and behavior* (pp. 39–72). Stamford, CT: Ablex.

Andersen, P. A. (1999a). *Nonverbal communication: Forms and functions.* Mountain View, CA: Mayfield.

Andersen, P. A. (1999b). 1999 WSCA Presidential address. *Western Journal of Communication, 63*, 339–543.

Andersen, P. A. (2000). Explaining intercultural differences in nonverbal communication. In L. A. Samovar & R. E. Porter (Eds.), *Intercultural communication: A reader* (9th ed., pp. 258–279). Belmont, CA: Wadsworth.

Andersen, P. A., & Bowman, L. (1999). Positions of power: Nonverbal influence in organizational communication. In L. K. Guerrero, J. A. DeVito, & M. L. Hecht (Eds.), *The nonverbal reader* (pp. 317–334). Prospect Heights, IL: Waveland Press.

Andersen, P. A., Hecht, M. L., Hoobler, G. D., & Smallwood, M. (2002). Nonverbal communication across culture. In B. Gudykunst & B. Mody (Eds.), *Handbook of international and intercultural communication* (pp. 89–106). Thousand Oaks, CA: Sage.

Andersen, P. A., & Leibowitz, K. (1978). The development and nature of the construct touch avoidance. *Environmental Psychology and Nonverbal Behavior, 3*, 89–106.

Andersen, P. A., Lustig, R., & Andersen, J. F. (1990). Changes in latitude, changes in attitude: The relationship between climate and interpersonal communication predispositions. *Communication Quarterly, 38*, 291–311.

Argyle, M. (1975). *Bodily communication.* New York: International Universities Press.

Barnland, D. C. (1978). Communication styles in two cultures: Japan and the United States. In A. Kendon, R. M. Harris, & M. R. Key (Eds.), *Organization of behavior in face to face interaction* (pp. 427–456). The Hague: Mouton.

Bellah, R. N., Madsen, R., Sullivan, W. M., Swidler, A., & Tipton, S. (1985). *Habits of the heart: Individualism and commitment in American life.* New York: Harper & Row.

Bem, S. L. (1974). The measurement of psychological androgyny. *Journal of Consulting and Clinical Psychology, 42,* 155–162.

Berger, C. R., & Gudykunst, W. B. (1991). Uncertainty and communication. In B. Dervin & M. Voigt (Eds.), *Progress in communication sciences* (Vol. 10, pp. 21–66). Norwood, NJ: Ablex.

Blieszner, R., & Adams, R. G. (1992). *Adult friendship*. Newbury Park, CA: Sage.

Bond, M. H. (1993). Emotions and their expression in Chinese culture. *Journal of Nonverbal Behavior, 17,* 245–262.

Brown, D. E. (1991). *Human universals*. Philadelphia: Temple University Press.

Brown, L. R., Kane, H., & Roodman, D. M. (1994). *Vital signs 1994: The trends that are shaping our future.* New York: W. W. Norton.

Bruneau, T. (1979). The time dimension in intercultural communication. In D. Nimmo (Ed.), *Communication yearbook 3* (pp. 423–433). New Brunswick, NJ: Transaction Books.

Buck, R. (1984). *The communication of emotion.* New York: Guilford Press.

Burgoon, J. (1985). Nonverbal signals. In M. L. Knapp & G. R. Miller (Eds.), *Handbook of interpersonal communication* (pp. 344–390). Beverly Hills, CA: Sage.

Burgoon, J., Buller, D., & Woodall, W. G. (1996). *Nonverbal communication: The unspoken dialogue* (2nd ed.). New York: McGraw-Hill.

Chinoy, E. (1967). *Society.* New York: Random House.

Condon, J. C., & Yousef, F. (1983). *An introduction to intercultural communication.* Indianapolis, IN: Bobbs-Merrill.

Cushner, K., & Brislin, R. (1996). *Intercultural interactions: A practical guide* (2nd ed.). Thousand Oaks, CA: Sage.

Ekman, P. (1972). Universal and cultural difference in the facial expression of emotion. In J. R. Cole (Ed.), *Nebraska symposium on motivation* (pp. 207–283). Lincoln: University of Nebraska Press.

Ekman, P., & Friesen, W. (1975). *Unmasking the face.* Englewood Cliffs, NJ: Prentice-Hall.

Ekman, P., & Oster, H. (1979). Facial expression of emotion. *Annual Review of Psychology, 30,* 527–554.

Elazar, D. J. (1972). *American federalism: A view from the states.* New York: Thomas P. Crowell.

Elliot, S., Scott, M. D., Jensen, A. D., & McDonough, M. (1982). Perceptions of reticence: A cross-cultural investigation. In M. Burgoon (Ed.), *Communication yearbook 5* (pp. 591–602). New Brunswick, NJ: Transaction Books.

Fernandez, D. R., Carlson, D. S., Stepina, L. P., & Nicholson, J. D. (1997). Hofstede's country classification 25 years later. *Journal of Social Psychology, 137,* 43–54.

Ford, J. G., & Graves, J. R. (1977). Differences between Mexican-American and white children in interpersonal distance and social touching. *Perceptual and Motor Skills, 45,* 779–785.

Gao, G., & Gudykunst, W. B. (1990). Uncertainty, anxiety, and adaptation. *International Journal of Intercultural Relations, 14,* 301–317.

Goldin-Meadow, S. (2003). *Hearing gestures.* Cambridge, MA: Belknap Press of Harvard University Press.

Gudykunst, W. B. (1993). Toward a theory of effective interpersonal and intergroup communication: An anxiety/uncertainty management (AUM) perspective. In R. L. Wiseman & J. Koester (Eds.), *Intercultural communication competence* (pp. 33–71). Newbury Park, CA: Sage.

Gudykunst, W. B. (1995). Anxiety/Uncertainty Management (AUM) theory: Current status. In R. L. Wiseman (Ed.), *Intercultural communication theory* (pp. 8–58). Thousand Oaks, CA: Sage.

Gudykunst, W. B., & Hammer, M. R. (1988). Strangers and hosts. In Y. Kim & W. Gudykunst (Eds.), *Cross-cultural adaptation* (pp. 106–139). Newbury Park, CA: Sage.

Gudykunst, W. B., & Kim, Y. Y. (1992). *Communicating with strangers: An approach to intercultural communication.* New York: Random House.

Gudykunst, W. B., Matsumoto, Y., Ting-Toomey, S., Nishida, T., Kim, K., & Heyman, S. (1996). Influence of cultural individualism–collectivism, self-construals, and individual values on communication styles across cultures. *Human Communication Research, 22,* 510–543.

Gudykunst, W. B., & Nishida, T. (1986). Attributional confidence in low- and high-context cultures. *Communication Research, 12,* 525–549.

Hall, E. T. (1959). *The silent language.* New York: Doubleday.

Hall, E. T. (1966a). *The hidden dimension* (2nd ed.). Garden City, NY: Anchor/Doubleday.

Hall, E. T. (1966b). A system of the notation of proxemic behavior. *American Anthropologist, 65,* 1003–1026.

Hall, E. T. (1976). *Beyond culture.* Garden City, NY: Anchor.

Hall, E. T. (1984). *The dance of life: The other dimension of time.* Garden City, NY: Anchor.

Hall, E. T., & Hall, M. (1987). *Hidden differences: Doing business with the Japanese.* Garden City, NY: Anchor/Doubleday.

Hecht, M. L., Andersen, P. A., & Ribeau, S. A. (1989). The cultural dimensions of nonverbal communication. In M. K. Asante & W. B. Gudykunst (Eds.), *Handbook of international and intercultural communication* (pp. 163–185). Newbury Park, CA: Sage.

Heslin, R., & Alper, T. (1983). Touch: A bonding gesture. In J. M. Wiemann & R. Harrison (Eds.), *Non-verbal interaction* (pp. 47–75). Beverly Hills, CA: Sage.

Hofstede, G. (1980). *Culture's consequences.* Beverly Hills, CA: Sage.

Hofstede, G. (1991). *Cultures and organizations: Software of the mind.* London: McGraw-Hill.

Hofstede, G. (1998). Masculinity/femininity as a dimension of culture. In G. Hofstede (Ed.), *Masculinity and femininity: The taboo dimension of national cultures* (pp. 3–28). Thousand Oaks, CA: Sage.

Hofstede, G. (2001). *Culture's consequences* (2nd ed.). Beverly Hills, CA: Sage.

Hofstede, G. J., Pedersen, P. B., & Hofstede G. (2003). *Exploring culture: Exercises, stories and synthetic cultures*. Yarmouth, ME: Intercultural Press.

Jones, S. E. (1994). *The right touch: Understanding and using the language of physical contact*. Cresshill, NJ: Hampton Press.

Jones, T. S., & Remland, M. S. (1982, May). *Cross-cultural differences in self-reported touch avoidance*. Paper presented at the annual convention of the Eastern Communication Association, Hartford, CT.

Jourard, S. M. (1966). An exploratory study of body-accessibility. *British Journal of Social and Clinical Psychology, 5,* 221–231.

Kowner, R., & Wiseman, R. (2003). Culture and status-related behavior: Japanese and American perceptions of interaction in asymmetric dyads. *Cross-Cultural Research, 37,* 178–201.

LaBarre, W. (1985). Paralinguistics, kinesics, and cultural anthropology. In L. A. Samovar & R. E. Porter (Eds.), *Intercultural communication: A reader* (4th ed., pp. 272–279). Belmont, CA: Wadsworth.

Lomax, A. (1968). *Folk song style and culture*. New Brunswick, NJ: Transaction Books.

Lustig, M. L., & Koester, J. (1999). *Intercultural competence: Interpersonal communication across culture*. New York: HarperCollins.

Marsh, A. A., Elfenbein, H. A., & Ambady, N. (2003). *Psychological Science, 14,* 373.

Martin, J. G., & Westie, F. R. (1959). The intolerant personality. *American Sociological Review, 24,* 521–528.

Matsumoto, D. (1991). Cultural influences on facial expressions of emotion. *Southern Communication Journal, 56,* 128–137.

McDaniel, E. R., & Andersen, P. A. (1998). Intercultural variations in tactile communication. *Journal of Nonverbal Communication, 22,* 59–75.

Mehrabian, A. (1971). *Silent messages*. Belmont, CA: Wadsworth.

Merritt, A. (2000). Culture in the cockpit: Do Hofstede's dimensions replicate? *Journal of Cross-cultural Psychology, 31,* 283–301.

Patterson, M. L. (1983). *Nonverbal behavior: A functional perspective*. New York: Springer-Verlag.

Pennebaker, J. W., Rimé, B., & Sproul, G. (1994). *Stereotype of emotional expressiveness of Northerners and Southerners: A cross-cultural test of Montesquieu's hypotheses*. Unpublished paper, Southern Methodist University, Dallas.

Porter, R. E., & Samovar, L. A. (1998). Cultural influences on emotional expression: Implications for intercultural communication. In P. A. Andersen & L. K. Guerrero (Eds.), *Handbook of communication and emotion: Research theory, applications and contexts* (pp. 451–472). San Diego, CA: Academic Press.

Remland, M. S. (2000). *Nonverbal communication in everyday life*. Boston: Houghton Mifflin.

Remland, M. S., Jones, T. S., & Brinkman, H. (1991). Proxemic and haptic behavior in three European countries. *Journal of Nonverbal Behavior, 15,* 215–232.

Samovar, L. A., & Mills, J. (1998). *Oral communication: Speaking across cultures*. Boston: McGraw-Hill.

Samovar, L. A., & Porter, R. E. (1985). Nonverbal interaction. In L. A. Samovar & R. E. Porter (Eds.), *Intercultural communication: A reader* (4th ed., pp. 252–255). Belmont, CA: Wadsworth.

Samovar, L. A., Porter, R. E., & Jain, N. C. (1981). *Understanding intercultural communication*. Belmont, CA: Wadsworth.

Samovar, P. A., Porter, R. E., & Stefani, L. A. (1998). *Communication between cultures*. Belmont, CA: Wadsworth.

Sapir, E. (1928). The unconscious patterning of behavior in society. In E. S. Drummer (Ed.), *The unconscious* (pp. 114–142). New York: Knopf.

Scheflen, A. E. (1972). *Body language and the social order.* Englewood Cliffs, NJ: Prentice-Hall.

Scheflen, A. E. (1974). *How behavior means*. Garden City, NY: Anchor.

Seager, J., & Olson, A. (1986). *Women in the world atlas*. New York: Simon & Schuster.

Shackleton, V. J., & Ali, A. H. (1990). Work-related values of managers: A test of the Hofstede model. *Journal of Cross-Cultural Psychology, 21,* 109–118.

Sheridan, J. H. (1978). Are you a victim of nonverbal "vibes"? *Industry Week, 198,* 36.

Sitaram, K. S., & Codgell, R. T. (1976). *Foundations of intercultural communication*. Columbus, OH: Charles E. Merrill.

Stafford, L. (1988, October). *Communication in long-distance relationships*. Paper presented at the annual convention of the Speech Communication Association, Chicago.

Ting-Toomey, S. (1999). *Communicating across cultures*. New York: Guilford Press.

Tomkins, S. S. (1984). Affect theory. In K. R. Scherer & P. Ekman (Eds.), *Approaches to emotion* (pp. 163–195). Hillsdale, NJ: Erlbaum.

Tung, R. (1994). Strategic management thought in East Asia. *Organizational Dynamics, 22,* 55–65.

Watzlawick, P., Beavin, J. H., & Jackson, D. D. (1967). *Pragmatics of human communication*. New York: W. W. Norton.

Wood, J. T. (1995). *Relational communication: Continuity and change in personal relationships*. Detroit: Wadsworth.

Concepts and Questions

1. What does Andersen mean when he writes that "the primary level of culture is communicated implicitly, without awareness, and chiefly by nonverbal means"?
2. Do you agree with Andersen that two of the most fundamental nonverbal differences in intercultural communication involve space and time? From your experiences, what two nonverbal areas have you found most troublesome when interacting with people from different cultures?
3. From your personal experiences, can you think of different ways in which people in various cultures greet, show emotion, and beckon?
4. Do you believe that intercultural communication problems are more serious when they involve nonverbal communication or verbal communication?
5. What is kinesic behavior? How does it vary from one culture to another? What types of communication problems can be caused by cultural differences in kinesic behavior?
6. The term *haptics* refers to patterns of tactile communication. How does tactile communication differ between cultures? Can you think of examples of how tactile communication differs among members of co-cultures? What type of communication problems might arise when people with different touching orientations interact?
7. How does physical appearance affect first impressions during interaction? How are expectations of physical appearance related to the informal–formal dimension of culture?
8. How does immediacy affect interpersonal interaction? What differences in behaviors would you expect from high- and low-contact cultures? In what way would violations of immediacy expectations affect intercultural communication?
9. How is the degree of individualism within cultures manifested in nonverbal behavior?

Japanese Nonverbal Communication: A Reflection of Cultural Themes

EDWIN R. MCDANIEL

Modern technological advances have made the world a much smaller place, promoting increased interactions between peoples of different nations and cultures. Growing international economic interdependencies and expanding multinational security alliances have significantly increased the importance of effective intercultural encounters. Individuals from diverse cultures are interacting with each other more and more frequently—in professional, diplomatic, and social venues.

The most critical aspect of this burgeoning transnational intercourse is, of course, communication. The ability to understand and be understood is central to successful cross-cultural activities. Comprehension, however, must go beyond a topical awareness of another culture's communicative practices and behaviors. An appreciation of the cultural antecedents and motivations shaping an individual's communication conventions is necessary for understanding *how* and *why* a particular practice is used.

An established method of explaining the cultural motivations of human behavior is to identify and isolate consistent themes among a social grouping. Anthropological writings have posited that each culture manifests a "limited number of dynamic affirmations" (Opler, 1945, p. 198), referred to as *themes*. According to Opler, these cultural themes promote and regulate human behavioral activities that are societally encouraged and condoned. To illustrate this approach, Opler used an examination of the social relations of the Lipan Apaches to demonstrate how thematic study could provide insight into cultural beliefs and behaviors.

 Edwin R. McDaniel teaches in the Department of Language Communication at Aichi Shukutoku University, Aichi, Japan.

In communication studies, the concept of thematic commonality has been used by Burgoon and Hale (1984, 1987) to help explicate relational communications. They conceptualized a series of "interrelated message themes" (Burgoon & Hale, 1987, p. 19), which have been purported to have application to both verbal and nonverbal exchanges. These proposed themes, or *topi,* have become a supposition cited in studies of interpersonal relations communication (e.g., Buller & Burgoon, 1986; Coker & Burgoon, 1987; Spitzberg, 1989).

Burgoon and Hale's (1984) concept of identifying consistent themes to assist in the explanation of a communication process possesses significant utility for additional, more comprehensive employment. The innovation has clear application to the study of culture-specific communication predispositions.

Using the Japanese as a cultural model, this essay makes practical application of the thematic consistency concept advanced by Opler (1945, 1946) and Burgoon and Hale (1984, 1987). The objective is to illustrate how nonverbal communication practices function as a reflection, or representation, of societal cultural themes. Employing a standard taxonomy of nonverbal communication codes and addressing each individually, the essay discusses cultural themes influencing and manifested by the code in a propositional format. Additionally, the essay strives to demonstrate how cultural influences can subtly shape a society's communication conventions.

JAPANESE CULTURAL THEMES

Japan's predominantly homogeneous population embodies a particularly rich array of cultural themes. The more prevalent themes include group affiliation (collectivism), hierarchy, social balance or harmony *(wa),* empathy, mutual dependency, perseverance and sacrifice *(gaman),* humility, and formality (ritual, tradition, and protocol) (Caudill, 1973; Lebra, 1976; Reischauer, 1988).

Confucian-based collectivism exerts a significant influence on Japanese communication patterns. The nation's racial and cultural homogeneity creates a strong identity bond and facilitates intragroup and interpersonal familiarity. This societal closeness promotes an instinctive, nonverbal understanding among Japanese people. Their cultural similitude abets an intuitive, nonverbal comprehension by diminishing the requirement to orally specify numerous details (Barnlund, 1989; Ishii, 1984; Kinosita, 1988; Kitao & Kitao, 1985; Morsbach, 1988a; Nakane, 1970; Westwood & Vargo, 1985; Yum, 1988).

The Japanese concept of collectivism is epitomized by their usage of the term *nihonjinron* to express self-perceived uniqueness as both a nation and a people. This idea of distinctive originality provides the Japanese with a focus for social cohesiveness. Their propensity for group affiliation has created a social context referred to as *uchi-soto,* or inside–outside. This context can also be viewed as in-group (possessing membership) and out-group (no involvement). Within the security of their respective in-groups *(uchi),* the Japanese can be quite expressive and display considerable nonverbal affiliation with other members. Much less interaction will occur in an out-group *(soto)* situation (Gudykunst & Nishida, 1984; Gudykunst, Nishida, & Schmidt, 1989; Gudykunst, Yoon, & Nishida, 1987; Lebra, 1976, 1993).

The hierarchical nature of Japanese society and an inexorable compulsion for social balance or harmony *(wa)* increase the reliance on nonverbal behaviors and concomitantly discourage verbal exchanges. A hierarchy exists in every instance of group or interpersonal interaction. In this superior–subordinate environment, the junior is socially compelled to assume a passive role, awaiting and hopefully anticipating the senior's desires or actions. The senior, desiring to exemplify humility and avoid any social or personal discord, will endeavor to nonverbally ascertain the junior's expectations.

The cultural pressure for social balance dictates the course of all Japanese activities and creates a pervasive acceptance of ambiguity and vagueness during any communication endeavor. Reluctant to arbitrarily advance personal opinions or attitudes, the Japanese will draw on the situational context and attempt to instinctively discern what the other person is thinking (Hall & Hall, 1990; Ishii, 1984; Ishii & Bruneau, 1991; Kitao & Kitao, 1985; Lebra, 1976; Morsbach, 1988a; Munakata, 1986; Reischauer, 1988).

The cultural trait of empathy *(omoiyari)* also lessens the Japanese reliance on verbal exchanges. In Japan, considerable value is placed on an individual's ability to empathetically determine the needs of another person. During interpersonal encounters, the Japanese often use indirect or vague statements and depend on the other person's sensitivity to ascertain the desired meaning of the interaction (Doi, 1988; Ishii, 1984; Lebra, 1976).

PROPOSITIONAL SURVEY

Considered in isolation, a nonverbal code normally provides only partial interpretation of the intended message. This study, however, is not concerned with the code's proposed message, but instead attempts to demonstrate how the code is culturally based and motivated. To this end, in each of the following propositions (denoted as P1, P2, etc.), specific nonverbal communication codes are shown to reflect one or more cultural themes common to Japanese society.

> P1: *Japanese kinesics reflect the cultural themes of (1) group orientation, (2) hierarchy, (3) social balance, (4) formality, and (5) humility.*

The Japanese employ a wide array of kinesic activities, especially gestures (Caudill & Weinstein, 1969; March, 1990; Seward, 1983). Usage, however, is situational and often limited to males (Richie, 1987). A Japanese manager, for instance, might rely on gestures to communicate with work subordinates (Sethi, 1974), thereby demonstrating the cohesive familiarity common among in-group *(uchi)* members.

The Japanese are more relaxed and expressive within their in-group. Away from the in-group, however, the use of body language is usually remarkably restrained (Cohen, 1991; Ishii, 1975). In public, it is common to see both Japanese men and women sitting quietly and unobtrusively, with hands folded (March, 1990). This self-restraint of body movement in out-group *(soto)* environments is designed to avoid attention and maintain situational harmony or balance.

As another example of concern for social balance, Japanese hand gestures are never used in reference to a person who is present at the time. Instead, they are employed when referring to some absent party (Richie, 1987). This behavior, quite naturally, reduces the opportunity for offending anyone present and helps sustain contextual harmony.

The most common activity associated with Japanese kinesics is the bow, which is an integral and repetitive part of daily social interaction. The Japanese bow is used when meeting someone, when asking for something, while apologizing, when offering congratulations, when acknowledging someone else, and when departing, to mention just a few instances. Historically a sign of submission, the bow is a contemporary ritual that continues to convey respect and denote hierarchical status. The junior person bows first, lowest, and longest. An improperly executed bow can be interpreted as a significant insult (Hendry, 1989; Ishii, 1975; Kitao & Kitao, 1987, 1989; Morsbach, 1988b; Ramsey, 1979; Richie, 1987; Ruch, 1984).

Traditional Japanese women exhibit a distinct kinesic activity by obscuring facial areas with their hands or some object[1] (Ishii, 1975; Ramsey, 1981). Ramsey's investigation of this phenomenon concluded that women utilized these adaptors for impression management. An explicit intent of these actions is to evoke a perception of humility when in the presence of a social superior.

> P2: *Japanese oculesics reflect the cultural themes of (1) hierarchy, (2) social balance, and (3) humility.*

In Japan, prolonged eye contact is considered rude, threatening, and disrespectful. The Japanese are taught, from childhood, to avert their gaze or look at a person's throat. When one is part of an audience, looking away or simply sitting silently with eyes closed indicates attention to, and possibly agreement with, the speaker. Direct, sustained eye contact is normally avoided, unless a superior wants to admonish a subordinate (Hall & Hall, 1990; Ishii, 1975; Kasahara, 1986; Kitao & Kitao, 1987, 1989; March, 1990; Morsbach, 1973; Richie, 1987; Ruch, 1984; Watson, 1970).

By avoiding eye contact, the participants in communication simultaneously evince an air of humility and sustain situational *wa.* The use of direct eye contact by a superior is a clear exercise of hierarchical prerogative (March, 1990).

> P3: *Japanese facial expressions reflect the cultural themes of (1) social balance and (2) gaman.*

As is common to all aspects of their social behavior, the Japanese do not normally evince any significant emotion through public facial displays. The most commonly observed expressions are either a placid, unrevealing countenance or a nondescript smile, whose actual meaning or intent may be totally indecipherable. A smile can indicate happiness or serve as a friendly acknowledgment. Alternatively, it may be worn to mask negative emotions, especially displeasure, anger, or grief (Gudykunst & Nishida, 1993; Kitao & Kitao, 1987, 1989; Matsumoto, 1996; Morsbach, 1973).

For the Japanese, the smile is simply a part of social etiquette, designed to help sustain harmony. In a social environment, the Japanese would consider it unpardonable to burden someone else with an outward show of elation, irritation, or anguish. Eschewing any external display of negative emotion is an example of perseverance or self-sacrifice *(gaman)* to avoid disrupting the social balance *(wa)*. The smile is also used to avoid conflict; a Japanese person might simply smile in order to avoid answering an awkward question or giving a negative answer (Ishii, 1975; Kitao & Kitao, 1987, 1989; Nakane, 1970; Ruch, 1984; Seward, 1972).

P4: *Japanese proxemic behaviors reflect the cultural themes of (1) in-group affinity, (2) hierarchy, and (3) balance.*

The Japanese attitude toward personal space is, on the surface, complex and often seemingly contradictory. In uncrowded situations, they assiduously strive to maintain personal space intervals that are even greater than those maintained by Americans. Conversely, when on a train or bus, they offer no resistance to frequent or even prolonged body contact with total strangers. Personal space is also close among friends or family members (Hall, 1990; Richie, 1987).

This apparent dichotomy is the result of their societal group orientation, vertical structure, and constant concern for social balance. In an uncrowded out-group environment, the Japanese maintain their personal space, which also provides a psychological barrier against the unknown, such as the hierarchical status and group affiliation of others (Ishii, 1975; Morsbach, 1973; Watson, 1970). If forced into proximity with an out-group member, the Japanese will assume a façade of imperturbable passivity in an effort to maintain situational harmony. I have often observed the Japanese projecting an air of composed detachment while being subjected to suffocating conditions in a crowded Tokyo subway car.

Among in-group members, where strong social ties exist, personal space is dramatically reduced. Traditionally, family members commonly slept in the same room, within easy touching distance of each other (Caudill & Plath, 1966). Male white-collar coworkers *(sarariman)* sitting close together and patting each other on the back during after-work drinking excursions are a common sight in Japanese bars.

Japanese proxemic behavior has been the subject of several investigations. In a study involving status manipulation, Japanese subjects exhibited signs of anxiety in reaction to an interviewer's forward lean (Bond & Shiraishi, 1974). Iwata's (1979) study of Japanese female students disclosed that individuals with high self-esteem evinced a negative reaction to crowding. This behavior is consistent with the Japanese concept of hierarchy. Self-esteem would be proportional with social status, which would predicate greater interpersonal distance in out-group situations.

P5: *Japanese tactile conventions reflect the cultural themes of (1) in-group affinity and (2) social balance.*

Studies of Japanese maternal care have disclosed that children experience considerable touch from their mothers (Caudill & Plath, 1966; Caudill & Weinstein, 1969). Even today, parents and their young children often share the same bed. The amount of public tactile interaction drops dramatically, however, after childhood, and the individual is expected to conform to societal nontouch standards (Barnlund, 1975; McDaniel & Andersen, 1998; Montague, 1978). Indeed, adult Japanese actively avoid public displays of interpersonal physical expressiveness (Barnlund, 1989) unless in a close-knit in-group setting.

For adults, in-group *(uchi)* touching is acceptable (Lebra, 1976). This is especially evident when male coworkers are drinking (Miyamoto, 1994). In an out-group *(soto)* situation, touch is uncommon unless it results inadvertently from crowding, and then it is simply ignored (Ishii, 1975; Morsbach, 1973; Ramsey, 1985). These conventions again indicate the value placed on group affiliation and harmony.

P6: *Japanese personal appearance reflects the cultural themes of (1) collectivism, (2) group affiliation, (3) social balance, and (4) hierarchy.*

The central theme of Japanese external appearance is, quite simply, group identity and status. The ubiquitous dark suit dominates the business world, and everyone, men and women alike, normally opts for conservative styles. Small lapel pins or badges identifying the individual's company are frequently worn.[2] Blue-collar workers normally wear a uniform (such as coveralls or smocks) distinctive to their corporation (Condon & Yousef, 1983; Hall, 1981; Harris & Moran, 1979; March, 1990; Morsbach, 1973; Ruch, 1984).

The general proclivity for conservative dress styles and colors emphasizes the nation's collectivism and, concomitantly, lessens the potential for social disharmony arising from nonconformist attire. Lapel pins and uniforms signal a particular group affiliation, which in turn helps determine a person's social position.

Although not specifically nonverbal, the Japanese business card, or *meishi,* must be discussed. It exerts considerable influence on Japanese nonverbal behavior and communication in general. The initial impression of an individual is derived from his or her *meishi.* The card must be of the appropriate size and color and, in addition to the individual's name, list the person's company and position. This facilitates rapid determination of the individual's group affiliation and personal station, which dictates the correct deportment and appropriate speech levels for participants engaging in interpersonal dialogue (Craft, 1986; Morsbach, 1973; Ruch, 1984).

P7: *Japanese use of space reflects the cultural themes of (1) hierarchy and (2) group orientation.*

The Japanese hierarchical contextualization of space is best exemplified by the standard spatial array of governmental and corporate offices. Numerous desks, occupied by lower-level employees, are lined, facing each other, hierarchically in rows in a large, common room, absent of walls or partitions. The supervisors and managers are positioned at the head of each row. This organization encourages the exchange of information, facilitates multitask accomplishment, promotes group cooperation and solidarity, and facilitates rapid discernment of the work-center rank structure. Seating arrangements at any formal or semi-formal function are also based on hierarchy (Hamabata, 1990; Ramsey, 1979; Ramsey & Birk, 1983; Ruch, 1984; Takamizawa, 1988).

In explaining the Japanese perception of space as a hierarchical concept, Hall (1990) offers an insightful illustration. Neighborhood houses in Japan are numbered in the order they are constructed, regardless of actual location along the street.

P8: *Japanese use of time reflects the cultural themes of (1) hierarchy, (2) group orientation, and (3) social balance.*

Hall and Hall (1990) have indicated that the Japanese use time polychronically among themselves and monochronically when conducting business with foreigners. The rigid adherence to schedules when dealing with foreigners is in contrast with the temporal flexibility exhibited during interactions with other Japanese. This demonstrates an ability to adjust to dynamic situations. For example, schedules may have to be altered in order to accommodate the desires of a senior, which reflects hierarchical sensitivities.

The Japanese decision-making process exhibits the influence of group orientation and social balance on the usage of time. In almost every interpersonal context, it is necessary to build a consensus before announcing a decision. This process, concerned with maintaining social balance among group members, can take days, weeks, or even months (Hall, 1988; Nakane, 1970; Stewart, 1993).

P9: *Japanese vocalics reflect the cultural themes of (1) hierarchy, (2) social balance, and (3) empathy.*

The Japanese make ample use of paralanguage in their conversations. During interpersonal discussions, the Japanese will constantly use small, culturally unique gestures *(aizuchi)* and utterances (e.g., *hai, soo, un,* or *ee*) to demonstrate their attentiveness (Harris & Moran, 1979; Nishida, 1996). These vocalics possess a cultural motivation. Hierarchy is demonstrated by the adjustment of voice tone and pitch to fit the speaker's position of junior or senior (Morsbach, 1973). Additionally, the feedback stream indicates that the listener is paying attention to the speaker, which helps maintain positive social relations *(wa)* between the two individuals.

For the Japanese, laughter can possess a variety of meanings. Laughter can signal joy, of course, but it is also used to disguise embarrassment, sadness, or even anger (Seward, 1972). Use of laughter in the latter modes is designed to maintain situational harmony and avoid any potential for interpersonal discord.

In a 1989 study, White analyzed tape-recorded English-language conversations of Americans and native Japanese. The Japanese participants used significantly more feedback responses than did the Americans. Unable to ascertain a linguistic reason for this greater use of vocalics, White (1989) concluded it was a cultural influence. The listener was believed to be exhibiting a sensitivity to the speaker's viewpoint and feelings (in other words, expressing empathy).

P10: *Japanese use of silence reflects the cultural themes of (1) hierarchy, (2) social balance, and (3) empathy.*

The salient role of silence in the Japanese communication process is attributed to a general mistrust of spoken words and an emphasis on emotionally discerning the other person's intentions (empathy). Silence is considered a virtue as well as a sign of respectability and trustworthiness (Burma, 1985; Cohen, 1991; Hall & Hall, 1990; Ishii, 1975, 1984; Lebra, 1976, 1993; Morsbach, 1988a).

A pronounced feature of Japanese conversations is the many short pauses or breaks, referred to as *ma*. According to Matsumoto (1988), the Japanese closely attend to these brief conversational breaks. The pauses may convey meaning, demonstrate respect, or be an attempt to assess the other person or the situation (Di Mare, 1990; Doi, 1973, 1988).

Instances of *ma* in Japanese discourse can impart a variety of messages, with the context supplying the actual meaning. Silence is used to tactfully signal disagreement, nonacceptance, or an uncomfortable dilemma. A period of silence can be used to consider an appropriate response or formulate an opinion. Also, a junior may remain silent in deference to a senior (Graham & Herberger, 1983; Morsbach, 1973; Ramsey & Birk, 1983; Ueda, 1974).

P11: *The Japanese use of olfactics reflects the cultural theme of social balance.*

Little information is available concerning the Japanese attitude toward odors. Kasahara (1986) asserted that the Japanese propensity for cleanliness creates a preference for an environment totally absent of odors. Although there is no supporting evidence, the near-ritualistic tradition of taking frequent baths and the desire to refrain from personal offense lends credence to this supposition.

CONCLUSIONS

The preceding propositions suggest that the use of and reliance on nonverbal communication are actually a part of Japanese behavioral psychology motivated by cultural imperatives. If this concept is accepted, the benefits of employing cultural motivations to investigate a society's nonverbal communication habits, or other communication patterns, become self-evident. Application of cultural themes to communicative dispositions could provide a salient methodology for examining and better understanding both culture-specific and intercultural communication phenomena.

Potential benefits derived from practical application of this approach are especially promising. Greater appreciation of the cultural imperatives behind communicative behaviors would directly enhance intercultural communication competence. An individual engaged in an intercultural communication exchange would better understand both *what* the other person was doing and *why* he or she was doing it.

The suggested design is not, however, free of limitations. Several perceived impediments exist that require additional investigation and clarification before implementation of wider theoretical application.

A particularly important aspect that demands greater inquiry relates to the identification of cultural themes. As discussed earlier, Japan presents an unusually homogeneous culture when compared with other nations. This societal similitude facilitates discernment of both cultural themes and their motivations. Moreover, the cultural themes can then be reliably applied across almost all dimensions of Japanese society.[3]

Other societies, such as the United States, do not have the degree of cultural congruency extant in Japan. For these cases, identification and application of consistent cultural themes to the composite ethnicities is fraught with considerable difficulty and potential peril. Any motivation to stereotype themes across an entire heterogeneous populace must be tempered by a resolve to treat ethnic divisions both as separate entities and as integral parts of the greater societal whole.

Another dilemma requiring meditation concerns units of measurement. The nonverbal communication patterns of a culture are largely observable and measurable. Culture, as an entity itself and as a motivator of communication behaviors, is not, however, readily quantifiable. Most studies dealing with cultural influences have relied on recounting of personal experiences and observations (anecdotal documentation).

Many studies incorporate "culture" as a somewhat ethereal, abstract manifestation of humankind's imagination. Others have approached "culture" empirically and attempted to employ scientific measurements. Hofstede, for instance, used survey questionnaires and statistical analysis in an effort to determine the role of culture in the formation of value systems that affect "human thinking, organizations, and institutions in predictable ways" (1980, p. 11). Similarly, Osgood, May, and Miron have made noteworthy progress in statistically quantifying intangible attributes, what they term "subjective culture" (1975, p. 4).

The progress of Hofstede (1980) and Osgood, May, and Miron (1975) suggests that culture is not entirely beyond the scope of objective quantification. Their achievements provide benchmarks for empirical examination of the influence of cultural themes on communication behaviors.

Thematic universality is also an area of potential peril for theoretical application of cultural themes to communicative practices. Specifically, the investigator must not axiomatically assume that similar themes beget similar behaviors when moving among cultures. A theme prompting a specific behavioral action in one culture may generate an entirely different pattern in another cultural environment. To obviate this possible pitfall, each culture must be examined as a unique entity. The identification of common cultural themes and communication practices across a substantial number of societies is needed before theoretical application can be made on unexamined cultures.

Further investigation is also needed to determine if any of the cultural themes are codependent. For example, if hierarchy is manifested by a culture, will formality or another theme also be present?

The preceding constraints should not be interpreted as a repudiation of the proposed approach to explaining communicative practices. Rather, they are simply areas of concern that must be investigated and clarified before cultural themes can be reliably employed to help discern and understand societal communication predispositions. Resolution of these concerns will instill the concept with increased application, additional rigor, and greater parsimony.

Notes

1. Although sometimes moving at a seemingly glacial pace, culture is actually a dynamic process, as individuals avail themselves of modern technologies they are exposed to and often adopt different social practices. This diffusion of cultural behaviors can and does exert change. With this in mind, we must recognize that the nonverbal communicative behaviors of the Japanese, as discussed in this article, are undergoing change. For example, except in rural areas, one seldom sees young Japanese women place their hand over their mouth. Direct eye contact is becoming increasingly common, especial in interactions with Westerners. Public touch is becoming more acceptable, and young Japanese couples can be seen cuddling in Tokyo's parks.
2. Even this established tradition is undergoing change. A recent article in a Japanese business newspaper bemoaned the fact that many of the younger employees were eschewing the company's lapel pins.
3. This is not to suggest that the Japanese are a wholly homogenous group uninfluenced by other cultures. For example, Japan has three large minority groups—Koreans, Ainu, and Burakumin—that possess distinct cultural characteristics. In recent years, the urban areas of Japan have also experienced a growing influx of foreign workers, coming from all parts of the globe. These immigrants bring their own values, beliefs, and behaviors, some of which are diffused, in varying degrees, into the Japanese culture.

References

Barnlund, D. (1975). *Public and private self in Japan and United States.* Tokyo: Simul.

Barnlund, D. (1989). *Communicative styles of Japanese and Americans.* Belmont, CA: Wadsworth.

Bond, M. H., & Shiraishi, D. (1974). The effect of body lean and status of an interviewer on the nonverbal behavior of Japanese interviewees. *International Journal of Psychology, 9*(2), 117–128.

Buller, D. B., & Burgoon, J. K. (1986). The effects of vocalics and nonverbal sensitivity on compliance. *Human Communication Research, 13,* 126–144.

Burgoon, J. K., & Hale, J. L. (1984). The fundamental topic of relational communication. *Communication Monographs, 51,* 193–214.

Burgoon, J. K., & Hale, J. L. (1987). Validation and measurement of the fundamental themes of relational communication. *Communication Monographs, 54,* 19–62.

Buruma, I. (1985). *A Japanese mirror.* New York: Penguin Books.

Caudill, W. (1973). General culture: The influence of social structure and culture on human behavior in modern Japan. *Journal of Nervous and Mental Disease, 157,* 240–257.

Caudill, W., & Plath, D. (1966). Who sleeps with whom? Parent–child involvement in urban Japanese families. *Psychiatry, 29,* 344–366.

Caudill, W., & Weinstein, H. (1969). Maternal care and infant behavior in Japan and America. *Psychiatry, 32,* 12–43.

Cohen, R. (1991). *Negotiating across cultures.* Washington, DC: U.S. Institute of Peace.

Coker, D. A., & Burgoon, J. K. (1987). The nature of conversational involvement and nonverbal encoding patterns. *Human Communication Research, 13,* 463–494.

Condon, J. C., & Yousef, F. (1983). *An introduction to intercultural communication.* Indianapolis, IN: Bobbs-Merrill.

Craft, L. (1986, May). All in the cards: The mighty *meishi. TOKYO Business Today,* 61–64.

Di Mare, L. (1990). *Ma* and Japan. *Southern Communication Journal, 55,* 319–328.

Doi, T. (1973). The Japanese patterns of communication and the concept of *amae. Quarterly Journal of Speech, 59,* 180–185.

Doi, T. (1988). Dependency in human relationships. In D. I. Okimoto & T. P. Rohlen (Eds.), *Inside the Japanese system:*

Readings on contemporary society and political economy (pp. 20–25). Stanford, CA: Stanford University Press.
Graham, I. L., & Herberger, R. A. (1983). Negotiations abroad: Don't shoot from the hip. *Harvard Business Review, 83,* 160–168.
Gudykunst, W. B., & Nishida, T. (1984). Individual and cultural influences on uncertainty reduction. *Communication Monographs, 51,* 23–36.
Gudykunst, W. B., & Nishida, T. (1993). Interpersonal and intergroup communication in Japan and the United States. In W. B. Gudykunst (Ed.), *Communication in Japan and the United States* (pp. 149–214). Albany: State University of New York Press.
Gudykunst, W. B., Nishida, T., & Schmidt, K. (1989). The influence of culture, relational, and personality factors on uncertainty reduction processes. *Western Journal of Speech Communication, 53,* 13–29.
Gudykunst, W. B., Yoon, Y. C., & Nishida, T. (1987). The influence of individualism–collectivism on perceptions of communication in ingroup and outgroup relationships. *Communication Monographs, 54,* 295–306.
Hall, E. T. (1981). *Beyond culture.* New York: Anchor Books, Doubleday. (Original work published 1976)
Hall, E. T. (1988). The hidden dimensions of time and space in today's world. In F. Poyatos (Ed.), *Cross-cultural perspectives in nonverbal communication* (pp. 145–152). Lewiston, NY: C. J. Hogrefe.
Hall, E. T. (1990). *The hidden dimension.* New York: Anchor Books, Doubleday. (Original work published 1966)
Hall, E. T., & Hall, M. R. (1990). *Hidden differences: Doing business with the Japanese.* New York: Anchor Books, Doubleday. (Original work published 1987)
Hamabata, M. M. (1990). *Crested kimono: Power and love in the Japanese business family.* Ithaca, NY: Cornell University Press.
Harris, P. R., & Moran, R. T. (1979). *Managing cultural differences.* Houston, TX: Gulf Publishing.
Hendry, J. (1989). *Becoming Japanese: The world of the pre-school child.* Honolulu: University of Hawaii Press. (Original work published 1986)
Hofstede, G. (1980). *Culture's consequence: International differences in work-related values.* Newbury Park, CA: Sage.
Ishii, S. (1975). Characteristics of Japanese nonverbal communicative behavior. *Occasional Papers in Speech.* Honolulu: University of Hawaii, Department of Speech.
Ishii, S. (1984). *Enyro-Sasshi* communication: A key to understanding Japanese interpersonal relations. *Cross Currents, 11,* 49–58.
Ishii, S., & Bruneau, T. (1991). Silence and silences in cross-cultural perspective: Japan and the United States. In L. A. Samovar & R. E. Porter (Eds.), *Intercultural communication: A reader* (6th ed., pp. 314–319). Belmont, CA: Wadsworth.
Iwata, O. (1979). Selected personality traits as determinants of the perception of crowding. *Japanese Psychological Research, 21,* 1–9.
Kasahara, Y. (1986). Fear of eye-to-eye confrontation among neurotic patients in Japan. In T. S. Lebra & W. P. Lebra (Eds.), *Japanese culture and behavior: Selected readings* (Rev. ed., pp. 379–387). Honolulu: University of Hawaii Press.
Kinosita, K. (1988). Language habits of the Japanese. *Bulletin of the Association for Business Communication, 51,* 35–40.
Kitao, K., & Kitao, S. K. (1985). *Effects of social environment on Japanese and American communication.* (ERIC Document Reproduction Service No. ED260579).
Kitao, K., & Kitao, S. K. (1987). *Differences in the kinesic codes of Americans and Japanese.* East Lansing, MI: Department of Communication, Michigan State University. (ERIC Document Reproduction Service No. ED282400).
Kitao, K., & Kitao, S. K. (1989). *Intercultural communication between Japan and the United States.* Tokyo: Eichosha Shinsha Co. (ERIC Document Reproduction Service No. ED321303).
Lebra, T. S. (1976). *Japanese patterns of behavior.* Honolulu: University of Hawaii Press.
Lebra, T. S. (1993). Culture, self, and communication in Japan and the United States. In W. B. Gudykunst (Ed.), *Communication in Japan and the United States* (pp. 51–87). Albany: State University of New York Press.
March, R. M. (1990/1989). The *Japanese negotiator: Subtlety and strategy beyond Western logic.* New York: Kondansha.
Matsumoto, M. (1988). *The unspoken way: "Haragei": Silence in Japanese business and society.* New York: Kondansha. (Original work published in 1984 in Japanese under the title *Haragei.)*
Matsumoto, D. (1996). *Unmasking Japan: Myths and realities about the emotions of the Japanese.* Stanford, CA: Stanford University Press.
McDaniel, E. R., & Andersen, P. A. (1998). International patterns of tactile communication: A field study. *Journal of Nonverbal Behavior, 22,* 59–75.
Miyamoto, M. (1994). *Straitjacket society: An insider's irreverent view of bureaucratic Japan.* New York: Kodansha International.
Montague, A. (1978). *Touching: The human significance of the skin* (2nd ed.). New York: Harper & Row.
Morsbach, H. (1973). Aspects of nonverbal communication in Japan. *Journal of Nervous and Mental Disease, 157,* 262–277.
Morsbach, H. (1988a). The importance of silence and stillness in Japanese nonverbal communication: A cross-cultural approach. In F. Poyatos (Ed.), *Cross-cultural perspectives in nonverbal communication* (pp. 201–215). Lewiston, NY: C. J. Hogrefe.

Morsbach, H. (1988b). Nonverbal communication and hierarchical relationships: The case of bowing in Japan. In F. Poyatos (Ed.), *Cross-cultural perspectives in nonverbal communication* (pp. 189–199). Lewiston, NY: C. J. Hogrefe.

Munakata, T. (1986). Japanese attitudes toward mental illness and mental health care. In T. S. Lebra & W. P. Lebra (Ed.), *Japanese culture and behavior: Selected readings* (Rev. ed.) (pp. 369–378). Honolulu: University of Hawaii Press.

Nakane, C. (1970). *Japanese society.* Berkeley: University of California Press.

Nishida, T. (1996). Communications in personal relationships in Japan. In W. B. Gudykunst, S. Ting-Toomey, & T. Nishida (Eds.), *Communication in personal relationships across cultures* (pp. 102–117). Thousand Oaks, CA: Sage.

Opler, M. E. (1945). Themes as dynamic forces in culture. *American Journal of Sociology, 51,* 198–206.

Opler, M. E. (1946). An application of the theory of themes in culture. *Journal of the Washington Academy of Sciences, 36,* 137–166.

Osgood, C. E., May, W. H., & Miron, M. S. (1975). *Cross-cultural universals of affective meaning.* Urbana: University of Illinois Press.

Ramsey, S. J. (1979). Nonverbal behavior: An intercultural perspective. In M. K. Asante, E. Newmark, & C. A. Blake (Eds.), *Handbook of intercultural communication* (pp. 105–143). Beverly Hills, CA: Sage.

Ramsey, S. J. (1981). The kinesics of femininity in Japanese women. *Language Sciences, 3,* 104–123.

Ramsey, S. J. (1985). To hear one and understand ten: Nonverbal behavior in Japan. In L. A. Samovar & R. E. Porter (Eds.), *Intercultural communication: A reader* (4th ed., pp. 307–321). Belmont, CA: Wadsworth.

Ramsey, S. J., & Birk, J. (1983). Training North Americans for interaction with Japanese: Considerations of language and communication style. In D. Landis & R. W. Brislin (Eds.), *The handbook of intercultural training: Vol. 3. Area studies in intercultural training* (pp. 227–259). New York: Pergamon Press.

Reischauer, E. O. (1988). *The Japanese today: Change and continuity.* Cambridge, MA: Belknap Press of Harvard University.

Richie, D. (1987). *A lateral view: Essays on contemporary Japan.* Tokyo: Japan Times.

Ruch, W. (1984). *Corporate communication: A comparison of Japanese and American practices.* Westport, CT: Quorum Books.

Sethi, S. P. (1974). Japanese management practices: Part I. *Colombia Journal of World Business, 9,* 94–104.

Seward, J. (1972). *The Japanese.* New York: William Morrow.

Seward, J. (1983). *Japanese in action* (Rev. ed.). New York: Weatherhill.

Spitzberg, B. H. (1989). Issues in the development of a theory of interpersonal competence in the intercultural context. *International Journal of Intercultural Relations, 13,* 241–268.

Stewart, L. P. (1993). Organizational communication in Japan and the United States. In W. B. Gudykunst (Ed.), *Communication in Japan and the United States* (pp. 215–248). Albany: State University of New York Press.

Takamizawa, H. (1988). *Business Japanese: A guide to improved communication.* New York: Kondansha International.

Ueda, T. (1974). Sixteen ways to avoid saying "no" in Japan. In J. C. Condon & M. Saito (Eds.), *Intercultural encounters with Japan* (pp. 185–192). Tokyo: Simul Press.

Watson, M. O. (1970). *Proxemic behavior: A cross-cultural study.* The Hague: Mouton.

Westwood, M. J., & Vargo, J. W. (1985). Counseling double-minority status clients. In R. J. Samuda (Ed.), *Intercultural counselling and assessment: Global perspectives* (pp. 303–313). Lewiston, NY: C. J. Hogrefe.

White, S. (1989). Backchannels across cultures: A study of Americans and Japanese. *Language in Society, 18,* 59–76.

Yum, Y. (1988). The impact of Confucianism on interpersonal relationship and communication patterns in East Asia. *Communication Monographs, 55,* 374–388.

Concepts and Questions

1. What are "cultural themes," and how might we benefit from their study?
2. What are the major Japanese cultural themes that influence intercultural communication?
3. Can you think of any American cultural themes that might influence how Americans use nonverbal communication?
4. How does Confucian-based collectivism help control Japanese nonverbal communication?
5. What cultural themes are seen as the basis for Japanese kinesic behavior? Are the same or different themes active in U.S. American nonverbal behavior?
6. What are the most obvious activities associated with Japanese kinesic behavior? What would be a U.S. American counterpart?
7. How does culture influence personal appearance in Japanese and U.S. American culture?
8. What are the cultural underpinnings of silence in Japan? How does the Japanese manipulation of silence affect intercultural communication?
9. Describe differences in the use of vocalics, or paralanguage, in Japan and the United States. How might these differences lead to misunderstandings during intercultural communication?

Cultural Contexts: The Influence of the Setting

6

He who would form a correct judgment of their tone must hear first one bell and then the other.

ITALIAN PROVERB

It should be clear at this stage of the book that communication involves much more than the sending and receiving of verbal and nonverbal messages. Human interaction takes place within a social and physical setting. That is to say, when you engage in a communication act, you do so within a specific environment or context. Whether you are in a classroom, dance club, doctor's office, business meeting, or church, the context or social environment influences how you and your communication partner perceive and respond to the interaction. How you dress, what you talk about, to whom you talk, and even the volume level of your voice is in some way determined by the context in which you find yourself. We call attention to the concept of social context because the setting is never neutral; it always influences, to some degree, how the communication participants behave. You have all learned appropriate patterns of communicative behavior for the various social contexts in which you normally find yourself. But, as with other aspects of intercultural communication, the patterns of behavior appropriate in various social contexts are culturally diverse. When you find yourself in an unfamiliar context without an internalized set of rules to govern your behavior or when you are interacting with someone who has internalized a different set of rules, communication problems frequently arise.

The sway of context is rooted in the following three interrelated assumptions.

1. *Communication is rule governed* (i.e., each encounter has implicit and explicit rules that regulate your conduct). These rules tell you everything from what is appropriate attire to what topics can be discussed.
2. *The setting helps you define what "regulations" are in operation.* Reflect for a moment on your own communication behavior as you move to and from the following arenas: classroom, courtroom, church, hospital, basketball game, and disco. Visualize yourself behaving differently as you proceed from place to place.
3. *Most of the communication rules you follow have been learned as part of cultural experiences.* Although cultures might share the same general settings, their specific notion of proper behavior for each context manifests the values and attitudes of that

culture. Concepts of turn taking, time, space, language, manners, nonverbal behavior, silence, and control of the communication flow are largely an extension of each culture.

In this chapter, we offer readings that demonstrate the crucial link that exists between context, culture, and communication. What emerges from these essays is the realization that to understand another culture you must appreciate the rules that govern that culture's behavior in a specific setting. Although intercultural communication occurs in a variety of contexts, we have selected three environments where you are most likely to be interacting with people from cultures different from your own. Those settings are the business, education, and health care environments.

As indicated, the readings that follow deal with cultural diversity in communication contexts. To improve the manner in which you communicate in those contexts, we will focus on a combination of international and domestic settings.

The growth of international business during the past 30 years has been astonishing. Overseas transactions that annually generated millions of dollars just a few decades ago are now multibillion-dollar operations. Furthermore, many national companies have become global, transnational companies with offices and production or service facilities located throughout the world. This trend has evolved for several reasons. One is the imposition of regulations that require some aspect of production to be done within a country if the product is to be marketed in that country, such as the assembly of Japanese automobiles in U.S. factories. A second way this trend has occurred is through mergers and acquisitions in which one company may buy or merge with another across national boundaries. A third impetus for the trend is the recognition that productivity increases come about with local presence. Finally, changes have occurred within the United States. In many geographic areas of the country, society has become pluralistic and multicultural. This has created a multicultural workforce in most companies, whether they are local, regional, national, or international organizations.

Because of this worldwide economic growth and the internationalization of business, people no longer have the comfort of dealing exclusively with those who possess the same cultural background and experiences. One's associates, clients, subordinates, and even supervisors are often from different countries and cultures. Many aspects of business life, such as methods of negotiation, decision making, policy formulation, marketing techniques, management structure, human resource management, gift giving, and patterns of communication, are now influenced by cultural diversity.

What is true about the expansion of intercultural business communication is also accurate when talking about the educational setting. That is to say, the forces of globalization, immigration, and population change have given classrooms both in the United States and elsewhere a new multicultural appearance. In the United States alone, nearly one in three students now identity themselves as African American, Latino, Asian, Pacific Islander, Arab, or American Indian. Because of the cultural experiences of these groups, schools are now experiencing a host of differences with regard to learning styles, interaction patterns, competition, the use of silence, the status and role of the teacher, and the like.

Exposure to global and multicultural populations has major implications for health care providers. This cultural context is important for a number of reasons. First, the promotion of health and the prevention of disease constitute an urgent need for any civilized culture. Second, diseases are often highly contagious and are transmitted into the host culture. Third, differences in the perception of the causes of illness and the treatment of illness are culture bound. And finally, cultures have varying communication patterns and styles when they are in the health care setting. Whereas members of one culture may talk openly and freely to a health care provider, members of another culture might be reluctant to reveal personal information.

As we have just highlighted, your understanding of how communication operates in the multicultural business setting, educational environment, and health care context is increasing in importance as cultural contact continues to intensify. In order for you to function successfully in these three arenas, we offer the following six essays.

We begin with two essays that involve a setting that is truly international—the world of business. It is obvious that all business activities encompass many forms of communication, and those forms reflect the attitudes, values, and communication patterns unique to each culture. Hence, our first two essays examine how cultural diversity touches nearly all aspect of the business setting.

With the proximity of Mexico to the United States and implementation of the North American Free Trade Agreement (NAFTA), business relationships between the United States and Mexico have increased dramatically. Both in terms of trade negotiations between the United States and Mexico and in the operation of U.S. businesses in Mexico, the need for better understanding of Mexican culture and the differences in U.S.–Mexican business practices has become an imperative. The importance of this relationship and the effect it is having on the cultures of both Mexico and the United States was examined in detail in a special issue of *Time* magazine in which the editors suggested that "along the U.S.–Mexican border, where hearts and minds and money and culture merge, the Century of the Americas is born" (June 11, 2001).

In their essay "U.S. Americans and Mexicans Working Together: Five Core Concepts," Sheryl Lindsley and Charles Braithwaite provide you with valuable insights into Mexican culture as it applies to the business environment. Lindsley and Braithwaite discuss five shared cultural patterns or core concepts common to doing business in Mexico: *confianza, simpatía, palanca, estabilidad,* and *mañana*. These are not mutually exclusive categories, but rather overlapping concepts reflecting deeply held values for many Mexicans. As these shared values make their way into the business environment, effective U.S. business managers and representatives must become aware of the influences these values have on behavior and communication.

In our next reading, the focus turns to doing business with the culture of India. As a country of more than 1 billion people, the major partner of American outsourcing, and a country that is becoming increasing modernized, you can see why India warrants your consideration. Suresh Gopalan and Angie Stahl analyze some important behavioral theories and practices in India and compare them with American management styles. They begin by offering what they call a "cultural profile" of American values. Their analysis uses the five cultural dimensions found in the writings of Kluckhohn and Strodtbeck: human nature, nature and supernatural elements, time, work, and relationships.

After discussing a particular dimension from an American point of view, they take that same dimension and apply it to India. For example, in writing about relationships in a particular culture, Gopalan and Stahl observe that in the workplace "American tend to be highly individualistic, autonomous, and egalitarian (non-hierarchical) in nature" and "stress independence over dependence and ascendancy of individual rights over group goals and aspirations." Specifically, some of these traits are manifested in management's having an "open door" policy, encouraging participative decision making, and promoting career advancement. You can see vast differences concerning the value of social relationships when Gopalan and Stahl turn to Indian management styles. They note that in India people are socialized in a culture in which an individual derives his/her identity from group affiliations based on family and caste membership. In the business setting, this means that age, seniority, and group status greatly contribute to an individual's success within the organization.

Finally, in order to help you gain further insight into the business context, we include an example of differences in culture and communication practices as they exist between American and northern European cultures. Hence, we turn to Robert A. Friday's article, "Contrasts in Discussion Behaviors of German and American Managers." Friday traces cultural expectations of both German and American managers across several dimensions, pointing out the differences and how they may lead to misunderstandings and ineffective communication. Specifically, he is concerned with cultural differences in business management approaches as they relate to (1) the perception of business, (2) interpersonal credibility, (3) assertiveness and fair play, (4) problem solving, and (5) education and training. Friday ends his essay by attempting to increase cultural understanding between German and American managers who share a common environment.

During our discussion we have referred to the idea that as the world figuratively shrinks, intercultural interaction increases. This proliferation of intercultural contact is evident in the health care setting as well as the business context. Hence, our next two selections emphasize the notion that a multicultural society strongly affects the health care setting. The reason is obvious: Cultural beliefs about health, disease, and caregiver–patient communication can differ significantly. In the first essay, Nagesh Rao reports the initial findings of an ongoing investigation into physician–patient communication across cultures. Through interviews conducted worldwide, Rao seeks to develop a base of information that will ultimately lead to a model of intercultural health care communication.

In his article "'Half-Truths' in Argentina, Brazil, and India: An Intercultural Analysis of Physician–Patient Communication," Rao provides an insightful view of how physicians from these cultures view the diversity within their countries. In addition, Rao shows how these physicians operating within a collectivist cultural environment would choose to reveal news of serious or terminal illness to patients.

Our next essay, "Exploring Culture in Nursing: A Theory-Driven Practice" by Brian E. Mendyka, is based on two interrelated premises, both of which are at the core of this book: first, "human illness is a cultural event"; and second, "cultural meanings should complement the nurse–patient relationships." It is Mendyka's view that the entire patient should be treated in a holistic manner. To accomplish this, a patient's culture becomes crucial. Hence, Mendyka offers suggestions that are both insightful and useful when patient and nurse are interacting. Although this essay is intended for nurses, Mendyka's advice regarding culture has merit for anyone interested in improving intercultural communication.

Mendyka offers numerous examples of how a lack of cultural understanding between patient and health care providers can create problems. By following the case of a single Native American patient, you can see how differences in time, perceptions of illness, family relationships, and perceptions of self can create problems. Mendyka believes the key to solving these and countless other patient–nurse difficulties is realizing that cultural experiences and meanings provide "a window" for understanding both the patient and the illness.

Classrooms represent yet another setting that is experiencing an explosion in intercultural contact. All over the world, the children of immigrants are now being educated. The faces of the people in these schools, and the languages they speak, have become as diverse as those found in the business and health care setting. And like the other two settings, classrooms represent yet another context in which the sway of culture is powerful. Although educational practices at any educational level of a multicultural society are affected by the cultural diversity found in each classroom, we believe that the practice of communication in the multicultural classroom is paramount. Traditional approaches to education and the use of single communication strategy are inadequate in a multicultural context. Cultural diversity affects thinking habits and strategies, communication patterns and styles, prejudice and stereotyping, educational expectations, approaches to learning, and classroom behavior—to name but a few cultural influences found in the educational setting.

In her article "Culture and Communication in the Classroom," Geneva Gay introduces the semiotic relationship that exists among communication, culture, teaching, and learning. She discusses some of the critical features and pedagogical potentials for different ethnic groups of color. Her discussion of culture and communication in this article first outlines some key assertions about culture and communication in teaching and learning in general. Gay then presents some of the major characteristics of the communicative modes of African, Native, Asian, and European Americans. Her focus throughout is on discourse dynamics—that is, who participates in communication, under what conditions, and how participation patterns are affected by culture.

Another approach to dealing with issues of the multicultural classroom is offered by Johann Le Roux in an essay titled "Social Dynamics of the Multicultural Classroom." What is interesting about this essay is that Le Roux is writing about schools in South Africa—a place that is also experiencing an increase in multicultural classrooms. His analysis, in the form of both citing problems and offering advice, is applicable to all multicultural classrooms.

The major premise behind Le Roux's paper is that the effective multicultural teacher must be sensitive to group and cultural affiliations. For Le Roux this means not only recognizing potential classroom problems but also developing the knowledge and skills to deal with these problems. Le Roux believes that frustration, misapprehension, and intercultural conflict will more frequently be the outcome when teachers do not deal with diversity in a sensitive manner. To avoid these negative consequences, Le Roux looks at the following problem areas: language, stereotyping, cultural expectations, self-concept, and conflict. Perhaps the preeminent feature of Le Roux's essay is the detailed advice he offers as a means of overcoming the five problems just cited. It is his belief, and ours, that unless culture is taken into consideration, and managed effectively, learning will not take place.

U.S. Americans and Mexicans Working Together: Five Core Concepts

SHERYL L. LINDSLEY
CHARLES A. BRAITHWAITE

> I was disadvantaged when I first came down here [to Mexico] because I didn't have the class [multicultural training]. I'm probably still doing some things wrong now. When I go to business meetings, I was raised in a culture where you just get out your reports and start talking about them and that's not how it is here. Here you talk about family and other things first. I often forget this and so one of my Mexican colleagues will remind me that I am violating this tradition by saying, "So, [name], how is your dog?" When I hear this then I know I'm not supposed to be talking about business. (Lindsley, 1995, p. 239)

This account by a U.S. American who lives and works in Mexico reflects the importance of adapting cultural behaviors to achieve communication competency in organizational settings. As an administrator who was transferred to Mexico more than eight years ago without any intercultural training, he's learned the hard way that lack of cultural knowledge and skills negatively affects organizational relationships, goals, and productivity. In this account, it appears that he still struggles to put aside that U.S. American "Let's get right down to business" orientation in order to prioritize personal relationships in meetings with his Mexican associates. A look at the literature on U.S. American experiences abroad tells us that his problems in intercultural communication are not unique.

Although U.S. American organizations are increasingly reliant on international liaisons to compete in the global economy, many have suffered failures as a result of inadequate managerial training for work abroad (Albert, 1994). These problems have resulted in tremendous financial losses to organizations as well as human costs by undermining job successes and increasing personal and familial suffering (Mendenhall, Dunbar, & Oddou, 1987). These international experiences demonstrate that one cannot simply export U.S. American ways of doing business to other countries. Rather, personnel in international organizations must understand the histories, cultures, and languages of the people with whom they work. This essay will review events affecting U.S.–Mexican economic relationships and then examine five Mexican cultural concepts influencing organizational effectiveness.

The historic ratification of the North American Free Trade Agreement (NAFTA) between the United States, Canada, and Mexico embodies both promises and problems. Government leaders who supported the bill promised increased competitiveness with other trade blocs such as the European Union (EU) and the Pacific Rim nations, along with larger consumer markets for good and services and, ultimately, increased prosperity (Weintraub, 1991). At the same time, this alliance created new problems and highlighted old ones that remain unresolved (Davidson, 2000). Critics have charged that the agreement promotes the interests of only large international and multinational firms, at the expense of smaller businesses and ordinary people in all three nations (Castañeda, 1995). In the United States, domestic manufacturers have problems competing with products made with inexpensive Mexican labor, and many citizens have lost jobs when factories relocated south of the border. In Mexico, many people fear increased national dependency on the United States for employment (Hansen, 1981; Sklair, 1993) and difficulties in competing with large U.S. multinationals in many service and product sectors (Batres, 1991; Hellman, 1994).

Finally, critics on both sides of the border have pointed to problems with several U.S.-owned assembly plants in Mexico that have exploited inexpensive labor (Prieto, 1997), failed to provide adequate health and safety conditions for workers, and polluted the borderlands and waterways (Fernandez-Kelly, 1983; Pena, 1997). Although a comprehensive review of international relationships between these two countries is beyond the scope of this article, it is important to understand these issues because they contribute to

---

 An earlier version of this article appeared in the ninth edition. The late Sheryl Lindsley taught at California State University, Stanislaus. Charles A. Braithwaite is Director of International Studies at the University of Nebraska–Lincoln.

the conditions in which businesses operate and the way people from both countries interpret each other's behavior in everyday work relationships.

In an environment characterized by anxiety about ongoing economic changes, the need for mutual understanding and respect is critical. One way for those who are unfamiliar with Mexican culture to begin to understand it is to examine some of the core cultural concepts that guide organizational relationships. Of course, it is essential to keep in mind that diversity exists within both U.S. American and Mexican societies related to socioeconomic class, ethnic origin, regional affiliation, gender, personal ideologies, and character. Thus, when the term *U.S. American* or *North American* culture is used, it refers to the dominant cultural characteristics—typically, middle-class—of the European American male. Among Mexicans, too, it is important to recognize that adherence to dominant cultural characteristics varies within the population, and although most Mexicans are *mestizos,* of both Spanish and indigenous origin, several ethnic groups have maintained aspects of their pre-colonial traditions. For example, more than 600,000 people who live on the Yucatan peninsula today speak predominantly Mayan languages among their family, friends, and community members. Because many Mayans learn Spanish as a second language to interact with other Mexicans, they often do not speak it with the same fluency as their first tongue, which likely influences satisfaction and effectiveness in interethnic work relationships (Love, 1994). Regional and ethnic differences also affect the structures of modern-day businesses. Although indigenous Mayans from Mexico's southern highlands emphasize corporate organization, northern Mexican businesses embody characteristics of traditional patronage systems (Alvarez & Collier, 1994).

Diversity notwithstanding, many behaviors that are typical of dominant cultural patterns in each country provide a useful starting point for developing intercultural awareness. These shared cultural patterns have been referred to as *core concepts.* Core concepts provide us with knowledge about appropriate and inappropriate cultural interactions in specific relationships and contexts (Lindsley, 1999b). Through an understanding of these concepts, one can choose from a myriad of ways of behaving in order to enhance intercultural work relationships and goals. Core concepts derived from research on doing business in Mexico include *confianza, simpatía, palanca, estabilidad,* and *mañana.* Throughout the discussion, it will be apparent that these are not mutually exclusive categories, but rather overlapping concepts that reflect deeply held values for many Mexicans.

CONFIANZA

In an interview with a Mexican production manager about communication with U.S. home office personnel, I asked her what she does when she thinks someone is wrong. She responded:

> Well, it's hard at first if someone is new, but after you establish trust and confidence, then it's easier. . . . I just make suggestions about things, but I don't tell people they are wrong, just give them information to make the decisions and then they are grateful and the relationship benefits from this. . . . When you just make suggestions and don't tell people what to do and let them learn and make decisions for themselves, then more confidence in the relationship develops and then they owe you. You didn't confront them, you treated them well, with respect, and now they owe you. (Lindsley & Braithwaite, 1996, p. 215)

According to this account, indirectness is appropriate in a situation in which another's face (or self-presentation) is vulnerable. Because relationships are generally more central to Mexican than U.S. American organizations, it is no surprise that relationships are carefully nurtured and safeguarded. One of the core aspects of a good relationship is the co-creation of *confianza,* or "trust," which is built through communicative behaviors that adhere to cultural norms for face saving. In addition, the aforementioned production manager's account reveals cultural norms for mutual obligation. There is an explicit reference to reciprocity—each party should protect the other's positive face in interaction.

The kinds of situations in which face concerns are primary include those that could possibly be threatening to one's own image or the other party with whom one is interacting. This means that communication of negative information (e.g., I don't understand; I made a mistake; I disagree with you; you made a mistake) is avoided or communicated indirectly. For example, a person's tone of voice may indicate that he or she is reluctant to adopt a new plan, even though this is not stated explicitly. Among the ways that U.S. American managers can adapt their own behaviors are avoiding displays of negative emotions, especially direct criticism, conveying receptivity to negative information, asking how they can help their employees, and paying close attention to nonverbal behaviors.

SIMPATÍA

In an interview with another Mexican production manager, he stated that the importance of good communication between managers and employees is not only in maintaining positive working relationships, but also in meeting productivity goals. He explained:

> When I have to discipline an employee, I start off by talking about the person's place in the corporation and what they are there for . . . what their role is in the plant. Then I talk to them about what they need to do. It is important not to hurt the employee, because once you do—[he shrugs, as if to say, "it's the end."] (Lindsley, 1999a, p. 24)

It is evident that this situation, in which the employee's behavior was not meeting organizational standards, was potentially face-threatening. In addressing the situation, the manager demonstrated adherence to the cultural script of *simpatía,* which emphasizes emotional support and self-sacrifice for the good of the group (Triandis, Marin, Lisansky, & Berancourt, 1984). The norm for "good communication" is evaluated through the types of interpersonal linkages that connect people in their familial, social, and organizational lives. Communication competency is described as developing over the course of long-term relationships, through interaction occurring both within and outside the plant. One Hermosillan manufacturing manager explained:

> Our communication is really good here. The informal communication is really the most important thing. A number of people here knew each other in high school, for example, I knew [name] in high school, I also knew the trainer [name] in high school, so we had known each other for a long time and done things together outside the plant. This is really important in contributing to the communication at the plant. (Lindsley, 1999a, p. 12)

The effects of this cultural script on communication include culturally normative behaviors that stress commitment to harmony and cooperation. Thus, communication that stresses the positive and minimizes negative feedback is emphasized. In this case, criticism is couched in terms of the individual's importance to the group (his or her role in the organization), which is stated in positive terms, showing concern for the employee's feelings. In Mexico, a person who is considered *simpático* "is sympathetic, understanding, pleasing, friendly, well-behaved, [and] trustworthy" (DeMente, 1996, p. 278). Being *simpático* is something to strive for in organizational relationships and is demonstrated through communication behaviors that show positive emotional connection with others.

PALANCA

The concept of *palanca* refers to leverage, or power derived from affiliated connections. It affects organizational relationships in terms of one's ability to get things done by virtue of one's official authority as well as through one's contacts with extensive networks of relationships among family members, relatives, former classmates, friends, and business associates. These connections are often built over many years and enable one to obtain favors that may transcend institutional rules and procedures or overcome scarcity of resources and services (Archer & Fitch, 1994). For example, interpersonal connections may allow one to receive "special" consideration for business transactions, faster service in obtaining government services, and personal recommendations for new jobs.

U.S. Americans may tend to evaluate these practices negatively as "corrupt" without reflecting on the similarities with their own organizational behaviors or without understanding the rationale for why these behaviors are functional in Mexican culture. It is typical in the United States for businesspeople to say, "Who you know is just as important, if not more so, than what you know," and to rely on personal affiliations for special introductions, advice, and information to promote their business goals. In Mexico, the importance of these interpersonal affiliations in business have been described as evolving from a history in which official authority was held for hundreds of years by descendants of Spanish colonial conquerors and government that were not representative of the majority of the people, but which served the interests of a small elite. Even today, one of the challenges of all presidential administrations is to establish a true representative democracy (Castañeda, 1995). Therefore, one of the ways that people work to protect themselves and promote their interests is through informal systems of affiliated connection. U.S. Americans often rely on a system of written laws and rules, but history has taught Mexicans that it is often more effective to rely on personal connections for social negotiation of written laws and rules to accomplish desired objectives.

Although the use of *palanca* is typical throughout Central and Latin America, it is important to differentiate it from *mordida* (paying a bribe) and to understand that both Mexican laws and U.S. American international laws (e.g., the Foreign Corrupt Practices Act) prohibit payments for certain kinds of services. Although the differentiation is murky, *palanca* embodies a system of mutual obligation and reciprocated favors, not necessarily money or gifts. In this matter, like all other aspects of culture, Mexican business practices are changing. In addition, there are differences among Mexicans in the way any particular behavior is evaluated.

For example, some individuals perceive that giving a small fee to a government worker for acting expeditiously is something positive and similar to the U.S. practice of tipping a food server for good service. Others might think it is inappropriate to give a "tip" but appropriate to reward good service by giving a gift afterward or simply making a point to tell that person's boss about how satisfied they are with the employee (Lindsley, 1995). In consideration of these issues, U.S. Americans need to be aware not only of the power of affiliated connections, but also of current laws and Mexicans' individual attitudes about special favors and consideration.

ESTABILIDAD

A common sentiment among many Mexicans is "The family is our first priority and must remain so for the future stability of our country" (Kras, 1989, p. 27). The need for *estabilidad* or "stability" reinforces the value of personal relationships and permeates organizational behaviors. It is reflected in the tendency for Mexicans to place relationships before tasks. This view is communicated through a wide range of behaviors, including asking questions about colleagues' families, discussing personal matters before business (e.g., at the beginning of a meeting), taking action to promote employees' personal well-being, including families in organizational activities, taking time off work to assist family members in need, and establishing, developing, and maintaining long-term interconnected networks of personal relationships. One Mexican manager explained the positive nature of familial stability as an adaptive force in an uncertain world. He said, "Families give us stability in Mexican culture. Men want stability in families because the Mexican economy and politics are sometimes not stable. In Mexico the family is the stable foundation" (Lindsley, 1995, p. 129).

Some of the ways that managers show responsibility for employees' well-being may be through *compadrazgo* and *comadrazgo* systems in which they become godfathers, godmothers, and mentors for their employees' children. This type of relationship, which dates back to the 16th century, is viewed as mutually beneficial because young people can rely on their mentors for advice, guidance, and financial, spiritual, and social support. In return, mentors can count on the loyalty of the young people throughout their lives.

These types of relationships exemplify the extent to which Mexican personal and organizational roles overlap, in contrast to U.S. roles that are typically more separate. American managers often criticize the reluctance to separate personal life from work life in Mexico. Kopinak (1996) describes an American manager being bothered by this characteristic because "I could argue with a person at work and still have a beer with him after work [in the U.S.] whereas the Mexicans wouldn't do this" (p. 55). The often-blurred distinction between familial and organizational life also means that Mexicans may give preference to hiring relatives over strangers, helping employees get a better education, or giving them small personal loans. These favors are often reciprocated with strong employee support and loyalty to the manager. For example, during financial hardships, the employee might continue working for his or her manager without a paycheck (Alvarez & Collier, 1994). Like other aspects of culture, this is an adaptive mechanism in Mexico—building stability through interconnected networks of familial and organizational relationships provides "social insurance" against the vagaries of uncertainty in economic and political structures.

Concerns for stability are also manifest in some Mexicans' negative attitudes about U.S. American investment in Mexico. Historically, U.S. Americans have often acted in ways that promote their own interests at the expense of Mexicans, which has led to criticism that U.S. involvement in Mexico threatens Mexican economic, political, and cultural stability. When U.S. American organizational personnel go to Mexico with attitudes of cultural superiority (e.g., "We're going to teach Mexicans how to do business"), negative stereotypes are reinforced about U.S. Americans as arrogant, exploitive, and self-centered. In this case, fear about threats to stability may emerge when U.S. Americans are in higher-power positions and try to use their authority to change Mexican culture, laws, policies, and so on. To establish positive working relationships, these stereotypes and the behaviors that reinforce them must be addressed. Although there are no guaranteed ways to combat stereotypes, a good beginning is awareness that these stereotypes exist. The next step, of course, is developing intercultural awareness and skills in order to adapt behaviors in ways that show an understanding of and respect for Mexican culture and language. Mexican and U.S. Americans can and do learn to appreciate aspects of each other's cultures, but this cannot be accomplished without mutual openness and trust based on true respect and understanding, not one-sided opportunistic motives.

MAÑANA

In intercultural interaction in organizations, Mexicans and U.S. Americans often find themselves at odds over different understandings and attitudes surrounding the concept of time. Misunderstandings may arise in intercultural interpretations of language:

> Spanish language dictionaries say that *mañana* means "tomorrow," and that is the meaning taught to foreign students in the language. But "tomorrow" is a literal translation, not the true cultural meaning of the word. In its normal cultural context *mañana* means "sometime in the near future, maybe." Behind the term are such unspoken things as "If I feel like it," "If I have the time," or "If nothing unexpected happens." (DeMente, 1996, p. 183)

U.S. Americans have the tendency to think about *mañana* as referring to some specific time period, beginning at 12 A.M. and running for 24 hours, because of a primarily external orientation toward time (clocks guide activities). Most Mexicans use time clocks but also consider time to be more interpersonally negotiable (relationships guide activities), and what counts as being "on time" can be mediated by unexpected events beyond one's control. In Mexico, organizational tasks are often not accomplished as quickly as in the United States because of infrastructural conditions (e.g., telephone service, roads, electricity, water, mail) and other structural elements (e.g., government bureaucracy) that can slow progress. Moreover, beyond the physical world, metaphorical forces influence people's lives. For example, events occur *"Si Dios quiere"* (God willing). Therefore, for Mexicans it is very adaptive in interaction to acknowledge that events occur that one cannot control and that influence the flow of organizational processes.

In addition, Mexicans' attitudes toward time differ from those of U.S. Americans because of relatively differing values that influence how one organizes one's behaviors. One Mexican manager explained to me, "In Mexico we have a saying, *'Salud, dinero, amor y tempo para disfrutarlos'* (Health, wealth, love and time for enjoying them)." He contrasted this concept with such American sayings as "Time is money." Thus, while Mexicans perceive time as functioning in a way that allows one to engage in behaviors that are part of a desirable life, U.S. Americans quantify time as a commodity that is most importantly viewed as related to profits. As one writer on border communication has noted:

> You may take much longer establishing a relationship with your Mexican prospects and you may spend hours talking about anything except the details of the purchase; but once you're in the door, you're likely to be their supplier for a long time . . . don't expect to get right down to business until you've established at least the beginnings of a friendship. (Webber, 1993, p. 20)

These contrasts in cultural orientation toward time can exacerbate problems in intercultural interaction. When U.S. Americans do not take time to develop and maintain good interpersonal relationships in business, Mexicans may think they do not care about people, only money. Likewise, when Mexicans do not complete tasks "on time," U.S. Americans may think they're lazy. To overcome these misunderstandings, U.S. Americans need to adapt their behaviors to respond to the recognition that personal relationships are the foundation of good business in Mexico and adjust their attitudes to recognize that Mexicans work very hard but have other priorities in life, too.

SUMMARY

U.S. organizations often have given employees foreign assignments based on technical expertise; however, experience shows that intercultural communication competency is critical to organization success. Through an understanding of the concepts of *confianza, simpatía, palanca, estabilidad,* and *mañana,* one can better adapt to working in Mexico. In business, cultural diversity can be a strength that managers can build on when personnel understand the ways that culture affects organizational lives. Thus, cultural contrasts in ways of doing business should not be viewed simply as a problem, but rather as an advantage in contributing to new understandings about ways of conducting business.

Significantly, U.S. Americans who learn to adapt their behaviors have reported enjoying the closeness of Mexican relationships and their emphasis on family values, as well as their hard work ethic and employee loyalty. Mexicans working in U.S. organizations have reported enjoying their career opportunities, learning efficiency in developing schedules, and training in new kinds of management philosophies. And many Mexicans understand the importance of such adaptation, as reflected in this common tale told by a Mexican administrator in a U.S.-owned maquiladora, which is an industry located along the border between the United States and Mexico:

> There is a mouse, a cat, and a dog that live together in the same house. The mouse has a child and is trying to teach the baby mouse how to survive. So the mom mouse tells her baby, "Listen before you go outside, and if you hear *meow-meow,* then don't go outside because it's the cat, and if you hear *hrrr-hrrr,* you can go outside because it's the dog." So one day, the baby mouse is listening at the door and it hears *hrrr-hrrr,* so, confident that it's the dog, he goes outside. . . . Unfortunately, it's the cat. The cat grins and says, "Isn't it great to be bilingual?" (Lindsley, 1995, p. 210)

References

Albert, R. D. (1994). Cultural diversity and international training in multinational organizations. In R. L. Wiseman & R. Shuter (Eds.), *Communicating in multinational organizations* (pp. 153–165). Thousand Oaks, CA: Sage.

Alvarez, R. R., & Collier, G. A. (1994). The long haul in trucking: Traversing the borderlands of the North and South. *American Ethnologist, 21,* 606–627.

Archer, L., & Fitch, K. L. (1994). Communication in Latin American multinational organizations. In R. L. Wiseman & R. Shurer (Eds.), *Communicating in multinational organizations* (pp. 75–93). Thousand Oaks, CA: Sage.

Batres, R. E. (1991). A Mexican view of the North American Free Trade Agreement. *Columbia Journal of Business, 26,* 78–81.

Casteñeda, J. G. (1995). *The Mexican shock: The meaning for the U.S.* New York: New Press.

Davidson, M. (2000). *Lives on the line: Dispatches from the U.S.–Mexico border.* Tucson: University of Arizona Press.

DeMente, B. L. (1996). *NTC's Dictionary of Mexican cultural code words.* Lincolnwood, IL: NTC.

Fernandez-Kelly, M. P. (1983). *For we are sold, I and my people: Women and industry in Mexico's frontier.* Albany: State University of New York Press.

Hansen, N. (1981). *The border economy.* Austin: University of Texas Press.

Hellman, J. A. (1994). *Mexican lives.* New York: New Press.

Kopinak, K. (1996). *Desert capitalism: Maquiladoras in North America's western industrial corridor.* Tucson: University of Arizon Press.

Kras, E. S. (1989). *Management in two cultures.* Yarmouth, ME: Intercultural Press.

Lindsley, S. L. (1995). *Problematic communication: An intercultural study of communication competency in maquiladoras.* Unpublished doctoral dissertation, Arizona State University, Tempe.

Lindsley, S. L. (1999a). Communication and "the Mexican way": Stability and trust as core symbols in maquiladoras. *Western Journal of Communication, 63,* 1–31.

Lindsley, S. L. (1999b). A layered model of problematic intercultural communication in U.S.-owned maquiladoras in Mexico. *Communication Monographs, 66,* 145–167.

Lindsley, S. L., & Braithwaite, C. A. (1996). "You should wear a mask": Facework norms in cultural and intercultural conflict in maquiladoras. *International Journal of Intercultural Relations, 20,* 199–225.

Love, B. (1994). *Mayan culture today.* Valladolid, Yucatan: ServiGraf Peninsular.

Mendenhall, M. E., Dunbar, E., & Oddou, G. R. (1987). Expatriate selection, training, and career-pathing: A review and critique. *Human Resource Management, 26,* 331–345.

Pena, D. G. (1997). *The terror of the machine: Technology, work, gender, and ecology on the US.–Mexico border.* Austin, TX: Center for Mexican American Studies.

Prieto, N. I. (1997). *Beautiful flowers of the maquiladora: Life histories of women workers in Tijuana* (Michael Stone with Gabrielle Winkler, Trans.). Austin: University of Texas Press.

Sklair, L. (1993). *Assembling for development: The maquila industry in Mexico and the United States.* San Diego: University of California at San Diego, Center for U.S.–Mexican Studies.

Triandis, H. C., Marin, G., Lisansky, J., & Berancourt, H. (1984). Simpatía as a cultural script of Hispanics. *Journal of Personality and Social Psychology, 47,* 1363–1375.

Webber, T. (1993, August). It's about time! *Twin Plant News,* 18.

Weintraub, S. (1991). *Trade opportunities in the Western Hemisphere.* Washington, DC: Woodrow Wilson Center for International Scholars.

Concepts and Questions

1. Describe some aspects of cultural diversity you may find in Mexico.
2. How is the core concept of *confianza* or trust manifested in Mexican human resources?
3. How can an American manager manifest *confianza* when dealing with Mexican workers?
4. What role does *simpatía* play in interpersonal relations among Mexicans?
5. What communication behaviors must an American manager display to establish that he or she is simpático?
6. *Palanca* refers to one's power derived from extensive networking among family members, relatives, former classmates, friends, and business associates. How, if at all, does the Mexican *palanca* differ from the American concept of the "good old boys" network?
7. How can an American manager in Mexico develop the relationships necessary to employ *palanca* as a tool?
8. How does *estabilidad* or stability reinforce the value of personal relationships and affect organizational behavior?
9. How do Mexican and American concepts toward time differ?
10. List several ways in which an American manager might misconstrue Mexican workers' behavior that reflects the cultural value *of mañana.*

Application of American Management Theories and Practices to the Indian Business Environment: Understanding the Impact of National Culture

SURESH GOPALAN

ANGIE STAHL

INTRODUCTION

Falling trade and economic barriers have increased global trade. Increasingly, South Asian countries like India which have embraced free market reforms are facing increased exposure to not only Western (particularly American) products and services, but also to their management philosophies, ideologies, and practices. According to Gopalan and Dixon (1996), the United States has emerged as a significant investor in India, accounting for more than 17% of all actual foreign direct investment from 1991 until 1994. Additionally, the Clinton Administration designated India as one of the world's "ten big emerging markets." Future projections indicate an increased U.S. presence and involvement in diverse areas ranging from telecommunications to consumer goods, power generation, financial services, software, and automobile manufacturing (Phillips, 1992).

Although some management ideas (especially those of a technical nature) are easily transferred across countries (i.e., they are culture free), a large number of American management ideas and practices are

 Suresh Gopalan is Assistant Dean in the School of Business and Economics at Winston-Salem State University.

"culture-specific" (Hofstede, 1980b; Jaeger & Kanungo, 1990). They cannot and should not be blindly imported to developing countries such as India where the cultural, social, political, economic, and judicial environments are vastly different from those of the United States. Unfortunately, this has not been the case, as the American business model is considered to be the paradigm for success. American management ideas and practices have been largely replicated with little or no modification in several developing countries including India (Jaeger, 1990).

American and Indian managers would benefit a great deal if they gained a better understanding of the cultural context in which American management theories originated. Such knowledge would enhance their ability to better discriminate and differentiate between management ideas that are culturally compatible and others that are incompatible (Davis & Rasool, 1988). Additionally, cultural awareness will enable managers from both countries to make suitable modifications and revisions to American management ideas and approaches in their application to the Indian business environment.

CAN BEHAVIORAL MODELS AND MANAGEMENT THEORIES BE UNIVERSALLY TRANSPLANTED? THE DEBATE WITHIN THE MANAGEMENT COMMUNITY

The majority of organizational behavioral theories (a) originate from the United States and (b) are for the most part based on samples consisting of Anglo-Saxon male managers who have been socialized in cultural, political, and economic environments that are vastly different from Asian and African cultures (Jaeger & Kanungo, 1990; Kanungo, 1983). Consequently, a question arises whether these management models can be transplanted universally. In other words, would such management theories be effective in countries where the sociocultural environments are vastly different from that of the United States?

There are three schools of thought that address the above mentioned question. Management scholars such as Weber (1958), Negandhi (1975), and Pascale and Maguire (1980) who advocate the "convergence perspective" (the first school of thought) contend that as countries across the world achieve similar levels of industrialization and standards of living, business behavior and thinking will become similar and come together (hence the term *convergence*). Under such circumstances, the effects of national culture will vastly diminish as managers will be thinking, speaking, and acting with common global business values, beliefs, and behaviors. In such situations, behavioral models and management theories may have universal application and relevance even if their origins are rooted in American culture.

Scholars who believe in the "divergence perspective" propose that national culture is (and will continue to be) the primary force in shaping the values, beliefs, and attitudes of managers within a country (Ottoway, Bhatnagar, & Korol, 1989; Hofstede, 1980a; Laurent, 1983). They reject the arguments of convergence and maintain that as long as countries have dissimilar values, management ideas and practices cannot be universally transplanted. These scholars maintain that although organizational structures and work processes may tend to converge with increasing levels of industrialization, the behavior of people within organizations will be largely influenced by the national culture.

More recently, the "cross-vergence" perspective has gained increasing attention from the management community (Bond & King, 1985; Ralston, Gustafson, Cheung, & Terpstra, 1993; Gopalan & Dixon, 1996). Management researchers have found that in many developing countries, a new management ideology has emerged over the last 10 years. The new management ideology appears to be a hybrid—one that combines both domestic and "imported" ideas. As managers in many developing countries have come into increased contact with international counterparts, they have learned to adapt by creating a management approach that blends the best elements of both their native and foreign cultures.

THE PRIMARY FOCUS OF THIS PAPER

Regardless of which school of thought one belongs to, it is important that both American and Indian managers develop a basic understanding of the national culture–management relationship. Therefore, this paper has two objectives. The first is to offer a comprehensive explanation of the cultural context and origins of American management practices, and the second is to examine the degree of their relevance and effectiveness with respect to the Indian business environment. Although a brief explanation of the Indian national culture is offered to facilitate comparison with that of American national culture, it is not the intent of this paper to focus on Indian national culture.

DESCRIPTION OF AMERICAN NATIONAL CULTURE AND ENSUING MANAGEMENT PRACTICES

Developing a cultural profile of any country is difficult because culture is a multidimensional and multilayered concept (Nahavandi & Malekzadeh, 1988; Schein, 1984). Additionally, culture is hard to define because of multiple definitions from several fields (Rousseau, 1990). Despite such difficulties, management scholars (Adler & Jelinek, 1986; Adler, 1997) are increasingly using five value orientations developed by two anthropologists, Kluckhohn and Strodtbeck (1961), to develop cultural profiles of countries. The basic assumption behind this framework is that in any country, there are fundamental assumptions and choices regarding the following:

- **Human nature.** Is human nature evil? Is it good? Is it a combination of good and evil? A separate but related issue is whether human nature can be fundamentally changed in this lifetime.
- **Natural and supernatural elements.** Are humans dominant over nature? Do humans live in harmony with nature? Do they subjugate themselves to nature?
- **Time.** Do we look to the past? Do we focus on the present? Is a future orientation the most important way to approach life?
- **Work.** Do people derive their identity from work, and is it a calling from God (a doing orientation)? Should we work just for meeting short-term needs necessary to enjoy life (a being orientation)? Should work be considered as a means of fulfilling one's duty, after which one should seek salvation as the ultimate goal (a being-in-becoming orientation)?
- **Relationships.** Should individualism and individual rights be the foundation for a society? Or should it be based on a lineal collective group-oriented approach? Or should it be based on an organized hierarchical structure with an elaborate definition of roles, duties, and responsibilities?

By identifying the preferred choice by the majority of the population for each of these five value orientations, it is possible to develop a cultural profile for any country. The Kluckhohn and Strodtbeck framework is used to describe value orientations that are typical of American national culture. This cultural profile may not represent the values of subcultural groups within the country whose cultural preferences may be markedly different from those of mainstream culture.

Human Nature Orientation

Americans tend to believe that humans have a combination of both good and evil qualities and that they are capable of evolving into better persons.

The majority of Americans believe that by appealing to the good nature within individuals, change and improvement is possible and desirable. Fundamental changes in human nature can be accomplished through a combination of right training, education, and exposure (Adler, 1997; Samovar, Porter, & Jain, 1981). The origin of such a belief can be traced to the Christian theological belief that "no matter how sinful you have been, you can be saved if you seek redemption by being born again."

Such beliefs affect business thinking considerably. Organizations spend millions of dollars annually in training seminars and other human resource development activities (Adler & Jelinek, 1986). Such seminars include a wide range of topics, from sexual harassment to diversity sensitivity, discrimination in the workplace, teamwork and team development, employee empowerment, leadership skills, improving speaking and other communication skills, positive thinking, and so forth.

The underlying principle behind such investments is that employees can "change," and that will result in a "better" and "improved" workforce. Alcoholism, for example, is considered to be a disease, and many organizations have employee assistance programs to help them kick the habit. Alcoholism is not considered a "moral lapse" or a "character flaw" in an organizational context. The focus is on helping the individual change his/her behavior instead of making moral judgments about his or her habits.

Companies large and small are actively involved in helping and interacting with the local community through organizations such as the United Way, which supports an umbrella of local agencies that help the sick, the young, the elderly, and the indigent. Executives volunteer time, effort, and other resources to help with many of the civic organizations in their city (Romano, 1994). More recently, several organizations have been in the forefront of promoting their employees' health by having "smoke-free" work environments. Smoking or use of tobacco items is prohibited inside office buildings; smokers have to go outside the building to smoke. A growing number are experimenting with policies that would ban smoking on company premises and property, including the parking lot. Smokers have to go outside the company's property if they have to light up! (McShulskis, 1996; Lang, 1992) Although some may consider such measures an intrusion on freedom and individual choice, the underlying assumption behind such actions is that "intervention can result in an improved society" and, by extension, that a healthier society is an improved society. From an organizational viewpoint, such interventionist measures translate into a healthier and more productive workforce, leading to higher job satisfaction in the long run (Sorohan, 1994; Wolfe & Johnson, 1993; Lau, 1990).

Most (not all) Indians believe that an individual's situation in this present life is largely a consequence of actions committed in a previous birth or births (in other words, life is predetermined) and that change is relatively difficult to accomplish (Saha, 1992; Kuppuswamy, 1994). Although a sizable number of Indians may not subscribe to this view, there is nevertheless a widespread sense of fatalism found in the Indian psyche that has been documented by Indian scholars (Srinivas, 1966; Kuppuswamy, 1994). For example, poverty in India is tolerated to a greater extent than in other cultures. It is endured, both by the observer and the person experiencing it, without widespread protest. Does such a sense of resignation result as a consequence of fatalism or apathy or a combination of both factors?

If the mindset stated earlier is true for the most part (i.e., life is predetermined), would Indian organizations be committed to investing in human resource development programs at a high level? Would senior managers believe that their junior managers can fundamentally change their belief systems and become beacons of change and progress after receiving the right training and education? Do hiring practices focus more on hiring the "right type" of people because once hired it may not be possible to "change" the individual to suit the organizational mold? Would a "Theory X" type of management approach be more suitable than a "Theory Y" type approach in the Indian environment?

Obviously, additional research is needed to answer these and other questions. But clearly one has to better understand the inherent differences underlying American and Indian value orientations about human nature before transferring American management ideas to India. It is possible that the contemporary Indian manager has moved away from traditional ideas such as the theory of karma and has evolved a more Western (Americanized) approach to the idea of human nature. This issue is worthy of further exploration.

Relationship to Nature and Supernatural Elements

The traditional American relationship to nature has been one of dominance, although there is an increasing emphasis on conservation and ecological awareness suggesting a trend toward living more in harmony with nature.

The traditional view toward nature has been one of dominance—exploiting natural resources is one of the primary reasons for the economic progress achieved by the United States (Kluckhohn & Strodtbeck, 1961; Stewart, 1972; Turner, 1920). The majority of Americans believe that natural resources and elements can and should be utilized for the benefit of humankind (Terpstra & David, 1991). Science and technology are considered allies used to minimize or mitigate the effects of disease, pestilence, drought, floods, earthquakes, and other natural catastrophes that have been the bane of humankind.

Only in recent years have Americans been concerned with issues of ecological preservation, conservation of resources, and the harmful effects of pollution. These concerns have influenced a somewhat paradoxical approach to the manipulation of nature. Advanced technology is developed to further maximize progress toward a higher future standard of living. Yet advancing technology is also expected to minimize depletion or destruction of ecological, environmental, or scarce natural resources requisitioned for use in past progress efforts (White, 1996; Barnett, Weathersby, & Aram, 1995; Goldsmith, 1993).

Dominance over nature and other elements has resulted in most Americans' having an internal locus of control (Stewart, 1972). In other words, they believe that they are in control of most if not all of life's events and that their individual actions and effort will make a difference in their personal lives. Responsibility and accountability lie with the individual, and outcomes, whether successful or unsuccessful, cannot be shifted to an unknown supernatural force.

Such a fundamental assumption is reflected in the goal-setting and motivational practices that have originated in the United States (Locke, Latham, & Erez, 1988; Locke & Latham, 1990). Central to the idea of any goal-setting theory is that if an individual expends the right type and degree of behavior, he or she can control and reasonably predict the outcome of his or her output. Although several factors can affect the effectiveness of goal-setting practices in organizations, one critical factor is an individual's internal locus of control. Individuals with a strong internal locus of control are more likely to actively pursue, and thus achieve, their goals than are those with an external locus of control.

Traditional cultures such as those found in India socialize people to have a predisposition toward an external locus of control. Individuals with an external locus of control believe that people are basically helpless in affecting life's events, which are largely controlled by fate and/or by supernatural forces that are largely beyond human control (Husain, 1961, Tripathi, 1988). Even if individuals in the Indian corporate environment can intellectually relate to and understand the basic premise behind goal-setting practices, to what extent will they be effective in implementing them over the long run if these practices are not positively reinforced by societal values? Can advanced education neutralize and overcome the notion of fatalism? Will exposure to international management practices neutralize the effects of national culture, allowing Indian employees to develop a stronger internal locus of control?

Although India has one of the largest pools of well-qualified and talented scientists, technicians, and other professionals in the world, it lags behind several countries in both basic and cutting-edge research in many areas. Although some may attribute this phenomenon to lack of resources and other structural issues, an alternative explanation may be that it could be due to a lack of adequate positive reinforcement from society (McClelland, 1961). It is reasonable to hypothesize that Indian scientists and other professionals working in the United States and other Western countries are able to have a high level of achievement not only because of access to superior resources but also because of the prevailing mindset found in both organizational and societal atmosphere that encourages and nurtures an internal locus of control.

Time Orientation

Americans are oriented toward the future with respect to both personal and business time orientations. The American notion of future is relatively short term oriented, extending at best from four months to a year.

The future time orientation results in several assumptions, two of which are discussed in this paragraph. These assumptions are true for most Americans in both their professional and personal lives (Hall & Hall, 1989; Weber, 1958). Time is viewed, first, as an asset with a perishable value and, second, as a linear entity that when utilized improperly or inefficiently is wasted. Time is compartmentalized wherein meeting deadlines, schedules, and appointments is emphasized. People are socialized to value punctuality and promptness and express strong disapproval toward latecoming, tardiness, and excessive delays. Lateness may be considered a reflection of rudeness and/or slothfulness.

These two key assumptions are building blocks for strategic management practices found in American organizations (Collins & Montgomery, 1997; Thompson & Strickland, 1996). Strategic management includes the development of (a) a vision and mission statement, (b) long-term goals and objectives spanning five or more years, (c) annual goals and objectives up to a year, and (d) monthly and weekly goals and objectives. The entire planning process is based on the assumptions that (a) "management is time-bound" and (b) unless critical targets and outcomes are achieved by a specified time period, organizational success will be severely compromised. Many seminars and workshops on time management are offered to American managers. These training sessions reinforce and strengthen the presuppositions of time management (Sunoo, 1996; Oshagbemi, 1995). Utility is gained and maximized by efficient use of time. As quantity of time is considered to be a limited and fixed resource, Americans tend to view time utilization as a zero sum game—time not used efficiently to gain maximum productivity is time wasted. Since most American employees profess the same time orientation in their personal and professional lives, they tend to exhibit required behaviors that conform to meeting organizational goals based on preestablished timetables (Adler, 1997; Hall & Hall, 1989).

Future time orientation also results in the belief that the future will be "bigger, "brighter," and "better" than either the present or the past. Consequently, not much emphasis is given in the United States to maintaining or upholding traditional customs or beliefs. The focus is not on maintaining the status quo—change is valued and embraced (Tocqueville, 1835/1945). One of the class assignments given by the first author to students over the past few years is the "Circle Test" developed by Tom Cottle (1967). This assignment requires students to draw three circles, representing the past, the present, and the future. Students are asked to draw these circles in any manner (including size and arrangement) they see fit. A trend emerged. The majority of American students tend to draw the circle representing the future as biggest in size and mostly unconnected with either the present or the past circles. Most students from Asian countries tend to assign a bigger size to the circle representing the past relative to Americans and to draw all three circles intersecting one another. Although this study is unscientific in nature, such pictorial representations of time reflect cultural patterns that are unconsciously embedded in the minds of young people from different backgrounds. Americans value the future and think that eventual outcomes are unconnected to either the present or the past. Asians tend to attach more importance to the past and believe that events are influenced and interconnected through the three time orientations (Trompenaars, 1993).

Despite the rhetoric of strategic management with long-term plans, in reality the focus of corporate America is on achieving short-term goals based on quarterly targets (Cavanagh, 1990). Companies that fail to declare dividends on a quarterly basis have seen their stock prices plummet in Wall Street and other capital markets. High-level management and CEO compensation plans, including bonuses, pay raises, and stock options, are often based on their firm's quarterly performance and stock price (Frazee, 1996; Dimma, 1996). Consequently, "making the numbers" is of paramount importance to American managers. This environment tends to promote a more impatient short-term orientation that focuses on "here-and-now" results rather than patient long-term thinking (Adler, 1997). This may be one of the many reasons why Americans have not been as effective as the Japanese in their approach to world markets. The Japanese are willing to wait for five or more years to see the results of an investment, but Americans tend to get impatient if no tangible returns are seen within a year.

Indian time orientation appears to be significantly different from that of the United States. Time is not viewed in a linear fashion, nor is it viewed as a commodity with perishable value (Sinha, 1990; Saha, 1992). Time is viewed as an infinite loop—one that has always been there and that will continue to exist. Consequently, Indian society has evolved with a more relaxed and reflective attitude toward time, one that is quite different from and at odds with the Indian corporate/business environment, which tends to be more similar to the American corporate environment. Additionally, Indians attach pride and importance to maintaining their heritage by following practices that are handed down from the past by tradition. Such past time orientation brings tremendous pressure to conform to time-honored practices and beliefs. Therefore, the focus may be on maintaining the status quo through perpetuation of the past, not change. The preference for planning, compartmentalizing, scheduling time, and a sense of urgency—key factors that enable the successful implementation of strategic planning and compensation practices characteristic of future-oriented societies such as the Untied States—may have to be extensively modified in India because of a different time orientation.

Approach to Work

A combination of historical and religious factors has led Americans to link individual identity with occupation/career. Additionally, work is considered an end to itself, not the means to an end.

Traditional American ideas of work are derived from a Protestant belief that considered work to be a calling from God, to be pursued for its own sake (Cavanagh, 1990). Individuals who became wealthy were considered to have been blessed or rewarded for their hard work, effort, dedication, and perseverance. Although the biblical origins of work are seldom consciously considered in contemporary living, the centrality of work to one's life is widely prevalent in the United States (Weber, 1958; Ferraro, 1990). Individuals derive their identity from work and will continue to work even after they have "retired." If you ask an American individual who he/she is, they will identify themselves by their occupation or profession (Adler, 1997).

Able-bodied individuals who remain poor over their lifetime are looked at with disdain, as they are perceived to be lazy—poverty in such situations is attributed to indolence and a lack of effort, not fate or chance. Social loafing is discouraged. Most Americans believe that all individuals, regardless of their background or origin, can become materially successful if they "work hard." Social welfare policies, though widespread, are increasingly coming under attack and are being scaled back because they are thought to perpetuate poverty instead of relieving it (Friedlander & Hamilton, 1996; Ullman, 1996).

The strong work ethic in the United States favors objectivity, competitiveness, and a need for achievement (Ferraro, 1990; McClelland, 1961). Consequently, the laws pertaining to hiring new employees are structured with the idea that the most qualified candidate should be hired for the job—not the owner's son or son-in-law. Individuals are respected for the quality of their work and the contribution they make to the organization—not for the status ascribed to them by caste membership or family connections. Such sentiments of anti-nepotism are reflected in human resource policies that prohibit family members such as husband and wife or father and son from working for the same organization (Reed & Cohen, 1989; Young, 1995). Although discrimination and favoritism do exist in corporate America to some extent, the nation's laws and popular sentiment are against such practices.

A flip side to the American approach to work is that loyalty from the employee to the organization or from the organization to the employee tends to be based on self-interest, and therefore is short-lived at best and nonexistent in most instances (Friedman & Friedman, 1980). Employees are loyal to their profession—not to their organization. Job hopping is fairly common, and layoffs are even more common. In most situations, employees work at the "will" and "pleasure" of the employer. If the employer no longer requires the services of any employee, the employer can "let him/her go." A two weeks' notice of termination from the employee's side is standard industry practice. Work relationships are relatively impersonal, legal, and contractual; nothing is implied or assumed—it has to be in the form of a written contract (Trompenaars, 1993). This type of atmosphere results in low trust and an "us" versus "them" mentality. Management operates from the assumption that the organization exists to provide a return to the stockholders, and that is their primary goal. If profits are at stake, management may resort to restructuring and downsizing (typically resulting in hundreds of employees' losing their jobs) to strengthen the bottom line. With managerial performance linked to financial performance of the firm (i.e., share valuation), it is reasonable to conclude that the primary focus is on meeting shareholder needs and not on providing employees with long-term employment. Employees likewise are under no obligation to stay with the organization even after receiving advanced technical or management training at the organization's expense. They are not required to sign a bond or compensate the organization and are free to leave anytime without any restraint or constraint. Freedom is a two-way street in the United States.

Motivational theories originating from the United States advocate that "job enrichment" is the primary way to motivate employees (Herzberg, 1968). In other words, the assumption is that individuals derive more satisfaction from job content, such as increased autonomy, responsibility, and recognition, and fewer fulfillments from contextual factors such as pay raises, bonuses, and relationships with bosses and coworkers. Managers are encouraged to enhance intrinsic factors at work to sustain worker motivation (Staw, 1976, 1977; Deci, 1975; Petty, McGee, & Cavender, 1984).

Space not does not permit a comprehensive assessment of the relevance of all American work-related practices. Suffice it to say that the widespread practice of layoffs and terminations will be highly unpopular in India for a variety of reasons (Bedi, 1995). Indian employers and employees are more inclined to exhibit feelings of loyalty and desire to have a long-term relationship relative to the United States, although job hopping has become increasingly common among the younger generation. Employment in India is also considered to be an extension of social justice (Khandwalla, 1990). For example, most (not all) Indian public sector organizations have been "running in the red" for several years. They continue to exist solely due to massive government subsidies, which are an indirect form of taxation paid by Indian citizens. Yet it is unthinkable to shut these organizations down or streamline their operations, as hundreds and thousands of workers would be laid off. Keeping people employed appears to be more important than achieving profitability in the Indian context.

Although Indian multinationals may be similar to their Western counterparts in hiring practices (reflecting impartiality and hiring people with the best credentials), this may not be reflected in family-owned organizations and public sector companies, where caste and family considerations along with political pressures may favor less qualified candidates (Khandwalla, 1990). Sinha (1990) noted that Indians have a strong distinction between "insiders" and "outsiders" and prefer loyalty and dependability over efficiency and independence. These preferences will certainly continue to make the hiring and promotion practices more "personal" than "impersonal." Motivational theories that focus on enhancing job content may have relevance in materially advanced and comparably wealthy countries such as the United States, but their widespread application may have to be examined with caution in developing countries such as India, where satisfaction of economic needs may be more important to many employees. So, focusing on contextual factors such as pay and bonus may be more relevant than increasing autonomy or independence at work. Additionally, most Indians value relationships that have been built over a lifetime and tend to display increased spiritualism and less emphasis on material goods as they get older. Therefore, work in an Indian context is a means to an end (for most if not all Indians).

People may approach work primarily for satisfying their family's needs; or for finding work for their relatives and friends, or because they like their superior and want to show their affection and regard for him/her (Sinha & Sinha, 1994). Once the primary needs are satisfied—for example, all the children are educated and married, a house has been constructed and fully paid for, and grandchildren are born—it is reasonable to expect the average Indian to shift his/her focus in life away from work toward other pursuits.

Relationships in Society

Americans tend to be highly individualistic, autonomous, and egalitarian (non-hierarchical) in nature. Socialization practices stress independence over dependence and ascendancy of individual rights over group goals and aspirations.

It would not be an exaggeration to state that Americans exhibit the highest individualism of any country in the world (Hofstede, 1980a; Adler, 1997). The focus is on maintaining and enhancing individual rights, liberties, goals, and aspirations. Parents encourage their children from a very young age to become "independent," and it is common practice for teens over 18 years to "leave" their parent's home and live by themselves. From their infancy, most children have their own room in their parents' home, which is considered their private space. It is customary for parents to knock and obtain permission before entering their children's rooms. Babies that are a few months old learn to sleep by themselves in a separate room—the practice of children sleeping with their parents in the same bed or room is atypical and uncommon. Elderly Americans often choose to live by themselves or in a retirement home rather than stay with their children; the preference is for independence and individuality over dependence and collectivism. Social relationships in the United States tend to be relatively transient and ephemeral, resulting in high divorce rates and large numbers of single parents.

Educational practices in schools and colleges encourage students to ask a lot of questions and express personal opinions. It is acceptable for students to disagree with their teachers as long as it is done in a polite manner. University-bound students do not have to choose a major area of specialization until the end of their second year (a bachelor's degree is typically obtained over four years). Once a major area of specialization is chosen, students are not "locked into" that particular choice for the rest of their lives—they have the option of changing their minds as many times as they want. Although they will certainly take a longer time to graduate in such situations, the choice of "who they want to be" is in their own hands. Interpersonal relationships between teachers and students tend to be relatively informal and casual. For example, students do not stand and greet the professor when he or she walks into the classroom, nor do they display a highly deferential manner of communication. In relating to one another, Americans display a strong streak of egalitarianism wherein social equality is desired and hierarchy downplayed (Cox, 1993).

Similarly, in workplace environments, there is a sizable and growing movement toward a form of egalitarianism in the workplace. Many employers encourage an "open door" policy that encourages employees to discuss issues or concerns with any member of management—not simply the employee's immediate supervisor. Additionally, American employers are generally more supportive of a participative management style that allows employees from all organizational levels to engage in managerial decisions and practices through direct input (Cox, 1993).

Socialization practices emphasize competitiveness over cooperation (Cox, 1993). Two assumptions prevail here. First, an individual's achievement must be measured by standards external to that individual (not by family connections or money) and second, an individual maximizes his/her talents and abilities to the fullest extent only in a competitive atmosphere. Notice that the emphasis is on developing the individual to the fullest extent—not the group or another collective entity. Athletic programs glorify the spirit of competitiveness. There are "little league" soccer teams where children as young as 4–5 years old compete with other teams. Even in team-oriented sports such as basketball and football, individuals are singled out for their proficiency and skill over their teammates.

These cultural practices have given rise to certain management practices, such as management by objectives (MBO), that have their origins in the United States. Implicit assumptions that serve as a foundation for MBO are that (a) subordinates can sit down with their superiors and have meaningful negotiations on future job performance (i.e., low power distance is present), (b) the superior welcomes and invites subordinates to participate in a joint management process, and (c) hierarchy is best when minimized. In such an organizational situation, both the supervisor and the employee are psychologically comfortable in coming together to initiate the MBO process (Drucker, 1954; McGregor, 1960; McClelland, 1961).

Human resource development (HRD) practices in the United States are driven by law with a strong emphasis on protecting individual rights and welfare. Two examples illustrate this point. The Americans with Disabilities Act considers employees infected with HIV and those with full-blown AIDS as "protected" workers who cannot be discriminated against in organizational recruitment, transfer, promotion, or termination practices (Gopalan & Summers, 1994). Organizations cannot require a blood test for HIV or AIDS as a condition of employment (for new employees), nor can they fire someone who is HIV positive (for current employees). If requested, reasonable accommodation must be made for such employees, such as a transfer from a field to a desk job. Managers are required not to discuss or disclose the medical condition of these employees with anyone, including their immediate superiors, unless the employee has authorized them to do so.

An increasing number of American organizations do not discriminate between heterosexual and homosexual lifestyles and extend health care, dental, and life insurance benefits to the gay and lesbian partners of their employees (Gopalan & Summers, 1994). Some communities in which these companies were located initially expressed their objections to such HRD practices, which, in the minds of some community members, contributed to encouraging "sinful" and "undesirable" lifestyles. Most organizations contended that their response was consistent in meeting their employees' changing needs and wants. In all such HRD practices, the reader will note that the focus is on meeting and enhancing individual (not a group's) needs.

Indians are socialized in a culture where an individual derives his/her identity based on family and caste membership. The group is considered to be more important than the individual (Prakash, 1994; Tripathi, 1994). Additionally, age and seniority are given great respect in Indian tradition. Children are raised to obey their elders and teachers, who are considered to be the "experts" having answers to all questions. In India, relationships are long lasting, organized on a hierarchical basis, and status oriented—husband over wife, elder brother over younger brothers and sisters, patriarchal side over matriarchal side, and so on (Sinha, 1988). It is not uncommon to see Indians sacrifice and/or defer their individual goals and desires for the collective goals and welfare of their family or a larger collective entity. The degree of psychological distance and social interactions between different groups in society is affected by a variety of factors, including but not limited to age, seniority, socioeconomic class, caste affiliation, and religion. It should be noted that there are subcultures within India whose relationship norms may deviate substantially from the description given here.

Nevertheless, it is obvious that socialization practices in India are vastly different from those of the United States. Given this situation, it is interesting to examine the degree of relevance of general management practices such as MBO and other American HRD practices mentioned earlier. Given the large power distance between superiors and subordinates in most social and organizational settings, would MBO or variations of MBO and participative management be truly effective in India? Would Indian managers and employees put aside feelings of hierarchy and status and relate to one another as equals? Would age and seniority take a backseat to knowledge and competence (even if coming from a younger person) in an organizational setting? Alternatively, would a benevolent and nurturing patriarchal style be more suitable for an Indian setting, as it may be more compatible with Indian culture where people do not relate as equals? A related but separate issue is the impact of regional cultures. Are there regional differences in the values emphasized in India? For example, is Western India more aggressive and risk embracing? Is Southern India more conservative and risk aversive? What part (or parts) of the country would be more inclined to be neutral to organizational policies that recognize gay and lesbian lifestyles? What part (or parts) of India would be more inclined to oppose such lifestyles? More important, would Indian society even tolerate such policies that deviate from "traditional" notions of family? Obviously, there are no easy answers to such questions, but they are raised to demonstrate the vacuity of replicating American management practices.

CONCLUSIONS AND SUGGESTIONS FOR FURTHER RESEARCH

The primary objective of this paper has been to trace the cultural origins of some of the behavioral theories and practices commonly found in American management approaches and to discuss their applicability to the Indian business environment. A profile of American cultural values has been presented through the Kluckhohn and Strodtbeck (1961) cultural profile, and has been juxtaposed with brief glimpses of Indian cultural values. The close relationship between American cultural values and management styles and practices has been illustrated through several examples. A number of questions have been offered to initiate discussion and offer suggestions for future research regarding relevancy and transferability of American management practices to India.

Globalization of business will have a tremendous impact on lifestyles and role relationships, especially in developing countries such as India. For example, as multinational companies (MNCs) establish operations in previously "closed economies," they will begin to affect tradition and culture. Compared to domestic companies, MNCs may be more inclined to hire women, pay them high salaries, and promote them to managerial positions. Under such conditions, economic disparities in earning capabilities between women and men are likely to disappear, allowing women to achieve a status equal to men. Increasing financial independence will enable Indian women to remove externally imposed constraints and become more assertive. This, in turn, will eventually cause women to reexamine traditional male–female role relationships, which have historically placed Indian males at the focus of power and control within the family. Therefore, we theorize that as we head through the 21st century, business institutions will continue to become more powerful in India, and international influences will be felt to a greater degree than ever before.

We speculate that along with the factors mentioned above, widespread usage of the English language, familiarity with Western modes of education, especially in urban areas in India, and the influence of the Internet may lead Indian management thinking to a state where some ideologies and approaches will reflect national culture while others will become more similar to Western practices and ideas (i.e., they will reject Indian national cultural values). Indian managers may develop and follow a hybrid, or cross-vergence, approach in the future, reflecting a combination of indigenous and imported approaches to managing people at work. For example, loyalty, which is an integral Indian value, may still be retained in Indian organizations, as it maintains and fosters an environment of trust necessary to build effective business relationships. On the other hand, exposure to equal employment opportunity practices may create a desire to hire the most qualified person for a job, as opposed to preferential hiring of family members or relatives. These issues are worthy of further exploration by cross-cultural researchers.

References

Adler, N. J. (1997). *International dimensions of organizational behavior.* Cincinnati, OH: South-Western.

Adler, N. J., & Jelinek, M. (1986). Is "organization culture" culture bound? *Human Resource Management, 25*(1), 73–90.

Barnett, J. H., Weathersby, R., & Aram, J. D. (1995). American cultural values: Shedding cowboy ways for global thinking. *Business Forum, 20*(1–2), 9–13.

Bedi, H. (1995). From blue chip to blue skies. *Asian Business, 31*(6), 45–47.

Bond, M., & King, A. (1985). Coping with the threat of Westernization in Hong Kong. *International Journal of Intercultural Relations, 9,* 351–364.

Cavanagh, G. F. (1990). *American business values*. Englewood Cliffs, NJ: Prentice-Hall.

Collins, D. J., & Montgomery, C. A. (1997). *Corporate strategy: Resources and the scope of the firm*. Chicago: McGraw-Hill.

Cottle, T. (1967). The circles test; an investigation of perception of temporal relatedness and dominance. *Journal of Projective Technique and Personality Assessments, 31,* 58–71.

Cox, T. (1993). *Cultural diversity in organizations: Theory, research, and practice*. San Francisco: Berrett-Koehler.

Davis, H. J., & Rasool, S. A. (1988). Values research and managerial behavior: Implications for devising culturally consistent managerial styles. *Management International Review, 28,* 11–20.

Deci, E. L. (1975). *Intrinsic motivation*. New York: Plenum Press.

Dimma, W. A. (1996). Executive compensation gets its share. *Business Quarterly, 61*(1), 77–80.

Drucker, P. (1954). *The practice of management*. New York: Harper & Row.

Ferraro, G. P. (1990). *The cultural dimensions of international business*. Englewood Cliffs, NJ: Prentice-Hall.

Frazee, V. (1996). Pay-for-performance bonuses are on the rise. *Personnel Journal, 75*(10), 22–23.

Friedlander, D., & Hamilton, G. (1996). The impact of a continuous participation obligation in a welfare employment program. *Journal of Human Resources, 31*(4), 734–756.

Friedman, M., & Friedman, R. (1980). *Free to choose: A personal statement*. New York: Harcourt Brace Jovanovich.

Goldsmith, E. (1993). *The way: An ecological worldview.* Boston: Shambhala.

Gopalan, S., & Dixon, R. (1996). An exploratory investigation of organizational values in the United States and India. *Journal of Transnational Management Development, 2*(2), 87–111.

Gopalan, S., & Summers, D. (1994). AIDS and the American manager: An assessment of management's response. *SAM Advanced Management Journal, 59*(4), 15–26.

Hall, E. T., & Hall, M. R. (1989). *Understanding cultural differences*. Yarmouth, ME: Intercultural Press.

Herzberg, F. (1968, January/February). One more time: How do you motivate employees? *Harvard Business Review,* 53–62.

Hofstede, G. (1980a). *Culture's consequences*. New York. Sage.

Hofstede, G. (1980b). Motivation, leadership, and organization: Do American theories apply abroad? *Organizational Dynamics, 9*(1), 42.

Husain, A. S. (1961). *The national culture of India*. Bombay: Asia Publishing House.

Jaeger, A. M. (1990). The applicability of Western management techniques in developing countries: A cultural perspective. In A. M. Jaeger & R. N. Kanungo (Eds.), *Management in developing countries*. New York: Routledge.

Jaeger, A. M., & Kanungo, R. N. (Eds.). *Management in developing countries*. New York: Routledge.

Kanungo, R. N. (1983). Work alienation: A pancultural perspective. *International Studies of Management and Organization, 13*(1–2), 119–138.

Khandwalla, P. N. (1990). Strategic developmental organizations: Some behavioral properties. In A. M. Jaeger & R. N. Kanungo (Eds.), *Management in developing countries*. New York: Routledge.

Kluckhohn, C. L., & Strodtbeck, E. L. (1961). *Variations in value orientations*. Evanston, IL: Row, Peterson.

Kuppuswamy, B. (1994). *Social change in India*. New Delhi: Konark.

Lang, N. (1992). The last gasp: Workplace smokers near extinction. *Management Review, 81*(2), 33–36.

Lau, B. (1990). Four key ways to protect your employees' health and productivity. *Management Quarterly, 31*(3), 51–53.

Laurent, A. (1983). The cultural diversity of Western conceptions of management. *International Studies of Management and Organization, 13*(1–2), 75–96.

Locke, E. A., & Latham, G. P. (1990). *A theory of goal setting and task performance*. Englewood Cliffs: NJ: Prentice-Hall.

Locke, E. A., Latham, G. P., & Erez, M. (1988). The determinants of goal commitment. *Academy of Management Review, 13*(1), 23–39.

McClelland, D. C. (1961). *The achieving society*. New York: Van Nostrand Reinhold.

McGregor, D. (1960). *The human side of enterprise*. New York: McGraw-Hill.

McShulskis, E. (1996). Smoke-free workplaces prevalent. *HR Magazine, 41*(6), 18.

Nahavandi, A., & Malekzadeh, A. R. (1988). Acculturation in mergers and acquisitions. *Academy of Management Review, 13*(1), 79–90.

Negandhi, A. R. (1975). Comparative management and organization theory: A marriage needed. *Academy of Management Journal, 18,* 334–344.

Oshagbemi, T. (1995). Management development and managers' use of their time. *Journal of Management Development, 14*(8), 19–34.

Ottoway, R., Bhatnagar, D., & Korol, T. (1989). A cross-cultural study of work related beliefs held by MBA students. In W. A. Ward & E. G. Gomolka (Eds.), *Proceedings of the 26th Annual Meeting of the Eastern Academy of Management,* 155–157.

Pascale, R. T., & Maguire, M. A. (1980). Comparison of selected work factors in Japan and the United States. *Human Relations, 33,* 433–455.

Petty, M. M., McGee, G. W, & Cavender, J. W (1984). A meta-analysis of the relationships between individual job satisfaction and individual performance. *Academy of Management Review, 9,* 712–721.

Prakash, A. (1994). Organizational functioning and values in the Indian context. In H. S. R. Kao, D. Sinha, & N. Sek-Hong (Eds.), *Effective organizations and social values* (pp. 193–201). New Delhi: Sage.

Phillips, E. J. (1992). India: The next manufacturing frontier. *Manufacturing Systems, 10*(7), 91–98.

Ralston, D. A., Gustafson, D. J., Cheung, F. M., & Terpstra, R. H. (1993). Differences in managerial values: A study of U.S., Hong Kong and PRC managers. *Journal of International Business Studies, 24*(2), 249–275.

Reed, C. M., & Cohen, L. J. (1989). Anti-nepotism rules: The legal rights of married co-workers. *Public Personnel Management, 18*(1), 37–44.

Romano, C. (1994). Pressed to service. *Management Review 83*(6), 37–39.

Rousseau, D. (1990). Assessing organizational culture: The case for multiple methods. In B. Schneider (Ed.), *Organizational climate and culture* (pp. 153–192). San Francisco: Jossey-Bass.

Saha, A. (1992). Basic human nature in India: Tradition and its economic consequences. *International Journal of Sociology and Social Policy, 12*(1–2), 1–50.

Samovar, L., Porter, R., & Jain, N. (1981). *Understanding intercultural communication.* Belmont, CA: Wadsworth.

Schein, E. H. (1984). Coming to a new awareness of organizational culture. *Sloan Management Review, 25*(3), 3–15.

Sinha, D. (1988). Basic Indian values and behaviour dispositions in the context of national development: An appraisal. In D. Sinha & H. S. R. Kao (Eds.), *Social values and development: An Asian perspective.* New Delhi: Sage.

Sinha, J. B. P. (1990). *Work culture in an Indian context.* New Delhi: Sage.

Sinha, J. B. P., & Sinha, D. (1994). Role of social values in Indian organizations. In H. S. R. Kao, D. Sinha, & N. Sek-Hong (Eds.), *Effective organizations and social values* (pp. 164–173). New Delhi: Sage.

Sorohan, E. G. (1994). Healthy companies. *Training and Development, 48*(3), 9–10.

Srinivas, M. N. (1966). *Social change in modern India.* Berkeley: University of California Press.

Staw, B. M. (1976). *Intrinsic and extrinsic motivation.* Morristown, NJ: General Learning Press.

Staw, B. M. (1977). Motivation in organizations: Toward synthesis and redirection. In B. M. Staw & G. R. Salancik (Eds.), *New directions in organizational behavior.* Chicago: St. Clair Press.

Stewart, E. (1972). *American cultural patterns: A cross-cultural perspective.* Pittsburgh, PA: Intercultural Communications Network.

Sunoo, B. P. (1996). This employee may be loafing: Can you tell? Should you care? *Personnel Journal, 75*(12), 54–62.

Terpstra, V., & David, K. (1991). *The cultural environment of international business.* Cincinnati, OH: South-Western.

Thompson, A., & Strickland, A. J. (1996). *Strategic management: Concepts and cases* (9th ed.). Chicago: Irwin.

Tocqueville, A. (1945). *Democracy in America.* New York: Knopf. (Original work published 1835)

Tripathi, R. C. (1988). Aligning development to values in India. In D. Sinha & H. S. R. Kao, (Eds.), *Social values and development: Asian perspectives.* New Delhi: Sage.

Tripathi, R. C. (1994). Interplay of values in the functioning of Indian organizations. In H. S. R. Kao, D. Sinha, & N. Sek-Hong (Eds.), *Effective organizations and social values* (pp. 174–192). New Delhi: Sage.

Trompenaars, E. (1993). *Riding the waves of culture: Understanding cultural diversity in business.* London: Nicholas.

Turner, F. J. (1920). *The frontier in American history.* New York: Holt.

Ullman, O. (1996, September 23). Good politics, bad policy: Tapping big business to fix welfare. *Business Week,* 49.

Weber, M. (1958). *The Protestant ethic and the spirit of capitalism.* New York: Scribner.

White, M. A. (1996). Valuing unique natural resources: Endangered species. *Appraisal Journal, 64*(3), 295–303.

Wolfe, R., & Johnson, T. (1993). Work, health, and productivity. *Academy of Management Review, 18*(1), 160–165.

Young, B. S. (1995). Family matters. *HR Magazine, 40*(11), 30–31.

Concepts and Questions

1. Can behavioral models of management be transferred from culture to culture?
2. What are some specific examples for each of Kluckhohn and Strodtbeck's five intercultural dimensions? Can you think of examples from the Indian culture using these same five dimensions?
3. How would an American manager deal with an employee that was using an Indian orientation to time?
4. How would Americans and Indians differ in their view of company loyalty?

5. How would you as a manager deal with difference between Americans and Indians with regard to socialization practices?
6. How could a manager adjust to differences between Americans and Indians as they relate to individualism and collectivism?

Contrasts in Discussion Behaviors of German and American Managers

ROBERT A. FRIDAY

AMERICAN MANAGERS' EXPECTATIONS

Business Is Impersonal

In any business environment, discussion between colleagues must accomplish the vital function of exchanging information that is needed for the solution of problems. In American business, such discussions are usually impersonal.[1] Traditionally, the facts have spoken for themselves in America. "When facts are disputed, the argument must be suspended until the facts are settled. Not until then may it be resumed, for all true argument is about the meaning of established or admitted facts" (Weaver, 1953) in the rationalistic view. Most of post–World War II American business decision making has been based on the quantitative MBA approach, which focuses on factual data and its relationship to the ultimate fact of profit or loss, writing strategy plans, and top-down direction. After all of the facts are in, the CEO is often responsible for making the intuitive leap and providing leadership. The power and authority of the CEO have prevailed in the past 40 years, with no predicted change in view (Bleicher & Paul, 1986, pp. 10–11). Through competition and contact with West Germany and Japan, the more personal approach is beginning to enter some lower-level decision-making practices (Peters & Waterman, 1982, pp. 35–118).

Another reason for the impersonal nature of American business is that many American managers do not identify themselves with their corporations. When the goals and interests of the corporation match up with those of the American manager, he or she will stay and prosper. However, when the personal agenda of the American manager is not compatible with that of the corporation, he or she is likely to move on to attain his or her objectives in a more conducive environment. Most American managers can disassociate themselves from their business identity, at least to the extent that their personal investment in a decision has more to do with their share of the profit rather than their sense of personal worth.

In contrast, "the German salesman's personal credibility is on the line when he sells his product. He spends years cultivating his clients, building long-term relationships based on reliability" (Hall, 1983, p. 67). This tendency on the part of Germans is much like American business in the early part of the 20th century.

The cohesiveness of the employees of most German businesses is evidenced in the narrow salary spread. Whereas in the United States the ratio of lowest paid to highest paid is approximately 1 to 80 [as of 2004, it is about 1 to 500], in Germany this ratio is 1 to 25 (Hall, 1983, p. 74).

GERMAN MANAGERS' EXPECTATIONS

Business Is Not As Impersonal

The corporation for most Germans is closely related to his or her own identity. German managers at Mobay are likely to refer to "Papa Bayer" because they perceive themselves as members of a corporate family that meets most of their needs. In turn, most German managers there, as elsewhere, have made a lifelong commitment to the larger group in both a social and economic sense (Friday & Biro, 1986–1987). In contrast to the American post–World War II trend is "the German postwar tradition of seeking consensus among a closely knit group of colleagues who have worked together for decades [which] provides a collegial harmony among top managers that is rare in U.S. corporations" (Bleicher & Paul, 1986, p. 12). Our interviews suggested that many German managers may enter a three-year-plus training program with the idea of moving on later to another corporation. This move rarely occurs.

While a three-year training program appears to be excessively long by American standards, one must understand that the longer training program works on several levels that are logical within the German culture. The three or more years of entry-level training is a predictable correlation to the German and U.S. relative values on the Uncertainty Avoidance Index[2] (Hofstede, 1984, p. 122). The longer training period is required to induct the German manager into the more formal decision-making rules, plans, operating procedures, and industry tradition (Cyert & March, 1963, p. 119), all of which focus on the short-run known entities (engineering/reliability of product) rather than the long-run unknowns problems (future market demand).

On another level, the "strong sense of self as a striving, controlling entity is offset by an equally strong sense of obligation to a code of decency" (McClelland, Sturr, Knapp, & Wendt, 1958, p. 252). Induction into a German company with an idealistic system of obligation requires a longer training period than the induction into an American company in which the corporate strategy for productivity is acquired in small group and interpersonal interaction.[3] The German manager who moves from one corporation to another for the purpose of advancement is regarded with suspicion partly because of his lack of participation in the corporate tradition, which could prove to be a destabilizing factor.

Our preliminary interview results suggested uncertainty avoidance (Hofstede, 1984, p. 130) in everyday business relationships, especially the German concern for security. For example, most of the transfer preparation from the German home office to the United States consists of highly detailed explanations of an extensive benefits package. Since the German manager sees a direct relationship between his or her personal security and the prosperity of his or her company, business becomes more personal for him or her. Similarly, Americans who work in employee-owned companies are also seeing a clear relationship between personal security and the prosperity of their company.

AMERICAN MANAGERS' EXPECTATIONS

Need to Be Liked

The American's need to be liked is a primary aspect of his or her motivation to cooperate or not to cooperate with colleagues. The arousal of this motivation occurs naturally in discussion situations when direct feedback gives the American the desired response, which indicates a sense or belongingness or acceptance. The American "envisions the desired responses and is likely to gear his actions accordingly. The characteristic of seeing others as responses is reflected in the emphasis on communication in interaction and in the great value placed on being liked. . . . [The] American's esteem of others is based on their liking him. This requirement makes it difficult for Americans to implement projects which require an 'unpopular' phase" (Stewart, 1972, p. 58).

For Americans, the almost immediate and informal use of a colleague's first name is a recognition that each likes the other. While such informality is common among American business personnel, this custom should probably be avoided with Germans. "It takes a long time to get on a first-name basis with a German; if you rush the process, you may be perceived as overly familiar and rude. . . . Germans are very conscious of their status and insist on proper forms of address. Germans are bewildered by the American custom of addressing a new acquaintance by his first name and are even more startled by our custom of addressing a superior by first name" (Hall, 1983, pp. 57–58). When such matters of decorum are overlooked during critical discussions, an "unpopular phase" may develop.

> The need to be liked is culturally induced at an early age and continued throughout life through regular participation in group activities. They [Americans] are not brought up on sentiments of obligation to others as the Germans are, but from kindergarten on they regularly participate in many more extracurricular functions of a group nature. In fact, by far the most impressive result . . . is the low number of group activities listed by the Germans (about 1, on the average) as compared with the Americans (about 5 on the average). In these activities the American student must learn a good deal more about getting along with other people and doing things cooperatively, if these clubs are to function at all. (McClelland et al., 1958, p. 250)

This cultural orientation in relation to group participation will be revisited later in the closing discussion on "learning styles, training, instruction, and problem solving."

GERMAN MANAGERS' EXPECTATIONS

Need to Be Credible

The German counterpart to the American need to be liked is the need to establish one's credibility and position in the hierarchy. The contrast between American informality and mobility and German formality and class structure is a reflection of the difference between these two needs. In the absence of a long historical tradition, Americans have developed a society in which friendships and residence change often, family histories (reputations) are unknown, and therefore, acceptance of what one is doing in the present and plans to do in the future is a great part of one's identity. In order to maintain this mobility of place and relationships, Americans rely on reducing barriers to acceptance through informality.

Germans, with their strong sense of history, tradition, family, and life-long friendships, tend to move much less often, make friendships slowly, and keep them longer than Americans. Because one's family may be known for generations in Germany, the family reputation becomes part of one's own identity, which in turn places the individual in a stable social position.[4]

The stability of the social class structure and, thus, the credibility of the upper class in Germany are largely maintained through the elitist system of higher education.

> Educational achievement has been a major factor in determining occupational attainment and socioeconomic status in the post–World War II era. University education has been virtually essential in gaining access to the most prestigious and remunerative positions. Some of the most enduring social divisions have focused on level of education. (Nyrop, 1982, p. 113)

A German's education most often places him or her at a certain level which, in turn, determines what he/she can and can't do. In Germany, one must present credentials as evidence of one's qualification to perform *any* task (K. Hagemann, personal communication, May–September 1987). Thus, the German societal arrangement guarantees stability and order by adherence to known barriers (credentials) that confirm one's credibility. In Germany, loss of credibility would be known in the manager's corporate and social group and would probably result in truncated advancement (not dismissal since security is a high value).

The rigid social barriers established by education and credentials stand in direct contrast to the concepts of social mobility in American society. "Our social orientation is toward the importance of the individual and the equality of all individuals. Friendly, informal, outgoing, and extroverted, the American scorns rank and authority even when [he or she] is the one with the rank. American bosses are the only bosses in the world who insist on being called by their first names by their subordinates" (Kohls, 1987, p. 8). When Germans and Americans come together in discussion, the German's drive is to establish hierarchy; the American's is to dissolve it.

AMERICAN MANAGERS' EXPECTATIONS

Assertiveness, Direct Confrontation, and Fair Play

In comparing Americans with Japanese, Edward Stewart relates the American idea of confrontation as "putting the cards on the table and getting the information 'straight from the horse's mouth.' It is also desirable to face people directly, to confront them intentionally" (Stewart, 1972, p. 52). This is done so that the decision makers can have all of the facts. Stewart contrasts this intentional confrontation of Americans to the indirection of the Japanese, which often requires the inclusion of an intermediary or emissary in order to avoid face-to-face confrontation and, thus, the loss of face. However, this view may leave the American manager unprepared for what he or she is likely to find in his or her initial discussion with a German manager.

The American manager is likely to approach his or her first discussion with German managers in an assertive fashion from the assumption that competition in business occurs within the context of cooperation (Stewart, 1972, p. 56). This balance is attained by invoking the unspoken rule of fair play.

> Our games traditions, although altered and transformed, are Anglo-Saxon in form; and fair play does mean for us, as for the English, a standard of behavior between weak and strong—a standard which is curiously incomprehensible to the Germans. During the last war, articles used to appear in German papers exploring this curious Anglo-Saxon notion called "fair play," reproduced without translation—for there was no translation.
>
> Now the element which is so difficult to translate in the idea of "fair play" is not the fact that there are rules. Rules are an integral part of German life, rules for behavior of inferior to superior, for persons of every status, for every formal situation. . . . the point that was incomprehensible was the inclusion of the other person's weakness inside the rules so that "fair play" included in it a statement of relative strengths of the opponents and it ceased to be fair to beat a weak opponent. . . . Our notion of fair play, like theirs [British], includes the opponent, but it includes him far more personally. (Mead, 1975, pp. 143–145)

I am not implying that the American is in need of a handicap when negotiating with Germans. It is important to note, however, that the styles of assertiveness under the assumption of American equality (fair play) and assertiveness under the assumption of German hierarchy may be very different. The general approach of the German toward the weaker opponent may tend to inspire a negative reaction in the American, thus reducing cooperation and motivation.

GERMAN MANAGERS' EXPECTATIONS

Assertiveness, Sophistication, and Direct Confrontation

The current wisdom either leaves the impression or forthrightly states that Americans and Germans share certain verbal behaviors that would cause one to predict that discussion is approached in a mutually understood fashion.

> If North Americans discover that someone spoke dubiously or evasively with respect to important matters, they are inclined to regard the person thereafter as unreliable, if not dishonest. Most of the European low-context cultures such as the French, the Germans, and the English show a similar cultural tradition. These cultures give a high degree of social approval to individuals whose verbal behaviors in expressing ideas and feelings are precise, explicit, straightforward, and direct. (Gudykunst & Kim, 1984, p. 144)

Such generalizations do not take into account the difference between *Gespräch* (just talking casually) and *Besprechung* (discussion in the more formal sense of having a discussion about an issue). *Besprechung* in German culture is a common form of social intercourse in which one has high-level discussions about books, political issues, and other weighty topics. This reflects the traditional German values, which revere education. Americans would best translate *Besprechung* as a high-level, well-evidenced, philosophically and logically rigorous debate in which one's credibility is clearly at stake—an activity less familiar to most Americans.

The typical language of most Americans is not the language many Germans use in a high-level debate on philosophical and political issues.

> In areas where English immigrants brought with them the speech of 16th and 17th century England, we find a language more archaic in syntax and usage than present-day English. Cut off from the main stream, these pockets of English have survived. But the American language, as written in the newspapers, as spoken over the radio (and television) . . . is instead the language of those who learned it late in life and learned it publicly, in large schools, in the factory, in the ditches, at the polling booth. . . . It is a language of public, external relationships. While the American-born generation was learning the public language, the private talk which expressed the overtones of personal relationships was still cast in a foreign tongue. When they in turn taught their children to speak only American, they taught them a one-dimensional public language, a language oriented to the description of external aspects of behavior, weak in overtones. To recognize this difference one has only to compare the vocabulary with which Hemingway's heroes and heroines attempt to discuss their deepest emotions with the analogous vocabulary of an English novel. All shares of passion, laughter close to tears, joy tremulous on the edge of revelation, have to be summed up in such phrases as: "They had a fine time." Richness in American writing comes from the invocation of objects which themselves have overtones rather than from the use of words which carry with them a linguistic aura. This tendency to a flat dimension of speech has not been reduced by the maintenance of a classical tradition. (Mead, 1975, pp. 81–82)

Since many Americans tend not to discuss subjects such as world politics or philosophical and ethical issues with a high degree of academic sophistication, a cultural barrier may be present even if the Germans speak American-style English. In a study of a German student exchange program, Hagemann (1986) observed that "it was crucial for the Germans, that they could discuss world-politics with their American counterparts, found them interested in environmental protection and disarmament issues and they could talk with them about private matters of personal importance. . . . If they met Americans who did not meet these demands the relationships remained on the surface" (p. 8).

This tendency not to enter into sophisticated discussion and develop deeper relationships may be a disadvantage for many Americans who are working with Germans (see Table 1). In addition, in a society in which one's intellectual credibility[5] establishes one's position in the group and thus determines what one can and can't do, *Besprechung* can become quite heated—as is the case in Germany.

FOCUS: WHEN *BESPRECHUNG* AND DISCUSSION MEET

The management style of German and American managers within the same multinational corporation is more likely to be influenced by their nationality than by the corporate culture. In a study of carefully matched national groups of managers working in the affiliated companies of a large U.S. multinational firm, "cultural differences in management assumptions were not reduced as a result of working for the same multinational firm. If anything, there was slightly more divergence between the national groups within this multinational company than originally found in the INSEAD multinational study" (Laurent, 1986, p. 95).

On the surface, we can see two culturally distinct agendas coming together when German and American managers "discuss" matters of importance. The American character, with its need to remain impersonal and to be liked, avoids *argumentum ad hominem*. Any attack on the person will indicate disrespect and promote a feeling of dislike for the other, thus promoting the "unpopular phase," which, as Stewart indicates, may destroy cooperation for Americans.

In contrast, the German manager, with a personal investment in his/her position and a need to be credible to maintain that position, may strike with vigor and

Table 1 *Development of Discussion Behavior at a Glance*

Focus	American	German
Relationship to business	Impersonal—act as own agent; will not move on when business does not serve his/her needs or when better opportunity arises	Not as impersonal—corporation is more cohesive unit; identity more closely associated with position, and security needs met by corporation
Personal need	Need to be liked—expressed through informal address and gestures	Need for order and establishment of place in hierarchy—expressed through formal address and gestures
Orientation to corporation	Short-term—largely informal; many procedures picked up in progress	Long-term training—formal, specific rules of procedure learned
Status	Based on accomplishment and image—underlying drive toward equality	Based on education and credentials—underlying drive toward hierarchy
Confrontation	Assertive, tempered with fair play—give benefit of doubt or handicap	Assertive—put other in his/her place
Common social intercourse	Discussion about sports, weather, occupation—what you do, what you feel about someone; logical, historical analysis rarely ventured; native language sophistication usually low	*Besprechung*—rigorous logical examination of the history and elements of an issue; politics favorite topic; forceful debate expected; native language sophistication high

enthusiasm at the other's error. The American manager, with his/her lack of practice in German-style debate and often less formal language, education, and training, may quickly be outmaneuvered, cornered, embarrassed, and frustrated. In short, he or she may feel attacked. This possible reaction may be ultimately important because it can be a guiding force for an American.

Beyond the question of character is the more fundamental question of the guidance system of the individual within his or her culture and what effect changing cultural milieu has on the individual guidance system. I define guidance system as that which guides the individual's actions. In discussing some of the expectations of German and American managers, I alluded several times to what could be construed as peer pressure within small groups. How this pressure works to guide the individual's actions, I will argue in the next section, has great implications for developing programs for American success in Germany.

Viewed as systems of argumentation, discussion and *Besprechung* both begin a social phase, even though Americans may at first view the forcefulness of the Germans as antisocial (Copeland & Griggs, 1985, p. 105). However, a dissimilarity lends insight into the difference in the guidance systems and how Germans and Americans perceive each other.

American discussion, with the focus on arriving at consensus, is based on the acceptance of value relativism (which supports the American value of equality and striving for consensus). The guidance system for Americans is partly in the peer group pressure, which the individual reacts to but may not be able to predict or define in advance of a situation. Therefore, some Americans have difficulty articulating, consciously conceiving, or debating concepts in their guidance system but rather prefer to consider feedback and adjust their position to accommodate the building of consensus without compromising their personal integrity.

German *Besprechung*, with the focus on arriving at truth or purer concepts, rejects value relativism in support of German values of fixed hierarchy and social order. The German *Besprechung* is argumentation based on the assumption that there is some logically and philosophically attainable truth. The guidance system for Germans is composed of concepts that are consciously taken on by the individual over years of formal learning (à la Hall) and debate. While a German makes the concepts his/her own through *Besprechung*, this position is not likely to shift far from a larger group pressure to conform to one hierarchical code.

The peer pressure of the immediate group can often become a driving force for Americans. The irony is that many Germans initially perceive Americans as conformists and themselves as individualists, stating that Americans can't act alone while Germans with their clearly articulated concepts do act alone. American, on the other hand, often initially perceive Germans as conformists and themselves as individualists, stating that Germans conform to one larger set of rules while Americans do their own thing.

LEARNING STYLES, TRAINING, INSTRUCTION, AND PROBLEM SOLVING

Education and Training

The ultimate functions of group process in American corporations are problem solving and individual motivation (being liked). For Germans, motivation is more of a long-term consideration such as an annual bonus or career advancement. Problem solving for Germans is more compartmentalized and individualized.

The contrasting elements discussed earlier and outlined in both "At a Glance" summaries (Tables 1 and 2) indicate that considerable cultural distance may have to be traveled by Germans and Americans before they can be assured that cooperation and motivation are the by-products of their combined efforts. The contrasting elements are, of course, a result of the organization and education—the acculturation—of the minds of Germans and Americans. In this section, I will examine the different cultural tendencies from the perspective of Hall's definitions of formal and informal culture and discuss some implications for intercultural training and education.

The first level of concern is general preparation for the managerial position. As an educator, I must take a hard look at the graduates of our colleges and universities as they compare to their German counterparts. I am not attempting to imply that Germans are better than Americans. All cultural groups excel in some area more than other cultural groups.

> Germans are better trained and better educated than Americans. A German university degree means more than its U.S. equivalent because German educational standards are higher and a smaller percentage of the population wins college entrance. Their undergraduate degree is said to be on par with our master's degree. It is taken for granted that men and women who work in business offices are well educated, able to speak a foreign language, and capable of producing coherent, intelligible, thoughtful communications. German business managers are well versed in history, literature, geography, music and art. (Hall, 1983, p. 58)

Americans tend to focus on the present as the beginning of the future, whereas Germans tend to "begin

Table 2 *Manager Background at a Glance*

Focus	American	German
Guidance system	Peer pressure of immediate group—reluctant to go beyond the bounds of fair play in social interaction; backdrop is social relativism	Peer pressure from generalized or larger social group—forceful drive to conform to the standard; backdrop is consistent and clearly known
Education	Generally weaker higher education—weak historical perspective and integrated thought; focus is on future results; get educational requirements out of the way to get to major to get to career success	Higher education standards generally superior—speak several languages, strong in history, philosophy, politics, literature, music, geography, and art
Problem solving	More group oriented—social phase develops into team spirit; individual strengths are pulled together to act as one	More individualized and compartmentalized—rely on credentialed and trained professional
Learning	Informal awareness—get the hang of variations; often unconscious until pointed out	Formal awareness—specific instruction given to direct behavior; one known way to act; highly conscious

every talk, every book, or article with background information giving historical perspective" (Hall, 1983, p. 20). While Hall makes a strong generalization, a contrary incident is rare. American college graduates are not known for having a firm or detailed idea of what happened before they were born. While some pockets of integrated sophisticated thinking exist, it is by no means the standard. Indeed, many American college students are unable to place significant (newsworthy) events within an overall political/philosophical framework two months after the occurrence.

In contrast, college-educated Germans tend to express a need to know why they should do something—a reasoning grounded in a logical understanding of the past. Compared to the rigorous German theoretical and concrete analysis of past events, Americans often appear to be arguing from unverifiable aspirations of a future imagined. While such vision is often a valuable driving force and the basis for American innovation and inventiveness, it may not answer the German need to explicitly know why and, thus, may fall short (from a German perspective) in group problem solving when these two cultures are represented. From the educational perspective, one must conclude that more than a few days of awareness training is needed before successful discussions can result between German and American managers, primarily because of what is not required by the American education system. The contrary may also be true in preparation of Germans to work with Americans. Tolerance for intuitive thinking may well be a proper focus in part of the German manager's training prior to working with American managers.

Formal and Informal Culture

The unannounced and largely unconscious agenda of small group process among Americans is usually more subtle than the German formal awareness but equally as important. American individuals come together in the initial and critical social phase, "size up" each other, and formally or informally recognize a leader. In a gathering of hierarchical equals, the first to speak often emerges as the leader. At this point, the embers of team spirit warm once again. As the group moves through purpose and task definition, members define and redefine their roles according to the requirements of the evolving team strategy. Fired with team spirit, inculcated through years of group activity and school sports, the group produces more than the sum of their individual promises.

"In the United States a high spontaneous interest in achievement is counterbalanced by much experience in group activities in which the individual learns to channel achievement needs according to the opinions of others. . . . Interestingly enough, the American 'value formula' appears to be largely unconscious or informally understood, as compared to the German one, at any rate" (McClelland et al., 1958, p. 252). Though this observation is over 30 years old, it still appears to be quite accurate. The use of modeling (imitation) as a way of acquiring social and political problem-solving strategies is also a way of adjusting to regionalisms. In taking on different roles, Americans become adept at unconsciously adjusting their character to meet the requirements of different situations. In short, says Hall, "compared to many other societies, ours does not invest traditions with an enormous weight. Even our most powerful traditions do not generate the binding force which is common in some other cultures. . . . We Americans have emphasized the informal at the expense of the formal" (Hall, 1973, p. 72).

The German learning style is often characterized by formal learning as defined by Hall (1973, p. 68). The characteristics of German frankness and directness are echoed in Hall's example of formal learning: "He will correct the child saying, 'Boys don't do that,' or 'You can't do that,' using a tone of voice indicating that what you are doing is unthinkable. There is no question in the mind of the speaker about were he stands and where every other adult stands" (Hall, 1973, p. 68). German formal awareness is the conscious apprehension of the detailed reality of history which forms an idealistic code of conduct that guides the individual to act in the national interest as if there were no other way.[6]

American informal awareness and learning are an outgrowth of the blending of many cultural traditions, in an environment in which people were compelled to come together to perform group tasks such as clearing land, building shelter, farming, and so on. The reduction of language to the basic nouns and functions was a requirement of communication for the multilingual population under primitive conditions. Cultural variations will always be a part of the vast American society. Americans have had to "get the hang of it" precisely because whatever *it* is, it is done with several variations in America.

In a sense, the informal rules such as "fair play" are just as prescriptive of American behavior as the system of German etiquette is prescriptive of much of German social interaction, including forms of address (familiar *Du* and the formal *Sie*). Even the rules for paying local taxes, entering children in school, or locating a reputable repair person vary by local custom in America and can only be known by asking.[7] The clear difference is that the rules are not overtly shared in America.

The American expectations or informal rules for group discussion are general enough to include the etiquette of American managers from different ethnic backgrounds. As long as notions of equality, being liked, respect, fair play, and so on guide behaviors, things run smoothly. "Anxiety, however, follows quickly when this tacit etiquette is breached. . . . What happens next depends on the alternatives provided by the culture for handling anxiety. Ours include withdrawal and anger" (Hall, 1973, p. 76). In the intercultural situation, the American who participates informally in group behavior may feel that something is wrong but may not be able to consciously determine the problem. Without the ability of bringing the informal into conscious awareness, which is a function of awareness and education, many Americans may flounder in a state of confusion, withdrawal, and anger.

CONCLUSION

What should become apparent to intercultural trainers working with companies that are bringing German and American personnel together is that they are working with two populations with distinct learning and problem-solving styles. The American is more likely to learn from an interactive simulation. Within the situation, the American can "get the hang of" working with someone who has a German style. Trainers and educators of American managers know that the debriefing of the role play, which brings the operative informal rules into conscious awareness, is the focus of the learning activity. The short-term immersion training so often used today can only supply some basic knowledge and limited role-play experience.

What must never be forgotten in the zeal to train American managers is that their basic guidance system in America is a motivation to accommodate the relative values of the immediate group. While the general cultural awareness exercises that begin most intercultural training may make Americans conscious of their internal workings, much more attention must be given to inculcate an understanding of German social order and the interaction permitted within it.

Knowledge of the language and an in-depth orientation to the culture for the overseas manager and spouse should be mandatory for American success in Germany and German success in the United States. "The high rate of marital difficulties, alcoholism and divorce among American families abroad is well known and reflects a lack of understanding and intelligent planning on the part of American business" (Hall, 1983, p. 88). In our pilot program, we became quite aware of the fact that German spouses require much more preparation for a sojourn to America. American short-term planning is in conflict with the long-term preparations needed for most Americans who are going to work with Germans. In Germany, the role of the spouse (usually the female) in business includes much less involvement than in the United States. We suspect this has much to do with the lack of attention to spouse preparations that we have observed thus far.

RECOMMENDATION

Long-term programs should be established that provide cultural orientation for overseas families at least three or four years before they start their sojourn, with beginning and increasing knowledge of the language as a prerequisite for entry. Such programs should attend to the general instructional deficiencies of Americans in the areas of history, philosophy, and politics as studied by Germans; prepare Germans to expect and participate in an informal culture guided by value relativism in a spirit of equality; and incorporate cultural sharing of German and American managers and their families in social settings so the sojourners can come together before, during, and after their individual experiences to establish a formal support network. Segments of such programs could be carried on outside the corporate setting to allow for a more open exchange of ideas. In America, colleges and universities could easily establish such programs. Many American colleges and universities that have served as research and development sites for business and industry are also developing alternative evening programs to meet the educational needs in the community. Also, corporate colleges are an ideal setting for extended in-house preparation. In such learning environments, professors can come together with adjunct faculty (private consultants and trainers) to produce a series of seminars that combine lecture instruction, small group intercultural interaction networking, media presentations, contact with multiple experts over time, and even a well-planned group vacation tour to the sojourner's future assignment site.

Part of the programs should be offered in the evening to avoid extensive interference with the employee's regular assignments and to take advantage of the availability of other family members who should be included in intercultural transfer preparation. Cost to the corporation would be greatly reduced in that start-up funds could be partly supplied through federal grants, travel costs would be lessened, and program costs would be covered under regular tuition and materials fees. As a final note, I strongly recommend that such programs for American managers be viewed as graduate-level education since they will be entering a society in which education is a mark of status.

Notes

1. Future references to America and Americans should be understood as referring to the Northeastern United States and the citizens thereof; references to Germany and Germans should be understood as West Germany and the citizens thereof.
2. Actual German values were 65, with a value of 53 when controlled for age of sample; the actual U.S. values were 46, with a value of 36 when controlled for age of sample.
3. For a quick overview of how small group and interpersonal communication is related to corporate success in America, see Peters and Austin, 1985, pp. 233–248.
4. These comparative descriptions correspond to the German social orientation and the American personal orientation discussed by Beatrice Reynolds (1984, p. 276) in her study of German and American values.
5. "In Germany, power can be financial, political, entrepreneurial, managerial or intellectual; of the five, intellectual powers seem to rank highest. Many of the heads of German firms have doctoral degrees and are always addressed as 'Herr Doktor'" (Copeland & Griggs, 1985, p. 120). While there may be exceptions to this rule, exceptions are few and hard to find.
6. "Yet this rigidity has its advantages. People who live and die in formal cultures tend to take a more relaxed view of life than the rest of us because the boundaries of behavior are so clearly marked, even to the permissible deviations. There is never any doubt in anybody's mind that, as long as he does what is expected, he knows what to expect from others" (Hall, 1973, p. 75).
7. The perplexing problem for German executives who are new in the United States is that in Germany everything is known; thus, you should not have to ask to find your way around. But in the United States, where change is the watchword, one has to ask to survive.

References

Bleicher, K., & Paul, H. (1986). Corporate governance systems in a multinational environment: Who knows what's best? *Management International Review, 26*(3), 4–15.

Copeland, L., & Griggs, L. (1985). *Going international: How to make friends and deal effectively in the global marketplace.* New York: Random House.

Cyert, R. M., & March, J. G. (1963). *A behavioral theory of the firm.* Englewood Cliffs, NJ: Prentice-Hall.

Friday, R. A. & Biro, R. (1986–1987). Pilot interviews with German and American personnel at Mobay Corporation (subsidiary of Bayer), Pittsburgh, PA. Unpublished raw data.

Gudykunst, W. B., & Kim, Y. (1984). *Communicating with strangers: An approach to intercultural communication.* Reading, MA: Addison-Wesley.

Hagemann, K. (1986). *Social relationships of foreign students and their psychological significance in different stages of the sojourn.* Summary of unpublished diploma thesis, University of Regensburg, Regensburg, Federal Republic of Germany.

Hall, E. T. (1973). *The silent language.* New York: Doubleday.

Hall, E. T. (1983). *Hidden differences: Studies in international communication—How to communicate with the Germans.* Hamburg, West Germany: Stern Magazine Gruner/Jahr AG & Co.

Hofstede, G. (1984). *Culture's consequences: International differences in work-related values.* Beverly Hills, CA: Sage.

Kohls, L. R. (1987, June). *Models for comparing and contrasting cultures.* A juried paper invited for submission to the National Association of Foreign Student Advisors.

Laurent, A. (1986). The cross-cultural puzzle of international human resource management. *Human Resource Management, 25,* 91–103.

McClelland, D. C., Sturr, J. F., Knapp, R. N., & Wendt, H. W. (1958). Obligations of self and society in the United States and Germany. *Journal of Abnormal and Social Psychology, 56,* 245–255.

Mead, M. (1975). *And keep your powder dry.* New York: William Morrow.

Nyrop, R. F. (Ed.). (1982). *Federal Republic of Germany: A country study.* Washington, DC: U.S. Government Printing Office.

Peters, T., & Austin, N. (1985). *A passion for excellence*. New York: Warner Communication.
Peters, T., & Waterman, R. (1982). *In search of excellence*. New York: Warner Communication.
Reynolds, B. (1984). A cross-cultural study of values of Germans and Americans. *International Journal of Intercultural Relations, 8,* 269–278.
Stewart, E. D. (1972). *American cultural patterns: A cross-cultural perspective*. Chicago: Intercultural Press.
Weaver, R. M. (1953). *The ethics of rhetoric*. South Bend, IN: Regnery/Gateway.

Concepts and Questions

1. How does the American expectation that business is impersonal differ from the corresponding German expectation? How might these differing expectations affect discussion behavior during American–German business discussions?
2. How does the German concept of corporate identity differ from the American? How does this affect entry-level training and career goals?
3. Compare and contrast an American manager's need to be liked with the German manager's need to be credible.
4. How might American and German styles of assertiveness differ? What cultural dynamics might account for these differences?
5. What is the German concept of *Besprechung*? How might Americans perceive this practice by Germans during business discussions? Do you believe that the typical American businessperson is adequately prepared to engage in *Besprechung*?
6. How do American and German managers differ in terms of the focus of their fundamental educational backgrounds? How does this influence their approaches to business discussions?
7. How would you suggest that American university policies be modified to produce graduates who are more competitive with their German counterparts?
8. Compare and contrast the formal and informal aspects of the German and American cultures as they relate to the conduct of business.
9. Differentiate between German "formal learning" and American "informal awareness and learning." How do these cultural dynamics affect each other's approaches to business discussions?
10. Considering Friday's recommendations about preparing American managers and their spouses for overseas assignments and the nature of American business orientations, what would be the most effective manner in which to train American businesspeople to interact effectively with German counterparts?

"Half-Truths" in Argentina, Brazil, and India: An Intercultural Analysis of Physician–Patient Communication

NAGESH RAO

> Mr. Akbar Ali, a 60-year-old Muslim from Pakistan, has been diagnosed as having insulin-dependent diabetes. Dr. Martin has prescribed insulin for him and instructed his family on how to administer it. However, when Mr. Ali returns for a checkup, Dr. Martin notices little improvement. Careful questioning of Mr. Ali's son reveals that Mr. Ali has not been taking his insulin, and when asked why, Mr. Ali sternly replies, "I am an Orthodox Muslim and would rather die than disobey Islam." Dr. Martin is puzzled and has no idea what Mr. Ali means. (Gropper, 1996)

Such instances are not uncommon when physicians[1] in the United States treat patients from diverse cultural backgrounds. In this case, it is likely that Mr. Ali has heard that insulin is made from the pancreas of a pig. A Muslim is expected to avoid any product of swine because it is considered unclean. Dr. Martin needs to explain that insulin can come from sheep or oxen too, and she would take care to make sure the insulin is not from a pig. This kind of problem, however, is not limited to situations in which the caregiver and the patient speak different languages and come from two different countries.

Helman (1994) aptly notes, "Physicians and patients, even if they come from the same social and cultural background, view ill-health in very different ways. Their perspectives are based on very different premises, employ a different system of proof, and

 Nagesh Rao teaches in the School of Interpersonal Communication, Ohio University, Athens, Ohio.

assess the efficacy of treatment in a different way" (p. 101). The following anecdote narrated by a patient named "Chris" is not uncommon even when the physician and patient perceive the other as having the same cultural background[2]:

> I was a sergeant in the army. I had been in the hospital, sick with fever for a week. I had lost 24 pounds (15% of my body weight) and the physicians could not find the cause of the illness. The physician read the results of some blood work that had been run the day before. Without preparing me for it, he casually said, "hmm . . . people with your white blood count normally have leukemia." He then started walking away. When I tried to stop him to ask questions, he reprimanded me for not calling him "sir"!

In this paper, we argue that the interaction between a physician and patient is inherently an *intercultural*[3] encounter even when the two parties *perceive* they are from the same culture. The distinction between illness and disease helps explain why every encounter between a physician and patient is intercultural. Rosen, Kleinman, and Katon (1982) define disease "as the malfunctioning of biological and/or psychological processes whereas illness may be defined as the perception, evaluation, explanation, and labeling of symptoms by the patient and his family and social network" (p. 496). Traditionally, physicians focus on the disease while patients are concerned with the illness. As du Pré (2000) adds, patients are operating with feelings while physicians are addressing evidence. Thus, in our anecdote, the physician is keen to diagnose the disease (possibly leukemia), while "Chris" is dealing with the psychological implications of having leukemia. This disparity in the physician's and patient's beliefs and value structures could create miscommunication between them and lead to ineffective medical care.

Recent research on physician–patient interaction also suggests the need to study the intercultural aspects of physician–patient communication. Physician–patient research generally falls into one of two broad areas: (1) research focusing on the interpersonal communication aspects of physician–patient interactions and identifying specific interpersonal skills for physicians to learn (e.g., Burgoon, Birk, & Hall, 1991; O'Hair, 1989; Ong, De Haes, Hoos, & Lammes, 1995; Roter, 2000; Sharf, 1990), and (2) scholarship focusing on the cross-cultural aspects of physician–patient communication to assist caregivers in being more culturally sensitive toward their patients (e.g., Baylav, 1996; Greengold & Ault, 1996; Rosenbaum, 1995; Young & Klingle, 1996). Both of these areas of research, however, fail to bring communication and culture together; the first concentrates on communication and not culture, and the second focuses on culture, but cross-culturally rather than interculturally. Kim et al. (2000) begin the quest to create an intercultural approach to physician–patient communication by analyzing how a patient's self-construal affects his or her verbal communication with a physician. Further, Geist (2000) offers an insightful analysis of the health challenges faced in dealing with co-cultural differences in the United States. In this chapter, as part of a five-year study to develop an *intercultural* model of physician–patient communication, we offer data from our interviews with physicians in Argentina, Brazil, and India.

In this essay, we begin with a literature review on the impact of culture on physician–patient communication and summarize the key findings. After offering a brief description of our methodology (see Rao & Beckett, 2000, for further information), we offer three key findings from our interviews with 91 physicians in Argentina, Brazil, and India. Finally, we highlight our main findings and discuss the implications for future research.

IMPACT OF CULTURE ON PHYSICIAN–PATIENT COMMUNICATION

Traditional medical literature increasingly stresses the importance of good physician communication skills (Burgoon et al., 1991; Cegala, McGee, & McNeils, 1996; O'Hair, 1989; Ong et al., 1995; Roter, 2000). Many factors that inhibit physician–patient communication have previously been documented. Although time limitations remain the number one reason given by providers for lack of communication, some posit that the qualities that earn respect from colleagues are very different from those that earn respect from patients (Welsbacher, 1998). With the exception of several key areas (e.g., care for refugees, using interpreters), the influence of culture(s) in health-related interactions has been largely glossed over. Considering the high rates of global migration, physicians from many different sociocultural backgrounds will find themselves serving an increasingly diverse patient population. Thus, it would seem that a major gap exists within mainstream medical literature.

However, there is one notable exception within the medical arena. Researcher-practitioners within the field of nursing have long advocated that health care providers become familiar with how patients of different cultures conceptualize the notions of "health" and "care." In particular, Madeline Leininger (1991) has been at the forefront of research dedicated to extrapolating these differences. According to her Theory of Culture Care Diversity and Universality, all cultures express care but attach different meanings to health-related practices. Within the health care context, meaning is shaped by technology, religion, cultural norms, economics, and education. Her work is critical in reminding providers that there is far more to culture than simple geography.

Several themes emerge from the nursing research. We are reminded that just as diversity exists across cultures, it also exists within cultural groups (Rosenbaum, 1995). These differences can be intensified by factors such as ethnicity, religion, education, age, sex, and acculturation. As Herselman (1996) aptly states, perceptions are influenced by individual experiences as well as cultural background. Thus, there is a great danger in relying on excessive generalizations (Meleis, 1996). For example, Denham (1996) explains that medical practitioners tend to believe that rural Appalachians are fatalistic in their outlook and in their health practices. However, Denham adds that a lot of variability occurs in rural Appalachians' fatalistic beliefs and health practices. Finally, if a health care provider is to understand how these variables influence a patient's ways of thinking and behaving, he or she must first be familiar with the patient's cultural background. One must also be aware of how the patient's cultural heritage intersects with the culture of the particular health care organization.

Language can provide a major barrier to culturally appropriate care because exploring goals and expectations can become difficult (Baylav, 1996). In her thesis, "When Yes Means No," Katalanos (1994) argues convincingly that South-East Asian (SEA) patients who are recent immigrants have health beliefs that are different from those held by health care professionals in the United States, and these differences are manifested in the communication behaviors of the two parties. Katalanos's (1994, p. 31) analyses of the communication patterns (see following section) show that there is significant misunderstanding between SEA patients and U.S.-trained health care providers, sometimes with serious consequences.

Physician Assistant: Are you happy here in America?

Vietnamese Patient: Oh yes. [meaning: I am not happy at all, but I do not want to hurt your feelings. After all, your country took me in.]

Further, "yes" may simply mean "I hear you, and I will answer your question," as the following exchange illustrates:

Physician Assistant: Did you take your medicine?

Vietnamese Patient: Yes. [I hear you.] No. [I did not take it.]

Physician Assistant: You did not take your medicine?

Vietnamese Patient: Yes. [I hear you] Yes. [I did not take it. The medicine was too strong.]

Physician Assistant: Ah, so you did not take it!

Vietnamese Patient: Yes. No.

These responses leave both the health care provider and the patient frustrated, as each person is operating out of her or his own paradigm—the U.S. provider paradigm of diagnosing the specific cause of illness and providing medication, and the SEA paradigm of being polite and not wanting to hurt the provider's feelings.

Medical jargon exacerbates linguistic barriers even further. Some measures that nurses have taken to compensate for these barriers include the use of interpreters, health education sessions run in conjunction with local service providers, ethnic recruiting, alternative medical services, cultural sensitivity training, multicultural videos/fliers, and cultural health care fairs (Baylav, 1996; Kothari & Kothari, 1997).

Research in nursing has also acknowledged the importance of culture in understanding a patient's attitudes toward birth, death, sex, relationships, and ritual (Mullhall, 1996). Treatments that are based on assumptions of how a patient regards such issues could potentially result in miscommunication, if not outright noncompliance. Spitzer et al. (1996) assert that expecting a patient to conform to a health care provider's orders is simply a cultural imposition rather than a joint process of discovering the best ways to treat certain ailments. Charonko (1992) also argues that the term "noncompliant" is biased toward preserving the power of the health care provider at the expense of his or her patient. From Charonko's perspective, it is the provider's responsibility to help patients live as productively as possible within *their* choices. Patient satisfaction, which depends heavily on communication, has been strongly correlated with compliance (Eraker, Kirscht, & Becker, 1984).

The traditional medical literature in the United States, however, is beginning to acknowledge the increasing diversity of the United States. Between 1990 and 1996, growth in Latino, African American, and Asian American populations accounted for almost two-thirds of the increase in the U.S. population (Bureau of the Census, 1996). While the patient population in the United States is growing more diverse, little is being done to prepare our physicians to work more effectively with these patients (Baylav, 1996; Greengold & Ault, 1996; Rao & Beckett, 2000; Rosenbaum, 1995).

For example, Drake and Lowenstein (1998) hold that California is an interesting case study because "minorities" (e.g., Latinos, Asians) will soon outnumber Caucasians.[4] Texas has also attracted attention as of late because of its ranking as the fifth most culturally diverse state (Kothari & Kothari, 1997). In either case, pronounced disparities exist between ethnicity and level of access to health care. The researchers do note that education, language, and literacy are major reasons why access to health care is limited among certain populations. Studies such as this dance around the issue of culture, but stop short of providing culturally specific care based on systematic research.

One area of medical research where culture is central, however, concerns health care for refugees. Although Kang, Kahler, and Tesar (1998) assert that there are 26 million refugees in the world, the crisis in Kosovo has surely increased these numbers. And the current problems in Afghanistan are creating additional refugees. Keeping this in mind, physicians will find themselves dealing with these issues increasingly often. Similarly, Obmans, Garret, and Treichel (1996) write that immigrants and refugees are often overrepresented in emergency room care. Interpreters are often necessary for physicians to provide care for refugees, yet many communication problems have been documented from this activity. Regardless of strategy, Obmans et al. write that negotiation and compromise will remain critical to culturally appropriate treatment.

Our succinct review suggests that culture impacts physician–patient communication in several significant ways. The key findings from research on physician–-patient communication can be summarized as follows. First, most physicians follow the biomedical approach, focusing more on the disease than on the person. Roter (2000) argues, rather persuasively, that as molecular and chemistry-oriented sciences gained prominence in the 20th century, the focus on communication as a central tenet in physician–patient relationships has declined. Second, there has been considerable research emphasizing the importance of several communication skills, such as empathy and active listening, in physician–patient communication (Burgoon et al., 1991; Ong et al., 1995; Roter & Hall, 1992). Third, research in nursing and counseling has emphasized the usefulness of focusing on the patient's culture in creating more effective encounters (Leininger, 1991). Fourth, patients are most satisfied when both task and relational dimensions of the relationship are addressed effectively in the physician–patient communication (Helman, 1991; Lochman, 1983; Stewart, 1995). Fifth, while most medical students enter medical school with an idealism to save lives, they often leave with "detached concern" because of the biomedical nature of the training (Miller, 1993). Finally, some medical schools train their students to communicate more effectively with their patients, but such models still focus on general communication and not on intercultural communication (Marshall, 1993).

It can be argued, therefore, that the research on physician–patient communication has focused on how to improve a physician's interpersonal and cross-cultural skills. Since there is limited research on the intercultural nature of this encounter, we are working on a systematic research program to create an intercultural communication model of physician–patient communication. In the next section, we focus on the first phase of our research project to answer the following research question: How do physicians in different countries communicate with culturally diverse patients? We administered the Medical Provider Questionnaire (MPQ) to 29 physicians in Campinas, Brazil; 30 physicians in Madras, India; and 32 physicians in Cordoba, Argentina.[5] Each interview was tape-recorded and ranged between 45 and 90 minutes in length. The

MPQ had several parts: (1) what motivated these physicians to join this profession; (2) what they liked and disliked about this profession; (3) how they communicated with culturally diverse patients; (4) the physician's response to the case study described in the first part of this article; (5) how physicians defined a successful encounter with a patient; and (6) what the physicians would change in the medical system if they were to go through medical school again. In this next section, we focus on the physicians' responses to questions 3 and 4. We first begin with how physicians defined cultural diversity in their context. Then, we focus on the three key findings: "half-truths," family as patient, and how physicians defined success.

Physicians' Definition of Culture

Almost without exception, the physicians in Argentina, Brazil, and India saw their countries as heterogeneous. This was not surprising by itself. However, what was surprising was how physicians defined diversity in these three countries. In Brazil, a few physicians divided patients along traditional race, ethnic, and national origin lines. One of our respondents, a resident in cardiology, explained:

> Oh, of course. No doubt about it because mainly the kind of settlement of people here in Brazil was in periods over these five centuries. So in the South region you have mostly a European settlement in the last century so Italians, Germans, many of these people. So in the North and Northeast mainly Portuguese and Indians and the slaves that were brought from Africa, so they are totally different.

Most of our Brazilian respondents, however, felt that their main cultural diversity was based on socioeconomic status. Brazil, according to them, had two distinctive cultures, the rich and the poor. For example, a cardiology resident summarized it rather succinctly:

> Oh, no, we have many cultures here. We have a statesman, a former minister of industry, economics, I don't know, and he always said Brazil is—was Belindia, I don't know if you ever heard of it—it's part of Belgium and part of India. You have many countries inside a country. I don't know if you have traveled for many states here. I don't know if you know the state of Maranhao. The Northeast region is the poorest region in the country. So our country is a mosaic, so if we are having problems here, you can imagine what they are having in the Northeast or the North region where we have the Amazon forest and many people don't have hospitals, don't have many roads because all of the transport system is water, it's rivers and boats and all of this, so the country is extremely, it's not homogeneous like you said.

Similarly, the physicians in Argentina saw their culture as heterogeneous. One senior female cardiologist noted:

> It [Argentina] is heterogeneous. People who formed this country have different origins, different customs, different traditions, and at the same time there were people who were from here.

Most Argentinean physicians focused primarily on education and socioeconomic status to describe the diversity in their country. One internist explained:

> No, it is heterogeneous. We have people very intellectual and with a lot of knowledge and people with a complete lack of education.

An ophthalmologist described Argentina with passion:

> I would say that it is heterogeneous but mainly because we have a huge difference between social classes. Instead of paying 20 dollars to go to a theater, you just think that you need food and clothing. There are many people here who are right now experiencing those kinds of problems.

Physicians in India also saw their country as diverse, but focused on different aspects of diversity—religion, language, socioeconomic status, north–south differences, and so on. A senior female general practitioner described India in the following manner:

> We have patients from all spectrums of life. When the patient's language is different, it is almost like they are from a different country. Their dress is different, language is different, and habits are different. The people in the south are much more humane.

A senior oncologist, working for a large private hospital, explained:

> In our setup here, we see really a cross section both geographically and culturally and even to some extent economically. It is not that only rich people

come here. Here patients know that there is better treatment available. So people come here selling all their belongings. Secondly, we see a lot of patients from the northeast. At least 30% of the patients come from that region.

It is intriguing that while Argentina, Brazil, and India have significant diversity based on immigration patterns, religion, languages, and so on, the physicians in Argentina and Brazil focused mainly on socioeconomic status and education as the main indicators of diversity. The Indian physicians represented the various aspects of India's diversity, including language, socioeconomic status, and the like. A physician in Brazil explained that because they speak Portuguese throughout the country, even though there is diversity, the common language takes care of cultural differences. This explanation is also viable in Argentina where Spanish is spoken throughout the country.

India, however, has 18 official languages, and it is difficult to ignore the cultural diversity. An Indian colleague often uses this analogy: "Think of India as a mini-Europe. You can travel 100 miles and speak a completely new language!" Thus, it is not surprising that the physicians in these cultures focused on different aspects of their country's diversity. These cultural differences also played a significant role in how they communicated with their patients.

"Half-Truths"

As part of the interview, we asked our respondents to read the following case study (cited previously) and asked them if the physician had responded appropriately.

> I was a sergeant in the army. I had been in the hospital, sick with fever for a week. I had lost 24 pounds (15% of my body weight) and the physicians could not find the cause of the illness. The physician read the results of some blood work that had been run the day before. Without preparing me for it, he casually said, "hmm . . . people with your white blood count normally have leukemia." He then started walking away. When I tried to stop him to ask questions, he reprimanded me for not calling him "sir"!

All 91 respondents indicated that the physician in this case study had responded inappropriately. We then asked the physicians to explain what they would have done if they had to tell a patient that he or she is terminally ill. Our data suggest that 90% of the physicians in these three countries engaged in what we have termed "half-truths," where physicians did not disclose the diagnosis immediately, described the diagnosis in doses over several visits, or informed a family member of the diagnosis first before telling the patient. In all these cases, the physicians explained that hearing such life-threatening news immediately would psychologically harm the patient, which, in turn, would reduce the patient's ability to fight the illness. In other words, the type of "half-truth" used was based on the psychological readiness of the patient. In 10% of the cases, the physicians insisted that they would tell the patient directly and immediately because that is what they would have liked. A cardiologist from India described his strategy:

> If I knew a patient had a terminal illness like leukemia, I would tell him that we have to do more tests before we can really be sure. If I tell him directly, he could die of the shock. If I think he is stronger, I may tell him that there are several possibilities and one could be cancer. If he is not strong, I would see which family member he has come with him and take them aside to tell them the news. We are very family oriented, and he has to get their support. So, better to tell them first. Also, they may have to make preparations.

A Brazilian physician, in response to the case study, offered a more direct example of "half-truths":

> It's completely crazy—unacceptable. First of all, because a blood exam is not enough to make a diagnosis of leukemia. It's more complicated; there are no justifications to answer this question in this way. I think the physician could hide the diagnosis in the start. If I was the physician I would try to hide my scared face. I would try not to reveal to the patient the situation and I would think more about it. I would ask for more tests, and when the diagnosis was certain, I would talk to the patient about the disease and about the treatment. Leukemia is not lethal and can be cured through chemotherapy.

A rheumatologist from Argentina described what he would do in this situation:

> One patient never comes alone, so I think that if I know the background and I recognize that the patient is unable to hear anything about himself, I first talk

> with the family if the background allows me to do that. If there is no family here, in the case of leukemia, sometimes you have to wait, just one day, two days, one week until you say to the patient, to know him better to know which words to use.

One Argentinean doctor, however, indicated that he would prefer to tell the patient directly:

> You have to tell the truth to a patient and tell what the patient wants to know. If the patient has leukemia, you have to explain to him that if you follow the treatment, you will be better. The patient knows that because you tell him about the several studies on this topic. You have to motivate the patient to do the treatment and keep on living.

In each of these cases, most of the physicians from Argentina, Brazil, and India chose to use "half-truths" to tell a patient that he or she is terminally ill. This phenomenon can be best explained by understanding collectivism and face-saving behaviors. Argentina, Brazil, and India are collective cultures where "[a] 'we' consciousness prevails: Identity is based on the social system; the individual is emotionally dependent on organizations and institutions; the culture emphasizes belonging to organizations; organizations invade private life and the clans to which individuals belong; and individuals trust group decisions even at the expense of individual rights" (Samovar & Porter, 2001, pp. 67–68). In these three cultures, the physicians are thinking of the patient's well-being within the context of his or her family and the larger community.

It is common to use face-saving behaviors like "half-truths" to comfort the patient and sustain the harmony of the group. Face-saving behaviors focus less on the veracity of a statement than what is culturally appropriate for the context. In our preliminary interviews in the United States, physicians were clear that they would tell only the patient and tell him or her directly. This is consistent with the individualistic nature of the United States, where direct and explicit communication is preferred. Du Pré (2000) notes that therapeutic privilege was a practice in the United States when physicians withheld information if they thought sharing the information would hurt the patient. However, Veatch (1991) argues that if we wish for patients to be informed partners in their health care, therapeutic privilege is counterproductive. Consistent with current legal expectation in medicine, there is an expectation that physicians in the United States inform the patient as soon as they know the diagnosis.

Family as Patient

Our analysis of "half-truths" indicated that physicians often chose to tell a family member rather than tell the patient. Further investigation suggested that even in regular health care visits, the physician had to treat the "family as patient," rather than focus just on the patient. When a patient was ill, the family members felt ill. When a patient recovered, the family members felt better too. We had explained earlier that Argentina, Brazil, and India are collectivistic cultures. People from these cultures also tend to have an interdependent self-construal (Markus & Kitayama, 1991), in which a person's identity is intrinsically connected with his or her family's identity. A person with an interdependent self-construal often makes decisions taking into consideration the needs of his or her family members, and family members often make decisions for him or her. Physicians described this interconnectedness in several ways. A cardiologist in India noted:

> Patients rarely come alone to the clinic. There are always two or three family members with them. I have to be careful to understand the family dynamics and understand how I should share the information. I will share certain kinds of information with the wife, some with the son, and may decide not to share anything with the uncle. I also know that the wife and the son feel the pain the patient is suffering from. When the patient feels better, I feel good too.

A senior cardiologist in Brazil explained how he would include the family so that they can make decisions for the patient:

> If the family were there, I would tell them together. If it were just the patient, I would contact the family. Why? The patient may not need to say anything. I would try to talk to the patient's spouse or child or parents. I would say, your son, your husband, your wife has this illness and we are going to treat it. In this situation, I would tell because the family has to prepare, there is going to be therapy, days when the patient is not feeling well, his diet will change, his hair will fall out. He needs the family's help.

An obstetrician in Argentina described how he would share the news with a patient that the baby in her womb is dead:

> The most common situation is to tell the news that the baby inside of the womb is dead. If I made the diagnosis, I won't tell her immediately. I will take a patient aside and, if she is alone, I wll try to call the family so she begins to suspect something is wrong. I allow that to happen because it helps me. If you tell her directly her baby is dead, she will be very hurt. Now she guesses and asks if her baby is dead. So the baby is dead, but that word might come from her mouth and not mine. Then I stay with her, I hold her arms and help her cry for a little while. If the husband comes later, which happens very often, I repeat the same exercise.

In all these cases, the family is an integral part of the healing process, being constantly present, making decisions, seeking advice, and protecting the patient. Our initial conversations with physicians in the United States suggest that patients generally come alone, and if family members are present, they respect the patient's space. Occasionally, the family member may seek clarification on behalf of the patient on certain issues.

Defining Success

We asked the physicians to explain when they had a successful interaction with a patient. In about two-thirds of our interviews, we asked the physician if it was a failure if their patient died. Every one of these physicians indicated that it was not a failure if the patient died, as long as they had done everything possible for the patient. Our preliminary conversations with physicians in the United States suggest that they would see it as a failure if the patient died. It is likely that the U.S. physicians, trained in the biomedical perspective, are focusing on curing the disease. If they cannot cure the patient, they have failed. Death is the ultimate failure with this perspective. Physicians in Argentina, Brazil, and India focused mostly on relational issues or relational plus task issues to define success, with a limited few focusing only on task-related issues (curing the patient). An emergency room physician summarized the task-oriented perspective by saying:

> I think I am always successful because I always give them a favorable solution. I try to help them. For example, when I am in the emergency room, I am there to give all I can so that a patient can leave the hospital with a treatment or with any response to her problem.

Most physicians, however, described the importance of building trust and strengthening the relationship with a patient as a key part of being successful. A second-year nuclear resident in Brazil defined success as follows:

> When he comes back with another patient. When he brings his uncle or daughter or wife. They would come over and say, "Oh, I knew that you were here; that is why I brought my grandmother. I wanted you to take a look at her." Probably the grandmother didn't have anything, but he wanted me to look at her. That is when I know a patient likes me.

A family practice physician in Madras described how she looked at both task and relational issues to define success:

> Early diagnosis. When we are able to pick up on traits and/or behaviors that might possibly cause illness. Success is also when a patient comes to you and says that they are happy with the treatment you have given them. You are building trust with a patient that will definitely help with the cure.

A senior physician of legal medicine in Argentina summarized the need to be aware of the patient's multiple needs by defining success as follows:

> In many moments, but especially when you have to transmit [to] a patient the information of an incurable disease, but not terminal. When sharing this information with the patient, if it ends up in improving the patient's wish to fight for his/her life and it has given the patient the possibility of living wonderful experiences that s/he has never lived before, I have allowed the patient a certain quality of life.

THE INTERCULTURAL JOURNEY CONTINUES

"The doctor is mean and the patient is dumb" (du Pré, 2000, p. 48) is a common response in the United States. In this essay, we have argued that it is not fruitful to assign blame to the physician or the patient when communication fails between these two parties.

While there is significant research on the interpersonal and cross-cultural aspects, there is little focus on the *intercultural* aspects of physician–patient communication. Our overall goal is to create such an intercultural model, drawing on literature from several disciplines and from original research. Our interviews with physicians in Argentina, Brazil, and India suggest that their collective orientation influences them to use unique communication strategies to deal with culturally diverse patients. They use "half-truths" to share challenging diagnoses, treat the family as the patient, and define success mostly along relational or relational and task objectives. Our results have several significant implications for studying the role of culture in physician–patient communication.

First, as Lienenger (1991) pointed out in her work, there is more to culture than just geography. Our respondents in Argentina and Brazil defined the country's cultural diversity mainly through socioeconomic and educational differences. Many of our respondents noted that having a common language (Portuguese or Spanish) reduced the impact of other cultural differences such as gender, age, ethnicity, religion, and so on. This is a particularly important finding since Bennett (1998) points out that people from most countries generally tend to focus on race, ethnicity, religion, and language when discussing cultural diversity.

Second, it is important to understand the communication strategies used by physicians in individualistic cultures. Toward this end, we are presently interviewing physicians in the United States to understand how they communicate with patients from culturally diverse backgrounds. Finally, since there are at least two people involved in a physician–patient communication, there are at least two cultural perspectives interacting in their communication. Therefore, it is no longer sufficient to conduct research from only the physician's or the patient's perspective; rather, the physician–patient communication must be analyzed as an *intercultural* phenomena.

To achieve this goal, in addition to our interviews with physicians, we have administered our Multicultural Health Beliefs Inventory (MBHI) to 600 patients in Argentina, Brazil, India, and the United States to explicate how they define good health (Rao, Beckett, & Kandath, 2000). The MBHI assesses respondents' perceptions of good health along five dimensions of health—physical, psychological, relational, spiritual, and lifestyle/environmental. Du Pré (2000) explains how the physician and the patient bring two opposing worldviews when they interact; the physician focuses on the disease (task) only, while the patient focuses on the illness (task plus relational dimension). By combining our data from physicians and patients from several cultures, our goal is to create an *intercultural* model of physician–patient communication that will have both theoretical and practical implications.

Notes

1. In our paper, the term *physicians* includes only Doctors of Medicine trained in the allopathic tradition.
2. We used this case study as a part of our Medical Provider Questionnaire to interview physicians.
3. Lustig and Koester (1999) explain that the term *intercultural* "denotes the presence of at least two individuals who are culturally different from each other on such important attributes as value orientations, preferred communication codes, role expectations and perceived rules of social relationships" (p. 60).
4. Since this research was conducted, Caucasians have become a minority in California.
5. We chose these three countries to compare how physicians in collectivistic cultures treated their patients as compared to physicians in the United States, an individualistic culture. For a more detailed explanation of our methodology, see Rao and Beckett (2000).

References

Baylav, A. (1996). Overcoming culture and language barriers. *The Practitioner, 240,* 403–406.

Bennett, M. J. (1998). *Basic concepts of intercultural communication.* Yarmouth, ME: Intercultural Press.

Bureau of the Census. (1996). *Statistical abstract of the United States* (116th ed.). Washington, DC: Author.

Burgoon, M., Birk, T. S., & Hall, J. R. (1991). Compliance and satisfaction with the physician–patient communication: An expectancy theory interpretation of gender differences. *Human Communication Research, 18,* 177–208.

Cegala, D. J., McGee, D. S., & McNeils, K. S. (1996). Components of patients and physicians perceptions of communication competence during a primary care medical interview. *Health Communication, 8,* 1–27.

Charonko, C. V. (1992). Cultural influences in "noncompliant" behavior and decision making. *Holistic Nursing Practice, 6,* 73–78.

Denham, S. (1996). Family health in a rural Appalachian Ohio county. *Journal of Appalachian Studies, 2,* 299–310.

Drake, M. V., & Lowenstein, D. H. (1998). The role of diversity in the health care needs of California. *Western Journal of Medicine, 168,* 348–354.

Du Pré, A. (2000). *Communication about health.* Mountain View, CA: Mayfield.

Eraker, S. A., Kirscht, J. P., & Becker, M. H. (1984). Understanding and improving patient compliance. *Annals of Internal Medicine, 100,* 258–268.

Geist, P. (2000). Communicating health and understanding in the borderlands of co-cultures. In L. A. Samovar & R. E. Porter (Eds.), *Intercultural communication: A reader* (9th ed., pp. 341–354). Belmont, CA: Wadsworth.

Greengold, N. L., & Ault, M. (1996). Crossing the cultural physician–patient barrier. *Academic Medicine, 71,* 112–114.

Gropper, R. C. (1996). *Cultural and the clinical encounter: An intercultural sensitizer for the health professions.* Yarmouth, ME: Intercultural Press.

Helman, C. G. (1991). Limits of biomedical explanation. *Lancet, 337,* 1080–1083.

Helman, C. G. (1994). *Culture, health and illness.* Boston: Butterworth-Heinemann.

Herselman, S. (1996). Some problems in health communication in a multi-cultural clinical setting: A South African experience. *Health Communication, 8,* 153–170.

Kang, D. S., Kahler, L. R., & Tesar, C. M. (1998). Cultural aspects of caring for refugees. *American Family Physician, 57,* 1245–1255.

Katalanos, N. L. (1994). *When yes means no: Verbal and nonverbal communication of Southeast Asian refugees in the New Mexico health care system.* Unpublished master's thesis, University of New Mexico, Albuquerque.

Kim, M., Klingle, R. S., Sharkey, W. F., Park, H., Smith, D. H., & Cai, D. (2000). A test of a cultural model of patients' motivation for verbal communication in physician–patient interactions. *Communication Monographs, 67,* 262–283.

Kothari, M. P., & Kothari, V. K. (1997). Cross-cultural healthcare challenges: An insight into small American community hospitals. *Journal of Hospital Marketing, 12,* 23–32.

Leininger, M. (1991). *Culture care diversity and universality: A nursing theory.* New York: National League for Nursing Press.

Lochman, I. E. (1983). Factors related to patients' satisfaction with their medical care. *Journal of Community Health, 9,* 91–109.

Lustig, M. W., & Koester, I. (1999). *Intercultural competence: Interpersonal communication across cultures* (3rd ed.). New York: Longman.

Markus, H. R., & Kitayama, S. (1991). Culture and the self: Implications for cognition, emotion, and motivation. *Psychological Review, 98,* 224–253.

Marshall, A. A. (1993). Whose agenda is it anyway? Training medical residents in patient-centered interviewing techniques. In E. B. Ray (Ed.), *Case studies in health communication* (pp. 15–30). Hillsdale, NJ: Erlbaum.

Meleis, A. I. (1996). Culturally competent scholarship: Substance and rigor. *Advances in Nursing Science, 19,* 1–16.

Miller, K. I. (1993). Learning to care for others and self: The experience of medical education. In E. B. Ray (Ed.), *Case studies in health communication* (pp. 3–14). Hillsdale, NJ: Erlbaum.

Mullhall, A. (1996). The cultural context of death: What nurses need to know. *Nursing Times, 92,* 38–40.

Obmans, P., Garrett, C., & Treichel, C. (1996). Cultural barriers to health care for refugees and immigrants: Provider perceptions. *Clinical and Health Affairs, 79,* 26–30.

O'Hair, D. (1989). Dimensions of relational communication control during physician–patient interactions. *Health Communication, 1,* 97–115.

Ong, L. M. L., De Haes, J. C. J. M., Hoos, A. M., & Lammes, F. B. (1995). Physician–patient communication: A review of the literature. *Social Science and Medicine, 40,* 903–918.

Rao, N., & Beckett, C. S. (2000). *"Half-truths" and analogies in doctor–patient communication: Dealing with culturally diverse patients in Brazil.* Paper presented at the Health Communication Division of the International Communication Association Conference, Washington, DC.

Rao, N., Beckett, C. S., & Kandath, K. (2000). *What is good health? Exploratory analyses of a multidimensional health beliefs scale in Brazil and in India.* Paper presented at the Health Communication Division of the National Communication Association Conference, Seattle.

Rosen, G., Kleinman, A., & Katon, W. (1982). Somatization in family practice: A biopsychosocial approach. *Journal of Family Practice, 14,* 493–502.

Rosenbaum, J. N. (1995). Teaching cultural sensitivity. *Journal of Nursing Education, 4,* 188–198.

Roter, D. (2000). The enduring and evolving nature of patient–physician relationship. *Patient Education and Counseling, 39,* 5–15.

Roter, D., & Hall, J. A. (1992). *Physicians talking with patients, patients talking with physicians.* Westport, CT: Auburn House.

Samovar, L. A., & Porter, R. E. (2001). *Communication between cultures* (4th ed.). Stamford, CT: Wadsworth.

Sharf, B. (1990). Physician–patient communication as interpersonal rhetoric: A narrative approach. *Health Communication, 2,* 217–231.

Spitzer, A., Kesselring, A., Ravid, C., Tamir, B., Granot, G., & Noam, R. (1996). Learning about another culture: Project and curricular reflections. *Journal of Nursing Education, 35,* 323–328.

Stewart, M. A. (1995). Effective physician–patient communication and health outcomes: A review. *Canadian Medical Association Journal, 152,* 1423–1433.

Veatch, R. M. (1991). *The patient–physician relation: Part 2. The patient as partner.* Bloomington: Indiana University Press.

Welsbacher, A. (1998). The give and take of physician–patient communication: Can you relate? *Minnesota Medicine, 81,* 15–20.

Young, M., & Klingle, R. S. (1996). Silent partners in medical care: A cross-cultural study of patient participation. *Health Communication, 8,* 29–53.

Concepts and Questions

1. How does Rao distinguish between the dynamics of illness and disease? In what manner may these dynamics be influenced by culture and affect physician–patient communication?
2. Describe several ways in which culture might inhibit physician–patient communication.
3. In what ways might cultural diversity in language affect physician–patient communication?
4. Rao makes the argument that effective physician–patient communication requires cultural knowledge as well as well-developed interpersonal communication skills. What justification is there for this position?
5. How do physician perceptions of cultural diversity in Argentina and Brazil seem to differ from those found in India?
6. What effect does the cultural dynamic of collectivism have on physician–patient communication in Argentina, Brazil, and India?
7. How does the collectivistic concept of family as patient differ from the individualistic approach often found in the United States?
8. In what way does building trust between physician and patient in Argentina, Brazil, and India differ from how it is achieved in the United States?
9. What does Rao mean when he refers to the *intercultural* aspects of physician–patient communication?
10. In what ways do the communication strategies of physicians in collectivistic cultures seem to differ from those of physicians in individualistic cultures?

Exploring Culture in Nursing: A Theory-Driven Practice

Brian E. Mendyka

Caring has emerged as one of the focus constructs of contemporary nursing (Dougherty & Tripp-Reimer, 1985; Leininger, 1994; Meisensholder & LaCharite, 1989; Rawnsley, 1990; Watson, 1979, 1985a, 1989), and it is viewed by many as the moral ideal of nursing (Watson, 1989, 1990). As such, caring behaviors in nursing practice customarily demonstrate transpersonal or intersubjective attempts that (1) protect, enhance, and preserve humanity by helping persons find meaning in their illness experiences (e.g., suffering, pain, existence) and (2) help others to gain self-knowledge, self-control, and self-healing as nurses move toward sharing human experiences with patients and their families (Watson, 1979, 1985b, 1989; Pettigrew, 1990; Smere, 1990).

For these reasons, Watson's (1979) Model of Human Care has been selected as a way to explore how to better understand culture for encouraging the development of holistic nursing practice. Furthermore, this model represents nursing as an interpersonal or intersubjective process, teaching us how to be more human by identifying ourselves through the experiences of others.

To further explain this idea, a clinical exemplar depicting the interaction between nurse and an American Indian seeking health care will focus on this process. Interpersonal aspects of caring often used by nurses to facilitate culturally unique and challenging care situations will be identified as seminal to understanding this process. It is hoped that this will shed light on the importance of trying to understand patient illness explanations and, thus, their cultural experience of illness. Understanding in this context is a meaning-filled event that shapes and complements nurse and patient as co-participants in the construction of holistic caring.

Finally, this exemplar will convey problems frequently encountered when trying to interpret any patient's illness explanations within the health care system. Differing points of view, clinical perceptions, and varying interpretations of culture and context from the standpoints of both nurse and patient oftentimes exacerbate these problems. Selected problem sections are enhanced by brief discussions of how Watson's Model of Human Care relates to nursing practice in these particular situations. Opportunities for more holistic care are offered as possible ways to help construct more culturally congruent nursing care.

CLINICAL EXEMPLAR

Problem: Gary is a 30-year-old self-identified American Indian who frequently travels between a small rural community and a major metropolitan area, where he receives medical treatment for his illness. Gary has known for more than two years that he is HIV seropositive and generally comes to the clinic for a physical examination every five to six weeks. Lately, Gary has been feeling well and occasionally skips some of his follow-up appointments. Gary's nurse practitioner wants him to come into the clinic for more frequent checkups; however, Gary wishes to spend time away from the city and on the reservation up north with family and friends. When he comes to the city, he does not want to sit around in what he calls a sterile clinic waiting to be seen by his health care provider.

This is one example of a conflict between the meaning of Gary's cultural experience of illness and its interpretation by his nurse practitioner. Implicit in the nurse practitioner's care recommendations is the belief that Gary makes more frequent outpatient visits to afford observation, monitoring, and management within the health care system. Gary, however, does not perceive himself to be at risk for illness and is presently asymptomatic without physical complaints. Yet for the nurse practitioner, there is the perception of risk for illness that she believes is in need of treatment. This perception essentializes Gary's situation and health care.

ESSENTIALIZING HOLISTIC CARE: THE MIND-BODY-SPIRIT AXIOM

In this situation, Gary's nurse practitioner presents an antithesis to holistic care by essentializing it. On the one hand, the challenge for achieving holistic care in nursing practice coincides with a definition of holism, stating that human beings are integrated systems who interface with their environments (Meleis, 1991). On the other hand, essentialism is an ideology that emphasizes the meaning of human "parts" over the meaning of the "whole." Thus, when nurses essentialize human beings for the sake of health care, they fail to adequately and consistently address patient and family health care concerns. This occurs when patient cultural models or explanations of illness meaning conflict with and become superseded by those explanations posed by care providers within the health care system.

An example of essentializing nursing care occurs when nurses exploit axioms like "mind-body-spirit" in practice. This axiom is often used to describe holistic care by nurses. By essentializing the meaning of holistic care with mind-body-spirit conceptions of human beings, nurses risk the reconfiguration of patient and family illness problems as nothing more than narrow technical issues, or "disease problems." This narrowness can produce a type of care that reduces, and even strips away, human uniqueness and diversity, relegating the cultural experience of the patient (the meanings of illness conceived by the sick person) to, at best, a secondary status in the care of the ill. One of the core tasks in the effective clinical care of the ill—one whose value is all too easy to underrate—is to affirm the patient's personal and cultural experience of illness as constituted by patient and family explanations and then use these illness explanations to cultivate therapeutic treatment (Kleinman, 1988). This is the holistic approach.

Holism in nursing practice has been criticized as ambiguous and nonambiticus (Owen & Holmes, 1993; Boschma, 1994; Iacono & Iacono, 1994). Applying nursing theory to such situations can help to dissect away some of the ambiguity and nonambition that frequently prevent the awakening of a more comprehensive and clear view of holistic care for nursing. In this situation, understanding how Watson's Model of Human Care applies to nursing practice can assist nurses to reduce obstacles to achieving holistic care, helping nurses to grasp a greater outlook of the patient as person, as cultural being, and as a member of larger phenomenologic systems (e.g., the family or community) and therefore reemphasize the meaning of the whole over human parts.

By "taking in" this fuller account of the patient, nurses can help to actualize holistic care through processes of human relating, such as the nurse–patient relationship, without privileging the placement of the objective reality of the nurse over the patient's subjective reality of the illness experience. With human care receiving less and less emphasis in the health care delivery system, Watson's model can offer a supportive paradigm for realizing patient cultural illness explanations and experiences as important and respected influences necessary for promoting and sustaining health.

Holistic Care Opportunity: Gary's nurse practitioner can address his care needs and promote holistic care in practice by actively listening to Gary's explanations of his cultural experience of illness. Frequent monitoring may be unnecessary at this time, or there may be alternative means to assess his health without requiring him to commute to and from the clinic. Through additional conversation with Gary, the nurse can expand on this and other health care issues regarding his personal experiences. Doing this can help offset any misconceptions, confusion, or ambiguity about the illness experience while helping to merge phenomenal fields of nurse and patient.

THE UNFOLDING OF PHENOMENAL FIELDS

Watson contends that this sense of confusion or ambiguity can be lessened and even avoided by understanding persons as phenomenal fields. A phenomenal field is "a person's frame of reference or subjective reality, composed of the totality of human experience" (1985a, p. 55). This definition includes a respect for a person's culture (worldviews), cultural meanings, and an appreciation of human beings as individuals who experience life. Furthermore, the meaning of what we see, touch, taste, smell, or hear contributes to a person's view of "context," and it must be noted that this view is shaped by culture (Schultz & Lavenda, 1998). People learn from their culturally shaped experiences and thus use preexisting categories to help interpret those new experiences. The same holds true for illness meaning and the experience of sickness.

Phenomenal fields can best be understood as "your entire life" and what it (life) brings to care situations between nurse and patient. Phenomenal fields of both nurse and patient eventually make up the interpersonal process of the nurse–patient relationship. According to Watson (1985b), as nurse and patient continue to share more illness meaning (often independent of time), they experience transpersonal caring. Transpersonal caring symbolizes a growing and spiritual awareness of the "therapeutic use of self" in the context of the illness experience of others (Watson, 1985b; Mendyka, 1993). This type of caring instills the idea that sharing human experience is indeed a unique privilege. Even so, one person's phenomenal field can never be entirely known by another person, although by extending empathy to another, one can begin to know another person's reality. Kleinman (1988) calls this "empathetic witnessing," whereas nurse scholars such as Pettigrew (1990) and Smere (1990) call this phenomenon "presencing" in nursing care situations.

The quality of the nurse–patient relationship (and the merging of patient and nurse phenomenal fields into a transpersonal caring relationship) is highly dependent on how interpersonal aspects of caring (domains of caring) are used by nurses and how they are perceived by patients. Because illness experiences are culturally shaped, it is equally important for nurses to make a conscious and concerted effort to actively listen and attune themselves to a patient's account of illness in light of their own cultural background and special interests (e.g., therapeutic, scientific, professional, financial, personal).

Patient accounts of illness generally constitute their cultural experience created by the sick person, family, and friends to make over an otherwise chaotic bio-occurrence into a more or less ritually controlled one (Kleinman, 1988). In any care situation, a lack or absence of affective characteristics such as genuineness and empathy can profoundly affect to what extent phenomenal fields merge between nurse and patient. Without this integration, holistic care becomes disabled. This eliminates any possibility of the nurse's ascertaining the patient's personal and cultural experience of illness. This can adversely affect the developmental course of the nurse–patient relationship.

Problem: The nurse practitioner tells Gary that he needs to come to the clinic more often because his past medical record shows that his "T-cell count" was lower on his last clinic visit. Also, she wants Gary's physician to consider ordering Gary HIV medications to prevent the possible emergence of full-blown AIDS. Gary is feeling good and says that it is unnecessary for him to take any prescribed medications. He tells the nurse practitioner that the medications make him sick, are poison, and that this poison is then recycled back into the earth. This greatly worries Gary. Furthermore, Gary tells the nurse practitioner that he is committed to going back to practicing some of his native traditional healing practices, including traditional prayer, sweat-lodge ceremony, herbal remedies, and spiritual transformation through a vision quest recommended by his medicine man. The nurse practitioner states that these things are not appropriate for treating HIV.

The meaning of Gary's personal behavior and cultural experience is steeped in his desire to cleanse himself and his body in culturally meaningful ways through native customs that emphasize the health of his entire self. The number of T-cells has less meaning for Gary but is meaningful to the health care provider in terms of the biomedical construction of HIV infection, which relates risk of experienced illness (Gifford, 1986) to correlated T-cell numbers. In this case, the nurse practitioner has simplified and reduced the meaning of Gary's cultural experience of sickness (HIV) to an illness based on technological laboratory findings and, thus, minimizes Gary's cultural experience of being HIV seropositive. She can prevent this by effectively using interpersonal aspects of caring while planning and implementing Gary's care.

INTERPERSONAL ASPECTS OF CARING

According to Watson, "human care can be effectively demonstrated and practiced only interpersonally" (1989, p. 222). This idea stresses the importance of nursing as a human endeavor. Furthermore, it teaches us how to be more human by identifying ourselves through the experiences of others through interpersonal aspects of caring. These aspects include cognitive, behavioral, and affective domains and are important for providing holistic care. Cognitive domains are the broad categories of intellectual, perceptual, and experiential nursing knowledge. This knowledge generally takes on such configurations as physiologic, psychologic, social, cultural, political, and economic dimensions. Behavioral domains are the technologic skills that nurses learn to apply for promoting compassionate and effective nursing care. Affective domains include the exercise and total expression of authenticity, congruence, empathy, genuineness, and nonpossessive warmth (Watson, 1979) in nursing care (see Table 1). In the case of Gary, the use of these interpersonal "aspects" together can assist in offsetting the deterioration of Gary's nursing care into a clinically confusing and nonambitious event. This is particularly true in the case of culture, where a patient's culture and cultural identity have been shown to add yet another complicating layer to the practice of nursing (Brink, 1990).

Holistic Care Opportunity: Here is an opportunity to learn more about Gary's cultural experience of illness while increasing the "shared meaning" that this experience holds for nurse and patient. Learning more about Gary's illness helps to move the nurse–patient relationship toward one based on transpersonal caring.

Table 1 *Affective Characteristics for Caring*

Authenticity	A human quality that evidences a commitment to sustaining human integrity
Congruence	A human quality that supports accurate, consistent, and faithful devotion to patient and family-centered goals
Empathy	A human quality that conveys the nurse's ability to experience another person's perceptions and feelings while communicating a high degree of understanding to the other person
Genuineness	A human quality evidenced by open honesty in care situations that transcends rigid role expectations to accommodate patient needs
Nonpossessive warmth	A compendium of human qualities that complement unconditional and nonjudgmental attitudes toward patients (e.g., comforting touch, soft tone of voice, facial expressions that evidence positive regard for the patient)

SOURCE: Adapted from J. Watson, *Nursing: The Philosophy and Science of Caring,* © 1979, Boston: Little, Brown and Company.

This kind of relationship stresses the simultaneous and spiritual union of "nurse–patient," and allows the patient to experience the release of feelings (Boyd & Mast, 1989).

Gary's nurse practitioner can further explore his feelings by using Watson's interpersonal aspects of caring to assist him to find meaning in his cultural experience of illness and, thus, expand the nurse–patient relationship. Exploring Gary's feelings about his illness experience in greater detail provides a welcoming opportunity for phenomenal fields of both nurse and patient to "move closer" together. At the same time, the nurse practitioner can further support Gary by respecting his choice of "alternative" or "complementary" therapies. (It must be noted by health care providers that labels like "alternative" or "complementary" can be inappropriate, even insulting, to many members of other cultures who define their personal modes of health care seeking as foremost to understand their personal experience of illness. For many, therapies such as sweat-lodge ceremony, the use of herbs, prayer, and spiritual transformation *are* the primary modes of therapy to treat illness, and, therefore, anything other than these patient-specific therapies [i.e., biomedicine] may be regarded as secondary sources of treatment. Even so, both ideologies generally essentialize health care treatment by giving preference for biomedicine over "alternative" or "complementary" and vice versa.) The nurse practitioner now has a unique opportunity to develop a healing relationship with Gary's medicine man. This relationship can help supplement Gary's need for personal meaning in his cultural experience of illness. Such liaisons have been quite useful in promoting more holistic and culturally meaningful health care treatment in a variety of community settings (Mendyka, 1994; Weidman, 1982), and more specifically among American Indians (Struthers & Littlejohn, 1999; Weaver, 1999; Upvall, 1997; Maclean & Bannelman, 1982; Mores, Young, & Swanz, 1991; Kimbrough & Drick, 1991).

CULTURAL MEANING AND CULTURAL BEINGS

According to both Watson (1979, 1985a, 1989) and Fitzpatrick (1989), meaning is the most crucial piece of human experience, and it is through human relating that meaning comes to life. Cultural meaning, in this instance, is a set of human phenomena that continually develops through the human senses and, as such, helps to frame, mesh, and interweave a person's life matrix, contributing to conceptions of illness meaning. Thus, cultural meanings can provide a "window" for understanding the meaning of the illness experience, while helping patients and families create, mediate, and shape their own perceptions of everyday life (through the phenomenal fields). Therefore, cultural meanings should complement the nurse–patient relationship.

The idea of culture adds to our cognizance of human meaning by providing us with a sort of template for understanding another's life context, while helping us picture a perception of humans as integral cultural beings. Cultural beings are persons who bring to nursing care situations differing values, beliefs, customs, and varying perspectives about illness causation, preferred methods of treatment, fears about illness, and expected outcomes of health care. Although the idea of culture does not completely explain human phenomena in their entirety, viewing humans as cultural beings can support the idea that

> humans cannot be separated and viewed apart from their cultural background. Humans need to be viewed and understood in their total context, and culture is the broadest and most holistic perspective that allows this to happen. (Luna & Cameron, 1989, p. 228)

This theoretical approach supports the view that cultural experiences of illness are indeed meaning-filled events conceived by nurse and patient through their phenomenal fields. The person no longer comes to be understood solely as a set of separate "attributes" (physical, psychologic, emotional, cultural, and spiritual) that require attention. The individual now becomes known by the nurse as an entire "life world," a world that exists in and outside of the health care delivery system. That is, people live the greater part of their lives in "everyday life," and this is something that can be more deeply explored by health care providers.

Problem: The nurse practitioner believes that Gary's healing experiences on the reservation are not as important as Gary's complying with health care treatment and starting HIV medications, and she insists that he take them. Gary tells her that he does not want the medication. Her response to Gary in this situation is: "You will die if you do not follow medical treatment and take the medications that are being prescribed for your benefit." Gary asks the nurse what she thinks will happen if he takes the medication, what kind of side effects he can expect, and whether taking them will help to prolong his life. She states that she cannot be sure what long-term effects taking or not taking the medications will have on Gary, although she gives him a list of common side effects often associated with the drugs. Furthermore, she cannot be certain how much remaining time Gary will have even if he chooses to take the medication. "So, what you are saying is that if I don't take the medication, I will die, and if I do take the medications, I will die anyway?" The nurse practitioner nods to this inquiry.

To this day, Gary refuses to take any HIV medications and practices native traditional healing offered by his medicine man. He remains asymptomatic and "feeling good." At this time, Gary does not suffer from the "treatment of risk" (Gifford, 1986), nor does he regard his cultural experience of illness as being separate from his own personal perceptions and definitions of cultural context and risk of illness (Odets, 1993; Bolton, 1992, 1995). This is in opposition with perceptions posed by his health care provider and the health care system, where the biomedical definition of illness risk and Gary's perceptions and definitions of cultural context and risk of illness are viewed as two distinct and conflicting entities.

Holistic Care Opportunity: If the nurse practitioner had taken previous opportunities to engage in a transpersonal caring relationship with Gary in an ongoing fashion, she could have situated herself in a unique position to share the intimate meanings of Gary's illness experience. In doing so, she could have worked with Gary, the medicine man, and others who have become a part of Gary's caring and healing system. She could have become more than a "mere advocate" within this health care system. She could have been a part of a special community of individuals who share the common goal of helping Gary understand the meaning of his illness and thus assist him to find the best possible means of achieving optimal health. Watson calls this achievement the actual caring occasion, in which human capacities of nurse and patient become expanded, and both experience new opportunities for greater knowledge of self and the universe (Boyd & Mast, 1989).

THE MORAL WORK OF NURSING AND HOLISTIC CARE

A fundamental feature of holistic care for nursing practice (which may add meaning to the cultural experience of illness) is the moral work of nursing—that is, helping patients find meaning in their illness experience. This feature can be actively channeled by nurses to protect and foster patient agency, particularly under conditions of patient vulnerability. Agency is defined here as "the capacity to initiate meaningful action" (Lischenko, 1994, p. 16) and is an essential and core feature for helping patients and families to find meaning during illness episodes.

The profession of nursing recognizes the need for helping all patients, and although discriminatory care and treatment do occur (McCann, 1999), the idea of agency is extremely pertinent to understanding how holistic care can be cultivated for nursing practice. It is

> not merely to help patients stay alive or even healthy, but in helping them to "have a life." To have a life is to have a sense of agency, to occupy social, cultural, and political space, to live a temporally structured existence, and to die. (Liaschenko, 1994, p. 23)

By helping patients to have a life, nurses can act for or on behalf of patients who are culturally different from themselves. According to Liaschenko (1995), acting for the patient is a matter of inherent ethical significance and carries the risk of instrumentality; that is, one person becomes the means to another's end.

If this is true, then how nurses comprehend "what is holistic" will have an impact on their ability to "act for" patients from diverse backgrounds during times of vulnerability and ultimately define how nurses go about helping patients from all walks of society to "have a life." Thus, it is imperative for nurses to recognize and respect, with their undying expertise and human sensitivities, the importance that culture and meanings of illness experience pose for those for whom they provide care. Using Watson's Model of Human Care in clinical practice can help nurses begin to comprehend the relevance of this all-important task.

In summary, nurses who hope to encourage holistic care in practice must first begin to recognize patients as integral cultural beings who possess unique phenomenal fields and who, as persons, have vital and inseparable physiologic, psychosocial, cultural, and spiritual dimensions. If the nurse and patient continue to effectively share illness meaning, they may experience a spiritual union or transpersonal caring relationship. This can lead to an understanding of culture as a contributing factor that holds care as a moral ideal (Watson, 1990; Boyd & Mast, 1989). Because culture provides a constant source of human meaning, nurses who strive to understand holistic care in practice fully recognize the patient's family, home life (e.g., pets, hobbies), work life, and friends within this context and know that these "vital constituents" exact major influences on the health status of the patient.

CONCLUSION

In conclusion, Watson's Model of Human Care offers a wonderful way to envision holistic care in nursing practice. And nursing theory can provide useful approaches when nurses are uncertain how to meet the particular needs of those who are different from themselves. In such instances, applying nursing theory to practice can act as a "blueprint" to help health care providers unveil more culturally appropriate and meaningful health care for patients and their families. This happens when all participants in the illness event "see" the value in exploring the cultural experience of illness together.

Finally, the usefulness that this care model bestows for understanding culture within the domain of holistic care calls into question the meaning of professionalism in nursing practice. Professionalism in nursing often implies that to achieve effective nursing care, nurses are required to practice "experience distant" versus "experience near" nursing. In other words, for a nurse to be effective in the administration of patient care, one must not "get too close to patients."

Often in health care matters, it is thought that the objective reality of the nurse should supersede the subjective reality of the patient. This presumption offsets the use of affective domains of caring and invalidates the patient's cultural experience of illness. And getting "too close to patients" assumes that nurses may risk losing their "objectivity" in practice. Watson's Model of Human Care offers a way to reexamine and balance the nurse–patient relationship by helping us view the value of this relationship through an intersubjective lens rather than through a plastic objective–subjective one. Intersubjectivity is a fluid process and implies the ability to construct nursing care with patients and families rather than for them. By adopting nursing care through intersubjectivity, one can engage the patient's cultural experience of illness, while inviting the patient and family to make their own health care decisions together. Thus, central to this feature is a prodigious opportunity for nurse, patient, and family to create many holistic care opportunities together by integrating the cultural experience of illness into nursing practice.

References

Bolton, R. (1992). AIDS and promiscuity: Muddles in the models of HIV prevention. *Medical Anthropology, 14,* 145–223.

Bolton, R. (1995). Rethinking anthropology: The study of AIDS. In H. Brummelhuis & G. Herdt (Eds.), *Culture and sexual risk: Anthropological perspective on AIDS.* Melbourne, Australia: Gordon and Breach.

Boschma, G. (1994). The meaning of holism in nursing: Historical shifts in holistic nursing ideas. *Public Health Nursing, 11,* 324–330.

Boyd, C., & D. Mast. (1989). Watson's model of human care. In J. J. Fitzpatrick & A. L. Whall (Eds.), *Conceptual models of nursing: Analysis and application* (2nd ed., pp. 371–383). Norwalk, CT: Appleton & Lange.

Brink, P. (1990). Cultural diversity in nursing: How much can we tolerate? In I. C. McCloskey & H. C. Grace (Eds.), *Current issues in nursing* (pp. 521–527). St. Louis, MO: Mosby.

Dougherty, M., & Tripp-Reimer, T. (1985). The interface of nursing and anthropology. In B. J. Siegel (Ed.), *Annual review of anthropology* (pp. 219–241). Palo Alto, CA: Annual Reviews.

Fitzpatrick, J. J. (1989). A life perspective rhythm model. In J. J. Fitzpatrick & A. L. Whall (Eds.), *Conceptual models of nursing: Analysis and application* (2nd ed., pp. 401–408). Norwalk, CT: Appleton & Lange.

Gifford, S. M. (1986). The meaning of lumps: A case study of the ambiguities of risk. In C. R. Lanes, R. Stall, & S. M. Gifford (Eds.). *Anthropology and epidemiology.* Boston: Reidel.

Iacono, B. J., & Iacono, J. J. (1994). How should holism guide the setting of educational standards? *Journal of Advanced Nursing, 19,* 342–346.

Kimbrough, K. L., & Drick, C. (1991). Traditional Indian medicine: Spiritual healing process for all people. *Journal of Holistic Nursing, 9,* 15–19.

Kleinman, A. (1988). *The illness narrative: Suffering, healing, and the human condition.* New York: Basic Books.

Leininger, M. (1994). Quality of life from a transcultural nursing perspective. *Nursing Science Quarterly, 7,* 22–28.

Liaschenko, J. (1994). The moral geography of home care. *Advances in Nursing Science, 17,* 16–26.

Liaschenko, I. (1995). Ethics in the work of acting for patients. *Advances in Nursing Science, 18,* 1–12.

Luna, L., & Cameron, C. (1989). Leininger's transcultural nursing. In J. J. Fitzpatrick & A. L. Whall (Eds.), *Conceptual modes of nursing: Analysis and application* (2nd ed., pp. 227–239). Norwalk, CT: Appleton & Lange.

Maclean, U., & Bannelman, R. H. (1982). Utilization of indigenous healers in national health delivery systems. *Social Sciences and Medicine, 16,* 1815–1816.

McCann, T. V. (1999). Reluctance amongst nurses and doctors to care for and treat patients with HIV/AIDS. *AIDS Care, 11,* 355–359.

Meisenholder, J. B., & LaCharite, C. L. (1989). *Comfort in caring: Nursing the person with HIV infection.* Glenview, IL: Scott, Foresman.

Meleis, A. I. (1991). *Theoretical nursing: Development and progress.* Philadelphia: Lippincott.

Mendyka, B. E. (1993). The dying patient in the intensive care unit: Assisting the family in crisis. *AACN Clinical Issues in Critical Care Nursing, 4,* 550–557.

Mendyka, B. E. (1994). The therapeutic syncretic process: Implications for nursing care delivery. *AACN Clinical Issues in Critical Care Nursing, 5,* 86–91.

Morse, J. M., Young, D. E., & Swanz, L. (1991). Cree Indian healing practices and Western health care: A comparative analysis. *Social Sciences and Medicine, 32,* 1361–1366.

Odets, W. (1993). *AIDS education and prevention: Why it has gone almost completely wrong and some things we can do about it.* Paper presented at the National Gay and Lesbian Health Conference, Houston, TX.

Owen, M. J., & Holmes, C. A. (1993). "Holism" in the discourse of nursing. *Journal of Advanced Nursing, 18,* 1688–1695.

Pettigrew, I. (1990). Intensive nursing care: The ministry of presence. *Critical Care Nursing Clinics of North America, 2,* 503–508.

Rawnsley, M. (1990). Of human bonding: The context of nursing as caring. *Advances in Nursing Science, 13,* 41–48.

Schultz, E. A., & Lavenda, R. H. (1998). *Cultural anthropology: A perspective on the human condition* (4th ed.). Mountain View, CA: Mayfield.

Smere, J. M. (1990). Ethical components of caring. *Critical Care Nursing Clinics of North America, 2,* 509–513.

Struthers, R., & Littlejohn, S. (1999). The essence of Native American nursing. *Journal of Transcultural Nursing, 10,* 131–135.

Upvall, M. I. (1997). Nursing perspectives of American Indian healing strategies. *Journal of Multicultural Nursing and Health, 3,* 29–34, 51.

Watson, I. (1979). *Nursing: The philosophy and science of caring.* Boston: Little, Brown.

Watson, I. (1985a). *Nursing: Human science and human care: A theory of nursing.* East Norwalk, CT: Appleton-Century-Crofts.

Watson, I. (1985b). *Nursing: The philosophy and science of caring.* Norwalk, CT: Appleton-Century-Crofts.

Watson, I. (1989). Watson's philosophy and theory of human caring in nursing. In J. P. Reihl-Sisca (Ed.), *Conceptual models for nursing practice* (pp. 219–235). Norwalk CT: Appleton & Lange.

Watson, I. (1990). Caring knowledge and informed moral passion. *Advances in Nursing Science, 13,* 15–24.

Weaver, H. N. (1999). Transcultural nursing with Native Americans: Critical knowledge, skills, and attitudes. *Journal of Transcultural Nursing, 10,* 197–202.

Weidman, H. H. (1982). Research strategies, structural alterations and clinically applied anthropology. In N. I. Chrisman & T. W. Maretzki (Eds.), *Clinically applied anthropology* (pp. 201–241). Dordrecht, The Netherlands: Reidel.

Concepts and Questions

1. What is meant by the phrase "nursing as an interpersonal process"?
2. Explain the following statement advanced by Mendyka: "Differing points of view, clinical perceptions, and varying interpretations of culture and context from the standpoints of both nurse and patient oftentimes exacerbate these problems."
3. What is meant by the phrase "cultural experiences of illness"?
4. Describe Mendyka's view of "holistic nursing."
5. Explain the idea that "humans cannot be separated and viewed apart from their cultural background."
6. Why does Mendyka advance the positive effects of "holistic nursing"?

Culture and Communication in the Classroom

GENEVA GAY

A semiotic relationship exists among communication, culture, teaching, and learning, and it has profound implications for implementing culturally responsive teaching. This is so because "what we talk about; how we talk about it; what we see, attend to, or ignore; how we think; and what we think about are influenced by our culture . . . [and] help to shape, define, and perpetuate our culture" (Porter & Samovar, 1991, p. 21). Making essentially the same argument, Bruner (1996) states that "learning and thinking are always situated in a cultural setting and always dependent upon the utilization of cultural resources" (p. 4). Culture provides the tools to pursue the search for meaning and to convey our understanding to others. Consequently, communication cannot exist without culture, culture cannot be known without communication, and teaching and learning cannot occur without communication or culture.

INTRODUCTION

The discussions in this article explicate some of the critical features and pedagogical potentials of the culture–communication semiotics for different ethnic groups of color. The ideas and examples presented are composites of group members who strongly identify and affiliate with their ethnic group's cultural traditions. They are not intended to be descriptors of specific individuals within ethnic groups, or their behaviors in all circumstances. If, how, and when these cultural characteristics are expressed in actual behavior, and by whom, are influenced by many different factors. Therefore, the ethnic interactional and communication styles described in this article should be seen as general and traditional referents of group dynamics rather than static attributes of particular individuals.

Students of color who are most traditional in their communication styles and other aspects of culture and ethnicity are likely to encounter more obstacles to school achievement than those who think, behave, and express themselves in ways that approximate school and mainstream cultural norms. This is the case for many highly culturally and ethnically affiliated African Americans. In making this point, Dandy (1991) proposes that the language many African Americans speak "is all too often degraded or simply dismissed by individuals both inside and outside the racial group as being uneducated, illiterate, undignified or simply non-standard" (p. 2). Other groups of color are "at least given credit for having a legitimate language heritage, even if they are denied full access to American life" (p. 2). Much of educators' decision making on the potential and realized achievement of students of color is dependent on communication abilities (their own and the students'). If students are not very proficient in school communication and teachers do not understand or accept the students' cultural communication styles, then their academic performance may be misdiagnosed or trapped in communicative mismatches. Students may know much more than they are able to communicate, or they may be communicating much more than their teachers are able to discern. As Boggs (1985, p. 301) explains, "The attitudes and behavior patterns that have the most important effect upon children . . . [are] those involved in communication." This communication is multidimensional and multipurposed, including verbal and nonverbal, direct and tacit, literal and symbolic, formal and informal, grammatical and discourse components.

The discussions of culture and communication in classrooms in this article are organized into two parts. The first outlines some key assertions about culture and communication in teaching and learning in general. These help to anchor communication within culturally responsive teaching. In the second part of the article, some of the major characteristics of the communication modes of African, Native, Latino, Asian, and European Americans are presented. The focus throughout these discussions is on discourse dynamics—that is, who participates in communicative interactions and under what conditions, how these participation

Reprinted by permission of the publisher from Geneva Gay, *Culturally Responsive Teaching* (New York: Teachers College Press, © 2000 by Teachers College, Columbia University. All rights reserved), 77–110.

patterns are affected by cultural socialization, and how they influence teaching and learning in classrooms.

RELATIONSHIP AMONG CULTURE, COMMUNICATION, AND EDUCATION

In analyzing the routine tasks teachers perform, Smith (1971) declares that "teaching is, above all, a linguistic activity" and "language is at the heart of teaching" (p. 24). Whether making assignments, giving directions, explaining events, interpreting words and expressions, proving positions, justifying decisions and actions, making promises, dispensing praise and criticism, or assessing capability, teachers must use language. And the quality of the performance of these tasks is a direct reflection of how well teachers can communicate with their students. Smith admonishes educators for not being more conscientious in recognizing the importance of language in the performance and effectiveness of their duties. He says, "It could be that when we have analyzed the language of teaching and investigated the effects of its various formulations, the art of teaching will show marked advancement" (p. 24). Dandy (1991) likewise places great faith in the power of communication in the classroom, declaring that "teachers have the power to shape the future, if they communicate with their students, but those who cannot communicate are powerless" (p. 10). These effects of communication skills are especially significant to improving the performance of underachieving ethnically different students.

Porter and Samovar's (1991) study of the nature of culture and communication, the tenacious reciprocity that exists between the two, and the importance of these aspects to intercultural interactions provides valuable information for culturally responsive teaching. They describe communication as "an intricate matrix of interacting social acts that occur in a complex social environment that reflects the way people live and how they come to interact with and get along in their world. This social environment is culture, and if we are to truly understand communication, we must also understand culture" (p. 10). Communication is dynamic, interactive, irreversible, and invariably contextual. As such, it is a continuous, ever-changing activity that takes place between people who are trying to influence each other; its effects are irretrievable once it has occurred, despite efforts to modify or counteract them.

Communication is also governed by the rules of the social and physical contexts in which it occurs (Porter & Samovar, 1991). Culture is the rule-governing system that defines the forms, functions, and content of communication. It is largely responsible for the construction of our "individual repertories of communicative behaviors and meanings" (p. 10). Understanding connections between culture and communication is critical to improving intercultural interactions. This is so because "as cultures differ from one another, the communication practices and behaviors of individuals reared in those cultures will also be different," and "the degree of influence culture has on intercultural communication is a function of the dissimilarity between the cultures" (p. 12).

Communication entails much more than the content and structure of written and spoken language, and it serves greater purposes than the mere transmission of information. Sociocultural context and nuances, discourse logic and dynamics, delivery styles, social functions, role expectations, norms of interaction, and nonverbal features are as important as (if not more so than) vocabulary, grammar, lexicon, pronunciation, and other linguistic or structural dimensions of communication. This is so because the "form of exchange between child and adult and the conditions in which it occurs will affect not only what is said, but how involved the child will become" (Boggs, 1985, p. 301). Communication is the quintessential way in which humans make meaningful connections with each other, whether in caring, sharing, loving, teaching, or learning. Montague and Matson (1979, p. vii) suggest that it is "the ground of [human] meeting and the foundation of [human] community."

Communication is also indispensable to facilitating knowing and accessing knowledge. This is the central idea of the Sapir–Whorf hypothesis about the relationship among language, thought, and behavior. It says that, far from being simply a means for reporting experience, language is a way of defining experience, thinking, and knowing. In this sense, language is the semantic system of meanings and modes of conveyance that people habitually use to code, analyze, categorize, and interpret experience (Carroll, 1956; Hoijer, 1991; Mandelbaum, 1968). In characterizing this relationship, Sapir (1968) explains that "language is a guide to 'social reality' . . . [and] a symbolic guide to culture. . . . It powerfully conditions all of our thinking about social problems and processes" (p. 162). People do not live alone in an "objectified world" or negotiate social realities without the use of language. Nor is language simply a "mechanical" instrumental tool for transmitting information. Instead, human beings are "very much at the mercy of the particular language which has become the medium of expression for their society" (p. 162). The languages used in different cultural systems strongly influence how people think, know, feel, and do.

Whorf (1952, 1956; Carroll, 1956), a student of Sapir, makes a similar argument that is represented by the "principle of linguistic relativity." It contends that the structures of various languages reflect different cultural patterns and values, and, in turn, affect how people understand and respond to social phenomena. In developing these ideas further, Whorf (1952) explains that "a language is not merely a reproducing instrument for voicing ideas but rather is itself the shaper of ideas, the program and guide for the individual's mental activity, for his analysis of impressions, for his synthesis of his mental stock in trade" (p. 5). Vygotsky (1962) also recognizes the reciprocal relationship among language, culture, and thought. He declares, as "indisputable fact," that "thought development is determined by language . . . and the sociocultural experience of the child" (p. 51).

Moreover, the development of logic is affected by a person's socialized speech, and intellectual growth is contingent on the mastery of social means of thought, or language. According to Byers and Byers (1985), "the organization of the processes of human communication in any culture is a template for the organization of knowledge or information in that culture" (p. 28). This line of argument is applied specifically to different ethnic groups by theorists, researchers, and school practitioners from a variety of disciplinary perspectives, including social and developmental psychology, sociolinguistics, ethnography, and multiculturalism. For example, Ascher (1992) applied this reasoning to language influences on how mathematical relationships are viewed in general. Giamati and Weiland (1997) connected it to Navajo students' learning of mathematics, concluding that the performance difficulties they encounter are "a result of cultural influences on perceptions rather than a lack of ability" (p. 27). This happens because of the reciprocal interactions among language, culture, and perceptions. Consistently, when these scholars refer to "language" or "communication," they are talking more about discourse dynamics than structural forms of speaking and writing.

Thus, languages and communication styles are systems of cultural notations and the means through which thoughts and ideas are expressively embodied. Embedded within them are cultural values and ways of knowing that strongly influence how students engage with learning tasks and demonstrate mastery of them. The absence of shared communicative frames of reference, procedural protocols, rules of etiquette, and discourse systems makes it difficult for culturally diverse students and teachers to genuinely understand each other and for students to fully convey their intellectual abilities. Teachers who do not know or value these realities will not be able to fully access, facilitate, and assess most of what these students know and can do. Communication must be understood to be more than a linguistic system.

CULTURALLY DIFFERENT DISCOURSE STRUCTURES

In conventional classroom discourse, students are expected to assume what Kochman (1985) calls a *passive-receptive* posture. They are told to listen quietly while the teacher talks. Once the teacher finishes, then the students can respond in some prearranged, stylized way—by asking or answering questions; validating or approving what was said; or taking individual, teacher-regulated turns at talking. Individual students gain the right to participate in the conversation by permission of the teacher. The verbal discourse is accompanied by nonverbal attending behaviors and speech-delivery mechanisms that require maintaining eye contact with the speaker and using little or no physical movement. Thus, students are expected to be silent and look at teachers when they are talking and wait to be acknowledged before they take their turn at talking. Once permission is granted, they should follow established rules of decorum, such as one person speaking at a time, being brief and to the point, and keeping emotional nuances to a minimum (Kochman, 1981; Philips, 1983).

These structural protocols governing discourse are expressed in other classroom practices as well. Among them are expecting students always to speak in complete sentences that include logical development of thought, precise information, appropriate vocabulary, and careful attention to grammatical features such as appropriate use of vocabulary and noun–verb agreement. Student participation in classroom interactions is often elicited by teachers asking questions that are directed to specific individuals and require a narrow range of information-giving, descriptive responses. It is important for individuals to distinguish themselves in the conversations, for student responses to be restricted to only the specific demands of questions asked, and for the role of speaker and audience to be clearly separated.

In contrast to the passive-receptive character of conventional classroom discourse, some ethnic groups have communication styles that Kochman (1985) describes as *participatory-interactive*. Speakers expect listeners to engage them actively through vocalized, motion, and movement responses *as they are speaking*. Speakers and listeners are action-provoking partners in the construction of the discourse. These communicative styles have been observed among African Americans, Latinos, and Native Hawaiians. As is the case with other cultural behaviors, they are likely to be more pronounced among individuals who strongly identify and affiliate with their ethnic groups and cultural heritages. For example, low-income and minimally educated members of ethnic groups are likely to manifest group cultural behaviors more thoroughly than those who are middle class and educated. This is so because they have fewer opportunities to interact with people different from themselves and to be affected by the cultural exchanges and adaptations that result from the intermingling of a wide variety of people from diverse ethnic groups and varied experiential backgrounds.

ETHNIC VARIATIONS IN COMMUNICATION STYLES

Among African Americans, the participatory-interactive style of communicating is sometimes referred to as *call-response* (Asante, 1998; Baber, 1987; Kochman, 1972, 1981, 1985; Smitherman, 1977). It involves listeners' giving encouragement, commentary, compliments, and even criticism to speakers *as they are talking*. The speaker's responsibility is to issue the "calls" (making statements), and the listeners' obligation is to respond in some expressive, and often auditory, way (e.g., smiling, vocalizing, looking about, moving around, "amening") (Dandy, 1991; Smitherman, 1977). When a speaker says something that triggers a response in them (whether positive or negative; affective or cognitive), African American listeners are likely to "talk back." This may involve a vocal or motion response, or both, sent directly to the speaker or shared with neighbors in the audience. Longstreet (1978) and Shade (1994) describe the practice as "breaking in and talking over." This mechanism is used to signal to speakers that their purposes have been accomplished or that it is time to change the direction or leadership of the conversation. Either way, there is no need for the speaker to pursue the particular discourse topic or technique further.

African Americans "gain the floor" or get participatory entry into conversations through personal assertiveness, the strength of the impulse to be involved, and the persuasive power of the point they wish to make, rather than waiting for an "authority" to grant permission. They tend to invest their participation with personality power, actions, and emotions. Consequently, African Americans are often described as verbal performers whose speech behaviors are fueled by personal advocacy, emotionalism, fluidity, and creative variety (Abrahams, 1970; Baber, 1987). These communication facilities have been attributed to the oral/aural nature of African American cultural and communal value orientations (Pasteur & Toldson, 1982; Smitherman, 1977). Many teachers view these behaviors negatively, as "rude," "inconsiderate," "disruptive," and "speaking out of turn," and they penalize students for them.

Native Hawaiian students who maintain their traditional cultural practices use a participatory-interactive communicative style similar to the call-response of African Americans. Called "talk-story" or "co-narrative," it involves several students working collaboratively, or talking together, to create an idea, tell a story, or complete a learning task (Au, 1980, 1993; Au & Kawakami, 1985, 1991, 1994; Au & Mason, 1981; Boggs, Watson-Gegeo, & McMillen, 1985). After observing these behaviors among elementary students, Au (1993) concluded that "what seems important to Hawaiian children in talk-story is not individual . . . but group performance in speaking" (p. 114). These communication preferences are consistent with the importance Native Hawaiian culture places on individuals' contributing to the well-being of family and friends instead of working only for their own betterment (Gallimore, Boggs, & Jordon, 1974; Tharp & Gallimore, 1988).

A communicative practice that has some of the same traits of call-response and talk-story has been observed among European American females. Tannen (1990) calls it "cooperative overlapping" and describes it as women "talking along with speakers to show participation and support" (p. 208). It occurs most often in situations where talk is casual and friendly. This *rapport-talk* is used to create community. It is complemented by other traditional women's ways of communicating, such as the following:

- Being "audience" more often than "speaker" in that they are recipients of information provided by males
- Deëmphasizing expertise and the competitiveness it generates
- Focusing on individuals in establishing friendships, networks, intimacy, and relationships more than exhibiting power, accomplishment, or control
- Negotiating closeness in order to give and receive confirmation, support, and consensus
- Avoiding conflict and confrontation (Belensky, Clinchy, Goldberger, & Tarule, 1986; Klein, 1982; Maltz & Borker, 1983; Tannen, 1990)

While these habits of "communal communication and interaction" are normal to the users, they can be problematic to classroom teachers. On first encounter, they may be perceived as "indistinguishable noise and chaos" or unwholesome dependency. Even after the shock of the initial encounter passes, teachers may still consider these ways of communicating socially deviant, not conducive to constructive intellectual engagement, rude, and insulting. They see them as obstructing individual initiative and preempting the right of each student to have a fair chance to participate in instructional discourse. These assessments can prompt attempts to rid students of the habits and replace them with the rules of individualistic, passive-receptive, and controlling communication styles predominant in classrooms.

Teachers may not realize that by doing this they could be causing irreversible damage to students' abilities or inclinations to engage fully in the instructional process. Hymes (1985) made this point when he suggested that rejecting ethnically different students' communication styles might be perceived by them as rejection of their personhood. Whether intentional or not, casting these kinds of aspersions on the identity and personal worth of students of color does not bode well for their academic achievement.

Problem Solving and Task Engagement

Many African American, Latino, Native American, and Asian American students use styles of inquiry and responding that are different from those employed most often in classrooms. The most common practice among teachers is to ask convergent (single-answer) questions and use deductive approaches to solving problems. Emphasis is given to details, to building the whole from the parts, to moving from the specific to the general. Discourse tends to be didactic, involving one student with the teacher at a time (Goodlad, 1984). In comparison, students of color who are strongly affiliated with their traditional cultures tend to be more inductive, interactive, and communal in task performance. The preference for inductive problem solving is expressed as reasoning from the whole to parts, from the general to the specific. The focus is on the "big picture," the pattern, the principle (Boggs et al., 1985; Philips, 1983; Ramirez & Castañeda, 1974; Shade 1989).

Although these general patterns of task engagement prevail across ethnic groups, variations do exist. Some teachers use inductive modes of teaching, and some students within each ethnic group of color learn deductively. Many Asian American students seem to prefer questions that require specific answers but are proposed to the class as a whole. Many Latino students may be inclined toward learning in group contexts, but specific individuals may find these settings distracting and obstructive to their task mastery.

In traditional African American and Latino cultures, problem solving is highly contextual. One significant feature of this contextuality is creating a "stage" or "setting" prior to the performance of a task. The stage setting is invariably social in nature. It involves establishing personal connections with others who will participate as a prelude to addressing the task. In making these connections, individuals are readying themselves for "work" by cultivating a social context. They are, in effect, activating their cultural socialization concept that an individual functions better within the context of a group. Without the group as an anchor, referent, and catalyst, the individual is set adrift, having to function alone.

These cultural inclinations may be operating when Latino adults begin their task interactions with colleagues by inquiring about the families of other participants and their own personal well-being or when African American speakers inform the audience about their present psychoemotional disposition and declare the ideology, values, and assumptions underlying the positions they will be taking in the presentation (i.e., "where they are coming from"). This "preambling" is a way for the speakers to prime the audience and themselves for the subsequent performance. Students of color may be setting the stage for their engagement with learning tasks in classrooms (e.g., writing an essay, doing seatwork, taking a test) when they seem to be spending unnecessary time arranging their tests, sharpening pencils, shifting their body postures (stretching, flexing their hands, arms, and legs, etc.), or socializing with peers rather than attending to the assigned task. "Preparation before performance" for these students serves a similar purpose in learning as a theater performer doing yoga exercises before taking the stage. Both are techniques the "actors" use to focus, to get themselves in the mood and mode to perform.

Those Asian Americans who prefer to learn within the context of groups use a process of *collaborative and negotiated problem solving*. Regardless of how minor or significant an issue is, they seek out opinions and proposed solutions from all members of the constituted group. Each individual's ideas are presented and critiqued. Their merits are weighed against those suggested by every other member of the group. Discussions are animated and expansive so that all parties participate and understand the various elements of the negotiations. Eventually, a solution is reached that is a compromise of several possibilities. Then more discussions follow to ensue that everyone is in agreement with the solution and understands who is responsible for what aspects of its implementation. These discussions proceed in a context of congeniality and *consensus building* among the many, not with animosity, domination, and the imposition of the will of a few.

A compelling illustration of the positive effects of this process on student achievement occurred in Treisman's (1985; Fullilove & Treisman, 1990) Mathematics Workshop Program at the University of California, Berkeley. He observed the study habits of Chinese Americans to determine why they performed so well in high-level mathematics classes and if he could use their model with Latinos and African Americans. He found what others have observed more informally—the Chinese American students always studied in groups, and they routinely explained to each other their understanding of the problems and how they arrived at solutions to them. Treisman attributed their high achievement to the time they devoted to studying and to talking through their solutions with peers. When he simulated this process with African Americans and Latinos, their achievement improved radically. Treisman was convinced that "group study" made the difference. Given other evidence that compatibility between cultural habits and teaching/learning styles improves student performance, this is probably what occurred. Communal problem solving and the communicative impulse were evoked, thus producing the desired results.

These are powerful but challenging pedagogical lessons for all educators to learn and emulate in teaching students of color. Collective and situated performance styles require a distribution of resources (timing, collective efforts, procedures, attitudes) that can collide with school norms; for instance, much of how student achievement is assessed occurs in tightly scheduled arrangements, which do not accommodate stage setting or collective performance. Students of color have to learn different styles of performing, as well as the substantive content, to demonstrate their achievement. This places them in potential double jeopardy—that is, failing at the level of both procedure and substance. Pedagogical reform must be cognizant of these dual needs and attend simultaneously to the content of learning and the processes for demonstrating mastery. It also must be bidirectional—that is, changing instructional practices to make them more culturally responsive to ethnic and cultural diversity while teaching students of color how to better negotiate mainstream educational structures.

Organizing Ideas in Discourse

In addition to mode, the actual process of discourse engagement is influenced by culture and, in turn, influences the performance of students in schools. Several elements of the dynamics of discourse are discussed here to illustrate this point: organizing ideas, taking positions, conveying imagery and affect through language, and gender variations in conversational styles.

How ideas and thoughts are organized in written and spoken expression can be very problematic to student achievement. Two techniques are commonly identified—*topic-centered* and *topic-associative,* or *topic-chaining,* techniques. European Americans seem to prefer the first while Latinos, African Americans, Native Americans, and Native Hawaiians (Au, 1993; Heath, 1983) are inclined toward the second.

In *topic-centered* discourse, speakers focus on one issue at a time; arrange facts and ideas in logical, linear order; and make explicit relationships between facts and ideas. In this process, cognitive processing moves deductively from discrete parts to a cumulative whole with a discernible closure. Quality is determined by clarity of descriptive details, absence of unnecessary or flowery elaboration, and how well explanations remain focused on the essential features of the issue being analyzed. The structure, content, and delivery of this discourse style closely parallel the expository, descriptive writing and speaking commonly used in schools. A classic example of topic-centered discourse is journalistic writing, which concentrates on giving information about who, what, when, where, why, and how as quickly as possible. Its purpose is to convey information and to keep this separate from other speech functions, such as persuasion, commentary, and critique. Another illustration is the thinking and writing associated with empirical inquiry, or critical problem solving. Again, there is a hierarchical progression in the communication sequence—identifying the problem, collecting data, identifying alternative solutions and related consequences, and selecting and defending a solution. There is a clear attempt to separate facts from opinions, information from emotions.

A *topic-associative style* of talking and writing is episodic, anecdotal, thematic, and integrative. More than one issue is addressed at once. Related explanations unfold in overlapping, intersecting loops, with one emerging out of and building on others. Relationships among segments of the discourse are assumed or inferred rather than explicitly established (Cazden, 1988; Lee & Slaughter-Defoe, 1995). Thinking and speaking appear to be circular and seamless rather than linear and clearly demarcated. For one who is unfamiliar with it, this communication style sounds rambling, disjointed, and as if the speaker never ends a thought before going to something else.

Goodwin (1990) observed topic-chaining discourse at work in a mixed-age (4- to 14-year-olds) group of African Americans in a Philadelphia neighborhood as they told stories, shared gossip, settled arguments, and negotiated relationships. She noted the ease and finesse with which a child could switch from a contested verbal exchange to an engaging story and dramatically reshape dyadic interactions into multiparty ones. Using a single utterance, the children could evoke a broad history of events, a complex web of identities and relationships that all participants understood without having elaborate details on any of the separate segments. The talk-story discourse style among Native Hawaiians operates in a similar fashion, which explains why Au (1993) characterizes it as a "joint performance, or the cooperative production of responses by two or more speakers" (p. 113).

Two other commonplace examples are indicative of a topic-chaining or associative discourse style. One is used by many African Americans, who literarily try to attach or connect the sentences in a paragraph to each through the prolific use of conjunctive words and phrases—for example, frequently beginning sentences with "consequently," "therefore," "however," thus," "moreover," "additionally," and "likewise." These sentences are in close proximity to each other—sometimes as often as four of every five or six.

The second example illuminates the storytelling aspect of topic-chaining discourse. African Americans (Kochman, 1981, 1985; Smitherman, 1977) and Native Hawaiians (Boggs, 1985) have been described as not responding directly to questions asked. Instead, they give narratives, or tell stories. This involves setting up and describing a series of events (and the participants) loosely connected to the questions asked. It is as if ideas and thoughts, like individuals, do not function or find meaning in isolation from context. A host of other actors and events are evoked to assist in constructing the "stage" upon which the individuals eventually interject their own performance (i.e., answer the question). This narrative-response style is also signaled by the attention given to "introductions" and preludes in writing. They are extensive enough to prompt such comments from teachers as "Get to the point" or "Is this relevant?" or "More focus needed" or "Too much extraneous stuff" or "Stick to the topic." The students simply think that these preludes are necessary to setting the stage for the substantive elements of the discourse.

Storytelling as Topic-Chaining Discourse

Speaking about the purposes and pervasiveness of storytelling among African Americans, Smitherman (1977) surmises that they allow many different things to be accomplished at once. These include relating information, persuading others to support the speaker's point of view, networking, countering opposition, exercising power, and demonstrating one's own verbal aestheticism. She elaborates further:

> An ordinary inquiry [to African American cultural speakers] is likely to elicit an extended narrative response where the abstract point or general message will be couched in concrete story form. The reporting of events is never simply objectively reported, but dramatically acted out and narrated. The Black English speaker thus simultaneously conveys the facts and his or her personal sociopsychological perspective on the facts. . . . This meandering away from the "point" takes the listener on episodic journeys and over tributary rhetorical routes, but like the flow of nature's rivers and streams, stories all eventually lead back to the source. Though highly applauded by blacks, this narrative linguistic style is exasperating to whites who wish you'd be direct and hurry up and get to the point. (pp. 161, 148)

It takes African American topic-chaining speakers a while to get to the point—to orchestrate the cast of contributors to the action. The less time they have to develop their storylines, the more difficult it is for them to get to the substantive heart of the matter. Frequently in schools, the time allocated to learning experiences lapses while African Americans are still setting up the backdrop for "the drama"—their expected task performance—and they never get to demonstrate what they know or can do on the proposed academic task.

Posed to an African American student who routinely uses a topic-chaining discourse style, a simple, apparently straightforward question such as "What did you do during summer vacation?" might prompt a response such as the following:

> Sometimes, especially on holidays, you know, like July 4, or maybe when a friend was celebrating a birthday, we go to the amusement park. It's a long ways from where I live. And, that is always a big thing, because we have to get together and form car caravans. Jamie and Kelly are the best drivers, but I preferred to ride with Aisha because her dad's van is loaded, and we be just riding along, chilling, and listening to tapes and stuff. Going to the amusement park was a kick 'cause we had to drive a long way, and when we got there people would stare at us like we were weird or something. And we would just stare right back at them. All but Dion. He would start to act crazy, saying things like "What you lookin' at me for? I ain't no animal in no zoo. I got as much right to be here as you do." You see, Dion gets hyped real quick about this racist thing. And we be telling him, "Man, cool it. Don't start no stuff. We too far from home for that." Then, we just go on into the park and have us a good time. We try to get all the rides before everything closes down for the night. Then, there's the trip home. Everybody be tired but happy. We do this three or four times in the summer. Different people go each time. But, you know something—we always run into some kind of funny stuff, like people expecting us to make trouble. Why is that so? All we doing is out for a good time. Dion, of course, would say it's a racist thing.

The narrator does eventually answer the question, but it is embedded in a lot of other details. In fact, there are stories within stories within stories (e.g., celebration rituals, friendships, drivers, the drive, racism, risk taking, activities at the amusement park, similarities and differences, continuity and change, etc.). These elaborate details are needed to convey the full meaning of the narrator's answer to the initial question. But to culturally uninitiated listeners or readers, such as many classroom teachers, the account sounds like rambling and unnecessarily convoluted information, or Smitherman's (1977) notion of "belabored verbosity" (p. 161).

Teachers seeking to improve the academic performance of students of color who use topic-associative discourse styles need to incorporate a storytelling motif into their instructional behaviors. This can be done without losing any of the substantive quality of academic discourses. Gee (1989) believes topic-associative talking is inherently more complex, literary, and enriching than topic-centered speech. The assertions are verified by the success of the Kamehameha Early Elementary Program, which produced remarkable improvement in the literacy achievement of Hawaiian students by employing their cultural and communication styles in classroom instruction. Boggs (1985) found that the performance of Native Hawaiian students on the reading readiness tests correlated positively with narrative abilities. The children who told longer narratives more correctly identified the picture prompts than those who responded to individually directed questions from adults.

Yet topic-associative discourse is troubling to many conventional teachers. Michaels and Cazden's (1986) research explains why. The European American teachers who participated in their study found this discourse style difficult to understand and placed little value on it. African American teachers gave equal positive value to topic-centered and topic-associative discourse. We should not assume that this will always be the case. Some African American teachers are as troubled by topic-chaining discourse among students as teachers from other ethnic groups. The ethnicity of teachers is not the most compelling factor in culturally responsive teaching for ethnically diverse students. Rather, it is teachers' knowledge base and positive attitudes about cultural diversity, and their recognition of diverse cultural contributions, experiences, and perspectives, that enhance their ability to teach ethnically diverse students effectively.

Taking Positions and Presenting Self

In addition to significant differences in the *organization* of thinking, writing, and talking, many ethnically diverse students *relate* differently to the materials, issues, and topic discussed or analyzed. Most of the information available on these patterns deals with African and European Americans. Not much research has been done on the discourse dynamics of Latinos and Native Americans. Deyhle and Swisher (1997) concluded their historical view of research conducted on Native Americans with a strong conviction that there are fundamental and significant linkages among culture, communication, and cognition that should help shape classroom instruction for ethnically diverse students. But they do not provide any descriptions of the discourse dynamics of various Native American groups. Fox (1994) examined the thinking, writing, and speaking behavior of international students from different countries in Africa, Asia, Latin America, and the Middle East studying in U.S. colleges and universities. She found that their cultural traditions valued indirect and holistic communication, wisdom of the past, and the importance of the group. Their cultural socialization profoundly affects how these students interact with professors and classmates, reading materials, problem solving, and writing assignments. How they write is especially important to their academic performance because, according to Fox (1994), "writing touches the heart of a student's identity, drawing its voice and strength and meaning from the way the student understands the world" (p. xiii).

Personalizing or Objectifying Communications

Kochman (1972, 1981, 1985), Dandy (1991), and Smitherman (1977) point out that African Americans (especially those most strongly affiliated with the ethnic identity and cultural heritage) tend to take positions of advocacy and express personal points of view in discussions. Facts, opinions, emotions, and reason are combined in presenting one's case. The worth of a particular line of reasoning is established by challenging the validity of oppositional ideas and by the level of personal ownership of the individuals making the presentations. Declaring one's personal position on issues, and demanding the same of others, is also a way of recognizing "the person" as a valid data source (Kochman, 1981). Publication is not enough to certify the authority of ideas and explanations, or the expertise of the people who author them. They must stand the test of critical scrutiny and the depth of personal endorsement.

Consequently, Kochman (1981) proposes that African Americans are more likely to challenge authority and expertise than students from other ethnic groups. He suggests the following reason for this:

> Blacks . . . consider debate to be as much a contest between individuals as a test of opposing ideas. Because it is a contest, attention is also paid to performance, for winning the contest requires that one outperform one's opponents; outthink, outtalk, and outstyle. It means being concerned with art as well as argument. . . . [B]lacks consider it essential for individuals to have personal positions on issues and assume full responsibility for arguing their validity. Otherwise, they feel that individuals would not care enough about truth or their own ideas to want to struggle for them. And without such struggle, the value of ideas cannot be ascertained. (pp. 24–25)

According to Kochman (1981), the discourse dynamics of European Americans are almost the opposite of African Americans. He says they relate to issues and materials as spokespersons, not advocates, and consider the truth or merits of an idea to be intrinsic, especially if the person presenting it has been certified as an authority or expert. How deeply individuals personally care about the idea is irrelevant. Their responsibility is to present the facts as accurately as possible. They believe that emotions interfere with one's capacity to reason and quality of reasoning. Thus, European Americans try to avoid or minimize opposition in dialogue (especially when members of ethnic minority groups are involved) because they assume it will be confrontational, divisive, and lead to intransigence or the further entrenchment of opposing viewpoints. They aim to control impulse and emotions, to be open-minded and flexible, and to engage a multiplicity of ideas. Since no person is privy to all the answers, the best way to cull the variety of possibilities is to ensure congeniality, not confrontation, in conversation. As a result of these beliefs and desires, the European American style of intellectual and discourse engagement "weakens or eliminates those aspects of character or posture that they believe keep people's minds closed and make them otherwise unyielding" (Kochman, 1981, p. 20).

Playing with and on Words

African American cultural discourse uses repetition for emphasis and to create a cadence in speech delivery that approximates other aspects of cultural expressiveness such as dramatic flair, powerful imagery, persuasive effect, and polyrhythmic patterns (Baber, 1987; Kochman, 1981; Smitherman, 1977). Some individuals are very adept at "playing on" and "playing with" words, thereby creating a "polyrhythmic character" to their speaking. It is conveyed through the use of nonparallel structures, juxtaposition of complementary opposites, inclusion of a multiplicity of "voices," manipulation of word meanings, poetic tonality, creative use of word patterns, and an overall playfulness in language usage. Although decontextualized, this statement written by a graduate student illustrates some of these tendencies: "The use of culturally consistent communicative competencies entails teachers being able to recognize the multitude of distinct methods of communication that African American students bring to the classroom." Another example of these discourse habits is the frequent use of verb pairs. Following are some samples selected from the writings of students:

- A number of public issues to be explored and represented
- Numerous factors have impacted and influenced
- Make an attempt to analyze and interpret
- No model is available to interpret and clarify
- Many ways of explaining and understanding
- A framework that will enable and facilitate
- Validity was verified and confirmed
- He will describe and give account

Two other examples are helpful in illustrating the dramatic flair and poetic flavor of playing with words that characterize African American cultural discourse. One comes from Smart-Grosvenor (1982), who describes African American cultural communication as "a metaphorical configuration of verbal nouns, exaggerated adjectives, and double descriptives" (p. 138). She adds (and in the process demonstrates that which she explains) that "ours is an exciting, practical, elegant, dramatic, ironic, mysterious, surrealistic, sanctified, outrageous and creative form of verbal expression. It is a true treasure trove of vitality, profundity, rhythm—and, yes, style" (p. 138). Smitherman (1972) provides a second example of African American discourse style and aestheticism. She writes:

> The power of the word lies in its enabling us to translate vague feelings and fleeting experiences into forms that give unity, coherence, and expression to the inexpressible. The process of composing becomes a mechanism for discovery wherein we may generate illuminating revelations about a particular idea or event. (p. 91)

Ambivalence and Distancing in Communication

Classroom experiences and personal conversations with Asian international and Asian American college students and professional colleagues reveal some recurrent communication features. These individuals tend not to declare either definitive advocacy or adversarial positions in either oral or written discourse. They take moderate stances, seek out compromise positions, and look for ways to accommodate opposites. They are rather hesitant to analyze and critique but will provide factually rich descriptions of issues and events. They also use a great number of "hedges" and conciliatory markers in conversations—that is, "starts and stops," affiliative words, and apologetic nuances interspersed in speech, such as "I'm not sure," "maybe . . . ," "I don't know, but . . . ," "I may be wrong, but. . . ." These behaviors give the appearance of tentative, unfinished thinking, even though the individuals using them are very intellectually capable and thoroughly prepared academically. And many Asian and Asian American students are virtually silent in classroom discussions.

I have observed Asian and Asian American students frequently interjecting laughter into conversations with me about their academic performance. This happens in instructional and advising situations in which students are having difficulty understanding a learning task that is being explained by the teacher. Rather than reveal the full extent of their confusion, or lack of understanding, students will interject laughter into the conversations. It functions to defuse the intensity of their confusion and give the impression that the problem is not as serious as it really is. Teachers who are unaware of what is going on may interpret these behaviors to mean the students are not taking their feedback or advice seriously. Or they may assume that the students understand the issue so completely that they have reached a point in their intellectual processing where they can relax and break the mental focus (signaled by laughter). When queried about this practice, students invariably say "It's cultural" and often add an explanation for it that invokes some rule of social etiquette or interpersonal interaction that is taught in their ethnic communities. Interestingly, Japanese, Chinese, Korean, Taiwanese, and Cambodians offer similar explanations about the motivation behind and meaning of this shared behavior. These students explain that "ritualized laughter" is a means of maintaining harmonious relationships and avoiding challenging the authority or disrespecting the status of the teacher.

These communication behaviors among students of Asian origin are consistent with those reported by Fox (1994). Hers were gleaned from observations, interviews, and working with students from non-Western cultures and countries (Fox refers to them as "world majority students") on their analytical writing skills in basic writing courses at the Center for International Education at the University of Massachusetts. Data were collected over three years. Sixteen graduate students from several different disciplines participated in the formal interviews. They represented 12 countries: Korea, Japan, the People's Republic of China, Nepal, Indonesia, Brazil, India, Chile, Sri Lanka, Cote d'Ivoire, Somalia, and Cape Verde. Faculty members who worked closely with these students were also interviewed. Additional information was derived from informal conversations and interactions with other students; analysis of writing samples; the teacher's notes about how she and the students worked through writing difficulties; and students' explanations about what they were trying to say in their writing, why assignments were misunderstood, and connections among language, culture, and writing.

Among these students from different countries, several common writing habits emerged that conflict with formal writing styles of academe, known variously as academic argument, analytical or critical writing, and scholarly discourse (Fox, 1994). The characteristics and concerns included:

- Much background information and imprecise commentary
- Exaggeration for effect
- Prolific use of transitional markers, such as "moreover," "nevertheless," and "here again"
- Preference for contemplative instead of action words
- Much meandering around and digressions from the primary topic of discussion
- Emphasis on surrounding context rather than the subject itself
- Being suggestive and trying to convey feelings instead of being direct and concise and providing proof or specific illustrations, as is the expectation of academic writing in the United States
- Tendency to communicate through subtle implications
- Great detail and conversational tonality
- Elaborate and lengthy introductions
- Reticence to speak out, to declare personal positions, and to make one's own ideas prominent in writing

Although all the students shared these communication tendencies, according to Fox's (1994) study, how they were expressed in actual behaviors varied widely. Culturally different meanings of "conversational tone" illustrate this point. Fox notes:

> In Spanish or Portuguese . . . speakers and writers may be verbose, rambling, digressive, holistic, full of

factual details, full of feeling, sometimes repetitious, sometimes contradictory, without much concern for literal meanings. In many Asian and African languages and cultures, metaphor, euphemism, innuendo, hints, insinuation, and all sorts of subtle nonverbal strategies—even silence—are used both to spare the listeners possible embarrassment or rejection, and to convey meanings that they are expected to grasp. (p. 22)

These descriptions of Asian American and non-Western student discourse are based on observations and conversations with a small number of people, in college classes and professional settings. How widespread they are across other educational settings, ethnic groups, generations of immigrants, and social circumstances is yet to be determined. Much more description and substantiation of these communicative inclinations are needed.

The explanation of Asian students that their discourse styles are cultural is elaborated by Chan (1991), Kitano and Daniels (1995), and Nakanishi (1994). They point to traditional values and socialization that emphasize collectivism, saving face, maintaining harmony, filial piety, interdependence, modesty in self-presentation, and restraint in taking oppositional points of view. Leung (1998) suggests some ways these values translate to behavior in learning situations, which underscore the observations made by Fox. Students socialized in this way are less likely to express individual thoughts, broadcast their individual accomplishments, and challenge or disagree with people in positions of authority, especially in public arenas. These interpretations echo the connections between Asian American culture and communicative styles provided by Kim (1978). She suggests that one of their major functions is to promote social harmony and build community. Consequently, many Asian American students may avoid confrontations as well as the expression of negative feelings or opinions in classroom discourse.

GENDER VARIATIONS IN DISCOURSE STYLES

Most of the detailed information on gender variations in classroom communication involves European Americans. Some inferences can be made about probable gender discourse styles among African, Latino, Native, and Asian Americans from their cultural values and gender socialization, since culture and communication are closely interrelated.

Females Communicate Differently from Males

Lakoff (1975) was among the first to suggest that different lexical, syntactical, pragmatic, and discourse features existed for females and males. She identified nine speech traits prolific among females that are summarized by L. Crawford (1993) as specialized vocabulary for homemaking and caregiving, mild forms of expletives, adjectives that convey emotional reactions but no substantive information, tag comments that are midway between questions and statements, exaggerated expressiveness, super polite forms, hedges or qualifiers, hypercorrect grammar, and little use of humor.

Other research indicates that European American females use more affiliating, accommodating, and socially bonding language mechanisms, while males are more directive, managing, controlling, task focused, and action oriented in their discourse styles. Girls speak more politely and tentatively, use less forceful words, are less confrontational, and are less intrusive when they enter into conversations. By comparison, boys interrupt more; use more commands, threats, and boast of authority; and give information more often (Austin, Salem, & Lefller, 1987; M. Crawford, 1995; Grossman & Grossman, 1994; Hoyenga & Hoyenga, 1979; Maccoby, 1988; Simkins-Bullock & Wildman, 1991; Tannen, 1994). Because of these gender patterns, Maccoby (1988) concludes that "speech serves more egotistic functions among boys and more socially binding functions among girls" (p. 758).

These general trends were substantiated by Johnstone (1993) in a study of spontaneous conversational storytelling of men and women friends. The women's stories tended to be about groups of people (women and men) engaged in supportive relationships and the importance of community building. The men's stories were more about conquests (physical, social, nature) in which individuals acted alone. Invariably, the characters were nameless men who did little talking but engaged in some kind of physical action. More details were given about places, times, and things than about people. Based on these findings, Johnstone suggests that women are empowered through cooperation, interdependence, collaboration, and community. For men, power comes from individuals "conquering" and acting in opposition to others.

Research by Gray-Schlegel and Gray-Schlegel (1995–1996) on the creative writing of third- and sixth-grade students produced similar results. They examined 170 creative writing samples of 87 students to determine if differences existed in how control, outcomes, relationships, and violence were used. Clear gender patterns emerged. Both boys and girls placed male characters in active roles more often than females, but this tendency increased with age only for the males. Females were more optimistic about the fate of their characters, while males were inclined to be cynical. Boys usually had their protagonists acting alone, while girls had them acting in conjunction with others. Regardless of age or the gender of the story character, boys included more crime and violence in their narratives.

Gender Communication Patterns Established Early in Life

These kinds of gender-related discourse patterns are established well before third grade, as research by Nicolopoulou, Scales, and Weintraub (1994) revealed. They examined the symbolic imagination of four-year-olds as expressed in the kinds of stories they told. The girls' stories included more order and social realism. These concepts were conveyed through the use of coherent plots with stable characters, continuous plot lines, and social and familial relationships as the primary topics of and contexts for problem solving. Their stories emphasized cyclical patterns of everyday domestic life, along with romantic and fairy tale images of kings and queens, princesses and princes. They were carefully constructed, centered, and coherent, with elaborate character and theme development, and were invariably directed toward harmonious conflict resolution.

Whenever threatening disruptive situations occurred, the girls were careful to reestablish order before concluding their stories. The boys' stories contained much more disorder and a picaresque, surrealistic aesthetic style. These traits were apparent in the absence of stable, clearly defined characters, relationships, and plots; large, powerful, and frightening characters; violence, disruption, and conflict; and a series of loosely associated dramatic images, actions, and events.

The boys were not concerned with resolving conflicts before their stories ended. Instead, action, novelty, excess, defiance, destruction, and often escalating and startling imagery drove their plots.

In summarizing differences between how boys and girls construct stories, Nicolopoulou and associates (1994) made some revealing observations that should inform instructional practices. They noted that the stories produced by girls focused on "creating, maintaining, and elaborating structure." In comparison, the stories boys told emphasized "action and excitement" and involved a restless energy that is often difficult for them to manage (p. 110). Furthermore, the boys and girls dealt with danger, disorder, and conflict very differently. The girls' strategy was *implicit avoidance* while the boys' technique was *direct confrontation.*

Another fascinating verification of theorized gender differences in communication is provided by Otnes, Kim, and Kim (1994). They analyzed 344 letters written to Santa Claus (165 from boys and 179 from girls). Although the age of the authors was not specified, they were probably eight years old or younger, since children stop believing in Santa Claus at about this time. The content of the letters was analyzed to determine the use of six kinds of semantic units, or meaning phrases: (1) polite or socially accepted forms of ingratiation, (2) context-oriented references, (3) direct requests, (4) requests accompanied by qualifiers, (5) affectionate appeals, and (6) altruistic requests of gifts for someone other than self. For the most part, results of the study confirmed the hypothesized expectations. Girls wrote longer letters, made more specific references to Christmas, were more polite, used more indirect requests, and included more expressions of affection. By comparison, boys made more direct requests. There were no differences between boys and girls in the number of toys requested or the altruistic appeals made. Findings such as these provide evidence about the extent and persistence of patterns of culturally socialized communicative behaviors.

Early gender patterns of communication may transfer to other kinds of social and educational interactions. They also can entrench disadvantages that will have long-term negative effects on student achievement. Interventions to achieve more comparable communications skills for male and female students should begin early and continue throughout the school years. Efforts should also be undertaken in both research and classroom situations to determine if or how communicative styles are differentiated by gender in ethnic groups other than European Americans.

Undoubtedly some differences do exist, since discourse styles are influenced by cultural socialization, and males and females are socialized to communicate differently in various ethnic groups.

Problems with Gendered Communication Styles

The "gendered" style of communication may be more problematic than the gender of the person doing the communicating. If this is so, then a female who is adept at using discourse techniques typically associated with males will not be disadvantaged in mainstream social interactions. Conversely, males who communicate in ways usually ascribed to females will lose their privileged status. Hoyenga and Hoyenga (1979) offer some support for this premise. In their review of research on gender and communication, they report that "feminine communication styles" are associated with less intelligence, passivity, and submissiveness, while "masculine styles" evoke notions of power, authority, confidence, and leadership.

However, M. Crawford (1995) suggests that some of the claims about female–male communication differences need to be reconsidered. For example, indirectness and equivocation in communication are not inherently strategies of female subordination or dominance. They can be tools of power or powerlessness as well. Interpretations of speech behaviors may depend more on the setting, the speaker's status and communicative ability, and the relationship to listeners rather than the person's gender per se (Tannen, 1994). Sadker and Sadker (1994) propose that males may be at greater *emotional risk* than females because of their role socialization. Girls are encouraged to be caring and emotionally expressive, but boys are taught to deny their feelings and to be overly cautious about demonstrating how deeply they care. Thus, male advantages in conventional conceptions of academic discourse may be countered somewhat by the psychoemotional and social advantages that females have in interpersonal relations.

CONCLUSION

Communication is strongly culturally influenced, experientially situated, and functionally strategic. It is a dynamic set of skills and performing arts whose rich nuances and delivery styles are open to many interpretations and instructional possibilities. Ethnic discourse patterns are continually negotiated because people talk in many different ways for many different reasons. Sometimes the purpose of talking and writing is simply to convey information. It is also used to persuade and entertain; to demonstrate sharing, caring, and connections; to express contentment and discontentment; to empower and subjugate; to teach and learn; and to convey reflections and declare personal preferences. In imagining and implementing culturally responsive pedagogical reform, teachers should not merely make girls talk more like boys, or boys talk more like girls, or all individuals within and across ethnic groups talk like each other. Nor should they assume that all gender differences in communication styles are subsumed by ethnicity or think that gender, social class, and education obliterate all ethnic nuances. Instead, we must be mindful that communication styles are multidimensional and multimodal, shaped by many different influences. Although culture is paramount among these, other critical influences include ethnic affiliation, gender, social class, personality, individuality, and experiential context.

The information in this essay has described some of the patterns, dynamics, and polemics of the discourse styles of different ethnicities and groups. Since communication is essential to both teaching and learning, it is imperative that it be a central part of instructional reforms designed to improve the school performance of underachieving African, Native, Asian, and European American students. The more teachers know about the discourse styles of ethnically diverse students, the better they will be able to improve academic achievement. Change efforts should attend especially to discourse dynamics as opposed to linguistic structures. The reforms should be directed toward creating better agreement between the communication patterns of underachieving ethnically diverse students and those considered "normal" in schools.

Knowledge about general communication patterns among ethnic groups is helpful, but it alone is not enough. Teachers need to translate it to their own particular instructional situations. This contextualization might begin with some self-study exercises in which teachers examine their preferred discourse modes and dynamics, and determine how students from different ethnic groups respond to them. They should also learn to recognize the discourse habits of students from different ethnic groups. The purposes of these analyses are to identify (1) habitual discourse features of ethnically diverse students; (2) conflictual and complementary points among these discourse styles; (3) how, or if, conflictual points are negotiated by students; and (4) features of the students' discourse patterns that are problematic for the teacher. The results can be used to pinpoint and prioritize specific places to begin interventions for change.

Whether conceived narrowly or broadly, and expressed formally or informally, communication is the quintessential medium of teaching and learning. It is also inextricably linked to culture and cognition. Therefore, if teachers are to better serve the school achievement needs of ethnically diverse students by implementing culturally responsive teaching, they must learn how to communicate differently with them. To the extent they succeed in doing this, achievement problems could be reduced significantly.

References

Abrahams, R. D. (1970). *Positively Black.* Englewood Cliffs, NJ: Prentice-Hall.

Asante, M. K. (1998). *The afrocentric idea* (Rev. and exp. ed.). Philadelphia: Temple University Press.

Ascher, M. (1992). *Ethnomathematics.* New York: Freeman.

Au, K. R. (1980). Participation structures in a reading lesson with Hawaiian children: Analysis of a culturally appropriate instructional event. *Anthropology and Education Quarterly, 11,* 91–115.

Au, K. R. (1993). *Literacy instruction in multicultural settings.* New York: Harcourt Brace.

Au, K. R., & Kawakami, A. J. (1985). Research currents: Talk story and learning to read. *Language Arts, 62,* 406–411.

Au, K. R., & Kawakami, A. J. (1991). Culture and ownership: Schooling of minority students. *Childhood Education, 67,* 280–284.

Au, K. R., & Kawakami, A. J. (1994). Cultural congruence in instruction. In E. R. Rolling, J. E. King, & W. C. Hayman (Eds.), *Teaching diverse populations: Formulating a knowledge base* (pp. 5–23). Albany: State University of New York Press.

Au, K. P., & Mason, I. M. (1981). Social organizational factors in learning to read: The balance of rights hypothesis. *Reading Research Quarterly, 17,* 115–152.

Austin, A. M. B., Salem, M., & Leflier, A. (1987). Gender and developmental differences in children's conversations. *Sex Roles, 16,* 497–510.

Baber, C. R. (1987). The artistry and artifice of Black communication. In G. Gay & W. L. Baber (Eds.), *Expressively Black: The cultural basis of ethnic identity* (pp. 75–108). New York: Praeger.

Belensky, M. F., Clinchy, B. M., Goldberger, N. R., & Tarule, I. M. (1986). *Women's ways of knowing: The development of self, voice, and mind.* New York: Basic Books.

Boggs, S. T. (1985). The meaning of questions and narratives to Hawaiian children. In C. B. Cazden, V. H. John, & D. Hymes (Eds.), *Functions of language in the classroom* (pp. 299–327). Prospect Heights, IL: Waveland.

Boggs, S. T., Watson-Gegeo, K., & McMillen, G. (1985). *Speaking, relating, and learning: A Study of Hawaiian children at home and at school.* Norwood, NJ: Ablex.

Bruner, I. (1996). *The culture of education.* Cambridge, MA: Harvard University Press.

Byers, P., & Byers, H. (1985). Nonverbal communication and the education of children. In C. B. Cazden, V. P. John, & D. Hymes (Eds.), *Functions of language in the classroom* (pp. 3–31). Prospect Heights, IL: Waveland.

Carroll, J. B. (Ed.). (1956). *Language, thought, and reality: Selected writings of Benjamin Lee Whorf.* Cambridge, MA: MIT Press.

Cazden, C. B. (1988). *Classroom discourse: The language of teaching and learning.* Portsmouth, NH: Heinemann.

Chan, S. (Ed.). (1991). *Asian Americans: An interpretative history.* Boston: Twayne.

Crawford, L. W. (1993). *Language and literacy learning in multicultural classrooms.* Boston: Allyn & Bacon.

Crawford, M. (1995). *Talking difference: On gender and language.* Thousand Oaks, CA: Sage.

Dandy, E. B. (1991). *Black communications: Breaking down the barriers.* Chicago: African American Images.

Deyhle, D., & Swisher, K. (1997). Research in American Indian and Alaska native education: From assimilation to self-determinations. In M. W. Apple (Ed.), *Review of research in education* (Vol. 22, pp. 113–194). Washington, DC: American Educational Research Association.

Fox, H. (1994). *Listening to the world: Cultural issues in academic writing.* Urbana, IL: National Council of Teachers of English.

Fullilove, R. E., & Treisman, P. U. (1990). Mathematics achievement among African Americans undergraduates at the University of California, Berkeley: An evaluation of the Mathematics Workshop Program. *Journal of Negro Education, 59,* 463–478.

Gallimore, R., Boggs, J. W., & Jordon, C. (1974). *Culture, behavior and education: A study of Hawaiian Americans.* Beverly Hills, CA: Sage.

Gee, J. P. (1989). What is literacy? *Journal of Education, 171,* 18–25.

Giamati, C., & Weiland, M. (1997). An exploration of American Indian students' perceptions of patterning, symmetry, and geometry. *Journal of American Indian Education, 36,* 27–48.

Goodlad, J. I. (1984). *A place called school: Prospects for the future.* New York: McGraw-Hill.

Goodwin, M. H. (1990). *He-said she-said: Talk as social organization among Black children.* Bloomington: Indiana University Press.

Gray-Schlegel, M. A., & Gray-Schlegel, T. (1995–1996). An investigation of gender stereotypes as revealed through children's creative writing. *Reading Research and Instruction, 35,* 160–170.

Grossman, H., & Grossman, S. H. (1994). *Gender issues in education.* Boston: Allyn & Bacon.

Heath, S. B. (1983). *Ways with words: Language, life, and work in communities and classrooms.* Cambridge, England: Cambridge University Press.

Hoijer, H. (1991). The Sapir–Whorf hypothesis. In L. A. Samovar & R. E. Porter (Eds.), *Intercultural communication: A reader* (6th ed., pp. 244–251). Belmont, CA: Wadsworth.

Hoyenga, K. B., & Hoyenga, K. T. (1979). *The question of sex differences: Psychological, cultural, and biological issues.* Boston: Little Brown.

Hymes, D. (1985). Introduction. In C. B. Cazden, V. P. John, & D. Hymes (Eds.), *Functions of language in the classroom* (pp. xi–xvii). Prospect Heights, IL: Waveland.

Johnstone, B. (1993). Community and contest: Midwestern men and women creating their worlds in conversational storytelling. In D. Tannen (Ed.), *Gender and conversational interaction* (pp. 62–80). New York: Oxford University Press.

Kim, B. L. (1978). *The Asian Americans: Changing patterns, changing needs.* Montclair, NJ: Association for Korean Christian Scholars of North America.

Kitano, H., & Daniels, R. (1995). *Asian Americans: Emerging minorities* (2nd ed.). Englewood Cliffs, NJ: Prentice-Hall.

Klein, S. S. (Ed.). (1982). *Handbook for achieving sex equity through education.* Baltimore: Johns Hopkins University Press.

Kochman, T. (Ed.). (1972). *Rappin' and stylin' out: Communication in urban Black America.* Urbana: University of Illinois Press.

Kochman, T. (1981). *Black and White styles in conflict.* Chicago: University of Chicago Press.

Kochman, T. (1985). Black American speech events and a language program for the classroom. In C. B. Cazden, V. P. John, & D. Hymes (Eds.), *Functions of language in the classroom* (pp. 211–261). Prospect Heights, IL: Waveland.

Lakoff, R. (1975). *Language and women's place.* New York: Harper & Row.

Lee, C. D., & Slaughter-Defoe, D. T. (1995). Historical and sociocultural influences on African American education. In J. A. Banks & C. A. M. Banks (Eds.), *Handbook of research on multicultural education* (pp. 348–371). New York: Macmillan.

Leung, B. P. (1998). Who are Chinese American, Japanese American, and Korean American children? In V. O. Pang & L-R. L. Cheng (Eds.), *Struggling to be heard: The unmet needs of Asian Pacific American children* (pp. 11–26). Albany: State University of New York Press.

Longstreet, W. (1978). *Aspects of ethnicity: Understanding differences in pluralistic classrooms.* New York: Teachers College Press.

Maccoby, E. E. (1988). Gender as a social category. *Developmental Psychology, 24,* 755–765.

Maltz, D. N., & Borker, R. A. (1983). A cultural approach to male–female miscommunication. In J. J. Gumperz (Ed.), *Communication, language, and social identity* (pp. 196–216). Cambridge, England: Cambridge University Press.

Mandelbaum, D. G. (Ed.). (1968). *Selected writings of Edward Sapir in language, culture and personality.* Berkeley: University of California Press.

Michaels, S., & Cazden, C. B. (1986). Teacher/child collaboration as oral preparation for literacy. In B. B. Schietfelin & P. Gilmore (Eds.), *The acquisition of literacy: Ethnographic perspectives* (pp. 132–154). Norwood, NJ: Ablex.

Montague, A., & Matson, F. (1979). *The human connection.* New York: McGraw-Hill.

Nakanishi, D. (1994). *Asian American educational experience.* New York: Routledge.

Nicolopoulou, A., Scales, B., & Weintraub, J. (1994). Gender differences and symbolic imagination in the stories of four-year-olds. In A. H. Dyson & C. Genishi (Eds.), *The need for story: cultural diversity in classroom and community* (pp. 102–123). Urbana, IL: National Council of Teachers of English.

Otnes, C., Kim, K., & Kim, Y. C. (1994). Yes, Virginia, there is a gender difference: Analyzing children's requests to Santa Claus. *Journal of Popular Culture, 28,* 17–29.

Pasteur, A. B., & Toldson, I. L. (1982). *Roots of soul: The psychology of Black expressiveness.* Garden City, NY: Anchor Press/Doubleday.

Philips, S. U. (1983). *The invisible culture: Communication in classroom and community on the Warm Springs Indian Reservation.* Prospect Heights, IL: Waveland.

Porter, R. E., & Samovar, L. A. (1991). Basic principles of intercultural communication. In L. A. Samovar & R. E. Porter (Eds.), *Intercultural communication: A reader* (6th ed., pp. 5–22). Belmont, CA: Wadsworth.

Ramirez, M., III, & Castañeda, A. (1974). *Cultural democracy, bicognitive development and education.* New York: Academic Press.

Sadker, M., & Sadker, D. (1994). *Failing at fairness: How our schools cheat girls.* New York: Touchstone.

Sapir, E. (1968). The status of linguistics as a science. In D. G. Mandelbaum (Ed.), *Selected writings of Edward Sapir in language, culture and personality* (pp. 160–166). Berkeley: University of California Press.

Shade, B. J. (Ed.). (1989). *Culture, style, and the educative process.* Springfield, IL: Thomas.

Shade, B. J. (1994). Understanding the African American learner. In E. R. Hollins, J. E. King, & W. C. Hayman (Eds.), *Teaching diverse populations* (pp. 175–189). Albany: State University of New York Press.

Simkins-Bullock, J. A., & Wildman, B. G. (1991). An investigation into the relationship between gender and language. *Sex Roles, 24,* 149–160.

Smart-Grosvenor, V. (1982). We got a way with words. *Essence, 13,* 138.

Smith, B. O. (1971). On the anatomy of teaching. In R. T. Hyman (Ed.), *Contemporary thought on teaching* (pp. 20–27). Englewood Cliffs, NJ: Prentice-Hall.

Smitherman, G. (1972). Black power is Black language. In G. M. Simmons, H. D. Hutchinson, & H. E. Summons (Eds.), *Black culture: Reading and writing Black* (pp. 85–91). New York: Holt, Rinehart & Winston.

Smitherman, G. (1977). *Talkin' and testifyin': The language of Black America.* Boston: Houghton Mifflin.

Tannen, D. (1990). *You just don't understand: Women and men in conversation.* New York: Morrow.

Tannen, D. (1994). *Gender and discourse.* New York: Oxford University Press.

Tharp, R. G., & Gallimore, R. (1988). *Rousing minds to life: Teaching, learning, and schooling in social context.* Cambridge, England: Cambridge University Press.

Treisman, P. U. (1985). *A study of the mathematics achievement of Black students at the University of California, Berkeley.* Unpublished doctoral dissertation, University of California, Berkeley.

Vygotsky, L. S. (1962). *Thought and language.* Cambridge, MA: MIT Press.

Whorf, B. L. (1952). *Collected papers on metalinguistics.* Washington, DC: Department of State, Foreign Service Institute.

Whorf, B. L. (1956). Language, mind, and reality. In J. B. Carroll (Ed.), *Language, thought and reality: Selected writings of Benjamin Lee Whorf* (pp. 246–270). Cambridge, MA: MIT Press.

Concepts and Questions

1. In what ways do students' communication abilities affect teachers' perceptions of students?
2. How important is language in the performance and effectiveness of teachers?
3. Beyond the transmission of information, what other purposes does Gay suggest that language serves?
4. What does Gay mean when she says "languages and communication styles are systems of cultural notations and the means through which thoughts and ideas are expressively embodied"?
5. What does Gay mean when she uses the term "discourse structures"?
6. Distinguish between *passive-receptive* and *participatory-interactive* styles of discourse.
7. Describe the methods employed by many African American students to gain entry into conversations. How does this style differ from the communication styles of Native Hawaiian students?
8. Describe differences in problem-solving styles among African Americans, Latinos, Native Americans, and Asian American students.
9. Distinguish between *topic-centered, topic-associative,* and *topic-chaining* techniques in organizing ideas in discourse. Which methods are associated with which cultural groupings of students?
10. How does the African American storytelling style function as topic-chaining discourse?
11. Distinguish between female and male communication styles.

Social Dynamics of the Multicultural Classroom

JOHANN LE ROUX

INTRODUCTION

Classrooms are social contexts where participants are in continual interaction. They are dynamic meeting spaces for teachers and learners alike. Not only these actors but also cultural and/or ethnic diversity and the curriculum interact here. Instruction and learning are socially embedded activities, where social forces such as classroom atmosphere, social feelings, cultural sentiments, prejudice and stereotyping, interpersonal relations, and expectations, as well as the reflection of social reality in the curriculum, all have a significant influence on the effectiveness of teaching and learning. A student's image of his or her self-worth is formed through interaction and feedback received from others. This, in turn, has a direct influence on relations, achievement, and social behaviour in multicultural classrooms. James (1890) first recognised the impact of others on the appraisal of the self:

> A man's social self . . . is the recognition which he gets from his mates . . . a man has as many social selves as there are individuals who recognise him and carry an image of him in their minds. To wound any of these images is to wound him.

LANGUAGE ISSUES IN MULTICULTURAL CLASSROOMS

In numerous schools the nonstandard language of marginalised ethnic and culture group students is used almost exclusively as a guide to their potential for academic achievement and to their worth as human beings. This is a reality in any diversified and stratified society where variations in vocabulary, syntax, accent, and discourse style are socially or culturally determined. In all multicultural societies around the world close-knit social or ethnic groups use a range of language varieties. Often many children arrive at school with little or no prior contact with the language medium of formal education. The result is that these children are penalised for not knowing the language variety that is accorded high status in the school. Discrimination against nonstandard language is quite common in various policies and school practices, even among those that call for linguistic tolerance. The evidence that language differences can serve to promote stereotypes and thus activate prejudices in multicultural classrooms is well documented in the scientific literature (Corson, 1998). The dangerous reality is that teacher perceptions of student ability are often influenced by the student's proficiency, or lack thereof, in terms of the standard language varieties that are prevalent in school and in society.

Educational success depends to a great extent on students' ability to "display" knowledge, usually through the spoken or written use of words in school. Young students' display of a language is often the first contact that classroom teachers have with them. Assessment of academic ability is based on verbal and written use of language on which the teacher (as the assessor) determines a student's academic fate. Formal education is to a large extent a process of teaching the rules of using words and other signs used in academic discourse. Assessment then becomes a formalised set of procedures used to judge how well those rules have been mastered. Language touches on every aspect of education. It is the medium of instruction, the content of instruction, and it provides the pedagogical means by which instruction is realised. Every outcome that schools attempt to achieve depends on the language ability of students. After the school period students' life chances will be determined by their ability to interact through language usage with different discourses around them. This means that language development is empowering for students, because the brain does not create language: language creates and actualises the brain's potential (Corson, 1998).

Educational success at school is affected by factors such as race, culture, gender, environmental influence, socioeconomic class, and genetic ability as well. Theoretically, if these variables could be taken out of the equation, the most important factor in academic success or failure would be a student's ability to have acquired and use written or spoken language in a functional manner.

In schools the culture-bound use of language, which is often unevenly distributed among different ethnic or cultural groups represented in class, is frequently applied as the sole determinant when assessing the quality of student thought and performance. A lack of an adequate English vocabulary severely affects the academic progress of many students from cultural and language groups other than the mainstream one. The danger is that language proficiency and not academic ability is being assessed in multicultural classrooms. Although the importance of language ability for academic success cannot be denied, it needs to be acknowledged by the multicultural teacher as one of a number of factors operating in the educational process. Lately, a good deal of concern has been expressed about the overemphasis on vocabulary skills in education (Garcia, 1991). Effective assessment of a diverse student population therefore has to make use of various assessment techniques and procedures to be applied on a continuous basis throughout the school year.

The relationship between language and sociocultural background needs to be emphasised: often people who are sociologically similar are linguistically similar as well. A school's academic culture is more linguistically similar to the dominant social groups in society than it is to ethnic or cultural minority groups present in a culturally diverse society. Differences in student vocabulary correlate directly with parental levels of education and with quality-of-life levels in general. Early achievement disparities tend to increase with age. It is an alarming reality that schools today do little to narrow these differential gaps in language ability and correlated academic achievement. Language enrichment sources and courses have to be made accessible to minority culture students, in order to be integrated into their own cultural meaning systems. Schools often tend to undervalue the richness of the cultural capital that students from diverse backgrounds bring to school. Reconstructing the school in a more student-accommodative way would accommodate student literacy needs more effectively as well.

Schools also need to support and encourage the value of minority cultures' native languages. It is understandable that no school can totally accommodate the often wide diversity of languages represented in multicultural schools. To expect minority languages to suddenly appear on every school's curriculum would be an idealistic and unrealistic expectation. However, schools can and should explicitly demonstrate appreciation and value for languages other than the mainstream languages in use. This is important, even in schools where English is the sole medium of instruction. To value a culture's language as an integral part of its cultural heritage is to demonstrate positive regard for that particular cultural group. This will positively affect the self-images of students from that particular culture and may enhance intercultural exchange and positive intercultural regard and appreciation in multicultural schools. When the school officially acknowledges students' native languages, it will impact in a positive way on social processes in the classroom (Corson, 1998; Auerbach, 1997) .

SOCIAL JUDGMENT AND STEREOTYPING IN THE MULTICULTURAL CLASSROOM

Social judgment and stereotyping are part of, and present in, all social encounters. Research has indicated, for instance, that teachers tend to award higher marks for the same assignment when submitted by a student with a particular name. Such research also shows that physically attractive persons are believed to have more desirable personalities, have higher (work and social) status, enjoy more fulfilling lives, and are better parents and students. Negative teacher attitudes towards the speech of culturally and socially different students in multicultural classrooms affect teacher expectations, which subsequently affect student academic performance. A long-standing finding of research (Corson, 1998) is that teachers' perceptions of students' speech leads to negative expectations about their personalities, social and cultural backgrounds, and academic abilities. Although teacher awareness of this key injustice stretches back over more than a generation, in practice it has not lessened the negative impact of such stereotyping in culturally diverse settings. The reality and severity of stereotyping become even more of a problem when the teacher is confronted by a classroom consisting of different ethnic or cultural groups.

According to Miller (in Foster, 1990), stereotyping as a concept refers to any generalisation about a particular social group, thus reflecting an inaccurate description of that group. More often, however, stereotyping refers to grossly inaccurate and exaggerated generalisations. Hewstone and Giles (1986) list the following descriptive aspects of stereotyping as they pertain to multicultural classrooms:

- Stereotyping stems from illusory correlation between students' group affiliations and their psychological attributes and traits.
- Stereotypes influence the way information is processed about members of groups. More favourable information is remembered about in-groups, while more unfavourable information is remembered about out-groups.
- Stereotypes create expectations about other people. The holders of stereotypes often search for information and behavioural patterns in others to confirm those expectations.
- Stereotypes restrict their holders' patterns of communication and promote communication that confirms the stereotypes held (and thus create self-fulfilling prophecies, described later in this section).

Evidence suggests that teachers' expectations can be influenced by the stereotypes they have of students in their classroom. Physical differences are often associated with particular ethnic or racial groups. In the United States research on prejudice shows that skin colour is the most salient characteristic that influences people's perception and judgment of each other. Students with a lighter skin tend to be more acceptable to teachers in multicultural classroom settings. Studies of classroom interaction in the United States (Bennett, 1990) have also demonstrated that teachers have higher expectations for and communicate more frequently with white students or those with a lighter complexion (than with a black, Hispanic, or other darker-skinned one). Although these teachers might be unaware of their unequal and dualistic treatment of students, they have accepted the racist view that a student's physical traits determine his or her social behaviour, intellectual abilities, and personality traits. This rigid form of prejudiced social judgment affects the formation of social relations in the classroom and impacts negatively on minority culture children's self-concepts and school achievement.

Clifford and Walster (1973) examined the effect of physical attractiveness on teacher expectations. It was found that a student's physical appearance is significantly related to the teacher's expectations of a student's intelligence and to predictions regarding academic success, as well as to predictions regarding the student's popularity and social attractiveness amongst the peer group. Communication skills and accents were also found to relate positively to particular negative teacher expectations and stereotypes. This has specific implications in the multicultural classroom where students often have to communicate in a language other than their mother tongue. Once students recognise that differences between people exist, a gradual belief can develop that these differences are important. Whereas one's in-group will tend to be viewed as "normal," others are viewed as "abnormal." Others are judged from the unique cultural context of the child, who uncritically adopts the in-group's values as objective reality and uses this as the context in order to judge other people and events. Prejudice literally means *judging in advance*. Negative attitudes towards other groups develop in the face of, or in the absence of, evidence to the contrary. Ethnocentrism, as a generalised attitude of preference for one's own group, develops and often leads to the stereotyping of others as being inferior or objects of contempt or hatred (Thomas, 1984).

Stereotyping involves grouping people, objects, and events around us into classes and responding to them in terms of their class membership rather than their uniqueness (Bruner, Goodnow, & Austin, 1956). People's evaluations of others different from themselves are influenced by their particular frames of reference that are usually culturally determined. These often inaccurate assumptions are usually viewed as fixed or absolute and influence communications towards and expectations of others. Often teachers fall into the pitfall of making unsubstantial generalisations about students and tend to categorise them and treat them accordingly. The labeling of students as "stupid," "difficult," "lazy," and the like usually results in images and behaviour from students to fit and "live" these (often ungrounded) images. Stereotyping or labeling is often situation or event specific with regard to one's own ethnic group and can be changed from one situation to the next. However, stereotypes with respect to race and ethnicity have proven especially difficult to change.

Numerous researchers have emphasised the reality of ethnic categorisation and stereotyping in multicultural school settings. Several arguments against the process of stereotyping have been developed in literature (Saunders, 1982):

- It is unacceptable from a humanistic view to categorise people.
- Often categorisation negates individualisation and differentiation.
- Stereotyping usually implies negative images based on inaccurate data.
- Stereotyping implies the categorisation of people based on inborn unchangeable characteristics.
- The assumption is that one's own group represents the norm from which others are judged.
- Categorisation leads to self-fulfilling prophecies.
- Stereotyping is objectionable to individuals who are stereotyped.
- Stereotyping is acquired through learning and can be unlearned.
- Stereotyping is not reconcilable with the principles of democracy, equality, and pluralism, especially in the multicultural class or societal contexts.

Although people cannot be regarded purely as individuals (thus detached from their group affiliated contexts), categorisation and the identification of similarities amongst students need to be managed with great care by teachers in multicultural classrooms. Categorisation is a necessary tool that allows teachers to deal with the complex world of education. Preparations and the implementation of strategies and teaching approaches take place on the basis of these categories. The effective classroom teacher demonstrates flexibility and makes continual adjustments, based on new insights and information gathered from external sources, but also from the students. Although grouping students with particular educational needs provides a forum for professional assistance and systematic classroom planning, individual differences must be respected and accommodated sufficiently. Stereotyping is unacceptable not merely because it implies generalisation and classification, but because of its hidden assumptions of superiority versus inferiority, its rigid structures, and its evaluative nature such that one's own culture becomes the relevant judgmental norm and any deviation is viewed as improper. A negative result of this process is that many students come to see themselves in the same negative way that they are portrayed by others and therefore act accordingly.

Effective teaching means that the teacher has to manage the social images and stereotyping that are prevalent in the multicultural class with great care and empathy. But a sensitivity to, and awareness of, one's own stereotypes and particular preconceptions needs to be developed as well. Because stereotypes form an integral part of our daily lives, it is the negative labeling of others that has to be avoided. Stereotypes determine how one views reality. They directly influence the teacher's interactions with his or her students, as well as expectations concerning academic success, ability, and social acceptability communicated on a continuous basis to all students. Stereotypes cannot be separated from expectations. Although negative stereotyping is usually based on inaccurate information and unsubstantiated generalisations, the stereotypes are perceived to be true.

Communicated expectations influence the self-expectations of students. Positive stereotyping can lead to positive (self-fulfilling) expectations, while negative labelling can lead to unsuccessful academic and socially unacceptable behaviour of students.

When teaching "race" or "ethnicity" issues, teachers usually adopt one of two teaching styles (Appiah, 1999). Some teachers present the material as yet another set of facts, theory, or discourse to be mastered or understood without any critical engagement. This occurs as a result of fear for conflict in the classroom. Other teachers merely create a "right on" politically correct culture where students are afraid to speak for fear of being labeled racist and/or ignorant. Gaine (1995) emphasises that teaching about race specifically lends itself to a teaching style that is both interactive and democratic, because race is a lived reality for both black and white students. Students must be allowed to converse at length in an atmosphere where they will feel free to speak, think aloud, and not feel put down. It is important that when teaching from multicultural standpoints, ground rules should be firmly established from the onset: everyone needs to feel safe, confident, and valued. Often teachers shy away from this because they may "fear that classrooms will be uncontrollable, that emotions and passions will not be contained. . . . there is always a possibility of confrontation, forceful expression of ideas, or even conflict" (hooks, 1994).

Effective education ought to be a strong counterforce to the development of negative stereotypes and racial prejudice. Prejudice involves an irrational system of beliefs and an emotional resistance to changing such beliefs. Through education, student commitment to reason and evidence needs to be developed. Students need to be taught to modify their beliefs in the light of new evidence. It is the teacher's task to get students to think for themselves, to be critical but fair, to be committed to reason, and to question without accepting everything merely on face value. In this process, student prejudices will be countered. In attaining this, teachers have to be open about discrimination and disadvantages by eliminating biases and negative stereotyping from their own teaching. This is an all-inclusive process of counteracting existing biases, both subtle and overt, in school textbooks, the curriculum, the school organisation, the whole school ethos, and in wider society ("Handbook for Teachers," 1983).

SOCIAL ATTRACTION, REPULSION, AND EXPECTATIONS IN THE MULTICULTURAL CLASSROOM

Researchers (e.g. Bennett, 1990) have discovered a positive relationship between a student's social acceptability (or popularity) and his/her social abilities, as well as a direct link between academic achievement and feelings of being acceptable amongst classroom peers. School and classroom climates of acceptance show a significant impact on the academic performance of especially minority culture students in a multicultural classroom setting. Students whose cultural or ethnic group represents a numerical minority in a culturally diverse class have been shown to achieve better in classroom climates of acceptance. Such a positive self-esteem-building atmosphere is furthermore conducive to the development of cross-cultural friendship patterns. On the other hand, in classrooms where low interracial acceptance is the norm, racial differences are very prominent, and groups tend to socialise almost exclusively within their own particular cultural or ethnic group. The pivotal role of the teacher as initiator, manager, and demonstrator of intergroup acceptance and positive regard of others different from oneself cannot be overemphasized.

A growing body of evidence indicates that many white school teachers often have lower expectations of nonwhite students than of students from their own ethnic or cultural group. Teacher interaction with low-expectation students is often intellectually limited, nonsupportive, and less stimulating when compared to the expectations communicated to majority culture students. Lower teacher expectations for a particular racial or ethnic group are usually based on erroneous judgment or ethnic prejudice. Often teachers are not aware of their prejudices and thus need guidelines in order to observe and interpret culturally different behaviour in an objective way. This is one of the fundamental premises and imperatives of a multicultural approach to education (Bennett, 1990). Unintentional racism is often the result of perceptions teachers have of particular groups in the classroom. These racially biased perceptions tend to develop into expectations that are implicitly—or worse, often explicitly and directly—communicated to students. The danger is that communicated expectations from teachers to students (realistic or not) tend to be realised. This is the so-called *"self-fulfilling prophecy"* effect, in which students tend to see themselves and their abilities in accordance with the way that the teacher conveys it to them. It simply means that students will behave and achieve in the manner that the teacher believes they will. When teachers demonstrate and communicate equal achievement expectations for all students in class, interracial friendship patterns among students tend to be influenced positively by the teacher. A classroom atmosphere of acceptance is related to increased student achievement, especially among minority culture students.

The idea of a self-fulfilling prophecy was first systematically expounded by the sociologist Thomas Merton in 1949 and has subsequently been developed in interactionist approaches to educational research. This theory (compare the work by Rosenthal & Jacobson, 1968; Brophy & Good, 1974) has been developed predominantly in the United States. Another theory, developed primarily in Britain, has focused on the link between *differentiation* and *polarisation* (compare Hargreaves, 1986; Lacey, 1970; Ball, 1981). Differentiation refers to ways in which teachers tend to evaluate students in terms of dominant school value systems of ability grouping, while polarisation describes student adaptation and subculture grouping as a reaction to differentiation. Such differentiation is usually based on academic achievement and behavioural conformity. Successful students are given high status and allocated to top school streams, while unsuccessful ones are socially neglected and academically marginalised. Those who are not successful tend to reject the school and its values. This amplifies the effect of existing class inequalities and the allocation of educational resources in ways similar to those outlined in the theory of the self-fulfilling prophecy. Once differentiated, students are categorised and labeled as either successes or failures. Ethnic minority students are predominantly allocated to low-status groups. Categories become the basis for the allocation of educational resources, for teacher expectations, and for subsequent treatment. Usually low-status students receive the least experienced teachers, they are given less demanding work, and lower standards are accepted from these students (Foster, 1990).

Once categorised, these minority culture students integrate into their self-image the lower expectations and negative attitudes held by their teachers. Teacher expectations therefore influence student self-expectations. Students labeled "poor" or "slow" tend to see themselves as failures, and their academic motivation and output suffer accordingly. This furthers educational inequalities and racially based self-fulfilling prophecies at school. There has been a great deal of concern recently about the educational underachievement of students from certain ethnic minorities and lower socioeconomic groups. It is therefore no coincidence that marginalised students from ethnic minority groups or those who are marginalised from mainstream culture because of limited financial and material means tend to fail academically at school. A variation of this theory is the notion that curriculum content and school ethos are essentially monocultural in nature. This implicitly (and sometimes even explicitly) denigrates or systematically ignores ethnic and cultural minorities' achievements and thus conveys a subtle message of cultural inferiority to students. As a result, such students become alienated from and negative towards their school and their teachers. This leads to poor school commitment, academic failure, and poor student–teacher relations (Foster, 1990). Other views are that a lack of cultural competence by the classroom teacher and the nonrepresentation of minority cultures in school curricula may enhance underachievement by minority culture students at school and thus contribute to the low social status and negative stereotyping and consequent treatment of such students. Teacher cultural incompetence thus limits the "cultural capital" needed by students to excel in the cognitive and social domains of the multicultural classroom.

Within every multicultural classroom we can find the dynamic interaction of attraction and repulsion at work. Some students are rated more highly and are more readily accepted by their classmates than others. Some are socially attractive, and others are socially rejected by most. It is significant that the academic achievement and social conduct of a student are closely associated with his or her experience of being socially acceptable or not. In the multicultural classroom, older learners tend to communicate acceptance *intraculturally,* while most cases of social rejection are transmitted *interculturally.* There is evidence to show that children's preferences for their own gender are much stronger than for their own racial group in the early years of schooling. However, once preference for one's own racial group starts appearing during the third or fourth school year, it tends to increase during the latter part of the student's school years. Neglected and rejected students are a source of concern for the classroom teacher. Research findings (e.g., Epstein, 1983) indicate that open classrooms that are characterised by cooperation among students and between students and teachers are more conducive to friendship formation and that fewer students are rejected or neglected by peers.

In terms of the social context of the culturally diverse classroom, and in particular regarding social acceptance, the following statement by Johnson and Johnson (1987) is noteworthy:

> Experiences with peers are not superficial luxuries to be enjoyed by some students and not by others. Student–student relationships are an absolute necessity for healthy cognitive and social development and socialisation.

Research reflects a culturally or ethnically determined preference for friendship. Numerous studies have used unknown children to generate ethnic attitudes. Children were merely asked to indicate their preference for photos of various children from different ethnic groups. Preferences related almost exclusively to in-group peers. This is particularly the case in secondary school and indicates the existence of prejudice regarding other groups and a clear preference for one's own group. The same tendency was found for preferential seating arrangements in class and socialisation on the school playground, as well as for classroom interaction. In racially mixed classrooms, the tendency was still to choose friends from one's own ethnic group, but significantly more cross-cultural friendship choices were made. This appears to hold true for both ethnic minorities and ethnic majority groups in a classroom. An important point needs to be made here: Children's racial attitudes are a critical issue in schools. Some researchers even claim that school-related experiences may influence the extent to which students exhibit an own-race preference. A failure to make deliberate and systematic attempts to promote cross-ethnic friendships may work to consolidate existing own-race preference friendships. Relationships between students of different ethnic backgrounds continue to pose challenges to school systems that aim for understanding and cooperation between students from different backgrounds (Cowie, Smith, Boulton, & Laver, 1994). The teacher's role in fostering a spirit of acceptance, respect, and cooperation among different groups cannot be overemphasised. This is underscored by Finkelstein and Haskins (1983):

> When teachers do influence the context of peer relations by assigning children to seats or work groups in the classroom, children exhibit a somewhat increased frequency of cross-colour interactions.

Teachers' attitudes towards students from cultural or ethnic groups other than their own tend to have a strong influence on peer relationships in the classroom. Students often echo perceived personal deficiencies, as when teachers do not involve some students in group discussions, ignore their attempts to contribute, lose patience with them, or treat them in a degrading manner. Schools can and should counteract the effect of racism through active commitment to policies that endorse all staff members. Pursuing a "colour-blind" approach and avoiding the reality that students are treated differently as a result of incipient racist attitudes is not the best way forward. Victimisation and racial harassment are daily realities that have to be actively addressed (Wright, 1992; Gillborn, 1990). Besag (1989) advocates the important role of the school in combating racism and thus creating a spirit of cross-cultural acceptance and friendship:

> Schools alone cannot combat racism. . . . schools can, however, escalate or deescalate the situation by the attitudes and practices at work within the school. . . . it is the quality of all daily interactions . . . which will be influential in bringing about a more positive situation. Social attitudes are man-made, they are the result of schooling in prejudice; therefore if a positive attitude is presented throughout all aspects of the school day, some inroads can be made to counteract the current situation.

The reality of social attraction and repulsion determines whether expectations that are communicated will be positive or negative. Teachers tend to be more positively inclined towards socially attractive learners, communicate more spontaneously with them, and have higher expectations of them. Inevitably, negative expectations are communicated more readily to social outcasts in class. The teacher has to promote acceptance of the culturally different students by demonstrating empathy and understanding. Often students tend to behave towards other cultural groups by following the teacher's example. Therefore the teacher has to encourage intercultural acceptance of those students who are socially marginalised, enhance feelings of self-worth by emphasising each student's positive qualities, and deliberately create opportunities for positive socialisation in the multicultural classroom. Social attraction or repulsion directly influences the communication of expectations in the multicultural classroom. This has the following important implications for teachers:

- Teacher expectations of a particular student influence communications with that student, as well as the self-concept and the achievements of that student.
- Teacher expectations give rise to self-expectations of learners, as perceived ability and anticipated success or failure.
- Teacher expectations of each student are based on particular information (school record, cultural perceptions, discussion amongst school staff members), stereotypes, cultural views, and previous intercultural experiences.
- Expectations of the teacher tend to be realised. This is the so-called self-fulfilling prophecy. This means that the set expectations of the teacher elicit conduct and performance from students which actualise the initial (true or false) expectations.

SELF-CONCEPT FORMATION IN MULTICULTURAL CLASSROOMS

Effective teaching in multicultural classes is directed at positively influencing students' self-concepts. *Self-enhancement theorists* claim that students' self-concepts influence their level of achievement. Therefore, in order to improve their academic achievement, their concepts of their ability must be made more favourable through various ways of reinforcement and positive feedback. Other theorists support the *skills development model* that claims that the self-concept of ability is the direct consequence of academic success. This could be attained; it is maintained through individualised instruction that recognises students' strengths and weaknesses. Recent follow-up research has in fact indicated a reciprocal interrelated relationship between self-images and scholastic success at school. No matter which theoretical approach is accepted, an important imperative for the teacher in a multicultural context is that students' self-concepts guide and sustain their learning success. Therefore, teachers have to take special care to enhance all students' self-concepts. In order to enhance the self-concepts of students, teachers in the multicultural classroom, the teacher has to:

- Create success patterns in the student's mind and purposefully create opportunities for success experiences
- Initiate and manage positive self-fulfilling predictions concerning all students in the classroom
- Create a favourable classroom atmosphere that is conducive to successful achievement and social relations
- Promote a climate of cooperation across ethnic and cultural boundaries in the classroom
- Create feelings and attitudes of mutual respect, understanding, unbiased outlooks, and human dignity
- Demonstrate sincere interest in the well-being of every student despite ethnic origin
- Be fair, consistent, open, and genuine in his/her approach towards and treatment of all students

Often self-images of students from minority cultures are directly affected by the whole structure and functioning of schools as well as curriculum content to which they are exposed. Often these aspects of the school are arranged and implemented in such a way as to sustain and reflect the majority culture (as superior in relation to minority groups). Various forms of behaviour are directly linked to or dependent on students' self-concepts (Wylie, 1961; Saunders, 1982):

- Performance in school learning tasks
- Self-regard and social adjustment in and out of the school
- Self-acceptance and acceptance of others of own and other groups
- Self-regard and ethnocentrism
- Self-regard and level of aspiration and personal motivation

Because self-attitudes are learned, they are also modifiable in a particular direction. The teacher always represents a particular model of the norms and values prevalent in society. This could be problematic if the teacher presents an image perceived as foreign to some minority students in class. As it is believed that multicultural education should permeate all aspects of school in a nondiscriminatory fashion, teachers should deliberately attempt to be positive role models for all students, despite their cultural or ethnic affiliations. The teacher with positive self-esteem usually communicates positive expectations to students and induces them to form positive self-concepts. The use of (alternative or additional) modeling as a teaching technique can enhance the self-concepts of minority children, particularly if the classroom teacher as a role model is not from the same ethnic or cultural group as the minority students present in the multicultural classroom (Saunders, 1982). Values associated with a particular ethnic group, as well as acceptable lifestyles prevalent in that particular group, can be influenced. If a teaching role model from the same ethnic or cultural group is not available, students with high prestige can fulfill a similar function. Such a role model should possess a high degree of competence and status, should encourage warm relations amongst students, and must be someone with whom students aspire to associate.

DEALING WITH CONFLICT IN MULTICULTURAL CLASSROOMS

Dealing with conflict situations is an essential life skill that is critical in any social context, especially in a culturally diverse setting such as a multicultural classroom. Conflict is an inescapable part of all interpersonal relationships in all classrooms. Everywhere people encounter potential differences of opinion, opposing views, miscommunication, and conflict. This is even more likely to occur in a class situation where pupils are characterised by different cultural backgrounds, family backgrounds, values in upbringing, and worldviews. Cultural pluralism among the individuals in a classroom creates many opportunities for mutual enrichment. But like all opportunities, there is the potential for either positive or negative outcomes. Diversity among students in a multicultural classroom can potentially lead to (when conflict is addressed):

- Increased achievement and productivity
- Creative problem-solving skills development
- Marked growth in cognitive and moral reasoning ability
- Increased perspective-taking ability
- Improved cross-cultural socialisation skills
- A general sophistication in interacting and working with peers from a variety of cultural and ethnic backgrounds (Johnson & Johnson, 1998)

Thus, from a positive point of view, if managed properly, conflict can serve as a purifying agent for strained relationships and is essential for a healthy climate in the classroom. Should the teacher ignore conflict in the classroom, or manage it in a negative way, students would indeed be deprived of these opportunities to learn about the cause, nature, dealing with, and peaceful resolution of conflict. Being able to deal with conflict in a mutually beneficial and constructive way should be a critical part of the student's total socialisation process towards being a responsible citizen in a future culturally diverse society.

Unfortunately, (potential) conflict is not usually addressed in a positive way. Ethnocentrism, ethnic and racial prejudices, and stereotyping serve to intensify intercultural conflict. This cultural alienation is overtly evident in interracial conflict. Multicultural classrooms place excessive demands on the teacher. Teachers need to be sensitised to the fact that diversity among students more often leads to negative outcomes relating to lower achievement, closed-minded rejection of new information about others different from oneself, and increased ethnocentrism. Such negative cross-cultural classroom interactions are detrimental to effective teaching and learning in class, and are usually characterised by hostility, rejection, divisiveness, "scapegoating," bullying, stereotyping, prejudice, and racism. Whether diversity among students will result in positive or negative outcomes will largely depend on the way that the teacher defines and manages the diverse classroom.

It needs to be emphasised that the existence of conflict is not the problem in culturally diverse classrooms. Conflicts can be part of the solution. Schools should therefore not be institutions where conflicts are suppressed, avoided, condemned, and discouraged. Rather, schools should be "conflict-positive" organisations in which constructive conflict management is encouraged and promoted and where procedures are purposefully taught to manage conflict in a constructive, mutually beneficial way. It could therefore be asked: Is the class atmosphere one of cooperation, or are individual achievement and competitiveness overemphasised? Does the classroom teacher handle the existing conflict potential in a positive and constructive way, or is it denied or managed destructively (Johnson & Johnson, 1995, 1998)?

The effective teacher in a multicultural class is capable of dealing with potentially destructive conflicts in a successful way. Constructive conflict offers ample opportunity for intercultural involvement, creativity, cooperative learning, and communication across cultural or ethnic boundaries. Heterogeneous groups promote constructive conflict. In such contexts, differences are regarded as solvable problems instead of barriers. Conflicting viewpoints are integrated into the problem-solving process, in which the student learns to appreciate the emotional and cognitive perspective of others. The positive value of conflict at school and in the classroom can be summarised as follows (Van Heerden, 1988):

- Conflict affords opportunity to alleviate stress.
- Conflict stimulates a quest for the actual facts.
- Conflict may promote change and progress.
- Conflict may enhance feelings of solidarity.
- Conflict may improve intercultural relationships.
- The proper management of conflict may improve academic achievement.
- Conflict serves as a functional basis for creativity, cooperation, mutual understanding, acceptance, and respect among different groups.

Schools need to be institutions where the positive outcomes of conflict can be instrumental in realising high-quality teaching and learning. In order to ensure this, students need to be taught procedures necessary for managing conflict in a constructive way. This is especially true and of value in the multicultural classroom, where the real value of diversity needs to be discovered and optimised.

CONCLUSION

For the classroom teacher, a relationship or social imperative exists regarding the multicultural classroom situation: The teacher needs to create positive and favourable relationships with all students. This is beneficial for their personality development and potential self-actualisation. The teacher should create a positive social climate for adequate communication (free, open, and supporting) in order to promote students' optimal mental health, personality development, and academic achievement. Respect for individual needs and interests should be demonstrated in a flexible way. Often students are labeled negatively as a result of inaccessible and negative attitudes of teachers, who fail to guide students to experience success, acceptance, and human dignity.

The effective "multicultural" teacher has to be concerned about each individual student, and must also be sensitive to the group and cultural affiliations of each of his or her students. Intercultural relations in the classroom may be a source of knowledge and mutual enrichment between culturally diverse learners if managed proactively by teachers, or a source of frustration, misapprehensions, and intercultural conflict if not dealt with appropriately. Teachers need to become aware of how racial awareness develops from the child's early years and often leads to prejudice and stereotyping of others who are different from oneself. This includes sensitivity to one's own prejudice regarding other ethnic groups. Attitudes are not innate, but are learned. Knowledge and feelings about others affect one's behaviour towards them. During the process of socialisation, intergroup attitudes form as the child gradually acquires beliefs about different groups, together with feelings and behaviour patterns towards them, usually adopted from the examples set by other members of one's in-group. The classroom situation should thus be defined in such a way that identifiable social dynamics (described above) are managed effectively and a social climate conducive to effective learning will be ensured.

References

Appiah, L. (1999). Race and ethnicity issues in the sociology curriculum. *Multicultural Teaching, 17*(2), pp. 24–29.

Auerbach, E. R. (1997). Family literacy. In V. Edwards & D. Corson (Eds.), *Literacy* (pp. 153–161). Boston: Kluwer.

Ball, S. J. (1981). *Beachside Comprehensive: A case study of secondary schooling.* Cambridge, England: Cambridge University Press.

Bennett, C. I. (1990). *Comprehensive multicultural education: Theory and practice* (2nd ed.). Boston: Allyn & Bacon.

Besag, V. E. (1989). *Bullies and victims in schools.* Milton Keynes, England: Open University Press.

Brophy, J. E., & Good, T. L. (1974). *Teacher–student relationships: Causes and consequences.* New York: Holt, Rinehart & Winston.

Bruner, J., Goodnow, J., & Austin, G. (1956). *A study of thinking.* New York: Wiley.

Clifford, M. M., & Waister, E. (1973). The effect of physical attractiveness on teacher expectation. *Sociology of Education, 46,* 248–258.

Corson, D. (1998) *Changing education for diversity.* London: Open University Press.

Cowie H., Smith, P., Boulton, M., & Laver, R. (1994). *Co-operation in the multi-ethnic classroom.* London: David Fulton.

Epstein, J. L. (1983). Selection of friends in differently organised schools and classrooms. In J. L. Epstein & N. Karewitt (Eds.), *Friends in school: Patterns of selection and influence in secondary schools.* New York: Academic Press.

Finkelstein, N. W., & Haskins, R. (1983). Kindergarten children prefer same-colour peers. *Child Development, 54,* 502–508.

Foster P. (1990). *Policy and practice in multicultural and anti-racist education.* New York: Routledge & Kegan Paul.

Gaine, C. (1995). *Still no problem here.* Staffordshire, England: Trentham Books.

Garcia, G. (1991). Factors influencing the English reading test performance of Spanish-speaking Hispanic students. *Reading Research Quarterly, 26,* 371–392.

Gillborn, D. (1990). *Race, ethnicity and education.* London: Unwin Hyman.

Handbook for Teachers in the Multicultural Society AFFOR. (1983). *Issues and Resources.* Birmingham, England: Russell Press.

Hargreaves, A. (1986). *Two cultures of schooling: The case of middle schools.* Lewes: Falmer Press.

Hewstone, M., & Giles, H. (1986). Social groups and social stereotypes in inter-group communication. In

W. Gudykunst (Ed.), *Inter-group Communication*. London: Edward Arnold.

hooks, b. (1994). *Teaching to transgress*. London: Routledge & Kegan Paul.

James, W. (1890). *Principles of psychology*. New York: Holt, Rinehart & Winston.

Johnson, D. W., & Johnson, R. T. (1987). *Learning together and alone*. Englewood Cliffs, NJ: Prentice Hall.

Johnson, D. W., & Johnson, R. T. (1995). *Teaching students to be peacemakers*. Edina, MN: Interaction.

Johnson, D. W., & Johnson, R. T. (1998). Teaching students to manage intercultural conflicts constructively. *European Journal of Intercultural Studies, 9*(2), 155–163.

Lacey, C. (1970). *Hightown Grammar: The school as a social system*. Manchester, England: Manchester University Press.

Rosenthal, R., & Jacobson, L. (1968). *Pygmalion in the classroom*. New York: Holt, Rinehart & Winston.

Saunders, M. (1982). *Multicultural teaching: A guide for the classroom*. London: McGraw-Hill.

Thomas, K. (1984). Intercultural relations in the classroom. In M. Craft (Ed.), *Education and cultural pluralism*. London and Philadelphia: Falmer Press.

Van Heerden, C. (1988). Stres en konflikhantrering. *Neon*, pp. 49–52.

Wright, C. (1992). *Race relations in the primary school*. London: David Fulton.

Wylie, R. (1961). *The self concept*. Lincoln: University of Nebraska Press.

Concepts and Questions

1. How does culture relate to the following statement advanced by Le Roux: "Classrooms are social contexts where participants are in continual interaction."?
2. Do you believe that schools have an obligation to support and encourage a minority culture's language?
3. What are some specific problems of cultural stereotyping as it applies to the multicultural classroom?
4. How can intercultural educators keep from stereotyping multicultural students?
5. Le Roux maintains that "many white school teachers often have lower expectations of nonwhite students." Do you agree? If so, why?
6. How does the notion of the "self-fulfilling prophecy" become manifested in the multicultural classroom?
7. According to Le Roux, how can teachers in the multicultural classroom enhance the self-concepts of their students?

7 Communicating Interculturally: Becoming Competent

Happy are they that hear their detractions
and can put them to mending.

William Shakespeare

In a sense, this entire volume has been concerned with helping you become competent in the practice of intercultural communication. We have introduced you to many diverse cultures and a host of communication variables that operate when people from different cultures attempt to interact. Our analysis so far, however, has been more theoretical than practical. Previous selections have concentrated primarily on the task of understanding the nature of intercultural communication. We have not yet dealt with the act of practicing intercultural communication.

We have already pointed out many of the difficulties that cultural diversity introduces into the communication process. And we have shown how awareness not only of other cultures but also of one's own culture can help mediate some of those difficulties. But intercultural communication is not exclusively a single-party activity. Like other forms of interpersonal communication, intercultural communication requires the reciprocal and complementary participation of all parties in the communication event in order to achieve its highest and most successful practice.

When elevated to its highest level, interpersonal communication becomes an act in which participants make simultaneous inferences not only about their own roles but also about the role of the other. This act of mutual role taking must exist before people can achieve a level of communication that results in mutual understanding. In intercultural communication, this means that you must know about both your own culture and the culture of the one with whom you are communicating. And that person also must know about his or her own culture and about your culture as well. Unless there is mutual acknowledgment of each other's cultures and a willingness to accept those cultures as a reality governing communicative interactions, then intercultural communication cannot rise to its highest potential.

In this chapter, we have slightly modified our orientation to discuss the activity of communication. The readings in this chapter will still increase your understanding, but their main purpose is to improve your behavior during intercultural communication.

As you approach this chapter we need to remind you that our primary purpose is to help you become a competent intercultural communicator. To this end, the readings throughout the text have offered you material that will increase your knowledge about culture in general and introduce you to the diversity found in many specific cultures. In this chapter we continue these two themes by offering you advice and counsel that apply both to all cultures and to specific cultures. The essays in Chapter 7 were selected specifically because the suggestions they advance are both universal and specific. Most of the selections discuss problems as well as solutions. Being alert to potential problems is the first step toward achieving intercultural communication competence. Once problems have been identified, it is easier to seek means of improvement—and improvement is at the heart of this chapter.

We begin this chapter with an essay that addresses the issue of intercultural awareness because we, as do the authors, see such awareness as the first step toward intercultural communication competency. The authors hold that intercultural awareness is one of three interrelated components of intercultural communication competence. In their essay "Intercultural Awareness," Guo-Ming Chen and William J. Starosta demonstrate that you must be able "to acknowledge, respect, tolerate, and integrate cultural differences" in order to become an enlightened global citizen. They define intercultural awareness as the "cognitive aspect of intercultural communication competence that refers to the understanding of cultural conventions that affect thinking and behavior." They identify three levels of intercultural awareness: *superficial cultural traits, awareness of significant and subtle cultural traits that contrast markedly with another's,* and *awareness of how another culture feels from the insider's perspective*. After discussing the components of intercultural awareness, Chen and Starosta provide examples of how you can study intercultural awareness and become cognizant of the various cultural dimensions that affect cultural awareness.

In our next reading, "Managing Intercultural Conflicts Effectively," Stella Ting-Toomey moves us from a general analysis of intercultural awareness to a specific topic associated with intercultural communication—intercultural conflict. The rationale behind this selection is clearly stated in the opening line of the essay: "Conflict is inevitable in all social and personal relationships." To preempt the problems created by interpersonal disharmony, particularly in the intercultural setting, Ting-Toomey maintains that conflict must be defined and managed. To help us improve our capacity to clarify and regulate conflict, the author explains three significant features of intercultural conflict. First, she advances a framework that uses low-context versus high-context and monochronic and polychronic time to demonstrate why and how cultures are different and similar. Second, she discusses some basic assumptions and factors that contribute to conflict. Finally, Ting-Toomey offers a series of skills that can help individuals manage conflict when it develops in the intercultural encounter.

Another approach to the topic of conflict is expressed in our next essay, "The Role of Dialogue in Managing Intergroup Conflict," by Abhik Roy and Bayo Oludaja. The motivation behind the authors' wanting you to improve your intercultural skills is expressed succinctly in the first five words of their essay: "We live in turbulent times." You need only look to Africa, the Middle East, and the former Yugoslavia or even to countless events within the United States to see the truth of Roy and Oludaja's assertion. Yet even after advancing such a gloomy declaration, the authors take an optimistic view toward human behavior and motives. They write: "We believe many of the conflicts that have involved violence and bloodshed within our world community could have been resolved through peaceful means if people had not taken polarized positions, precipitating such communicative crisis." For Roy and Oludaja, "dialogical communication" is the most effective means for dealing with the communicative crisis they are referring to. This type of communication is best described "as a meeting of persons, a fostering of understanding based on realities within and beyond each individual's stand, and a forging of authentic human relationships." At the core of this positive view is the idea that, regardless of the cultures involved, the authors believe that there are essential qualities that humans share regardless of their culture or group affiliation. Drawing on the work of four well-known philosophers (Buber, Jaspers, Gadamer, and Habermas), the authors present a detailed explanation of what dialogue is and how it can be adapted to the intercultural venue. Roy and Oludaja, because of their keen interest in intercultural matters, suggest that if intergroup conflicts are to be overcome using the dialogue method, communicators must, among other behaviors, strive for openness, mutuality, respect, fairness, equality (perceive people as equals), directness, honesty, and truth, be flexible, and confront personal prejudices.

When we travel to a foreign culture, we often encounter for the first time a new and often confusing environment. Our ability to interact effectively in a new cultural environment depends on our ability to adapt. In our next article, "Sojourner Adaptation," Polly Begley draws on her extensive international travel experiences to offer insights and strategies for living, learning, and adapting in global communities. After introducing us to both the characteristics and the effects of culture shock and the challenges associated with adapting to another cultural environment, she reviews the changes and adaptations one must make as a sojourner in another culture. Begley suggests that ethnocentrism, language disequilibrium, length of stay, and level of knowledge are the major factors that affect our ability to adapt to a foreign culture. She then provides us with several useful strategies to assist in cultural adaptation.

Two themes recurring throughout this book have been the notions that our world is figuratively shrinking and that the U.S. population is rapidly becoming more diverse and multicultural. Worldwide, as the figurative distance among diverse cultures continues to decrease, and as our own population continues to reflect greater cultural diversity, our proximity to cultural differences grows closer. This nearness demands that we develop intercultural understanding and sensitivity if we are to live peacefully among and interact successfully with others who reflect unique and different cultures.

Intercultural Awareness

Guo-Ming Chen
William J. Starosta

Globalization creates a world in which people of different cultural backgrounds increasingly come to depend on one another. Understanding and accepting cultural differences becomes an imperative in order to become an effective intercultural communicator in a global society. According to Chen and Starosta (1997, 2000), technology development, especially communication and transportation technology, over the last decades is the main reason the world now engages in intercultural communication on a daily basis. Communication and transportation technology not only enable people to easily and efficiently move from continent to continent to encounter others in face-to-face communication, but also bring about other impacts, including increasing domestic cultural diversity and globalization of the economy. As a result, the need for intercultural knowledge and skills that lead to intercultural communication competence becomes critical for leading a productive and successful life in the 21st century.

Interculturally competent persons know how to elicit a desired response in interactions and to fulfill their own communication goals by respecting and affirming the worldview and cultural identities of the interactants. In other words, intercultural communication competence is the ability to acknowledge, respect, tolerate, and integrate cultural differences that qualifies one for enlightened global citizenship. Intercultural communication competence comprises three interrelated components: intercultural sensitivity, intercultural awareness, and intercultural adroitness (Chen & Starosta, 1996). *Intercultural sensitivity* is the affective aspect of intercultural competence, and refers to the development of a readiness to understand and appreciate cultural differences in intercultural communication. *Intercultural awareness* is the cognitive aspect of intercultural communication competence that refers to the understanding of cultural conventions that affect thinking and behavior. *Intercultural adroitness* is the behavioral aspect of intercultural communication competence that stresses those skills that are needed for us to act effectively in intercultural interactions.

Unfortunately, although the three concepts are closely related, most research tends to mingle them without clearly distinguishing them from each other. This chapter attempts to alleviate this problem of conceptual ambiguity and confusion by conceptualizing and operationalizing intercultural awareness through synthesizing existing literature.

INTERCULTURAL AWARENESS: WHY AND WHAT?

Globalization of the world community inevitably leads to cultural diversity or multiculturalism in all aspects of life. In other words, the changing cultural characteristics of neighborhoods, schools, the workforce, and social and political life make cultural diversity the norm rather than the exception of life in most countries, especially the United States. According to Belay (1993), the trend will nourish multiple identities for citizens in terms of culture, race, ethnicity, gender, religion, and nationality. To be aware of the relevant multiple identities of another is the first step to becoming an enlightened global citizen who tolerates cultural differences and shows mutual respect among cultures in order to practice a multicultural coexistence in a "global civic culture" (Boulding, 1988). Thus, intercultural awareness functions as the minimum condition for an interculturally competent individual in the global society.

The importance of intercultural awareness in the modern world is reflected in the increasing demands of intercultural training programs. Scholars and experts have developed numerous intercultural training programs to develop intercultural awareness (Landis & Bhagat, 1996; Yum, 1989). A common goal of intercultural training is to increase awareness of cultural differences in order to develop one's communication

This original article first appeared in the 10th edition. An earlier version of this paper appeared in the Winter 1998/Spring 1999 edition of *Human Communication,* a journal of the Pacific and Asian Communication Association. Guo-Ming Chen teaches at the University of Rhode Island, Kingston. William J. Starosta teaches at Howard University, Washington, D.C.

skills while lessening the likelihood of misunderstandings in intercultural interactions (Seidel, 1981). Among the six most common intercultural training programs, including affective training, cognitive training, behavioral training, area simulation training, cultural awareness training, and self-awareness training, only cognitive training, cultural awareness, and self-awareness are directly concerned with intercultural awareness (Brislin, Landis, & Brandt, 1983; Gudykunst & Hammer, 1983).

According to Gudykunst, Ting-Toomey, and Wiseman (1991), cognitive training promotes understanding of cultural differences and similarities. Cultural awareness training requires participants to understand the aspects of culture that are universal and specific. Finally, self-awareness training helps participants identify attitudes, opinions, and biases embedded in their own culture that influence the way they communicate. Thus, intercultural awareness requires individuals to understand, from their own cultural perspective, that they are cultural beings and to use this understanding as a foundation to further figure out the distinct characteristics of other cultures in order to effectively interpret the behavior of others in intercultural interactions (Triandis, 1977). It refers to the understanding of cultural conventions that affect how people think and behave.

Intercultural awareness is, therefore, the cognitive perspective of intercultural communication. It emphasizes the changing of personal thinking about the environment through an understanding of the distinct characteristics of one's own and the other's cultures (Triandis, 1977). It furnishes an opportunity to develop an understanding of cultural dynamics by reducing the level of situational ambiguity and uncertainty in intercultural interactions. With little visible discomfort, little confusion, and little nervousness in a new environment, individuals can adapt to situational demands with no noticeable personal, interpersonal, or group consequences and can cope with the changing environment rapidly and comfortably (Ruben, 1976; Ruben & Kealey, 1979).

Thus, understanding the dimensions of cultural variability provides ways to identify how communication differs across cultures. Because each culture tends to favor certain forms of processing surrounding data, problems occur in intercultural communication when newcomers misunderstand such thought patterns. Therefore, learning the preferences of a culture for supporting arguments and determining knowledge becomes one key to effective intercultural interaction (Glenn & Glenn, 1981; Harris & Moran, 1989; Oliver, 1962). In other words, one must understand cultural variability in order to modify communication patterns to be congruent with the cues of unfamiliar interactants (Hall, 1959, 1976; Hall & Whyte, 1963). Changing behaviors to be congruent with that of our counterparts helps in reaching a mutual understanding and maintaining a multicultural coexistence.

Finally, intercultural awareness resembles the ideas of "cultural map" (Kluckhohn, 1948), "cultural theme" (Turner, 1968), or "cultural grammars" (Colby, 1975) that emphasize the importance of cultural knowledge for being competent in intercultural communication. Kluckhohn (1948) asserts that cultural awareness requires understanding the "cultural map"; "if a map is accurate, and you can read it, you won't get lost; if you know a culture, you'll know your way around in the life of a society" (p. 28). If a point in reality consistently corresponds to points on a mental map, the map is said to be "isomorphic" with reality. Thus, isomorphic attribution becomes a level of cognitive awareness. Turner (1968) indicates that to be aware of a culture means to catch the "culture theme"—the thread that goes through a culture and organizes a culture as a recognizable system. It acts as a guideline to people's thinking and behavior, and appears repeatedly in daily life.

LEVELS OF INTERCULTURAL AWARENESS

Intercultural awareness can be considered a process of attitudinally internalizing "insights about those common understandings held by groups that dictate the predominant values, attitudes, beliefs, and outlooks of the individual" (Adler, 1987). This process can be integrated into three levels: (1) awareness of superficial cultural traits, (2) awareness of significant and subtle cultural traits that contrast markedly with another's, and (3) awareness of how another culture feels from the insider's perspective (Hanvey, 1987).

The first level is the understanding of another culture based mainly on stereotypes. The awareness in this level tends to be superficial and often partial. Information about the culture comes from the media, tourism books, textbooks, or the first impression. For example, U.S. Americans are perceived as outgoing, friendly, loud, hardworking, wasteful, wealthy people by foreigners (Kohls, 1988). Chen and Starosta (1998) also report some of the first impressions of U.S. Americans made by Japanese visitors. They include that Americans walk very fast, are always in a hurry, always try to talk everything out, and don't respect teachers in school. In this level, one tends to understand a culture or its people by the most visible characteristics it possesses. Then some of these characteristics are applied to the whole group. For example, Asian students with a high GPA in American colleges are often incorrectly considered as science and math majors because the media report that Asian students often do better in those areas. Finally, the same treatment is given to each member of the group by saying, for example, "You are Japanese; you must be smart."

The second level of intercultural awareness shows how significant and subtle cultural traits differ sharply from one's own through direct or secondhand experience. This level has two phases. The first phase approaches intercultural awareness through culture-conflict situations and the second through intellectual analysis. Although the media, tourism books, or textbooks may provide contrasting information, one does not fully feel or grasp the real meaning of the cultural differences except through experience by direct or indirect interactions with people of another culture. In the first phase of this level, the experience of cultural conflict may lead to depression, helplessness, hostility, anxiety, withdrawal, or disorientation, but at the same time it provides the chance to further recognize and understand another's culture. The feeling in this phase resembles culture shock in the process of intercultural adjustment (Oberg, 1960).

Many sojourners, such as Peace Corps volunteers and foreign students, experience stress during this phase of intercultural awareness. If they are unable to overcome the symptoms of culture shock, then development of intercultural awareness will be halted in this frustrating stage, and culture-conflict situations will continue to exist in which they feel alienated and marginalized (Mansell, 1981). At this point, the conflict situations that lead to culture shock may impede the process of being aware of the host culture. For example, as Draguns (1977) indicates, experiencing something unbalancing may be detrimental to the psychological growth of some learners or sojourners. Moreover, cognitively and perceptually, some sharp cultural differences are considered bizarre or idiosyncratic. It may take a long time or may prove impossible for learners or sojourners to sort through their feelings about cultural differences. This, in turn, leads them to judge the unfamiliar more harshly and irrationally than they did in the first level of intercultural awareness.

In the second phase of the second level of intercultural awareness, through rational and intellectual analysis, one comes to understand that cultural differences can be justified from the other culture's perspective. In other words, differences in cultural traits begin to make sense. Differences then become believable and acceptable (Bennett, 1986). This believability through understanding helps sojourners fully adjust to the host culture. In this phase sojourners begin to appreciate and respect the new culture and to develop sensitivity toward cultural differences. Cultural differences in this phase are processed with a positive affect. This provides motivational force to move one forward to a higher level of intercultural awareness. In addition, intercultural understanding in this phase results from drawing comparisons and contrasts. This practice promotes the learning of cultures that have not yet been experienced (Adler, 1987; Hall, 1976; Stewart & Bennett, 1991). While a few scholars argue that some people reach this kind of intellectual understanding even before they move into the first phase of this level (Hanvey, 1987), research on intercultural adjustment portrays it as a process that all sojourners must experience, although the duration of each phase may vary.

Finally, the third level of intercultural awareness requires the ability to see the culture from an insider's perspective through empathy. The believability through understanding explicated in phase two of the second level is enhanced by intellectual analysis and by subjective familiarity (Hanvey, 1987). In other words, one needs to foster the power of flexibility to make psychic shifts. The power of flexibility is nourished by empathy and "transspection." Empathy helps one to estimate what is inside another's mind and to share the other's experience (Barnlund, 1989). This selfless and affectively or telepathically sensitive process helps one to more accurately estimate behaviors or internal states of mind in counterparts that are different from one's own (Campbell, Kagan, & Krathwohl, 1971; Gardner, 1962). The latent capacity of empathy can be activated through the process of "transspection." The term was coined by Maruyama (1970), who indicates that "transspection" is an understanding by practice.

Empathy is the ability to project feelings to others with a shared epistemology, whereas "transspection" is a trans-epistemological process of temporarily believing whatever counterparts believe by trying to learn their beliefs, their assumptions, their perspectives, their feelings, and the consequences of such feelings in their context. This parallels the stage of duality or biculturalism in the intercultural adjustment process through which the fully developed autonomy provides us with the freedom and ability to approach dual cultural identity, awareness of being in control of creative enjoyment, aesthetic appreciation for the contrasts of cultures, development of satisfactory interpersonal relationships, and a high level of commitment toward both cultural contexts (Mansell, 1981). Whether this stage can be fully achieved or only approximated is still an open question (Chen & Starosta, 1998).

The developmental levels show that intercultural awareness is a learning process by which one becomes aware of his or her own cognitive growth, learning, and change regarding a set of cultural situations and cultural principles stemming from intercultural communication. It is a part of cognitive function regarding the knowing of how people's outlook, attitudes, values, and behavior are based on cultural dispositions. Thus, intercultural awareness involves change and movement from one cultural frame of reference to another and provides unlimited opportunity for contrast and comparison resulting from cultural differences. A clearer picture of cultural maps, cultural themes, or cultural grammars emerges through this process.

APPROACHES TO THE STUDY OF INTERCULTURAL AWARENESS

Culture-general and culture-specific are two approaches used to demystify the process of intercultural awareness. A culture-general approach aims to understand culture's global influence on human behavior. Through different learning techniques, one comes to know the possible variations in culture. For example, cultural assimilators and baFa baFa simulation (Shirts, 1973) are common techniques used in intercultural training programs to help participants learn about the general influence of culture. Cultural assimilators require participants to answer a question by selecting the best from the four or five possible answers about a critical incident regarding a specific culture. The critical incident has been demonstrated to produce variant cultural interpretations. This kind of attribution training not only helps participants recognize that the way they think is not always the way other cultural groups think, but also helps them understand that certain experiences are common to all intercultural interactions (Albert, 1986; Cushner, 1989; Cushner & Brislin, 1995).

BaFa baFa is a simulation game that divides participants into Alphas and Betas—cultural groups representing two distinct sets of values and communication patterns. Members of each group are sent to the other group to collect information about the culture. The ensuing exchange gives participants a chance to play a new role in a different cultural setting and to experience the inevitable communication frustration, confusion, and anxiety caused by the different cultural orientations. An understanding of the general influence of culture on its members is therefore reached.

The culture-specific approach aims to impart information about a specific culture and cultural guidelines for interacting with people in a specified culture. In addition to cultural assimilators that can help participants learn about the specific characteristics of a culture, role plays and area studies are commonly used to enhance culture-specific understanding. Role plays allow participants to gain insight into the experiences of people of different cultures. Through playing the role of a host national in a situation that is problematic because of cultural differences, learners are transformed from observers of a culture into participants in another culture. The process can develop greater understanding of the thinking and behavioral patterns of people from different cultures and can further augment and enhance intercultural communication skills (Barnak, 1980; Seidel, 1981). Area studies usually employ a lecture to present information about a particular country and its people and culture. For example, environmental briefings or cultural orientations are used to describe facts such as the locale, history, politics, or economics of a particular cultural group. A "dos and don'ts" format is often used to help learners obtain specific data that can be assembled to develop a holistic picture of the culture.

Both culture-specific and culture-general approaches indicate that intercultural awareness can be reached through didactic and experiential learning. Didactic learning is implemented through traditional academic methods in which, for example, the lecture format is used to disseminate cultural information and characteristics of another culture to learners. Didactic learning is commonly used in the first level of intercultural awareness. Experiential learning involves participants intellectually, emotionally, and behaviorally in a simulated environment of role play (Cargile & Giles, 1996). It aims to reach intercultural awareness through interactions. The second level of intercultural awareness, especially the second phase, demands that participants learn, respect, and accept sharp cultural differences through this kind of interactional experience with people from or representing the target culture.

MODELS FOR THE STUDY OF INTERCULTURAL AWARENESS

What constitutes the components of "cultural map," "cultural theme," or "cultural grammars" that embody a comprehensive knowledge of a culture? From the discussions of the levels of and approaches to the study of intercultural awareness are derived two categories of cultural components: basic factual information and deep structured cultural values. The basic factual information concerns the profile of the culture or nation regarding history, geography, family and social organization, art, or political system. It concerns the "what" aspect of the culture that can be obtained through reading, didactic learning, or other media without the need to interact with people from the target culture for collecting the information. For example, Saville-Troike (1978) proposed 20 categories for learning about the basic factual information of a culture. Such learning also proceeds incidentally and stereotypically from viewing mass media productions. Fact learning includes asking general questions about what are "traditional" or "typical" cultural beliefs or behaviors, family structure and relationships, food, dress, and personal appearance. Similar to this approach, Kohls (1988) also pointed out 10 basic areas that constitute foundational cultural factual information.

In addition, *Culturegram,* a series published by the David M. Kennedy Center for International Studies, classifies the understanding of a nation into four categories: customs and courtesies, the people, the lifestyle, and the nation. Harris and Moran (1989), by contrast, used a coordinated systems approach to divide the unitary whole of a culture into eight systems: kinship system, educational system, economic system, political system, religious system, association system, health system, and recreational system.

Although the basic factual information of a culture tends to be easier to approach and acquire, the deep structure of the culture is much more difficult to attain. Cultural values are the most fundamental framework of the deep structure of a culture. They concern the "why" aspect of a culture. They justify why people of the culture think or practice as learned in the "what" aspect: why do people of the culture dress like that, celebrate that, communicate in that way, or have that kind of religious belief? Cultural values dictate what one ought or ought not to do. In other words, they are a set of explicit or implicit conceptions that distinguish an individual or characteristic of a group from another. According to Sitaram and Haapanen (1979), cultural values are communicated through verbal and nonverbal symbols. For example, the proverb "A man's home is his castle" explicates the U.S. American emphasis on "privacy" and hints at male dominance, while the custom of exchanging gifts in Japanese society reflects the cultural values of reciprocity and generosity. Moreover, cultural values determine our communication patterns. For example, the emphasis on "harmony" in the Chinese culture leads Chinese people to exhibit minimal displays of public emotion and to avoid saying "no" in interactions (Chen, 2001). Thus, understanding cultural values through direct and indirect experience with people is the key to the awareness, respect, and acceptance of the contrasting cultural practices.

Much research has been conducted to examine cultural values. Among them, models developed by Parsons, Kluckhohn and Strodtbeck, Condon and Yousef, Hall, Hofstede, and Schwartz are commonly mentioned. Parsons' (1951) model consisted of five categories: (1) the gratification–discipline dilemma: affectivity vs. affective neutrality, (2) the private vs. collective interest dilemma: self-orientation vs. collectivity orientation, (3) the choice between types of value-orientation standards: universalism vs. particularism, (4) the choice between "modalities" of the social object: achievement vs. ascription, and (5) the definition of scope of interest in the object: specificity vs. diffuseness.

Kluckhohn and Strodtbeck's (1961) model assumed that all human societies must face universal problems, and the ways used to solve these universal problems are limited and different for each society. Based on this assumption, they proposed five universal problems faced by human societies that form the basic dimensions of cultural values: human nature, human–nature relationship, sense of time, activity, and social relations.

Based on Kluckhohn and Strodtbeck's model, Condon and Yousef (1975) extended the categories of cultural values to cover the six basic spheres of human societies—the self, the family, society, humanity, nature, and the supernatural—and attached four or five universal problems to each sphere, which makes the model a highly comprehensive one. Hall (1976) classified culture into high-context culture and low-context culture, in which people demonstrate different thinking patterns and communication styles. Hofstede's (1983, 1984) model stipulated five dimensions of cultural values from the organizational perspective: individualism–collectivism, power distance, uncertainty avoidance, masculinity–femininity, and Confucian dynamism.

Finally, aiming to improve the problem of dichotomous categorization of cultural values, Schwartz (1990, 1992; Schwartz & Bilsky, 1987, 1990; Schwartz & Sagiv, 1995) argued that many universal values, such as power, achievement, and hedonism, exist in different cultures. In other words, in order to reach intercultural awareness, one must also seek universal commonalities of human behaviors.

In sum, the study of cultural values is the most important gateway to reach intercultural awareness. The models discussed not only provide us with a structured way to tackle the complexity of cultural values, but they also offer the potential for further examining different aspects of human society.

Nevertheless, the great potential for the application of cultural values to reach intercultural awareness is not without its limitations and inherent problems. In addition to the misperception of the dichotomy of cultural values such as high-context versus low-context culture and individualism versus collectivism, we must understand that all models used for the study of cultural values are incomplete and show the scholars' biases. Furthermore, the categories used to explain the models tend to break the concepts and components of cultural values into fragments. In other words, the cultural values approach to cultural classification is only for the purpose of illustration. In real-life situations, cultural values are meaningful only when the categories are treated or examined in combination rather than in isolation (Condon & Yousef, 1975) and are viewed within specified contexts.

ASSESSMENT OF INTERCULTURAL AWARENESS

Because intercultural awareness aims to unveil the "cultural map," "cultural theme," or "cultural grammar," the next question will be how to extract empirical indicators from the process of operationalization. In other words, the question is about how to measure or assess intercultural awareness. Although a thorough literature review shows that presently there is no instrument used to directly measure intercultural awareness in the field, measurements have been developed to assess our understanding of the basic factual information of the culture and cultural values. Four measurements regarding the basic factual information or knowledge of a culture are Saville-Troike's Questions to Ask about Culture, Kitao's Test of American Culture, Kohls's Fifty Questions about Culture, and Harris and Moran's Pre-deployment Area Questionnaire.

Saville-Troike (1978) proposed 20 categories for learning about the basic factual information of a culture. For each category, the author created three to ten open-ended questions that reflect the understanding of the basic information of the category. For example, the category of communication asks "What languages, and varieties of each language, are used in the community? By whom? When? Where? For what purposes?" A total of 128 questions are attached to the 20 categories. Kitao's (1981) Test of American Culture is a specific measurement used to test participants' knowledge of basic traits of American culture. The test contains 100 multiple-choice questions about 49 different areas of American culture. Examples of questions include "The Gettysburg Address was given by: (a) Abraham Lincoln, (b) Patrick Henry, (c) Daniel Boone, (d) Martin Luther King, Jr." and "Common speaking distance is: (a) 1 ft, (b) 1.5 ft, (c) 2 ft, (d) 3 ft."

Kohls's (1984) Fifty Questions were developed to help sojourners better know their host country and culture. The author claims that if sojourners know the answers to the 50 open-ended questions, they have moved well beyond the beginner stage of intercultural adaptation. Representative questions include "Who are the country's national heroes and heroines?" and "What are the most important religious observances and ceremonies? How regularly do people participate in them?"

Finally, Harris and Moran's (1989) questionnaire was designed to help a global manager who is planning to go abroad on an extensive foreign assignment be familiar with the host culture. Ninety-two "yes" or "no" questions were used to reflect different aspects of the culture that are closely related to the business interaction. For example, one question asks about an aspect of social structure, "Does dress reflect social or economic status?" and a question about the roles of men and women queries, "Are there differences between male and female roles in business?"

While these measurements can be used to assess and help people understand the basic cultural information or traits, they suffer from two main weaknesses. First, the complexity of a culture requires a large volume of questions to catch different nuances of cultural characteristics. It is not uncommon to have more than 100 items in a single measurement. This often leads to the problem of efficiency in the process of measurement. Thus, these tools are more appropriate to be applied to the didactic learning settings in which participants are gradually learning to know the basic information or traits of a culture, rather than to assess a person's ability in terms of the degree of understanding of a specific culture. Second, culture is dynamic. Some of the basic information or traits of a culture tend to change in a short period of time. This leads to the problem of content validity of the measurement. For example, the answer for a question such as "Minimum wage per hour: (1) $1.60, (b) $2.00, (c) $2.20, (d) not specified" in Kitao's Test may be subject to change several times in a few years.

Studies that measure values are not scarce in the literature. Two representative measurements are Allport, Vernon, and Lindzey's (1960) study of values and Rokeach's (1967, 1973) value survey. The two measurements are highly reliable and valid and have been widely used to assess values. Unfortunately, the measurements approach values from the psychological rather than the cultural perspective. Their applications to the assessment of intercultural awareness are limited.

Three measurements are more helpful for the assessment of intercultural awareness. First, Kluckhohn and Strodtbeck's (1961) categories of cultural value orientations were used as an index for deriving instruments in written questionnaires (Platt, 1985; Triandis, Leung, Villareal, & Clark, 1985). For each universal problem, a case is created and explanations for the three value orientations are listed. Participants are then asked to choose which explanation is the most appropriate for answering the case. This kind of questionnaire can reflect value orientations of a culture in terms of human nature, humans and nature, time perception, human activity, and social relation. The weakness is that it takes too much time and energy to create a case for each universal problem and explanations of the three value orientations attached to each universal problem. It is also a time-consuming process for participants to answer all of the questions.

Second, Gilgen and Cho (1979) revised and simplified Kluckhohn and Strodtbeck's original measures by using a Likert scale to answer statements that represent all cultural value orientations. For example, participants were asked to answer how much they agree or disagree with each of the statements, such as "I do not believe in a personal god" and "Man should strive to free himself from the uncompromising forces of nature," by using a five-point scale.

Finally, Chen (1995) generated 15 items of cultural value orientations from Kluckhohn and Strodtbeck's and Condon and Yousef's models. Participants are also asked to use five-point Likert scales to indicate the degree to which they agree or disagree with each of the statements, such as "<u>Americans</u> see themselves as individualists," and "<u>Americans</u> tend to express their opinions openly and directly." The instrument has been applied to assess participants' degree of intercultural awareness in international electronic communication settings. The nation underlined in the instrument can be changed to any nation to fit the purpose of the study. Both Gilgen and Cho's and Chen's instruments have a great potential for the assessment of intercultural awareness because of their preciseness and ease of operation. However, more empirical testing is needed to assess the validity of the instruments before they are widely applied.

CONCLUSION

The trend of global interdependence has created an ever-shifting cultural, economic, ecological, and technological reality that defines the shrinking world of the 21st century. Globalization demands the enhancement of intercultural communication among people from diverse cultures in order for us to survive in the 21st century. As a component of intercultural communication competence, intercultural awareness is an indispensable element for us to reach this global mindset. This article makes an effort to synthetically delineate the concept.

In this article we have first conceptualized and explained why it is important to develop intercultural awareness in the global society. Three levels of intercultural awareness have been discussed. Then two approaches for the study of intercultural awareness and models for learning the basic cultural knowledge and cultural values have been explicated and evaluated. Finally, instruments used to assess intercultural awareness have been discussed and appraised. In conclusion, the indispensability of intercultural awareness for living meaningfully in global society demands that intercultural communication scholars further explore and expand the scope and functions of the concept. Understanding a culture through cognitive learning should be the foundation for individuals to reach intercultural communication competence. Accompanied with the abilities of intercultural sensitivity and intercultural adroitness, intercultural awareness can help us develop multiple cultural identities that transform us from single-culture-minded beings into "multiple persons." This approach will, in turn, ensure our ability to integrate various communication demands in the web of culture, ethnicity, race, gender, and religion.

References

Adler, P. S. (1987). Culture shock and the cross-cultural learning experience. In L. F. Luce & E. C. Smith (Eds.), *Toward internationalism* (pp. 24–35). Cambridge, MA: Newbury.

Albert, R. D. (1986). Conceptual framework for the development and evaluation of cross-cultural orientation programs. *International Journal of Intercultural Relations, 10,* 197–213.

Allport, G. W., Vernon, P. E., & Lindzey, G. (1960). *Study of values: Manual and test booklet.* Boston: Houghton Mifllin.

Barnak, P. (1980). Role-playing. In D. S. Hoopes & P. Ventura (Eds.), *Intercultural sourcebook: Cross-cultural training methodologies* (pp. 7–10). Washington DC: Society for Intercultural Education, Training, and Research.

Barnlund, D. S. (1989). *Communication styles of Japanese and Americans: Images and reality.* Belmont, CA: Wadsworth.

Belay, G. (1993). Toward a paradigm shift for intercultural and international communication: New research directions. *Communication Yearbook, 16,* 437–457.

Bennett, M. J. (1986). A developmental approach to training for intercultural sensitivity. *International Journal of Intercultural Relations, 10,* 179–196.

Boulding, E. (1988). *Building a global civic culture.* New York: Teachers College Press.

Brislin, R. W., Landis, D., & Brandt, M. E. (1983). Conceptualizations of intercultural behavior and training. In D. Landis & R. W. Brislin (Eds.), *Handbook of intercultural training* (Vol. 1, pp. 1–35). New York: Pergamon.

Campbell, R. J., Kagan, N., & Krathwohl, D. R. (1971). The development and validation of a scale to measure affective sensitivity (empathy). *Journal of Counseling Psychology, 18,* 407–412.

Cargile, A. C., & Giles, H. (1996). Intercultural communication training: Review, critique, and a new theoretical framework. *Communication Yearbook, 19,* 385–424.

Chen, G. M. (1995). *International e-mail debate and intercultural awareness.* Manuscript prepared for the grant project sponsored by FIPSI.

Chen, G. M. (2001). Towards transcultural understanding: A harmony theory of Chinese communication. In V. H. Milhouse, M. K. Asante, & P. O. Nwosu (Eds.), *Transcultural realities: Interdisciplinary perspectives on cross-cultural relations* (pp. 55–70). Thousand Oaks, CA: Sage.

Chen, G. M., & Starosta, W. I. (1996). Intercultural communication competence: A synthesis. *Communication Yearbook, 19,* 353–384.

Chen, G. M., & Starosta, W. I. (1997). Chinese conflict management and resolution: Overview and implications. *Intercultural Communication Studies, 7,* 1–16.

Chen, G. M., & Starosta, W. I. (1998). *Foundations of intercultural communication.* Boston: Allyn & Bacon.

Chen, G. M., & Starosta, W. I. (2000). Communication and globalization: An overview. In G. M. Chen and W. I. Starosta (Eds.), *Communication and globalization* (pp. 1–16). New York: Peter Lang.

Colby, B. N. (1975). Culture grammars. *Science, 187,* 913–919.

Condon, I. C., & Yousef, F. (1975). *An introduction to intercultural communication.* Indianapolis: Bobbs-Merrill.

Cushner, K. (1989). Assessing the impact of a culture-general assimilator. *International Journal of Intercultural Relations, 13,* 125–146.

Cushner, K., & Brislin, R. W. (1995). *Intercultural interactions: A practical guide.* Thousand Oaks, CA: Sage.

Draguns, I. G. (1977). Problems of defining and comparing abnormal behavior across cultures. In L. L. Adler (Eds.), *Issues in cross-cultural research* (pp. 664–675). New York: New York Academy of Science.

Gardner, G. H. (1962). Cross-cultural communication. *Journal of Social Psychology, 58,* 241–256.

Gilgen, A. R., & Cho, I. H. (1979). Questionnaire to measure Eastern and Western thought. *Psychological Reports, 44,* 835–841.

Glenn, E. S., & Glenn, C. G. (1981). *Man and mankind: Conflict and communication between cultures.* Norwood, NJ: Ablex.

Gudykunst, W. B., & Hammer, M. R. (1983). Basic training design: Approaches to intercultural training. In D. Landis & R. W. Brislin (Eds.), *Handbook of intercultural training* (Vol. 1, pp. 118–154). New York: Pergamon.

Gudykunst, W. B., Ting-Toomey, S., & Wiseman, R. (1991). Taming the beast: Designing a course in intercultural communication. *Communication Quarterly, 40,* 272–286.

Hall, E. T. (1959). *The silent language.* Garden City, NY: Doubleday.

Hall, E. T. (1976). *Beyond culture.* Garden City, NY: Anchor.

Hall, E. T., & Whyte, W. F. (1963). Intercultural communication: A guide to men of action. *Practical Anthropology, 9,* 83–108.

Hanvey, R. G. (1987). Cross-culture awareness. In L. F. Luce & E. C. Smith (Eds.), *Toward internationalism* (pp. 13–23). Cambridge, MA: Newbury.

Harris, R. H., & Moran, R. T. (1989). *Managing cultural differences.* Houston, TX: Gulf.

Hofstede, G. (1983). National cultures in four dimensions. *International Studies of Management and Organization, 13,* 46–74.

Hofstede, G. (1984). *Culture's consequences.* Beverly Hills, CA: Sage.

Kitao, K. (1981). The test of American culture. *Technology and Mediated Instruction, 15,* 25–45.

Kluckhohn, F. K. (1948). *Mirror for man.* New York: HarperCollins.

Kluckhohn, F. K., & Strodtbeck, F. L. (1961). *Variations in value orientations.* Evanston, IL: Row, Peterson.

Kohls, L. R. (1984). *Survival kit for overseas living.* Yarmouth, ME: Intercultural Press.

Kohls, L. R. (1988). Models for comparing and contrasting cultures. In I. M. Reid (Ed.), *Building the professional dimension of educational exchange* (pp. 137–153). Yarmouth, ME: Intercultural Press.

Landis, D., & Bhagat, R. S. (1996). A model of intercultural behavior and training. In D. Landis & R. S. Bhagat (Ed.), *Handbook of intercultural training* (pp. 1–16). Thousand Oaks, CA: Sage.

Mansell, M. (1981). Transcultural experience and expressive response. *Communication Education, 30,* 93–108.

Maryuma, M. (1970). *Toward a cultural futurology.* Cultural Futurology Symposium, American Anthropology Association national meeting, Training Center for Community Programs, University of Minnesota.

Oberg, K. (1960). Culture shock: Adjustment to new cultural environments. *Practical Anthropology, 7,* 177–182.

Oliver, R. T. (1962). *Culture and communication: The problem of penetrating national and cultural boundaries.* Springfield, IL: Thomas.

Parsons, T. (1951). *The social system.* Glencoe, IL: Free Press.

Platt, S. D. (1985). A subculture of parasuicide? *Human Relations, 38,* 257–297.

Rokeach, M. (1967). *Value survey.* Sunnyvale, CA: Halgren Tests.

Rokeach, M. (1973). *The nature of human values.* New York: Free Press.

Ruben, B. D. (1976). Assessing communication competency for intercultural adaptation. *Group and Organization Studies, 1,* 334–354.

Ruben, B. D., & Kealey, D. J. (1979). Behavioral assessment of communication competency and the prediction of cross-cultural adaptation. *International Journal of Intercultural Relations, 3,* 15–47.

Saville-Troike, M. (1978). *A guide to culture in the classroom.* Rosslyn, VA: InterAmerica Research Associates.

Schwartz, S. (1990). Individualism–collectivism. *Journal of Cross-Cultural Psychology, 21,* 139–157.

Schwartz, S. (1992). Universals in the content and structure of values: Theoretical advances and empirical tests in 20 countries. In M. Zanna (Ed.), *Advances in experimental social psychology* (pp. 1–65). Orlando, FL: Academic Press.

Schwartz, S., & Bilsky, W. (1987). Toward a psychological structure of human values. *Journal of Personality and Social Psychology, 53,* 850–862.

Schwartz, S., & Bilsky, W. (1990). Toward a theory of the universal content and structure of values: Extensions and cross-cultural replications. *Journal of Personality and Social Psychology, 58,* 878–891.

Schwartz, S., & Sagiv, L. (1995). Identifying culture-specifics in the content and structure of values. *Journal of Cross-Cultural Psychology, 26,* 92–116.

Seidel, G. (1981). Cross-cultural training procedures: Their theoretical framework and evaluation. In S. Bochner (Ed.), *The mediating person: Bridge between cultures.* Cambridge, MA: Schenkman.

Shirts, G. (1973). *BaFa baFa: A cross-cultural simulation.* Delmar, CA: Simile.

Sitaram, K. S., & Haapanen, L. W. (1979). The role of values in intercultural communication. In M. K. Asante & C. A. Blake (Eds.), *The handbook of intercultural communication* (pp. 147–160). Beverly Hills, CA: Sage.

Stewart, E. C., & Bennett, M. J. (1991). *American cultural patterns.* Yarmouth, ME: Intercultural Press.

Triandis, H. C. (1977). Theoretical framework for evaluation of cross-cultural training effectiveness. *International Journal of Intercultural Relations, 1,* 195–213.

Triandis, H. C., Leung, K., Villareal, M. J., & Clark, F. L. (1985). Allocentric versus idiocentric tendencies: Convergent and discriminate validation. *Journal of Research in Personality, 19,* 395–415.

Turner, C. V. (1968). The Sinasina "big man" complex: A central cultural theme. *Practical Anthropology, 15,* 16–22.

Yum, J. O. (1989). *Communication sensitivity and empathy in culturally diverse organizations.* Paper presented at the 75th Annual Conference of Speech Communication Association, San Francisco.

Concepts and Questions

1. How do Chen and Starosta define intercultural communication competence? What are the three interrelated components of intercultural communication competence?
2. Why is intercultural awareness important to intercultural communication competence? How might you learn to increase your level of intercultural awareness?
3. What do Chen and Starosta mean when they say "intercultural awareness is, therefore, the cognitive perspective of intercultural communication"?
4. What are the three levels of intercultural awareness? How do you achieve the highest of the three levels?
5. How does understanding the dimensions of cultural variability provide ways to identify how communication differs across cultures?
6. How might the experiential level of developing intercultural awareness lead to depression, helplessness, hostility, or disorientation?
7. Which do you believe would be the most useful means of developing intercultural awareness: experiential means or intellectual means? Why?
8. What are the differences between culture-general and culture-specific approaches to developing intercultural awareness?
9. What models are available for the study of intercultural awareness? How might these various models help you develop such awareness?

Managing Intercultural Conflicts Effectively

STELLA TING-TOOMEY

Conflict is inevitable in all social and personal relationships. The Latin root words for conflict, *com* and *fligere,* mean "together" and "to strike," or more simply, "to strike together." Conflict connotes a state of dissonance or collision between two forces or systems. This state of dissonance can be expressed either overtly or subtly. In the context of intercultural encounters, *conflict* is defined in this article as the perceived and/or actual incompatibility of values, expectations, processes, or outcomes between two or more parties from different cultures over substantive and/or relational issues. Such differences are often expressed through different cultural conflict styles. Intercultural conflict typically starts off with miscommunication. Intercultural miscommunication often leads to misinterpretations and pseudoconflict. If the miscommunication goes unmanaged or unclarified, however, it can become actual interpersonal conflict.

This article is developed in three sections: (1) A cultural variability perspective that emphasizes identity construal variations, low-context versus high-context, and monochronic and polychronic time patterns is presented; (2) assumptions and factors leading to conflict induced by violations of expectations are explained; and (3) effective conflict management skills in managing intercultural conflicts are discussed.

A CULTURAL VARIABILITY PERSPECTIVE

To understand differences and similarities in communication across cultures, it is necessary to have a framework to explain why and how cultures are different or similar. A cultural variability perspective refers to how

---

 Stella Ting-Toomey teaches at California State University, Fullerton.

cultures vary on a continuum of variations in accordance with some basic dimensions or core value characteristics. Although cultures differ on many dimensions, one that has received consistent attention from both cross-cultural communication researchers and psychologists around the world is individualism–collectivism. Countless cross-cultural studies (Chinese Culture Connection, 1987; Gudykunst & Ting-Toomey, 1988; Hofstede, 1980, 1991; Hui & Triandis, 1986; Schwartz & Bilsky, 1990; Triandis, Brislin, & Hui, 1988; Wheeler, Reis, & Bond, 1989) have provided theoretical and empirical evidence that the value orientations of individualism and collectivism are pervasive in a wide range of cultures. Ting-Toomey and associates (Ting-Toomey, 1988, 1991; Ting-Toomey et al., 1991; Trubisky, Ting-Toomey, & Lin, 1991) have related individualism–collectivism to conflict styles, providing clear research evidence that the role of cultural variability is critical in influencing the cross-cultural conflict negotiation process. The cultural socialization process influences individuals' basic assumptions and expectations, as well as their process and outcome orientations in different types of conflict situations. The dimension of individualism–collectivism, as a continuum of value tendency differences, can be used as a beginning point to understand some of the basic differences and similarities in individual-based or group-based cultures. Culture is defined as a system of knowledge, meanings, and symbolic actions that is shared by the majority of the people in a society.

Individualism–Collectivism Value Tendencies

Basically, *individualism* refers to the broad value tendencies of a culture to emphasize the importance of individual identity over group identity, individual rights over group rights, and individual needs over group needs. In contrast, *collectivism* refers to the broad value tendencies of a culture to emphasize the importance of the "we" identity over the "I" identity, group obligations over individual rights, and in-group-oriented needs over individual wants and desires. An *in-group* is a group whose values, norms, and rules are deemed salient to the effective functioning of the group in the society, and these norms serve as the guiding criteria for everyday behaviors. On the other hand, an *out-group* is a group whose values, norms, and rules are viewed as inconsistent with those of the in-group, and these norms are assigned a low priority from the in-group standard. Macro-level factors such as ecology, affluence, social and geographic mobility, migration, cultural background of parents, socialization, rural or urban environment, mass media exposure, education, and social change have been identified by Triandis (1988, 1990) as some of the underlying factors that contribute to the development of individualist and collectivistic values. High individualistic values have been found in the United States, Australia, Great Britain, Canada, the Netherlands, and New Zealand. High collectivistic values have been uncovered in Indonesia, Colombia, Venezuela, Panama, Ecuador, and Guatemala (Hofstede, 1991).

In intercultural communication research (Gudykunst & Ting-Toomey, 1988), Australia, Canada, and the United States have been consistently identified as cultures high in individualistic value tendencies, while strong empirical evidence has supported that China, Taiwan, Korea, Japan, and Mexico can be clearly identified as collectivistic, group-based cultures. Within each culture, different ethnic communities can also display distinctive individualistic and collectivistic value tendencies. For example, members of first-generation Asian immigrant cultures in the United States may retain some basic group-oriented value characteristics.

The core building block of individualism–collectivism is its relative emphasis on the importance of the "autonomous self" or the "connected self" orientation. In using the terms *independent construal of self* and *interdependent construal of self* to represent individualist versus group-oriented identity, Markus and Kitayama (1991) argue that the placement of our self-concept in our culture has a profound influence on our communication with others. They argue that the sense of individuality that accompanies the independent construal of self includes a sense of

> oneself as an agent, as a producer of one's actions. One is conscious of being in control over the surrounding situation, and of the need to express one's own thoughts, feelings, and actions to others. Such acts of standing out are often intrinsically rewarding because they elicit pleasant, ego-focused emotions (e.g., pride) and also reduce unpleasant ones (e.g., frustration). Furthermore, the acts of standing out themselves form an important basis of self-esteem. (p. 246)

Conversely, the self-concept that accompanies an interdependent construal of self includes an

> attentiveness and responsiveness to others that one either explicitly or implicitly assumes will be reciprocated by these others, as well as the willful management of one's other-focused feelings and desires so as to maintain and further the reciprocal interpersonal relationship. One is conscious of where one belongs with respect to others and assumes a receptive stance toward these others, continually adjusting and accommodating to these others in many aspects of behavior. Such acts of fitting in and accommodating are often intrinsically rewarding, because they give rise to pleasant, other-focused emotions (e.g., feeling of connection), while diminishing unpleasant ones (e.g., shame) and, furthermore, because the self-restraint required in doing so forms an important basis of self-esteem. (p. 246)

Thus, the cultural variability of independent versus interdependent construal of self frames our existential experience and serves as an anchoring point in terms of how we view our communicative actions and ourselves. For example, if we follow an independent construal of self orientation, our communicative action will tend to be more self-focused, more ego-based, and more self-expressive. Concurrently, the value we place on our particular self-conception also influences the criteria we use to perceive and evaluate others' communicative actions. To illustrate, if we follow an interdependent construal of self orientation, we will tend to use group norms, group interests, and group responsibilities to interpret and evaluate others' conflict behaviors. Overall, the cultural variability dimension of individualism–collectivism and the independent and interdependent construal of self help us to "make sense" or explain why people in some cultures are more likely to prefer certain approaches or modes of conflict negotiation than people in other cultures.

Low Context and High Context

In addition to individualism–collectivism, Edward T. Hall's (1976, 1983) low-context and high-context communication framework helps enrich our understanding of the role of communication in individualistic and collectivistic cultures. According to Hall (1976), human transaction can be basically divided into low-context and high-context communication systems:

> HC [high-context] transactions feature preprogrammed information that is in the receiver and in the setting, with only minimal information in the transmitted message. LC [low-context] transactions are the reverse. Most of the information must be in the transmitted message in order to make up what is missing in the context. (p. 101)

Although no culture exists exclusively at one extreme of the communication context continuum, in general, low-context communication refers to communication patterns of linear logic interaction approach, direct verbal interaction style, overt intention expressions, and sender-oriented value (Ting-Toomey, 1985). High-context communication refers to communication patterns of spiral logic interaction approach, indirect verbal negotiation mode, subtle nonverbal nuances, responsive intention inference, and interpreter-sensitive value (Ting-Toomey, 1985). Low-context (LC) communication patterns have typically been found in individualistic cultures, and high-context (HC) communication patterns have typically been uncovered in collectivistic cultures.

For individualistic, LC communicators, the bargaining resources in conflict typically revolve around individual pride and self-esteem, individual ego-based emotions, and individual sense of autonomy and power. For collectivistic, HC interactants, the negotiation resources in conflict typically revolve around relational "face" maintenance and group harmony, group-oriented status and self-esteem, face-related emotions, and a reciprocal sense of favors and obligations. For individualistic, LC negotiators, conflict typically arises because of incompatible personalities, beliefs, or goal orientations. For collectivistic, HC negotiators, conflict typically arises because of incompatible facework or relational management.

The concept of face is tied closely to the need people have to a claimed sense of self-respect in any social interactive situation (Ting-Toomey, 1985, 1988, 1994; Ting-Toomey & Cole, 1990). As human beings, we all like to be respected and feel approved in our everyday communicative behaviors. However, how we manage face and how we negotiate "face loss" and "face gain" in a conflict episode differ from one culture to the next. As Cohen (1991) observes:

> Given the importance of face, the members of collectivistic cultures are highly sensitive to the effect of what they say on others. Language is a social instrument—a device for preserving and promoting social interests as much as a means for transmitting information. [Collectivistic], high-context speakers must weigh their words carefully. They know that whatever they say will be scrutinized and taken to heart. Face-to-face conversations contain many emollient expressions of respect and courtesy alongside a substantive element rich in meaning and low in redundancy. Directness and especially contradiction are much disliked. It is hard for speakers in this kind of culture to deliver a blunt "no." (p. 26)

M-Time and P-Time

Finally, the concept of time in the conflict-negotiation process also varies in accordance with the individualism–collectivism dimension. Time is reflective of the psychological and the emotional environment in which communication occurs. Time flies when two friends are enjoying themselves and having a good time. Time crawls when two enemies stare at each other and have nothing more to say to one another. Time influences the tempos and pacings of the developmental sequences of a conflict-negotiation session. It also influences the substantive ideas that are being presented in a conflict bargaining episode.

Hall (1983) distinguished two patterns of time that govern the individualistic and collectivistic cultures: monochronic time schedule (M-time) and polychronic time schedule (P-time). According to Hall (1983):

> P-time stresses involvement of people and completion of transactions rather than adherence to preset schedules. Appointments are not taken as seriously and, as a consequence, are frequently broken. P-time is treated as less tangible than M-time. For polychronic people, time is seldom experienced as "wasted" and is apt to be considered a point rather than a ribbon or a road, but that point is often sacred. (p. 46)

For Hall (1983), Latin American, Middle Eastern, African, Asian, French, and Greek cultures are representatives of P-time patterns, whereas northern European, North American, and German cultures are representatives of M-time patterns. M-time patterns appear to predominate in individualistic, low-context cultures, and P-time patterns appear to predominate in group-based, high-context cultures. People who follow individualistic, M-time patterns usually compartmentalize time schedules to serve individualistic-based needs, and they tend to separate task-oriented time from socioemotional time. In addition, they are more future conscious of time than centered in the present or the past. People who follow collectivistic, P-time patterns tend to hold more fluid attitudes toward time schedules, and they tend to integrate task-oriented activity with socioemotional activity. In addition, they are more past and present conscious than future oriented.

Members of individualistic, M-time cultures tend to view time as something that can be possessed, drained, and wasted, while members of collectivistic, P-time cultures tend to view time as more contextually based and relationally oriented. For individualistic, M-time people, conflict should be contained, controlled, and managed effectively within certain frames or within certain preset schedules. For collectivistic, P-time people, the clock time in resolving conflict is not as important as is taking the time to really know the parties who are involved in the dispute. For P-time individuals, the time spent in synchronizing the implicit interactional rhythms between people is much more important than any preset, objective timetable.

In sum, in individualistic cultures, people typically practice "I" identity-based values, low-context direct interaction, and M-time negotiation schedules. In collectivistic cultures, people typically treasure "we" identity-based values, high-context indirect interaction, and P-time negotiation rhythms.

VIOLATIONS OF CONFLICT EXPECTATIONS

Drawing from the key ideas of the cultural variability perspective, we can now apply these concepts to understanding the specific conflict assumptions, conflict issues and process factors, and the conflict interaction styles that contribute to intercultural miscommunication or intercultural conflict. When individuals from two contrastive cultures meet one another, especially for the first time, they typically communicate out of their culturally based assumptions and beliefs, stereotypical images of each other, and habitual communication patterns. These assumptions create expectations for others' conflict behavior.

It is inevitable that we hold anticipations or expectations of how others should or should not behave in any communicative situation. These expectations, however, are grounded in the social norms of the culture and also depend on the symbolic meanings individuals assign to behaviors (Burgoon, 1991). Intercultural miscommunication or intercultural conflict often occurs because of violations of normative expectations in a communication episode. Expectation violations occur frequently, especially if one party comes from an individualistic-based culture and the other party comes from a collectivistic-based culture.

Cultural Conflict Assumptions

Different cultural value assumptions exist as the meta-conflict issues in framing any intercultural conflict episode. Based on the individualism–collectivism dimension, we can delineate several cultural assumptions concerning LC and HC communicators' basic attitudes toward conflict. For individualistic, LC communicators, conflict typically follows a "problem-solving" model: (1) Conflict is viewed as an expressed struggle to air out major differences and problems; (2) conflict can be both dysfunctional and functional; (3) conflict can be dysfunctional when it is repressed and not directly confronted; (4) conflict can be functional when it provides an open opportunity for solving problematic issues; (5) substantive and relational issues in conflict should be handled separately; (6) conflict should be dealt with openly and directly; and (7) effective management of conflict can be viewed as a win-win problem-solving game.

For the collectivistic, HC interactants, their underlying assumptions of conflict follow a "face maintenance" model: (1) Conflict is viewed as damaging to social face and relational harmony and should be avoided as much as possible; (2) conflict is, for the most part, dysfunctional; (3) conflict signals a lack of self-discipline and self-censorship of emotional outbursts, and hence, a sign of emotional immaturity; (4) conflict provides a testing ground for a skillful facework negotiation process; (5) substantive conflict and relational face issues are always intertwined; (6) conflict should be dealt with discreetly and subtly; and (7) effective management of conflict can be viewed as a win-win face negotiation game.

In the conflict as a "problem-solving" model, conflict is viewed as potentially functional, personally liberating, and an open forum for "struggling against" or "struggling with" one another in wrestling with the conflict issues at hand. In the conflict as a "face maintenance" model, conflict is viewed as primarily dysfunctional, interpersonally embarrassing and distressing, and a forum for potential group-related face loss and face humiliation. These fundamental cultural conflict assumptions influence the mindsets and attitudinal level of the conflict parties in terms of how they should approach an interpersonal conflict episode. Appropriate and inappropriate conflict behaviors, in short, are grounded in the basic value assumptions of the cultural conflict socialization process.

Conflict Issues and Process Violations

Every conflict entails both substantive and relational issues. Individualistic conflict negotiators typically attend to the objective, substantive issues more than the relational, socioemotional issues. Collectivistic conflict negotiators, in contrast, typically attune to the relational, affective dimension as the key issue in resolving task-related or procedural-related conflict. When collectivistic communicators are in sync with one another and their nonverbal rhythms harmonize with one another, peaceful resolutions can potentially follow. When individualistic communicators are able to rationalize the separation of the people from the problems, and emphasize compartmentalizing affective issues and substantive issues, conflict can be functional.

In reviewing diplomatic negotiation case studies between individualistic, low-context (United States) and collectivistic, high-context (China, Egypt, India, Japan, and Mexico) cultures, Cohen (1991) concludes:

> Individualistic, low-context negotiators can be described as primarily problem oriented and have the definition of the problem and the clarification of alternative solutions uppermost in their thoughts; [collectivistic] high-context negotiators are seen to be predominantly relationship oriented. For them, negotiation is less about solving problems (although,

obviously, this aspect cannot be dismissed) than about attending a relationship. For interdependent cultures it is not a conflict that is resolved but a relationship that is mended. . . . In international relations the consequence is concern both with the international relationship and with the personal ties between the interlocutors. (p. 51)

In individualistic, LC cultures such as Australia and the United States, control of one's autonomy, freedom, territory, and individual boundary is of paramount importance to one's sense of self-respect and ego. In collectivistic, HC cultures such as Japan and Korea, being accepted by one's in-group members and being approved by one's superiors, peers, and/or family members is critical to the development of one's sense of self-respect. Thus, conflict issues in individualistic cultures typically arise through the violation of autonomous space, privacy, individual power, and sense of individual fairness and equity. In collectivistic cultures, conflict issues typically revolve around the violation of in-group or out-group boundaries, norms of group loyalty and commitment, and reciprocal obligations and trust.

In terms of different goal orientations in intercultural conflict, individualists' conflict management techniques typically emphasize a win-win goal orientation and the importance of a tangible outcome action plan. For collectivists, typically time and energy are invested in negotiating face loss, face gain, and face protection issues throughout the various developmental phases of conflict. Whereas individualists tend to be highly goal or result oriented in conflict management, collectivists tend to emphasize heavily the relational or facework process of conflict resolution. This collectivistic conflict facework negotiation process can also take place beyond the immediate conflict situation.

Several writers (Cohen, 1991; Leung, 1987, 1988; Ting-Toomey, 1985) indicate that collectivists tend to display a stronger preference for informal third-party conflict mediation procedure than individualists. For example, in the Chinese culture, conflict is typically defused through the use of third-party intermediaries. However, there exists a key difference in the use of third-party mediation between the individualistic, Western cultures and the collectivistic, Asian cultures. In the Western cultures, conflict parties tend to seek help from an impartial third-party mediator (such as a professional mediator or family therapist). In many Asian cultures, conflict parties typically seek the help of an older (and hence assumed to be wiser) person who is related to both parties. It is presumed that the informal mediator has a richer database to arbitrate the conflict outcome. Expectations may be violated when an individualistic culture sends an impartial third party to arbitrate an international conflict with no prior relationship-building sessions. Conflict process violations also arise if an individualistic culture sends an intermediary who is perceived to be of lower rank or lower status than the representative negotiators of the collectivistic culture. Conversely, a collectivistic culture tends to violate the individualistic fairness norm when it sends an "insider" or in-group person to monitor or arbitrate the conflict outcome situation.

The concept of power in a conflict negotiation situation also varies from an individualistic culture to a collectivistic culture. Power, in the context of individualistic culture, often means tangible resources of rewards and punishments that one conflict party has over another. Power, in the context of collectivistic culture, often refers to intangible resources such as face loss and face gain, losing prestige or gaining reputation, and petty-mindedness versus benevolent generosity as displayed in the conflict anxiety-provoking situation.

Finally, the interpretation of conflict resolution rhythm also varies along the individualism–collectivism dimension. For individualistic, M-time people, conflict resolution processes should follow a clear agenda of opening, expressing conflicting interests, negotiating, and closing sequences. For collectivistic, P-time people, conflict facework processes have no clear beginning and no clear end. For M-time individuals, conflict resolution time should be filled with decision-making activities. For P-time individuals, time is a "being" construct that is governed by the implicit rhythms in the interaction between people. Whereas M-time negotiators tend to emphasize agenda setting, objective criteria, and immediate, future-oriented goals in the conflict negotiation process, P-time negotiators typically like to take time to engage in small talk, to delve into family or personal affairs, and also to bring in the historical past to shed light on the present conflict situation. As Cohen (1991) observes:

[North] Americans, then, are mostly concerned with addressing immediate issues and moving on to new challenges, and they display little interest in (and sometimes little knowledge of) history. The idea that something that occurred hundreds of years ago might be

> relevant to a pressing problem is almost incomprehensible. . . . In marked contrast, the representatives of non-Western societies possess a pervasive sense of the past. . . . This preoccupation with history, deeply rooted in the consciousness of traditional societies, cannot fail to influence diplomacy. Past humiliations for these societies (which are highly sensitive to any slight on their reputations) are not consigned to the archives but continue to nourish present concerns. (p. 29)

The arbitrary division of clock time or calendar time holds little meaning for collectivistic, P-time people. For them, a deadline, in one sense, is only an arbitrary human construct. For P-time individuals, a deadline is always subject to revision and renegotiation. Graceful handling of time pressure is viewed as much more important than a sense of forceful urgency. In sum, people move with different conflict rhythms in conflict negotiation sessions. For M-time individuals, a sense of timeline and closure orientation predominate in their mode of conflict resolution. For P-time individuals, a sense of the relational commitment and synchronized relational rhythm signal the beginning stage of a long-term, conflict-bargaining process.

Expectation violations often occur when a person from an individualistic culture engages a person from a collectivistic culture in an interpersonal conflict situation. Different cultural conflict assumptions lead to different attitudes toward how to approach a basic conflict episode. Miscommunication often gives rise to escalatory conflict spirals or prolonged misunderstandings. Although common feelings of anxiety, frustration, ambivalence, and a sense of emotional vulnerability typically exist in individuals in any conflict situation, how we go about handling this sense of emotional vulnerability varies from one culture to the next. Individualists and collectivists typically collide over their substantive orientation versus relational face maintenance orientation, goal orientation versus process orientation, formal versus informal third-party consultation process, tangible versus intangible power resources, and different time rhythms that undergird the conflict episode. In addition, the verbal and nonverbal messages they engage in, and the distinctive conflict styles they carry with them, can severely influence the overall outcome of the conflict dissonance process.

Cross-Cultural Conflict Interaction Styles

In a conflict situation, individualists typically rely heavily on direct requests, direct verbal justifications, and upfront clarifications to defend their actions or decisions. In contrast, collectivists typically use qualifiers ("Perhaps we should meet this deadline together"), tag questions ("Don't you think we might not have enough time?"), disclaimers ("I'm probably wrong but . . ."), tangential responses ("Let's not worry about that now"), and indirect requests ("If it won't be too much trouble, let's try to finish this report together") to make a point in the subtle, conflict face-threatening situation. From the collectivistic orientation, it is up to the interpreter of the message to pick up the hidden meaning or intention of the message and to respond either indirectly or equivocally. In addition, in an intense conflict situation, many collectivists believe that verbal messages can often compound the problem. However, by not using verbal means to explain or clarify a decision, collectivists are often viewed as "inscrutable."

Silence is viewed as demanding immense self-discipline in a collectivistic conflict situation. On the other hand, silence can be viewed as an admission of guilt or incompetence in an individualistic culture. In addition, whereas open emotional expression during a stressful conflict situation is often viewed as a signal of caring in an individualistic culture, proper emotional composure and emotional self-restraint are viewed as signals of a mature, self-disciplined person in most collectivistic Asian cultures. In comparing verbal and nonverbal exchange processes in Japan and the United States, Okabe (1983) summarizes:

> The digital is more characteristic of the [North] American mode of communication. . . . The Japanese language is more inclined toward the analogical; its use of ideographic characters . . . and its emphasis on the nonverbal aspect. The excessive dependence of the Japanese on the nonverbal aspect of communication means that Japanese culture tends to view the verbal as only a means of communication, and that the nonverbal and the extra-verbal at times assume greater importance than the verbal dimension of communication. This is in sharp contrast to the view of Western rhetoric and communication that the verbal, especially speech, is the dominant means of expression. (p. 38)

In short, in the individualistic cultures, the conflict management process relies heavily on verbal offense and defense to justify one's position, to clarify one's opinion, to build up one's credibility, to articulate one's emotions, and to raise objections if one disagrees with someone else's proposal. In collectivistic conflict situations, ambiguous, indirect verbal messages are often used with the intention of saving mutual face, saving group face, or protecting someone else's face. In addition, subtle nonverbal gestures or nonverbal silence is often used to signal a sense of cautionary restraint toward the conflict situation. The use of deep-level silence can also reflect a sense of resignation and acceptance of the fatalistic aspect of the conflict situation. The higher the person is in positional power in a collectivistic culture, the more likely she or he will use silence as a deliberate, cautionary conflict strategy.

In terms of the relationship between the norm of fairness and cross-cultural conflict interaction style, results from past research (Leung & Bond, 1984; Leung & Iwawaki, 1988) indicate that individualists typically prefer to use the equity norm (self-deservingness norm) in dealing with reward allocation in group conflict interaction. In comparison, collectivists often prefer to use the equality norm (the equal distribution norm) to deal with in-group members and thus avoid group disharmony. However, like their individualistic cohorts, collectivists prefer the application of the equity norm (the self-deservingness norm) when competing with members of out-groups, especially when the conflict involves competition for scarce resources in the system.

Findings in many past conflict studies also indicate that individuals do exhibit quite consistent cross-situational styles of conflict negotiation in different cultures. Although dispositional, relationship, or conflict salient factors also play a critical part in conflict management patterns, culture assumes the primary role in the conflict style socialization process. Based on the theoretical assumptions of the "I" identity and the "we" identity, and the concern of self face maintenance versus mutual face maintenance in the two contrasting cultural systems, findings across cultures (China, Japan, Korea, Taiwan, Mexico, and the United States) clearly indicate that individualists tend to use competitive control conflict styles in managing conflict, whereas collectivists tend to use integrative or compromising conflict styles in dealing with conflict. In addition, collectivists also tend to use more obliging and avoiding conflict styles in task-oriented conflict situations (Chua & Gudykunst, 1987; Leung, 1988; Ting-Toomey et al., 1991; Trubisky et al., 1991).

Different results have also been uncovered concerning in-group and out-group conflict in the collectivistic cultures. For example, Cole's (1989) study reveals that Japanese students in the United States tend to use obliging strategies more with members of in-groups than with members of out-groups. They also tend to use more competitive strategies with out-group members than with in-group members. In addition, the status of the in-group person plays a critical role in the collectivistic conflict process.

Previous research (Ting-Toomey et al., 1991) suggests that status affects the conflict management styles people use with members of their in-group. For example, in a collectivistic culture, although a high-status person can challenge the position or opinion of a low-status person, it is a norm violation for a low-status person to directly rebut or question the position or the opinion of the high-status person, especially in the public arena. Again, the issue of face maintenance becomes critical in high- versus low-status conflict interaction. The low-status person should always learn to "give face" or protect the face of the high-status person in times of stressful situations or crises. In return, the high-status person will enact a reciprocal face protection system that automatically takes care of the low-status person in different circumstances.

Overall, the preferences for a direct conflict style, for the use of the equity norm, and for the direct settlement of disputes reflect the salience of the "I" identity in individualistic, HC cultures; whereas preferences for an indirect conflict style, for the use of the equality norm, and for the use of informal mediation procedures reflect the salience of the "we" identity in collectivistic, HC cultures. In individualistic, LC cultures, a certain degree of conflict in a system is viewed as potentially functional and productive. In collectivistic, HC cultures, in which group harmony and consultative decision making are prized, overt expressions of interpersonal conflict are highly avoided and suppressed. Instead, nonverbal responsiveness, indirect verbal strategies, the use of informal intermediaries, and the use of cautionary silence are some of the typical collectivistic ways of dealing with interpersonal conflict.

EFFECTIVE CONFLICT MANAGEMENT

Effective conflict management requires us to communicate effectively, appropriately, and creatively in different conflict interactive situations. Effective conflict management requires us to be knowledgeable and respectful of different worldviews and ways of dealing with a conflict situation. It requires us to be sensitive to the differences and similarities between low-context and high-context communication patterns and to attune to the implicit negotiation rhythms of monochronic-based and polychronic-based individuals.

Effective conflict management also requires the awareness of the importance of both goal-oriented and process-oriented conflict negotiation pathways, and requires that we pay attention to the close relationship between cultural variability and different conflict communication styles. For both individualists and collectivists, the concept of "mindfulness" can serve as the first effective step in raising our awareness of the differences and similarities in cross-cultural conflict negotiation processes. Langer's (1989) concept of mindfulness helps individuals to tune in conscientiously to their habituated mental scripts and expectations. According to Langer, if mindlessness is the "rigid reliance on old categories, mindfulness means the continual creation of new ones. Categorization and recategorization, labeling and relabeling as one masters the world are processes natural to children" (p. 63). To engage in a mindfulness state, an individual needs to learn to (a) create new categories, (b) be open to new information, and (c) be aware that multiple perspectives typically exist in viewing a basic event (Langer, 1989, p. 62).

Creating new categories means that one should not be boxed in by one's rigid stereotypical label concerning cultural strangers. One has to learn to draw out commonalties between self and cultural strangers and to appreciate the multifaceted aspects of the individuals to whom the stereotypical label is applied. In order to create new categories, one has to be open to new information. New information relies strongly on responsible sharing and responsive listening behavior.

Some specific suggestions can be made based on differences in individualistic and collectivistic styles of conflict management. These suggestions, however, are not listed in order of importance. To deal with conflict effectively in the collectivistic culture, individualists need to:

1. Be mindful of the face maintenance assumptions of conflict situations that take place in this culture. Conflict competence resides in the strategic skills of managing the delicate interaction balance of humiliation and pride, shame and honor. The face moves of one-up and one-down in a conflict episode, the use of same-status negotiators, and the proprieties and decorum of gracious "face fighting" have to be strategically staged with the larger group audience in mind.
2. Be proactive in dealing with low-grade conflict situations (such as by using informal consultation or the "go-between" method) before they escalate into runaway, irrevocable, mutual face loss episodes. Individualists should try to realize that by helping their opponent to save face, they might also enhance their own face. Face is, intrinsically, a bilateral concept in the group-based, collectivistic culture.
3. "Give face" and try not to push their opponent's back against the wall without any room for maneuvering face loss or face recovery. Learn to let their opponent find a gracious way out of the conflict situation if at all possible, without violating the basic spirit of fundamental human rights. They should also learn self-restraint and try not to humiliate their opponent in the public arena or slight her or his public reputation. For collectivists, the concept of "giving face" typically operates on a long-range, reciprocal interaction system. Bilateral face giving and face saving ensure a continuous, interdependent networking process of favor giving and favor concessions—especially along a long-term, historical timeline.
4. Be sensitive to the importance of quiet, mindful observation. Individualists need to be mindful of the historical past that bears relevance to the present conflict situation. Restrain from asking too many "why" questions. Since collectivistic, LC cultures typically focus on the nonverbal "how" process, individualists need to learn to experience and manage the conflict process on the implicit, nonverbal pacing level. Use deep-level silence, deliberate pauses, and patient conversational turn taking in conflict interaction processes with collectivists.

5. Practice attentive listening skills and feel the co-presence of the other person. In Chinese characters, hearing or *wun* (聽) means "opening the door to the ears," and listening or *ting* (聞) means attending to the other person with your "ears, eyes, and heart." Listening means, in the Chinese character, attending to the sounds, movements, and feelings of the other person. Patient and deliberate listening indicates that one person is attending to the other person's needs, even if it is an antagonistic conflict situation.
6. Discard the Western-based model of effective communication skills in dealing with conflict situations in collectivistic, HC cultures. Individualists should learn to use qualifiers, disclaimers, tag questions, and tentative statements to convey their point of view. In refusing a request, learn not to use a blunt "no" as a response because the word "no" is typically perceived as carrying high face threat value in the collectivistic culture. Use situational or self-effacing accounts ("Perhaps someone else is more qualified than I am in working on this project"), counterquestions ("Don't you feel someone else is more competent to work on this project?"), or conditional statements ("Yes, but . . .") to convey the implicit sense of refusal.
7. Let go of a conflict situation if the conflict party does not want to deal with it directly. A cooling period may sometimes help to mend a broken relationship, and the substantive issue may be diluted over a period of time. Individualists should remember that avoidance is part of the integral, conflict style that is commonly used in the collectivistic, LC cultures. Avoidance does not necessarily mean that collectivists do not care to resolve the conflict. In all likelihood, avoidance is strategically used to avert face-threatening interaction and is meant to maintain face harmony and mutual face dignity.

In sum, individualists need to learn to respect the HC, collectivistic ways of approaching and handling conflicts. They need to continuously monitor their ethnocentric biases on the cognitive, affective, and behavioral reactive levels; learn to listen attentively; and observe mindfully and reflectively.

Some specific suggestions also can be made for collectivists in handling conflict with individualists. When encountering a conflict situation in an individualistic, LC culture, collectivists need to:

1. Be mindful of the problem-solving assumptions. The ability to separate the relationship from the conflict problem is critical to effective conflict negotiation in an individualistic, LC culture. Collectivists need to learn to compartmentalize the task dimension and the socioemotional dimension of conflict.
2. Focus on resolving the substantive issues of the conflict, and learn to openly express opinions or points of view. Collectivists should try not to take the conflict issues to the personal level, and learn to maintain distance between the person and the conflict problem. In addition, try not to be offended by the upfront, individualistic style of managing conflict. Learn to emphasize tangible outcomes and develop concrete action plans in implementing the conflict decision proposal.
3. Engage in an assertive, leveling style of conflict behavior. Assertive style emphasizes the rights of both individuals to speak up in a conflict situation and to respect each other's right to defend her or his position. Collectivists need to learn to open a conflict dialogue with an upfront thesis statement and then develop the key points systematically, with examples, evidence, figures, or a well-planned proposal. In addition, collectivists need to be ready to accept criticisms, counterproposals, and suggestions for modification as part of the ongoing group dialogue.
4. Own individual responsibility for the conflict decision-making process. Owning responsibility and using "I" statements to describe feelings in an ongoing conflict situation constitute part of effective conflict management skills in an individualistic, LC culture. Collectivists need to learn to verbally explain a situation more fully and learn not to expect others to infer their points of view. Assume a sender-based approach to resolving conflict; ask more "why" questions, and probe for explanations and details.
5. Provide verbal feedback and engage in active listening skills. Active listening skills, in the individualistic, LC culture, means collectivists have to engage in active verbal perception checking and ensure that the other person is interpreting points

accurately. Collectivists need to use verbal paraphrases, summary statements, and interpretive messages to acknowledge and verify the storyline of the conflict situation. Learn to occasionally self-disclose feelings and emotions; they cannot rely solely on nonverbal, intuitive understanding to "intuit" and evaluate a situation.

6. Use direct, integrative verbal messages that clearly convey their concern over both the relational and substantive issues of a conflict situation. Collectivists should also not wait patiently for clear turn-taking pauses in the conflict interaction because individualistic conversation typically allows overlap talks, simultaneous messages, and floor-grabbing behavior. Collectivists also may not want to engage in too many deliberate silent moments because individualists will infer incompetence or an inefficient use of time.
7. Commit to working out the conflict situation with the conflict party. Collectivists should learn to use task-oriented integrative strategies and try to work out a collaborative, mutual goal dialogue with the conflict party. Work on managing individual defensiveness and learn to build up trust on the one-to-one level of interaction. Finally, confirm the conflict person through explicit relationship reminders and metacommunication talks, while simultaneously working on resolving the conflict substantive issues, responsibly and constructively.

In sum, collectivists need to work on their ethnocentric biases as much as the individualists need to work on their sense of egocentric superiority. Collectivists need to untangle their historical sense of cultural superiority—especially in thinking that their way is the only "civilized" way to deal appropriately with conflict. Both individualists and collectivists need to be mindful of the cognitive, affective, and behavioral blinders they bring into a conflict mediation situation. They need to continuously learn new and novel ideas in dealing with the past, present, and the future for the purpose of building a peaceful community that is inclusive of all ethnic and cultural groups.

In being mindful of the potential differences between individualistic, LC and collectivistic, HC conflict styles, the intercultural peacemaking process can begin by affirming and valuing such differences as diverse human options in resolving some fundamental human communication phenomena. Although it is not necessary to completely switch one's basic conflict style in order to adapt to the other person's behavior, mutual attuning and responsive behavior in signaling a willingness to learn about each other's cultural norms and rules may be a major first step toward a peaceful resolution process. In addition, conflicting parties from diverse ethnic or cultural backgrounds can learn to work on collaborative task projects and strive toward reaching a larger-than-self, community goal.

To be a peacemaker in the intercultural arena, one has to be first at peace with oneself and one's style. Thus, the artificial switching of one's style may only bring artificial results. Creative peacemakers must learn first to affirm and respect the diverse values that exist as part of the rich spectrum of the basic human experience. They may then choose to modify their behavior to adapt to the situation at hand. Finally, they may integrate diverse sets of values and behaviors, and be able to move in and out of different relational and cultural conflict boundaries. Creative peacemakers can be at ease and at home with the marginal stranger in their search toward common human peace. Peace means, on a universal level, a condition or a state of tranquility—with an absence of oppressed thoughts, feelings, and actions, from one heart to another, and from one nation state to another nation state.

References

Burgoon, J. (1991). Applying a comparative approach to expectancy violations theory. In J. Blumer, J. McCleod, & K. Rosengren (Eds.), *Communication and culture across space and time.* Newbury Park, CA: Sage.

Chinese Culture Connection. (1987). Chinese values and search for culture-free dimensions of culture. *Journal of Cross-Cultural Psychology, 18,* 143–164.

Chua, E., & Gudykunst, W. (1987). Conflict resolution style in low- and high-context cultures. *Communication Research Reports, 4,* 32–37.

Cohen, R. (1991). *Negotiating across cultures: Communication obstacles in international diplomacy.* Washington, DC: U.S. Institute of Peace.

Cole, M. (1989, May). Relational distance and personality influence on conflict communication styles. Unpublished master's thesis, Arizona State University, Tempe.

Gudykunst, W., & Ting-Toomey, S. (1988). *Culture and interpersonal communication.* Newbury Park, CA: Sage.

Hall, E. T. (1976). *Beyond culture.* New York: Doubleday.

Hall, E. T. (1983). *The dance of life.* New York: Doubleday.
Hofstede, G. (1980). *Culture's consequences: International differences in work-related values.* Beverly Hills, CA: Sage.
Hofstede, G. (1991). *Cultures and organizations: Software of the mind.* London: McGraw-Hill.
Hui, C., & Triandis, H. (1986). Individualism–collectivism: A study of cross-cultural researchers. *Journal of Cross-Cultural Psychology, 17,* 225–248.
Langer, E. (1989). *Mindfulness.* Reading, MA: Addison-Wesley.
Leung, K. (1987). Some determinants of reactions to procedural models for conflict resolution: A cross-national study. *Journal of Personality and Social Psychology, 53,* 898–908.
Leung, K. (1988). Some determinants of conflict avoidance. *Journal of Cross-Cultural Psychology, 19,* 125–136.
Leung, K., & Bond, M. (1984). The impact of cultural collectivism on reward allocation. *Journal of Personality and Social Psychology, 47,* 793–804.
Leung, K., & Iwawaki, S. (1988). Cultural collectivism and distributive behavior. *Journal of Cross-Cultural Psychology, 19,* 35–49.
Markus, H., & Kitayama, S. (1991). Culture and the self: Implications for cognition, emotion, and motivation. *Psychological Review, 2,* 224–253.
Okabe, R. (1983). Cultural assumptions of East–West: Japan and the United States. In W. Gudykunst (Ed.), *Intercultural communication theory.* Beverly Hills, CA: Sage.
Schwartz, S., & Bilsky, W. (1990). Toward a theory of the universal content and structure of values. *Journal of Personality and Social Psychology, 58,* 878–891.
Ting-Toomey, S. (1985). Toward a theory of conflict and culture. In W. Gudykunst, L. Stewart, & S. Ting-Toomey (Eds.), *Communication, culture, and organizational processes* (pp. 71–86). Beverly Hills, CA: Sage.
Ting-Toomey, S. (1988). Intercultural conflict styles: A face-negotiation theory. In V. Kim & W. Gudykunst (Eds.), *Theories in intercultural communication.* Newbury Park, CA: Sage.
Ting-Toomey, S. (1991). Intimacy expressions in three cultures: France, Japan, and the United States. *International Journal of Intercultural Relations, 15,* 29–46.
Ting-Toomey, S. (Ed.). (1994). *The challenge of face-work: Cross-cultural and interpersonal issues.* Albany: State University of New York Press.
Ting-Toomey, S., & Cole, M. (1990). Intergroup diplomatic communication: A face-negotiation perspective. In F. Korzenny & S. Ting- Toomey (Eds.), *Communicating for peace: Diplomacy and negotiation.* Newbury Park, CA: Sage.
Ting-Toomey, S., et al. (1991). Culture, face maintenance, and styles of handling interpersonal conflict: A study in five cultures. *International Journal of Conflict Management, 2,* 275–296.
Triandis, H. (1988). Collectivism vs. individualism: A reconceptualization of a basic concept in cross-cultural psychology. In G. Verma & C. Bagley (Eds.), *Cross-cultural studies of personality, attitudes and cognition.* London: Macmillan.
Triandis, H. (1990). Cross-cultural studies of individualism and collectivism. In J. Berman (Ed.), *Nebraska Symposium on Motivation.* Lincoln: University of Nebraska Press.
Triandis, H., Brislin, R., & Hui, C. H. (1988). Cross-cultural training across the individualism–collectivism divide. *International Journal of Intercultural Relations, 12,* 269–289.
Trubisky, P., Ting-Toomey, S., & Lin, S. L. (1991). The influence of individualism–collectivism and self-monitoring on conflict styles. *International Journal of Intercultural Relations, 15,* 65–84.
Wheeler, L., Reis, H., & Bond, M. (1989). Collectivism–individualism in everyday social life: The middle kingdom and the melting pot. *Journal of Personality and Social Psychology, 57,* 79–86.

Concepts and Questions

1. How does Ting-Toomey define conflict?
2. In what way does the cultural socialization process relate to different forms of intercultural conflicts?
3. From the perspective of intercultural conflict, how may in-group and out-group differences contribute to such conflict?
4. How can differences between high- and low-context cultures contribute to intercultural conflict?
5. How can an awareness of expectations help mediate intercultural conflict?
6. How do differences along the individualistic–collectivist scale of cultural differences contribute to intercultural conflict? What would you suggest to minimize these influences?
7. In what ways can differences in cross-cultural conflict interaction styles affect intercultural communication?
8. What role does silence play in intercultural conflict reduction?
9. What differences are there between individualistic and collectivist conflict management styles?
10. What does Ting-Toomey suggest is necessary for effective intercultural conflict management?

The Role of Dialogue in Managing Intergroup Conflict

Abhik Roy
Bayo Oludaja

We live in turbulent times. The unspeakable horror and tragedies in the Congo, India, Rwanda, former Yugoslavia, Indonesia, the Middle East, and Nigeria, among others, have left a profound impression on us. Furthermore, the violence that was unleashed against the Muslim community and other minority groups in the United States after the September 11 terrorist attacks is etched vividly in our memory. We believe many of the conflicts that have involved violence and bloodshed within our world community could have been resolved through peaceful means if people had not taken polarized positions, precipitating such communicative crisis. On the communicative crisis facing us today, Martin Buber, once said:

> Man is more than ever inclined to see his own principle in its original purity and the opposing one in its present deterioration, especially if the forces of propaganda confirm his instincts in order to make better use of them. . . . He is convinced that his side is in order, the other side fundamentally out of order, that he is concerned with the recognition and realization of the right, his opponent with the masking of his selfish interest. Expressed in modern technology, he believes that he has ideas, his opponent only ideologies. The obsession feeds the mistrust that incites the two camps. (cited in Arnett, 1986, p. 15)

Thus, polarized positions can be explained as the refusal to consider one's own opinion as in error and the other's view as truth. With such polarized positions, the communication that takes place typically becomes a discourse of "we" are right and "they" are wrong. We are on "god's side" while they are on the "side of the devil."

It is against the background of the communicative crisis facing us that we write this essay about human dialogue. We draw on the ideas of four philosophers—Martin Buber, Karl Jaspers, Hans-Georg Gadamer, and Jürgen Habermas—to explain how productive dialogue can help us reach common understanding with others in intergroup conflicts. Several communication scholars have examined the importance of dialogue from an interpersonal communication perspective (e.g., Anderson & Cissna, 1996, 1997; Anderson, Cissna, & Arnett, 1994; Arnett, 1981, 1982, 1986, 1989, 1992, 2001; Baxter & Montgomery, 1996; Cissna & Anderson, 1990, 1994, 1996, 1997, 1998, 2002; Johannesen, 1971, 2000; Poulakos, 1974; Stewart, 1978; Stewart & Zediker, 2000), but to date, no study has examined the implications of dialogical communication for managing intergroup conflicts. Hence, this essay seeks to bring in a philosophical/theoretical perspective about dialogical communication and how it can be a productive force in dealing with intergroup conflicts. We will briefly discuss Buber's notion of authentic dialogue, to be followed by Jaspers,' Gadamer's, and Habermas' ideas of dialogical communication. Finally, we will synthesize the key ideas of Buber, Jaspers, Gadamer, and Habermas about dialogue and extract some key principles that we believe are applicable to managing intergroup conflict.

Although at first glance this group may appear to be an odd quartet, they share some common traits. For example, all four have expressed a deep understanding and appreciation of dialogical communication. The quartet has also profoundly influenced our theorizing about dialogical communication, especially in interpersonal contexts. In differing ways, the four philosophers conceive of dialogue as a meeting of persons, a fostering of understanding based on realities within and beyond each individual's stand, and a forging of authentic human relationships. The significance of their contribution lies in their focus on the essential qualities that humans share regardless of their culture or group affiliations. Focusing on those qualities can result in authentic dialogue that in turn can enable us to celebrate our similarities as well as appreciate how our differences can be mutually enriching. The four philosophers share the view that intergroup problems and difficulties are not detrimental to genuine relationships as long as we are committed to

---

This original essay appears here in print for the first time. Abhik Roy teaches at Howard University, Washington, D.C., and Bayo Oludaja teaches at Northwest Missouri State University, Maryville, Missouri.

upholding the essential human qualities in the process of engaging those problems or communicating about them with one another. Thus, an understanding of their position can help us strive for the happy medium between cultural insensitivity and cultural pandering in intergroup conflict situations.

MARTIN BUBER'S PHILOSOPHY OF DIALOGUE

Martin Buber (1878–1965), in *Ich und Du (I and Thou)*, has asserted that dialogue is at the heart of every human existence. Buber's philosophical writings have served as a catalyst for other European philosophers on dialogue. Based on his major writings, we have identified five major characteristics that Buber has consistently emphasized in his notion of dialogue.

I-It versus I-Thou. According to Buber (1970), there are two primary attitudes and relations: I-Thou and I-It. In I-It relation, a person uses and experiences the other person as an object for his/her profit or self-interest. The I-Thou relation is based on "mutuality, directness, presentness, intensity, and ineffability" (Friedman, 1960, p. 57). Similarly, Johannesen (1971) characterizes Buber's I-Thou dialogue between two individuals as "open-heartedness, honesty, spontaneity, frankness, lack of pretense, nonmanipulative intent, communion, intensity, and love in the sense of responsibility of one human for another" (p. 375). Thus, Buber's I-Thou relation is one in which an individual is appreciated in all her/his uniqueness and is not objectified.

For Buber (1970), it is the dialogic relationship of I-Thou that helps humans attain their completeness by understanding one another in a spirit of authenticity. In such an authentic dialogue, a person reaches out toward the "other" in a spontaneous and unaffected fashion. This kind of authentic dialogue is one in which one partner affirms the other. Unity in a dialogue with someone who is a "stranger" to us cannot be achieved by distancing ourselves from the other person; neither can it be accomplished by objectifying the other person, who is different from us on account of her/his race, ethnicity, or culture. For Buber, "genuine conversation, and therefore, every actual fulfillment of relation between men, means acceptance of otherness" (1998, p. 59). In a Buberian I-Thou dialogue, an individual does not try to influence the "other," nor does s/he intend to change the "other"; neither does s/he want to inject her/his rightness into the other person. It means recognizing and affirming the "elemental otherness of the other" in such a manner that both the individuals "confirm one another in their individual being by means of genuine meetings" (Buber, 1998, p. 59).

Confirming the Other. Buber's dialogue calls for genuine acceptance of the other, even in conflict. In conflict, when you meet the person in dialogue, you meet in wholeness and concreteness; you truly confirm the other person. True confirmation for Buber means that you accept the other party in the conflict as your own partner even when you oppose him or her (Friedman, 1960). You legitimize her/his claims as you would expect the other person to value and respect yours. Most important, in such a dialogue both parties have to trust and act toward each other as genuine partners who are seeking a resolution in this conflict. Buber also underscores the need for both parties in conflict to "imagine the real," which requires them to imagine what the other party at that very moment is "wishing, feeling, perceiving, thinking," not in a detached but in an involved manner (Buber, 1998, p. 60).

Unfolding versus Imposing. During the dialogical encounter, the interactants do not seek to influence each other. Neither do they "inject" their "rightness" onto each other. Instead they help to see each other's perspective without any kind of manipulation. In this kind of dialogue, both parties let each other realize her/his potential. Genuine dialogue, even in times of conflict, permits issues and ideas to unfold rather than imposing or pushing one's ideas or perspective on the other.

Being versus Seeming. In all dialogical encounters, Buber exhorts us to remain true, honest, and authentic with others, even in situations of conflict. He advocates striving for a life of "being," which involves the spontaneous and unreserved presentation of who one really is, as opposed to a life of "seeming," which is concerned with one's image and how others perceive one.

Confronting the Truth. In Buber's mode of "being," one constantly has to strive for the truth even when it causes pain and discomfort. In any conflict, both parties who are involved in dialogue should pursue truth boldly and relentlessly. Arnett (1980) points out that in dialogue both parties stand firm while both affirm each other's right to the same privilege. An individual in conflict has the right to disagree with the other person's view of the situation, but her/his right to hold that view is supported. The final resolution in such dialogue may happen through a synthesis of opposing perspectives, or one party may persuade the other to accept the viewpoint she or he once resisted, or a solution may emerge from the dialogue that was not even considered previously (Arnett, 1980).

Buber describes dialogue as the unity of contraries because an individual must stand her/his ground and at the same time remain open to the other. When there is genuine dialogue to resolve a conflict, both parties must walk on a "narrow ridge" between two extreme opposites: (1) the urge to refuse to understand and appreciate the other's perspective of the conflict, and (2) giving up one's ground and blindly accepting the other's viewpoint. In genuine dialogues, both parties must give up their extreme positions. They have no choice but to participate in what Buber describes as a "holy insecurity" that does not choose one extreme position or the other. Arnett (1980) explains that a person "walks a narrow ridge in a holy insecurity that requires him to stand between the extremes of stubbornly standing his ground and blindly following his partner's direction."

KARL JASPER'S PHILOSOPHY OF LIMITLESS COMMUNICATION

Karl Jaspers (1883–1969) drew upon his power of observation and used it to harness the forces of science, faith, and language in crafting his philosophy. His recognition of the limits of scientific knowledge and methodology led to his pursuit of answers to the questions of the origin and purpose of human existence. His focus was the authenticity of the human situation. In his introduction to the second volume of Jaspers' *Philosophy* (1970), Ashton notes that the volume "contains the thought which made Jaspers one of existential philosophy's founding fathers" (inside flap). A major theme of his philosophy is limitless communication, which is very similar to Buber's notion of dialogue. But before turning to the theme of communication, we briefly outline some recurring elements that form the building blocks of Jaspers' philosophy.

The Encompassing. Jaspers refers to his conception of the absolute unity of Being as the Encompassing. He identifies several modes of encompassing. Existence, as a mode of the Encompassing, refers to the empirical world in which we live. It is the mode by which the individual derives sensations from the empirical world. Another mode is consciousness-as-such. This is the realm of cognition, a realm in which "everything which exists for us must take on that form in which it can be thought or experienced by consciousness" (Jaspers, 1955, p. 55). The other mode is spirit, the sum total of the individual's Idea. "It is the process of fusing and reconstructing all totalities in a present which is never finished yet always fulfilled" (p. 57). This is the mode by which the individual reflects on things within and without. It is the level at which the individual seeks to establish coherence by relating to "everything which is comprehensible to us" (p. 58). Another mode is *Existenz* which Jaspers describes as "the self-being that stands in relation to itself and thereby to transcendence; it knows itself as given to itself through, and bases itself on, transcendence" (Ehrlich, Ehrlich, & Pepper, 1986, p. 140).

Reason. The glue that holds the different modes of the Encompassing together is reason. For Jaspers, reason means more than "clear, objective thinking" or "the life of the Idea"; it is "what goes beyond all limits, the omnipresent demand of thought." Although reason moves within the modes of the Encompassing, it transcends the limits of the modes by continually pushing on. Reason is "the binding, recollecting, and progressive power whose contents are always derived from its own limits and which passes beyond every one of these limits, expressing perpetual dissatisfaction" (Jaspers, 1955, p. 66). Reason is drawn toward everything that can be expressed. It is "the total will to communication" (Ehrlich et al., 1986, p. 181).

Communication. For Jaspers, communication is the origin of self-being. It is in human relations that we realize our existence. He writes:

> "I am only in communication with another" is a statement that can, of course, be taken to refer objectively and subjectively to our existence, to our connecting links of understanding and of action, and in that case its meaning is definite and demonstrable in facts of human cohabitation. (Jaspers, 1970, p. 47)

Human relations require clarification, for "true communication, in which I begin to know my being as I bring it about jointly with another, does not exist empirically. Its elucidation is a philosophical task" (Jaspers, 1970, p. 48). In undertaking this philosophical task, Jaspers posits that communication engenders self-revelation and self-realization. Self-realization requires a willingness to risk oneself "completely in communication." It is a process that "occurs only with another" and constitutes "a unique struggle, combative and loving at once," a struggle that entails "the fighting, clear-sighted love of possible *Existenz* tackling another possible *Existenz*, questioning it, challenging it, making things hard for it" (pp. 59–60). Participants in the loving struggle do not employ the tools of deceit and manipulation. Instead, they embrace forthrightness, equality, and vulnerability. In addition, the struggle is characterized by self-abandonment, solidarity, and mutual transparency, a readiness to "put everything at the other's disposal" (p. 61). Ultimately, it is a struggle in which both parties join forces to "fight against oneself and the other, but solely for the truth" (p. 59).

Truth

In an effort to address the dissolution of unity resulting from exclusionary truth claims, Jaspers conceived a theory of truth that would ground "the multiplicity of human realizations in an open-ended unity" (Ehrlich et al., 1986, p. 230). Human beings live by multiple shades of truth, and in its unity, truth is transcendent. Jaspers' commitment to transcendent truth led him to the concept of cipher-language, a notion that Ehrlich (1975) has described as "one of his most distinct and original achievements in the clarification of the meaning and possibility of metaphysics" (p. 4). Ciphers are means of apprehending transcendent truth either by direct impression or through symbols. He contends that truth and communication are inseparable. Communication is so fundamental to human nature that "both what man is and what is for him are in some sense bound up with communication." Truth "only appears in time as a reality-through-communication. Abstracted from communication, truth hardens into an unreality" (Jaspers, 1955, p. 79). Truth, in time, has as many meanings "as there are modes of communication in which it arises" (p. 80). So truth is relative and changing, and a point of view that one may consider wrong today may become relevant tomorrow, given a change in situation. His theory of truth allows for people to seek the path of their truth in "unfanatical absoluteness, in a decisiveness which remains open" (p. 76). But it also requires compromise, and "Compromise is the truth which does not forget that every standpoint, no matter how right it seems, can also be refuted through the very fact of process" (p. 82). The danger is not in challenging one another's truth but in ceasing to talk. "To stop talking is politically unjustifiable even if the opponent does not use language to seek a meeting of minds; for talk among men always offers a chance of finally meeting in truth" (Jaspers, 1961, p. 107). Thus, humans can discover unity in truth through authentic existential communication that, according to Gordon (2000), "requires equality, mutual recognition, affirmation, solidarity, questioning, abandonment of ego, no quest for victory, unlimited clarification, and no sophistry" (p. 113). It is this concept of communication that forms the basis of Jaspers' philosophy.

HANS-GEORG GADAMER'S PERSPECTIVE OF DIALOGICAL COMMUNICATION

Since the publication of Hans-Georg Gadamer's *Wahrheit und Methode (Truth and Method)* in 1960, Gadamer's ideas have appealed to academicians of varied backgrounds. Similar to Buber and Jaspers, Hans-Georg Gadamer (1900–2002) was also interested in how people could come to a mutual understanding through dialogue. Gadamer (1960/1989) views dialogue as a "process of coming to an understanding" where two people can make themselves understood (p. 385). Understanding requires openness to the possible truth claims of the other party as well as to the potential challenge these claims pose to one's own viewpoints. Gadamer explains, "It belongs to any true conversation that each person opens himself up to the other, truly accepts his point of view as valid and transposes himself into the other to such an extent that he understands not the particular individual but what he says" (p. 385). Here we will briefly discuss four important elements of Gadamerian dialogue.

I-Thou Relationship. Like Buber, Gadamer also advocated an I-Thou relationship that is based on a position of symmetry of claims and is characterized by nondomination (Scheibler, 2000). This is a relation that is based on open-mindedness and mutuality and a willingness to listen to the claims of the other with an eye to their possible validity and to allow oneself to be open to the possibility that the other person's viewpoint is right while mine is wrong. Gadamer (1960/1989) explains his notion of I-Thou relationship thus:

> In human relations the important thing is, as we have seen, to experience the Thou truly as a Thou–i.e., not to overlook his claims but to let him really say something to us. Here is where openness belongs. But ultimately this openness does not exist only for the person who speaks; rather, anyone who listens is fundamentally open. Without such openness to one another there is no genuine human bond. (p. 361)

Socratic Question and Answer. Gadamer believes that by determining the question to which another person's statement responds, one's understanding of an issue is enhanced. For Gadamer (1976), understanding is possible because "nothing that is said [in a dialogue] has its truth simply in itself, but refers backward and forward to what is unsaid. Every assertion is motivated, that is, one can sensibly ask of everything said, 'Why do you say that?'" (p. 67). Gadamer (1960/1989) explains that "a person who wants to understand must question what lies behind what is said. He must understand it is an answer to a question" (p. 370).

In addressing the issue of questions, Gadamer makes a distinction between appropriate questions versus rhetorical ones. An appropriate question opens up the subject matter so that a dialogue can emerge. A person who raises a good question opens the dialogue to explore the issues under consideration. Gadamer says that the person who knows how to ask questions preserves an orientation toward openness. The art of thinking acknowledges that to ask a question requires a person to admit ignorance. It also requires that the person wants to know. Legitimate questions and the art of asking these questions show us that understanding requires a context of openness. This openness enables the thinker to meet something that addresses him or her and to respond to that address. It is this kind of openness that results in authentic dialogue.

The Role of Prejudice in Understanding. Instead of prejudice being something to be avoided or minimized, Gadamer views human prejudice as the basis of all understanding. Prejudice, for Gadamer, actually means "prejudgment"; prejudice can be either positive or negative, and to assume that all prejudices are illegitimate and misleading represents simply a "prejudice against prejudice" (Gadamer, 1960/1989, p. 270). Therefore, in order to gain an understanding every individual undergoes a process of projecting his/her prejudices. Gadamer points out that communicative understanding requires:

> the suspension of one's prejudices, whether this involves another person through whom one learns one's own nature and limits, or an encounter with a work of art, or a text; always something more is demanded than to understand the other, that is to seek and acknowledge the immanent coherence contained within the meaning claim of the other. (Gadamer, 1987, p. 87)

In order to understand, one opens him/herself to other possibilities (or prejudices). Being open does not mean starting from no prejudice or bias; rather, one learns to differentiate productive prejudices from those that are unproductive or counterproductive. Deetz (1978) observes, "the person who imagines himself free from prejudices not only becomes unconsciously dominated by them but cuts himself [herself] off from their positive insight" (p. 18). The positive insight of prejudice is that other people become a means for us to correct our understanding (White, 1994). Thus, Gadamer's hermeneutic approach, instead of adopting an objective and neutral stance, calls for bracketing of all presumptions and biases and qualifying them as such in order to understand others' perspectives compared to one's own prejudices. Instead of prejudice being something to be avoided or minimized, Gadamer views it as the basis of all understanding. It is not to be condemned, and rather than trying to eliminate or minimize it, Gadamer asks communicators to be aware of its existence and use it productively.

Understanding. Gadamer perceives understanding as a *fusion of horizons* of the parties in dialogue. In genuine dialogue, the participants will be able to weigh counterarguments while holding onto their own viewpoints. This willingness to listen to the other person's views requires each participant to consider seriously the claims of the other, all the while defining and testing one's prejudices against such claims and counterclaims and reaching a new understanding of the subject matter at hand (White, 1994).

Closely related to Gadamer's concept of understanding is the process of experience. In order to explain the process of experience, Gadamer (1960/1989) uses the German word, *Erfahrung*. *Erfahrung* is the kind of experience that *happens* to one. According to Gadamer, a person who is considered experienced has become so "not only *through* experiences but is also open *to* new experiences" (p. 355). An experienced person has the qualities of openness, flexibility, and humility. Gadamer sums up the qualities of an experienced person in the following way:

> "Being experienced" does not consist in the fact that someone already knows everything and knows better than anyone else. Rather, the experienced person proves to be, on the contrary, someone who is radically undogmatic; who, because of the many experiences he has had and the knowledge he has drawn from them, is particularly well equipped to have new experiences and to learn from them. (p. 355)

Gadamer states that language helps communicators to understand one another and to establish and maintain interhuman contact. To actually experience communication is to take part in "communion" with another. In Gadamer's words, "To reach an understanding in a dialogue is not merely a matter of putting oneself forward and successfully asserting one's own point of view, but being transformed into a communion in which we do not remain what we were." Dialogue does not simply involve understanding what the other person says and how s/he feels, but coming to grips with one another. It is this shared understanding in the dialogical process that helps the parties in conversation to transcend to a higher level that "overcomes not only one's own particularity, but that of the other as well" (Roy & Starosta, 2001, p. 10).

JÜRGEN HABERMAS, COMMUNICATIVE ETHICS, AND IDEAL SPEECH SITUATION

Jürgen Habermas (1929–) is a philosopher whose writings on communicative ethics have had a profound influence in both the social sciences and humanities. His philosophical ideas about communicative ethics and the accompanying liberal virtues of universal freedom, openness, mutual recognition, and respect for one another have appealed to numerous scholars in the field of communication studies. Like Buber, Jaspers, and Gadamer, Habermas also views dialogical communication as teleologically oriented toward a state of mutual recognition and respect for persons.

According to Habermas, every communicative utterance can be divided into three general categories based on the validity claims they raise: truth, rightness, and claims to truthfulness (Habermas, 1979). Constative speech acts are associated with truth claims, regulatives with normative rightness, and avowals with claims to truthfulness (Cooke, 1998). In a constative speech act, a person has to demonstrate the truth of her/his claim. On the other hand, in a regulative speech act, s/he has to meet the criterion of appropriateness. And for the expressive speech acts (avowals), the individual has to demonstrate that s/he is sincere or truthful. In a communicative action, it is quite common that all three claims to validity are raised. However, when there is an intergroup conflict, one generally finds that the claims to truth and normative rightness are more salient than the one concerning truthfulness. When a speaker's claim to validity in any of the three areas, or all of them, is challenged, it can be resolved in a dialogue, which Habermas calls a "discourse," so that the parties concerned can offer arguments to demonstrate the validity of their claim or claims. Habermas argues that the moot point of trying to come to an understanding with someone is "to bring about an agreement that terminates in the intersubjective mutuality of reciprocal understanding, shared knowledge, mutual trust, and accord with one another" (p. 3).

Habermas believes that claims to truth or rightness can be settled in a dialogue on the basis of consensus theory of truth (Burleson & Kline, 1979). He opines that it is the "force of the better argument" that will determine the truth or appropriateness of the issue that is under challenge. In a dialogue, both parties in conflict are required to have "substantive arguments" that are based on sound evidence. Thus, it will be the cogency of arguments, soundness, deductive or inductive strength that will enable the parties to accept a truth claim or a claim to appropriateness (Burleson & Kline, 1979).

Habermas has laid down stringent guidelines for conducting a dialogue when parties are in conflict concerning a validity claim or claims. It is only when these stipulations are met that participants are in what Habermas describes as the "Ideal Speech Situation." The following are some of the conditions of the ideal speech situation:

1. The speakers cannot contradict themselves.
2. The speakers are required to assert only what they believe.
3. Every person who has the competence to speak and act must be allowed to participate in the discourse.
4. Everyone is permitted to question any assertion.
5. Everyone is allowed to introduce any assertion into the discourse.
6. Everyone is allowed to express his/her attitudes, desires, and needs.
7. There should not be any kind of internal or external coercion that prevents the speakers from exercising their rights as stipulated in 3 and 4.

Habermas emphasizes that an "ideal speech situation must not only guarantee unlimited discussion but must also insure that discussion is free from distorting influences stemming from domination, strategic behavior, or self-deception" (Burleson & Kline, 1979, p. 423).

When writing about the "Conflict of Beliefs," Habermas (2001) underscores the need for intercultural understanding that will help us to "foster the mutual esteem of alien cultures and ways of life" despite differences in fundamental value orientations (p. 43). He believes that this kind of understanding and appreciation of cultural differences in times of conflict cannot be present unless certain preconditions are met. Habermas (2001) sums up four conditions that are essential to having an authentic dialogue in handling conflicts concerning cultural beliefs:

1. The parties must renounce the violent imposition of their convictions—an imposition by military, governmental, or terrorist means.
2. They must acknowledge each other as partners with equal rights, regardless of their reciprocal evaluations of traditions and forms of life.
3. They must also acknowledge each other as participants in a discussion in which each party can learn from the other.
4. There must be openness and willingness by both parties to view things from the perspective of the other.

Very much akin to Buber, Jaspers, and Gadamer, Habermas' notion of discourse is based on the virtues of respect, recognition, tolerance, and openness, as well as the principles of freedom of expression and equal access to the dialogue. In "Israel or Athens," Habermas (2001) quotes Johann Baptist Metz, exhorting us to "seek freedom and justice for all" and to be guided by "a culture of the recognition of the other in his otherness" (p. 88).

IMPLICATIONS FOR CONFLICT MANAGEMENT

From the preceding discussion of dialogue by Buber, Jaspers, Gadamer, and Habermas, some major principles of authentic dialogue emerge. Among them are openness, mutuality, respect, fairness, equality, directness, honesty, and truth. The underlying theme is that if parties in a conflict are willing and ready to conduct themselves in an appropriate manner and to listen to each other's position while remaining open to the possibility of changing one's views if found to be incorrect, they can have a productive dialogue with one another. It is only then that the power of dialogue can help bring about understanding and harmony. So, we offer the following suggestions for harnessing the power of dialogue in managing intergroup conflict.

First, learn to acknowledge the other participants in the encounter as equals. Equality does not mean sameness, but it does mean extending to the other participants equal right and responsibility for the dialogue. It means acknowledging each party as human beings on an equal footing to contribute to the dialogue.

Second, approach the conflict with openness. Recognize that there is much to learn about the other participants as persons and about the worldview that has shaped their position. Be open to the possibility of being informed and enriched by the other party's perspective on the issue at hand. Openness does not mean abandoning one's point of view; rather, it means recognizing that however brilliant that point of view might appear to be, it is at best a slice of the truth and not the whole truth. It is therefore subject to modification or enrichment through dialogue.

Third, confront your prejudices. The important thing is to be aware of biases so that the other person in the dialogical encounter can present his/her ideas in all its otherness. Since prejudice is a basic human condition, the prejudices of all the interactants in the dialogue should be subjected to "openness."

Fourth, affirm the other party. One of the best ways to affirm is to listen with genuine care to the concern of the other party. Resist the temptation to filter everything only through your own definition of reality. Instead, listen to and sense the other party's definition of reality. Although one may disagree with the other party's ideas, listening genuinely to those ideas shows respect for self and others.

Fifth, use questioning as a means of dialogical exploration of the issues rather than make dogmatic assertions. Proper use of questions has a way of inviting the other party to collaborate in the search for Truth. Conversely, dogmatic assertions may be seen as an imposition of one's cultural truth. Such imposition is often met with resistance and defensiveness.

Sixth, be flexible. Genuine dialogue requires time and flexibility. Flexibility enables dialogue to function as a process by which creative minds meet to provide some synergistic answers to a problematic situation. Not all conflicts can be resolved, but flexibility allows for dialogue to continue and thus prevents conflicts from escalating into violence.

In summary, our discussions of Buber, Jaspers, Gadamer, and Habermas indicate that not only did they all view dialogue from a philosophical and pragmatic perspective, but they also recognized the special potential that human dialogue holds as a concrete, life-sustaining force. All four philosophers have grounded dialogue in *praxis,* which is inherently ethical. As Carr (1995) points out, *praxis* involves "morally informed or morally committed action" (p. 68). Thus, by making dialogue prescriptive and praxical, all four philosophers have underscored the ethical implications that are involved in the communication process. The praxical dimension of dialogue involves our making moral judgments and decisions that have moral consequences. Stewart and Zediker (2000) remind us that when "one chooses to engage dialogically, he or she not only becomes an active agent shaping the quality of the relationship, but also assumes responsibility for the ways in which communicative practice facilitates relation" (p. 240). When dialogue is envisioned as a communicative ideal, as it is by all four philosophers we have discussed, it can pull communication that emerges in a conflict situation toward a collaborative, cooperative engagement with the potential for harmony and peaceful resolution. Although it is true that the conditions of having genuine dialogue to manage intergroup conflict as envisioned by Buber, Jaspers, Gadamer, and Habermas are not always present and may not always be possible to achieve in all real-life situations, human dialogical process nevertheless creates and sustains all human communities. It is these principles of human dialogue that constitute the teleological and normative dimensions of communicative practice, and thus dialogical communication is worthy of serving as an ideal in dealing with intergroup conflicts. The principles of human dialogue, such as mutual recognition and respect, freedom, equality, solidarity, and civility, are "inherent to the universal human practice of persons coming together in solidarity to discuss, debate, and understand the world in which they live. These principles are constitutive of a conception of justice centered around the integrity of the human being" (Fairfield, 1999, p. 161).

It is our position that the principles outlined in the works of Buber, Jaspers, Gadamer, and Habermas coalesce around four essential values: Communication, Self, Other, and Truth. Positive commitment to all four is necessary for managing intergroup conflict. In some form or another, all conflicts are a contest of truth claims. The way the claims are communicated reveals something about the Self and how the Self perceives the Other. Managing intergroup conflict effectively does not necessarily mean reaching agreement on truth claims. But it does mean valuing Communication, valuing Self, and valuing the Other, all in the pursuit of Truth. Authentic communication brings about genuine knowledge of Self and Other. Genuine understanding of Self reveals the limit of one's knowledge and opens the possibility of learning something from an Other in the journey toward Transcendent Truth. Thus, Truth is seen as relational.

The pursuit of Truth at the expense of relationship results in destructive dogma. Conversely, the pursuit of relationship at the expense of Truth leads to deceptive harmony. But the pursuit of Truth as relational becomes a process of courtship in which parties woo and tease one another in the hope of reaching a union that itself becomes the ground of further positive and enriching confrontation, a confrontation in which the Other is no longer seen as being *apart* from the Self, but rather as being *a part* of the Self, in the sense of connectivity. Thus we conclude that while truth claims will always remain a source of conflict, the achievement of genuine knowledge of Self and of Other through Communication (dialogue) will diminish fear. And where fear is reduced, the potential for fighting will decrease; instead, debating becomes normal and the contests for Truth, relational.

References

Anderson, R., & Cissna, K. N. (1996). Criticism and conversational texts: Rhetorical bases of role, audience, and style in the Buber–Rogers dialogue. *Human Studies, 19,* 85–118.

Anderson, R., Cissna, K. N., & Arnett, R. C. (Eds.). (1994). *The reach of dialogue: Confirmation, voice, and community.* Cresskill, NJ: Hampton Press.

Anderson, R., & Cissna, K. N. (1997). *The Martin Buber–Carl Rogers dialogue: A new transcript with commentary.* Albany: State University of New York Press.

Arnett, R. C. (1980). Loving the stranger: A discussion guide based on the book *Dwell in Peace.* Nyack, NY: US–USSR Reconciliation Program, Fellowship of Reconciliation.

Arnett, R. C. (1981). Toward a phenomenological dialogue. *Western Journal of Speech Communication, 45,* 201–212.

Arnett, R. C. (1982). Rogers and Buber: Similarities, yet fundamental differences. *Western Journal of Speech Communication, 46,* 358–372.

Arnett, R. C. (1986). *Communication and community: Implications of Martin Buber's dialogue.* Carbondale & Edwardsville: Southern Illinois University Press.

Arnett, R. C. (1989). What is dialogic communication? Friedman's contribution and clarification. *Person-Centered Review, 4,* 42–60.

Arnett, R. C. (1992). *Dialogic education: Conversation about ideas and between people.* Carbondale: Southern Illinois University Press.

Arnett, R. C. (2001). Dialogic civility as pragmatic ethical praxis: An interpersonal metaphor for the public domain. *Communication Theory, 11,* 315–338.

Baxter, L. A., & Montgomery, B. M. (1996). *Relating: Dialogues and dialectics.* New York: Guilford Press.

Buber, M. (1970). *I and Thou* (W. Kauffman, Trans.). New York: Scribner's.

Buber, M. (1998). *The knowledge of man: Selected essays* (M. Friedman, Ed.; M. Friedman & R. G. Smith, Trans.). New York: Humanity Books.

Burleson, B. R., & Kline, S. L. (1979). Habermas' theory of communication: A critical explication. *Quarterly Journal of Speech, 65,* 412–428.

Carr, W. (1995). *For education: Towards critical educational inquiry.* Buckingham: Open University Press.

Cissna, K. N., & Anderson, R. (1990). The contributions of Carl Rogers to a philosophical praxis of dialogue. *Western Journal of Speech Communication, 54,* 125–147.

Cissna, K. N., & Anderson, R. (1994). The 1957 Martin Buber–Carl Rogers dialogue, as dialogue. *Journal of Humanistic Psychology, 34,* 11–45.

Cissna, K. N., & Anderson, R. (1996). Dialogue in public: Looking critically at the Buber–Rogers dialogue. In M. Friedman (Ed.), *Martin Buber and the human sciences* (pp. 191–206). Albany: State University of New York Press.

Cissna, K. N., & Anderson, R. (1997). Carl Rogers in dialogue with Martin Buber: A new analysis. *Person-Centered Journal, 4,* 4–13.

Cissna, K. N., & Anderson, R. (1998). Theorizing about dialogic moments: The Buber–Rogers position and postmodern times. *Communication Theory, 8,* 63–104.

Cissna, K. N., & Anderson, R. (2002). *Moments of meeting: Buber, Rogers, and the potential for public dialogue.* Albany: State University of New York Press.

Cooke, M. (1998). Introduction. In *On the pragmatics of communication* (pp. 1–19). Cambridge, MA: MIT Press.

Deetz, S. (1978). Conceptualizing human understanding: Gadamer's hermeneutics and American communication research. *Communication Quarterly, 26,* 12–23.

Ehrlich, L. (1975). *Karl Jaspers: Philosophy as faith.* Amherst: University of Massachusetts Press.

Ehrlich, E., Ehrlich, H. E., & Pepper, G. B. (Eds., Trans.). (1986). *Karl Jaspers: Basic philosophical writings.* Atlantic Highlands, NJ: Humanities Press.

Fairfield, P. (1999). Hermeneutical ethical theory. In G. B. Madison & M. Fairbairn (Eds.), *The ethics of postmodernity: Current trends in continental thought* (pp. 138–162). Evanston, IL: Northwestern University Press.

Friedman, M. S. (1960). *Martin Buber: The life of dialogue.* New York: Harper Torchbooks.

Gadamer, H.-G. (1976). *Philosophical hermeneutics* (D. E. Linge, Trans.). Berkeley: University of California Press.

Gadamer, H.-G. (1989). *Truth and method.* (J. Weinsheimer & D. G. Marshall, Trans.). New York: Crossroad. (Original work published 1960)

Gordon, R. D. (2000). Karl Jaspers: Existential philosopher of dialogical communication. *Southern Communication Journal, 65,* 105–118.

Habermas, J. (1979). *Communication and the evolution of society* (T. McCarthy, Trans.). Boston: Beacon Press.

Habermas, J. (2001). *The liberating power of symbols* (P. Dewes, Trans.). Cambridge, MA: MIT Press.

Jaspers, K. (1955). *Reason and Existenz* (W. Earle, Trans.). New York: Noonday Press.

Jaspers, K. (1961). *Atombombe und die Zukunft des Menschen* [Atom bomb and the future of mankind] (E. B. Ashton, Trans.). Chicago: University of Chicago Press.

Jaspers, K. (1970). *Philosophy: Vol. II.* (E. B. Ashton, Trans.). Chicago: University of Chicago Press.

Johannesen, R. L. (1971). The emerging concept of communication as dialogue. *Quarterly Journal of Speech, 57,* 373–382.

Johannesen, R. L. (2000). Nel Nodding's uses of Martin Buber's philosophy of dialogue. *Southern Communication Journal, 65,* 151–160.

Poulakos, J. (1974). Components of dialogue. *Western Speech, 38,* 199–212.

Roy, A., & Starosta, W. J. (2001). Hans-Georg Gadamer, language, and intercultural communication. *Language and Intercultural Communication, 1,* 6–20.

Scheibler, I. (2000). *Gadamer: Between Heidegger and Habermas.* Lanham, MD: Rowman and Littlefield.

Stewart, J. (1978). Foundations of dialogic communication. *Quarterly Journal of Speech, 64,* 83–201.

Stewart, J., & Zediker, K. (2000). Dialogue as tensional, ethical practice. *Southern Communication Journal, 65,* 224–241.

White, K. W. (1994). Hans-Georg Gadamer's philosophy of language: A constitutive-dialogic approach to interpersonal understanding. In K. Carter & M. Presnell (Eds.), *Interpretive approaches to interpersonal communication* (pp. 83–114). Albany: State University of New York Press.

Concepts and Questions

1. Why do Roy and Oludaja believe that polarization of ideas is such a serious problem? Do you agree? If so, why?
2. Is dialogue, as discussed by Roy and Oludaja, possible in today's world?
3. What solutions to conflict do you believe would be more effective than dialogue?
4. Give an example of each of Buber's five major characteristics of dialogue.
5. What is the role of compromise in human dialogue?
6. According to Gadamer, what is the major distinction between appropriate questions and rhetorical questions?
7. Would you add any items to the Roy and Oludaja list of characteristics that are part of successful dialoguing? If so, what characteristics?

Sojourner Adaptation

POLLY A. BEGLEY

I am not an Athenian or a Greek, but a citizen of the world.

SOCRATES

What does it mean to be a global citizen when world economic markets change by the minutes or seconds, rebels plot in online chat rooms to overthrow oppressive governmental regimes, and borders on a map mean nothing as deadly "greenhouse" gasses and diseases permeate the planet? Economic, political, environmental, and cultural interdependence have made humanity aware that no one nation can meet the challenges of the current global frontier alone.

Former Citicorp chairman, Walter Wriston, described globalization as a world that is "tied together in a single electronic market moving at the speed of light" (A. T. Kearney Inc., 2001, p. 58). The economic statistics are staggering as we witness 1.5 trillion U.S. dollars moving around the world daily. Specifically, advanced technology allows bonds and equities to flow across U.S. borders at a rate 54 times faster than in 1970, 55 times faster in Japan, and 60 times faster in Germany.

Technology is also changing the landscape of global politics. Literally thousands of Internet sites have been created to disseminate information for "Free Tibet" and "Free Burma" campaigns. Nobel Peace Prize winner Aung San Suu Kyi was under house arrest in Burma, but everyone still had access to her letters and speeches on the Web. The Zapatista National Liberation Army fighting government oppression in southern Mexico shouted "Ya Basta!" (Enough is enough!) across the world through such Internet sites as "Zapatistas in Cyberspace" (2001).

The United Nations (UN) climate summit at The Hague in 2000 failed to produce an accord to decrease greenhouse gas emissions. The facts are disturbing, as scientists find more evidence of global warming and overall climate disruption caused by environmental pollution. "The United States, with its wasteful lifestyle, annually pours 5.4 tons of carbon dioxide

---

 Polly Begley teaches at Fresno City College, Fresno, California.

per capita into the atmosphere—20 times what an African produces" (Radford, 2000, p. 9). Melting ice caps, droughts, and rising sea levels are just a few possible environmental disasters humanity can look forward to because of increasing global temperatures.

Diseases that know no boundaries also threaten the citizens of the planet. AIDS has caused 20 million deaths, and infection rates in some African countries have risen to more than 35% of the adult population (Singer, 2000, p. 50). Fidler notes the importance of "disease diplomacy" as people "spread shigella and malaria while fleeing across borders to business travelers and vacationers who carry pathogenic microbes on intercontinental flights" (2001, p. 80). The global spread of infectious diseases has made communication across borders a necessity for human survival.

Global instability stems from clashes between cultures as humankind creates catastrophes that are far worse than natural disasters. Human beings have to cope with living in harmony on a planet with a volatile international economy, too many people arguing over shrinking resources, mounting environmental contamination, and epidemics without borders. International travelers and tourists represent "almost 3 million people daily—up from only one million per day in 1980" (A. T. Kearney Inc., 2001, p. 57). Global citizens must learn how to communicate effectively wherever they are in the world.

This article examines challenges and strategies for living, learning, and adapting in global communities. Specifically, this is a review of the changes or adaptations that occur when a sojourner crosses cultural boundaries. First, the terms *culture shock* and *adaptation* will be defined. Second, this review will focus on the challenges associated with adapting to another cultural environment, such as ethnocentrism, language barriers, disequilibrium, length of stay, and level of knowledge. Finally, previous preparation, certain personality characteristics, personal determination, and the amount of time spent communicating are presented as possible strategies for effective adaptation.

SOJOURNERS, CULTURE, AND ADAPTATION

People who cross cultural boundaries are referred to as *sojourners*. This term includes immigrants, refugees, business executives, students, or tourists. People enter a cultural region with diverse experiences, backgrounds, knowledge, and goals, but every sojourner must adjust or adapt his or her communication for the particular cultural setting. The term *culture shock* was coined by Oberg (1960) and included a four-stage model of cultural adjustment. These stages referred to the progression of experiences throughout intercultural interactions. Culture shock occurs in the second stage and is characterized by hostility and stereotypes. Although it is generally accepted that individuals experience shocks or stress as they learn to communicate with people of another culture, the term *shock* had a negative connotation. Researchers began to utilize other terms that described the shocks, stress, rewards, and growth process of sojourners who work, travel, or live in another country.

Cross-cultural *adaptation* refers to how a sojourner chooses to cope with cultural changes. *Adaptation* is an umbrella term that encompasses culture shock, assimilation, adjustment, acculturation, integration, and coping. A sojourner's coping mechanism can include seeking out specific cultural knowledge, adopting a different style of communication, reserving judgment on unfamiliar cultural practices, or withdrawing from intercultural interactions (Witte, 1993). Adaptation is a complex and dynamic process that is an inevitable part of intercultural interactions. When a sojourner is faced with diverse cultural practices and habits, then his or her assumed cultural training and self-identity are questioned, reevaluated, and adapted for the cultural environment. For example, assertive and task-oriented communication is a positive attribute in the United States but may be considered rude or selfish in China. The process of learning new greetings, responses, or communication styles while maintaining a balanced cultural and personal identity is part of the adaptive challenges faced by a sojourner.

CHALLENGES

Challenges to sojourner adaptation include ethnocentrism, language barriers, disequilibrium, length of stay, and level of knowledge.

Ethnocentrism

A photographer uses a green or yellow filter to enhance the natural hues of a landscape. Similarly, humans have "cultural filters" that influence the ways in which they see the world around them. *Ethnocentrism* refers to a bias leading people to judge another culture's habits and practices as right or wrong, good or bad according to their own cultural attitudes, beliefs, and values. Patricia Neil Warren used another analogy to describe ethnocentric thinking. When researchers study, "the peoples of ancient times, they believe that they understand the 'circle' mind. But they underestimate that their thinking is square. So they translate everything through the square" (Krebs, 1999, p. 98). Americans are astonished that some people consume dogs or cats. Hindus in India are dismayed by societies that eat cows. Taiwanese favor jade talismans and are shocked to discover that some Americans carry a severed animal's paw in their pockets for good luck (a rabbit's foot).

Likewise, expelling mucus on a public street corner in China is acceptable behavior, but the American practice of blowing the nose into a handkerchief, then saving it in the pocket would astound many Chinese. Islamic countries have been criticized for supposedly subordinating women (e.g., female veiling practices and segregation), but Turkey is a predominantly Muslim country where about half of all stockbrokers, doctors, lawyers, professors, and bankers are women. A young Turkish stockbroker, Esra Yoldas, jokes, "Maybe the abnormal situation is not here, but in Christian countries where stockbrokers are mostly male" (Pope, 1997, p. A8). Ethnocentric attitudes limit the mind, preventing people from seeing beyond perceptions of right and wrong when in fact there are countless appropriate ways to accomplish the same goal.

Sojourners must be willing to reserve judgment and to accept that different is not automatically negative when they encounter diverse customs and habits. People may choose to eat cows, dogs, cats, or no meat at all. The range of acceptable and unacceptable behavior and communication styles varies from culture to culture. Ethnocentric attitudes can become barriers to the development of international business deals, meaningful relationships, and intercultural understanding. A key to effective adaptation is for a sojourner not to allow his or her cultural biases to influence communication with people from another culture.

Language Barriers

Learning to speak to someone in her or his native language is an indisputable part of the adaptation process. Previous research studies link language skills with adaptation effectiveness (DeVerthelyi, 1995). Long-term sojourners and immigrants in the United States who cannot speak English experience social isolation and are segregated "into fields that require less mastery of the English language and less interpersonal interaction" (Leong & Chou, 1994, p. 165). Many subtle nuances of life in a particular culture can be conveyed only through the unique words of the people living in the region. A friendly sojourner in northern Canada would be surprised when he or she cannot say "come to my place" in the Inuktitut language because Inuits never lived by themselves (Nolen, 2000, p. 37). Sojourners who do not take the time to learn and understand the words of others will experience more difficulty adapting their communication patterns to the environment.

Disequilibrium

Adaptation involves a choice of how or what to adapt to or change to fit into the host culture. An encounter with changing communication patterns, a new language, or ethnocentrism can be a stressful experience. "It is estimated that one in seven UK managers fail on international assignments and this figure is even higher for US managers, with an estimated failure rate of 25–40 percent" (Marx, 1999, p. xiii).

Sojourners are "at least temporarily, in a state of disequilibrium, which is manifested in many emotional 'lows' of uncertainty, confusion, and anxiety" (Kim, 1995, p. 177). The degree of anxiety depends on whether the person feels able to cope with a situation. A goal-oriented international manager would feel frustrated when things do not run on a strict schedule at the factory. An ambitious new employee might experience anxiety when political undercurrents or previously established relationships prevent him or her from accomplishing a task. A sojourner would also have to relearn everyday jobs such as how to order a meat-free meal in Mexico City or how to turn on the phone in a Tokyo apartment. Learning proper ways to accept or reject requests, local greetings, and polite conversational behavior can be confusing. Our own cultural habits and practices are questioned and modified as we adapt and learn to interact effectively in a different context. The adaptation process is typically characterized by "ups" and "downs" or incidents of effective and ineffective communication as cultural learning advances.

Length of Stay

The length of time spent in a different culture influences the adaptation process. A person who plans a short-term sojourn acquires less specific cultural knowledge and practical interactive experience, and is less motivated to make drastic adaptive changes to fit into the dominant culture. Tourists on a two-week tour need to know an occasional phrase in the local language and only a few details about their destination. In contrast, individuals who seek long-term business relations, work, travel, or residence are motivated to make significant changes in their communicative styles. Longer sojourns are characterized by less "social difficulty" and increasingly effective adaptations (Ward & Kennedy, 1993). Shorter sojourns are characterized by more uncertainty, confusion, or mistakes concerning appropriate communication behavior and practices.

Level of Knowledge

Should I shake hands, bow, hug, or kiss when I meet someone? Should I show enthusiasm when I speak or control my facial expressions? What kinds of topics are appropriate for initial meetings? A sojourner needs to learn many cultural customs and norms before and during a sojourn. A person's level of general and specific cultural knowledge can contribute to the adaptation process. For example, a sojourner bargaining in the Middle East should understand when to start with a conservative quote (Bedouin style) or to begin with an outrageously high number (*suk*/market style). In China, a public altercation with witnesses is one way to preserve the reputation and respect of the concerned parties. Countless international marketing campaigns have failed because companies failed to understand local values and beliefs. Negotiations stall between leaders of nations because there is insufficient understanding of appropriate communication or differing interactive styles. Incorrect information, broad cultural generalizations, or stereotypes are also destructive and may lead to misunderstandings.

STRATEGIES

Possible strategies for effective adaptation include previous preparation, certain personality characteristics, personal determination, and the amount of time spent communicating.

Preparation

Previous examples show the importance of acquiring the appropriate knowledge before intercultural contact. Sojourners should never assume that their communicative behavior would be appropriate in every cultural environment. The culture-specific and culture-general are two commonly used approaches to understanding interactive customs and behavior. The culture-specific approach focuses on one or a limited number of cultures. A culture-general approach explores "cultural traits and behaviors that are common to all cultures" (Samovar & Porter, 1995, p. 277).

Communication competence across cultures can benefit from a more general approach. Milhouse (1996) argues that students learn from general discussions of cross-cultural differences and similarities, rather than unique cultural details. One must be aware that knowing when to bow or shake hands does not guarantee communicative competence, but understanding that greetings vary according to culture helps us speak with people from diverse backgrounds. The general approach provides students with a broader base of knowledge.

The general approach can also take the focus away from differences. An emphasis on teaching regional differences perpetuates stereotypes and discourages people from realizing that each person is unique. A common focus during culture-specific intercultural training is the characteristics of the group, and individuality is ignored. It would be incorrect to assume that all Americans have blond hair, eat at McDonald's restaurants, wear jeans, and drink Coca-Cola. Every population is characterized by diversity, and generalizations can only represent certain tendencies (but not rules) within a group. Individuals are influenced by culture, as well as genetic makeup, personal experiences, and gender. The culture-general approach can teach us to reject false generalizations and to recognize the unique and exceptional characteristics of each person.

Language skills are crucial to learning and adapting to another culture. Too many people assume and fear that English has become too much of a world standard. For instance, the aboriginal languages of Canada have been reduced from 60 to 4 commonly spoken in the last century, and the Ministry of Culture has just begun several linguistic preservation projects (Nolen, 2000). Hope may be in the form of "millions of young men and women around the globe [who] have responded to the challenges of globalization by learning Japanese, German, Mandarin, Cantonese, Russian, and French" (Llosa, 2001, p. 70).

Classes, books, videotapes, or audiotapes are effective ways to study a new language; however, common words and slang terms may have to be learned in the country of origin. The common language and accent may differ slightly according to region. Taiwanese students study English for approximately 10 years, but they frequently admit that communication with speakers of English is difficult. The reason for this difficulty stems from the dichotomy between "textbook language" and the "everyday language" that contains inside references, slang, and other regional differences. The most successful communicators take every opportunity to learn new vocabulary, ask questions, and practice their new language skills. Sojourners also demonstrate an interest and appreciation for a culture by attempting to learn the language. For example, a well-timed response of *"Insha' allah"* (a common Arabic expression translated as "If God wills it") can elicit applause, lower prices from merchants, or better business relations in Egypt.

Personality Characteristics

Personality characteristics such as openness and strength of personality are influential determinants of cross-cultural adaptation effectiveness. Openness, and the related concept of flexibility, refers to a willingness to suspend judgment regarding another group's communication habits or practices. This implies a flexible attitude toward change and diverse viewpoints.

Openness and flexibility are the antithesis of ethnocentrism and are based on the assumption that there is more than one way to reach our goals. Sojourners must recognize that there is more than one path to truth or understanding. A person may choose to improve his or her life by hiring a *feng shui* (wind and water) expert to rearrange furniture or add elements of wood and water to achieve balance and harmony in the home. Another person buys a red convertible car and an expensive gold watch to improve his or her life. Both people chose different paths to reach the same goal, but only they can judge if their efforts were successful.

Personal Determination

Personal determination can stem from external factors or internal factors. *External factors* refer to the length of stay, the purpose of the visit, or the attitude of the local culture. These factors may or may not be under the control of the sojourner. Entry permits limit the amount of time for business or tourist purposes. Companies often decide the agenda for executives. In some cases, cultural differences are tolerated within a society, but in other countries the sojourner is pressured to adopt the melting pot ideology of cultural sameness. If the society exhibits high levels of conformity pressure, then visitors have little choice but to emulate communicative patterns to fit into that cultural group. A major disadvantage of the melting pot idea is that it does not allow people to "treasure their uniqueness, which, for many, evolves from ethnic, cultural or spiritual history" (Krebs, 1999, p. 16).

Internal factors include the ability to think across cultures and a value of multiculturalism. Anxiety or disequilibrium may cause sojourners to reduce stress by becoming overly critical of their surroundings and others, by attempting only monocultural solutions, or by withdrawing from the situation (e.g., locking themselves in a luxury hotel room or seeking out culturally similar people). The person who develops an ability to think across cultures meets "a complex foreign environment with an equally complex range of interpretations" (Marx, 1999, p. 61). This person does not withdraw when experiencing stress, but rather utilizes coping strategies to manage the situation and ultimately find alternative ways to communicate effectively. For example, international students who make friends with members of multiple cultural groups tend to develop a broader worldview and express higher levels of satisfaction with their exchange experiences. Multiculturalism is characterized by "understanding and accepting the values and perspectives of both [or multiple] cultures" (Marx, 1999, p. 68). Multiculturalism rejects the melting pot and isolation ideologies while embracing the idea that people do not have to choose between cultures. Finally, sojourners must understand that the adaptation process is not a predictable or linear experience. A sojourner may experience stressful conditions prompting her or him to withdraw from cross-cultural contact one day, and then the next day is able to devise more effective ways to interact with the local population.

Amount of Time Spent Communicating

The most important factor predicting adaptation is the frequency of host communication participation. The proverb "Practice makes perfect" is never truer than for the sojourner. Although insight and knowledge can be gained through prior intercultural study, additional practical wisdom is attained through everyday conversations with people from other cultures. Practical interactions or extroversion is associated with an increase in "opportunities for cultural learning" (Ward & Kennedy, 1993, p. 240). The implication is that information pertaining to cultural communicative rules, nonverbal cues, and common customs can be learned and used during communication. Practical communicative experiences contribute to overall understanding and effective adaptations.

Although there is no substitute for face-to-face interactions with locals, mediated communication can also be an important source of intercultural knowledge and language skills. A sojourner can watch TV programs or listen to radio to learn a language and gain experience about additional cultural situations or events. Popular local programs can be a good topic of conversation. Jordanians especially appreciate the soap opera *The Bold and the Beautiful* and are eager to discuss plot developments with visiting Americans. The Chinese kung-fu movie star Jackie Chan is well known in Hong Kong, Taiwan, and the United States. The royal family of Britain, World Cup soccer, video games, Pokemon cartoons, and internationally known pop singer Michael Jackson are all topics that have inspired conversations all over the world.

CONCLUSION

An economic recession in one country causes a financial downturn in other countries. The depletion of a rainforest in South America can influence the world's supply of clean air. A nuclear mishap creates a cloud that causes a path of destruction across the globe. Distance and seas no longer keep people at home as more of the world's population is on the move, seeking trade, work, knowledge, or adventure. Sojourners who cross cultural boundaries encounter challenges and initiate strategies to adapt to different cultural settings. This article has reviewed the terms and concepts associated with the coping process during a sojourn as well as specific challenges and strategies to increase adaptation effectiveness. Intercultural adaptation is a crucial area of interest for people of every nation who wish to live in a healthy and harmonious world.

References

A. T. Kearney Inc. & The Carnegie Endowment for International Peace. (2001, January/February). Measuring globalization. *Foreign Policy,* 56–64.

DeVerthelyi, R. F. (1995). International students' spouses: Invisible sojourners in the culture shock literature. *International Journal of Intercultural Relations, 19,* 387–411.

Fidler, D. P. (2001, January/February). The return of "microbialpolitik." *Foreign Policy,* 80–81.

Kim, Y. Y. (1995). Cross-cultural adaptation: An integrative theory. In R. L. Wiseman (Ed.), *Theories in intercultural communication* (pp. 170–193). Thousand Oaks, CA: Sage.

Krebs, N. B. (1999). *Edgewalkers: Defusing cultural boundaries on the new global frontier.* Far Hills, NJ: New Horizon.

Leong, F. T., & Chou, E. L. (1994). The role of ethnic identity and acculturation in the vocational behavior of Asian Americans: An integrative review. *Journal of Vocational Behavior, 44,* 155–172.

Llosa, M. V. (2001, January/February). The culture of liberty. *Foreign Policy,* 66–71.

Marx, E. (1999). *Breaking through culture shock: What you need to succeed in International business.* London: Nicholas Brealey.

Milhouse, V. A. (1996). Intercultural communication education and training goals, content, and methods. *International Journal of Intercultural Relations, 20,* 69–95.

Nolen, S. (2000, July 25). Can the Inuit keep their voice? *Globe and Mail.* In *World Press Review* (2001, February), 8–9.

Oberg, K. (1960). Culture shock: Adjustment to new cultural environment. *Practical Anthropology, 7,* 177–182.

Pope, H. (1997, March 14). The new middle: Turks add their voices to contest of generals and fundamentals. *Wall Street Journal,* pp. A1, A8.

Radford, T. (2000, November 15). The future of global warming: A grim picture. *The Guardian.* In *World Press Review* (2001, February), 8–9.

Samovar, L. A., & Porter, R. E. (1995). *Communication between cultures* (2nd ed.). Belmont, CA: Wadsworth.

Singer, P. (2000). How are your morals? *The World in 2001 (The Economist)*, p. 50.

Ward, C., & Kennedy, A. (1993). Where's the "culture" in cross-cultural transition? Comparative studies of sojourner adjustment. *Journal of Cross-Cultural Psychology, 24,* 221–249.

Witte, K. (1993). A theory of cognition and negative affect: Extending Gudykunst and Hammer's theory of uncertainty and anxiety reduction. *International Journal of Intercultural Relations, 17,* 197–215.

Zapatistas in cyberspace: A guide to analysis and resources. (2001). Available at http://www.eco.utexas.edu/Homepages/Faculty/Cleaver/zapsincyber.html

Concepts and Questions

1. What does Begley mean by the term *sojourner?*
2. What is culture shock? How does it affect a sojourner?
3. In what ways can ethnocentrism affect the adaptation of a sojourner to a new cultural environment?
4. How does reserving judgment help a sojourner deal with her or his ethnocentrism?
5. It is unusual for a sojourner to be fully fluent in the language of another culture he or she may be visiting, so what steps may be taken to help overcome language barriers?
6. What characterizes a "state of disequilibrium"? How can a sojourner minimize the disequilibrium effect?
7. How does the intended length of stay in a new culture affect a sojourner's experiences in that culture?
8. What strategies does Begley recommend for a sojourner to prepare for entry into a different culture?
9. How does an individual's personality affect interpersonal interactions in another culture?
10. What role can personal determination play in adapting to another culture?

8 Ethical Considerations: Prospects for the Future

What is the freedom of the most free?
To do what is right.

GOETHE

The goal of this book has been to help you understand intercultural communication and to assist you in appreciating the issues and problems inherent in interactions involving people from cultures different from your own—whether those cultures be across the street or across the ocean. To this end, we have presented a series of essays that examine some of the diverse variables influencing intercultural encounters. In previous chapters we have looked at what seems to be known about intercultural communication. We now shift our emphasis to focus on issues that are much more speculative and harder to pin down, yet issues that are just as important. We now move to questions concerning what is right and what is wrong, what is good and what is evil.

Most cultures recognize an ethical dimension of communication. This recognition exists at both the legal and the interpersonal level. In the United States, for example, legal recognition of communication ethics is manifest in libel, slander, truth-in-advertising, and political campaign practice laws. At the interpersonal level, there is an inherent need to be accountable for your communication acts. Whether the consequences of your messages be simple or profound, you cannot hide from the fact that your actions affect other people. As Shakespeare once put it in his *Comedy of Errors*, "Every why hath a wherefore." We now ask you to think about "why" and "wherefore."

These kinds of questions deal with the ethical considerations that are part of every intercultural encounter. For when you interact with others, your words and actions have the potential to change their behavior, attitudes, and beliefs. The changes might be short-term or long-term, immediate or delayed, but you are having an affect and an influence on another person. The very fact that your message is having an impact carries an ethical responsibility. This chapter examines that responsibility. In short, we now look at some of the questions you must confront as you have contact with people from cultures that are different from your own. As noted, this contact raises both ethical and philosophical issues about the question of how people from diverse cultures can live together without destroying themselves and the planet. In short, what sort of interpersonal and intercultural ethic must we develop if we are to practice the art and science of intercultural communication?

To set the tone for this final chapter, we begin with two essays that examine the issue of diversity and offer insight into both its importance and its limitations. The first essay, "Cultural Diversity: A World View," by Thomas Sowell, seeks "to separate the issue of the general importance of cultural diversity—not only in the United States but in the world at large—from the more specific, more parochial, and more ideological agendas that have become associated with that word in recent years."

Sowell begins by speaking about the worldwide importance of cultural diversity over centuries of human development. He believes that the whole rise of humankind "has been marked by transfers of cultural advances from one group to another and from one civilization to another." He relates how many accepted parts of Western society had their origins in the Middle East or Asia. Such vital parts of Western civilization as paper and printing had their origins in China, and the worldwide numbering system in use today originated in India. Sowell also shows how aspects of some cultures are superior to those of other cultures. For instance, once paper and printing from China became the norm in Western society, the keeping of precious records, knowledge, and thought on scrolls disappeared because books were clearly superior. He holds that "a given culture may not be superior for all things in all settings, much less remain superior over time, but particular cultural features may nevertheless be clearly better for some purposes—not just different."

Sowell insists that just like civilizations, social groups differ in their effectiveness in different fields of endeavor. He then discusses the strong sociopolitical resistance to accepting the reality of different levels and kinds of skills, interests, habits, and orientations among different groups of people. To support his position, Sowell traces American immigration patterns and shows how various cultural groups have moved and developed in their new homes.

The second essay, by Harlan Cleveland, is titled "The Limits to Cultural Diversity." Cleveland eloquently alerts us to some of the problems associated with cultural diversity while offering us guidance for the future. The basic problem brought about by increased cultural contact is clear for Cleveland: Ethnic and religious diversity is creating painful conflicts around the world. Too often these clashes turn one culture against another in ideological disputes. When this happens, according to Cleveland, "'culture' is being used . . . as an instrument of repression, exclusion, and extinction." Cleveland fears that when people see the chaos created by alien cultures, they believe that their best haven of certainty and security is a group based on ethnic similarity, common faith, economic interest, or political like-mindedness. Cleveland rejects this "single culture" hypothesis and recommends a counterforce of wider views, global perspectives, and more universal ideas. This universal view, according to Cleveland, rests in a philosophy that has civilization (universal values, ideas, and practices) as the basic core for all humanity. In this analysis, culture represents the "substance and symbols of the community," while civilization is rooted in compromise and built on "cooperation and compassion." With this orientation, people can deal with each other in ways that respect cultural differences while granting essential overarching values. Cleveland's optimism is clearly stated in his conclusion: "For the 21st century, this 'cheerful acknowledgment of difference' is the alternative to a global spread of ethnic cleansing and religious rivalry."

Our next essay, "Intercultural Personhood: An Integration of Eastern and Western Perspectives," by Young Yun Kim, is based on one of the central themes of this book—the idea that today's interconnected and fast-changing world demands that you change your assumptions about culture and your place within that culture. Recognizing these changes, Kim advances a philosophical orientation that she calls "intercultural personhood." For Kim, intercultural personhood combines the key attributes of Eastern and Western cultural traditions. She presents a model that uses these attributes and considers the basic modes of consciousness, cognitive patterns, personal and social values, and communication behavior. The notion of intercultural personhood also leads us into the concept of the multicultural person, as set forth in the next two essays.

Communication in any form has the potential to affect others. An ethical dimension must therefore be present in communication to minimize the chance of causing harm to others. In intercultural settings, where our ethnocentrism, prejudices, and lack of understanding about other cultures may influence our perceptions of others, the need for an ethical dimension in communicative interaction is paramount.

The next two essays focus directly on the issue of ethics in intercultural communication. The first, by Sam Dragga, is titled "Ethical Intercultural Technical Communication: Looking through the Lens of Confucian Ethics." Dragga's concern is with technical communicators who find themselves in a multicultural, intercultural situation "engaging issues of translation, interpretation, and localization." Dragga believes this situation holds potential peril for technical communicators because there is little guidance to identify ethical practices in intercultural technical communication. In his essay, Dragga turns to the ethics of Chinese philosophy to develop a clear picture of the different perspectives toward ethics found in the United States and China.

Dragga begins with a discussion of Confucian ethics which contain the elements of goodness, righteousness, wisdom, faithfulness, reverence, and courage. He then turns to Taoist thought, which encourages the isolation of the individual to a contemplative union with the natural world. The Taoist position is quite different from the Confucian, which requires individuals to "immerse themselves within a society of reciprocal human relationships."

Dragga demonstrates the application of ethical considerations through an analysis of the marketing approach taken to introduce Kellogg's Coco Pops in a Chinese market, examining the rhetorical strategies that involved persuasion, instruction, and education. He shows how the marketing campaign, when viewed through a Confucian lens, addressed the issues of goodness, righteousness, wisdom, faithfulness, reverence, and courage. Thus, the buying and use of this foreign product by Chinese consumers was the result of a moral decision on their part.

The last essay in this chapter is "Business Ethics and Intercultural Communication: Exploring the Overlap Between Two Academic Fields," by Johannes Brinkmann. Here, Brinkmann bridges the disciplines of business ethics and intercultural communication in order to incorporate an important ethical aspect. He believes that when companies operate in different countries, where company ownership resides in different cultures, and where norms and values reflect and are affected by cultural differences, an ethical dimension is a vital component of the communication process.

To accomplish his goals, Brinkmann introduces basic ethical definitions through classic case examples followed by a consideration of selected important issues relevant to business ethics. He then addresses cultural and ethical relativism through reference to a fourfold illustration that combines both types of relativism to form a process model. His model departs from cultural and moral relativism and describes how communicators can transcend such relativism. He concludes with a list of ten theses that summarize the use of ethical considerations in intercultural business communication.

One final note: Much of what we offer in this chapter is subjective and may even appear naive to some readers. Neither the authors nor we apologize for maintaining that in intercultural contacts each person should aim for the ideal. What we introduce here are suggestions for developing new ways of perceiving yourself and others. In so doing, we can all help make this complex and shrinking planet a more habitable and peaceful place for its more than 6.5 billion residents.

Cultural Diversity: A World View

THOMAS SOWELL

Diversity has become one of the most often used words of our time—and a word almost never defined. Diversity is invoked in discussions of everything from employment policy to curriculum reform, from entertainment to politics. Nor is the word merely a description of the long-known fact that the U.S. population is made up of people from many countries, many races, and many cultural backgrounds. All that was well known long before the word *diversity* became an insistent part of our vocabulary, an invocation, an imperative, or a bludgeon in ideological conflicts.

The very motto of the United States—*E Pluribus Unum*—recognizes the diversity of the American people. For generations, this diversity has been celebrated, whether in comedies like *Abie's Irish Rose* (the famous play featuring a Jewish boy and an Irish girl) or in patriotic speeches on the Fourth of July. Yet one senses something very different in today's crusades for "diversity"—certainly not a patriotic celebration of America and often a sweeping criticism of the United States, or even a condemnation of Western civilization as a whole.

At the very least, we need to separate the issue of the general importance of cultural diversity—not only in the United States but in the world at large—from the more specific, more parochial, and more ideological agendas that have become associated with that word in recent years. I would like to talk about the worldwide importance of cultural diversity over centuries of human history before returning to the narrower issues of our time.

The entire history of the human race, the rise of man from the caves, has been marked by transfers of cultural advances from one group to another and from one civilization to another. Paper and printing, for example, are today vital parts of Western civilization—but they originated in China centuries before they made their way to Europe. So did the magnetic compass, which made possible the great ages of exploration that put the Western Hemisphere in touch with the rest of mankind. Mathematical concepts likewise migrated from one culture to another: Trigonometry came from ancient Egypt, and the whole numbering system now used throughout the world originated among the Hindus of India, though Europeans called this system Arabic numerals because the Arabs were the intermediaries through which these numbers reached medieval Europe. Indeed, much of the philosophy of ancient Greece first reached Western Europe in Arabic translations, which were then retranslated into Latin or into the vernacular languages of the Western Europeans.

Much that became part of the culture of Western civilization originated outside that civilization, often in the Middle East or Asia. The game of chess came from India, gunpowder from China, and various mathematical concepts from the Islamic world, for example. The conquest of Spain by Moslems in the eighth century A.D. made Spain a center for the diffusion into Western Europe of the more advanced knowledge of the Mediterranean world and of the Orient in astronomy, medicine, optics, and geometry. The later rise of Western Europe to world preeminence in science and technology built upon these foundations, and then the science and technology of European civilization began to spread around the world, not only to European offshoot societies such as the United States and Australia but also to non-European cultures, of which Japan is perhaps the most striking example.

The historic sharing of cultural advances until they became the common inheritance of the human race implied much more than cultural diversity. It implied that some cultural features were not only different from others but *better* than others. The very fact that people—all people, whether Europeans, Africans, Asians, or others—have repeatedly chosen to abandon some feature of their own culture in order to replace it with something from another culture implies that the replacement served their purposes more effectively: Arabic numerals are not simply different from Roman numerals; they are *better* than Roman numerals. This is shown by their replacing Roman numerals in many countries whose own cultures derived from Rome, as well as in other countries whose respective numbering systems were likewise superseded by so-called Arabic numerals.

Reprinted from *The American Enterprise*, Vol. 2, No. 3, 1991, pp. 43–55. Thomas Sowell is at the Hoover Institute, Stanford University, Stanford, California.

It is virtually inconceivable today that the distances in astronomy or the complexities of higher mathematics could be expressed in Roman numerals. Merely to express the year of American independence—MDCCLXXVI—requires more than twice as many Roman numerals as Arabic numerals. Moreover, Roman numerals offer more opportunities for errors, as the same digit may be either added or subtracted, depending on its place in the sequence. Roman numerals are good for numbering kings or Super Bowls, but they cannot match the efficiency of Arabic numerals in most mathematical operations—and that is, after all, why we have numbers at all. Cultural features do not exist merely as badges of "identity" to which we have some emotional attachment. They exist to meet the necessities and forward the purposes of human life. When they are surpassed by features of other cultures, they tend to fall by the wayside or to survive only as marginal curiosities, like Roman numerals today.

Not only concepts, information, products, and technologies transfer from one culture to another. The natural produce of the Earth does the same. Malaysia is the world's leading grower of rubber trees—but those trees are indigenous to Brazil. Most of the rice grown in Africa today originated in Asia, and its tobacco originated in the Western Hemisphere. Even a great wheat-exporting nation like Argentina once imported wheat, which was not a crop indigenous to that country. Cultural diversity, viewed internationally and historically, is not a static picture of differentness but a dynamic picture of competition in which what serves human purposes more effectively survives and what does not tends to decline or disappear.

Manuscript scrolls once preserved the precious records, knowledge, and thought of European or Middle Eastern cultures. But once paper and printing from China became known in these cultures, books were clearly far faster and cheaper to produce and drove scrolls virtually into extinction. Books were not simply different from scrolls; they were *better* than scrolls. The point that some cultural features are better than others must be insisted on today because so many among the intelligentsia either evade or deny this plain reality. The intelligentsia often use words like "perceptions" and "values" as they argue, in effect, that it is all a matter of how you choose to look at it.

They may have a point in such things as music, art, and literature from different cultures, but there are many human purposes common to peoples of all cultures. They want to live rather than die, for example. When Europeans first ventured into the arid interior of Australia, they often died of thirst or hunger in a land where the Australian aborigines had no trouble finding food or water. Within that particular setting, at least, the aboriginal culture enabled people to do what both aborigines and Europeans wanted to do—survive. A given culture may not be superior for all things in all settings, much less remain superior over time, but particular cultural features may nevertheless be clearly better for some purposes—not just different.

Why is there any such argument in the first place? Perhaps it is because we are still living in the long, grim shadow of the Nazi Holocaust and are understandably reluctant to label anything or anyone "superior" or "inferior." But we don't need to. We need only recognize that particular products, skills, technologies, agricultural crops, or intellectual concepts accomplish particular purposes better than their alternatives. It is not necessary to rank one whole culture over another in all things, much less to claim that they remain in that same ranking throughout history. They do not.

Clearly, cultural leadership in various fields has changed hands many times. China was far in advance of any country in Europe in a large number of fields for at least a thousand years and as late as the 16th century had the highest standard of living in the world. Equally clearly, China today is one of the poorer nations of the world and is having great difficulty trying to catch up to the technological level of Japan and the West, with no real hope of regaining its former world preeminence in the foreseeable future.

Similar rises and falls of nations and empires have been common over long stretches of human history. Examples include the rise and fall of the Roman Empire, the "golden age" of medieval Spain and its decline to the level of one of the poorest nations in Europe today, and the centuries-long triumphs of the Ottoman Empire—intellectually as well as on the battlefields of Europe and the Middle East—and then its long decline to become known as "the sick man of Europe." But although cultural leadership has changed hands many times, that leadership has been real at given times, and much of what was achieved in the process has contributed enormously to our well-being and opportunities today. Cultural competition is not a zero-sum game. It is what advances the human race.

If nations and civilizations differ in their effectiveness in different fields of endeavor, so do social groups.

Here there is especially strong resistance to accepting the reality of different levels and kinds of skills, interests, habits, and orientations among different groups of people. One academic writer, for example, said that 19th-century Jewish immigrants to the United States were fortunate to arrive just as the garment industry in New York began to develop. I could not help thinking that Hank Aaron was similarly fortunate—that he often came to bat just as a home run was due to be hit. It might be possible to believe that these Jewish immigrants just happened to be in the right place at the right time if you restrict yourself to their history in the United States. But, again taking a world view, we find Jews prominent, often predominant, and usually prospering, in the apparel industry in medieval Spain, in the Ottoman Empire, in the Russian Empire, in Argentina, in Australia, and in Brazil. How surprised should we be to find them predominant in the same industry in the United States?

Other groups have also excelled in their own special occupations and industries. Indeed, virtually every group excels at something. Germans, for example, have been prominent as pioneers in the piano industry. American piano brands such as Steinway and Schnabel, not to mention the Wurlitzer organ, are signs of the long prominence in this industry of Germans, who produced the first pianos in colonial America. Germans also pioneered in piano building in czarist Russia, Australia, France, and England. Chinese immigrants have, at one period of history or another, run more than half the grocery stores in Kingston (Jamaica) and Panama City and conducted more than half of all retail trade in Malaysia, the Philippines, Vietnam, and Cambodia. Other groups have dominated retail trade in other parts of the world—the Gujaratis from India in East Africa and in Fiji and the Lebanese in parts of West Africa, for example.

Nothing has been more common than for particular groups—often a minority—to dominate particular occupations or industries. Seldom do they have any ability to keep out others—and certainly not to keep out the majority population. They are simply *better* at the particular skills required in that occupation or industry. Sometimes we can see why. When Italians have made wine in Italy for centuries, it is hardly surprising that they should become prominent among wine makers in Argentina or in California's Napa Valley. Similarly, when Germans in Germany have been for centuries renowned for their beer making, how surprised should we be that in Argentina they became as prominent among beer makers as the Italians were among wine makers? How surprised should we be that beer making in the United States arose where there were concentrations of German immigrants—in Milwaukee and St. Louis, for example? Or that the leading beer producers to this day have German names like Anheuser-Busch and Coors, among many other German names?

Just as cultural leadership in a particular field is not permanent for nations or civilizations, neither is it permanent for racial, ethnic, or religious groups. By the time the Jews were expelled from Spain in 1492, Europe had overtaken the Islamic world in medical science, so that Jewish physicians who sought refuge in the Ottoman Empire found themselves in great demand in that Moslem country. By the early 16th century, the sultan of the Ottoman Empire had on his palace medical staff 42 Jewish physicians and 21 Moslem physicians. With the passage of time, however, the source of the Jews' advantage—their knowledge of Western medicine—eroded as successive generations of Ottoman Jews lost contact with the West and its further progress. Christian minorities within the Ottoman Empire began to replace the Jews, not only in medicine but also in international trade and even in the theater, once dominated by Jews. The difference was that these Christian minorities—notably Greeks and Armenians—maintained their ties in Christian Europe and often sent their sons there to be educated. It was not race or ethnicity as such that was crucial, but maintaining contacts with the ongoing progress of Western civilization. By contrast, the Ottoman Jews became a declining people in a declining empire. Many, if not most, were Sephardic Jews from Spain—once the elite of world Jewry. But by the time the state of Israel was formed in the 20th century, those Sephardic Jews who had settled for centuries in the Islamic world now lagged painfully behind the Ashkenazic Jews of the Western world—notably in income and education. To get some idea of what a historic reversal that has been in the relative positions of Sephardic and Ashkenazic Jews, one need only note that Sephardic Jews in colonial America sometimes disinherited their own children for marrying Ashkenazic Jews.

Why do some groups, subgroups, nations, or whole civilizations excel in some particular fields rather than others? All too often, the answer to that question must be: Nobody really knows. It is an unanswered question largely because it is an *unasked* question. It is an uphill struggle merely to get acceptance of the fact that large differences exist among peoples, not just in specific skills in the narrow sense (computer science, basketball, or brewing beer) but more fundamentally in different interests, orientations, and values that determine which particular skills they seek to develop and with what degree of success. Merely to suggest that these internal cultural factors play a significant role in various economic, educational, or social outcomes is to invite charges of "blaming the victim." It is much more widely acceptable to blame surrounding social conditions or institutional policies.

But if we look at cultural diversity internationally and historically, there is a more basic question whether blame is the real issue. Surely, no human being should be blamed for the way his culture evolved for centuries before he was born. Blame has nothing to do with it. Another explanation that has had varying amounts of acceptance at different times and places is the biological or genetic theory of differences among peoples. I have argued *against* this theory in many places but will not take the time to go into these lengthy arguments here. A world view of cultural differences over the centuries undermines the genetic theory as well. Europeans and Chinese, for example, are clearly genetically different. Equally clearly, China was a more advanced civilization than Europe in many scientific, technological, and organizational ways for at least a thousand years. Yet over the past few centuries, Europe has moved ahead of China in many of these same ways. If those cultural differences were due to genes, how could these two races have changed positions so radically from one epoch in history to another?

All explanations of differences between groups can be broken down into heredity and environment. Yet a world view of the history of cultural diversity seems, on the surface at least, to deny both. One reason for this is that we have thought of environment too narrowly—as the immediate surrounding circumstances or differing institutional policies toward different groups. Environment in that narrow sense may explain some group differences, but the histories of many groups completely contradict that particular version of environment as an explanation. Let us take just two examples out of many that are available.

Jewish immigrants from Eastern Europe and Italian immigrants from southern Italy began arriving in the United States in large numbers at about the same time in the late 19th century, and their large-scale immigration also ended at the same time, when restrictive immigration laws were passed in the 1920s. The two groups arrived here in virtually the same economic condition—namely, destitute. They often lived in the same neighborhoods, and their children attended the same schools, sitting side by side in the same classrooms. Their environments—in the narrow sense in which the term is commonly used—were virtually identical. Yet their social histories in the United States have been very different.

Over the generations, both groups rose, but they rose at different rates, through different means, and in a very different mixture of occupations and industries. Even wealthy Jews and wealthy Italians tended to become rich in different sectors of the economy. The California wine industry, for example, is full of Italian names like Mondavi, Gallo, and Rossi, but the only prominent Jewish wine maker—Manischewitz—makes an entirely different kind of wine, and no one would compare Jewish wine makers with Italian wine makers in the United States. When we look at Jews and Italians in the very different environmental setting of Argentina, we see the same general pattern of differences between them. The same is true if we look at the differences between Jews and Italians in Australia, or Canada, or Western Europe.

Jews are not Italians, and Italians are not Jews. Anyone familiar with their very different histories over many centuries should not be surprised. Their fate in America was not determined solely by their surrounding social conditions in America or by how they were treated by American society. They were different before they got on the boats to cross the ocean, and those differences crossed the ocean with them.

We can take it a step further. Even among Ashkenazic Jews, those originating in Eastern Europe have had significantly different economic and social histories from those originating in Germanic Central Europe, including Austria as well as Germany itself. These differences have persisted among their descendants not only in New York and Chicago but as far away as Melbourne and Sydney. In Australia, Jews from Eastern Europe have tended to cluster in and around Melbourne, while Germanic Jews have settled in and around Sydney. They even have a saying among themselves that Melbourne is a cold city with warm Jews while Sydney is a warm city with cold Jews.

A second and very different example of persistent cultural differences involves immigrants from Japan. As everyone knows, many Japanese Americans were interned during World War II. What is less well known is that there is and has been an even larger Japanese population in Brazil than in the United States. These Japanese, incidentally, own approximately three-quarters as much land in Brazil as there is in Japan. (The Japanese almost certainly own more agricultural land in Brazil than in Japan.) In any event, very few Japanese in Brazil were interned during World War II. Moreover, the Japanese in Brazil were never subjected to the discrimination suffered by Japanese Americans in the decades before World War II. Yet, during the war, Japanese Americans overwhelmingly remained loyal to the United States, and Japanese American soldiers won more than their share of medals in combat. But in Brazil, the Japanese were overwhelmingly and even fanatically loyal *to Japan*. You cannot explain the difference by anything in the environment of the United States or the environment of Brazil. But if you know something about the history of those Japanese who settled in these two countries, you know that they were culturally different *in Japan, before* they ever got on the boats to take them across the Pacific Ocean—and they were still different decades later.

These two groups of immigrants left Japan during very different periods in the cultural evolution of Japan itself. A modern Japanese scholar has said: "If you want to see Japan of the Meiji era, go to the United States. If you want to see Japan of the Taisho era, go to Brazil." The Meiji era was a more cosmopolitan, pro-American era; the Taisho era was one of fanatical Japanese nationalism.

If the narrow concept of environment fails to explain many profound differences between groups and subgroups, it likewise fails to explain many very large differences in the economic and social performance of nations and civilizations. An 18th-century writer in Chile described that country's many natural advantages in climate, soil, and natural resources—and then asked in complete bewilderment why it was such a poverty-stricken country. That same question could be asked of many countries today. Conversely, we could ask why Japan and Switzerland are so prosperous when they are both almost totally lacking in natural resources. Both are rich in what economists call "human capital"—the skills of their people. No doubt there is a long and complicated history behind the different skill levels of different peoples and nations. The point here is that the immediate environment—whether social or geographic—is only part of the story.

Geography may well have a significant role in the history of peoples, but perhaps not simply by presenting them with more or fewer natural resources. Geography shapes or limits peoples' opportunities for cultural interactions and the mutual development that comes out of that. Small, isolated islands in the sea have seldom been sources of new scientific advances or technological breakthroughs—regardless of where such islands were located and regardless of the race of the people on these islands. There are islands on land as well. Where soil fertile enough to support human life exists only in isolated patches, widely separated, there tend to be isolated cultures (often with different languages or dialects) in a culturally fragmented region. Isolated highlands often produce insular cultures, lagging in many ways behind the cultures of the lowlanders of the same race—whether we are talking about medieval Scotland, colonial Ceylon, or the contemporary Montagnards of Vietnam.

With geographical environments as with social environments, we are talking about long-run effects, not simply the effects of immediate surroundings. When Scottish highlanders, for example, immigrated to North Carolina in colonial times, they had a very different history from that of Scottish lowlanders who settled in North Carolina. For one thing, the lowlanders spoke English while the highlanders spoke Gaelic—on into the 19th century. Obviously, speaking only Gaelic—in an English-speaking country—affects a group's whole economic and social progress.

Geographical conditions vary as radically in terms of how well they facilitate or impede large-scale cultural interactions as they do in their distribution of natural resources. We are not even close to being able to explain how all these geographical influences have operated throughout history. That too is an unanswered question largely because it is an unasked question—and it is an unasked question because many are seeking answers in terms of immediate social environment or are vehemently insisting that they have already found the answer in those terms.

How radically do geographic environments differ—not just in terms of tropical versus arctic climates but also in the very configuration of the land and how that helps or hinders large-scale interactions among peoples? Consider one statistic: Africa is more than twice the size of Europe, and yet Africa has a shorter coastline than Europe. That seems almost impossible. But the reason is that Europe's coastline is far more convoluted, with many harbors and inlets being formed all around the continent. Much of the coastline of Africa is smooth—which is to say, lacking the harbors that make large-scale maritime trade possible by sheltering the ships at anchor from the rough waters of the open sea. Waterways of all sorts have played a major role in the evolution of cultures and nations around the world. Harbors on the sea are not the only waterways. Rivers are also very important. Virtually every major city on Earth is located on either a river or a harbor. Whether it is such great harbors as those in Sydney, Singapore, or San Francisco, London on the Thames, Paris on the Seine, or numerous other European cities on the Danube, waterways have been the lifeblood of urban centers for centuries. Only very recently has man-made, self-powered transportation like automobiles and airplanes made it possible to produce an exception to the rule like Los Angeles. (There a Los Angeles River, but you don't have to be Moses to walk across it in the summertime.) New York has both a long and deep river and a huge sheltered harbor.

None of these geographical features in themselves create a great city or develop an urban culture. Human beings do that. But geography sets the limits within which people can operate—and in some places it sets those limits much wider than in others. Returning to our comparison of the continents of Europe and Africa, we find that they differ as radically in rivers as they do in harbors. There are entire nations in Africa without a single navigable river—Libya and South Africa, for example. "Navigable" is the crucial word. Some African rivers are navigable only during the rainy season. Some are navigable only between numerous cataracts and waterfalls. Even the Zaire River, which is longer than any river in North America and carries a larger volume of water, has too many waterfalls too close to the ocean for it to become a major artery of international commerce. Such commerce is facilitated in Europe not only by numerous navigable rivers but also by the fact that no spot on the continent, outside of Russia, is more than 500 miles from the sea. Many places in Africa are more than 500 miles from the sea, including the entire nation of Uganda.

Against this background, how surprised should we be to find that Europe is the most urbanized of all inhabited continents and Africa the least urbanized? Urbanization is not the be-all and end-all of life, but certainly an urban culture is bound to differ substantially from nonurban cultures, and the skills peculiar to an urban culture are far more likely to be found among groups from an urban civilization. (Conversely, an interesting history could be written about the failures of urbanized groups in agricultural settlements.)

Looking within Africa, the influence of geography seems equally clear. The most famous ancient civilization on the continent arose within a few miles on either side of Africa's longest navigable river, the Nile, and even today the two largest cities on the continent, Cairo and Alexandria, are on that river. The great West African kingdoms in the region served by the Niger River and the long-flourishing East African economy based around the great natural harbor on the island of Zanzibar are further evidence of the role of geography. Again, geography is not all-determining—the economy of Zanzibar has been ruined by government policy in recent decades—but, nevertheless, geography is an important long-run influence on the shaping of cultures as well as in narrowly economic terms.

What are the implications of a world view of cultural diversity on the narrower issues being debated under that label in the United States today? Although "diversity" is used in so many different ways in so many different contexts that it seems to mean all things to all people, a few themes appear again and again. One of these broad themes is that diversity implies organized efforts at the preservation of cultural differences, perhaps governmental efforts, perhaps government subsidies to various programs run by the advocates of "diversity."

This approach raises questions as to what the purpose of culture is. If what is important about cultures is that they are emotionally symbolic, and if differentness is cherished for the sake of differentness, then this particular version of cultural "diversity" might make some sense. But cultures exist even in isolated societies where there are no other cultures around—where there is no one else and nothing else from which to be different. Cultures exist to serve the vital, practical requirements of human life—to structure a society so as to perpetuate the species, to pass on the hard-learned knowledge and experience of generations past and centuries past to the young and inexperienced in order to spare the next generation the costly and dangerous process of learning everything all over again from scratch through trial and error—including fatal errors. Cultures exist so that people can know how to get food and put a roof over their heads, how to cure the sick, how to cope with the death of loved ones, and how to get along with the living. Cultures are not bumper stickers. They are living, changing ways of doing all the things that have to be done in life.

Every culture discards over time the things that no longer do the job or that don't do the job as well as things borrowed from other cultures. Each individual does this, consciously or not, on a day-to-day basis. Languages take words from other languages, so that Spanish as spoken in Spain includes words taken from Arabic, and Spanish as spoken in Argentina has Italian words taken from the large Italian immigrant population there. People eat Kentucky Fried Chicken in Singapore and stay in Hilton Hotels in Cairo.

This is *not* what some of the advocates of "diversity" have in mind. They seem to want to preserve cultures in their purity, almost like butterflies preserved in amber. Decisions about change, if any, seem to be regarded as collective decisions, political decisions. But that is not how any cultures have arrived where they are. Individuals have decided for themselves how much of the old they wished to retain, how much of the new they found useful in their own lives. In this way, cultures have enriched each other in all the great civilizations of the world. In this way, great port cities and their crossroads of cultures have become centers of progress all across the planet. No culture has grown great in isolation—but a number of cultures have made historic and even astonishing advances when their isolation was ended, usually by events beyond their control.

Japan was a classic example in the 19th century, but a similar story could be told of Scotland in an earlier era, when a country where once even the nobility were illiterate became—within a short time, as history is measured—a country that produced world pioneers in field after field: David Hume in philosophy, Adam Smith in economics, Joseph Black in chemistry, Robert Adam in architecture, and James Watt, whose steam engine revolutionized modern industry and transport. In the process, the Scots lost their language but gained world preeminence in many fields. Then a whole society moved to higher standards of living than anyone had ever dreamed of in their poverty-stricken past.

There were higher standards in other ways as well. As late as the 18th century, it was considered noteworthy that pedestrians in Edinburgh no longer had to be on the alert for sewage being thrown out the windows of people's homes or apartments. The more considerate Scots yelled a warning, but they threw out the sewage anyway. Perhaps it was worth losing a little of the indigenous culture to be rid of that problem.

Those who use the term *cultural diversity* to promote a multiplicity of segregated ethnic enclaves are doing an enormous harm to the people in those enclaves. However they live socially, the people in those enclaves are going to have to compete economically for a livelihood. Even if they were not disadvantaged before, they will be very disadvantaged if their competitors from the general population are free to tap the knowledge, skills, and analytical techniques that Western civilization has drawn from all the other civilizations of the world, while those in the enclaves are restricted to what exists in the subculture immediately around them.

We need also to recognize that many great thinkers of the past—whether in medicine or philosophy, science or economics—labored not simply to advance whatever particular group they happened to have come from but to advance the human race. Their legacies, whether cures for deadly diseases or dramatic increases in crop yields to fight the scourge of hunger, belong to all people—and all people need to claim that legacy, not seal themselves off in a dead-end of tribalism or in an emotional orgy of cultural vanity.

Concepts and Questions

1. How does Sowell's treatment of the notion of diversity differ from the general usage in the United States today?
2. What benefits derive from the meeting of various cultures and their inherent diversity?
3. How does cultural leadership in various fields of human endeavor change from time to time? What are the advantages and/or disadvantages of this activity?
4. Sowell asserts that some groups, subgroups, nations, or whole civilizations excel in some particular fields rather than others. What explanations does he provide to justify this assertion?
5. Sowell asserts that explanations of differences between groups can be broken down into heredity and environment. Do you agree or disagree? Why?
6. What role does geography play in developing diversity among groups?
7. Sowell differentiates between a wide view and a narrow view of diversity. What implications does he advance when people take the narrow view of diversity?
8. Do you believe, as Sowell asserts, that some people use the term *cultural diversity* to promote a multiplicity of segregated ethnic enclaves?

The Limits to Cultural Diversity

Harlan Cleveland

I'm engaged just now in an effort to think through the most intellectually interesting, and morally disturbing, issue in my long experience of trying to think hard about hard subjects. I call it "The Limits of Cultural Diversity." If that seems obscure, wait a moment.

After the multiple revolutions of 1989, it began to look as if three ideas we have thought were Good Things would be getting in each other's way, which is not a Good Thing. What I have called the "triple dilemma," or "trilemma," is the mutually damaging collision of individual human rights, cultural human diversity, and global human opportunities. Today the damage from that collision is suddenly all around us.

In 1994, in the middle of Africa, ethnicity took over as an exclusive value, resulting in mass murder by machete. In ex-Yugoslavia (and too many other places), gunpowder and rape accomplish the same purpose: trampling on human rights and erasing human futures. Even on the Internet, where individuals can now join global groups that are not defined by place names or cordoned off by gender or ethnicity, people are shouting at each other in flaming, capital-letters rhetoric.

Look hard at your hometown, at the nearest inner city; scan the world by radio, TV, or newspapers and magazines. What's happened is all too clear: Just when individual human rights have achieved superstar status in political philosophy, just when can-do information technologies promise what the UN Charter calls "better standards of life in larger freedom," culture and diversity have formed a big, ugly boulder in the road called Future.

"If we cannot end now our differences, at least we can help make the world safe for diversity." That was the key sentence in the most influential speech of John F. Kennedy's presidency: his commencement address at American University on June 10, 1963. That speech led directly (among other things) to the first nuclear test ban treaty. For most of the years since then, we were mesmerized by the threat of strategic nuclear war, but now a big nuclear war has become the least likely eventuality among the major threats to human civilization. And that brings us face to face with the puzzle identified in Kennedy's speech: how to make diversity safe.

But is "cultural diversity" really the new Satan in our firmament? Or does it just seem so because "culture" is being used—as Culture has been used in other times and places—as an instrument of repression, exclusion, and extinction?

AN EXCESS OF CULTURAL IDENTITY

In today's disordered world, the collision of cultures with global trends is in evidence everywhere. Ethnic nations, fragmented faiths, transnational businesses, and professional groups find both their inward loyalties and their international contacts leading them to question the political structures by which the world is still, if tenuously, organized. The results are sometimes symbolic caricatures ("In Rome, can a Moslem minaret be built taller than St. Peter's dome?") and sometimes broken mosaics like the human tragedy in what used to be Yugoslavia.

More people moved in 1994 than ever before in world history, driven by fear of guns or desire for more butter and more freedom. (This was true even before a couple of million Rwandans left their homes in terror—and some were floated out of the country as cadavers.) This more mobile world multiplies the incentives for individuals to develop "multiple personalities," to become "collages" of identities, with plural loyalties to overlapping groups. Many millions of people believe that their best haven of certainty and security is a group based on ethnic similarity, common faith, economic interest, or political like-mindedness.

Societies based on fear of outsiders tend toward "totalitarian" governance. Fear pushes the culture beyond normal limits on individuals' behavior. "To say that you're ready to *die* for cultural identity," said one of my colleagues at a workshop of the World Academy of Art and Science in Romania last year, "means that you're also ready to kill for cultural identity." Said another: "The ultimate consequence of what's called 'cultural identity' is Hutus and Tutsis murdering each other."

From *The Futurist,* March–April 1995, pp. 23–26. Reprinted by permission of the World Future Society. Harlan Cleveland is immediate past president of the World Academy of Art and Science.

The fear that drives people to cleave to their primordial loyalties makes it harder for them to learn to be tolerant of others who may be guided by different faiths and loyalties. But isolating oneself by clinging to one's tribe is far from a stable condition; these days, the tribe itself is highly unstable. Differences in birthrates and pressures to move will continue to mix populations together. So ethnic purity isn't going to happen, even by forcible "cleansing."

Besides, cultures keep redefining themselves by mixing with other cultures, getting to know people who look, act, and believe differently. In today's more open electronic world, cultures also expose themselves to new faiths and fashions, new lifestyles, work ways, technologies, clothing, and cuisines.

The early stage of every realization of "cultural identity," every assertion of a newfound "right" of differences, does create a distinct group marked by ethnic aspect ("black is beautiful"), gender ("women's lib"), religion ("chosen people"), or status as a political minority. But when members of a group insisting on the group's uniqueness do succeed in establishing their own personal right to be different, something very important happens: They begin to be treated *individually* as equals and tend to integrate with more inclusive communities. Traditions of separateness and discrimination are often persistent, but they are never permanent and immutable. The recent history of South Africa bears witness.

Before the fighting in Yugoslavia, the most tolerant people in that part of the world were seen by their close neighbors to be the Serbs, Croats, and Moslems living together in Bosnia and Herzegovina, with the city of Sarajevo as a special haven of mutual tolerance.

The problem does not seem to be culture itself, but cultural overenthusiasm. Cultural loyalties, says one European, have the makings of a runaway nuclear reaction. Without the moderating influence of civil society—acting like fuel rods in a nuclear reactor—the explosive potential gets out of hand. What's needed is the counterforce of wider views, global perspectives, and more universal ideas.

Post-communist societies, says a resident of one of them, have experienced a loss of equilibrium, a culture shock from the clash of traditional cultures, nostalgia for the stability of Soviet culture, and many new influences from outside. What's needed, he thinks, is cultural richness without cultural dominance, but with the moderating effect of intercultural respect.

CULTURE AND CIVILIZATION

We have inherited a fuzzy vocabulary that sometimes treats *culture* as a synonym for *civilization*. At a World Academy workshop, my colleagues and I experimented with an alternative construct. In this construct, *civilization* is what's universal—values, ideas, and practices that are in general currency everywhere, either because they are viewed as objectively "true" or because they are accepted pragmatically as useful in the existing circumstances. These accepted "truths" offer the promise of weaving together a civitas of universal laws and rules, becoming the basis for a global civil society.

What is sometimes called "management culture" appears to be achieving this kind of universal acceptance, hence becoming part of global "civilization." But nobody has to be in charge of practices that are generally accepted. For instance, the international exchange of money—a miracle of information technologies—is remarkably efficient, daily moving more than a trillion dollars' worth of money among countries. Yet no one is in charge of the system that makes it happen. Recently, the puny efforts of governments to control monetary swings by buying and selling currencies have only demonstrated governments' incapacity to control them.

If civilization is what's universal, *culture* is the substance and symbols of the community. Culture meets the basic human need for a sense of belonging, for participating in the prides and fears that are shared with an in-group. Both culture and civilization are subject to continuous change. In our time, the most pervasive changes seem to be brought about by the spread of knowledge, the fallout of information science and information technologies.

Civil society consists of many structures and networks, cutting across cultural fault lines, brought into being by their ability to help people communicate. They are not very dependent on public authority for their charters or their funding, increasingly taking on functions that used to be considered the responsibility of national governments.

Many of these "nongovernments"—such as those concerned with business and finance, scientific inquiry, the status of women, population policy, and the global environmental common—have become effective users of modern information technologies. In consequence, they are providing more and more of the policy initiative both inside countries and in world affairs.

Civilization is rooted in compromise—between the idea of a democratic state and a strong state, between a free-market economy and a caring economy, between "open" and "closed" processes, between horizontal and vertical relationships, between active and passive citizenship. The required solvent for civilization is *respect for differences.* Or, as one of my World Academy colleagues puts it, we need to learn *how to be different together.*

Civilization will be built by cooperation and compassion, in a social climate in which people in differing groups can deal with each other in ways that respect their cultural differences. "Wholeness incorporating diversity" is philosopher John W. Gardner's succinct formulation. The slogan on U.S. currency is even shorter, perhaps because it's in Latin: *E pluribus unum* ("from many, one").

LESSONS FROM AMERICAN EXPERIENCE

We Americans have learned, in our short but intensive 200-plus years of history as a nation, a first lesson about diversity: that it cannot be governed by drowning it in "integration."

I came face to face with this truth when, just a quarter century ago, I became president of the University of Hawaii. Everyone who lives in Hawaii, or even visits there, is impressed by its residents' comparative tolerance toward each other. On closer inspection, paradise seems based on paradox: Everybody's a minority. The tolerance is not despite the diversity but because of it. It is not through the disappearance of ethnic distinctions that the people of Hawaii achieved a level of racial peace that has few parallels around our discriminatory globe. Quite the contrary. The glory is that Hawaii's main ethnic groups managed to establish the right to be separate. The group separateness, in turn, helped establish the rights of individuals in each group to equality with individuals of different racial aspect, different ethnic origin, and different cultural heritage.

Hawaii's experience is not so foreign to the transatlantic migrations of the various more-or-less white Caucasians. On arrival in New York (passing that inscription on the Statue of Liberty, "Send these, the homeless, tempest-tost, to me"), the European immigrants did not melt into the open arms of the white Anglo-Saxon Protestants who preceded them. The reverse was true. The new arrivals stayed close to their own kind, shared religion and language and humor and discriminatory treatment with their soul brothers and sisters, and gravitated at first into occupations that did not too seriously threaten the earlier arrivals.

The waves of new Americans learned to tolerate each other—first as groups, only thereafter as individuals. Rubbing up against each other in an urbanizing America, they discovered not just the old Christian lesson that all men are brothers, but the hard, new, multicultural lesson that all brothers are different. Equality is not the product of similarity; it is the cheerful acknowledgment of difference.

What's so special about our experience is the assumption that people of many kinds and colors can together govern themselves without deciding in advance which kinds of people (male or female, black, brown, yellow, red, white, or any mix of these) may hold any particular public office in the pantheon of political power.

For the 21st century, this "cheerful acknowledgment of difference" is the alternative to a global spread of ethnic cleansing and religious rivalry. The challenge is great, for ethnic cleansing and religious rivalry are traditions as contemporary as Bosnia and Rwanda in the 1990s and as ancient as the Assyrians who, as Byron wrote, "came down like a wolf on the fold" but, says the biblical Book of Kings, were prevented by sword-wielding angels from taking Jerusalem.

In too many countries there is still a basic if often unspoken assumption that one kind of people is anointed to be in general charge. Try to imagine a Turkish chancellor of Germany, an Algerian president of France, a Pakistani prime minister of Britain, a Christian president of Egypt, an Arab prime minister of Israel, a Jewish president of Syria, a Tibetan ruler in Beijing, anyone but a Japanese in power in Tokyo.

Yet in the United States during the 20th century, we have already elected an Irish Catholic as president, chosen several Jewish Supreme Court justices, and racially integrated the armed forces right up to chairman of the Joint Chiefs of Staff. We have not yet adjusted—as voters in India, Britain, and Turkey have done—to having a woman atop the American political heap. But early in the 21st century, that too will come. And during that same new century, which will begin with "minorities" as one in every three Americans, there is every prospect that an African American, a Latin American, and an Asian American will be elected president of the United States.

I wouldn't dream of arguing that we Americans have found the Holy Grail of cultural diversity when in fact we're still searching for it. We have to think hard about our growing pluralism. It's useful, I believe, to dissect in the open our thinking about it, to see whether the lessons we are trying to learn might stimulate some useful thinking elsewhere. We do not yet quite know how to create "wholeness incorporating diversity," but we owe it to the world, as well as to ourselves, to keep trying.

Concepts and Questions

1. What does Cleveland mean when he speaks of making diversity safe?
2. What does Cleveland imply when he refers to "an excess of cultural identity"?
3. How does loyalty to one's own cultural identity make it difficult to be tolerant of others?
4. What is meant by the term *cultural overenthusiasm?* How does it affect intercultural relations?
5. How does Cleveland differentiate between the concepts of *culture* and *civilization?*
6. What are the hallmarks of civilization? How can they be maintained?
7. What does Cleveland imply when he states that diversity cannot be governed by drowning it in integration?

Intercultural Personhood: An Integration of Eastern and Western Perspectives

Young Yun Kim

We live in a time of clashing identities. As the tightly knit communication web has brought all cultures closer than ever before, rigid adherence to the culture of our youth is no longer feasible. Cultural identity in its "pure" form has become more a nostalgic concept than a reality. As Toffler (1980) noted, we find ourselves "[facing] a quantum leap forward. [We face] the deepest social upheaval and creative restructuring of all time. Without clearly recognizing it, we are engaged in building a remarkable new civilization from the ground up" (p. 44). Yet the very idea of cultural identity, coupled with rising nationalism and xenophobic sentiments, looms over much of today's fractious world landscape. Can the desire for some form of collective uniqueness be satisfied without resulting in divisions and conflicts among groups? Can individuals who are committed to communal values and responsibilities transcend allegiance to their own people?

This essay addresses these issues by proposing the concept of *intercultural personhood*—a way of life in which an individual develops an identity and a definition of self that integrates, rather than separates, humanity. Intercultural personhood projects a kind of self–other orientation that is open to growth—a growth beyond the perimeters of one's own cultural upbringing.[1] In making a case for the viability of intercultural personhood, we will first survey some of the core elements in the two seemingly incompatible cultural traditions of the East and the West. We will focus on the cultural apriority, or "root ideas," that define these

---

This article first appeared in the ninth edition, and has been revised for this edition. Young Yun Kim teaches at the University of Oklahoma, Norman, Oklahoma.

philosophical perspectives. A case will be made that certain aspects of these two traditions, often considered unbridgeably incompatible, are profoundly complementary and that such complementary elements can be creatively integrated into a model of human development for the 21st century, intercultural personhood. We will then examine how the process of building an intercultural personhood is actually played out in the lives of people whose life experiences span both cultural worlds.

The author's conception and discussion of intercultural personhood in this essay owes much to the writings of several prominent thinkers of the 20th century who have explored ideologies larger than national and cultural interests and that embrace all humanity. One such work is Northrop's *The Meeting of East and West* (1966), in which an "international cultural ideal" was presented as a way to provide intellectual and emotional foundations for what he envisioned as "partial world sovereignty." Inspiration has also been drawn from the work of Thompson (1973), which explored the idea of "planetary culture," or how Eastern mysticism was integrated with Western science and rationalism. The primary sources for the current analysis of Eastern and Western cultural traditions also include Nakamura's *Ways of Thought of Eastern People* (1964), Campbell's *The Power of Myth* (1988), Gulick's *The East and the West* (1963), Oliver's *Communication and Culture in Ancient India and China* (1971), Capra's *The Tao of Physics* (1975), and Hall's *Beyond Culture* (1976) and *The Dance of Life* (1983).

EASTERN AND WESTERN CULTURAL TRADITIONS

Traditional cultures throughout Asia, including India, Tibet, Japan, China, Korea, and those in Southeast Asia, have been influenced by such religious and philosophical systems as Buddhism, Hinduism, Taoism, and Zen. On the other hand, Western Europe has mainly followed the Greek and Judeo-Christian traditions. Of course, any attempt to present the cultural assumptions of these two broadly categorized civilizations inevitably sacrifices specific details and the uniqueness of variations within each tradition. No two individuals or groups hold identical beliefs and manifest uniform behaviors, and whatever characterizations we make about one culture or cultural group must be thought of as normative tendencies that vary rather than monolithic and uniform attributes. Nevertheless, several key elements distinguish each group from the other. To specify these elements is to indicate the general interconnectedness of different nations that constitute either the Eastern or the Western cultural world.

Universe and Nature

A fundamental way in which culture shapes human existence is through the explicit and implicit teachings about our relationships to the nature of the universe and the human and nonhuman realms of the world. Traditional Eastern and Western perspectives diverge significantly with respect to basic premises about these relationships. As Needham (1951) noted in his article "Human Laws and the Laws of Nature in China and the West," people in the West have conceived the universe as having been initially created and, since then, externally controlled by a divine power. As such, the Western worldview is characteristically dualistic, materialistic, and lifeless. The Judeo-Christian tradition sets "God" apart from this reality; having created it and set it into motion, God is viewed as apart from "His" creation. The fundamental material of the universe is conceived to be essentially nonliving matter, or elementary particles of matter, that interact with one another in a predictable fashion. It is as though the universe is an inanimate machine wherein humankind occupies a unique and elevated position among the life-forms that exist. Assuming a relatively barren universe, it seems only rational that humans make use of the lifeless material universe (and the "lesser" life-forms of nature) on behalf of the most intensely living—humankind itself.

Comparatively, the Eastern worldview is more holistic, dynamic, and inwardly spiritual. From the Eastern perspective, the entirety of the universe is viewed as a vast, multidimensional, living organism consisting of many interdependent parts and forces. The universe is conscious and engaged in a continuous dance of creation: The cosmic pattern is viewed as self-contained and self-organizing. It unfolds itself because of its own inner necessity and not because it is "ordered" by any external volitional power. What exists in the universe are manifestations of a divine life force. Beneath the surface appearance of things, an ultimate reality is continuously creating, sustaining, and infusing our worldly experience. The all-sustaining life force that creates our manifest universe is not apart from humans and their worldly existence. Rather, it is viewed as dynamic and intimately involved in every aspect of the cosmos—from its most minute details to its grandest features.

The traditional Eastern worldview, then, reveres the common source out of which all things arise. As Campbell (1990) noted, "people in Eastern culture—whether they are Indians, Japanese, or Tibetan—tend to think that the real mystery is in yourself . . . finding the divine not only within you, but within all things. . . . And what the Orient brings is a realization of the inward way. When you sit in meditation with your hands in your lap, with your head looking down, that means you've gone in and you're coming not just to a soul that is disengaged from God: you're coming to that divine mystery right there in yourself" (p. 89).

This perspective recognizes that everything in this world is fluid, ever-changing, and impermanent. In Hinduism, all static forms are called *maya,* which exists only as illusory concepts. This idea of the impermanence of all forms is the starting point of Buddhism. Buddhism teaches that "all compounded things are impermanent" and that all suffering in the world arises from our trying to cling to fixed forms—objects, people, or ideas—instead of accepting the world as it moves. This notion of impermanence of all forms and the appreciation of the aliveness of the universe in the Eastern worldview contrasts with the Western emphasis on the definitive forms of physical reality and their improvement through social and material progress.

Knowledge

Because the East and the West have different views of cosmic patterns, we can expect them to have different approaches to knowledge. In the East, because the universe is seen as a harmonious organism, there is a corresponding lack of dualism in epistemological patterns. The Eastern view emphasizes perceiving and knowing things synthetically, rather than analytically. The ultimate purpose of knowledge is to transcend the apparent contrasts and "see" the interconnectedness of all things. When the Eastern mystics tell us that they experience all things as manifestations of a basic oneness, they do not mean that they pronounce all things to be same or equal. Instead, they emphasize that all differences are relative within an all-encompassing phenomenon. Indeed, the awareness that all opposites are polar and, thus, a unity is one of the highest aims of knowledge. As Suzuki (1968) noted: "The fundamental idea of Buddhism is to pass beyond the world of opposites, a world built up by intellectual distinctions and emotional defilements, and to realize the spiritual world of non-distinction, which involves achieving an absolute point of view" (p. 18).

Because all opposites are interdependent, their conflict can never result in the total victory of one side but will always be a manifestation of the interplay between the two sides. A virtuous person is not one who undertakes the impossible task of striving for the "good" and eliminating the "bad," but rather one who is able to maintain a dynamic balance between the two. Transcending the opposites, one becomes aware of the relativity and polar relationship of opposites. One realizes that good and bad, pleasure and pain, life and death, winning and losing, light and dark, are not absolute experiences belonging to different categories, but merely two sides of the same reality—extreme parts of a single continuum. The Chinese sages in their symbolism of the archetypal poles, yin and yang, have emphasized this point extensively. And the idea that opposites cease to be opposites is the very essence of *Tao.* To know the Tao, the illustrious way of the universe, is the highest aim of human learning.

This holistic approach to knowledge in the East is pursued by means of "concepts by intuition," a sense of the aesthetic components of things. A concept by intuition is something immediately experienced, apprehended, and contemplated. Northrop (1966) described it as the "differentiated aesthetic continuum" within which there is no distinction between subjective and objective. The aesthetic continuum is a single all-embracing continuity. The aesthetic part of the self is also an essential part of the aesthetic object, whether the object is a flower or a person. Taoism, for example, pursues an undifferentiated aesthetic continuum as it is manifested in the differentiated, sensed aesthetic qualities in nature. The Taoist claim is that only if we take the aesthetic continuity in its all-inclusiveness as ultimate and irreducible, will we properly understand the meaning of the universe and nature. Similarly, Confucianism stresses the all-embracing aesthetic continuum with respect to its manifestations in human nature and its moral implications for human society: Only if we recognize the all-embracing aesthetic manifold to be an irreducible part of human nature will we have compassion for human beings other than ourselves.

As such, the undifferentiated aesthetic continuum is the Eastern conception of the constituted world. The differentiations within it, such as particular scenes, events, or persons, are not irreducible atomic identities, but merely arise out of the undifferentiated ground-level reality of the aesthetic continuum. Sooner or later, they fade back into it again. They are transitory and impermanent. Thus, when Eastern sages insist that one must become *selfless,* they mean that the self consists of two components: one a differentiated, unique element, distinguishing one person from any other person, and the other the all-embracing, aesthetically immediate, compassionate, and undifferentiated component. The former is temporary and transitory, and the cherishing of it, the desire for its immortality, is a source of suffering and selfishness. The part of the self that is not transitory is the aesthetic component of the self, which is identical not merely in all persons, but in all aesthetic objects throughout the universe.

Whereas the Eastern knowledge tradition has concentrated its mental processes on the holistic, intuitive, aesthetic continuum, the Western pursuit of knowledge has been based on a doctrinally formulated dualistic worldview. In this view, because the world and its various components came into existence through the individual creative acts of a god, the fundamental question is, "How can I reach out to the external inanimate world or to other people?" In this question, there is a basic dichotomy between the knower and the things to be known. Accompanying this epistemological dualism is the emphasis on rationality in the pursuit of knowledge. Since the Greek philosopher Plato "discovered" reason, virtually all subsequent Western thought—its themes, questions, and terms—has relied on an essential rational basis (Wei, 1980).

Even Aristotle, the great hero of all anti-Platonists, was not an exception. Although Aristotle did not propose, as Plato did, a realm of eternal essences ("really real") to justify the primacy of reason, he was by no means inclined to deny this primacy. This is an indication that, while the East has tended to emphasize the direct experience of oneness via intuitive concepts and contemplation, the West has viewed the faculty of the intellect as the primary instrument of worldly mastery. Compared with Eastern thought, which tends to conclude in more or less vague, imprecise statements consistent with its existential flexibility, Western thought emphasizes clear and distinct categorization and the linear, analytic logic of syllogism. Whereas the Eastern cultural drive for human development is aimed at spiritual attainment of oneness with the universe, the Western cultural drive finds its expression in its drive for material and social progress.

Time

Closely parallel to differences between the two cultural traditions regarding the nature of knowledge are differences in the perception and experience of time. Along with the immediate, undifferentiated experiencing of here and now, the Eastern time orientation can be portrayed as a placid, silent pool within which ripples come and go. Historically, the East has tended to view worldly existence as cyclical and has often depicted it with metaphors of movement such as a wheel or an ocean: The "wheel of existence" or the "ocean of waves" appears to be in a continual movement but is "not really going anywhere." Although individuals living in the world may experience a rise or fall in their personal fortunes, the lot of the whole is felt to be fundamentally unchanging. As Northrop (1966) observed, "the aesthetic continuum is the greater mother of creation, giving birth to the ineffable beauty of the golden yellows on the mountain landscape as the sun drops low in the late afternoon, only a moment later to receive that differentiation back into itself and to put another in its place without any effort" (p. 343).

Because worldly time is not experienced as going anywhere and because in spiritual time there is nowhere to go but the eternity within the now, the future is expected to be virtually the same as the past. Recurrence in both cosmic and psychological realms is very much a part of Eastern thought. Thus, the individual's aim is not to escape from the circular movement into linear time, but to become a part of the eternal through the aesthetic experience of the here and now and the conscious evolution of spirituality to "know" the all-embracing, undifferentiated wholeness. In contrast, the West has represented time either with an arrow or as a moving river that comes out of a distant place and past (which are not here and now) and that goes into an equally distant place and future (which also are not here and now). In this view of time, history is conceived of as goal-directed and gradually progressing in a certain direction (toward the universal salvation and second coming of Christ or, in secular terms, toward an ideal state such as boundless freedom or a classless society).

Closely corresponding to the above comparison is Hall's (1976, 1983) characterization of Asian cultures as "polychronic" and Western cultures as "monochronic" in their respective time orientations. Hall explained that individuals in a polychronic system are less inclined to adhere rigidly to time as a tangible, discrete, and linear entity; instead, they emphasize completion of transactions in the here and now, often carrying out more than one activity simultaneously.

Comparatively, according to Hall, a monochronic system emphasizes schedules, segmentation, promptness, and standardization of activities. We may say that the Eastern polychronic time orientation is rooted in the synchronization of human behavior with the rhythms of nature, whereas the Western time orientation is driven by the synchronization of human behavior with the rhythms of the clock or machine.

Communication

The historical ideologies examined so far have shaped the empirical content of the East and the West. The respective Eastern and Western perspectives on the universe, nature, knowledge, and time are reflected in many of the specific activities of individuals as they relate themselves to fellow human beings—how individuals view self and the group, and how they use verbal and nonverbal symbols in communication.

First, the view of self and identity cultivated in the Eastern tradition is embedded within an immutable social order. People tend to acquire their sense of identity from an affiliation with, and participation in, a virtually unchanging social order. As has been pointed out in many of the contemporary anthropological studies, the self that emerges from this tradition is not the clearly differentiated existential ego of the West, but a less distinct and relatively unchanging *social ego*. Individual members of the family tend to be more willing to submit their own self-interest for the good of the family. Individuals and families are often expected to subordinate their views to those of the community or the state. The Eastern tradition also accepts hierarchy in social order. In a hierarchical structure, individuals are viewed as differing in status, although all are considered to be equally essential for the total system and its processes. A natural result of this orientation is the emphasis on authority—the authority of the parents over the children; of the grandparents over their descendants; of the official head of the community, the clan, and the state over all its members. Authoritarianism is an outstanding feature of Eastern life, not only in government, business, and family, but also in education and in beliefs. The more ancient a tradition, the greater is its authority.

The Eastern view further asserts that who "we" are is not limited to our physical existence. Consciousness is viewed as the bridge between the finite and differentiated (one's sense of uniqueness) and the infinite and undifferentiated (the experience of wholeness and eternity). With sufficient training, each person can discover that who he or she is correlates with nature and the divine. All are one and the same in the sense that the divine, undifferentiated, aesthetic continuum of the universe is manifested in each person and in nature. Through this aesthetic connection, individuals and nature are none other than the Tao, the Ultimate Reality, the divine life force, Nirvana, God.

Comparatively, the Western view, in which God, nature, and humans are distinctly differentiated, fosters the development of autonomous individuals with strong ego identification. The dualistic worldview is manifested in an individual's view of his or her relationship to other persons and nature. Interpersonal relationships are essentially egalitarian—cooperative arrangements between two equal partners in which the personal needs and interests of each party are more or less equally respected, negotiated, or resolved by compromise. Whereas the East emphasizes submission (or conformity) of the individual to the group, the West encourages individuality and individual needs to drive the group. If the group no longer serves the individual needs, then it (not the individual) must be changed. The meaning of an interpersonal relationship is decided on primarily by the functions that each party performs in satisfying the needs of the other. A relationship is regarded as healthy to the extent that it serves the expected function for all parties involved. As extensively documented in anthropology and cross-cultural psychology (e.g., Hsu, 1981; Kluckhohn & Strodtbeck, 1960; Triandis, 1995), individualism is the central theme of the Western personality distinguishing the Western world from the collectivistic non-Western world.

This pragmatic interpersonal orientation of the West can be contrasted with the Eastern tradition, in which group membership is taken as given and therefore unchallenged, and in which individuals must conform to the group in case of conflicting interest. Members of the group are encouraged to maintain harmony and minimize competition. Individuality is discouraged, while moderation, modesty, and the bending of one's ego are praised. In some cases, both individual and group achievement (in a material sense) must be forsaken to maintain group harmony. In this context, the primary source of interpersonal understanding is the unwritten and often unspoken norms, values, and ritualized mannerisms pertinent to a particular situation. Rather than relying heavily on explicit and logical verbal expressions, the Eastern communicator grasps the aesthetic essence of the communication dynamic by observing subtleties in nonverbal and circumstantial cues. Intuition, rather than rational thinking, plays a central role in the understanding of how one talks, how one addresses the other, under what circumstances, on what topic, in which of various styles, with what intent, and with what effect.

These implicit communication patterns are reflected in the Eastern fondness for verbal hesitance and ambiguity out of fear of disturbing or offending others (Cathcart & Cathcart, 1982; Doi, 1982; Kincaid, 1987). Even silence is sometimes preferred to eloquent verbalization in expressing strong compliments or affection. Easterners are often suspicious of the genuineness of excessive verbal praises or compliments because, to their view, truest feelings must be intuitively apparent and therefore do not need to be, and cannot be, articulated. As a result, the burden of communicating effectively is shared by both the speaker and the listener, who is expected to "hear" the implicit messages through empathic attentiveness. In contrast, the Western communicative mode is primarily direct, explicit, and verbal, relying on logic and rational thinking. Participants in communication are viewed as distinctly different individuals, and their individuality has to be expressed through accurate verbal articulation. Inner feelings are not to be intuitively understood but to be honestly and assertively verbalized and discussed. Here, the burden of communicating effectively lies primarily with the speaker. The preceding characterization of Eastern and Western communication patterns is largely consistent with observations made by other scholars such as Hall (1976, 1983), Kincaid (1987), Robinson (2003), and Yum (1994). Hall, in particular, has depicted Asian cultures as *high-context* in comparison with the low context cultures of the West. The focal point of Hall's cross-cultural comparison is "contexting"—that is, the act of taking into account information that is either embedded in physical or social context (which includes nonverbal behaviors) or internalized in the communicator. In this scheme, low-context communication, which is more prevalent in the West, is observed when most interpersonal information is expressed by explicit, verbalized codes.

BEYOND CULTURAL DIFFERENCES

As has been pointed out, many of the specific differences that we observe between Eastern and Western societies hinge upon their respective worldviews. Based on an organic, holistic, and cyclic worldview, the East has followed an epistemology that emphasized direct, immediate, and aesthetic components in human experience of the world. The ultimate aim of human learning is to transcend the immediate, differentiated self and to develop an integrative perception of the undifferentiated universe. The goal is to be spiritually one with the universe and to find the eternal within the present moment, which is a reflection of the eternal. Alternatively, the eternal resides in the present moment. The Western tradition, in contrast, is rooted in the cosmology of dualism, determinism, and materialism. It engenders an outlook that is rational, analytic, and indirect. History is conceived as a linear progression from the past into the future. The pursuit of knowledge is not so much a pursuit of spiritual enhancement as a quest to improve the human condition.

These different worldviews, in turn, are reflected in the individual's conception of the self, the other, and the group. While the East has stressed the primacy of the group over the individual, the West has stressed the primacy of the individual over the group. Interpersonally, the East views the self as deeply merged in the group ego, while the West encourages distinct and autonomous individuality. Explicit, clear, and logical verbalization is a salient feature in the Western communication system, as compared to the emphasis on implicit, intuitive, and nonverbal messages in the Eastern tradition.

The cultural premises of the East and the West that we have examined suggest the areas of vitality, as well as areas of weakness, that are characteristic of each civilization. The Western mechanistic and dualistic worldview has helped to advance scientific efforts to describe systematically and explain physical phenomena, leading to extremely successful technological advancements. The West has learned, however, that the mechanistic worldview and the corresponding communication patterns may not adequately illuminate the rich, complex, and often paradoxical nature of life and human relationships and that such an epistemological constraint can cause alienation from self and others. The West has seen that its dualistic distinction between humanity and nature brings about alienation from the natural world. Even as the analytical mind of the West has led to modern science and technology, it also has brought about knowledge that is often fragmented and detached from the totality of reality.

In comparison, the East has not experienced the level of alienation that the West has. At the same time, however, the East has not seen as much material and social development. Its holistic and aesthetic worldview has not been conducive to the development of science or technology. Its hierarchical social order and binding social relationships have not fostered the civic-mindedness, worldly activism, humanitarianism, and volunteerism that flourish in the West. Many Asian societies continue to struggle to institute democratic political systems that are based on the rights and responsibilities of individuals.

It should be stressed at this time that the Western emphasis on logical, theoretic, dualistic, and analytic thinking does not suggest that it has been devoid of intuitive, direct, purely empirical, aesthetic elements. Conversely, emphasizing the Western contributions of socio-material development is not meant to suggest that the East has been devoid of learning in these areas. The differences that have been pointed out do not represent diametric opposition, but rather differences in emphasis that are nonetheless significant and observable. Clearly, the range of sophistication of Western contributions to the socio-material domain far exceeds that of contributions from the East. However, the Eastern emphasis on aesthetic and holistic self-mastery offers a system of life philosophy that touches on the depth of human experience vis-à-vis other humans, the natural world, and the universe.

Indeed, many have expressed increasing realization of limitations in the Western worldview. Using the term "extension transference," for instance, Hall (1976) pointed out the danger of the common intellectual maneuver in which technological "extensions" including language, logic, technology, institutions, and scheduling—are confused with or take the place of the process extended. We observe the tendency in the West to assume that the remedy for problems arising from technology should be sought not in the attempt to rely on an ideal minimum of technology, but in the development of even more technology. Burke (1974) called this tendency "technologism": "[There] lie the developments whereby 'technologism' confronts its inner contradictions, a whole new realm in which the heights of human rationality as expressed in industrialism readily become 'solutions' that are but the source of new and aggravated problems" (p. 148).

Self-criticisms in the West have also been directed to the rigid scientific dogmatism that insists on the discovery of truth based on mechanistic, linear causality and objectivity. In this regard, Thayer (1983) commented:

> What the scientific mentality attempts to emulate, mainly, is the presumed method of laboratory science. But laboratory science predicts nothing that it does not control or that is not otherwise fully determined. . . . One cannot successfully study relatively open systems with methods that are appropriate only for closed systems. Is it possible that this is the kind of mentality that precludes its own success? (p. 88)

Similarly, Hall (1976) has pointed out that the Western emphasis on logic as synonymous with the "truth" denies that part of human self that integrates. Hall sees that logical thinking is only a small fraction of our mental capabilities and that there are many different and legitimate ways of thinking that have tended to be less emphasized in Western cultures (p. 9).

The criticisms raised by these and other critics of scientific epistemology do not deny the value of the rational, inferential knowledge. Rather, they are directed to the error of Western philosophy in regarding concepts that do not adhere to its mode as invalid. They refer to the arrogance or overconfidence in believing that scientific knowledge is the only way to discover truth, when, in reality, the very process of doing science requires an immediate, aesthetic experience of the phenomenon under investigation. Without the immediately apprehended component, the theoretical hypotheses proposed could not be tested empirically with respect to their truth or falsity and would lack relevance to the corresponding reality. As Einstein once commented:

> Science is the attempt to make the chaotic diversity of our sense-experience correspond to a logically uniform system of thought. In this system single experiences must be correlated with the theoretic structure in such a way that the resulting coordination is complete and convincing. (quoted in Northrop, 1966, p. 443)

In this description of science, Einstein is careful to indicate that the relation between the theoretically postulated component and the immediately experienced aesthetic component is one of correspondence. The wide spectrum of our everyday life activities demands both scientific and aesthetic modes of apprehension: critical analysis as well as perception of wholes; doubt and skepticism as well as unconditional appreciation; abstraction as well as concreteness; perception of the general and regular as well as the individual and unique; the literalism of technical terms as well as the power and richness of poetic language, silence, and art; relationships with casual acquaintances as well as intimate personal engagement. If we limit ourselves to the dominant scientific mode of apprehension and do not value the aesthetic mode, then we are making an error of limiting the essential human to only a part of the full span of life activities.

One potential benefit of incorporating the Eastern aesthetic orientation into Western cultural life is a heightened sense of freedom. The aesthetic component of human nature is in part indeterminate, and the ambiguity of indetermination is the basis of our freedom. We might also transcend the clock-bound worldly time to the "eternal now," the "timeless moment" that is embedded within the center of each moment. By occasionally withdrawing into the indeterminate, aesthetic component of our nature, away from the determinate, transitory circumstances, we could overcome the pressures of everyday events as a basis for renewal of our human spirit. The traditional Eastern practice of meditation is designed primarily for the purpose of moving one's consciousness from the determinate to the indeterminate, freer state.

Second, incorporation of the Eastern view could bring the West to a greater awareness of the aliveness and wholeness of the universe we inhabit and the life we live. The universe is engaged in a continuous dance of creation at each instant of time. Everything is alive, brimming with a silent energy that creates, sustains, and infuses all that exists. With the expanded perspective on time, we would increase our sensitivity to the rhythms of nature such as the seasons and the cycles of birth and decay. This integrative worldview is one that pacifies us. Because of its all-embracing oneness and unity, the indeterminate aesthetic continuum helps us to cultivate compassion and intuitive sensitivity, not only for other humans but also for all of nature's creatures. In this regard, Maslow (1971) referred to Taoistic receptivity or "let-be" as an important attribute of self-actualizing persons:

> We may speak of this respectful attention to the matter-in-paradigm as a kind of courtesy or deference (without intrusion of the controlling will) which is akin to "taking it seriously." This amounts to treating it as an end, something per se, with its own right to be, rather than as a means to some end other than itself; i.e., as a tool for some extrinsic purpose. (p. 68)

Such aesthetic perception is an instrument of intimate human meeting, a way to bridge the gap between individuals and groups. In dealing with each other aesthetically, we do not subject ourselves to a rigid scheme, but do our best in each new situation, listening to the silence as well as the words, and experiencing the other person as a whole living entity with less infusion of our own egocentric and ethnocentric demands. A similar attitude can be developed toward the physical world, as is witnessed in the rising interest in the West in ecological integrity and holistic medicine (see Brody, 1997; Wallis, 1996).

What the preceding considerations suggest is that many Eastern and Western philosophical premises offer views of reality that are not competitive, but complementary. Of course, the entire values, norms, and institutions of the West cannot, and should not, be substituted for their Eastern counterparts, and vice versa. The West may no more adopt the worldview of the East than the East may adopt the worldview of the West. Rather, we need to recognize that a combination of rational and intuitive modes of experiencing life leads to a life that is more real and more meaningful. With this understanding, we see the interrelatedness and reconciliation of the two seemingly incompatible perspectives.

Our task, then, is to reach for the unity in human experiences and simultaneously to express diversity. A general synthesis of East and West is neither possible nor desirable: The purpose of evolution is not to create a homogeneous mass, but to continuously unfold an ever diverse and yet organic whole. Yet knowledge of differing cultural traditions can help each society move toward greater collective self-understanding, especially by revealing blind spots that can be illuminated only by adopting a vastly different way of seeing. Each tradition can play a necessary and integral part in the continuing evolution of humanity, out of which another birth, a higher integration of human consciousness, may arise.

EMERGENCE OF INTERCULTURAL PERSONHOOD

The task of synthesizing elements of Eastern and Western cultural traditions is undertaken not merely to satisfy an esoteric academic curiosity but also out of keen relevance to the everyday realities of numerous individuals whose life experiences extend beyond their primary cultural world. Through extensive and prolonged experiences of interfacing with other cultures, they have embarked on a personal evolution, creating a new culture of their own, fusing diverse cultural elements into a single personality. As Toffler (1980) noted, they have created a new personal culture that is "oriented to change and growing diversity" that attempts "to integrate the new view of nature, of evolution and progress, the new, richer conceptions of time and space, and the fusion of reductionism and wholism, with a new causality" (p. 309).

Identity Transformation

The emergence of intercultural personhood is a direct function of dramatically increasing intercultural communication activities—from the personal experiences of diverse people and events through direct encounters to observations via various communication media such as books, magazines, television programs, movies, magazines, art museums, music tapes, and electronic mail. Communicating across cultural identity boundaries is often challenging because it provokes questions about our presumed cultural premises and habits, as well as our inevitable intergroup posturing and the us-and-them psychological orientation (Kim, 1991). Yet it is precisely such challenges that offer us openings for new cultural learning, self-awareness, and personal growth (Adler, 1982; Kim, 1988, 1995, 2001). The greater the severity of intercultural challenges, the greater is the potential for reinvention of an inner self that goes beyond the boundaries of our original cultural conditioning.

In this process, our identity is transformed gradually and imperceptibly from an ascribed or assigned identity to an achieved or adopted identity—that is, an emergent intercultural personhood at a higher level of integration (Grotevant, 1993). Such an identity transformation takes place in a progression of stages. In each stage, new concepts, attitudes, and behaviors are incorporated into an individual's psychological makeup. As previously unknown life patterns are etched into our nervous systems, they become part of our new psyches. The evolution of our identity from cultural to intercultural is far from smooth or easy. Moments of intense stress can reverse the process at any time because individuals may indeed regress toward re-identifying with their origins, having found the alienation and malaise involved in maintaining a new identity too much of a strain (De Vos & Suarez-Orozco, 1990). Such strain may take various forms of an identity crisis (Erickson, 1968) and cultural marginality (Stonequist, 1964; Taft, 1977). Yet the stress experience also challenges individuals to accommodate new cultural elements and become more capable of making deliberate and appropriate choices about action as situations demand.

The emerging "intercultural personhood" (Kim, 1988, 1995, 2001; Kim & Ruben, 1988), then, is a special kind of mindset that promises greater fitness in our increasingly intercultural world. It represents a continuous struggle of searching for the authenticity in self and others within and across cultural groups. It is a way of existence that transcends the perimeters of a particular cultural tradition, and one that is capable of embracing and incorporating seemingly divergent cultural elements into one's own unique worldview. The process of becoming intercultural affirms the creative courage and resourcefulness of humans because it requires discovering new symbols and new patterns of life. This creative process of identity development speaks to a uniquely human plasticity, "our relative freedom from programmed reflexive patterns . . . the very capacity to use culture to construct our identities" (Slavin & Kriegman, 1992, p. 6). It is the expression of normal, ordinary people in the act of "stretching" themselves out of their habitual perceptual and social categories. In Adler's (1982) words, the development of an intercultural identity and personhood places strangers in a position of continually "negotiating ever new formations of reality" (p. 391).

This kind of human development echoes one of the highest aims of humans in the spiritual traditions of the Eastern cultures. Suzuki (1968) writes, "The fundamental idea of Buddhism is to pass beyond the world of opposites, a world built up by intellectual distinctions and emotional defilements, and to realize the spiritual world of non-distinction, which involves achieving an absolute point of view" (p. 18). A virtuous person in this tradition is not one who undertakes the impossible task of striving for the good and eliminating the bad, but rather one who is able to maintain a dynamic balance between good and bad. This Eastern notion of dynamic balance is reflected in the symbolic use by Chinese sages of the archetypal poles of yin and yang. These sages call the unity lying beyond yin and yang the Tao and see it as a process that brings about the interplay of the two poles. Yoshikawa (1988) described this development as a stage of "double-swing" or "transcendence of binary opposites" (p. 146). With this transcendental understanding, intercultural persons are better able to conciliate and reconciliate seemingly contradictory elements and transform them into complementary, interacting parts of a single whole.

An Illustration

Many people have been able to incorporate experiential territories seldom thought possible, attainable, or even desirable. In doing so, they have redrawn the lines of their original cultural identity boundary to accommodate new life patterns. Numerous firsthand accounts are available that bear witness to the reality of intercultural personhood. Such accounts have appeared in case studies, memoirs, biographical stories, and essays of self-reflection and self-analysis, as well as survey interviews (see, for instance, Keene, 1994; Kim, Lujan, & Dixon, 1998; O'Halloran, 1994; Ramos, 2002). Many of these accounts present vivid insights into the emotional ebb and flow of the progress toward intercultural transformation.

An illustration of intercultural synthesis is offered by Duane Elgin, who was born and raised in the United States as a Christian and studied Buddhism in Tibet and Japan for many years. In his book *Voluntary Simplicity* (1981), Elgin integrated the philosophical ideas of Eastern and Western worldviews into his concept of "voluntary simplicity." He presented this idea as "global common sense" and as a practical lifestyle to reconcile the willful, rational approach to life of the West and the holistic, spiritual orientation of the East. Examining historical trends, cycles of civilizations, and related ecological concerns, Elgin proposed voluntary simplicity as a goal for all of humanity. The main issue Elgin addresses is how humans can find ways to remove, as much as possible, the nonessential "clutters" of life. He suggests, for example, that one own or buy things based on real need and consider the impact of one's consumption patterns on other people and on the earth. Before purchasing nonessential items, one should ask oneself if these items promote or compromise the quality of one's nonmaterial life. One could also consciously simplify communications by making them clearer, more direct, and more honest, eliminating idle, wasteful, and manipulative speech. One should also respect the value of silence and nonverbal actions.

Perhaps one of the most succinct and eloquent testimonials to the present conception of intercultural personhood was offered by Muneo Yoshikawa (1978). As someone who had lived in Japan and in the United States, Yoshikawa offered the following insight into his own psychic development—an insight that captures the very essence of what it means to be an intercultural person:

> I am now able to look at both cultures with objectivity as well as subjectivity; I am able to move in both cultures, back and forth without any apparent conflict. I think that something beyond the sum of each [cultural] identification took place, and that it became something akin to the concept of "synergy"—when one adds 1 and 1, one gets 3, or a little more. This something extra is not culture-specific but something unique of its own, probably the emergence of a new attribute or a new self-awareness, born out of an awareness of the relative nature of values and of the universal aspect of human nature. . . . I really am not concerned whether others take me as Japanese or as American; I can accept myself as I am. I feel I am much freer than ever before, not only in the cognitive domain (perception, thoughts, etc.), but also in the affective (feeling, attitudes, etc.) and behavioral domains. (p. 220)

Suggested in these and other personal stories are some common patterns associated with the development of intercultural personhood. One such pattern is a mindset that is less parochial and more open to different perspectives. This outlook has been referred to as a "third-culture" orientation that enables us to transcend the "paradigmatic barrier" (Bennett, 1976) between divergent philosophical perspectives.

Development of an intercultural personhood leads to a "cultural relativistic insight" (Roosens, 1989) or "moral inclusiveness" (Opotow, 1990) that is based on an understanding of the profound similarities in human conditions as well as recognition of important differences between and among human groups. In becoming intercultural, then, we can rise above the hidden grips of our childhood culture and discover that there are many ways to be "good," "true," and "beautiful." In this process, we can attain a *wider circle of identification,* approaching the limits of many cultures and, ultimately, of humanity itself. This process is not unlike climbing a mountain. As we reach the mountaintop, we see that all paths below lead to the same summit and that each path offers unique scenery. Likewise, the process of becoming intercultural leads to an awareness of ourselves as being part of a larger, more inclusive whole and gives us a greater empathic capacity to "step into and imaginatively participate in the other's world view" (Bennett, 1976, p. 49).

Such developments, in turn, endow us with a special kind of *freedom* and *creativity,* with which we can make deliberate choices about action in specific situations rather than have these choices simply be dictated by habitual conventions of thought and action. This personal evolution presents the potential for achieving what Harris (1979) defined as "optimal communication competence." An optimally competent communicator, according to Harris, has a sophisticated "meta system" for critiquing his or her own managing system and interpersonal system. The very existence of the meta system makes the difference between the optimal level and the other two levels of competence a qualitative one.

In the end, it is people such as Elgin and Yoshikawa who constitute the sustaining core or "cross-links" of our intercultural world. They provide an infrastructure of moral cement that helps hold together the human community and discourage excessive identity claims to the exclusion of other identities. They are among the ones who can best meet the enormous challenge that confronts us all—that is, "to give not only yourself but your culture to the planetary view" (Campbell, 1990, p. 114).

Note

1. The term *intercultural personhood* represents other similar terms such as "multicultural man" (Adler, 1982), "universal man" (Tagore, 1961; Walsh, 1973), "international man" (Lutzker, 1960), and "species identity" (Boulding, 1990), as well as "meta-identity" and "transcultural identity."

References

Adler, P. (1982). Beyond cultural identity: Reflections on cultural and multicultural man. In L. Samovar & R. Porter (Eds.), *Intercultural communication: A reader* (3rd ed., pp. 389–408). Belmont, CA: Wadsworth.

Bennett, J. (1976). *The ecological transition: Cultural anthropology and human adaptation.* New York: Pergamon.

Boulding, E. (1990). *Building a global civic culture.* Syracuse, NY: Syracuse University Press.

Brody, J. (1997, November 6). U.S. panel on acupuncture calls for wider acceptance. *New York Times,* p. A10.

Burke, K. (1974). Communication and the human condition. *Communication, 1,* 135–152.

Campbell, J. (1988). *The power of myth* (with B. Moyers). New York: Doubleday.

Campbell, J. (1990). *An open life* (in conversation with M. Toms). New York: Harper & Row.

Capra, F. (1975). *The Tao of physics.* Boulder, CO: Shambhala.

Cathcart, D., & Cathcart, R. (1982). Japanese social experience and concept of groups. In L. Samovar & R. Porter (Eds.), *Intercultural communication: A reader* (3rd ed., pp. 120–127). Belmont, CA: Wadsworth.

De Vos, G., & Suarez-Orozco, M. (1990). *Status inequality: The self in culture.* Newbury Park, CA: Sage.

Doi, T. (1982). The Japanese patterns of communication and the concept *of amae.* In L. Samovar & R. Porter (Eds.), *Intercultural communication: A reader* (3rd ed., pp. 218–222). Belmont, CA: Wadsworth.

Elgin, D. (1981). *Voluntary simplicity.* New York: Bantam Books.

Erickson, E. (1968). *Identity, youth, and crisis.* New York: Norton.

Grotevant, H. (1993). The integrative nature of identity: Bridging the soloists to sing in the choir. In J. Kroger (Ed.), *Discussions on ego identity* (pp. 121–146). Hillsdale, NJ: Erlbaum.

Gulick, S. (1963). *The East and the West.* Rutland, VT: Charles E. Tuttle.

Hall, E. (1976). *Beyond culture.* Garden City, NY: Anchor Books.

Hall, E. (1983). *The dance of life: The other dimension of time.* Garden City, NY: Anchor Press.

Harris, L. (1979, May). *Communication competence: An argument for a systemic view.* Paper presented at the annual meeting of the International Communication Association, Philadelphia.

Hsu, F. (1981). *The challenges of the American dream.* Belmont, CA: Wadsworth.

Keene, D. (1994). *On familiar terms: A journey across cultures.* New York: Kodansha International.

Kim, Y. (1988). *Communication and cross-cultural adaptation: An integrative theory.* Clevedon, UK: Multilingual Matters.

Kim, Y. (1991). Intercultural communication competence. In S. Ting-Toomey & F. Korzenny (Eds.), *Cross-cultural interpersonal communication* (pp. 259–275). Newbury Park, CA: Sage.

Kim, Y. (1995). Identity development: From cultural to intercultural. In H. Mokros (Ed.), *Information and behavior: Vol. 6. Interaction and identity* (pp. 347–369). New Brunswick, NJ: Transactions.

Kim, Y. (2001). *Becoming intercultural: An integrative theory of communication and cross-cultural adaptation.* Thousand Oaks, CA: Sage.

Kim, Y., Lujan, P., & Dixon, L. (1998). "I can walk both ways": Identity integration of American Indians in Oklahoma. *Human Communication Research, 25*(2), 252–274.

Kim, Y., & Ruben, B. (1988). Intercultural transformation. In Y. Kim & W. Gudykunst (Eds.), *Theories in intercultural communication* (pp. 299–321). Newbury Park, CA: Sage.

Kincaid, L. (1987). Communication East and West: Points of departure. In L. Kincaid (Ed.), *Communication theory: Eastern and Western perspectives* (pp. 331–340). San Diego, CA: Academic Press.

Kluckhohn, F., & Strodtbeck, F. (1960). *Variations in value orientations.* New York: Row, Peterson.

Lutzker, D. (1960). Internationalism as a predictor of cooperative behavior. *Journal of Conflict Resolution, 4,* 426–430.

Maslow, A. (1971). *The farther reaches of human nature.* New York: Viking.

Nakamura, H. (1964). *Ways of thought of Eastern peoples.* Honolulu: University of Hawaii Press.

Needham, J. (1951). Human laws and laws of nature in China and the West. *Journal of the History of Ideas, 12.*

Northrop, F. (1966). *The meeting of the East and the West.* New York: Collier Books. (Original work published 1946).

O'Halloran, M. (1994). *Pure heart, enlightened mind.* Boston: Charles E. Tuttle.

Oliver, R. (1971). *Communication and culture in ancient India and China.* New York: Syracuse University Press.

Opotow, S. (1990). Moral exclusion and inclusion. *Journal of Social Issues, 46*(1), 1–20.

Ramos, J. (2002). No *borders: A journalist's search for home.* New York: Rayo.

Robinson, J. (2003). Communication in Korea: Playing things by eye. In L. Samovar & R. Porter (Eds.), *Intercultural communication: A reader* (10th ed., pp. 57–64). Belmont, CA: Wadsworth.

Roosens, E. (1989). *Creating ethnicity: The process of ethnogenesis.* Newbury Park, CA: Sage.

Slavin, M., & Kriegman, D. (1992). *The adaptive design of the human psyche.* New York: Guilford.

Stonequist, E. (1964). The marginal man: A study in personality and culture conflict. In E. Burgess & D. Bogue (Eds.), *Contributions to urban sociology* (pp. 327–345). Chicago: University of Chicago Press.

Suzuki, D. (1968). *The essence of Buddhism.* Kyoto, Japan: Hozokan.

Taft, R. (1977). Coping with unfamiliar culture. In N. Warren (Ed.), *Studies in cross-cultural psychology* (Vol. 2, pp. 121–153). London: Academic Press.

Tagore, R. (1961). *Toward universal man.* New York: Asia Publishing House.

Thayer, L. (1983). On "doing" research and "explaining" things. *Journal of Communication, 33*(3), 80–91.

Thompson, W. (1973). *Passages about earth: An exploration of the new planetary culture.* New York: Harper & Row.

Toffler, A. (1980). *The third wave.* New York: Bantam Books.

Triandis, H. (1995). *Individualism and collectivism.* Boulder, CO: Westview Press.

Wallis, C. (1996, June 24). Healing. *Time,* 58–64.

Walsh, J. (1973). *Intercultural education in the community of man.* Honolulu: University of Hawaii Press.

Wei, A. (1980, March). *Cultural variations in perception.* Paper presented at the Sixth Annual Third World Conference, Chicago.

Yoshikawa, M. (1978). Some Japanese and American cultural characteristics. In M. Prossor, *The cultural dialogue: An introduction to intercultural communication* (pp. 220–239). Boston: Houghton Mifflin.

Yoshikawa, M. (1988). Cross-cultural adaptation and perceptual development. In Y. Kim & W. Gudykunst (Eds.), *Cross-cultural adaptation: Current approaches* (pp. 140–148). Newbury Park, CA: Sage.

Yum, J. (1994). The impact of Confucianism on interpersonal relationships and communication patterns in East Asia. In L. Samovar & R. Porter (Eds.), *Intercultural communication: A reader* (7th ed., pp. 75–86). Belmont, CA: Wadsworth.

Concepts and Questions

1. What is meant by the term *intercultural personhood?*
2. How do Eastern and Western teachings about humankind's relationship to the nature of the universe differ?
3. In what major ways do Eastern and Western approaches to knowledge differ?
4. How do Eastern time orientations differ from those found in the West?
5. How do differences in Eastern and Western views of self and identity affect intercultural communication?
6. What are the major differences between Eastern and Western modes of communication?
7. What strengths and weaknesses are found in Eastern and Western worldviews?
8. How could an integration of Eastern and Western perspectives benefit both Eastern and Western cultural life?
9. What conditions are required for the emergence of intercultural personhood?
10. What benefits accrue to both society and the individual from the development of an intercultural personhood perspective?

Ethical Intercultural Technical Communication: Looking Through the Lens of Confucian Ethics

SAM DRAGGA

Given the collapse of communism and the geographical expansion of capitalism and democracy, more and more organizations have committed themselves to developing their international potential. Today's technical communicator, as a consequence, is often a multicultural, intercultural communicator engaging issues of translation, interpretation, and localization. In this situation, however, is a potential peril for technical communicators because little research or guidance is available to identify the practices of ethical intercultural technical communication.

Ordinarily, the research on intercultural communication does a good job of encouraging sensitivity to international audiences, chiefly by isolating communication behaviors that reveal cultural differences (e.g., Alred, 1997; Artemeva, 1998; Boiarsky, 1995; Forman, 1998; Hagen, 1998; Rodman, 1996; Ulijn, 1996) and by describing various coarse filters (such as "high context" versus "low context") for categorizing disparate cultures (e.g., Hall, 1976; Hofstede, 1980; Kluckhohn & Strodtbeck, 1961; Trompenaars, 1994; Varner & Beamer, 1995). This research is a necessary starting point for appreciating the diverse practices that might disrupt intercultural communication but eludes the philosophical perspectives that inspire such practices (Irwin, 1996, pp. 58–59). For example, we might observe that Chinese people give and receive business cards using both hands, answer a compliment with a denial (e.g., "No, I am really a poor writer"), are "indirect" in their style of speaking and writing, or have a "collectivist" culture, but still unexplained in

Reprinted from *Technical Communication Quarterly,* Vol. 8, Issue 4, 1999, pp. 365–381. © 1999 Lawrence Erlbaum Associates. Reprinted with permission. Sam Dragga teaches at Texas Tech University.

this listing and sorting are the ideals driving and unifying their communication behaviors. And if we simply acquiesce to sporadic insights and polarizing categories, Chinese culture and Chinese writers and readers will always be to us curious, mysterious, and foreign. To achieve effective and ethical intercultural technical communication, I believe, requires of us the heavy lifting of studying and explicating the ethics of individual civilizations.

In this article, I try to exemplify the tighter and crisper focus that I believe is necessary to advance research on intercultural technical communication. Specifically, I look at the ethics of China. I start by explaining the diversity of Chinese philosophy and proceed to offer a basic introduction to Confucian thought and the virtues that according to Confucius constitute ethical behavior. I also briefly discuss opposing philosophies. I conclude by analyzing a salient artifact of intercultural communication according to Confucian ethics. I believe this analysis demonstrates that Americans and Chinese come to the subject of ethics from different perspectives and that unless we develop a comprehensive understanding of such differences, effective and ethical communication is unlikely to occur.

THE CHINESE PHILOSOPHICAL TRADITION

Unlike the United States with a heritage that is chiefly Judeo-Christian, China adopts a philosophical perspective that is primarily Confucian or Neo-Confucian. (See also Tu's brief history of Confucianism, 1990, including the contributions of such major thinkers as Mencius, Hsun Tzu, and Chu Hsi.) Please keep in mind, however, that multiple schools of thought operate in China, such as Taoist, Buddhist, Maoist, and anti-Confucian (rejecting Confucian philosophy as a barrier to progress and looking to European and American ideals). Little is monolithic or homogeneous to China, and no single philosophy could identify or explain all of China's distinguishing characteristics. With 1.3 billion people, virtually every generalization is a sweeping generalization that likely omits at least 10% of the population (i.e., the equivalent of 50% of the population of the United States).

Nevertheless, Chinese philosophy is almost always a practical vehicle for self-realization or self-cultivation. Human beings are considered capable of attaining perfection without divine intervention within a process that proceeds from perfection of the individual to perfection of the world, from personal improvement to social and political efficacy (Cheng, 1991, p. 85): "Individuals are endowed with innate capacities to transform themselves and induce the transformation of others in the domain of moral relationships and moral virtues" (Cheng, p. 26).

I would emphasize, however, that Chinese people are, like all people, neither always ethical nor always meticulous in their philosophy or practice of ethics. Grievous economic and political conditions encourage a survivor's mentality, and immorality is often justified as necessary or appropriate because society itself is immoral (De Mente, 1989, p. 96). It is thus impossible to promise that a specific individual within a specific situation will be chiefly motivated by a specific ethical perspective; it is only possible to describe the potential influence of ethics on the individual's communication behaviors. (See also Yuan's, 1997, caution on the serious limitations of emphasizing intercultural communication versus individual communication.)

THE ETHICS OF CONFUCIUS

To Confucius (i.e., Kong Fuzi or Master Kong), the ethical individual cultivates and exercises several key virtues—chiefly, goodness (*ren*), righteousness (*yi*), wisdom (*zhi*), faithfulness (*xin*), reverence (*jing*), and courage (*yong*). This cultivation and exercise of virtue is achieved through obedience to the rituals (*li*)—specific traditions regarding virtually all human behavior, from the etiquette of eating and drinking to the propriety of family relations and the operations of political institutions (Huang, 1997, p. 20). Confucius also emphasizes the individual's social relations and social responsibility over self-consciousness: people perceive themselves according to their social relationships and responsibilities as opposed to their individual being. Ethical action is only possible within a society, in the relationships among people (Huang, Andrulis, & Chen, 1994, 71–72).

Goodness

Goodness (benevolence, love, or humanity) is the most important of the virtues. Ethical individuals desire for others that which they desire for themselves, treating others as they would like others to treat them. The goodness offered to others is determined, however, according to the benefits one has received from others. Thus, the obligation to one's mother and father (who have given life itself) exceeds one's obligation to brothers and sisters, friends and neighbors, city and country (Lau, 1979, pp. 18–19).

The hierarchy of relationships thus has clear levels: family, colleagues, friends and neighbors, and indirect relationships (e.g., the sister of one's neighbor) (Huang et al., pp. 43–44). Family, however, always has priority.

This definition of goodness inspires Chinese society to operate on a rule of people exercising benevolence instead of a rule of law. Morality is perceived as superior to legality: rule by people preserves the humanity of society whereas rule by law is mechanical (Huang et al., pp. 155–156).

Individuals with whom Chinese people have an existing relationship will thus usually be preferred to those who are strangers. Fairness (or being ethical) requires Chinese people to give special privilege to family and friends. Treating all people the same (family and friends as well as strangers) would be to ignore the goodness received from family and friends; treating all people the same, as a consequence, would be unfair and unethical. Thus behavior that foreigners might interpret as either prejudice or favoritism, Chinese people perceive as the simple exercise of goodness (Yum, 1998, pp. 378–379).

In doing business in China, for example, foreigners are likely victims of the virtue of goodness because Chinese people are disposed to privilege Chinese friends (or friends of friends) as opposed to foreigners (Tung, 1996, pp. 239–241). It is not impossible to penetrate the concentric circles of obligation, but it is important that foreigners realize that they start on the outside circle, that it will take them considerable time and effort to work toward the center, and that they will never arrive at the center (because it is occupied by family).

To do business in China, nevertheless, requires the ethical positioning of oneself as a friend instead of a stranger. Communication in China, as a consequence, is often considered "indirect" by foreigners because initial attention is dedicated to the establishing of a personal relationship among the parties to a business transaction. A meeting or a letter, for example, might start with discussion of family or social pursuits prior to addressing pertinent business issues. To Chinese people, this practice is ethical.

The virtue of goodness is also inextricably linked to food in Chinese society. In the United States, the foundation of goodness is the right to individual liberty, especially through the virtually unrestricted exchange of ideas. A good government, for example, provides its people individual liberty. In China, however, it is the right to food that ordinarily drives the ethical agenda, and all other rights are subservient to this principle: that the function of political institutions is to promote the good of the people, starting with the food necessary to nourish life itself.

This difference in definitions of goodness is a consequence of geography. In the United States, the land is fertile and crops are plentiful; food is abundant and efficiently distributed. In China, however, the territory is huge, but the land is chiefly deserts and mountains; habitable land is small (De Mente, 1989, p. 2) and subject to periodic flooding. In China, 1.3 billion people live and die and raise their crops and chickens and pigs on land that is roughly the size of the continental United States—east of the Mississippi River.

China's priority is thus the human right to food—to life as opposed to liberty. (I offer no excuse for the genuine abuses of human liberty that plague China, but it is also important to acknowledge the emphasis on a different human right.) Food—its acquisition, preparation, and consumption—is a chief focus of Chinese attention, unlike Americans who assume that food will be readily available and who proudly claim the invention and worldwide dissemination of fast-food restaurants. (The popularity of such restaurants must be understood, in part, as a sign of prosperity—a visible demonstration that individuals and peoples never have to occupy themselves with the acquisition and preparation of food. And genuine liberty can be understood, in part, as liberation from continuous anxiety over the acquisition of food.)

The virtue of goodness, however, also has negative influences on Chinese society. The ethical obligations to parents and grandparents lead to a respect for age and seniority over intelligence, initiative, and ingenuity, creating a more conservative society (De Mente, 1989, pp. 85–86). And though the ideal is a pliable exercise of benevolence, a rule of people is easily corrupted by the avaricious, the despotic, and the arbitrary (De Mente, p. 160).

Righteousness

The moral philosophy of Confucius espouses *yi*, righteousness or propriety, as the chief criterion of human behavior, as a "guiding principle in all human relations" (Huang, 1997, p. 5). Righteousness is consistently doing the right thing, choosing morality over profit or success, trying only to be as good a man or woman as possible without regard for fortune or reward in this or any other possible life.

The virtue of righteousness constitutes "the fundamental principle of morality" as it "forms the necessary component of a virtuous life and restrains the inclinations towards material goods and desires of pleasure and comfort" (Cheng, 1991, p. 234).

Righteousness asks the individual to derive significance from a specific situation, integrating the individual and his or her circumstances, to determine ethical action (Hall & Ames, 1987, p. 96):

> *Yi* has normative force without itself actually constituting a norm. The actions that realize *yi* are not performed in accordance with strict guidelines. . . . This means that *yi* is as much the consequence of a particular decision or action as its cause. The normative force of *yi* exists in spite of its inchoate character at the beginning of *yi* acts. The articulation of *yi* with respect to a given situation involves the emerging awareness of what is or is not appropriate in that situation and how one might act so as to realize this appropriateness in its highest degree. (Hall & Ames, p. 102)

Righteousness also inspires the rituals *(li)*, the 300 major rules and 3,000 minor rules regarding appropriate behavior. The rituals are "patterns of behavior initiated and transmitted in order to refine and enhance life in a community" (Hall & Ames, 1987, p. 89). The rituals are thus the heuristics of righteousness: "A person in learning and reflecting upon these ritual actions seeks in them the *yi* contributed by his precursors, and in so doing, stimulates, develops, and refines his own sensitivities" (Hall & Ames, p. 99). Social practices and traditions such as the exchange of greetings or business cards, the giving of gifts, and the offering of food or drink to guests possess genuine ethical implications. Each is a vehicle for self-cultivation and the exercise of righteousness.

According to Confucius, superior human beings (*chün-tze*) are motivated by righteousness and inferior people by profit. The tension of righteousness versus profit encourages a denigration of business people and a veneration of the political and academic professions (Huang et al., 1994, pp. 30–33). Emphasis on business is considered a necessary but obvious moral degeneration (Huang et al., p. 166).

In business transactions, morality over profit is the ideal: buyers want a low enough price so that they can buy all the things they need, but sellers want a high enough price so that they can cover their expenses, buy the things they need themselves, and buy more things to sell. Righteousness is the balance between the buyer's needs and the seller's needs; righteousness is always considering the opposing perspective and trying to achieve a situation in which both sides are satisfied (Huang et al., 1994, pp. 191–192).

Greed and glory, as a consequence, are inappropriate as motivators. Money is earned and success is sought chiefly for the benefit it can bring to your family and friends and to fulfill the ethical obligations of goodness. That is, it would be unethical to encourage selfish desires: "If we do business together, you will make a lot of money and be able to buy yourself a fancy new sports car." But espousing the exercise of goodness would be ethical: "If we do business together, you will make enough money to afford the finest schools for your children."

Self-promotion, similarly, is considered unethical. Righteousness dictates that people be modest regarding their abilities and achievements. The writing of a résumé or letter of job application, for example, is a rhetorical activity of obvious delicacy. In a job interview, if a Chinese candidate is asked if he or she is a good teacher, the ethical answer despite years of education and experience is "No, I am still learning to be a teacher."

In addition, compliments are ordinarily received with denials. The ethical answer to "You are doing a good job" is "No, I make a lot of mistakes" or "No, I could do better" because glory, however gratifying or merited, is itself never a righteous objective. You do a good job for neither praise nor profit, but because it is the ethical thing to do. A sincere compliment, nevertheless, deserves repetition following the denial: "No. I don't see mistakes. You are doing a good job."

The negative impact of righteousness on Chinese society, however, is the possibility of blind obedience to the rituals. The denigration of business also has the potential of driving ethical people from the field and leaving it to the unscrupulous.

Wisdom

Wisdom is the key to self-improvement. It is achieved through learning, with schooling considered superior to experience. Formal education and degrees thus offer a higher level of authority and credibility relative to on-the-job experience (Lau, 1979, p. 23). Education is a vehicle for understanding right behavior; it has less to do with the acquisition of knowledge and more to do with the cultivation of morality (Leys, 1997, p. xxix). It also has a lot to do with identifying the things you know and admitting the things you still have to learn (Lau, p. 23).

Confucius identifies four levels of people: at the highest level is the extraordinary individual with innate knowledge, followed by the individual who studies to avoid making mistakes, the individual who studies after making mistakes, and the individual who never studies after making mistakes (Lau, 1979, p. 23).

Of all wisdom, the most critical is a knowledge of people (i.e., being a good judge of character) because human behavior is the chief variable in one's preparation for the future (Lau, 1979, p. 22). Instruction in the humanities, as a consequence, is considered superior to investigation of science and engineering (Huang, 1997, p. 11).

This definition of wisdom also has a negative side, equating education and moral superiority. The privileging of the humanities also has the potential to divert creativity and ingenuity to artistic purposes only and thus slow scientific and technological progress.

Faithfulness

Faithfulness or trustworthiness is matching one's words (*yan*) with one's deeds (*xing*), thus establishing both credibility and reliability. Failure to deliver on a promise is thus a failure of morality. The ethical individual, as a consequence, is slow to speak and never makes claims or promises until a deed is already or almost accomplished (Lau, 1979, p. 25).

In business negotiations, for example, the Chinese will ordinarily resist making promises or commitments, especially in the absence of a previous or existing relationship. In contracts and proposals, similarly, the Chinese will hesitate to specify budgets and schedules, but consider it easier to detail their track record on earlier projects.

Eloquence is also distrusted, and a rhetoric of the implicit is privileged (Leys, 1997, p. xxx). The ethical communicator is thus advised to "say what you need to say, not what you want to say" (Huang et al., 1994, p. 167). While loquacious foreigners might perceive themselves as candid and gregarious, for example, the Chinese could interpret their behavior as inanity or insincerity. Brevity, however, isn't necessarily virtuous: the "direct" style of writing practiced by Americans—getting straight to the point without polite socializing—is obviously succinct, but omits the humanizing information that the Chinese consider crucial to a working relationship.

The risk to Chinese society of this virtue of faithfulness, however, is passivity. In the desire to prove credible and reliable, the timid individual might neither speak nor act, neither promise nor deliver. By thus doing nothing, he or she does nothing wrong.

Reverence

Reverence or seriousness is "moral alertness" (Cheng, 1991, p. 50) or awareness of one's social responsibilities and a sincere devotion to discharging one's responsibilities. Self-cultivation through schooling, for example, is a conscientious pursuit of manifest intensity; it is the individual's necessary contribution to his or her community. Service to family, friends, supervisors, and officials, similarly, inspires the highest levels of dedication and diligence. Inattention to one's obligations or inability to meet one's obligations is a genuine ethical failure, a moral disgrace.

A teacher's job of instructing his or her students, for example, is never simply a professional responsibility: it is also a moral obligation. A cavalier attitude regarding this job, however poorly paid, would be unethical. And though dull students or ineffective administrators might bruise a teacher's devotion to duty, the ethical teacher persists in the exercise of reverence. Ethical students, similarly, exhibit reverence by committing themselves to learning from every teacher, including the irascible and the insipid.

Such devotion to social duties, however, could lead to a deleterious single-mindedness and servility.

Courage

Courage is self-sacrifice in the pursuit of goodness. Courage is only a virtue if the individual is also guided by righteousness (Huang, 1997, p. 21). For example, it is courageous for employees to criticize their employer, thus risking their jobs, if their criticism is motivated by a genuinely unselfish desire to benefit the company. And it is courageous for the employer, risking his or her power and prestige, to consider such criticism with a receptive heart and mind. Similarly, it is courageous for business people to acknowledge a deficiency in their products or services, risking a loss of profit and reputation, to keep faith with their customers or clients. It is also courageous for customers or clients to accept lesser products or services, risking a loss of satisfaction, to support such candid and caring business people.

Courage is different, however, from simple audacity or daring. It is courageous to meet one's obligations to family and friends. It is daring to establish new relationships or to offer goodness out of proportion to the goodness received. Supporting the business proposal of a friend, for example, is courageous; supporting a stranger's is audacious. Foreigners who would like to do business with the Chinese, as a consequence, try to establish a relationship of reciprocal obligations (e.g., by gift giving, by offering concessions) so that business emerges from the exercise of courage, from the Chinese meeting their obligations to their new foreign friends.

This definition of courage allows the Chinese to shield family and friends from dangerous foreigners and inhibits aggressive international exploits, but also has the potential to reinforce parochial and isolationist attitudes and policies.

CHALLENGES TO CONFUCIAN THOUGHT

Classical Confucianism is challenged by the Taoist thought of the Lao Tzu and Chang Tzu schools. According to Lao Tzu, *tao* is the indefinable, inexhaustible, indeterminate, and dynamic void that is the source of all that is finite; *tao* is the unity of opposites, the change from negative to positive, from *yin* to *yang*, from tranquility to action. To act deliberately is to make oneself an object of action and thus exhaust the potential for action. Remaining at the point of potential stimulates awareness of the *tao* and cultivates the *tao*. The ideal action is the action that arises spontaneously and naturally from that point of potential (Cheng, 1991, pp. 72–74). According to Chuang Tzu, however, *tao* is the relativity and relation of all things. Cultivating this understanding of the *tao* allows human beings to see the variety of possible perspectives from which life might be lived, thus leading to a natural and spontaneous life (Cheng, pp. 74–75). Both schools espouse a degree of passivity or resignation to existing social and political conditions. And Taoist thought encourages the isolation of the individual to achieve a contemplative union with the natural world, whereas Confucian thought requires individuals to immerse themselves within a society of reciprocal human relationships.

In the Buddhist philosophy of China, both the world and the mind have reality, both the ontological and the phenomenological, and "enlightenment is a dynamic unification of the objective with the subjective, that is, of the known object with the knowing subject" (Cheng, 1991, p. 78). Each incident is the consequence of "innumerable causes interacting and interpenetrating each other" (Chang & Holt, 1991, p. 33), and human life is thus essentially inexplicable because of the "inability to see all causative and conditioning factors" (p. 34). While Confucians claim that virtues are innate and require only cultivation, Buddhists perceive a void: the mind is disciplined by meditation and studies and thus delivered from meaninglessness and suffering. Especially distressing for the Confucians is that Buddhism is a philosophy of foreign origin. In addition, it establishes the ideal of the monastic pursuit of truth—the individual who leaves his or her family, violating existing ethical obligations, to join a religious community separated from the wider society (Tillman, 1992, pp. 16–17).

Neo-Confucian philosophy incorporates Taoist and Buddhist influences, newly interpreting the classic writings of Confucius according to a metaphysical principle: "a thing comes into existence and has its being through the interaction of the two material forces, *yin*, the cosmic force of tranquility, and *yang*, the cosmic force of activity" (Chan, 1967, p. xxi). All things are explained by this principle, including the relationship of cause and effect as well as of right and wrong (Chan, p. xxi). The exercise of virtue serves to harmonize human life to this principle of existence. Nevertheless, Neo-Confucian philosophy preserves the traditional emphasis on the cultivation of virtues by individuals operating within concentric circles of human relationships.

Anti-Confucian philosophy, however, emerged during the 1800s as the Chinese came to question their poor economic and political conditions relative to the superior resources of the Europeans and Americans (who were dictating foreign policy to China, addicting its people to opium, and seizing its territory). New thinking espoused ideals of democracy as well as capitalist principles of business and denounced Confucian and Neo-Confucian philosophy as a chief contributor to political corruption and the decay of scientific learning and technological progress. With the collapse of the empire and the rise of the republic in the early 1900s, anti-Confucian thought had a major political impact on China. In the guidance of family, social, and business relationships, however, Confucian ideals continued to be the dominant philosophy.

The communists of the People's Republic of China initially emphasized the compatibility of Confucian philosophy and communism, chiefly as a way to give communism credibility and adapt traditional morality to socialist ethics (Kam, 1980, pp. 44–45). In the years of the radical communists, 1966 to 1976, however, Confucian thought was rejected as a competitor to Maoist principles (Kam, p. 91). The teachings of Confucius on the virtue of wisdom, for example, privileging academic learning and putting the uneducated on the lowest level of society, were newly interpreted by Mao Zedong as oppressive of the lower classes (Kam, pp. 105–106). In a specific repudiation of Confucian ideals, Mao denigrated scholars and teachers: "the lowly are the most intelligent and the elite are the most ignorant" (Kam, p. 128). In the years following Mao, however, the effort to eradicate Confucian ideals came to be widely recognized as futile.

In China today, Confucian thought again prevails, but often filtered by Taoist, Buddhist, Maoist, and especially anti-Confucian influences. The drive to modernize, liberalize, and democratize China is often synonymous with a rejection or revision of the Confucian traditions of Chinese society (Irwin, 1996, pp. 114–115).

ETHICAL ANALYSIS OF INTERCULTURAL COMMUNICATION

As I mentioned earlier, Chinese philosophy is never speculative, but always a practical vehicle for solving real dilemmas. In that spirit, I investigate a relatively simple artifact of intercultural communication to determine the degree to which it is effective and ethical from the chiefly Confucian perspective of the target audience. Specifically, I analyze a breakfast cereal box created by Kellogg's® as it tried to introduce ready-to-eat cereal, specifically Coco Pops®, to the Chinese.

I acquired this artifact in 1994 during a visit to Hong Kong; it carries a 1989 copyright. I would like to display here the image of the box, but the nice people at Kellogg's® denied my permissions request.

I will readily admit that I don't know the full origins of this cereal package. I do know it was manufactured in Australia for distribution to Hong Kong, Singapore, and Taiwan, all locations of chiefly Chinese populations. I don't know the people who designed the box, their professional experience, level of education, philosophical orientation, ethical intentions, language abilities, or racial heritage. And neither would the people buying this box of cereal. Such information regarding authorship is immaterial to the impact of the box on the reading public.

In addition, though I offer my reading of this box from a Confucian perspective, I can't promise that it is the only reading possible from a Confucian perspective or from a Chinese perspective. It is, however, according to my studies of the people and their philosophical literature, a credible reading.

Though displaying both English and Chinese writing, the box is clearly addressed to a Chinese audience unfamiliar with ready-to-eat cereal. A traditional Chinese breakfast might be noodles or rice; ready-to-eat cereal is decidedly foreign. So the technical communicator has to offer both persuasive and instructional information—persuasive to convince people that eating ready-to-eat cereal is a desirable thing to do, and instructive to explain to people how to eat it. To accomplish this objective, the Kellogg's® cereal package conveys two different messages: the first reinforces Chinese traditions, emphasizing how Kellogg's® Coco Pops® accords with conventional foods and cultural practices, and the second challenges those traditions to create a space for the admission of a foreign product and its accompanying cultural practices. Both rhetorical strategies raise important ethical questions.

Persuasion

The right side of the cereal box displays two persuasive messages. One emphasizes tradition: "Kellogg's Coco Pops is a crisp nutritious breakfast cereal food that retains the delicious flavour of rice." This message emphasizes the similarity of the new food to the traditional Chinese food: eating this cereal is really like eating rice. The specific wording, however, is a potential mistake: if the individual decides that Coca Pops® tastes less like rice and more like cocoa and sugar, Kellogg's® credibility could be jeopardized. Kellogg's® could be perceived as violating the virtue of faithfulness or trustworthiness. The desired link to tradition could as easily be achieved with a definitive claim such as "Kellogg's Coco Pops is a crisp and nutritious rice cereal."

The other message emphasizes tradition, but also faithfulness, thus reinforcing the credibility of the earlier claim:

> The trustworthy sign of quality which is famous around the world. This red trademark of Kellogg's has a long history and is well-known by all families. It was originally the autograph of the founder of the Kellogg Company, W. K. Kellogg. It has been a guarantee of quality of each Kellogg's product since 1906. Now, it has become synonymous with "Good taste & nutrition in breakfast cereal in over 130 countries throughout world. If you are not satisfied with the quality of this product, please return the entire package with your name, address, reasons, where purchased, date and price paid. Our company will mail you another package as compensation.

The "red trademark" (i.e., the Kellogg's signature is always displayed in red) is mentioned because red in China is the color of good luck: according to Chinese rituals, red brings prosperity. The trustworthiness of the Kellogg's family is also emphasized by citing the trademark's long history and its worldwide recognition by "all families" as a symbol of quality. The promise of quality and compensation for dissatisfaction proves the reverence or seriousness of the company in meeting its obligations.

The implication on this side of the box is clear: eating this cereal is a good thing to do because it accords with Chinese tradition, brings good luck, and comes from a sincere and credible company.

Instruction

On the opposite side of the box are verbal and visual instructions on how to serve ready-to-eat cereal: four small numbered pictures followed by four corresponding instructions. The first picture shows cereal being poured into a clear glass bowl (as opposed to the traditional ceramic bowl); the corresponding instruction is "Put 4oz of nutritious Kellogg's Coco Pops into a clean bowl." A "clean bowl" is specified because of the Chinese practice of eating different foods in succession from the same bowl during a meal with several courses. This instruction thus poses a challenge to existing Chinese tradition. Similarly, each individual is instructed to create his or her own small bowl of cereal, as opposed to the Chinese practice of preparing a large common bowl of food from which individuals serve themselves into their smaller bowls. The designation of a specific quantity of cereal gives this instruction almost empirical precision, which coupled with the word "nutritious" and the repetition of "Kellogg's Coco Pops" has obvious persuasive implications: this ready-to-eat cereal, however new or different, is good food.

The second picture shows milk being added to the cereal, and the corresponding instruction is "Pour milk (fresh, long life, powdered, or soy)." Given that 80 to 90 percent of Chinese people are lactase-deficient and thus lactose-intolerant, their consumption of animal milk with this cereal could lead to abdominal pain, diarrhea, and malnutrition. In a culture that privileges the right to life-sustaining food, the omission of cautionary information on the package could be perceived as unethical—a failure of reverence and courage. Although a detailed (and unappetizing) explication of the hazards of animal milk consumption might prove displeasing, a simple and discreet advisory is possible: "For better digestion, soy milk is recommended."

The third picture simply shows the cereal and milk sitting in the bowl with the non-instruction "Ready to serve." Because no action is specified here, either visually or verbally, a technical communicator would ordinarily omit this information (i.e., ready-to-serve cereal is really only a three-step process), but it does serve to emphasize the readiness of the cereal once the milk is added. The simplicity of preparation thus challenges the ritual complexity of Chinese cooking (i.e., the characteristic cutting and chopping, boiling and frying).

The fourth picture shows a silver spoon filled with cereal and positioned over the glass bowl. The corresponding instruction is "Eat and enjoy Kellogg's® Coco Pops®." The use of a silver spoon in the picture (instead of a traditional ceramic spoon) once again challenges existing Chinese practices. And the repetition of the name of the cereal reinforces the source of that challenge.

The instructions on this side of the box thus push aside Chinese traditions to create a space in Chinese culture for this foreign food. In doing so, the instructions could be perceived as violating righteousness by putting the pursuit of profits over the practice of ethical behavior. The failure to offer a caution regarding animal milk, in particular, could be perceived as evidence of insincerity or cowardice, a casual attitude or timidity about meeting one's ethical obligations, and ignorance of or indifference to the people buying one's product.

Education

While the sides of the box address adult audiences, the back of the box tries to engage Chinese boys and girls, offering both persuasive and instructional information through the "Kellogg's Nutrition Classroom." This information, offering a simplified explanation of nutrition, adds to the credibility of Kellogg's® and Kellogg's® Coco Pops® by its explicit invocation of the virtue of wisdom and the principle of formal education. The "classroom" metaphor here is especially significant because the traditional Chinese classroom is a highly authoritarian environment in which teachers are never challenged or questioned. In the nutrition classroom, the lesson is taught by a cartoon character, a bright-eyed smiling monkey, who also appears on the front of the box eating Kellogg's® Coco Pops® from a silver spoon. This Kellogg's® Coco Pops® monkey thus aspires to a level of credibility similar to that characteristic of teachers. And Kellogg's® Coco Pops® aspires to be both academically and physically nourishing: food for the mind and the body.

The lesson starts with the following advice: "There are many different kinds of nutrition, and you can find all in many different kinds of food. So be sure to eat a balanced diet. Now, let me introduce my nutrition friends."

In a series of eight captioned drawings of cartoon characters, the Kellogg's® Coco Pops® monkey proceeds to introduce

- Mr. Protein, who "does important work making muscles, bones, and blood" and "helps you when you get sick"
- Mr. Carbohydrate, who "turns into calories, power, and energy" inside your body
- Ms. Fat, who "works making energy"
- Mr. Vitamin A, who will "help you grow" and is "good for your eyes"
- The Vitamin B family, who "help you get energy from your food and improve your appetite" as well as "help make strong bones and teeth"
- Ms. Vitamin C, who will "make the walls of your arteries and veins strong" and "make your teeth and gums healthy" as well as "help you get well" from cuts or burns
- Vitamin D, who will "help you get strong bones and teeth"
- Mr. Mineral (Iron), who "carries oxygen throughout your body and makes your blood thick"

The Kellogg's® Coco Pops® monkey also lists the various foods in which the nutrition friends "live," including Kellogg's® Coco Pops®. For example, he teaches that Mr. Protein "lives in meat, fish, milk, and beans" and Mr. Carbohydrate is located "in bread, Coco Pops, rice, and sweet things." (Milk—clearly necessary to Kellogg's® Coca Pops®—is promoted as housing three of the nutrition friends, including Vitamin D. In truth, however, Vitamin D is really available from simple sunlight; it occurs in milk as a chemical additive.)

By personifying the constituents of nutrition, the Kellogg's® Coca Pops® monkey establishes a series of social relationships for the young audience. Through the "classroom" experience, each boy and girl comes to know his or her nutrition friends and appreciate their important service in sustaining life. Each boy and girl thus discovers a moral obligation to the friends as well as to the teacher, the Kellogg's® Coca Pops® monkey. And how is this moral obligation satisfied? The teacher's lesson concludes with the following advice:

> Now you see why it's important to get many kinds of nutrition. Did you know that the Kellogg's Coco Pops you like so much contain a good balance of vitamins, iron, protein and other nutrition? Have delicious Kellogg's at breakfast every morning and you'll get energy to start the busy day.

The Chinese traditions of privileging education and establishing social obligations are elicited here to build allegiance to a foreign food and foreign eating practices.

THE LENS OF ETHICS

Viewed through a Confucian lens, the cereal package addresses issues of goodness, righteousness, wisdom, faithfulness, reverence, and courage. Buying and using this foreign product thus constitutes for the target audience a moral decision. This cultural artifact has ethical implications that a technical communicator might be oblivious to unless he or she is familiar with the dominant beliefs and practices of China. A technical manual, research report, or business proposal is likely to be at least as ethically treacherous as the relatively simple package.

The lens of ethics thus offers a vital perspective for technical communicators. If intercultural technical communication is to be ethical as well as effective, teachers and researchers of technical communication ought to fortify their sweeping surveys of intercultural technical communication and analyses of illustrative case studies with focused research on the morality or moralities driving the communication practices of specific civilizations.

Acknowledgments

I am grateful to the anonymous reviewers of TCQ, who offered important insights and advice, and to my colleague and friend Gwendolyn Gong of The Chinese University of Hong Kong, who inspired my visits to China and my research on international technical communication.

References

Alred, Gerald J. (1997). Teaching in Germany and the rhetoric of culture. *Journal of Business and Technical Communication, 11,* 353–378.

Artemeva, Natasha. (1998). The writing consultant as cultural interpreter: Bridging cultural perspectives on the genre of the periodic engineering report. *Technical Communication Quarterly, 7,* 285–299.

Boiarsky, Carolyn. (1995). The relationship between cultural and rhetorical conventions: Engaging in international communication. *Technical Communication Quarterly, 4,* 245–259.

Chan, Wing-Tsit. (1967). *Reflections on things at hand: The Neo-Confucian anthology compiled by Chu Hsi and Lü Tsu-Ch'ien.* New York: Columbia University Press.

Chang, Hui-Ching, & Holt, G. Richard. (1991). The concept of *Yuan* and Chinese interpersonal relationships. In Stella Ting-Toomey & Felipe Korzenny (Eds.), *International and intercultural communication annual: Vol. 15. Cross-cultural interpersonal communication* (pp. 28–57). Newbury Park, CA: Sage.

Cheng, Clung-Ying. (1991). *New dimensions of Confucian and Neo-Confucian philosophy.* Albany: State University of New York Press.

De Mente, Boye Lafayette. (1989). *Chinese etiquette and ethics in business.* Lincolnwood, IL: NTC Business Books.

Forman, Janis. (1998). Corporate image and the establishment of Euro Disney: Mickey Mouse and the French press. *Technical Communication Quarterly, 7,* 247–248.

Hagen, Patricia. (1998). Teaching American business writing in Russia: Cross-cultures/cross-purposes. *Journal of Business and Technical Communication, 12,* 109–126.

Hall, David L., & Ames, Roger T. (1987). *Thinking through Confucius.* Albany: State University of New York Press.

Hall, Edward T. (1976). *Beyond culture: Into the cultural unconscious.* Garden City, NY: Anchor Books.

Hofstede, Geert. (1980). *Culture's consequences: International differences in work-related values.* Beverly Hills, CA: Sage.

Huang, Chichung (Trans. and Ed.). (1997). *The Analects of Confucius: Lun Yu.* New York: Oxford University Press.

Huang, Quanyu, Andrulis, Richard S., & Chen, Tong. (1994). *A guide to successful business relations with the Chinese: Opening the Great Wall's gate.* New York: International Business Press.

Irwin, Harry. (1996). *Communicating with Asia: Understanding people and customs.* St. Leonards, Australia: Allen & Unwin.

Kam, Louie. (1980). *Critiques of Confucius in contemporary China.* Hong Kong: Chinese University of Hong Kong Press.

Kluckhohn, Florence Rockwood, & Strodtbeck, Fred L. (1961). *Variations in value orientations.* Evanston, IL: Row, Peterson.

Lau, D. C. (Trans. and Ed.). (1979). *The Analects* [Confucius]. New York: Penguin.

Leys, Simon (Trans. and Ed.). (1997). *The Analects of Confucius.* New York: W. W. Norton.

Rodman, Lilita. (1996). Finding new communication paradigms for a new nation: Latvia. In Deborah Andrews (Ed.), *International dimensions of technical communication* (pp. 111–121). Arlington, VA: Society for Technical Communication.

Tillman, Hoyt Cleveland. (1992). *Confucian discourse and Chu Hsi's ascendancy.* Honolulu: University of Hawaii Press.

Trompenaars, Fons. (1994). *Riding the waves of culture: Understanding diversity in global business.* Burr Ridge, IL: Irwin.

Tu, Wei-Ming. (1990). The Confucian tradition in Chinese history. In Paul S. Ropp (Ed.), *Heritage of China: Contemporary perspectives on Chinese civilization* (pp. 112–137). Berkeley: University of California Press.

Tung, Rosalie L. (1996). Managing in Asia: Cross-cultural dimensions. In Pat Joynt & Malcolm Warner (Eds.), *Managing across cultures: Issues and perspectives* (pp. 233–245). London: International Thompson Business Press.

Ulijn, Jan M. (1996). Translating the culture of technical documents: Some experimental evidence. In Deborah

Andrews (Ed.), *International dimensions of technical communication* (pp. 69–86). Arlington, VA: Society for Technical Communication.

Varner, Iris I., & Beamer, Linda. (1995). *Intercultural communication in the global workplace.* Chicago: Irwin.

Yuan, Rue. (1997). Yin/yang principle and the relevance of externalism and paralogic rhetoric to intercultural communication. *Journal of Business and Technical Communication, 11,* 297–320.

Yum, June Ock. (1998). The impact of Confucianism on interpersonal relationships and communication patterns in East Asia. *Communication Monographs, 55,* 374–388.

Concepts and Questions

1. Why does Dragga believe it necessary to unite the fields of business ethics and intercultural communication?
2. Explain why Dragga believed Confucian ethics would be a proper model for intercultural communication ethics.
3. What is the Confucian concept of goodness, and how does it apply to intercultural communication?
4. According to Confucius, what is the motivating force for superior human beings? How does it relate to intercultural communication?
5. How does the Confucian principle of faithfulness relate to intercultural business negotiations?
6. How did the Kellogg Company use "persuasion" as a tool in marketing Coco Pops to a Chinese consumer base?
7. Why is it important to include education in an intercultural marketing campaign?
8. How does the lens of Confucian ethics offer a vital perspective for technical intercultural communicators?

Business Ethics and Intercultural Communication: Exploring the Overlap Between Two Academic Fields[1]

JOHANNES BRINKMANN

The main intention of this paper is to demonstrate that intercultural communication as an academic field should incorporate business ethics concepts and theory.[2] Business ethics is a well-institutionalized[3] academic field, too, which deals with the moral dimension of business activity.[4] This paper offers a brief presentation of business ethics and how this field approaches the moral dimension of cross-cultural business activity. (For a broader presentation of business ethics as an academic field, see Brinkmann 2001a; for a more skeptical one, see Brinkmann, 2001b.)

The field's key terms, *morality* and *ethics,* both refer to acceptable, correct behavior, and are often used synonymously.[5] A clear distinction between these two terms can be useful, and is a question of how precisely "correct" or "acceptable" is defined, and by whom. A behavior that most insiders in a given culture or subculture accept or reject ("morality") is not necessarily considered the same way by a neutral, critical outsider. For this and other reasons, many writers distinguish clearly between morality on the one hand, and ethics on the other.

Such a sharp distinction can help with sorting a whole range of closely related phenomena: *real worlds* of "morality" as a question of practice and subcultural identity versus *preferred worlds* of "ethics" as a question of ideals and of critical argument as formulated, for example, by moral philosophy. Or, to quote an example of this distinction in prose:

From *The Journal of Intercultural Communication,* No. 5 (2002). http://www.immi.se/intercultural/nr5/brinkman.rtf. Reprinted with permission. Johannes Brinkmann teaches at the Norwegian School of Management, BI, Oslo, Norway.

> Ethics is concerned with the *justification* of actions and practices in specific situations. Ethics generally deals with the reasoning process and is a philosophical *reflection* on the moral life and the principles embedded in that life. . . . Morality . . . generally refers to *traditions* or beliefs that have evolved over several years or even centuries in societies concerning right and wrong conduct. Morality can be thought of as a social institution that has a history and a *code of conduct* that are implicit or explicit about how people ought to behave. (Buchholz & Rosenthal, 1998, p. 4, italics added)

In this quotation, morality and ethics are defined in relation to one another, as a *continuum* with a real-practical and an ideal-theoretical, a descriptive and a normative, extreme point. One could also extend this continuum by including the "bad neighbor" of morality, moralism. In such a case morality represents a neutral term, with moralism as its preaching and stigmatizing extension and ethics as its constructive-critical extension. Whereas moralism is often self-righteous and looks for sinners and chases them, ethics integrates people by seeking a consensus around good principles and procedures. In other words, moralism lacks the self-criticism of morality that defines ethics. In terms of such a distinction, morality can degenerate to moralism and is exposed to potential ethical criticism. Proper critical evaluation requires sufficient knowledge and understanding of morality and moralism, respectively.

In addition to such a moralism–ethics dimension, one could also try to understand morality and ethics in their contrast to positive, formal law and individual, private conscience. Morality and ethics seem to be located somewhere between conscience and law in several respects, being less emotional, private, and inner-directed than conscience and less formal, predictable, public, and outer-directed than law. Because of such a middle position on several dimensions, morality and ethics can potentially serve as bridge builders and substitutes whenever individual conscience or positive law cannot be relied upon (see Jensen et al., 1990, p. 38). On the other hand, for the same reason, there is less need for ethics and morality as long as individual conscience and positive law guarantee similar control (see Exhibit 1; also Brinkmann, 2001b, fig. 1, table 3).

Exhibit 1 *Understanding Morality in Its Relationship to Ethics and Moralism, Law, and Conscience.*

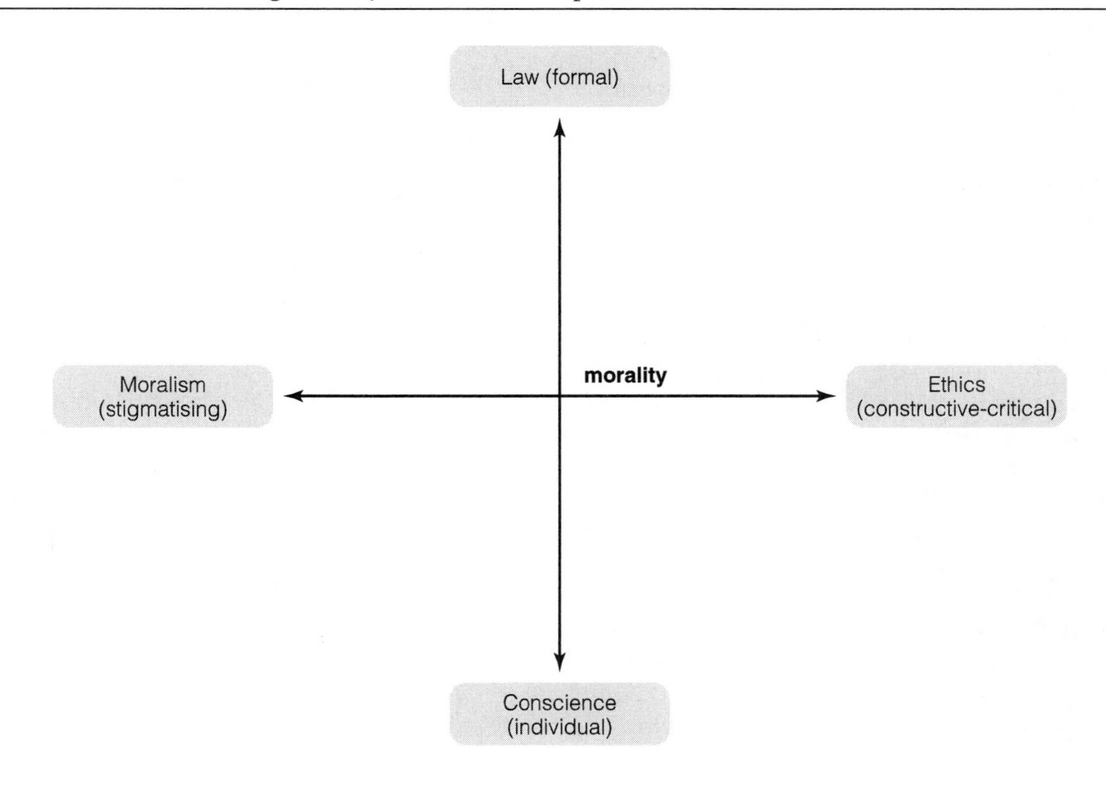

Still another way of structuring and presenting the field is by means of moral-philosophical schools or approaches. Utilitarianism versus deontology (associated with names such as J. Bentham or J. S. Mill versus I. Kant or W. D. Ross) is a standard dichotomy, often with other schools mentioned in addition (e.g., J. Rawls' *justice ethics,* M. Weber's *responsibility ethics,* or J. Habermas' *consensus-by-communication* ethics). Deontology asks idealistically if a societal status quo or a given action is consistent with universal principles, such as human duties and rights. If there is no other way out, principles are focused on at the expense of holistic consequence analyses and compromises. Utilitarianism is more pragmatic in its search for maximized total utilities of a societal status quo or a given action, for the "greatest good for the greatest number of people." If there is no other way out, welfare maximization is primarily at the expense of any other principles. The communication ethics approach questions the authority of the positions defining principles or welfare and believes in consensus building by fair and open communication among all the stakeholders affected. Such a standpoint of "communication as a principle" welcomes deontological and or utilitarianist arguments, together with other ones.[6]

> "Ethics" most often refers to a domain of inquiry, a discipline, in which matters of right and wrong, good and evil, virtue and vice, are systematically examined. "Morality," by contrast, is most often used to refer not to a discipline but to patterns of thought and action that are actually operative in everyday life. In this sense, morality is what the discipline of ethics is about. And, so business morality is what business ethics is about. (Goodpaster, 1992, p. 111)

In this and similar quotations,[7] *business ethics* is presented as a special case of ethics. And business ethics contains a similar ambiguity of everyday moral practice versus ethics—that is, theorizing, discussing, and agreement about such practice—and of ethics versus moralism. There are gray zones toward law and conscience, and there are different schools or approaches. In addition to such rather general, perhaps too general, quotations with low awareness of intercultural connotation differences, one can distinguish between talking of business ethics, business ethical practice, and theorizing about business ethics (Enderle, 1996, p. 34).

CROSS-CULTURAL BUSINESS ETHICS: CLASSIC CASES AND IMPORTANT ISSUES

Cross-cultural business ethics addresses moral issues that emerge when companies operate in different countries, when stakeholders live in different societies, and when norms and values reflect and are affected by cultural differences. In addition to such a working definition, a number of classic case examples and some of the most important issues in cross-cultural business ethics can be described briefly, with references added for further reading and discussion.

- *The* classical case is probably Nestlé Infant Formula marketing in less developed countries, where Nestlé was held responsible for marketing a risky or unsafe product—if mothers stopped breast-feeding or, even worse, if infants died when Nestlé's breast milk substitute was prepared without available clean drinking water (see Beauchamp & Bowie, 1993, pp. 590–591, or French & Granrose, 1995, 197–199).
- The Union Carbide incident in Bhopal, India, in which thousands of people were killed and injured, is basically about the issue of whether Western companies can defend working with legal but lower health, environment, and safety standards in developing countries (see Boatright, 1997, pp. 370–372; DeGeorge, 1995, pp. 473–475; Donaldson, 1989, pp. 109–128).
- The story of how ITT and other U.S. companies in the early 1970s participated actively in overthrowing the Allende government in Chile represents one of the classic cases in which multinational companies have deliberately destabilized legitimate political systems (see, e.g., DesJardins & McCall, 1996, p. 502, or French & Granrose, 1995, pp. 176–177).
- During the apartheid period in South Africa, many political groups claimed that businesses had a moral duty to boycott the apartheid regime—that is, either not to enter or to pull out—while others, and in particular "staying" companies, claimed that they were obliged to use their influence to better the life situation for the country's discriminated-against majority (see DeGeorge, 1995, chap. 19, or French & Granrose, 1995, pp. 181–183).
- How typically Western is the issue of female self-determined abortion? What about birth control and

population growth control, looked at from different standard of living and worldview angles? Does a multinational company have a right or even a moral obligation to make an assumed lower-risk abortion possible for developing country women? What about making forced abortions easier in the People's Republic of China? Or giving in to an expected boycott from U.S. pro-life organizations? In this situation French Roussell-Uclaf faced a choice between marketing or not marketing an abortion pill, a choice cutting across a wide range of moral and cultural issues (see Harvey et al., 1994, pp. 11–12, 128–158).

- Is a multinational company that is doing business with a developing country ruled by a repressive regime co-responsible for human rights violations in such a country—for example, in the case of Shell and other oil companies operating in Nigeria (see, e.g., Livesey, 2001, with further references)?
- Is child labor unacceptable independent of circumstances, or acceptable if, for example, the only alternative would be child prostitution? If circumstances matter, under which conditions is which type of child labor acceptable? (See DesJardins & McCall, 1996, pp. 540–541, or http://www.ilo.org/public/English/standards/ipec/.)
- Should gift giving in the context of business transactions follow local culture? Is there any situation or none in which bribery could be acceptable in international business? (See Ferrell & Fraedrich, 1997, pp. 209–210; Beauchamp & Bowie, 1993, pp. 591–592.)
- Should respect for faith and beliefs or principles of free expression be primary criteria when deciding if Rushdie's *Satanic Verses* should be sold and marketed? How should one respond to terror possibilities against shops carrying the book, with a risk to employees' and customers' health and lives? (See Smith & Quelch, 1993, pp. 507–512.)
- Can the northern Norwegian tradition of minke whaling be defended for cultural and environmental reasons, even if this communicates a bad example for international bans on whaling? Should local or global stakeholders go first? (See Brinkmann, 1996.)

These cases and similar ones can be sorted into at least one of the following issue categories:[8]

- Health, environment, and safety (local versus global standards)
- International marketing issues, including bribery
- Multinational company size, power, and responsibility
- Code of conduct development (in particular if there is a legal vacuum)
- Outsourcing, slave, and child labor
- Arms trade
- Co-responsibility for human rights violation
- Interference with political stability and self-determination
- Non-ethnocentric handling of norm and value diversity

CULTURAL AND ETHICAL RELATIVISM

Cultural relativism is a worldview and standpoint that no culture as such is superior to any other one, and that any culture deserves to be described, understood, and judged on its own premises. (The opposite is ethnocentrism,[9] where one culture judges other cultures.) Ethical relativism[10] as a worldview and standpoint claims that there is no culture-free, universal morality and therefore no way of ranking moral views and practices as more or less right, at least across cultures.

Both relativisms have been criticized as extreme positions, but are at the same time widely used in their respective parent disciplines, social anthropology and moral philosophy, as basic labels of theoretical orientation. Since cultural relativism is less normative and much less controversial than ethical relativism, a listing of the most important arguments against the latter is sufficient here:[11]

- Obvious empirical differences of moral beliefs and practices do not prove that they are all right.
- One should not give up "because some justifiable practices vary from place to place"; "surrender of principles in the face of disagreement" hurts integrity.
- Cultural relativism and cultural tolerance should not be confused (tolerance and respect for diversity create rather than remove the right to have justified standpoints).
- Disagreement about judgments does not necessarily prove disagreement about the principles on which such judgments are based.

- Relativism can confuse behavior and analysis rather than enlighten them.
- There is no moral-free space, but there are many moral gray zones.

What is needed (and sufficient) is an intercultural moral consensus about an ethical minimum. For addressing and handling such criticisms, problems, and questions, a few conventions seem useful:

- One should keep cultural and ethical relativism apart conceptually.[12] Unprejudiced empirical description and understanding (i.e., cultural relativism) is not the same as a denial of any moral or cultural outsider criticism of non-acceptable practices (i.e., ethical relativism).
- One should reserve the term *ethics* for a qualified consensus about moral issues, brought about by fair dialogue (or defendable by fair dialogue), interculturally or intraculturally.[13]
- Cultural and ethical relativism are counter-positions to assumed cultural superiority (or ethnocentrism) and to top-down moralism (in other words, it is sometimes easier to be against the enemies of relativism than to take a relativist position).
- Individual conscience, moral customs, and positive law vary more interculturally than minimum ethics.

THE INDIVIDUAL-LEVEL IDEAL: OPEN-MINDEDNESS AND MORAL INTEGRITY

In education or recruitment situations, cultural and ethical relativism turns into a question of individual attitudes and capabilities and how such qualities can be assessed. Three examples of assessment instruments in this field can be briefly referred to. J. Koester and M. Olebe have suggested and developed a rather broad *Behavioral Scale for Intercultural Competence* (BASIC) which focuses on intercultural open-mindedness—or, as they call it, intercultural communication skills—by using eight categories (Lustig & Koester, 1996, p. 329, with further references):

- Display of respect
- Orientation to knowledge
- Empathy
- Task role behavior
- Relational role behavior
- Interaction management
- Tolerance for ambiguity
- Interaction posture

Most of such an instrument's categories seem to be indicators of individual cultural relativism. Another, more one-dimensional instrument is M. J. Bennett's *Developmental Model of Intercultural Sensitivity* (DMIS; see Exhibit 2). As the name of this model suggests, there is a learning process assumption from lower to higher stages, such as growing into a culture and replacing biased and superficial understanding of a culture by an in-depth understanding of such a culture's "emics" (see also Segall et al., 1990, pp. 48–66; Bennett, 1998, pp. 191–214).

The third example is Lawrence Kohlberg's classic continuum of moral sensitivity and judgment maturity[14] (see, e.g., 1972, 1985; see Exhibit 3, using J. Rest's reformulations).

Kohlberg's interest and assumptions concern individual moral maturity development and assessment.[15] In our context one could consider reading the Kohlberg model as a continuum of cultural-moral opportunism, with a ("relativist") position of choosing ways of least resistance at the one end, and non-resignation in the face of moral controversy and defiance of integrity at the other end.

Exhibit 2 *M. J. Bennett's DMIS Model (1998, 26, slightly modified).*

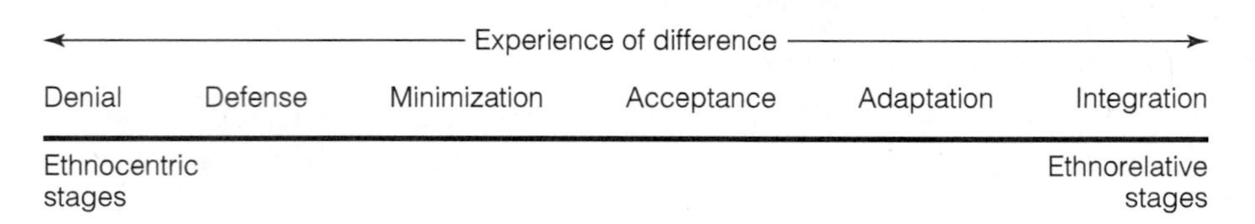

Exhibit 3 *Kohlberg's Six Stages (following Rest and Narváez 1994, 5).*

Preconventional	Stage 1	The morality of obedience: Do what you're told.
	Stage 2	The morality of instrumental egoism and simple exchange: Let's make a deal.
Conventional	Stage 3	The morality of interpersonal concordance: Be considerate, nice, and kind: you'll make friends.
	Stage 4	The morality of law and duty to social order: Everyone in society is obliged to and protected by the law.
Postconventional	Stage 5	The morality of consensus-building procedures: You are obligated by the arrangements that are agreed to by due process procedures.
	Stage 6	The morality of nonarbitrary social cooperation: Morality is defined by how rational and impartial people would ideally organize cooperation.

Exhibit 4 *Four Combination Types of Relativism.*

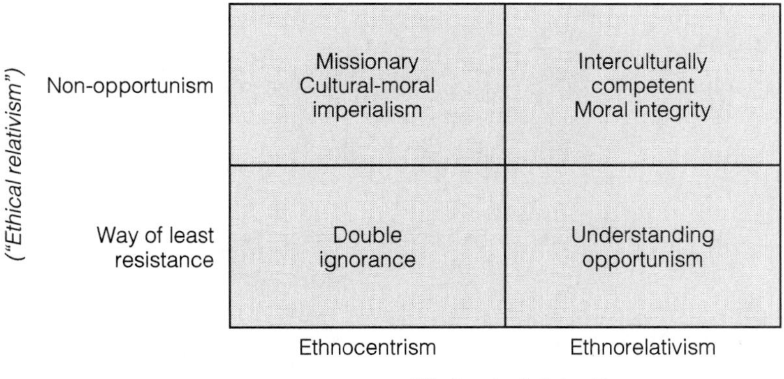

DIALECTICS OF CULTURAL AND ETHICAL RELATIVISM

Cultural and moral relativism are different, but interdependent. One can understand a culture on its own premises without accepting it, and one can accept it without understanding it (see, e.g., Eriksen, in Brinkmann & Eriksen, 1996, p. 25). One can be a tolerant and empathetic ethnorelativist and at the same time have a postconventional or conventional, non-opportunistic approach to morality. Such difference *and* interdependence ("dialectics") can be illustrated by a fourfold table with both relativisms as independent dimensions (see Exhibit 4). Obviously, one should avoid double ignorance and try to move toward the ideal—that is, aim at a high score on both dimensions.

From such references, one would assume that

- Business ethics potentially can profit from more intercultural communication competence.
- Intercultural communication can learn from ethics how to identify and defend moral standpoints worth defending.
- Cultural and moral relativism can be fruitful points of departure when analyzing or when communicating about ethical dilemmas or intercultural moral standpoint differences,[16] *as long as the aim is to transcend such relativism during such analysis and communication.* (See Lustig & Koester's D-I-E tool,[17] 1996, pp. 333–336; see Exhibit 5.)

Exhibit 5 *A Virtuous (but Vulnerable) Circle of Delaying Judgement and Transcending Ethical Relativism.*

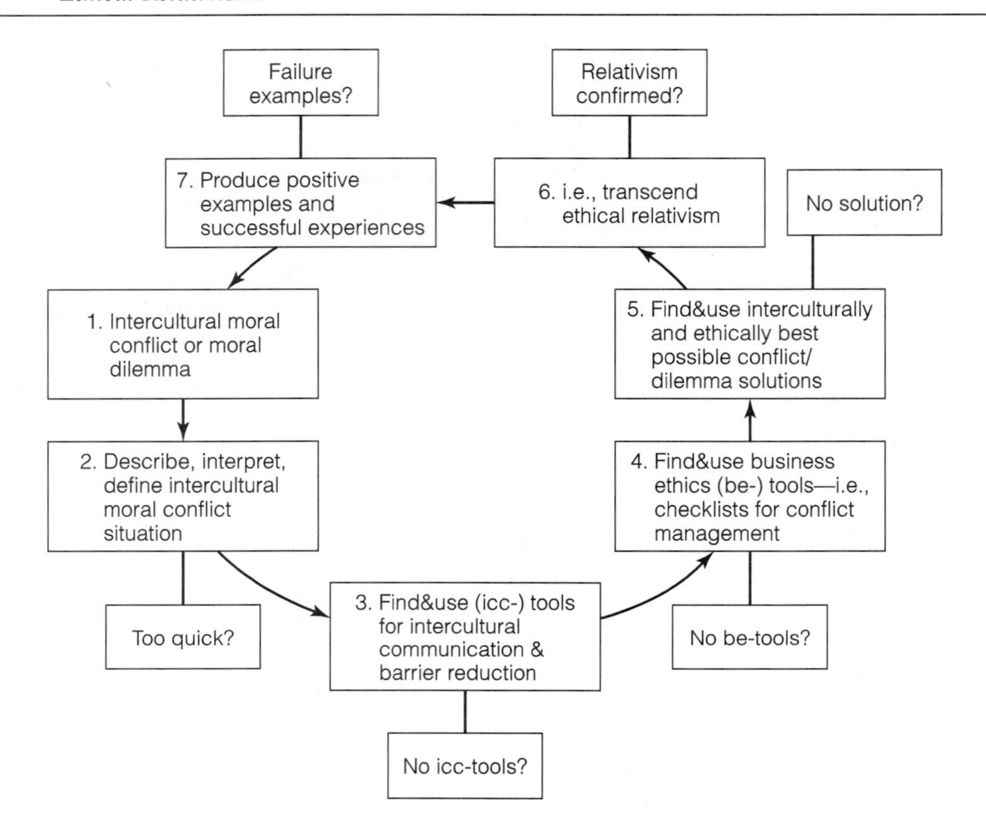

ETHICAL DILEMMA HANDLING

The last point can be illustrated as a possible virtuous circle that can easily turn into a vicious one (see Exhibit 5). Or in prose: If a moral conflict or dilemma is faced in an intercultural setting (1), intercultural communication, ideally, could contribute with unprejudiced, non-ethnocentric description and interpretation (2), with tools for communication and barrier reduction (3), while ethics would focus on moral and value conflicts (4) and on possibilities for solutions, preferably consensus-building (5). Such an interdisciplinary mix of competencies could then reach a preliminary minimum consensus, a first step toward transcending ethical relativism (6), and produce positive examples and experiences for future situations (7). Such idealism—that is, a virtuous circle—is not only self-reinforcing once it works, but is also vulnerable; it can fail or even turn into a vicious circle (see indications of potential traps in Exhibit 5).

As a next step after such general observations and assumptions, one can recommend a brief look at textbooks and casebooks in business ethics with conflict management checklists[18] and so-called codes of conduct for inventories of universal norms and, hopefully, for conflict prevention (see, e.g., Ferrell & Fraedrich, 1997, pp. 201–206).

TEN THESES AS A SUMMARY AND INSTEAD OF A CONCLUSION

1. There is an important distinction between morality and ethics—that is, between empirical description and understanding of moral phenomena and their critical-normative evaluation.
2. Two ("moralistic") dangers must be observed: the use of moral perspectives where other perspectives would be equally or even more appropriated, and a reduction of moral analysis to an identification of sinners.

3. While Western cultures tend to remove moral issues (and to turn them into private conscience and/or positive law issues), this might not be the case in other cultures.
4. Case examples and issues within cross-cultural business ethics seem to have at least two common denominators: power and moral judgment insecurity. On the one hand, globalization of business creates power and legal vacuum situations where mega-size company power can't be matched by small countries. More company power and more stakeholder powerlessness create more moral responsibility. On the other hand, cultural and moral relativism become at the same time more tempting and more exposed to criticism.
5. Cultural and ethical relativism should not be mixed up but treated as dialectic—that is, different, interdependent, and conflicting. A simplified fourfold table can be useful as a start (see again Exhibit 4).
6. Moral standpoints and moral conflicts should not be sacrificed for the benefit of intercultural understanding. Cultural relativism does not necessarily imply moral opportunism. The right order of procedure is crucial: nonbiased description and understanding should always come before critical evaluation (see again Exhibit 5).
7. Individuals, groups, or organizations should ask themselves and be prepared to be asked critical questions about their moral acceptability and responsibility thresholds—for example, core human rights, child labor, health, environment, and safety.[19]
8. When it comes to moral conflict management, there is no moral alternative to fair and open intercultural communication, along with, for example, J. Habermas' ideals (see Habermas, 1990; with reference to business ethics, see French & Granrose, 1995, pp. 148–154, 214–215, or more practically, Brown, 1996).
9. The more its issues are clearly intercultural or intersubcultural, the more can business ethics as an academic field profit from intercultural communication competence.
10. Intercultural communication as an academic field can profit from using highly controversial business ethics cases for testing its competence and for staying humble.

REMAINING QUESTIONS

At least three questions remain for further discussion, related to the cases mentioned perviously, or not.

- What should one do if at least one party to an intercultural moral conflict declines to discuss the issue?
- How should one handle moral conflict situations if there is no minimum consensus, such as a willingness to coexist peacefully and to live constructively with disagreement?
- Would you be willing to fight for intercultural tolerance and consensus ethics, and if yes, how?

Notes

1. A previous version of this paper has appeared, under another title, as "Cross-Cultural Business Ethics," in M. Isaksson and F. A. Rokaas (Eds.), *Conflicting Values: An Intercultural Challenge* (Selected papers from the 1999 NIC Symposium in Oslo, Norway, Norwegian School of Management BI, Sandvika 2000), pp. 177–192.
2. Business ethics should incorporate intercultural communication concepts and theory, too, but that is not the primary concern of this paper.
3. Institutionalization or establishment indicators are, for example, professional organization size, number of full professor positions, textbook shelf-meters, number and prestige of academic journals, international conference activity, and the like.
4. The multilevel and multidimensional complexity of such a task requires interdisciplinarity, with all its strengths and weaknesses. A diversity of intellectual backgrounds often creates a more open and low-threat communication climate of mutual learning, in particular if there are shared problem experiences and ambitions. A potential danger is that academics from different fields meet, develop a common rhetoric, and then do the same at a level of lowest common denominator. The challenge, therefore, is always to start by asking oneself critically about the unique competence with which one's own home discipline could contribute. In other words, a wise division of labor can often be more important than cooperation.
5. Compare the Greek distinction between "ethos" with a short e, ____ (habits) and "ethos" with a long e, ____ (virtue). Latin has only one word for both, "mos." See Brinkmann, 1994, with an inventory of antonyms in table format.
6. See the following references for further elaboration: Hoffman et al., 2001, pp. 1–43; Frankena, 1973;

DeGeorge, 1995, chap. 3 and 4; Beauchamp and Bowie, 1993, pp. 20–42; French and Granrose, 1995, esp. chap. 7.

7. For example: "Business ethics is concerned with the application of moral standards to the conduct of individuals involved in organisations through which modern societies produce and distribute goods and services. . . . It is a type of applied ethics concerned with clarifying the obligations and dilemmas of managers and other employees who make business decisions" (Buchholz, 1989, p. 4). "Business ethics deals with the behaviour, responsibilities and motives of business organisations and their effects on the "social partners" of firms—their employees, managers, shareholders, suppliers, customers, communities, and governments" (Harvey, in Steinmann & Löhr, 1991, p. 482).
8. See, for example, DeGeorge, 1993, 1995; Donaldson, 1989; Donaldson and Dunfee, 1999; Buchholz and Rosenthal, 1998; Hoffman et al., 2001.
9. Or similar terms, such as cultural absolutism or cultural imperialism.
10. As morality has been introduced above, the poles are cultural and ethical relativism—morality *is* culturally relative; right and wrong are ethically relative.
11. See in particular DeGeorge, 1993; DeGeorge, 1995, chap. 2; Donaldson, 1989; Donaldson and Dunfee, 1999; DesJardins and McCall, 1996; Falkenberg and Nordenstam, 1998, pp. 182–189. For a more general summary of various relativisms, see Harré and Krausz, 1996; Frankena, 1973, pp. 109–110.
12. Donaldson, 1989, pp. 14–19, for example, does not and loses important points.
13. One could almost say that intercultural moral conflict-handling issues represent a good and necessary test of intercultural communication competence (otherwise the field would be "for good weather only").
14. James R. Rest (in Rest & Narváez, 1994, pp. 22–25) suggests that one should distinguish between moral sensitivity (the ability to see moral issues), moral evaluation (the ability to judge right versus wrong, Kohlberg's domain according to Rest), moral motivation, and moral character. In this paper, we assume the Kohlberg model covers both sensitivity and judgment.
15. C. Gilligan has criticized Kohlberg for a focus on male rule-oriented ethics while females instead understand ethics as a question of caring or empathy. There is no space here to discuss if a caring approach to ethics would offer better bridge-building possibilities to a need of intercultural empathy (not "sympathy," Bennett would remark, 1998, p. 191).
16. A. Sohn-Rethel would have called this a "necessary false consciousness."
17. Description —> Interpretation —> Evaluation
18. See, for example, Blanchard and Peale's three simple questions—is it legal? is it fair? how does it feel? (1989, pp. 16–22)—or the more detailed lists of H. van Luijk (in the European casebook edited by Harvey et al., 1994, pp. 8–9) or L. Nash (see Smith & Quelch, 1993, p. 18). An interesting meta-checklist question would then be whether these checklists are interculturally sensitive.
19. See http://www.cepa.org for more information about the Social Accountability 8000 (SA 8000) standard, or P. Adamcik's presentation of the SA 8000 standard in "Menneskerettigheter," 1999, pp. 118–123.

References

Beauchamp, Tom L., & Bowie, Norman E. (1993). *Ethical theory and business.* Englewood Cliffs, NJ.

Bennett, Milton J. (Ed.). (1998). *Basic concepts of intercultural communication.* Yarmouth, ME.

Blanchard, K. H., & Peale, N. V. (1988). *The poser of ethical management.* New York: W. Morrow.

Boatright, John R., 1997. *Ethics and the conduct of business.* Upper Saddle River, NJ.

Brinkmann, Johannes. (1994). Moral, Ethik und Wirtschaft [Morals, ethics, and business]. *Management Review, 3,* 181–190.

Brinkmann, Johannes. (1996). Sustainability—Yes. But how? Norwegian minke whaling as a case. *European Environment, 6,* 6–13.

Brinkmann, Johannes. (2001a). *Etikk for næringslivet: Perspektiver og praksis* [Ethics for business: Perspectives and practice]. Oslo: Unipub.

Brinkmann, Johannes. (2001b). On business ethics and moralism. *Business Ethics: A European Review, 10*(4), 311–319.

Brown, Marvin T. (1996). *The ethical process.* Upper Saddle River, NJ.

Buchholz, Rogene A. (1989). *Business ethics.* Englewood Cliffs, NJ.

Buchholz, Rogene A., & Rosenthal, Sandra B. (1998). *Business ethics.* Englewood Cliffs, NJ.

DeGeorge, Richard. (1993). *Competing with integrity in international business.* New York.

DeGeorge, Richard. (1995). *Business ethics* (4th ed.). Englewood Cliffs, NJ.

DesJardins, Joseph R., & McCall, John J. (1996). *Contemporary issues in business ethics.* Belmont, CA.

Donaldson, Thomas. (1989). *The ethics of international business.* New York.

Donaldson, Thomas, & Dunfee, Thomas W. (1999). When ethics travel: The promise and peril of global business ethics. *California Management Review, 41*(4), 45–63.

Enderle, Georges. (1996). A comparison of business ethics in North America and continental Europe. *Business Ethics: A European Review, 5,* 33–46.

Enderle, Georges. (1997). A worldwide survey of business ethics in the 1990s. *Journal of Business Ethics, 16,* 1475–1483.

Falkenberg, Andreas, & Nordenstam, Tore. (1998). *Etikk i næringslivet* [Ethics in business]. Oslo.

Ferrell, O. C., & Fraedrich, J. (1997). *Business ethics.* Boston.

Frankena, William K. (1973). *Ethics* (2nd ed.). Englewood Cliffs, NJ.

French, Warren A., & Granrose, John. (1995). *Practical business ethics.* Englewood Cliffs, NJ.

Goodpaster, Kenneth R. (1992). Business ethics. In L. C. Becker & C. B. Becker (Eds.), *Encyclopedia of ethics* (pp. 111–115). New York.

Habermas, Jürgen. (1990). Morality, society and ethics [Interview by Torben Hviid Nielsen]. *Acta sociologica, 33,* 93–114.

Harré, Rom, & Krausz, Michael. (1996). *Varieties of relativism.* Oxford and Cambridge, MA.

Harvey, Brian, et al. (Eds.). (1994). *A European casebook on business ethics.* Hemel Hempstead.

Hoffman, W. Michael, et al. (Eds.). (2001). *Business ethics: Readings and cases in corporate morality.* New York.

Jensen, Hans S., et al. (1990). *Den etiske udfordring* [The ethical challenge]. Copenhagen.

Kohlberg, Lawrence (1972). Moral development. In David L. Sills (Ed.), *International encyclopedia of the social sciences.* New York: Macmillan.

Kohlberg, Lawrence. (1985). A current statement on some theoretical issues. In I. S. Mogill & C. Mogill (Eds.), *Lawrence Kohlberg: Consensus and controversy* (pp. 485–546). Philadelphia.

Livesey, Sharon M. (2001). Eco-identity as discursive struggle: Royal Dutch/Shell, Brent Spar, and Nigeria. *Journal of Business Communication, 38*(1), 58–91.

Lustig, Myron W., & Koester, Jolene. (1996). *Intercultural competence.* New York.

Rest, James, & Narváez, Darcia. (Eds.). (1994). *Moral development in the professions: Psychology and applied ethics.* Hillsdale, NJ.

Segall, Marshall H., et al. (Eds.). (1990). *Human behavior in a global perspective.* Boston.

Smith, N. Craig, & Quelch, John A. (1993). *Ethics in marketing.* Burr Ridge, IL.

Steinmann, Horst, & Löhr, Albert (Eds.). (1991). *Unternehmensethik.* Stuttgart. (Original work published 1989)

Concepts and Questions

1. Why does Brinkmann believe it necessary to unite business ethics and intercultural communication?
2. How does Brinkmann distinguish between ethics and morality?
3. In the classical case of Nestlé Infant Formula, what do you believe should have been the proper intercultural message to send to mothers about the risks involved in using the product?
4. How do you feel about U.S. companies doing business in other cultures engaging in gift giving or bribery if that is the custom of that culture?
5. What ethical rules do you believe should be applied to international marketing practices?
6. What does Brinkmann mean by the term *cultural and ethical relativism?*
7. Brinkmann asserts the need for an intercultural moral consensus about an ethical minimum. What would you propose as set of conditions to achieve this ethical goal?
8. How does Brinkmann use the principle of dialectics to address the issues of cultural and ethical relativism?
9. How would you propose to invoke an ethical-moral dimension in intercultural business communication?

Index